Lecture Notes in Computer Science 16832

The series Lecture Notes in Computer Science (LNCS), including its subseries Lecture Notes in Artificial Intelligence (LNAI) and Lecture Notes in Bioinformatics (LNBI), has established itself as a medium for the publication of new developments in computer science and information technology research, teaching, and education.

LNCS enjoys close cooperation with the computer science R & D community, the series counts many renowned academics among its volume editors and paper authors, and collaborates with prestigious societies. Its mission is to serve this international community by providing an invaluable service, mainly focused on the publication of conference and workshop proceedings and postproceedings. LNCS commenced publication in 1973.

Nadia El Mrabet · Loubna Ghammam ·
Francisco Rodríguez-Henríquez
Editors

Progress in Cryptology - AFRICACRYPT 2026

17th International Conference on Cryptology in Africa
Hammamet, Tunisia, July 8–10, 2026
Proceedings

Springer

Editors
Nadia El Mrabet
EMSE
Gardanne, France

Loubna Ghammam
ITK Engineering GmbH (Bosch)
Rülzheim, Germany

Francisco Rodríguez-Henríquez
Technology Innovation Institute (TII)
Abu Dhabi, United Arab Emirates

ISSN 0302-9743 ISSN 1611-3349 (electronic)
Lecture Notes in Computer Science
ISBN 978-3-032-31129-0 ISBN 978-3-032-31130-6 (eBook)
https://doi.org/10.1007/978-3-032-31130-6

This Springer imprint is published by the registered company Springer Nature Switzerland AG
The registered company address is: Gewerbestrasse 11, 6330 Cham, Switzerland

Preface

This volume contains the papers accepted for presentation at Africacrypt 2026, the 17th International Conference on the Theory and Application of Cryptographic Techniques in Africa. The aim of this conference series is to provide an international forum for practitioners and researchers from industry, academia, and government agencies to discuss all aspects of cryptography and its applications. The Africacrypt conference series was launched in 2008, when the first edition was held in Morocco. Subsequent editions have taken place in Tunisia, South Africa, Senegal, Morocco, Egypt, and Cameroon.

Africacrypt 2026 was organized by the University of Tunis, the Military Research Center, and Tunisian Mathematical Society, in cooperation with the International Association for Cryptologic Research (IACR). The conference was held in Hammamet from July 8 to 10.

We received 57 submissions from researchers around the world. After a double-blind reviewing process that included online discussions and involved 50 Program Committee members and 26 external reviewers, we decided to accept 19 papers, resulting in an acceptance rate of approximately 33%. All submitted papers received at least three reviews. We thank the Program Committee members and the external reviewers for their diligent work and fruitful discussions, and we thank all authors who submitted papers for their support of the conference.

The Best Paper Award went to Marcus Dansarie, Gregor Leander, Shahram Rasoolzadeh, Lukas Stennes, and Cihangir Tezcan for their paper "Ciphertext-Only Attack on HALFLOOP-24". The runner-up went to Alice Pellet-Mary and Michel Seck for their paper "On the Properties of HighBits and LowBits Functions and their Applications"

The conference program featured three keynote speakers: Elena Kirshanova from the Technology Innovation Institute, United Arab Emirates; María Naya-Plasencia from Inria Paris, France; and Peter Schwabe from the Max Planck Institute for Security and Privacy, Germany, and Radboud University, the Netherlands. We were delighted that they agreed to attend the conference in person and deliver their keynote lectures.

A post-quantum cryptography summer school was also held in Hammamet on July 6–7 as an IACR Cryptology School. The event was very successful, bringing together 80 participants, including students, faculty members, and representatives from industry and government.

The General Chairs, Leila Ben Abdelghani from the University of Monastir, Tunisia, and Ines Saihi from the University of Tunis El Manar, Tunisia, did a fantastic job with the local organization of the conference. It was a pleasure to work with them toward this event and to enjoy the results of our joint efforts during the conference.

We thank the staff at Springer for their help with the production of the proceedings. Without the support of all our sponsors, both local (various research laboratories and universities) and international (Duokey, Mines Saint-Étienne, Symbolic Software, and

Technology Innovation Institute), the support provided to the speakers and the local organization would not have been possible. We are deeply grateful to them.

Serving as Program Chairs for Africacrypt 2026 was a privilege and a rewarding experience. We thank everyone who helped make the conference a great success.

July 2026

Nadia El Mrabet
Loubna Ghammam
Francisco Rodríguez-Henríquez

Organization

General Chairs

Leila Ben Abdelghani	University of Monastir, Tunisia
Ines Saihi	University of Tunis El Manar, Tunisia

Program Committee Chairs

Nadia El Mrabet	Mines Saint-Étienne, CEA-LETI, Centre CMP, Equipe commune SAS, France
Loubna Ghammam	ITK Engineering GmbH (Bosch), Germany
Francisco Rodríguez-Henríquez	Technology Innovation Institute, UAE

Steering Committee

Lina Mortajine	ITK Engineering GmbH (Bosch), Germany
Souheib Yousfi (Chair)	University of Carthage, Tunisia

Program Committee

Gora Adj	Technology Innovation Institute, UAE
Kevin Atighehchi	École de l'air et de l'espace, France
Anubhab Baksi	Wallenberg AI, Sweden, Nanyang Technological University, Singapore
Morgan Barbier	ENSICAEN, France
Sonia Belaïd	CryptoExperts, France
Alexandre Berzati	Thales, France
Slim Bettaieb	Technology Innovation Institute, UAE
Olivier Blazy	École Polytechnique, France
Sébastien Canard	Télécom Paris, France
Guilhem Castagnos	Université de Bordeaux, France
Joan Daemen	Radboud University, The Netherlands
Luca De Feo	IBM Research Europe, Switzerland
Laurent-Stéphane Didier	University of Toulon, France
Christoph Dobraunig	Radboud University, The Netherlands

Fangan Yssouf Dosso	Seal SQ, France
Sylvain Duquesne	University Rennes 1, France
Laila El Aimani	University of Cadi Ayyad, Morocco
Nadia El Mrabet	École des Mines de Saint-Étienne, France
Muhammad Elsheikh	National Institute of Standards, Egypt
Fouotsa Emmanuel	University of Bamenda, Cameroon
Georgios Fotiadis	University of Luxembourg, Luxembourg
Essam Ghadafi	Newcastle University, UK
Loubna Ghammam	ITK Engineering GmbH, Germany
Javier Herranz	Universitat Politècnica de Catalunya, Spain
Sorina Ionica	University of Versailles Saint-Quentin-en-Yvelines, France
Tetsu Iwata	Nagoya University, Japan
Samuel Jaques	University of Waterloo, Canada
Nadim Kobeissi	Cure53 and Symbolic Software, France
Juliane Krämer	University of Regensburg, Germany
Péter Kutas	University of Birmingham, UK
Pascal Lafourcade	LIMOS, University Clermont Auvergne, France
Xiangyu Liu	Purdue University, USA
Marine Minier	LORIA, Nancy, France
Lina Mortajine	ITK Engineering GmbH, Germany
Svetla Nikova	KU Leuven, Belgium
Abderrahmane Nitaj	LMNO, University of Caen Normandie, France
Chinenye Okafor	Purdue University, USA
Nicola Pace	NXP Semiconductors, Germany
Yanbin Pan	Academy of Mathematics and Systems Science, China
Christophe Petit	University of Birmingham, UK and Université libre de Bruxelles, Belgium
Vincent Rijmen	Katholieke Universiteit Leuven, Belgium
Jean-Marc Robert	University of Toulon, France
Francisco Rodríguez-Henríquez	Technology Innovation Institute, UAE
Simona Samardjiska	Radboud University, The Netherlands
Palash Sarkar	Indian Statistical Institute, Kolkata, India
El Mamoun Souidi	Mohammed V University, Morocco
Bruno Sterner	University of Waterloo, Canada
Vanessa Vitse	University of Grenoble, France

Additional Reviewers

Adam Oumar Abdel-Rahman
Abdelrahaman Aly
Harrison Banda
Andersson Calle Viera
Sofia Celi
Axel Durbet
Yansong Feng
Antoine Gansel
Valerie Gilchrist
Louis Goubin
Guillaume Hanrot
David Heath
Elena Kirshanova
Barry van Leeuwen
Baiyu Li
Dhekra Mahmoud
Fabrice Mouhartem
Mickael Montessinos
Léo Noël
Renaud Sirdey
Jenit Tomy
Stefan Winderl
Yingfei Yan
Leila Zahhafi

Contents

Symmetric Cryptography and Implementation Security

ECC, Pairings, and RSA

Advanced Signatures

Lattice-Based and Post-quantum Cryptography

Lightweight Lattice-Based Single-Party Public-Key Authenticated Key Exchange

Alex Aïdan[1], Sébastien Canard[2(✉)], Emmanuel Fouotsa[3], and Melchisedech Mbeng Nyiang[3]

[1] Université Paris-Saclay, CEA, List, Palaiseau, France
alex.aidan@cea.fr
[2] LTCI, Télécom Paris, Institut Polytechnique de Paris, Palaiseau, France
sebastien.canard@telecom-paris.fr
[3] Center for Cybersecurity and Mathematical Cryptology, The University of Bamenda, P.O.Box 39, Bambili, Cameroon
{emmanuel.fouotsa,nyiang.mbeng}@uniba.cm

Abstract. Authenticated Key Exchange (AKE) is a cornerstone of secure communication, especially in resource-constrained IoT environments where lightweight and post-quantum security are paramount. While lattice-based cryptography offers promising solutions, existing post-quantum AKE protocols often prioritize strong security notions, such as the use of an IND-CCA encryption scheme, incurring overheads incompatible with IoT devices. This raises a critical question: Can one-way security (OW), a weaker but potentially more efficient notion, suffice for secure AKE in the post-quantum era? We address this challenge by revisiting the ALIKE framework (ISO/IEC 29192-4), which achieves OW-CCA-based AKE using deterministic RSA. However, RSA's quantum vulnerability and the lack of lattice-based OW-CCA schemes hinder its applicability today. Our work bridges this gap through three key contributions. First, we prove that the Hash-Before-Encrypt (HBE) paradigm generically transforms deterministic OW-CPA schemes into OW-CCA-secure ones. Second, we modify Bai et al.'s efficient lattice-based OW-CPA scheme to a deterministic variant and rigorously prove its security. Third, we generalize the SPAKE framework to support our OW-CCA construction, enabling post-quantum AKE with minimal assumptions, implement and benchmark the resulting protocol, demonstrating state-of-the-art efficiency for lightweight, quantum-resistant AKE. By relaxing security requirements from IND-CCA to OW-CCA while preserving adaptive security we achieve a practical balance between robustness and performance, paving the way for deployable solutions in constrained environments like IoT and connected vehicles.

1 Introduction

Authenticated key exchange (AKE) stands as a cornerstone of modern cryptography, enabling secure communication between two parties over insecure channels by ensuring both confidentiality and mutual authentication. Its importance

N. El Mrabet et al. (Eds.): AFRICACRYPT 2026, LNCS 16832, pp. 3–28, 2026.
https://doi.org/10.1007/978-3-032-31130-6_1

is further amplified in the era of the Internet of Things (IoT) and connected devices, where vehicles, sensors, and embedded systems routinely exchange sensitive data. In these resource-constrained environments such as smart cities, industrial IoT, and autonomous vehicles the deployment of robust yet efficient cryptographic mechanisms is critical. Many IoT devices and connected systems operate with limited computational power, memory, and energy, making the lightweight aspect of cryptographic protocols not just desirable, but essential. Traditional AKE schemes, while secure, often impose prohibitive overheads on such devices, necessitating the design of protocols that balance security with practical feasibility. In this paper, we focus on a special case of AKE, called Single-party Public-key Authenticated Key Exchange (SPAKE), which is a two-party cryptographic protocol played between a Prover and a Verifier. In this case, the Verifier authenticates the Prover using public key cryptography (hence relative to a certification authority) and the Prover and the Verifier establish a session key later used for secure messaging [17]. We remark that the Prover does not authenticate the Verifier, implying that any attacker can fake a Verifier and establish a session key with the Prover. Hence, the security model is less strong than traditional AKE.

In IoT and connected vehicle environments, such a single-party authentication model offers a compelling balance between security and efficiency. Unlike traditional mutual AKE, this approach eliminates the need for the Prover to verify the Verifier, significantly reducing computational overhead, latency, and energy consumption. This is critical for battery-powered devices or real-time applications like contactless access control, toll systems, or vehicle-to-infrastructure (V2I) communication, where the Prover (e.g., an RFID tag or onboard unit) operates under strict resource constraints. By leveraging lightweight public-key cryptography, SPAKE-like protocols ensure provable security while avoiding the complexity of symmetric key management or bidirectional authentication. The model's simplicity also enables low-cost, SAM-less readers, making it scalable for large-scale deployments such as smart cities or fleet management, where fast transaction times and minimal bandwidth usage are essential.

However, the advent of quantum computing poses an existential threat to classical cryptographic primitives, rendering widely used algorithms like RSA and ECC vulnerable to Shor's algorithm. This looming quantum threat has spurred the development of post-quantum cryptographic solutions, which rely on mathematical problems believed to be resistant to quantum attacks. Among these, lattice-based, code-based, hash-based, and multivariate approaches have emerged as leading candidates. However, lattice-based cryptography has gained particular prominence due to its versatility, efficiency, and strong security guarantees. It supports a wide range of cryptographic primitives, including AKE and their variants, and offers a compelling combination of theoretical robustness and practical performance. Hence, we focus on lattice-based constructions in the sequel. As the cryptographic community transitions toward a post-quantum future, the challenge lies in designing AKE-like protocols that are not only quantum-resistant but also lightweight enough to be deployed on constrained devices. This paper addresses this dual challenge, proposing a Single-party Public-key AKE scheme that meets both post-quantum security requirements and the stringent resource limitations of IoT and connected systems.

1.1 Related Work on Lattice-Based AKE

A natural approach to constructing an AKE protocol is to leverage public-key encryption (PKE) schemes, where one party encrypts a shared secret under the other's public key, and authentication is achieved through digital signatures or certificates. In this paradigm, the security of the key exchange relies on the underlying PKE scheme's security properties. Classical security notions for PKE include one-wayness (OW) and indistinguishability (IND) under two different kinds of attacks: chosen-plaintext attacks (CPA), and the stronger chosen-ciphertext attacks (CCA). It is well-established that IND-CPA security is enough for passively secure AKE, while CCA security is necessary to resist adaptive adversaries, who may exploit decryption oracles or side-channel information to break weaker schemes (see for example [24,36] in the lattice seting). A foundational result in this context is the Fujisaki-Okamoto transform [25], which generically converts an IND-CPA scheme into an IND-CCA one, albeit at a cost in efficiency.

In [23], Fujioka et al. have proposed a generic way to go from a OW-CCA secure Key Encapsulation Message (KEM) to reach a so-called CK^+ secure AKE. Such a property permits to manage weak perfect forward secrecy, resilience to key compromise impersonation, and resilience to maximal exposure attacks. But their result if far from being "lightweight", executing several times the key generation, the encapsulation and the decaspulation algorithms by both parties.

In the post-quantum setting, Kyber (now standardized as ML-KEM) is a leading lattice-based key encapsulation mechanism (KEM) achieving IND-CCA security. However, its efficiency while acceptable for many applications remains a bottleneck for resource-constrained IoT devices. Recent works have explored optimizing this trade-off. For instance, Düzlü et al. [22] propose a modified Kyber variant that achieves IND-CPA security and demonstrates that, when combined with a clever adaptation of the Fujisaki-Okamoto (FO) transform, the resulting scheme can both lead to a secure AKE scheme but also improve side-channel resistance without significant overhead. However, the efficiency gains are modest, as the transform itself introduces computational and communication costs.

An alternative direction is pursued by Kundu et al. [29], who introduce a new lattice-based PKE scheme natively achieving IND-CCA security. While their construction offers competitive performance, it still adheres to the IND-CCA paradigm, leaving open the question of whether weaker security notions could suffice for AKE in practice.

More recently, the PQuAKE protocol [8], proposed as an IETF Internet-Draft, introduces a lightweight authenticated key exchange mechanism based on ML-KEM and ML-DSA, specifically targeting constrained environments. They are only considering IND-CCA secure KEM, and they additionally need a digital signature. Although this is still a work in progress, with which it is difficult to draw comparisons at this stage, this draft reflects current trends toward reducing communication and computational overhead in post-quantum AKE design.

Following [22], one idea would be to further reduce the requirements on the encryption system used, in order to be able to use instantiations that could be considered as "lightweight". This raises a critical research question:

Can the security requirements for the underlying PKE be relaxed to One-Wayness (OW) while still ensuring the overall security of the AKE protocol?

If so, lattice-based OW candidates potentially more efficient than their IND-CCA counterparts could enable lighter AKE protocols. Exploring this possibility could yield significant efficiency improvements, particularly for IoT deployments where every cycle and byte counts. Focusing on single-party public key AKE, this paper investigates whether OW security is sufficient for this case in the post-quantum setting and identifies promising lattice-based candidates that balance minimal security assumptions with practical performance.

1.2 Our Approach

A pioneering work by Coron et al. [17] demonstrates that one-way security under chosen-ciphertext attacks (OW-CCA) can indeed suffice for secure SPAKE, even against adaptive adversaries. Their construction, ALIKE (later standardized as ISO/IEC 29192-4), achieves this by leveraging the deterministic nature of RSA-OAEP. However, RSA's vulnerability to quantum attacks renders this approach obsolete in the post-quantum era. This begs the question:

Can their framework be generalized to a SPAKE-like construction compatible with any OW-CCA scheme, and can lattice-based primitives fill this role?

Positively answering those questions could provide an interesting trade-off between security and efficiency for IoT devices. It would allow the use of OW-CCA schemes instead of their more secure but more costly IND-CCA counterparts. To date, no lattice-based public-key encryption scheme is known to natively achieve both one-way (OW) security and chosen-ciphertext (CCA) security.

Achieving OW-CCA from IND-CPA. A first strategy to reach OW-CCA, is to start from and IND-CPA-secure KEM or PKE, as it has been done in [23] for their CK^+ AKE. Using [26] who proves that IND-CPA with a sufficiently large message space implies OW-CPA (in the quantum random oracle model), and then through the Fujisaki-Okamoto transform [25], we get OW-CCA, as expected. This could then be applied to any IND-CPA-secure KEM, such as [33] and [38], as proposed in [23], but also to Kyber [9], Lizard-based constructions [13], SABER [20], Peikert's proposals [36], etc.

We consider this way to proceed as not optimal for two reasons: (i) using IND to reach OW is like using a sledgehammer to crack a nut and (ii) using the Fujisaki-Okamoto transform leads to additional computational and communication costs, which is not relevant in our lightweight setting. Hence, in this paper, we consider another alternative.

Achieving OW-CCA from OW-CPA. The second natural way to proceed is to start from a OW-CPA-secure scheme. Several recent lattice-based candidates achieve OW-CPA security, including works by Bai et al. [2] and Cong et al. [15]. Again, applying the Fujisaki-Okamoto transform to upgrade OW-CPA to OW-CCA would work, but would also introduce prohibitive overhead, undermining the lightweight goal.

Instead, we propose a novel adaptation of the techniques in [17] to probabilistic encryption, providing a new way to design lattice-based OW-CCA PKE (and KEM). This approach consists in hashing before encryption. More precisely, from a message m and a hash function H, we compute $h = H(m)$ and then use the OW-CPA encryption scheme to encrypt $m\|h$. This enables a ALIKE-inspired SPAKE protocol that retains both post-quantum security and efficiency, addressing the gap left by prior work.

Our Contributions. Given all that, our contributions are threefold.

- Generic transformation for OW-CCA security: We formally prove that the Hash-Before-Encrypt (HBE) paradigm enables a generic transformation of any deterministic OW-CPA-secure encryption scheme into an OW-CCA-secure variant, preserving efficiency while strengthening security guarantees. This subject has been extensively studied in the case of indistinguishability [19,25,34] but, to the best of our knowledge, has never been studied in the case of one-wayness.
- Deterministic lattice-based OW-CPA scheme: We adapt the probabilistic OW-CPA scheme of Bai et al. [2] to a deterministic setting and provide a rigorous security proof for the resulting construction, bridging a critical gap in lattice-based primitives.
- Efficiency benchmarking: Building on these results, we propose PQ-ALIKE, a post-quantum version of ALIKE [17]. It demonstrates the compatibility with modern AKE protocols while maintaining post-quantum security. We implement and evaluate our PQ-ALIKE construction, showing that it achieves state-of-the-art efficiency among lightweight, post-quantum SPAKE protocols, validating its practicality for resource-constrained environments.

The paper is now organised as follows. We first give in Sect. 2 all the material we need for public-key encryption schemes. We then provide in Sect. 3 our first results on the Hash-Before-Encryption paradigm. In Sect. 4, we give all the details of our second contribution on the lattice-based OW-CCA encryption scheme we propose. Section 5 recalls the notion of Single-party Public Key AKE and then gives the (PQ-)ALIKE generic construction. Eventually, we terminate by Sect. 6 by describing our implementation of PQ-ALIKE and the benchmarking we have obtained.

2 One-Way Secure Encryption

In this section, we give the security definition for encryption schemes, and one-way security. We then provide some new results about the security, and several ways to go from CPA (Chosen Plaintext Attack) security to CCA (Chosen Ciphertext Attack) security.

2.1 Encryption Schemes

Public-key encryption schemes form the foundation for secure communication in authenticated key exchange protocols. An encryption scheme can be either probabilistic or deterministic, depending on how randomness is managed during encryption. We introduce both notions below.

Definition 1 (Public-Key Encryption Scheme). *A public-key encryption scheme* Π *is defined by the three following procedures, where* $\mathcal{M}$ *is the set of accepted messages.*

- $\mathcal{K}$ *is the key generation. It takes as input the security parameter* 1^λ *and outputs a private key* sk *and the corresponding public key* pk*. We consider that the security parameter is now included in the public key.*
- $\mathcal{E}$ *is the encryption algorithm. It takes as input the public key* pk *and a message* $m \in \mathcal{M}$*, and outputs a ciphertext* c*. The encryption algorithm may be probabilistic, taking additional randomness* $r \in \mathcal{R}$ *(denoted* $\mathcal{E}(pk, m; r)$ *in the sequel), or deterministic (denoted* $\mathcal{E}(pk, m)$ *in the sequel).*
- $\mathcal{D}$ *is the decryption algorithm. It takes as input a ciphertext* c *and a secret key* sk *and outputs a message* m*.*

Remark. A well-known technique to obtain deterministic encryption from probabilistic schemes is derandomization. Instead of sampling fresh randomness $r \in \mathcal{R}$ for each encryption, the randomness is derived deterministically from the message. Throughout this paper, we employ derandomization to convert our base probabilistic encryption scheme into a deterministic one that achieves OW-CCA security, as detailed in Sect. 3.

2.2 One-Way Security

We present the one-way security notions for public-key encryption schemes. Let $\Pi = (\mathcal{K}, \mathcal{E}, \mathcal{D})$ be a public-key encryption scheme defined by $\mathcal{K}, \mathcal{E}$, and $\mathcal{D}$. We now define the two usual notions of one-wayness that differ in the adversarial capabilities.

One-Way Security under Chosen Plaintext Attack (OW-CPA). We first consider an adversarial model in which the adversary does not have access to an encryption oracle.

Definition 2 (OW-CPA Security). *A public-key encryption scheme* $\Pi = (\mathcal{K}, \mathcal{E}, \mathcal{D})$ *is* (t, ε)*-OW-CPA secure if for any adversary* $\mathcal{A}$ *running in time at most* t*, the probability of recovering the message* m *from a challenge ciphertext* $c = \mathcal{E}nc(\mathsf{pk}, m)$ *is less than or equal to* ε*. Formally:*

$$\Pr\left[(\mathsf{pk}, \mathsf{sk}) \leftarrow \mathcal{K}(1^\lambda); m \leftarrow \mathcal{M}; c \leftarrow \mathcal{E}(\mathsf{pk}, m); m' \leftarrow \mathcal{A}(\mathsf{pk}, c) : m' = m\right] \leq \varepsilon$$

where the adversary $\mathcal{A}$ *only has access to the public key pk and the challenge ciphertext* c*.*

In the public-key setting, having access to the public key *pk* means the adversary has the ability to encrypt any message of its choice. Therefore, OW-CPA security captures the scenario where the adversary can compute encryptions of arbitrary plaintexts but must still find it infeasible to decrypt a challenge ciphertext.

One-Way Security under Chosen Ciphertext Attack (OW-CCA). Secondly, we consider the strongest one-way security notion where the adversary has access to a decryption oracle, except for the challenge ciphertext itself.

Definition 3 (OW-CCA Security). *A public-key encryption scheme* $\Pi = (\mathcal{K}, \mathcal{E}, \mathcal{D})$ *is* (t, ε)*-OW-CCA secure if for any adversary* $\mathcal{A}$ *running in time at most* t *and having access to a decryption oracle (except for the challenge ciphertext), the probability of recovering the message* m *from a challenge ciphertext* c *is less than or equal to* ε*. Formally:*

$$\Pr\left[(\mathsf{pk}, \mathsf{sk}) \leftarrow \mathcal{K}(1^\lambda); m \leftarrow \mathcal{M}; c \leftarrow \mathcal{E}(\mathsf{pk}, m); m' \leftarrow \mathcal{A}^{\mathcal{D}(\cdot, \mathsf{sk})}(\mathsf{pk}, c) : m' = m\right] \leq \varepsilon$$

where $\mathcal{A}^{\mathcal{D}ec(\cdot, \mathsf{sk})}$ *denotes that* $\mathcal{A}$ *has access to a decryption oracle that it can query on any ciphertext* $c' \neq c$ *to get the message* $m' = \mathcal{D}(c', \mathsf{sk})$*.*

The OW-CCA notion models active adversaries who can manipulate ciphertexts and observe the results of decryption, making it a much stronger security requirement than OW-CPA. An encryption scheme that achieves OW-CCA security provides strong guarantees even against sophisticated adaptive attacks.

3 From OW-CPA to OW-CCA Security

OW-CCA security is more challenging to obtain than OW-CPA security since the adversary has access to a decryption oracle and can adaptively query the oracle during the attack. In this paper, we study two generic transformations that upgrade OW-CPA secure schemes to OW-CCA security: the Fujisaki-Okamoto (FO) transformation and the Hash-Before-Encryption (HBE) transformation. Both transformations work in the random oracle model and use derandomization to achieve deterministic encryption with strong security guarantees. As the FO transform is obviously less efficient that the HBE approach, we focus on the latter in this paper.

3.1 Hash-Before-Encryption Transform

The Hash-Before-Encryption (HBE) transformation provides an alternative method to achieve OW-CCA security that is more efficient than FO for schemes with derandomization. The HBE technique has been analyzed in the context of symmetric authenticated-encryption [37] and for specific schemes like RSA [17]. We present a generalization that works for any OW-CPA secure public-key encryption scheme with derandomization, providing a formal security proof that extends beyond the RSA setting.

The key advantage of HBE over FO is efficiency: HBE avoids the re-encryption check during decryption, requiring only hash verification. This saves one encryption operation per decryption, which is significant for computationally intensive schemes like lattice-based encryption.

Let $\Pi = (\mathcal{K}, \mathcal{E}, \mathcal{D})$ be a public-key encryption scheme with derandomization (i.e., $\mathcal{E}(pk, m)$ computes $r = G(m, pk)$ and encrypts using derived randomness). The HBE-transformed scheme $\Pi_{HBE} = (\mathcal{K}_{HBE}, \mathcal{E}_{HBE}, \mathcal{D}_{HBE})$ is constructed as described in Fig. 1.

- **Key Generation** $\mathcal{K}_{HBE}(1^\lambda)$:
  1. Run $(pk, sk) \leftarrow \mathcal{K}(1^\lambda)$
  2. Return (pk, sk)
- **Encryption** $\mathcal{E}_{HBE}(pk, m)$:
  1. Compute hash of message: $h \leftarrow H(m)$ where $H : \{0,1\}^* \to \{0,1\}^t$ is a hash function modeled as a random oracle
  2. Concatenate message with hash: $m' \leftarrow m \| h$
  3. Derive randomness: $r \leftarrow G(m', pk)$ where G is another hash function
  4. Encrypt: $c \leftarrow \mathcal{E}(pk, m'; r)$ using the derived randomness
  5. Return c
- **Decryption** $\mathcal{D}_{HBE}(sk, c)$:
  1. Decrypt $m^* \leftarrow \mathcal{D}(sk, c)$
  2. If $m^* = \perp$, return $\perp$ (or pseudorandom value derived from c
  3. Parse m^* as $m \| h$ (split into message and hash components)
  4. Re-compute hash $h' \leftarrow H(m)$
  5. If $h' \neq h$, return $\perp$ (or pseudorandom value)
  6. If verification succeeds, return m

Fig. 1. Hash-Before-Encryption transform

Properties of the HBE Transform. The HBE transformation has two advantages compare to the FO transform: (i) it naturally permit to use derandomization (using $r = G(m', pk)$) and (ii) it requires fewer operations during decryption (1 hash vs 2 hashes + re-encryption).

3.2 Security Proof

We now prove that the HBE transformation can convert any OW-CPA secure deterministic encryption scheme into an OW-CCA secure scheme.

Theorem 1 (HBE Transform: OW-CPA to OW-CCA for Deterministic Encryption). *Let* $\Pi = (KeyGen, Encrypt, Decrypt)$ *be a* (t', ε')*-OW-CPA secure public-key encryption scheme. Then the hash-before-encrypting variant* $\Pi_{HBE} = (KeyGen, Encrypt_{HBE}, Decrypt_{HBE})$ *is* (t, ε)*-OW-CCA secure in the random oracle model, with*

$$Encrypt_{HBE}(pk, m) = Encrypt(pk, m \| H(m)) \tag{1}$$

$$Decrypt_{HBE}(sk, c) \text{ first decrypts to } m' \| h, \text{ then verifies } H(m') = h \tag{2}$$

$$\varepsilon = q_h \cdot \varepsilon' + q_c \cdot 2^{-t} \tag{3}$$

where q_h *is the number of hash queries,* q_c *is the number of ciphertext queries,* ε' *is the base security bound, and* t *is a security parameter determining the length of the hash output.*

Proof. Assume that there exists an adversary $\mathcal{A}$ that breaks the OW-CCA security of Π_{HBE} with probability at least ε in time t, making at most q_h hash queries and q_c decryption queries. We construct an adversary $\mathcal{B}$ that breaks the OW-CPA security of the base encryption scheme Π.

Setup. Adversary $\mathcal{B}$ receives a public key pk and a challenge ciphertext

$$c^* = \text{Encrypt}(pk, m^* \| h^*)$$

for an unknown message m^*, where $h^* = H(m^*)$. Adversary $\mathcal{B}$ gives (pk, c^*) to $\mathcal{A}$ as the challenge ciphertext in the OW-CCA game and simulates the random oracle and the decryption oracle.

Random Oracle Simulation. $\mathcal{B}$ maintains a table $\mathcal{T}$ of pairs (m, h). When $\mathcal{A}$ queries $H(m)$:

1. If (m, h) already appears in $\mathcal{T}$, return h.
2. Otherwise choose $h \xleftarrow{\$} \{0,1\}^t$, store (m, h) in $\mathcal{T}$ and return h.

Decryption Oracle Simulation. When $\mathcal{A}$ submits a ciphertext c:

1. If $c = c^*$, return $\perp$.
2. Otherwise, for each (m, h) in $\mathcal{T}$, compute $c' = \text{Encrypt}(pk, m \| h)$. If $c' = c$, return m.
3. If no match is found, return $\perp$.

The simulation may differ from the real decryption oracle only if $\mathcal{A}$ submits a valid ciphertext $c = \text{Encrypt}(pk, m \| H(m))$ without querying $H(m)$ (item 3. above). This requires guessing the random oracle value $H(m)$, which occurs with probability at most $q_c 2^{-t}$, which will be taken into account in the below analysis.

Analysis. We distinguish two cases.

Type 1 adversary. Suppose that $\mathcal{A}$ never queries $H(m^*)$. Then the value $h^* = H(m^*)$ remains completely random from $\mathcal{A}$'s point of view. For $\mathcal{A}$ to succeed it must produce a valid ciphertext containing the correct value h^*. The probability of guessing this value is at most 2^{-t} per decryption query, hence

$$\Pr[\text{Type 1 success}] \leq q_c \cdot 2^{-t}.$$

Type 2 adversary. Otherwise, $\mathcal{A}$ queries $H(m^*)$ at some point. Since the two cases are mutually exclusive,

$$\Pr[\text{Type 2 success}] \geq \varepsilon - q_c 2^{-t}.$$

If this occurs, the value m^* necessarily appears among the q_h hash queries. Adversary $\mathcal{B}$ chooses uniformly at random one of these q_h queries and outputs its argument as its guess for m^*. Hence

$$\Pr[\mathcal{B} \text{ succeeds} \mid \text{Type 2}] = \frac{1}{q_h}.$$

Therefore

$$\Pr[\mathcal{B} \text{ succeeds}] \geq \frac{\varepsilon - q_c 2^{-t}}{q_h}.$$

Conversely, if Π is (t', ε')-OW-CPA secure, we must have

$$\varepsilon \leq q_h \varepsilon' + q_c 2^{-t}.$$

This proves that Π_{HBE} is OW-CCA secure in the random oracle model. □

As we will see in our implementation analysis, HBE is very efficient for decryption, making it well-suited for applications where decryption performance is critical, such as authenticated key exchange in resource-constrained environments [5].

4 Our Post-Quantum OW-CCA Encryption Scheme

In this section, we present our deterministic version of the compact encryption scheme given in [2]. We first present the security asumption we will use, then we describe the scheme, and finally, we show its OW-CCA security.

4.1 Assumptions

Setting. We work over the polynomial ring:

$$R_q = \mathbb{Z}_q[X]/(X^n + 1) \tag{4}$$

where n is a power of 2 (typically $n = 384, 512$, or 768) and q is a prime modulus. Elements of R_q are polynomials of degree at most $n-1$ with coefficients in $\mathbb{Z}_q$. For a positive integer d (the module rank), we work with the module:

$$R_q^d = \underbrace{R_q \times R_q \times \cdots \times R_q}_{d\text{times}} \tag{5}$$

Module-NTRU. Module-NTRU improves upon classic NTRU by using module lattices (rather than ideal lattices) to mitigate potential attacks exploiting the algebraic structure, while preserving NTRU's advantages of small key sizes and fast operations [11]. It is based on the following probability distributions.

Definition 4 ($\mathsf{MNTRU}_{R_q,k,\chi_{\mathbf{F}},\chi_{\mathbf{g}}}$ Distribution). *Let R_q be a quotient polynomial ring, k be a positive integer, and $\chi_{\mathbf{F}}, \chi_{\mathbf{g}}$ be distributions defined over $R_q^{k\times k}$ and R_q^k, respectively. The $\mathsf{MNTRU}_{R_q,k,\chi_{\mathbf{F}},\chi_{\mathbf{g}}}$ distribution is defined as:*

$$\left\{\mathbf{h} = \mathbf{F}^{-1}\mathbf{g} \mid \mathbf{F} \leftarrow \chi_{\mathbf{F}},\ \mathbf{F} \text{ invertible},\ \mathbf{g} \leftarrow \chi_{\mathbf{g}}\right\}.$$

This now gives us the following definition for the Decisonal MNTRU problem.

Definition 5 (Decisional $\mathbf{MNTRU}_{R_q,k,\chi_{\mathbf{F}},\chi_{\mathbf{g}}}$ Problem). *Let $R_q, k, \chi_{\mathbf{F}}, \chi_{\mathbf{g}}$ be defined as above. The Decisional $\mathsf{MNTRU}_{R_q,k,\chi_{\mathbf{F}},\chi_{\mathbf{g}}}$ problem asks to distinguish between:*

- *Arbitrarily many independent samples from the $\mathsf{MNTRU}_{R_q,k,\chi_{\mathbf{F}},\chi_{\mathbf{g}}}$ distribution,*
- *The same number of independent uniform samples on R_q^k.*

The best known attacks on Module-NTRU are lattice reduction algorithms (BKZ, sieving) that attempt to find short vectors in $\Lambda_{\mathbf{h}}$. While there is no known polynomial-time reduction from worst-case SVP to average-case NTRU, the problem has resisted cryptanalysis for long, providing strong empirical confidence in its hardness. Hence, the $\mathsf{MNTRU}_{R_q,k,\chi_{\mathbf{F}},\chi_{\mathbf{g}}}$ assumption states that no probabilistic polynomial-time (PPT) algorithm can solve the decisional MNTRU problem with non-negligible advantage over a random guess.

Module-LWE. The Module-LWE (MLWE) problem introduced in [30] can be considered as a balanced solution that interpolates the parameters used in-between Ring-LWE and LWE. It is based on the following distribution.

Definition 6 ($\mathsf{MLWE}_{R_q,k,\mathbf{s},\chi_e}$ Distribution). *Let R_q be a quotient polynomial ring, k be a positive integer, $\mathbf{s} \in R_q^k$, and χ_e be a distribution on R_q. The $\mathsf{MLWE}_{R_q,k,\mathbf{s},\chi_e}$ distribution is defined as:*

$$\left\{(\mathbf{a}, \langle \mathbf{a}, \mathbf{s}\rangle + e) \mid \mathbf{a} \leftarrow R_q^k,\ e \leftarrow \chi_e\right\}.$$

And the corresponding search version of the MLWE problem is then defined as follows.

Definition 7 (Search$\mathsf{MLWE}_{R_q,k,\chi_s,\chi_e}$ Problem). *Let R_q, k be defined as above, and χ_s, χ_e be two distributions on R_q. The Search $\mathsf{MLWE}_{R_q,k,\chi_s,\chi_e}$ problem asks to recover the secret $\mathbf{s}$ given arbitrarily many samples from the $\mathsf{MLWE}_{R_q,k,\mathbf{s},\chi_e}$ distribution, where $\mathbf{s} \leftarrow \chi_s^k$.*

The MLWE assumption states that no PPT algorithm can solve the search $\mathsf{MLWE}_{R_q,k,\chi_s,\chi_e}$ problem with non-negligible advantage.

4.2 Our Deterministic OW-CPA Scheme

We present our compact encryption scheme based on the Module-NTRU problem, based on an initial scheme proposed by Bai et al. in [2]. We first describe our to modify it to a deterministic OW-CPA-secure scheme under the Module-NTRU assumption (Sect. 4.1). We then show that applying the Hash-Before-Encryption transformations from Sect. 3 directly yields a OW-CCA secure variant.

Scheme description. We first modify the proposal by Bai et al. [2] so that it becomes deterministic, using differently a trick given in [5] and adapted to the case of lattices in [9]. Let $R_q = \mathbb{Z}_q[X]/(X^n + 1)$ be defined as above. Let k be a positive integer where $k + 1$ denotes the module rank, q be a prime denoting the ciphertext modulus and p be a prime denoting the plaintext modulus with $p < q$. Let χ_f, χ_g, χ_r be distributions over R_q. Finally, let H and G be two hash functions, seen as random oracles. Our resulting complete scheme is given in Fig. 2 and provide below some details.

At first, the key generation samples an invertible matrix $\{f_{ij}\}_{i,j \in [k]} \leftarrow \chi_f^{k \times k}$ with $\mathbf{F}$ having the following structure to ensure invertibility:

$$\mathbf{F} = \begin{bmatrix} pf_{11}+1 & pf_{12} & pf_{13} & \cdots & pf_{1k} \\ f_{21} & pf_{22}+1 & pf_{23} & \cdots & pf_{2k} \\ f_{31} & f_{32} & pf_{33}+1 & \cdots & pf_{3k} \\ \vdots & \vdots & \vdots & \ddots & \vdots \\ f_{k1} & f_{k2} & f_{k3} & \cdots & pf_{kk}+1 \end{bmatrix} \tag{6}$$

The diagonal entries $pf_{ii} + 1$ ensure that $\mathbf{F}$ is invertible modulo q with high probability.

Then, the critical difference from standard probabilistic Module-NTRU-based encryption scheme [2] is the deterministic randomness derivation. While the initial scheme samples $\mathbf{r} \leftarrow \chi_r^k$ freshly for each encryption, we here compute $\mathbf{r} = G(H(pk), m)$ deterministically from the message, using hash functions $G : \{0,1\}^* \to \chi_r^k$ and $H : \{0,1\}^* \to \{0,1\}^{256}$. This modification, initially proposed in [5], and adapted to the case of lattices in [9], ensures the same message always produces the same ciphertext under a given public key. This is essential for applying the HBE transformation s described in Sect. 3.

As we will see in our implementation section, the resulting encryption scheme possesses two key properties:

1. **Compact ciphertexts**: Unlike standard Module-LWE schemes that require rank-$(k+1)$ ciphertexts, our scheme achieves rank-1 ciphertexts (single polynomial) by using the Module-NTRU structure. This results in ciphertext sizes of approximately 1024 bytes for NIST Level 3 security [2].
2. **Efficient Module-NTRU structure**: Operating over polynomial rings $R_q = \mathbb{Z}_q[X]/(X^n + 1)$ with module rank k, the scheme enables efficient NTT-based multiplication for fast operations [14].

- **KeyGen**$(R, q, p, k, \chi_f, \chi_g)$:
  1. Sample $\{f_{ij}\}_{i,j\in[k]} \leftarrow \$\chi_f^{k\times k}$ and construct $\mathbf{F}$ by Eq. (6) until $\mathbf{F}$ is invertible in $R_q^{k\times k}$
  2. Sample $\mathbf{g} \leftarrow \$\chi_g^k$
  3. Compute $\mathbf{h} = \mathbf{F}^{-1} \cdot \mathbf{g} \bmod q$
  4. Return $pk := \mathbf{h} \in R_q^k, \quad sk := \det(\mathbf{F})$
- **Encryption**$(pk = \mathbf{h}, m)$:
  1. Compute $h_{pk} = H(pk)$
  2. Derive randomness $\mathbf{r} = G(h_{pk}, m) \in \chi_r^k$
  3. Return $c = p \cdot \mathbf{h}^T\mathbf{r} + m \bmod q$
- **Decryption**$(sk = (\det(\mathbf{F}), \mathbf{h}), c)$:
  1. Return $m = c \cdot \det(\mathbf{F}) \bmod p$

Fig. 2. Deterministic Module-NTRU-based (OW-CPA-secure encryption scheme)

Correctness. As the definition of r isn't involved in the proof of correctness given in [2] for $k = 2$, the property still holds with our modification.

Security. Under the Module-NTRU assumptions and modeling G and H as random oracles, the base scheme achieves OW-CPA security. More precisely, we have the following theorem.

Theorem 2 (OW-CPA Security of Base Scheme). *The deterministic encryption scheme given in Fig. 2 achieves OW-CPA security in the random oracle model, under the $\mathsf{MNTRU}_{R_q,k,\chi_\mathbf{F},\chi_\mathbf{g}}$ and the $\mathsf{MLWE}_{R_q,k,\chi_s,\chi_e}$ assumptions.*

Proof. The proof follows the same principle as the one given in [2], except that we have to manage the random oracle for both G and H. More precisely, assume $\mathcal{A}$ can break the OW-CPA security of our scheme with non-negligible advantage. The goal of the proof is to construct a simulator $\mathcal{B}$ that uses $\mathcal{A}$ to solve the Search MLWE problem. Hence, $\mathcal{B}$ receives Search MLWE samples $(\mathbf{a}_i, b_i)$ and simulates the public key pk by setting $\mathbf{h}_i = \mathbf{a}_i/p \pmod q$. By the Decisional MNTRU assumption, $\mathbf{h}_i$ is computationally indistinguishable from a genuine public key.

To recover $\mathbf{s}$, $\mathcal{B}$ invokes $\mathcal{A}$ at least k times to collect k linear equations. For each MLWE sample $(\mathbf{a}_i, b_i)$, $\mathcal{B}$ proceeds as follows to generate the challenge ciphertext.

1. Select a message $m_i \in R_p$.
2. Request the random oracle H on input $\mathbf{h}_i$ to get a random value $\mathbf{r}_{\mathbf{h}_i}$.
3. Request the random oracle G on input $r_{\mathbf{h}_i} \| m_i$ to get a random value $\mathbf{r}_{m_i}$.
4. Constructs a ciphertext $c_i = p \cdot \mathbf{h}_i^T \mathbf{r}_{m_i} + m_i \pmod q$

As we are in the random oracle model, the adversary is not able to distinguish $\mathbf{r}_{m_i}$ from a true random value in χ_r^k. Hence, a ciphertext in our scheme is exactly similar to a ciphertext in [2]. We can then obviously proceed as in the initial paper.

After all the executions with $\mathcal{A}$, if the obtained linear system is non-singular, we can recover the secret by linear algebra, hence breaking the Search MLWE problem. The probability of seeing a non-singular matrix of dimension k over R_q is given in Lemma 3.7 in [2]. We also need to take care of the fact that the OW-CPA adversary $\mathcal{A}$ is seeing samples with the same secret, which mean that we needs to re-randomize the MLWE secret, which is done using a Rényi divergence argument provided in Lemma 3.5 of [2]. □

4.3 Our OW-CCA Scheme

Given the above deterministic OW-CPA secure scheme, we can now apply the HBE transform from Sect. 3 to get a OW-CCA-secure scheme. The resulting final scheme is given in Fig. 3.

- **KeyGen**: Same as base scheme (Figure 2)
- **Encryption**$_{HBE}(pk = \mathbf{h}, m)$:
  1. Compute hash: $h = H(m) \in \{0,1\}^{256}$
  2. Augment message: $m' = m \| h$
  3. Derive randomness $\mathbf{r} = G(H(pk), m') \in \chi_r^k$
  4. Return $c = p \cdot \mathbf{h}^T \mathbf{r} + m' \bmod q$
- **Decryption**$_{HBE}(sk = (\det(\mathbf{F}), \mathbf{h}), c)$:
  1. Compute $m^* = (c \cdot \det(\mathbf{F})) \bmod p$
  2. Parse m^* as $(m \| h)$
  3. Recompute hash $h' = H(m)$
  4. If $h' \neq h$, return $\perp$
  5. Return m

Fig. 3. Module-NTRU-based OW-CCA-secure encryption scheme

Security Arguments. Correctness is obvious, based on the one of the OW-CPA version. Additionally, based on Theorem 1 and Theorem 2, we directly get the following corollary.

Corollary 1 (OW-CCA Security with HBE Transform). *The HBE-transformed scheme given in Fig. 3 achieves OW-CCA security in the random oracle model, under the* $\mathsf{MNTRU}_{R_q,k,\chi_{\mathbf{F}},\chi_{\mathbf{g}}}$ *and the* $\mathsf{MLWE}_{R_q,k,\chi_s,\chi_e}$ *assumptions.*

5 The SPAKE Framework

This section recalls the notion of Single-party Public Key AKE, and provides the description of the SPAKE framework, as given in [17]. We recall the main ingredients of the protocol, then show its description and we finally talk about the obtained security.

Remark. A perfectly valid alternative to our decision to work on the SPAKE framework and the ALIKE protocol could have been to build on the work of Fujioka et al. [23] to derive a CK^{+}-secure AKE scheme. Our OW-CCA-secure post-quantum encryption scheme is fully compatible with this framework too.

5.1 Single-party Public Key Authenticated Key Exchange

As defined in [17], a Single-party Public Key Authenticated Key Exchange is made of two parts: a key generation procedure and an interactive protocol between two parties, a Prover $\mathcal{P}$ and a verifier $\mathcal{V}$.

Procedures. More formally, we have the following procedures.

- KeyGen is a key generation procedure executed by $\mathcal{P}$, which given a security parameter λ generates a key pair $(\mathsf{sk}, \mathsf{pk})$.
- An interactive protocol executed by both $\mathcal{P}$ and $\mathcal{V}$, with the following algorithms.
  - Commit is executed by $\mathcal{P}$ which on input sk outputs a commitment , and some auxiliary information denoted $\mathsf{aux}_{\mathcal{P}}$.
  - $\mathsf{Challenge}$ is executed by $\mathcal{V}$ which on input $(\mathsf{pk}, ,)$ outputs a challenge chal which is sent to $\mathcal{P}$, and some auxiliary information aux_{calV}.
  - $\mathsf{Response}$ is executed by $\mathcal{P}$ which on input $(\mathsf{sk}, \mathsf{chal})$ outputs a response res and a key k.
  - Verif is executed by $\mathcal{V}$ which on input $(\mathsf{chal}, \mathsf{res}, \mathsf{aux})$ outputs k'. If $\mathsf{k}' = \perp$, then it aborts the protocol.

For simplicity, we assume that the public key pk is certified and that $\mathcal{V}$ always checks such a certificate sent by $\mathcal{P}$.

Correctness. We require that $\mathsf{KeyGen}(1^{\lambda}) = (\mathsf{sk}, \mathsf{pk})$. $\mathsf{Commit}(\mathsf{sk}) = (, , \mathsf{aux}_{\mathcal{P}})$, $\mathsf{Challenge}(\mathsf{pk}, ,) = (\mathsf{chal}, \mathsf{aux})$ and $\mathsf{Response}(\mathsf{sk}, \mathsf{chal}) = (\mathsf{res}, \mathsf{k})$ it follows that $\mathsf{Verif}(\mathsf{chal}, \mathsf{res}, \mathsf{aux}) = \mathsf{k}$.

Security. We expect two properties for this primitive [17]. Unforgeability means that no attacker can impersonate a prover without knowing $\mathcal{P}$'s private key sk. Next, channel secrecy expects that no attacker can recover the session key k of an eavesdropped transaction.

Attack model. An adversary $\mathcal{A}$ can be *passive* (eavesdropping only) or *active* (interacting with the prover $\mathcal{P}$). Note that server $\mathcal{V}$ authentication is **not** required, so active attackers can trivially impersonate a reader. Thus, we only analyze **passive attacks** for key secrecy. We first provide the below game, where $\mathcal{C}$ is a challenger, and $\mathcal{A}$ is an adversary.

Security game:

1. $\mathcal{C}$ generates a key pair $(\mathsf{pk}, \mathsf{sk})$ and sends pk to $\mathcal{A}$.
2. Using sk, $\mathcal{C}$ simulates n protocol executions between a prover and a verifier, and sends the protocol transcripts $(T_1, \ldots, T_n)$ to $\mathcal{A}$.
3. $\mathcal{A}$ can request any of the session keys used in the transcripts $(T_1, \ldots, T_n)$.
4. **(Active attack).** $\mathcal{A}$ can engage in up to n protocol executions with $\mathcal{C}$, who plays the role of the prover $\mathcal{P}$. $\mathcal{C}$ answers using sk. At the end of each protocol execution, $\mathcal{A}$ obtains the corresponding session key k.
5. **(Secrecy).** $\mathcal{A}$ outputs one of the session keys matching the protocol transcripts $(T_1, \ldots, T_n)$, not previously revealed in step 3.
6. **(Unforgeability).** $\mathcal{C}$ plays the role of the verifier $\mathcal{V}$ and $\mathcal{A}$ plays the role of the prover $\mathcal{P}$. $\mathcal{A}$ must output res such that $\mathsf{Verif}(\mathsf{chal}, \mathsf{res}, \mathsf{aux}) \neq \perp$.

Definition 8 ([17]). *A* SPAKE *protocol is said to be* (t, ε)-secure *if no adversary running in at most* t *elementary steps can impersonate a prover* $\mathcal{P}$ *or recover the session key of an observed transaction with probability greater than* ε.

5.2 Description of ALIKE

We now provide the description of the generic construction which is given in [17], and called ALIKE in ISO/IEC 29192-4. Additionally to a OW-CCA secure public key encryption scheme $\Pi = (\mathcal{K}, \mathcal{E}, \mathcal{D})$ as described in Sect. 2, ALIKE requires the use of a block cipher $\mathsf{B} = (\mathcal{K}, \mathcal{E}, \mathcal{D})$. In the security proof [17], it is necessary to see it as ideal, using the *Ideal Cipher Model* (ICM), equivalent to the Random Oracle Model as shown in [18].

Instantiated with our lattice-based OW-CCA-secure encryption scheme, we get a quantum-safe version of ALIKE, that we call PQ-ALIKE in the sequel.

Key generation. During KeyGen, we consider that the prover $\mathcal{P}$ executes the $\Pi.\mathcal{K}$ algorithm to get a key pair $(\mathsf{sk}_i, \mathsf{pk}_i)$ for the public key encryption scheme. We also assume that the public key is certified by some Certification Authority.

Interactive Protocol. The protocol between two parties $\mathcal{P}$ and $\mathcal{V}$ is given in Fig. 4.

5.3 Security

In [17], the following two theorems are proven.

Theorem 3 (Active Unforgeability [17]**).** *The (PQ-)ALIKE scheme is* (t, ϵ)*-secure against unforgeability under active attacks, in the ideal cipher model, assuming that* Π *is* (t', ϵ')*-OW-CCA, where* $t = t' - \mathsf{poly}(\lambda, q, n)$ *and* $\epsilon = \epsilon' + 2 - \beta$*, where* q *is the number of queries to the ideal cipher, and* n *is the number of protocol transcripts.*

$\mathcal{P}$		$\mathcal{V}$
Commit:		
$k \leftarrow \mathsf{B}.\mathcal{K}(1^\lambda)$		
$y = \mathsf{B}.\mathcal{E}(k, 0)$		
$\mathsf{com} = \mathsf{pk} \| y$	$\xrightarrow{\mathsf{com}}$	Challenge:
		$r \leftarrow \{0,1\}^\alpha$
Response:	$\xleftarrow{\mathsf{chal}}$	$\mathsf{chal} = \Pi.\mathcal{E}(\mathsf{pk}, r)$
$r = \Pi.\mathcal{D}(\mathsf{sk}, c)$		
if $r = \perp$, then abort		
$\mathsf{res} = \mathsf{B}.E(r, k)$		
$\mathcal{K} = r \oplus k$	$\xrightarrow{\mathsf{res}}$	Verif:
		$k = \mathsf{B}.D(r, \mathsf{res})$
		if $\mathsf{B}.\mathcal{E}(k, 0) \neq y$, then reject
		$\mathcal{K} = r \oplus k$

Fig. 4. ALIKE Protocol

Theorem 4 (Passive Channel Secrecy [17]**).** *The (PQ-)ALIKE scheme is (t, ϵ)-passively secure against secrecy, in the ideal cipher model, assuming that Π is (t', ϵ')-OW-CPA, where $t = t' - \mathsf{poly}(\lambda, q, n)$ and $\epsilon = n \cdot \epsilon' + n \cdot 2^{-\alpha}$, where q is the number of queries to the ideal cipher, and n is the number of protocol transcripts.*

6 Implementations

Our implementation of PQ-ALIKE, a lightweight, post-quantum single-party public-key authenticated key exchange (SPAKE) protocol marks a significant advancement for resource-constrained environments such as IoT and connected vehicles. By combining the *Hash-Before-Encryption* (HBE) paradigm with a deterministic variant of the Module-NTRU scheme, we deliver a solution that achieves quantum resistance, computational efficiency, and minimal memory footprint. This section details our optimization strategies, concrete performance benchmarks on an embedded platform, and the security guarantees provided by PQ-ALIKE. Our benchmarks were conducted on a STM32F4-DISCOVERY board (ARM Cortex-M4 at 120 MHz), demonstrating the efficiency of our implementation in a lightweight environment.

6.1 Parameter Selection and Rationales

To strike an optimal balance between security and performance, we selected parameters compatible with the Number Theoretic Transform (NTT), enabling fast and efficient polynomial operations. The parameter sets, summarized in

Table 1, are optimized for NIST-equivalent security levels while minimizing resource consumption.

In addition to NTT compatibility, the choice of the modulus q is driven by both correctness and security considerations. In particular, q is selected such that the noise growth during encryption and decryption remains well below q/2, ensuring a negligible decryption failure probability. At the same time, q directly influences the hardness of the underlying Module-NTRU problems: choosing q too large may weaken resistance to lattice reduction attacks, while choosing it too small increases the risk of decryption errors. The specific q values used in Table 1 therefore represent a trade-off between these constraints and differ slightly from those in [3] to better match the targeted implementation and NTT efficiency requirements.

Table 1. Parameter sets for the Module-NTRU implementation ($k = 2$, $p = 3$).

Parameter Set	n	k	q	NIST Level
II-NTRU(a)	512	2	32,257	L3
II-NTRU(b)	512	2	51,713	L3
III-NTRU	1024	2	119,809	L5 (future work)

The parameters were chosen to (i) minimize key and ciphertext sizes as public keys and ciphertexts are compact (e.g., 1920 bytes for II_ntru(a)), reducing communication overhead, (ii) optimize cryptographic operations as the modulus q satisfies the condition $n|(q-1)$, ensuring the existence of primitive n-th roots of unity and enabling efficient polynomial multiplication via NTT, while also being chosen to balance noise growth and security requirements, (iii) ensure robust security as decryption failure probability is negligible, and resistance to lattice reduction attacks is based on the assumed hardness of the Module-NTRU problems, (iv) reach a fully plausible security level for real-life applications.

We estimated the concrete security of each parameter set using the lattice estimator of Albrecht et al. [1], evaluating the cost of primal uSVP, BDD, BDD-hybrid, BDD-MITM-hybrid, and DSD attacks under the classical gate cost model ($2^{0.292\beta}$). NIST security levels are defined in terms of classical security: Level 3 requires at least 2^{192} classical operations (equivalent to AES-192 exhaustive key search) and Level 5 requires 2^{256}. Since our scheme is a Module-NTRU construction with rank $k = 2$, the effective lattice dimension input to the estimator is $k \cdot n$. The dominant attack across all parameter sets is the BDD attack. For II-NTRU(a) ($n = 512$, $q = 32{,}257$) the estimator yields $2^{207.1}$ classical operations, and for II-NTRU(b) ($n = 512$, $q = 51{,}713$) it yields $2^{198.8}$, both exceeding the Level 3 threshold by 15.1 and 6.8 bits respectively. For III-NTRU ($n = 1024$, $q = 119{,}809$) the estimator yields $2^{392.1}$, far exceeding the Level 5 threshold. The reduced margin of II-NTRU(b) relative to II-NTRU(a) is expected: a larger q moves closer to the NTRU overstretching boundary while remaining necessary for correct decryption. Both Level 3 variants nonetheless satisfy their claimed security level.

6.2 Optimization Techniques

To achieve state-of-the-art performance on resource-constrained platforms, our implementation leverages several advanced optimization strategies, each tailored to exploit the unique properties of lattice-based cryptography and the target hardware.

Number Theoretic Transform (NTT). The core of our polynomial arithmetic relies on the Number Theoretic Transform (NTT), a specialized variant of the Fast Fourier Transform (FFT) adapted for finite rings. NTT enables efficient polynomial multiplication in $O(n \log n)$ time, a critical requirement for lattice-based schemes where polynomial operations dominate the computational cost. Our implementation employs a radix-2 NTT with degree-2 splitting, as described in [6], to minimize the number of modular reductions and memory accesses. To further accelerate the transform, we use Barrett reduction for base multiplication, a technique that replaces expensive division operations with multiplications and shifts, as detailed in [4]. This approach is particularly effective on microcontrollers lacking hardware support for 64-bit division. Additionally, we precompute the roots of unity (zetas) and their inverses, storing them in static memory to eliminate redundant calculations during runtime. The NTT butterflies are unrolled in a 4-way loop where beneficial, reducing loop overhead and improving instruction cache utilization. The inverse NTT is optimized by fusing the final normalization step, as suggested in [32], to minimize the number of passes over the polynomial coefficients.

Memory Management and Efficient Sampling. Memory efficiency is critical for embedded systems with limited RAM. To avoid dynamic allocation and heap fragmentation, all working buffers (including those required for NTT, polynomial inversion, and key generation) are statically allocated in the Binary Static Section (BSS). This ensures deterministic memory usage and prevents runtime overhead associated with heap management. For polynomial sampling, we use a hardware-based random number generator (RNG) via the STM32's built-in RNG peripheral, which provides cryptographically secure randomness without software delays. The sampling process follows a rejection sampling approach with constant-time loops, as recommended in [16], to mitigate timing side-channel attacks. The public key is stored in its NTT-transformed form immediately after generation, eliminating the need for repeated forward NTT operations during encryption. This optimization is inspired by the "lazy reduction" technique used in Kyber [9], where precomputed representations of polynomials are reused to minimize redundant computations.

6.3 Concrete Performance Benchmarks

In this section, we provide the concrete performance results we obtained on STM32L4R5 (NUCLEO-L4R5ZI board), starting with the encryption system (see Sect. 4) and continuing with a complete version of our SPAKE protocol (see Sect. 5).

Our OW-CCA encryption scheme. Regarding our base OW-CCA-secure encryption scheme, Table 2 compares computational costs for key operations, while Table 3 details key and ciphertext sizes. Those performances have been obtained through a mean (min-max) over 100 execution of each process. Key generation is dominated by the polynomial inversion. While this operation is computationally intensive, accounting for the majority of the ~18.8 million cycles required, its impact on real-world performance is mitigated by the fact that key generation is a one-time operation performed during device initialization, especially in PQ-

Table 2. Performance comparison on ARM Cortex-M4 (cycles $\times 10^3$). Our scheme runs at 120 MHz. Saber [28] on Cortex-M4 as well as NTRU-HPS-677 [27]. ML-KEM (FIPS 203 [35]) cycle counts measured by wolfSSL [39] on STM32 NUCLEO-F439ZI, Cortex-M4 @ 168 MHz. Cycle counts are frequency-independent.

Scheme	Level	Type	KeyGen	Enc/ Encap	Dec/ Decap
Kyber-768 (v2) [10]	L3	IND-CCA KEM	947	1,113	1,059
Saber [28]	L3	IND-CCA KEM	1,147	1,444	1,543
ML-KEM-768 [39]	L3	IND-CCA KEM	1,095	1,104	1,400
NTRU-HPS-677 [27]	L3	IND-CCA KEM	144,383	956	837
Ours – II-NTRU(a)	L3	OW-CCA PKE	18,803	342	266
Ours – II-NTRU(b)	L3	OW-CCA PKE	18,830	341	266

† ML-KEM cycle counts converted from milliseconds reported in [39] at 168 MHz. Kyber-768 [10] and ML-KEM [35] are based on the same scheme; both are included as they represent optimised implementations from 2019 and 2025 respectively.

Table 3. Key and ciphertext sizes in bytes. Lizard [13] targets 128-bit classical security. ML-KEM sizes are from FIPS 203 [35].

Scheme	NIST Level	Public Key	Secret Key	Ciphertext
Saber [21]	L3	992	2,304	1,088
ML-KEM-768 [35]	L3	1,184	2,400	1,088
Lizard [13]	128-bit cl.	1,622,000	34,000	955
NTRU-HPS-677 [12]	L3	930	1234	930
Ours – II-NTRU(a)	L3	1,920	6,144	1,024
Ours – II-NTRU(b)	L3	2,048	6,144	1,024

ALIKE construction. Once generated, keys are reused for many encryption and decryption operations, making the amortized cost negligible in practice.

PQ-ALIKE over HBE Module-NTRU. Our proposed OW-CCA-secure encryption scheme has then be integrated into our PQ-ALIKE protocol, providing lightweight, quantum-resistant authentication. The performance of the full protocol is summarized in Table 4.

Table 4. PQ-ALIKE protocol phase performance on ARM Cortex-M4 @ 120 MHz (mean over 100 runs). Commit includes key generation. Challenge is performed by the Verifier. Response and Verify are performed by the Prover.

Scheme	Commit (cycles)	Challenge (cycles)	Response (cycles)	Verify (cycles)	Prover Total (cycles)
II-NTRU(a)	~18,835,099	1,195,936	380,630	39,502	420,132
II-NTRU(b)	~18,860,584	1,193,336	380,071	39,488	419,559

Note on Commit cycles: The Commit phase consists of a lightweight randomness generation step (7,985 / 7,981 cycles) followed by key generation (~18.8M cycles). The total Commit cost is therefore dominated by key generation, as reported above. Prover Total combines Response and Verify ($\approx$ 3.50 ms at 120 MHz).

6.4 Comparison

Our implementation demonstrates significant performance and memory advantages compared to leading post-quantum lattice-based schemes optimised for embedded platforms. We benchmark against five proposals: Kyber-768 as implemented by Botros et al. [10] and its NIST-standardised successor ML-KEM (FIPS 203 [35]) benchmarked by wolfSSL [39]—both included as they represent 2019 and 2025 state-of-the-art optimisations of the same underlying scheme—Saber on ARM Cortex-M4 by Karmakar et al. [28], NTRU-HPS-2048-677 from pqm4 [27], and the lightweight identification protocol by Düzlü et al. [22]. Rudraksh [29] targets NIST Level 1 security exclusively and is implemented on FPGA only; it is therefore excluded from all comparisons.

Kyber-768 cycle counts are taken from Botros et al. [10] at 168 MHz. Saber cycle counts are from Karmakar et al. [28] on Cortex-M4. ML-KEM cycle counts are from wolfSSL benchmarks on an STM32 NUCLEO-F439ZI (Cortex-M4 @ 168 MHz) [39], converted from milliseconds using the platform frequency. NTRU-HPS-2048-677 cycle counts are from the pqm4 project [27] at 168 MHz. Since cycle counts are frequency-independent, differences in clock speed do not affect the validity of these comparisons. Düzlü et al. report cycles at 24 MHz on the same Cortex-M4 platform; the same reasoning applies.

Encryption and Decryption. Our OW-CCA-secure encryption scheme outperforms all compared schemes in both encryption and decryption. Against Kyber-768 [10], we achieve a 69.4% reduction in encryption cycles (341K vs. 1,113K) and a 75% reduction in decryption cycles (265K vs. 1,059K). Against Saber (speed-optimised) [28], our scheme is 4.2× faster in encryption (342K vs. 1,444K) and 5.8× faster in decryption (266K vs. 1,543K). Against ML-KEM-768 [39], the gains are 3.2× in encryption (342K vs. 1,104K) and 5.3× in decryption (266K vs. 1,400K). This efficiency stems from the compact rank-1 ciphertext structure of Module-NTRU, which requires fewer polynomial multiplications than the rank-$(k+1)$ other designs. Düzlü et al. [22] focuses on identification rather than key exchange; direct comparison is therefore not meaningful.

Key Generation. Our key generation requires approximately 18.8M cycles at both security levels, which is higher than LWE/LWR-based schemes such as Kyber and Saber. This is an inherent characteristic of NTRU-family lattices: the standard NTRU-HPS-2048-677 at the same NIST Level 3 requires 143.7M cycles for key generation [27], more than 7.6× our cost. Our Module-NTRU construction therefore achieves significantly faster key generation than classical NTRU while preserving the structural advantages of the NTRU lattice. In the SPAKE protocol, key generation is performed only once per session by the Prover, while encryption and decryption are repeated across protocol steps. Optimising key generation further remains future work.

Key and Ciphertext Sizes. Our scheme achieves a public key of 1.9 KB for II-NTRU(a) compared to Kyber-768 (1.2 KB) [10] and Saber (1.3 KB) [21]. Ciphertext sizes are competitive: 960 bytes for II-NTRU(a) vs. 1,088 bytes for Kyber-768 and 1,088 bytes for ML-KEM-768 [35]. The larger public key of our scheme is a known characteristic of NTRU-based constructions and remains acceptable for the IoT settings targeted by this work, where computation cost outweighs communication overhead. Düzlü et al.'s protocol [22] offers smaller keys but lacks full AKE functionality.

Memory Usage. In terms of RAM and flash usage, our implementation (208 KB RAM, 53.5 KB flash) is competitive with Botros et al.'s Kyber optimisation (210 KB RAM, 55 KB flash) [10]. Düzlü et al. [22] do not report RAM or flash consumption for their Cortex-M4 implementation. Our memory efficiency is attributed to static buffer allocation and reuse of NTT-transformed keys, which minimises runtime overhead.

Table 5 compares communication costs. Then, NTRU-HPS-677 [12] achieves the lowest cost (14,880 bits); our scheme requires 23,040 bits (II-NTRU(a)) and 24,576 bits (II-NTRU(b)), remaining below all post-quantum instantiations of [23] and uniquely providing a Cortex-M4 implementation without the FO transform.

6.5 Future Directions for Optimization

While our current implementation achieves competitive performance, further optimizations are possible. One promising avenue is the integration of **fast divstep** algorithms, such as those proposed in [7], which could reduce the cost

Table 5. Communication cost per protocol exchange (bits). Fujioka et al. [23] costs are theoretical (from their Table 1); all others computed as (pk+ct)×8. Only post-quantum instantiations of [23] are included.

Scheme	Assumption	Model	Comm. Cost (bits)
Fujioka et al. [23], Ring-LWE	Ring-LWE	ROM	≈80,600
Fujioka et al. [23], Codes	Code-based	ROM	≈52,320
Fujioka et al. [23], NTRU	NTRU	ROM	≈19,756
Saber [21]	Module-LWR	ROM	16,640
ML-KEM-768 [35]	Module-LWE	ROM	18,176
NTRU-HPS-677 [12]	NTRU	ROM	14,880
Ours – II-NTRU(a)	Module-NTRU	ROM	23,040
Ours – II-NTRU(b)	Module-NTRU	ROM	24,576

of polynomial inversion by up to 30%. Another direction is the adoption of NTT-friendly primes that enable more efficient modular reduction, as explored in [31]. For high-security applications, we could also add some masking techniques to protect against side-channel attacks. Finally, the use of hardware acceleration such as custom instructions for NTT or modular arithmetic could provide significant speedups on platforms that support it.

Acknowledgments. We would like to thank anonymous reviewers for their helpful discussions and valuable comments. Third author is funded by the ARES PRD PFS 2022 2027 Programme on Cybersecurity and Cryptology at The University of Bamenda in Cameroon. The work of the second author has been conducted within the Intelligent Cybersecurity for Mobility Systems (ICMS) research chair at Télécom Paris, founded by Ampere, BCG, IRT SystemX, Renault, Solent, Thales, Valeo, and ZF Group, and supported by the Fondation Mines-Télécom.

References

1. Albrecht, M.R., et al.: Estimate all the LWE, NTRU schemes! In: Catalano, D., De Prisco, R. (eds.) SCN 18, volume 11035 of LNCS, pp. 351–367. Springer, Cham (2018)
2. Bai, S., Jangir, H., Lin, H., Ngo, T., Wen, W., Zheng, J.: Compact encryption based on module-NTRU problems. In: Saarinen, M.-J., Smith-Tone, D. (eds.) Post-quantum cryptography - 15th international workshop. PQCrypto 2024, Part I, pp. 371–405. Springer, Cham (2024)
3. Bai, S., Jangir, H., Lin, H., Ngo, T., Wen, W., Zheng, J.: Compact encryption based on module-NTRU problems. Cryptology ePrint Archive, Report 2024/732 (2024)
4. Barrett, P.: Implementing the rivest shamir and adleman public key encryption algorithm on a standard digital signal processor. In: Odlyzko, A.M. (ed.) CRYPTO'86. LNCS, vol. 263, pp. 311–323. Springer, Berlin, Heidelberg (1987)

5. Bellare, M., Boldyreva, A., O'Neill, A.: Deterministic and efficiently searchable encryption. In: Menezes, A. (ed.) CRYPTO 2007. LNCS, vol. 4622, pp. 535–552. Springer, Berlin, Heidelberg (2007)
6. Bernstein, D.J.: Fast multiplication and its applications. Math. Sci. Res. Institute Publications, Cambridge University Press , 325–384 (2008)
7. Bernstein, D.J., Yang, B.-Y.: Fast constant-time GCD computation and modular inversion. IACR TCHES **2019**(3), 340–398 (2019)
8. Blumenthal, U., Luo, B., O'Melia, S., Torres, G., Wilson, D.A.: PQuAKE - post-quantum authenticated key exchange. Internet-Draft draft-uri-lake-pquake-00, IETF Secretariat (2025)
9. Bos, J.W., et al.: CRYSTALS - Kyber: A CCA-secure module-lattice-based KEM. In: 2018 IEEE European Symposium on Security and Privacy, pp. 353–367. IEEE Computer Society Press (2018)
10. Botros, L., Kannwischer, M.J., Schwabe, P.: Memory-efficient high-speed implementation of kyber on cortex-M4. In: Buchmann, J., Nitaj, A., Rachidi, T. (eds.) AFRICACRYPT 2019. LNCS, vol. 11627, pp. 209–228. Springer, Cham (2019). https://doi.org/10.1007/978-3-030-23696-0_11
11. Boudgoust, K., Jeudy, C., Roux-Langlois, A., Wen, W.: Entropic hardness of module-LWE from module-NTRU. In: Isobe, T., Sarkar, S. (eds.) INDOCRYPT 2022. LNCS, vol. 13774, pp. 78–99. Springer, Cham (2022)
12. Chen, C., et al.: NTRU. technical report, national institute of standards and technology (2020). https://csrc.nist.gov/projects/post-quantum-cryptography/post-quantum-cryptography-standardization/round-3-submissions
13. Cheon, J.H., Kim, D., Lee, J., Song, Y.: Lizard: cut off the tail! a practical post-quantum public-key encryption from LWE and LWR. In: Catalano, D., De Prisco, R. (eds.) SCN 18. LNCS, vol. 11035, pp. 160–177. Springer, Cham (2018)
14. Chuengsatiansup, C., Prest, T., Stehlé, D., Wallet, A., Xagawa, K.: ModFalcon: compact signatures based on module-NTRU lattices. In: Sun, H.-M., Shieh, S.-P., Gu, G., Ateniese, G. (eds.) ASIACCS 20, pp. 853–866. ACM Press, Oct. (2020)
15. Cong, K., Cozzo, D., Maram, V., Smart, N.P.: Gladius: LWR based efficient hybrid public key encryption with distributed decryption. In: Tibouchi, M., Wang, H. (eds.) ASIACRYPT 2021. Part IV, volume 13093 of LNCS, pp. 125–155. Springer, Cham (2021)
16. Coron, J.-S.: Resistance against differential power analysis for elliptic curve cryptosystems. In: Koç, Ç.K., Paar, C. (eds.) CHES 1999. LNCS, vol. 1717, pp. 292–302. Springer, Heidelberg (1999). https://doi.org/10.1007/3-540-48059-5_25
17. Coron, J.-S., Gouget, A., Paillier, P., Villegas, K.: SPAKE: A single-party public-key authenticated key exchange protocol for contact-less applications. In: Sion, R., et al. (eds.) FC 2010 Workshops. LNCS, vol. 6054, pp. 107–122. Springer, Berlin, Heidelberg (2010)
18. Coron, J.-S., Patarin, J., Seurin, Y.: The random oracle model and the ideal cipher model are equivalent. In: Wagner, D. (ed.) CRYPTO 2008. LNCS, vol. 5157, pp. 1–20. Springer, Berlin, Heidelberg (2008)
19. Cramer, R., Shoup, V.: A practical public key cryptosystem provably secure against adaptive chosen ciphertext attack. In: Krawczyk, H. (ed.) CRYPTO'98. LNCS, vol. 1462, pp. 13–25. Springer, Berlin, Heidelberg (1998)
20. D'Anvers, J.-P., Karmakar, A., Roy, S.S., Vercauteren, F.: Saber: module-LWR based key exchange, CPA-secure encryption and CCA-secure KEM. In: Joux, A., Nitaj, A., Rachidi, T. (eds.) AFRICACRYPT 18. LNCS, vol. 10831, pp. 282–305. Springer, Cham (2018)

21. D'Anvers, J.-P., et al.: SABER. technical report, national institute of standards and technology (2020). https://csrc.nist.gov/projects/post-quantum-cryptography/post-quantum-cryptography-standardization/round-3-submissions
22. Düzlü, S., Krämer, J., Pöppelmann, T., Struck, P.: A lightweight identification protocol based on lattices. In: Boldyreva, A., Kolesnikov, V. (eds.) PKC 2023. Part I, volume 13940 of LNCS, pp. 95–113. Springer, Cham (2023)
23. Fujioka, A., Suzuki, K., Xagawa, K., Yoneyama, K.: Practical and post-quantum authenticated key exchange from one-way secure key encapsulation mechanism. In: Chen, K., Xie, Q., Qiu, W., Li, N., Tzeng, W.-G., (eds.), ASIACCS 13, pp. 83–94. ACM Press (2013)
24. Fujioka, A., Suzuki, K., Xagawa, K., Yoneyama, K.: Strongly secure authenticated key exchange from factoring, codes, and lattices. DCC **76**(3), 469–504 (2015)
25. Fujisaki, E., Okamoto, T.: Secure integration of asymmetric and symmetric encryption schemes. In: Wiener, M.J. (ed.) CRYPTO'99. LNCS, vol. 1666, pp. 537–554. Springer, Berlin, Heidelberg (1999)
26. Jiang, H., Zhang, Z., Chen, L., Wang, H., Ma, Z.: IND-CCA-secure key encapsulation mechanism in the quantum random oracle model, revisited. In: Shacham, H., Boldyreva, A. (eds.) CRYPTO 2018. Part III, volume 10993 of LNCS, pp. 96–125. Springer, Cham (2018)
27. Kannwischer, M.J., Rijneveld, J., Schwabe, P., Stoffelen, K.: PQM4: testing and benchmarking NIST PQC on ARM Cortex-M4. Cryptology ePrint Archive, Report 2019/844 (2019)
28. Karmakar, A., Mera, J.M.B., Roy, S.S., Verbauwhede, I.: Saber on ARM CCA-secure module lattice-based key encapsulation on ARM. Cryptology ePrint Archive, Report 2018/682 (2018)
29. Kundu, S., Ghosh, A., Karmakar, A., Sen, S., Verbauwhede, I.: Rudraksh: a compact and lightweight post-quantum key-encapsulation mechanism. IACR TCHES **2025**(2), 647–680 (2025)
30. Langlois, A., Stehlé, D.: Worst-case to average-case reductions for module lattices. DCC **75**(3), 565–599 (2015)
31. Liu, Z., Longa, P., Pereira, G.C.C.F., Reparaz, O., Seo, H.: Four$\mathbb{Q}$ on embedded devices with strong countermeasures against side-channel attacks. In: Fischer, W., Homma, N. (eds.) CHES 2017. LNCS, vol. 10529, pp. 665–686. Springer, Cham (2017)
32. Longa, P., Naehrig, M.: Speeding up the number theoretic transform for faster ideal lattice-based cryptography. In: Foresti, S., Persiano, G. (eds.) CANS 16. LNCS, vol. 10052, pp. 124–139. Springer, Cham (2016)
33. Lyubashevsky, V., Peikert, C., Regev, O.: On ideal lattices and learning with errors over rings. In: Gilbert, H. (ed.) EUROCRYPT 2010. LNCS, vol. 6110, pp. 1–23. Springer, Heidelberg (2010). https://doi.org/10.1007/978-3-642-13190-5_1
34. Naor, M., Yung, M.: Public-key cryptosystems provably secure against chosen ciphertext attacks. In: 22nd ACM STOC, pp. 427–437. ACM Press (1990)
35. National institute of standards and technology. In: FIPS 203: Module-Lattice-Based Key-Encapsulation Mechanism Standard (2024). https://doi.org/10.6028/NIST.FIPS.203. Federal Information Processing Standards Publication
36. Peikert, C.: Lattice cryptography for the internet. In: Mosca, M. (ed.) Post-Quantum Cryptography - 6th International Workshop. PQCrypto 2014, pp. 197–219. Springer, Cham (2014)

37. Sabt, M., Traoré, J.: Breaking into the keystore: a practical forgery attack against android keystore. In: Askoxylakis, I.G., Ioannidis, S., Katsikas, S.K., Meadows, C.A. (eds.) ESORICS 2016. Part II, volume 9879 of LNCS, pp. 531–548. Springer, Cham (2016)
38. Stehlé, D., Steinfeld, R.: Making NTRU as secure as worst-case problems over ideal lattices. In: Paterson, K.G. (ed.) EUROCRYPT 2011. LNCS, vol. 6632, pp. 27–47. Springer, Berlin, Heidelberg (2011)
39. wolfSSL Inc. Updated post-quantum benchmarks for ML-KEM and ML-DSA on STM32 (2025). https://www.wolfssl.com/updated-post-quantum-benchmarks-for-ml-kem-and-ml-dsa-on-stm32/. STM32 NUCLEO-F439ZI, Cortex-M4 @ 168 MHz

New Post-quantum IBE Leveraging Maturity, Efficiency and Security of Standard Schemes

Julien Cam[1,2](✉)

[1] Kudelski Group, Phoenix, USA
[2] University of Rennes, CNRS, IRMAR - UMR 6625, 35000 Rennes, France
julien.cam@nagra.com

Abstract. Many Identity-Based Encryption (IBE) schemes rely on the hardness of the Discrete Logarithm Problem, making them vulnerable to quantum attacks. In recent years, lattice-based cryptography has emerged as a source of Post-Quantum cryptosystems, for example with Kyber, Dilithium and Falcon chosen by NIST to be standardized as ML-KEM, ML-DSA and FN-DSA. Some IBEs have also been proposed over lattices, but they can still be considered as interesting theoretical constructions, the community's attention having been more on the NIST competition than on optimizing IBEs, assessing their security, and protecting them against physical attacks. So, in this paper, we build a new IBE scheme from the basic blocks of the highly studied ML-KEM, ML-DSA and ModFalcon, to put both their maturity and efficiency at the benefits of IBE. More precisely, we leverage the Module-NTRU trapdoor from ModFalcon to enable extraction of secret keys, we use the encryption and decryption algorithms from ML-KEM, and the modular arithmetic and Number-Theoretic Transform from ML-DSA. Therefore, being able to reuse code from widely deployed schemes, our IBE is much easier to implement and maintain in practice, and can benefit from existing (and future) optimizations, hardware accelerators, and side-channel protections, with very little to no additional work. We also prove the IND-sID-CPA-security of our scheme under standard assumptions, and precisely describe the algorithms and the choice of concrete parameters.

Keywords: Post-Quantum Cryptography · Identity-Based Encryption · ML-KEM · ML-DSA · ModFalcon

1 Introduction

1.1 Identity-Based Encryption

Let's consider two people (Alice and Bob as usual) wanting to establish a shared secret over a public channel. To do that, they will use public-key cryptography, so each of them needs to have a secret key, and to know the other's public key. However, because they don't trust the network, reliably learning the other's public key is a challenge. In practice, they mainly have two solutions: either a Public-Key Infrastructure (PKI) or an Identity-Based Encryption (IBE) scheme.

N. El Mrabet et al. (Eds.): AFRICACRYPT 2026, LNCS 16832, pp. 29–56, 2026.
https://doi.org/10.1007/978-3-032-31130-6_2

PKI: This requires a trusted Certification Authority (CA), securely connected to every participant, whose verification key is known by everyone. Having generated a key pair, Alice asks the CA to sign a *certificate* containing both her identity and her public key. Once Bob has gone through the same process, they can exchange their certificates and verify them with the CA's public key, to reliably know the other's public key.

IBE: This requires a trusted Private Key Generator (PKG), securely connected to every participant, able to compute a secret key from an identity. Then, each participant can compute the other's public key from their known identity.

Comparison: First, IBE reduces the number of messages exchanged over the network, since it does not require any certificate to be sent. Then, it uses fewer cryptographic algorithms: an IBE scheme is self-sufficient, while a PKI requires a Digital Signature Algorithm to exchange public keys (with integrity), and another scheme to exchange a shared secret (with confidentiality). Moreover, since its first proposal by Shamir in 1984, Identity-Based Cryptography has given simple solutions to many specific problems that would have been hard to solve with a PKI [Sha84]. For example, the users can send ciphertexts without having first to receive a certificate, bringing resiliency to congestion and disruption, enabling deferred delivery, and improving real-time communication [AKG+07,Nat16,Gro12]. IBE can also enable encrypted messaging inside an organization (government, company...) while allowing a unique authority to audit the communications if and when needed [Nat16]. As another example, broadcast encryption can leverage the ability to choose the public key to set it to a policy, only giving the appropriate users the corresponding secret key [TWZL08].

The Quantum Threat: The first IBE schemes were proposed in 2001, based on bilinear pairings over elliptic curves and quadratic residues [BF01,Coc01]. However, they could be efficiently broken by Shor's quantum algorithm [Sho94]. With the current fast development of quantum computing, we would rather follow the global transition to post-quantum schemes, for which we don't know any algorithm (neither classical nor quantum) that would break them.

1.2 Lattice-Based IBE Schemes

Lattice-based cryptography has emerged as a good candidate to replace number-theoretic-based cryptography in a world where attackers have (or will have) access to quantum computers. Indeed, this field has already allowed to efficiently instantiate a wide range of schemes, such as Key Encapsulation Mechanisms or Digital Signature Algorithms. In particular, Kyber, Dilithium and Falcon are three lattice-based schemes that have been chosen by the US National Institute of Standards and Technology to be standardized, as ML-KEM, ML-DSA and FN-DSA [SAB+22,LDK+22,PFH+22,Nat24b,Nat24a].

Moreover, several lattice-based IBE schemes have been proposed, relying on problems like Learning With Errors (LWE), or NTRU. In 2008, Gentry, Peikert and Vaikuntanathan proposed a generic framework to build an IBE scheme from a trapdoored one-way function [GPV08]. This framework could be instantiated, but that led to schemes that were not practical due to the size of the keys.

In 2014, Ducas, Lyubashevsky and Prest used an NTRU trapdoor to instantiate this framework, leading to the first practical lattice-based IBE [DLP14]. Although it is still one of the most efficient IBE schemes, it suffers from the inflexibility in the choice of parameters inherent to the ring setting. In an attempt to solve that, Cheon, Kim, Kim and Son tried to generalize the NTRU trapdoor to the module setting [CKKS19]. However, their work has been aborted because this generalization was concurrently proposed to improve the flexibility of the choice of parameters in Falcon, resulting in the ModFalcon scheme [CPS+20].

In parallel to the work conducted with NTRU trapdoors, Micciancio and Peikert proposed a notion of gadget trapdoors in 2012 [MP12]. The efficiency of such trapdoors have been improved in 2018 by Chen, Genise and Mukherjee, who introduced the notion of approximate trapdoors [CGM19]. Since these works also suffered from the drawbacks of the ring setting, they were extended to the module setting in 2023 by Izabachène, Prabel and Roux-Langlois, who used them to build an IBE scheme [IPR23]. However, since no standardized scheme use such approximate gadget trapdoors, these schemes have been less studied than the NTRU-based ones, which benefitted from the focus on Falcon. In this paper, we thus focus on the NTRU-based family, and more particularly [DLP14], since it is still the most practical lattice-based IBE scheme.

1.3 Contributions

Although some existing IBEs (including [DLP14,CKKS19,IPR23]) are practical, they have some drawbacks, that we detail below. We address them by building an IBE from standardized schemes, in order to leverage their maturity and efficiency, but also to minimize the engineering cost of deploying an IBE scheme in practical applications, by enabling it to reuse code and scientific knowledge from widely adopted schemes. More precisely, we propose a new IBE based on ML-KEM, with some parameters and algorithms from ML-DSA, leveraging the MNTRU trapdoor from ModFalcon to enable secret key extractions.

Strong Security via Tight Reduction: Because of their similar structure inherited from the GPV framework and (M)NTRU trapdoor, our IBE, [DLP14, CKKS19] all achieve the same security properties. However, this paper uses a different approach to assess the security level of an instantiation.

Indeed, the security of [DLP14,CKKS19] is analyzed via ad-hoc cryptanalysis, against the best attack found by the authors. So, the IND-ID-CPA-security of their parameters is not proven, it was believed by the authors at publication time. The problem can be illustrated by [CKKS19] proposing insecure parameters, analyzed against a non-optimal attack (see Sect. 5).

Although the same approach can apply to our IBE, we rather chose to give a tight proof of its security under standard assumptions, in the `IND--sID-CPA` model. Since our proof can also apply to [DLP14,CKKS19], we emphasize that the difference lies in the paper's redaction, not in the schemes' security.

Simple Security Analysis: Beyond the stronger theoretical guarantee, our approach also has practical advantages. Indeed, while the security analysis of previous NTRU-based IBEs is a manual process, we can perform the analysis via a well-maintained and open-source tool, LatticeEstimator [APS15]. When a new attack is proposed against a lattice-based problem, we must manually assess the impact on the parameters of [DLP14], while we can simply use up-to-date LatticeEstimator to assess the impact on our instantiation. This is especially relevant because of the quick evolution of lattice-based cryptanalysis, that makes the original parameters of [DLP14] currently insecure (from LatticeEstimator).

Straightforward to Implement: We build and describe our scheme in a way that makes it easy to implement. For example, all of our keys are byte-strings, and not abstract mathematical objects. In [DLP14,CKKS19], the master public key contains integers, which does not exist on a computer (knowing at best "integers on a fixed number of bits"). Moreover, byte-strings make the size estimations more direct and accurate. As an independent advantage of our design, while all of the above schemes have to be implemented from scratch, ours reuses code from standardized (thus widely-implemented) schemes.

Number Theoretic Transform: The NTT is a crucial operation for the efficiency of lattice-based schemes. In [DLP14], the conditions on the modulus to be compatible with NTT are presented, but the implementation provided by the authors does not use NTT, defining the modulus to be a power-of-two, incompatible with that operation. The implementation of [CKKS19] follows the same path, and the paper does not even mention NTT. Conversely, our scheme uses parameters that are fully compatible with NTT, and all of its algorithms explicitly use it to improve their efficiency.

Optimization and Securing: If we choose to use an IBE scheme, it may need (for example) to run faster, to use less memory, or to resist to physical attacks (side-channel/fault-injection), depending on its application context. To achieve that, the scheme has to go through a careful (thus long and costly) analysis, to determine what is the bottleneck/leakage/vulnerability, and how we should modify the code, or which hardware we would need. Since our scheme is built to reuse existing blocks of standardized implementations, it also allows to reuse the optimizations, the hardware and the countermeasures that have been developed for it, making the above process a lot easier, or even free, in practice.

Efficiency: Our goal is to design an IBE scheme that is able to reuse as much existing code as possible. In particular, we did not try to reduce data sizes, or to increase efficiency, so we can wonder if the resulting scheme is practical or not. Fortunately, a side effect of our design is that our scheme is also close to standardized schemes in terms of efficiency (because we reuse their code) and sizes (because we reuse their formats). Since the standardized schemes have been designed to be efficient and small, our scheme inherits these good aspects.

1.4 Paper Organization

We will begin with some preliminaries in Sect. 2. This will enable fixing the notation, introducing constants, and defining the mathematical spaces and probability distributions, so that the reader can fully understand the rest of the paper.

To transform ML-KEM into an IBE scheme, we first have to define how to map any identity to a valid public key. Then, we must enable the PKG (and only the PKG) to generate a secret key associated with such a public key. We thus introduce a secret trapdoor in the public matrix, that allows to "invert" the key generation function of ML-KEM. These two steps are described in Sect. 3.

Beyond theory, one contribution of this paper is to give a very detailed and "implementation-friendly" description of the algorithms, treating keys as byte-strings, and explicitly leveraging NTT, which is achieved in Sect. 4. In a nutshell (it is of course not so simple in practice), the `Setup` and `Extract` algorithms come from ModFalcon, and `Encrypt` and `Decrypt` are from ML-KEM.

In Sect. 5, we will use this good description of the real operation of the scheme to analyze its security. More precisely, we will give a tight reduction from the decisional variants of the Ring-LWE and Module-NTRU problems to the `IND--sID-CPA` security of our IBE, in the Random Oracle Model.

Finally, we describe our choice of parameters in Sect. 6. We first present all the constraints that guide this choice, and then perform some experiments to determine the optimal values. In particular, we found parameters that allow to reach a standard level of provable security, to achieve negligible failure probability, and to mostly reuse existing code from standardized schemes.

2 Preliminaries

2.1 Constants, Parameters and Spaces

We introduce here some constants and parameters without giving them specific values for now, and refer to Sect. 6 for how to give them accurate values. We let d_{SK}, d_u, d_v, η_1, η_2, k, n and q denote positive integers such that n is a power of two and q is prime. Moreover, we let σ denote a positive real number. With these parameters, we are able to define some useful spaces:

- $K = \mathbb{Q}[X]/_{(X^n+1)}$ is the cyclotomic field of degree n [CPS+20].
- $R = \mathbb{Z}[X]/_{(X^n+1)}$ is the ring of integers of K [CPS+20].
- $R_q = \mathbb{Z}_q[X]/_{(X^n+1)} = R/_{qR}$ is used in the algorithms for efficiency.

- T_q is the image of R_q under the NTT (see [Nat24a, Nat24b]).
- $\mathbb{B} = \mathbb{Z}_{256}$ is the set of the possible values for a byte [Nat24a, Nat24b].
- For a ring A and $m \in \mathbb{N}^*$, A^m is the set of column vectors of size m over A.

2.2 Matrices

We will use the common notation $\mathrm{GL}_k(R_q)$ to denote the set of invertible matrices of size k over R_q. For the rest of this section, we let A be in $R^{k\times k}$.

We let A^{T} denote the transpose of A. If A is invertible, we also let $A^{-\mathrm{T}}$ denote its inverse transpose $(A^{-1})^{\mathrm{T}} = (A^{\mathrm{T}})^{-1}$. Moreover, we let $\mathrm{adj}\,(A)$ denote the adjugate of A, such that: $\mathrm{adj}\,(A) \times A = A \times \mathrm{adj}\,(A) = \det(A)I$.

The lattice $\Lambda(A) = \{Ax\}_{x\in R^k}$ is called the lattice generated by A. The column vectors of A, denoted $(a_i)_{i\in[\![1,k]\!]}$, form a basis of $\Lambda(A)$. The Gram-Schmidt orthogonalization of $(a_i)_{i\in[\![1,k]\!]}$ is denoted $(\tilde{a}_i)_{i\in[\![1,k]\!]}$. We also define the Gram-Schmidt norm of A, which is a crucial quantity for the security of the trapdoor sampling, to be the norm of the largest vector in the Gram-Schmidt basis $(\tilde{a}_i)_{i\in[\![1,k]\!]}$, and we will denote it $\|A\|_{\mathrm{GS}} = \max\limits_{i\in[\![1,k]\!]} \|\tilde{a}_i\|$ [GPV08].

2.3 Random Distributions

In order to rely on standardized schemes, our IBE will sample random elements from uniform distributions (used in ML-KEM), Centered Binomial Distributions (used in ML-KEM) and discrete Gaussian distributions (used in Falcon).

For any finite set $\mathcal{X}$, we let $x \overset{\$}{\leftarrow} \mathcal{X}$ denote the uniform sampling of an element x in $\mathcal{X}$, meaning that each element in $\mathcal{X}$ is sampled with probability $(\#\mathcal{X})^{-1}$.

For any $\eta \in \mathbb{N}^*$, we define CBD_η as the distribution of the sum of η independent random variables, each of them being the difference between two independent Bernoulli-distributed random variables [Nat24b].

For any lattice $\Lambda \subset \mathbb{Z}^m$ and any $(c, \sigma) \in \mathbb{Z}^m \times \mathbb{R}_+^*$, the distribution $\mathcal{N}_{\Lambda,c,\sigma}$ assigns to any $x \in \Lambda$ a probability proportional to the evaluation of the gaussian density function on x, that is: $\exp\left(-\|x-c\|^2/(2\sigma^2)\right)$ [CPS+20].

2.4 Trapdoor Sampling

To extract secret keys, we need to sample from discrete Gaussian distributions over lattices. This is a common practice in lattice-based cryptography, and we present our sampler in Algorithm 1, based on the most standard one [GPV08].

Algorithm 1. `GaussianSampler`

Input: A matrix $M \in R^{m \times m}$, for some integer m
Input: A center $c \in R^m$
Input: A standard deviation $\sigma \in \mathbb{R}_+^*$
Output: $s \in \Lambda(M)$ sampled from $\mathcal{N}_{\Lambda(M),c,\sigma}$

Build $B \in \mathbb{Z}^{nm \times nm}$ by replacing each element of M by its anti-circulant matrix
Build $x_{nm} \in \mathbb{Z}^{nm}$ as the concatenation of the coordinate vectors of c's elements
for $i = nm$ down to 1 **do**
    Sample $z_i \in \mathbb{Z}$ from $\mathcal{N}_{\mathbb{Z},c_i,\sigma_i}$, with $c_i = \frac{\langle x_i | \tilde{b}_i \rangle}{\langle \tilde{b}_i | \tilde{b}_i \rangle}$ and $\sigma_i = \frac{\sigma}{\langle \tilde{b}_i | \tilde{b}_i \rangle}$
    Compute $x_{i-1} = x_i - z_i \times b_i$
end for
return $x_{nm} - x_0$

3 Overview of the Scheme

3.1 Building an IBE from ML-KEM

The Key-Encapsulation Mechanism ML-KEM is derived from the Public-Key Encryption scheme K-PKE via the Fujisaki-Okamoto transform [SAB+22, FO99]. In this paper, we build an Identity-Based Encryption scheme, which can also be transformed into an Identity-Based KEM by similar techniques. So, our goal is to build an IBE scheme such that the encryption and decryption functions are the same as those of K-PKE [Nat24b]. At a high level, this IND-CPA-secure encryption scheme can be summarized as follows:

- K-PKE.`KeyGen`()
  - Sample $A \in R_q^{k \times k}$ from uniform and $e \in R_q^k$ and $s \in R_q^k$ from CBD_{η_1}.
  - With $t = A \times s + e$, output $pk = (A, t)$ and $sk = s$.
- K-PKE.`Encrypt`$((A,t), m)$
  - Sample $y \in R_q^k$ from CBD_{η_1} and $e_1 \in R_q^k$ and $e_2 \in R_q$ from CBD_{η_2}.
  - Output $\begin{cases} u = A^{\mathrm{T}} \times y + e_1 \\ = t^{\mathrm{T}} \times y + e_2 + \lfloor q/2 \rceil m \end{cases}$
- K-PKE.`Decrypt`$(s, (u, v)) = \lfloor (v - s^{\mathrm{T}} \times u) / \lfloor q/2 \rceil \rceil$.

A natural way to define the keys for our IBE is to use A as the PKG's public key, and (t, s) as the user's key pair. However, for correctness, s and $t - A \cdot s$ must be short vectors. This means that, for any $t \in R_q^k$, the PKG must find a short $s \in R_q^k$ such that $t - A \cdot s$ is short, which is known as the Module-LWE problem. Since solving that for a uniform matrix A is hard, the public matrix of the PKG must be constructed together with a trapdoor for the Module-LWE problem (which will be the secret key of the PKG), while looking like a uniform matrix. Finally, the operation of our IBE scheme will look like this:

- `Setup`()
  - Sample a uniform-looking $PK \in R_q^{k \times k}$ with a LWE-trapdoor SK.

- `Extract`$(SK, \texttt{ID})$
  - Compute $pk \in R_q^k$ from `ID`.
  - Use SK to find a short vector $sk \in R_q^k$ such that $pk - PK \cdot sk$ is short.
- `Encrypt`$(PK, \texttt{ID}, m) =$ K-PKE.`Encrypt`$((PK, pk), m)$.
  With $pk \in R_q^k$ computed from `ID` as in `Extract`.
- `Decrypt`$(sk, c) =$ K-PKE.`Decrypt`(sk, c).

3.2 Mapping an Identity to a Public Key

The goal of an IBE scheme is that a user's public key can be derived from their identity. So, we must specify what is an identity and how to derive a public key from it. Usually, we consider identities as bit-strings, to include any data that can be handled by a computer, we hash it, and encode it into a valid public key in the corresponding domain [GPV08].

So, we must publicly encode a bit-string into a valid public key for ML-KEM. However, for a given $A \in R_q^{k \times k}$, such a valid public key is any $pk \in R_q^k$ that can be written as $pk = A \times sk + e_k$, with some very short $sk \in R_q^k$ and $e_k \in R_q^k$. Therefore, a valid public key is a vector that is very close to a small multiple of A, and the associated secret key is the lattice element close to this vector. Unfortunately, we cannot publicly know where are the vectors close to these elements without knowing which is this close element.

The solution is to allow larger sk and e_k [DLP14]. That way, valid public keys are vectors father away from higher multiples of A, multiplying their number until they fill the whole space. This idea is illustrated in Fig. 1, using toy parameters to compare the situations in ML-KEM (valid public keys are sparse) and in our scheme (any vector is a valid public key).

The advantage of this approach is that any encoding of a bit-string into a vector actually maps an identity to a valid public key, so we decided to reuse the `SampleNTT` function from ML-KEM, which maps a bit-string to a uniform vector in $T_q^k \simeq R_q^k$, via a cryptographic hash function. The drawback is that both the secret key sk and the error term e_k will be much larger than in ML-KEM, increasing the probability of a decryption failure. This explains why IBEs must use a larger modulus than ML-KEM [DLP14, CKKS19].

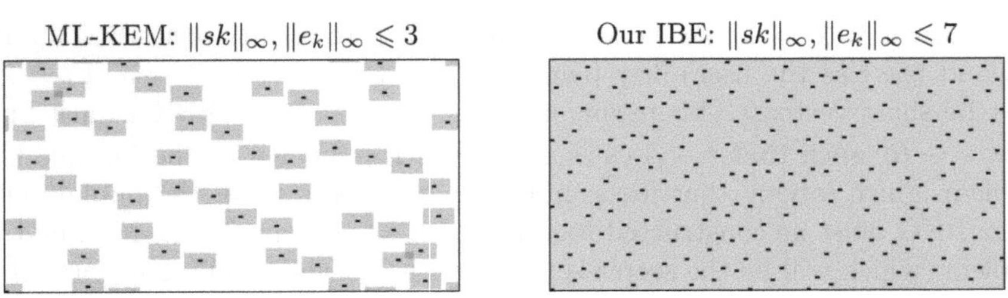

Fig. 1. Illustration of the sparsity of public keys with toy parameters ($q = 101$)

3.3 The Module-NTRU Trapdoor

During the extraction of a user's secret key, the PKG must use a trapdoor to invert the Module-LWE function $s \mapsto As + e$. We leverage the Module-NTRU (MNTRU) trapdoor introduced in [CPS+20, CKKS19].

In a nutshell, the generation of this trapdoor is as follows. First, we sample the coefficients of $(f, g) \in R^{k\times k} \times R^k$ from narrow centered gaussians, and we compute the public key as $h = f^{-\mathrm{T}} \times g \mod q$. Then, we compute a short solution $(F, G) \in R^k \times R$ to the MNTRU equation:

$$\det_K(f) \times G - g^{\mathrm{T}} \times \operatorname{adj}(f) \times F = q$$

The key property is that $B_{f,g}$ is a good basis of the MNTRU lattice $\Lambda_{h,q}$, with:

$$B_{f,g} = \begin{pmatrix} g^{\mathrm{T}} & G \\ -f & -F \end{pmatrix} \quad \text{and} \quad \Lambda_{h,q} = \left\{(u, v) \in R^{k+1},\ u + hv = 0 \mod q\right\}$$

Compared to an NTRU trapdoor (the special case $k = 1$), a MNTRU trapdoor is bigger, but allows to use a smaller standard deviation σ in the `Extract` algorithm. Indeed, σ is lower-bounded by some quantity roughly proportional to $q^{1/(k+1)}$. For our chosen modulus q, using $k = 1$ would not allow to achieve negligible decryption failure probability, so we instead use $k = 2$, at the price of about doubling the data sizes (see Sect. 6 for more details).

4 The Operation of the Scheme

4.1 Setup

This algorithm basically consists in the generation of a MNTRU trapdoor. First, we sample the coefficients of $f \in R^{k\times k}$ and $g \in R^k$ from narrow integral Gaussian distributions, and we restart until $f \in \mathrm{GL}_k(R_q)$ and the MNTRU equation has a solution. Then, we complete $B_{f,g}$ with a solution of that equation, restarting if $\|B_{f,g}\|_{\mathrm{GS}}$ is too high, and finally compute $PK = f^{-\mathrm{T}} \times g \mod q$ [CPS+20].

Sampling f and g: From the original IBE over NTRU lattices, there has always been the idea to sample the coefficients of f and g from narrow integral Gaussian distributions, whose standard deviations are chosen to minimize $\|B_{f,g}\|_{\mathrm{GS}}$ [DLP14]. The authors there conjectured that we can optimally hope for $\|B_{f,g}\|_{\mathrm{GS}} \leqslant 1.17\sqrt{q}$, where the value 1.17 was determined from experiments. This was generalized to the MNTRU case for [CKKS19] and ModFalcon. Both agree that we can reach $\|B_{f,g}\|_{\mathrm{GS}} \leqslant \mathrm{GS\_SLACK}_k \times q^{1/(k+1)}$, where $\mathrm{GS\_SLACK}_k$ is a function of k such that $\mathrm{GS\_SLACK}_1 = 1.17$. However, they disagree on the value of $\mathrm{GS\_SLACK}_2$ (1.2 vs 1.17) [CKKS19, CPS+20]. From our experiments, we found that $\mathrm{GS\_SLACK}_2 = 1.2$ gives the best results.

Solving the MNTRU Equation: Our IBE scheme directly uses the MNTRU solver from ModFalcon [CPS+20], which is a slight modification of the NTRU solver from Falcon [PFH+22, Algorithm 6]. More precisely, this MNTRU solver first computes $\alpha = \det_K(f)$ and sets β to be the first coordinate of $g^{\mathrm{T}} \operatorname{adj}(f)$, and then uses the NTRU solver to find a short solution (F_0, G) to the NTRU equation: $\alpha \times G - \beta \times F_0 = q$. Finally, defining $F = (F_0, 0, \cdots, 0) \in R^k$, the pair (F, G) is a short solution to the MNTRU equation.

Computing the Gram-Schmidt Norm of the Trapdoor: For security reasons, the standard deviation σ used to extract secret keys is lower-bounded by a function of $\|B_{f,g}\|_{\mathrm{GS}}$. There, we can use the fact (explained above) that we can expect $\|B_{f,g}\|_{\mathrm{GS}} \leqslant \mathrm{GS\_SLACK}_k \times q^{1/(k+1)}$ with good probability. So, we can instead lower-bound σ by a function of $\mathrm{GS\_SLACK}_k \times q^{1/(k+1)}$, allowing this parameter to be independent of the secret trapdoor. Thus, in practice, we should ensure that the above inequality holds, restarting if it does not. However, solving the MNTRU equation is a costly operation. Fortunately, the MNTRU structure allows to compute $\|B_{f,g}\|_{\mathrm{GS}}$ only from f and g, allowing to restart before pointlessly solving the equation if it is too high [CPS+20].

Encoding the Master Secret Key: In many lattice-based IBE schemes, the master secret key is a matrix of (theoretically unbounded) integers. This poses problems for implementation, as it is not clear how to represent such objects on a computer. For that reason, we choose to instead encode the master secret key as a byte array. To do that, we leverage the encoding function already defined in ML-KEM, allowing to encode a list of integers into a byte array, using a predefined number of bits per integer [Nat24b]. So, we need to tell the encoder in advance the number d_{SK} of bits it should use to encode each coefficient of the master secret key. Unfortunately, the coefficients of f and g are unbounded, since they are sampled from Gaussian distributions over the integers.

One solution is to bound the tail of a Gaussian distribution, which allows us to choose d_{SK} to make the probability of an overflow negligible. However, we now face another problem on F and G. These are a solution to the MNTRU equation, and not the output of a Gaussian sampler with known parameters. For that reason, we use the same approach as in Falcon [PFH+22, Section 4.4.3]: we run the MNTRU solver on a large number of pairs (f, g), and define d_{SK} as the maximum bit-size of the coefficients of F and G. The results on our parameters can be found in Sect. 6.

Another problem we encounter when encoding the coefficients of the master secret key is that they can either be positive or negative, while the encoder from ML-KEM expects non-negative integers. To fix that, we add $2^{d_{SK}-1}$ to each coefficient. We restart the `Setup` if the result is outside $[\![0, 2^{d_{SK}} - 1]\!]$, and, otherwise, we encode it into d_{SK} bits.

Finally, ML-KEM only specifies the encoding of a vector of polynomials. So, we need to give an order for encoding the polynomial matrix f. In our scheme, we chose to use row-major order, i.e., we first encode the coefficients of the first row, then the second row, and so on. We can also note that, since the MNTRU solver outputs F as a vector with only one non-zero coordinate, we can only encode F_0 into the key.

The Number-Theoretic Transform: The use of NTT accelerates polynomial multiplications, so it is used in the format of the public matrix in ML-KEM. Therefore, we want (and need) to output the master public key in NTT domain, so that it can directly be used as a ML-KEM public matrix.

Algorithm 2. `Setup`

Output: A master secret key $SK \in \mathbb{B}^{(k+1)^2\, n\, d_{SK}/8}$
Output: A master public key $PK \in \mathbb{B}^{kn\lfloor \log_2()q+1\rfloor/8}$

```
repeat
    repeat
        repeat
            for j = 1 to k do
                Sample g_j ∈ R from N_{Z,σ_j}, with σ_j = (GS_SLACK_k × q^{1/(k+1)}) / sqrt(n(k − j + 2))
                for i = 1 to k do
                    Sample the coefficients of f_{i,j} ∈ R from N_{Z,σ_j}
                end for
            end for
        until ||B_{f,g}||_GS ⩽ GS_SLACK_k × q^{1/(k+1)} and f ∈ GL_k(R_q)
    until ⊥ ≠ SolveMNTRU(f, g) = (F, G)
    Define (f', g', F'_0, G') by adding 2^{d_SK − 1} to every coefficient of (f, g, F_0, G)
until Every coefficient of (f', g', F'_0, G') is in [[0, 2^{d_SK} − 1]]
Compute h = f^{−T} × g mod q
Compute SK = ByteEncode_{d_SK}(f', g', F'_0, G')
Compute PK = ByteEncode_{⌊log_2()q+1⌋}(NTT(h_1), ··· , NTT(h_k))
return SK and PK
```

4.2 Extract

On input a public key $pk \in R_q$ derived from an identity, the goal of the `Extract` algorithm is to find a secret key $sk \in R_q^k$ such that both sk and $pk - PK^{\mathrm{T}} \times sk$ are small polynomials. Our algorithm follows the usual approach of trapdoor sampling, first finding an arbitrary solution to the equation, and then using the trapdoor to reduce that solution while preserving the equation [GPV08].

More precisely, we search for a small $s \in R_q^{k+1}$ such that: $pk = (1, PK)^{\mathrm{T}} \times s$. To do that, we will first remark that $t = (pk, 0, \cdots, 0) \in R_q^{k+1}$ is such that: $(1, PK)^{\mathrm{T}} \times t = pk$. Then, we will use the MNTRU trapdoor SK, which is a good basis of $\Lambda = \{(u, v) \in R \times R^k,\ u + PK^{\mathrm{T}} \times v = 0 \mod q\}$, to sample a

$c \in \Lambda$ that is close to t. Finally, we will compute $s = (s_0, \cdots, s_k) = t - c \mod q$ and $sk = (s_1, \cdots, s_k)$. That way, we will have:

$$\begin{aligned} s_0 + PK^{\mathrm{T}} \times sk &= (1, PK)^{\mathrm{T}} \times s \\ &= (1, PK)^{\mathrm{T}} \times t - (1, PK)^{\mathrm{T}} \times c \\ &= pk - 0 \mod q \end{aligned}$$

For security, it is important to never issue two different secret keys for a single public key. Indeed, the difference between two such secret keys would be a short element of Λ. The simplest (from a theoretical point of view) way to tackle this is to remember every generated secret key, although a pseudo-random Gaussian sampler would be much better (simpler, lighter, and more secure).

Moreover, the output of the trapdoor sampler must be indistinguishable from a discrete Gaussian distribution that is independent of the trapdoor, to guarantee that the sampler does not leak the trapdoor. We will refer to ModFalcon, that uses a Rényi divergence argument to prove this if the standard deviation σ is greater than some multiple of $\|SK\|_{\mathrm{GS}}$ [CPS+20].

For compatibility with encryption and decryption from ML-KEM, and in order to optimize these algorithms, we directly compute the public key pk (from ID) in NTT domain, and we also output the secret key sk in NTT domain.

Algorithm 3. Extract

Input: A master secret key $SK \in \mathbb{B}^{(k+1)^2\, n\, d_{SK}/8}$
Input: A user identity $\mathtt{ID} \in \mathbb{B}^{32}$
Output: A user secret key $sk \in \mathbb{B}^{kn\lfloor \log_2()q+1 \rfloor/8}$

1: **if** ID has already been queried **then**
2:     **return** The previously computed sk
3: **end if**
4: $pk = \mathtt{SampleNTT}(\mathtt{ID} \parallel 0 \parallel 0)$.
5: $t = (\mathtt{NTT}^{-1}(pk), 0, \cdots, 0) \in R^{k+1}$
6: Subtract $2^{d_{SK}-1}$ from each coefficient of $\mathtt{ByteDecode}_{d_{SK}}(SK)$ and build $B_{f,g}$
7: With $c \leftarrow \mathtt{GaussianSampler}(B_{f,g}, t, \sigma)$, compute $s = (s_0, \cdots, s_k) = t - c \mod q$
8: **return** $sk = \mathtt{ByteEncode}_{\lfloor \log_2()q+1 \rfloor}(\mathtt{NTT}(s_1), \cdots, \mathtt{NTT}(s_k))$

4.3 Encrypt

The original encryption algorithm from [CKKS19] is based on a usual Ring-LWE encryption [LPR12]. More precisely, it first samples small polynomials $y \in R_q$, $e_1 \in R_q^k$ and $e_2 \in R_q$, and then computes the ciphertext as:

$$\left(y \times PK + e_1,\ y \times pk + e_2 + \lfloor q/2 \rceil\ \mathrm{m}\right) \in R_q^k \times R_q$$

Our original objective is to reuse the `Encrypt` and `Decrypt` from ML-KEM. However, in the K-PKE encryption scheme, the ciphertext is rather computed by sampling small $y \in R_q^k$, $e_1 \in R_q^k$ and $e_2 \in R_q$, and then computing [Nat24b]:

$$\left(A^{\mathrm{T}} \times y + e_1,\ t^{\mathrm{T}} \times y + e_2 + \lfloor q/2 \rceil \ \mathrm{m}\right) \in R_q^k \times R_q$$

In order to reuse the `Encrypt` from ML-KEM to compute a ciphertext for our IBE, we use a little trick: if the first row of A (resp. t) is PK (resp. pk), and the other rows are all zeros, then we can check that the ciphertext computed by ML-KEM indeed corresponds to the ciphertext from [CKKS19] described above.

Moreover, in ML-KEM, the public matrix A is expanded to a uniform matrix from a seed in the public key. In an IBE scheme, that is not possible, because the authority must know a trapdoor for this matrix. However, finding a trapdoor for a uniform matrix A is a hard problem (lattice reduction), and finding a seed that generates a chosen matrix A is also hard (inverting a hash function). Consequently, our scheme cannot use the same format to store the public matrix, and the construction of the matrix will be a little different.

Algorithm 4. `Encrypt`

Input: A master public key $PK \in \mathbb{B}^{kn\lfloor \log_2()q+1 \rfloor/8}$
Input: A user identity $\mathtt{ID} \in \mathbb{B}^{32}$
Input: A message $m \in \mathbb{B}^{n/8}$
Output: A ciphertext $c \in \mathbb{B}^{n(d_u k + d_v)/8}$

Create $\hat{A} \in T_q^{k \times k}$, whose first row is $\mathtt{ByteDecode}_{\lfloor \log_2()q+1 \rfloor}(PK) \in T_q^k$
Create the vector $\hat{t} \in T_q^k$, whose first element is $\mathtt{SampleNTT}(\mathtt{ID} \parallel 0 \parallel 0) \in T_q$
for $i = 1$ to k **do** ▷ Sample y and e_1 in R_q^k
  $y_i \leftarrow \mathtt{SamplePolyCBD}_{\eta_1}$
  $e_{1,i} \leftarrow \mathtt{SamplePolyCBD}_{\eta_2}$
end for
$e_2 \leftarrow \mathtt{SamplePolyCBD}_{\eta_2}$
$\hat{y} = \mathtt{NTT}(y)$
$u = \mathtt{NTT}^{-1}(\hat{A}^{\mathrm{T}} \circ \hat{y}) + e_1$
$\mu = \mathtt{Decompress}_1(\mathtt{ByteDecode}_1(m))$
$v = \mathtt{NTT}^{-1}(\hat{t}^{\mathrm{T}} \circ \hat{y}) + e_2 + \mu$
$c_1 = \mathtt{ByteEncode}_{d_u}(\mathtt{Compress}_{d_u}(u))$
$c_2 = \mathtt{ByteEncode}_{d_v}(\mathtt{Compress}_{d_v}(v))$
return $c = (c_1 \parallel c_2)$

4.4 Decrypt

The `Decrypt` algorithm is already the exact same in ML-KEM and [CKKS19], so we can simply pass our ciphertext encrypted like in [CKKS19] to the `Decrypt` algorithm of ML-KEM.

Algorithm 5. `Decrypt`

Input: A user secret key $sk \in \mathbb{B}^{kn\lfloor\log_2()q+1\rfloor/8}$
Input: A ciphertext $c \in \mathbb{B}^{n(d_u k+d_v)/8}$
Output: A message $m \in \mathbb{B}^{n/8}$

1: $c_1 = c[0 : d_u \times k \times n \,/\, 8]$
2: $c_2 = c[d_u \times k \times n \,/\, 8 : n \times (d_u \times k + d_v) \,/\, 8]$
3: $u' = \texttt{Decompress}_{d_u}(\texttt{ByteDecode}_{d_u}(c_1))$
4: $v' = \texttt{Decompress}_{d_v}(\texttt{ByteDecode}_{d_v}(c_2))$
5: $\hat{s} = \texttt{ByteDecode}_{\lfloor\log_2()q+1\rfloor}(sk)$
6: $w = v' - \texttt{NTT}^{-1}(\hat{s}^{\mathrm{T}} \circ \texttt{NTT}(u'))$
7: **return** $m = \texttt{ByteEncode}_1(\texttt{Compress}_1(w))$

4.5 Proof-of-Concept Implementation

We implemented the algorithms described in the previous subsections in Python, and the result is available on a public GitHub repository [Cam25]. This clean proof-of-concept implementation has several purposes: illustrate how easy it is to implement this IBE from standardized schemes, check that everything works as expected, and give a (very rough) idea of the running time. Indeed, even if a C implementation would be needed to precisely measure the running time and memory usage, this Python implementation still allows to check that our scheme is roughly practical, since encryption and decryption both take approximately 15ms on a laptop with a 12th gen Intel Core i7 (2.2GHz).

5 Provable Security

In this section, we tightly bound our IBE's security to standard problems over lattices. To achieve that, we will extensively use security games, which oppose a challenger $\mathcal{C}$ generating a random instance of some problem or scheme, and an adversary $\mathcal{A}$ trying to solve the problem or to break some security property. At the end of the game, the challenger outputs $\top$ if the adversary succeeded, and $\bot$ otherwise. In this paper, the adversary will have to guess a bit $b \in \{0,1\}$. So, we define the (normalized) advantage of an adversary $\mathcal{A}$ in a game $\mathcal{G}$ as:

$$\mathrm{Adv}_{\mathcal{G}}(\mathcal{A}) = 2\left|\mathbb{P}(\top) - 1/2\right|$$

A problem is said to be hard, or a scheme is said to be secure (for some definition of security), if no polynomial-time adversary has non-negligible advantage in the corresponding game [BF01].

5.1 Security Models for IBE

The definition of the game is what defines the security property, which is denoted by an acronym containing first the target of the adversary (what they try to do), and then their possibilities (how they can do it).

Regarding encryption, there mainly are two targets that are used in practice. One-Wayness (OW) is the weakest security property (it is the hardest to break, so the easiest to achieve), asking $\mathcal{A}$ to recover the message hidden in a random ciphertext c. Indistinguishability (IND) is the stronger property that we want in practice. Here, $\mathcal{A}$ first chooses two messages m_0 and m_1 and sends them to the challenger. $\mathcal{C}$ picks a random bit b and sends an encryption c of m_b. The goal of $\mathcal{A}$ is then to guess the value of b.

In any security game related to public-key cryptography, $\mathcal{C}$ generates a key pair and gives the public key to $\mathcal{A}$. Then, for usual Public-Key Encryption, we mainly have two possibilities. In a Chosen-Plaintext Attack (CPA), $\mathcal{A}$ can only use the public key they received to encrypt messages. In the stronger Chosen-Ciphertext Attack (CCA) model, $\mathcal{A}$ is given access to a so-called decryption oracle, which means that $\mathcal{A}$ can ask $\mathcal{C}$ to decrypt any ciphertext (except c).

When considering Identity-Based Encryption, $\mathcal{A}$ can choose the challenge identity ID* that $\mathcal{C}$ will use to encrypt the challenge ciphertext, but we have here two possible security models. In the Selective-Identity model (sID), $\mathcal{A}$ chooses ID* at the very beginning of the game, before $\mathcal{C}$ has even generated a key pair. In the stronger Full-Identity model (ID), $\mathcal{A}$ chooses ID* just before receiving the challenge ciphertext c. Regardless of this choice, $\mathcal{A}$ is given access to an extraction oracle, which means that $\mathcal{A}$ can ask $\mathcal{C}$ to get the secret key associated to any identity (except ID*) [GH05].

In our paper, we leverage the widely-used Random Oracle Model, which is a way to handle an ideal hash function in security proofs. Concretely, we assume the underlying hash functions to be cryptographically-secure, preventing $\mathcal{A}$ from relying on any particular structure on their outputs. Therefore, we model that by giving $\mathcal{A}$ access to a so-called random oracle, which means that $\mathcal{A}$ can ask $\mathcal{C}$ for the hash of any identity [BR93].

Putting it all together, the strongest security model for a PKE scheme is IND-CCA. However, in 1999, Fujisaki and Okamoto proposed a way to build an IND-CCA-secure scheme given an IND-CPA-secure one, with little impact on performances [FO99]. Therefore, many Key-Establishment Mechanisms, including ML-KEM, are built from an IND-CPA-secure PKE scheme with this transform [Nat24b]. Since it also applies to IBE, we can focus on the CPA model like it was done for [DLP14].

Therefore, regarding IBE, we would want to prove the IND-ID-CPA-security, enabling to reach IND-ID-CCA-security via the FO-transform. However, this model is not really convenient for security proofs. This mainly comes from the impossibility for $\mathcal{C}$ to choose a special value for the hash of the challenge identity, since $\mathcal{A}$ could query the hash of ID* before sending it to $\mathcal{C}$.

One solution can be to try to guess which of the queried identity will be the challenge, but this engenders a loss in the tightness of the reduction [GPV08]. Another solution can be to analyze the best attack we find against the scheme, but this results in a (debatable) empirical hint, not a proof [DLP14]. For example, [CKKS19] based its security on a non-optimal attack, leading to an overly optimistic analysis of the security level (more details in Sect. 5.2). In [DLP14], the best attack directly tries to decrypt the challenge ciphertext, without leveraging any oracle, nor the ability to choose the challenge identity according to the public key and the previous answers of the oracles. Strictly speaking, their analysis is therefore more related to the weakest model (OW-sID-CPA) than to the strong target IND-ID-CPA. Since their analysis also applies to our scheme, this suggests that stronger adversaries have no further possibilities in practice.

In this paper, we prove that our scheme is IND--sID-CPA-secure as soon as the decisional variants of the Ring-LWE and Module-NTRU problems are hard. Interestingly, [DLP14] and our IBE being very similar, they satisfy the same security properties in practice. So, our proof also applies for the IND--sID-CPA-security of [DLP14] (replacing MNTRU by NTRU), as well as the analysis from [DLP14] also gives the same confidence in the IND-ID-CPA-security of our IBE.

5.2 The Underlying Hard Problems

The security of our IBE scheme relies on the decisional variants of two lattice-related problems: Ring-LWE and Module-NTRU. These two problems are currently conjectured post-quantum because we don't know any algorithm able to win the game with non-negligible advantage, neither for a classical nor for a quantum computer.

Decisional Ring-LWE

- $\mathcal{C}^{\text{RLWE}}$ samples uniform $a \in R_q^{k+1}$.
- $\mathcal{C}^{\text{RLWE}}$ samples uniform $c \in \{0, 1\}$.
- If $c = 0$:
  - $\mathcal{C}^{\text{RLWE}}$ samples uniform $b \in R_q^{k+1}$.
- If $c = 1$:
  - $\mathcal{C}^{\text{RLWE}}$ samples $s \in R_q$ from CBD_{η_1}.
  - $\mathcal{C}^{\text{RLWE}}$ samples $e \in R_q^{k+1}$ from CBD_{η_2}.
  - $\mathcal{C}^{\text{RLWE}}$ computes $b = a \times s + e$.
- $\mathcal{C}^{\text{RLWE}}$ sends a and b to $\mathcal{A}^{\text{RLWE}}$.
- $\mathcal{A}^{\text{RLWE}}$ sends $c' \in \{0, 1\}$ to $\mathcal{C}^{\text{RLWE}}$.
- $\mathcal{C}^{\text{RLWE}}$ outputs $\top$ if $c = c'$, and $\bot$ otherwise.

Decisional Module-NTRU

- $\mathcal{C}^{\text{MNTRU}}$ samples uniform $c \in \{0, 1\}$.
- If $c = 0$:
  - $\mathcal{C}^{\text{MNTRU}}$ samples uniform $h \in R_q^k$.
- If $c = 1$:
  - $\mathcal{C}^{\text{MNTRU}}$ computes $h \in R_q^k$ as in Algorithm 2.
- $\mathcal{C}^{\text{MNTRU}}$ sends h to $\mathcal{A}^{\text{MNTRU}}$.
- $\mathcal{A}^{\text{MNTRU}}$ sends $c' \in \{0, 1\}$ to $\mathcal{C}^{\text{MNTRU}}$.
- $\mathcal{C}^{\text{MNTRU}}$ outputs $\top$ if $c = c'$, and $\bot$ otherwise.

The Role of the Dimension Parameter. We want to highlight here the ambiguous role of k in the previously defined problems, and the implications for the security of schemes based upon them.

The Module-NTRU problem can be solved by modelling it as a lattice-reduction problem, where the lattice dimension is proportional to nk. Since the hardness of lattice reduction increases with the dimension, the security increases together with k. This fact explains why ModFalcon becomes harder to break when k grows.

However, regarding Ring-LWE, k corresponds to the number of samples given to the adversary. As a consequence, increasing k gives more knowledge to the adversary, and thus the security can only decrease. This explains why an IBE based on Ring-LWE encryption and MNTRU trapdoor becomes no more secure when k increases (contrary to what is stated in [CKKS19]), especially since the best attack is to break the Ring-LWE encryption itself.

5.3 Game 0 - The IND-sID-CPA Security Model

The security property that we want our IBE scheme to achieve is called "*Indistinguishability of ciphertexts under a selective identity chosen plaintext attack*", and is denoted `IND--sID-CPA` [GH05]. We describe the associated security game in Fig. 2. In that model, the adversary can query the random oracle and the extraction oracle in any order and as many times as needed, before choosing the challenge messages and after having received the challenge ciphertext.

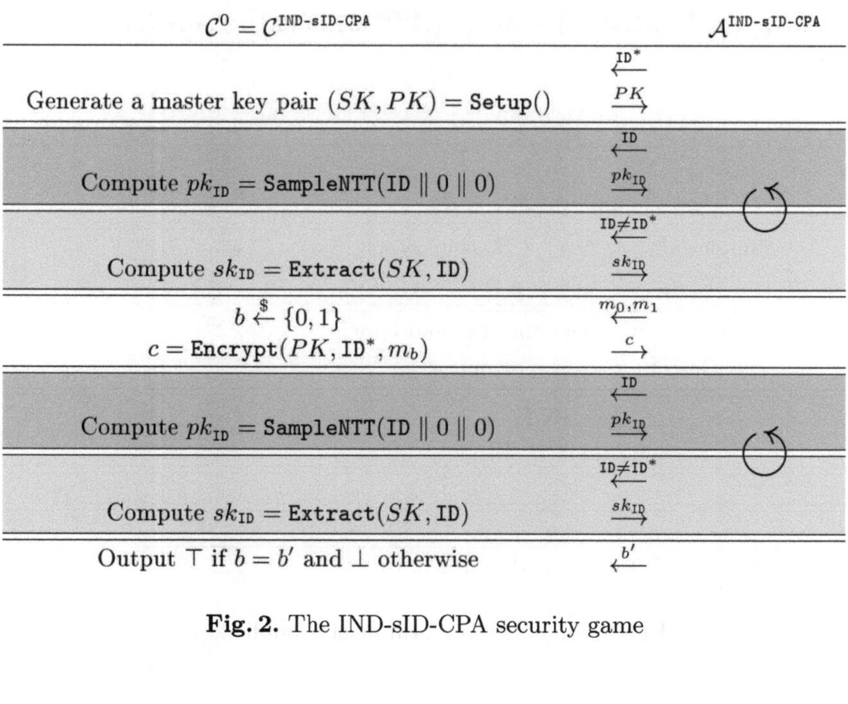

Fig. 2. The IND-sID-CPA security game

5.4 Game 1 - Not Using the Trapdoor

When asked for the hash of a new identity ID, the new challenger $\mathcal{C}^1$ samples small $sk_{\mathtt{ID}} \in R_q^k$ and $e \in R_q$ from discrete Gaussian distribution $\mathcal{N}_{R,\sigma}$, and computes the public key $pk_{\mathtt{ID}} = PK \cdot sk_{\mathtt{ID}} + e$. Finally, $\mathcal{C}^1$ stores $(\mathtt{ID}, pk_{\mathtt{ID}}, sk_{\mathtt{ID}})$ in a hash table $\mathscr{H}$, and sends $pk_{\mathtt{ID}}$ to $\mathcal{A}^{\mathtt{IND}\text{-}}$-sID-CPA. When asked for the hash of an identity that is already in $\mathscr{H}$, $\mathcal{C}^1$ answers with the corresponding $pk_{\mathtt{ID}}$.

When asked for a secret key associated to an identity $\mathtt{ID} \neq \mathtt{ID}^*$, $\mathcal{C}^1$ checks if ID is already in $\mathscr{H}$. If not, it executes the random oracle as described above. Then, it sends the corresponding $sk_{\mathtt{ID}}$ to $\mathcal{A}^{\mathtt{IND}\text{-}}$-sID-CPA.

The fact that the adversary cannot tell which of $sk_{\mathtt{ID}}$ or $pk_{\mathtt{ID}}$ has been generated from the other comes from how close the output of the trapdoor sampler is from a discrete Gaussian. In Sect. 6, we will choose parameters so that the distance between these two distributions is below $2^{-\lambda}$, where λ is the security parameter. Therefore, we can write:

$$\left|\mathrm{Adv}_{\mathcal{G}_1}\left(\mathcal{A}^{\mathtt{IND}\text{-}}\text{-}\mathtt{sID}\text{-}\mathtt{CPA}\right) - \mathrm{Adv}_{\mathcal{G}_0}\left(\mathcal{A}^{\mathtt{IND}\text{-}}\text{-}\mathtt{sID}\text{-}\mathtt{CPA}\right)\right| \leqslant 2^{-\lambda}$$

5.5 Game 2 - Sampling the Master Public Key at Random

This game changes the generation of the master key pair. Since $\mathcal{C}^2$ (like $\mathcal{C}^1$ before) does not need to really extract keys, we can forget the unused SK. Then, the real difference from Game 1 is that PK is generated uniformly at random. The fact that the adversary cannot tell the difference comes from the Decisional-MNTRU problem. More precisely, we have:

$$\left|\mathrm{Adv}_{\mathcal{G}_2}\left(\mathcal{A}^{\mathtt{IND}\text{-}}\text{-}\mathtt{sID}\text{-}\mathtt{CPA}\right) - \mathrm{Adv}_{\mathcal{G}_1}\left(\mathcal{A}^{\mathtt{IND}\text{-}}\text{-}\mathtt{sID}\text{-}\mathtt{CPA}\right)\right| \leqslant \mathrm{Adv}\left(\mathcal{A}^{\mathrm{MNTRU}}\right)$$

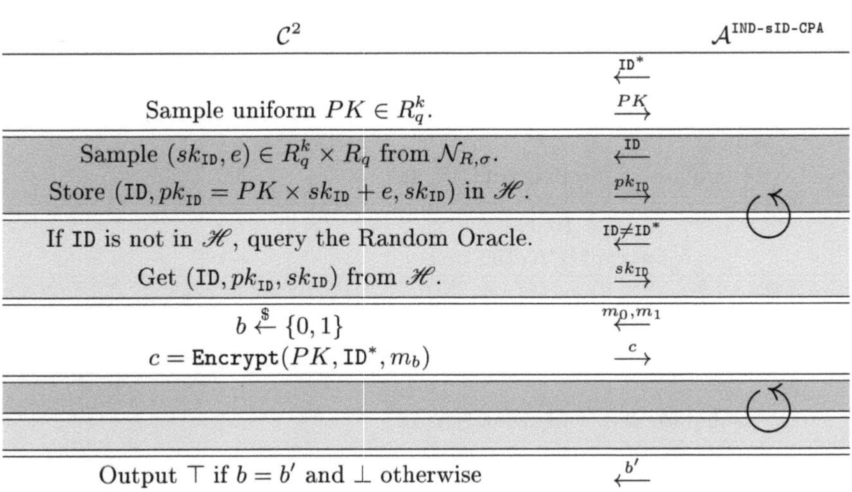

Fig. 3. Game 2 - Uniform master public key

5.6 Game 3 - Reduction from Decisional-RLWE

In Fig. 4, we describe how a reduction $\mathcal{R}$ attacking the Decisional-RLWE problem can emulate the challenger $\mathcal{C}^2$ in order to leverage $\mathcal{A}^{\texttt{IND-sID-CPA}}$ (Fig. 3).

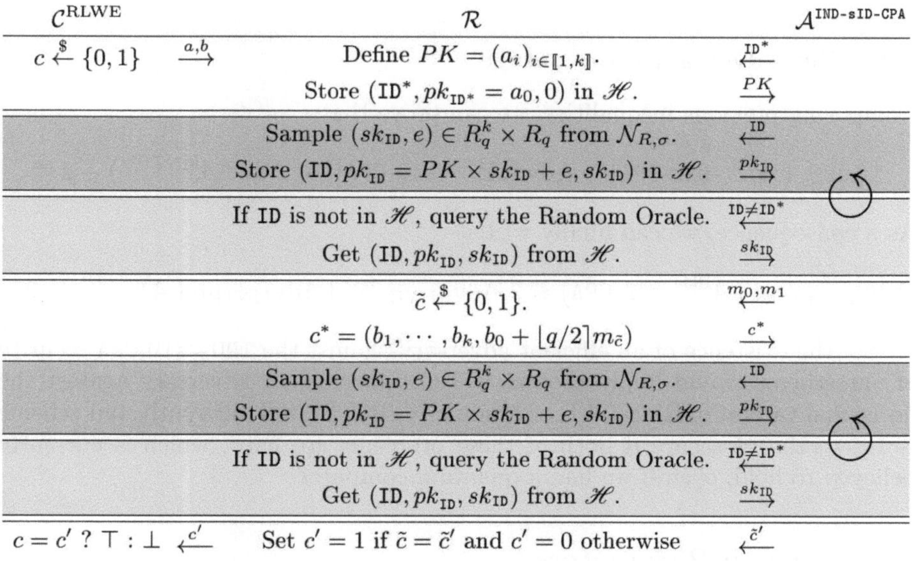

Fig. 4. Game 3 - Reduction from Decisional-RLWE

The main subtlety lies in the computation of c^*, which should be a valid encryption of the challenge message if $c = 1$. In that case, since $b = as + e'$, we can denote $y = s$, $e_1 = (e'_i)_{i \in [\![1,k]\!]}$ and $e_2 = e'_0$. Then, we indeed have:

$$(u, v) = \left(PK^{\mathrm{T}} \times y + e_1,\ pk_{\texttt{ID}^*}^{\mathrm{T}} \times y + e_2 + \lfloor q/2 \rceil m_{\tilde{c}}\right) = \left((b_i)_{i \in [\![1,k]\!]},\ b_0 + \lfloor q/2 \rceil m_{\tilde{c}}\right)$$

The advantage of $\mathcal{R}$ in solving the decisional version of the Ring-LWE problem can be expressed as follows:

$$\begin{aligned}
\text{Adv}_{\text{RLWE}}(\mathcal{R}) &= 2\,|\mathbb{P}(\top) - 1/2| \\
&= 2\,|\mathbb{P}(c = 0) \times \mathbb{P}(\top \mid c = 0) + \mathbb{P}(c = 1) \times \mathbb{P}(\top \mid c = 1) - 1/2| \\
&= |\mathbb{P}(\top \mid c = 0) + \mathbb{P}(\top \mid c = 1) - 1| \\
&= |\mathbb{P}(\tilde{c} \neq \tilde{c}' \mid c = 0) + \mathbb{P}(\tilde{c} = \tilde{c}' \mid c = 1) - 1|
\end{aligned}$$

If $c = 0$, then $\mathcal{A}^{\texttt{IND-sID-CPA}}$ faces a theoretically-secure one-time pad, so its probability to find the value of the bit $\tilde{c}$ is strictly equal to $1/2$.

If $c = 1$, then $\mathcal{A}^{\texttt{IND-sID-CPA}}$ faces Game 2, so its probability to find $\tilde{c}$ is related to its advantage in that game.

Finally, we obtain the following result:

$$\begin{aligned}\mathrm{Adv}_{\mathrm{RLWE}}(\mathcal{R}) &= \left|1/2 + \mathbb{P}(\tilde{c} = \tilde{c}' \mid c = 1) - 1\right| \\ &= 2\left|\mathbb{P}(\tilde{c} = \tilde{c}' \mid c = 1) - 1/2\right|/2 \\ &= \mathrm{Adv}_{\mathcal{G}_2}\left(\mathcal{A}^{\texttt{IND-}}\texttt{-sID-CPA}\right)/2\end{aligned}$$

5.7 The Adversary's Advantage

Composing previous inequalities, we can prove that:

$$\left|\mathrm{Adv}_{\mathcal{G}_2}\left(\mathcal{A}^{\texttt{IND-}}\texttt{-sID-CPA}\right) - \mathrm{Adv}\left(\mathcal{A}^{\texttt{IND-}}\texttt{-sID-CPA}\right)\right| \leqslant \mathrm{Adv}\left(\mathcal{A}^{\mathrm{MNTRU}}\right) + 2^{-\lambda}$$

As a consequence, we can finally write:

$$\mathrm{Adv}_{\texttt{IND--sID-CPA}}\left(\mathcal{A}^{\texttt{IND-}}\texttt{-sID-CPA}\right) \leqslant 2\ \mathrm{Adv}_{\mathrm{RLWE}}(\mathcal{R}) + \mathrm{Adv}_{\mathrm{MNTRU}}\left(\mathcal{A}^{\mathrm{MNTRU}}\right) + 2^{-\lambda}$$

So, the existence of an efficient adversary against the IND--sID-CPA security of our scheme would imply the existence of an efficient adversary against the decisional variant of Ring-LWE or Module-NTRU. Stated differently, our scheme is IND--sID-CPA-secure if both of these problems are hard, which is currently believed to hold, even if we had a quantum computer.

6 Concrete Parameters

As in [DLP14], we focus on the CPA-secure IBE for simplicity and fair comparison. To choose concrete parameters, we must take into account some criteria. Some of them are common to all cryptosystems (security, data sizes, running time), some are specific to lattice-based cryptosystems (NTT, failure probability), and some are specific to our scheme, or our target use-case (code-reusability).

6.1 The Security of the Scheme

The first criterion is of course that the security must be sufficient (we target here a security level of 128 bits, comparable to ML-KEM-512). To check that, we leverage the reduction from Ring-LWE and Module-NTRU from Sect. 5, and LatticeEstimator, a tool that evaluates the security of an instance of some problem over lattices [APS15, commit 6b25d9d]. Indeed, since we know that our scheme is at least as secure as the corresponding instances of Ring-LWE and Module-NTRU, we can use LatticeEstimator to evaluate the security of these instances, to get a lower bound on the security of our scheme. We target here a security level of 128 bits (comparable to ML-KEM-512), but we can apply the same methodology to choose parameters for any security level.

6.2 The Reusability of the Key Functions

Modular arithmetic is present all over our scheme, and it can be a crucial point for the efficiency of the implementation. The choice of the modulus q is thus important, all the more since some operations could be protected or optimized specifically for some moduli. Following our goal of reusing the existing optimizations and protections, we want to use a standard modulus q, namely either $3\,329$ (from ML-KEM) or $8\,380\,417$ (from ML-DSA).

The Number Theoretic Transform, or NTT, is also a core operation in our scheme. It uses a primitive m-th root ζ of -1 modulo q to quickly split a polynomial in $R_q = \mathbb{Z}_q[X]/_{\langle X^n+1\rangle}$ into a tuple of m lower-degree polynomials in $T_q = \prod \mathbb{Z}_q[X]/_{\langle X^{n/m}-\zeta^{\alpha}\rangle}$. To use NTT, there must exist such a ζ in $\mathbb{Z}_q$, which only depends on n and q. More precisely, we can only find a primitive m-th root of -1 (i.e. a primitive $2m$-th root of 1) for m up to 128 modulo $3\,329$, and for m up to $4\,096$ modulo $8\,380\,417$. Since both ML-KEM and ML-DSA use $n = 256$, this means we are able to split an element of $R_{8\,380\,417}$ into n scalars, but we can only split an element of $R_{3\,329}$ into $n/2$ degree-1 polynomials.

Since the main use of NTT is to quickly multiply polynomials, its characteristics mainly influence the `BaseCaseMultiply` function, used to multiply two polynomials in NTT domain, of degree n/m. In ML-DSA, this function performs $n = 256$ products of two degree-0 polynomials, and in ML-KEM, it performs $n/2 = 128$ products of two degree-1 polynomials. In order to reuse that code, we must find parameters that allow splitting to degree at most 1. Stated differently, we need that $n/m \in \{1, 2\}$, which means that we need $n \leqslant 256$ with $q = 3\,329$, or $n \leqslant 8\,192$ with $q = 8\,380\,417$.

Moreover, NTT seems to be a great target for physical attacks, as illustrated in [Car24]. Protections are thus being developed for ML-KEM and ML-DSA, and we want to be able to reuse them in our IBE, even if they protect the `BaseCaseMultiply` function.

6.3 The Failure Probability

Last but not least, we must check that the failure probability is negligible. While there is no universal definition of "negligible", we use the same target as ML-KEM, which is "under 2^{-128}". The failure probability estimation notably allows to define the compression level of the ciphertext. Indeed, ML-KEM allows to reduce each coefficient (which is in $\mathbb{Z}_q$) of u (resp. v) to d_u (resp. d_v) bits.

First, we must validate that our choice of n and q can achieve negligible failure probability. To do that, we estimate that probability when there is no ciphertext compression, i.e. with $d_u = d_v = \lfloor \log_2 () \, q + 1 \rfloor$. If it is indeed negligible, then our choice of parameters is compatible with negligible failure probability. We can then enable some compression of the ciphertext, by (basically) dropping some low-order bits of its coefficients. To parameterize that, we follow the same approach as in previous NTRU-based IBE schemes, which only keep 3 bits of each coefficient of the vector v [DLP14, CKKS19].

6.4 The Final Choice of Parameters

The Degree n and Modulus q: As explained before, we want q to be either 3 329 or 8 380 417, and n to be a power of 2 such that the NTT is compatible with an existing one. We thus summarize some possible combinations in Table 1.

Table 1. Choosing parameters to reuse the Number Theoretic Transform

n	q	$\mathbb{Z}_q$ arithmetic	NTT domain T_q	`BaseCaseMultiply`	Security
256	3 329	ML-KEM	$\prod_{i=0}^{127} \mathbb{Z}_q[X]/\langle X^2-17^{2i+1}\rangle$	ML-KEM	69 bits
256	8 380 417	ML-DSA	$\prod_{i=0}^{255} \mathbb{Z}_q[X]/\langle X-1753^{2i+1}\rangle$	ML-DSA	40 bits
1 024	8 380 417	ML-DSA	$\prod_{i=0}^{1023} \mathbb{Z}_q[X]/\langle X-1306^{2i+1}\rangle$	ML-DSA	140 bits

First, we can see that the ideal case, with the standardized degree $n = 256$, does not provide enough security in our scheme, with any of our two modulus of interest, so we must increase n. However, as explained before, using $q = 3\,329$ would require a new implementation of `BaseCaseMultiply`. Therefore, we will set $q = 8\,380\,417$, which requires to increase n to 1 024 for security.

Fortunately, the existence of the primitive 2 048-th root of unity $\zeta = 1\,306$ in $\mathbb{Z}_q$ allows to reuse the implementation of `BaseCaseMultiply` from ML-DSA, with $n/m = 1$. Interestingly, we can also set $\zeta = 10\,730$ if we prefer to reuse the implementation of `BaseCaseMultiply` from ML-KEM, with $n/m = 2$.

The Standard Deviation σ: Now that we have chosen n and q such that the encryption itself is secure, we must also consider the security of another important feature: the trapdoor sampling. Indeed, the output distribution must be wide enough so that the discreteness of the secret lattice remains hidden to the adversary. To do that, a classical approach is to prove that the output distribution differs negligibly from a Gaussian distribution that is independent of the trapdoor [GPV08]. For ModFalcon, this is proved using the Rényi divergence between the two distributions, which requires [CPS+20]:

$$\sigma \geqslant \frac{\text{GS\_SLACK}_k \times q^{1/(k+1)}}{\pi} \times \sqrt{\frac{\log_2()\,2(k+1)n(1+4\sqrt{256\times 2^{64}})}{2}}$$

In the meantime, the larger the σ, the larger the failure probability, so we will use the lowest integer satisfying this security condition. For now, we have fixed n and q but not k, so we will consider σ as a function of k until this parameter is assigned a value. In practice, we set σ to the ceiling of the above right term.

The Encryption Noise (η_1 and η_2): To stay as close as possible to the encryption algorithm of ML-KEM, we use Centered Binomial Distributions, with parameters η_1 and η_2. We ran experiments with LatticeEstimator, and found out that these parameters don't seem to have a significant impact on security. Moreover, these parameters influence the failure probability of the scheme. So, we decided to take the values from ML-KEM-512: $(\eta_1, \eta_2) = (3, 2)$.

The Dimension k Over Polynomial Rings: An unfortunate relation is that k has opposite impacts on sizes and failure probability. Indeed, σ mainly depends on $q^{1/(k+1)}$, so increasing k leads to decrease the failure probability. At the same time, since it represents the number of polynomials in many objects, increasing k makes the keys and ciphertext bigger. Therefore, we would want to use $k = 1$ to minimize the size of the data (which would correspond to an NTRU trapdoor, as used in [DLP14]). However, the decryption failure probability of our scheme would then be too high, even without compressing the ciphertext. So, we set $k = 2$, which reaches negligible failure probability with $\sigma = 325$.

The Ciphertext Compression (d_u and d_v): At this point, the failure probability only depends on how much we compress the ciphertext, which is parameterized by d_u and d_v. As explained previously, we used the same technique as in prior NTRU-based IBE schemes, keeping only the 3 highest-order bits of the coefficients of v, which corresponds to $(d_u, d_v) = (23, 3)$. We can also note that this is consistent with what is performed in ML-KEM, where each coefficient of v is also compressed into only a few bits.

The Compression of the Master Secret Key: At the end of `Setup`, each coefficient of each polynomial in the mathematical master secret key (f, g, F, G) is encoded into d_{SK} bits to form the computer-friendly byte array SK, the algorithm restarting if any coefficient is too large. So, in order to reduce the size of SK, we want d_{SK} to be as small as possible. However, it must remain high enough so that the algorithm does not restart too often. Regarding f and g, we can apply the Chernoff bound to their known Gaussian distributions to ensure that all their (signed) coefficients will fit in 8 bits with probability at least $1 - 2^{-406}$. For F and G, we generated 100 master secret keys, and observed that all the absolute values of their 204 800 coefficients fit in 16 bits. We thus use $d_{SK} = 17$, but we could also decrease the size of SK by using $d_{SK} = 8$ for f and g, and $d_{SK} = 17$ for F and G.

Finally, we summarize in Table 2 the parameters that we have chosen to instantiate our scheme, the Gram-Schmidt slack resulting of these choices, and the security level achieved by this parameter set.

Table 2. The parameters of our scheme

n	q	k	η_1	η_2	σ	d_{SK}	d_u	d_v	GS_SLACK$_k$	Security
1024	8380417	2	3	2	325	17	23	3	1.2	140 bits

6.5 Data Sizes

We summarize in Table 3 the sizes of the keys and ciphertexts in our IBE scheme. We compare them to the sizes resulting of the parameter set of [DLP14] that was originally announced to provide a security level of 192 bits, since LatticeEstimator currently estimates its level of provable security to about 118 bits. We don't compare to [CKKS19], as we estimated the provable security level of its only parameter set to about 82 bits. Since the master secret key of [DLP14] contains integers, we were not able to give it a precise size, highlighting one of the benefits of our encoding to byte arrays.

We can see that our IBE, while not beating the [DLP14] scheme in terms of sizes, is still in the same order of magnitude (while being more secure), even if it was not the original objective. Therefore, the simplicity to implement, optimize and protect our scheme in a device that already embeds standardized lattice-based schemes, possibly with some existing hardware accelerators and countermeasures, can be worth the extra size of the keys and ciphertexts.

Table 3. Sizes of the keys and ciphertexts

Element	Size in our scheme (bytes)	[DLP14]
Master secret key	$(k^2 + k + 2) \times n \times d_{SK} \,/\, 8 \;=\; 17\,408$	Undefined
Master public key	$k \times n \times \lfloor \log_2 ()\, q + 1 \rfloor \,/\, 8 \;=\; 5\,888$	3 456
User secret key	$k \times n \times \lfloor \log_2 ()\, q + 1 \rfloor \,/\, 8 \;=\; 5\,888$	3 456
User public key (ID)	32	32
Ciphertext	$(k \times n \times d_u + n \times d_v) \,/\, 8 \;=\; 6\,272$	3 750

Even if Identity-Based Encryption has always been bigger than usual Public-Key Encryption, its properties can be interesting in specific use-cases (see Sect. 1). However, it is important that its cost remains acceptable in practice. That is why we compare the communication costs of our IBE to the one of ML-KEM, even if these are different kind of schemes enabling different features. For that comparison, we must consider a complete establishment of a shared secret. Indeed, while our scheme allows to directly send a ciphertext, ML-KEM requires an additional certificate. In the simple case where a (Post-Quantum) certificate (with 128-bit security) contains an identity, a public key for ML-KEM and a ML-DSA signature from the Certification Authority, then its size is $32 + 800 + 2\,420 = 3\,252$ bytes, and then the total communication cost with ML-KEM is $3\,252 + 768 = 4\,020$ bytes. This means that our scheme is again in the same order of magnitude, with a total communication only containing one ciphertext, of size 6 272 bytes. The benefits of Identity-Based Encryption can be worth this additional communication cost, in application contexts which leverage some of its special properties.

7 Future Perspectives

We created a clean Python implementation of our IBE to illustrate its ability to reuse blocks from standardized schemes and to give a rough idea about its running time. Deriving a C implementation from reference codes of standards would further demonstrate our IBE's practicality, and give more accurate runtime.

Like prior IBEs, we estimated the failure probability via theoretical approximations, and set up ciphertext compression relying on existing NTRU-based IBE schemes. At the opposite, Kyber's authors estimated the failure probability via a concrete computation, using a program they designed [SAB+22, CRY21]. However, the time taken by that program grows quadratically with the modulus, making it hard to use with our parameters. So, the analysis could be refined by some optimized version of that tool, which could reduce the ciphertext size.

8 Conclusion

We built a post-quantum IBE scheme over the standardized ML-KEM and ML-DSA, and the variant ModFalcon of Falcon, under standardization.

Any method that can assess the security of one of our IBE, [DLP14] or [CKKS19] can apply to the others, so the schemes all satisfy the same security properties. However, while their parameters were analyzed against the best attack found by their authors, ours rely on a tight reduction from Ring-LWE and Module-NTRU (from Sect. 5). This allows our scheme to have high security guarantees, in addition to being similar to well-trusted standardized schemes. For comparison, via our evaluation technique based on LatticeEstimator, our scheme reaches a security level of 140 bits, while the highest parameter set of [DLP14] reaches 118 bits, and the instantiation in [CKKS19] only reaches 82 bits.

Our scheme can easily be instantiated with concrete parameters according to some targets, in terms of security and decryption failure probability. Targeting security above 128 bits and failure probability below 2^{-128}, our scheme is comparable in sizes to [DLP14], while being more secure and easier to deploy.

While previous schemes leave some blank space about how to concretely implement them (how to represent an integer, what precise parameters should be used), our paper gives a detailed description of the algorithms and their implementations (from Sect. 4) and a precise analysis of our scheme's parameters (from Sect. 6). All our algorithms input and output byte-strings, making both concrete implementation and sizes estimation easy.

If we want to use any of the previously existing lattice-based IBE, the chosen scheme should be implemented, optimized and protected from scratch, requiring lot of time and work, and thus being costly. Conversely, we built our scheme so that it can reuse existing code from standardized schemes, making it easy to implement and allowing it to benefit from any optimization or protection that can be applied to these well-studied standardized schemes.

Finally, in order to check that everything works as announced, that the scheme indeed inherits much of its code from standardized schemes, to measure the running time, or for any other purpose, we provide a clean open-source implementation of our scheme in Python [Cam25].

Acknowledgments. This work was supported in part by French projects ANR-11-LABX-0020-01 "Centre Henri Lebesgue" and ANR-18-EURE-0004 "Cyberschool".

Disclosure of Interests. The authors have no competing interests to declare that are relevant to the content of this article.

References

AKG+07. Asokan, N., Kostiainen, K., Ginzboorg, P., Ott, J., Luo, C.: Applicability of identity-based cryptography for disruption-tolerant networking. In: Proceedings of the 1st International MobiSys Workshop on Mobile Opportunistic Networking, MobiOpp '07, pp. 52–56, New York, NY, USA (2007). Association for Computing Machinery. https://doi.org/10.1145/1247694.1247705

APS15. Albrecht, M.R., Player, R., Scott, S.: On the concrete hardness of Learning with Errors. J. Math. Cryptology **9**(3), 169–203 (2015). https://doi.org/10.1515/jmc-2015-0016

BF01. Boneh, D., Franklin, M.: Identity-based encryption from the Weil pairing. In: Kilian, J. (ed.) CRYPTO 2001. LNCS, vol. 2139, pp. 213–229. Springer, Heidelberg (2001). https://doi.org/10.1007/3-540-44647-8_13

BR93. Bellare, M., Rogaway, P.: Random oracles are practical: a paradigm for designing efficient protocols. In: Denning, D.E., Pyle, R., Ganesan, R., Sandhu, R.S., Ashby, V. (eds.) ACM CCS 93, pp. 62–73. ACM Press (1993). https://doi.org/10.1145/168588.168596

Cam25. Cam, J.: A python implementation of the current IBE scheme (2025). https://github.com/JCamCrypto/ID-ML-KEM_MNTRU_Python

Car24. Rodriguez, R.C.: Study of the resistance to side-channel attacks of cryptographic primitives based on lattices for post-quantum cryptography. PhD thesis, Université de Montpellier (2024). https://ged.scdi-montpellier.fr/florabium45/jsp/nnt.jsp?nnt=2024UMONS058

CGM19. Chen, Y., Genise, N., Mukherjee, P.: Approximate trapdoors for lattices and smaller hash-and-sign signatures. In: Galbraith, S.D., Moriai, S. (eds.) ASIACRYPT 2019. LNCS, vol. 11923, pp. 3–32. Springer, Cham (2019). https://doi.org/10.1007/978-3-030-34618-8_1

CKKS19. Cheon, J.H., Kim, D., Kim, T., Son, Y.: A new trapdoor over module-NTRU lattice and its application to ID-based encryption. Cryptology ePrint Archive, Report 2019/1468 (2019). https://eprint.iacr.org/2019/1468

Coc01. Cocks, C.: An identity based encryption scheme based on quadratic residues. In: Honary, B. (ed.) Cryptography and Coding 2001. LNCS, vol. 2260, pp. 360–363. Springer, Heidelberg (2001). https://doi.org/10.1007/3-540-45325-3_32

CPS+20. Chuengsatiansup, C., Prest, T., Stehlé, D., Wallet, A., Xagawa, K.: ModFalcon: compact signatures based on module-NTRU lattices. In: Sun, H.-M., Shieh, S.-P., Gu, G., Ateniese, G. (eds.) ASIACCS 20, pp. 853–866. ACM Press (2020). https://doi.org/10.1145/3320269.3384758

CRY21. CRYSTALS team. Security estimation scripts for Kyber and Dilithium (2021). https://github.com/pq-crystals/security-estimates

DLP14. Ducas, L., Lyubashevsky, V., Prest, T.: Efficient identity-based encryption over NTRU lattices. In: Sarkar, P., Iwata, T. (eds.) ASIACRYPT 2014. LNCS, vol. 8874, pp. 22–41. Springer, Heidelberg (2014). https://doi.org/10.1007/978-3-662-45608-8_2

FO99. Fujisaki, E., Okamoto, T.: Secure integration of asymmetric and symmetric encryption schemes. In: Wiener, M. (ed.) CRYPTO 1999. LNCS, vol. 1666, pp. 537–554. Springer, Heidelberg (1999). https://doi.org/10.1007/3-540-48405-1_34

GH05. Galindo, D., Hasuo, I.: Security notions for identity based encryption. Cryptology ePrint Archive, Report 2005/253 (2005). https://eprint.iacr.org/2005/253

GPV08. Gentry, C., Peikert, C., Vaikuntanathan, V.: Trapdoors for hard lattices and new cryptographic constructions. In: Ladner, R.E., Dwork, C. (eds.) 40th ACM STOC, pp. 197–206. ACM Press (2008). https://doi.org/10.1145/1374376.1374407

Gro12. Groves, M.: MIKEY-SAKKE: Sakai-Kasahara Key Encryption in Multimedia Internet KEYing (MIKEY). RFC 6509 (2012). https://www.rfc-editor.org/info/rfc6509, https://doi.org/10.17487/RFC6509

IPR23. Izabachène, M., Prabel, L., Roux-Langlois, A.: Identity-based encryption from lattices using approximate trapdoors. In: Simpson, L., Baee, M.A.R. (eds.) ACISP 23, volume 13915 of LNCS, pp. 270–290. Springer, Cham (2023). https://doi.org/10.1007/978-3-031-35486-1_13

LDK+22. Lyubashevsky, V., et al.: CRYSTALS-DILITHIUM. Technical report, National Institute of Standards and Technology (2022)

LPR12. Lyubashevsky, V., Peikert, C., Regev, O.: On ideal lattices and learning with errors over rings. Cryptology ePrint Archive, Report 2012/230 (2012). https://eprint.iacr.org/2012/230

MP12. Micciancio, D., Peikert, C.: Trapdoors for lattices: simpler, tighter, faster, smaller. In: Pointcheval, D., Johansson, T. (eds.) EUROCRYPT 2012. LNCS, vol. 7237, pp. 700–718. Springer, Heidelberg (2012). https://doi.org/10.1007/978-3-642-29011-4_41

Nat16. National Cyber Security Center. The development of MIKEY-SAKKE (2016). https://www.ncsc.gov.uk/information/the-development-of-mikey-sakke

Nat24a. National Institute of Standards and Technology. Module-Lattice-Based Digital Signature Standard. (Department of Commerce, Washington, D.C.), Federal Information Processing Standards Publication (FIPS) NIST FIPS 204 (2024). https://doi.org/10.6028/NIST.FIPS.204

Nat24b. National Institute of Standards and Technology. Module-Lattice-Based Key-Encapsulation Mechanism Standard. (Department of Commerce, Washington, D.C.), Federal Information Processing Standards Publication (FIPS) NIST FIPS 203 (2024). https://doi.org/10.6028/NIST.FIPS.203

PFH+22. Prest, T., et al.: FALCON. Technical report, National Institute of Standards and Technology (2022)

SAB+22. Schwabe, P., et al.: CRYSTALS-KYBER. Technical report, National Institute of Standards and Technology (2022)

Sha84. Shamir, A.: Identity-based cryptosystems and signature schemes. In: Blakley, G.R., Chaum, D. (eds.) CRYPTO 1984. LNCS, vol. 196, pp. 47–53. Springer, Heidelberg (1985). https://doi.org/10.1007/3-540-39568-7_5

Sho94. Shor, P.W.: Algorithms for quantum computation: discrete logarithms and factoring. In: 35th FOCS, pp. 124–134. IEEE Computer Society Press (1994). https://doi.org/10.1109/SFCS.1994.365700

TWZL08. Tan, C.C., Wang, H., Zhong, S., Li, Q.: Body sensor network security: an identity-based cryptography approach. In: Proceedings of the First ACM Conference on Wireless Network Security, WiSec '08, pp. 148–153, New York, NY, USA (2008). Association for Computing Machinery. https://doi.org/10.1145/1352533.1352557

First-Order Masked Fine-Shuffling Implementation Against Side-Channel Attacks with Application to ML-KEM

Noura Ait Manssour[1], Souhayl Ben El Haj Soulami[1,2(✉)], Sylvain Duquesne[2], and Guillaume Fumaroli[1]

[1] Valeo, Créteil, France
{noura.ait-manssour,souhayl.ben-el-haj-soulami, guillaume.fumaroli}@valeo.com
[2] Univ Rennes, CNRS, IRMAR - UMR 6625, 35000 Rennes, France
sylvain.duquesne@univ-rennes.fr

Abstract. In 2020, Ravi *et al.* [23] published three shuffling variants with each offering a different performance-security trade-off for protecting the Numeric theoretic Transform (NTT). Among them, the *fine-shuffling* was proposed as the lightweight variant. The idea is to randomise the order of loading and storing the operands of the butterfly computation using conditional swapping based on random control bit. However, as noted by the authors themselves, *basic-fine-shuffling* implementation suffered from an obvious attack on the conditional swapping mask. So they introduced the *bitwise-fine-shuffling* to fix this issue. In this paper, we break this implementation using a template attack. The idea is to aggregate the leakage from the 16 bitwise AND operations used to construct the swap mask. The attack has been performed both on simulation and on a STM32F303 target. Then, we propose a *masked fine-shuffling* variant to protect the *fine-shuffling* operation. The idea is to mask the secret-dependent memory accesses and apply the swap mask over its boolean sharing instead. The implementation is proven secure against first-order attacks in the probing model. The implementation has been benchmarked on an ARM-Cortex-M4 processor and incurs a total overhead of 25% on the entire ML-KEM768 decapsulation algorithm, compared with 51% overhead for the defeated *bitwise-fine-shuffling* of [23].

Keywords: ML-KEM · Shuffling · Side-channel Attack · Number Theoretic Transform · Countermeasures · Lattice-based cryptography

1 Introduction and Related Work

Physical attacks pose a serious threat to cryptographic implementations. They can be divided into fault-injection attacks and side-channel attacks. Introduced by Paul Kocher in [15], side-channel attacks rely on physical measurements

N. El Mrabet et al. (Eds.): AFRICACRYPT 2026, LNCS 16832, pp. 57–83, 2026.
https://doi.org/10.1007/978-3-032-31130-6_3

leaked by hardware circuits such as power consumption [17], electromagnetic emanation [16], execution time [5] or cache access time [6], to extract information about sensitive values. The most widely adopted countermeasure is masking. The idea is to split the secret variable into random multiple shares and do the computations over these shares instead to break the correlation between the secret and the power consumption [4]. Masking offers an exponential security growth with the masking order d (the number of traces required for a successful attack grows as $\mathcal{O}(N^d)$, where N depends on the noise level). Notwithstanding, it is important to combine it with shuffling. The idea of the shuffling is to randomise the execution order of the sensitive operations in order to make it harder for the attacker to identify the power consumption related to the targeted operation on a trace. This helps prevent highly sophisticated attacks such as Soft-Analytical-Side-Channel-Attacks (SASCA) [21,22]. These attacks exploit the algebraic structure of masked implementations by leveraging knowledge of the algorithm's data flow. For statistically advanced attacks rely on the hypothesis that traces are well aligned. The effort of traces alignment due to the shuffling scales exponentially with the order of masking used. However, it is important to securely implement the shuffling to achieve the desired security level. While combining masking and shuffling provides strong theoretical security, recent works [3,14] demonstrate that attackers can break each countermeasure separately, significantly reducing the attack complexity. For instance, Jendal *et al.* [14] use fault injection to bypass shuffling before attacking the masking with deep learning analysis, while Backlund *et al.* [3] recover the shuffling permutation via side-channel observations to realign traces before attacking the masking. The present work addresses this attack path by proposing a shuffling implementation where the permutation itself is protected through masking. Furthermore, piling up countermeasures comes with a significant cost. Hence, it is paramount to propose robust and fast shuffling implementations especially for embedded devices. In this context, previous research tried to answer the following challenges in different ways:

Reduce the Space of Permutations. The polynomials involved in ML-KEM and ML-DSA have a size of 256. This means that the shuffled polynomials can be executed in 256! possible orders, which is astronomically beyond the desired security requirement. Therefore, Ravi *et al.* [23] proposed to reduce the space of permutations to gain in efficiency by introducing three shuffling variants in the context of ML-KEM and ML-DSA with each one of them offering a different trade-off between security and performance: *coarse shuffling*, *coarse-in-group shuffling* and *fine-shuffling*.

Improving the Quality of the Random Number Generator (RNG). The shuffling uses random generators to generate the permutations. Sampling uniformly at random from such very large spaces in an unbiased way can be challenging in practice. Ziljstra *et al.* [27] use Linear-Feedback-Shift-Register (LFSR). Ravi [23] proposes to use the well-established FY algorithm. While Park [18] insists on the necessity of abandoning cheap solutions such as the biased modular reduction or low entropy algorithms such as cyclic shifts. Moreover, in

[19], Park *et al.* provide a fast statistical verification method to identify the bias in RNGs.

Design Hardware Accelerators for the Shuffling Operation. The purpose of hardware acceleration is to maximise parallelisation and data reuse. Ziljstra *et al.* [27] proposed to use *Benes networks* instead of FY algorithm to increase data parallelisation. Xu *et al.* in [26] introduced a FY implementation tailored for ML-KEM. Indeed, FY has an intrinstic problem which is to generate random indices with dynamic range. This is particularly a bottleneck in the hardware. Instead, they used a fixed-width RNG to generate random numbers and modulo reductions to map these to the current valid range.

Security Evaluation of Shuffled Operations. Despite the theoretical proofs on the shuffling, shuffled implementations are still vulnerable. In [11], Hermelink *et al.* shows that under an expanded attacker model, it is possible to break the *fine-shuffling* and *coarse-in-group* shuffling variants with using SASCA. However, the attacks were limited to simulation. In [3], Backlund *et al.* break the *coarse-shuffling* in ML-KEM by targeting the computation of the swap index inside the FY implementation first to descramble the traces, then perform a classical SASCA attack on unshuffled traces. Goy *et al.* in [10] performed a similar work on HQC and concludes that the fine-shuffling is inherently weak in the case of HQC.

1.1 Contributions

The contributions of this article are the following:

1. **Security analysis of *bitwise-fine-shuffling*.** In [11], Hermerlink *et al.* carried out the attack using SASCA focusing on the random bit used to load the data. The attack was only carried out on simulation and trained the system to directly learn on the masked and shuffled traces. In this work, we attack at a different angle. We perform a template attack by aggregating the leakage from all the bitwise `AND` loop, and validate the attack on a real device (`STM32F303` with electromagnetic measurements) to confirm our theoretical analysis. Our attack strategy differs from [11] in that we first recover the shuffling permutation to realign the traces, rather than attacking the masked and shuffled traces simultaneously. This two-stage approach significantly reduces the training complexity.
2. **`cswap` gadget.** We introduce a new first-order secure conditional swapping gadget (`cswap`) that operates on arithmetic shares of the control bit. This gadget can be used to protect fine-shuffling in ML-KEM and is applicable to other cryptographic contexts requiring masked conditional operations.
3. ***Masked fine-shuffling* implementation.** We introduce an original *masked fine-shuffling* implementation using the `cswap` gadget and we prove it secure against first-order attacks in the probing model. The implementation is secure against the attack we performed on the *bitwise fine shuffling* implementation and also against the attack described in [11]. We bench-marked the solution on an embedded device and quantified the overhead compared with the

unprotected version of ML-KEM768. The implementation we proposed is more secure and faster than the one from the state-of-the art.
Note that we mask the permutation used in the shuffling, not the data being shuffled. Our method is however fully compatible with such data masking, a technique extensively discussed in the literature. We focus on masking the permutation because it is the specific novel part and we want to specifically measure the associated overhead.

Outline. The rest of the paper is organised as follows: Sect. 2 describes the NTT operation in the context of ML-KEM and introduces the different shuffling variants, Sect. 3 introduces the attack on the *bitwise-fine shuffling* variant. In Sect. 4, we introduce our new masked shuffling method and Sect. 5 concludes the article.

2 NTT Operation and Its Different Shuffling Variants

Among the lattice-based algorithms, there is a family of algorithms whose security relies on the hardness of Module-Learning-with-Error (MLWE) and Module-Short-Integer-Solution (MSIS) over lattices, such as ML-KEM and ML-DSA. The public, private key and shared keys are represented as polynomials in $\mathcal{R}_q$ or vectors of polynomials in $\mathcal{R}_q^k$. The key generation, encryption and decryption operations involve performing polynomial multiplications over these keys. For that purpose we use the NTT because it has a low algorithmic complexity of $O(n \log n)$ and offers a significant speedup compared with the schoolbook multiplication [1]. The leakage in the NTT has lead to full secret key recovery in ML-KEM as shown in previous works [20,21]. Hence, it is relevant to mask and shuffle this operation.

2.1 Shuffling as a Countermeasure

Performing power analysis requires attacking operations that depend on some parts of the secret key. Therefore, it is important to know the exact moment where these operations happen to capture the power consumption at the right time. The idea of the shuffling is to break the correspondance between the time-points and the operations that are being executed. This goes by randomising the order of execution of the operations. The order is randomly generated at each execution. For example, the AES involves the performing SBOX operation on each of the 16 bytes of the key. So instead of applying the SBOX in a predictable order,

$$\texttt{SBOX}[state[0]],\ \texttt{SBOX}[state[1],\ \ldots,\ \texttt{SBOX}[state[15]]]$$

one can apply the states in a random order.

$$\texttt{SBOX}[state[7]],\ \texttt{SBOX}[state[2],\ \ldots,\ \texttt{SBOX}[state[3]]]$$

Notice that there are two conditions for the shuffling to be effective: the shuffled operations shall be independent to preserve the correctness of the algorithm.

Moreover, they should have similar power consumption and execution time, because otherwise, the order of the execution can be recovered simply using Simple Power Analysis (SPA) *i.e.* the naked eye.

2.2 Description of the NTT

To deeply understand the mechanisms of the NTT we refer the reader to [25]. In this section, we briefly recall the algorithm of the NTT (cf. Algorithm 1) and focus on the different shuffling strategies.

The algorithm operates over a polynomial represented as an array of 256 coefficients and outputs its NTT representation in a bit-reversed order. The algorithm follows a hierarchichal structure with three nested loops:

1. Stage loop (Line 2): Iterates over $\log_2(256) = 8$ stages with len halving the size of the butterfly blocks at each iteration. We call a block of butterflies at a specific stage, the set of butterfly operations that share the same *twiddle factor* ζ^k.
2. Block loop (Line 3): For each stage, we process $\frac{128}{len}$ independent blocks of size $2 \cdot len$.
3. Butterfly loop (Line 5): Within each block, we perform len butterfly operations on coefficients $p[j]$ and $p[j+len]$. A butterfly operation takes two inputs, multiplies one by a root-of-unity called a *twiddle factor* using Montgomery reduction and outputs their modular sum and difference efficiently mixing the pair as a building block of the transform.

Algorithm 1. In-Place Number Theoretic Transform NTT

Require: Array $p[0 \dots 255]$
Ensure: p contains the NTT in bit-reversed order
1: $k \leftarrow 1$
2: **for** $len \leftarrow 128$ **downto** 2 **by** halving **do** ▷ NTT stages
3:     **for** $start \leftarrow 0$ **to** 255 **step** $2 \cdot len$ **do** ▷ Block loop
4:         $k \leftarrow k + 1$ ▷ Load twiddle factor
5:         **for** $j \leftarrow start$ **to** $start + len - 1$ **do** ▷ Butterflies inside block
6:             $t \leftarrow \textsc{MontgomeryMul}(\zeta^k, p[j + len])$
7:             $p[j + len] \leftarrow p[j] - t$
8:             $p[j] \leftarrow p[j] + t$
9:         **end for**
10:     **end for**
11: **end for**

So, we identify the following independent operations:

- In each stage, the butterfly operations rely on the input from the previous stages, therefore, butterfly operations belonging to different stages cannot be shuffled (cf. Fig. 1).

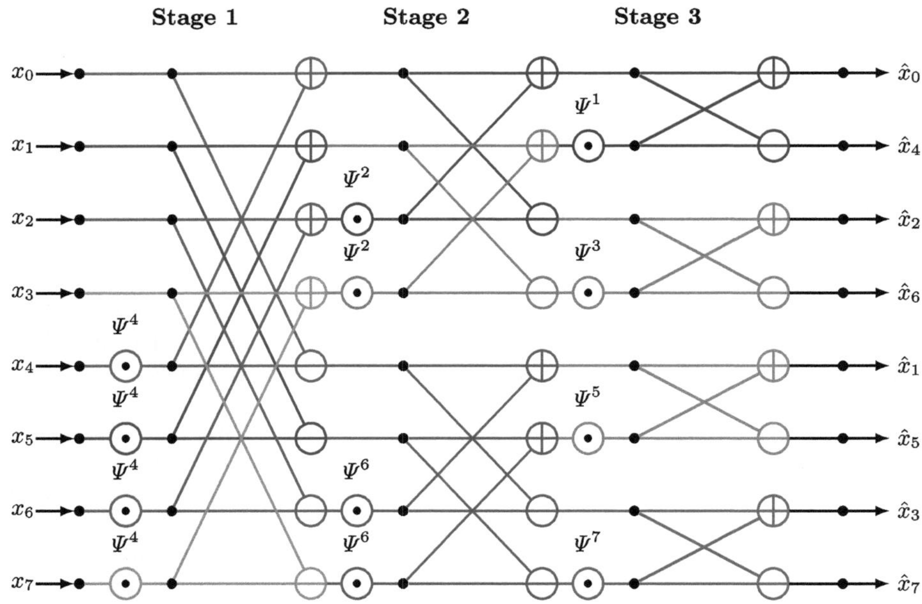

Fig. 1. Data flow graphs of NTT operation following Cooley-Tukey implementation for $n = 3$ stages.

- Within the same stage, the blocks are completely independent, therefore, the execution can happen at any order.
- Within the same block, all the butterfly operations are independent from one another, therefore they can be shuffled.

2.3 Shuffling Variants of the NTT

In light of the data-dependency analysis in the previous section, three variants have been proposed in [23] and each one of them offers a different level of trade-off between security and optimisation.

1. *coarse NTT shuffling*: The idea is to permute all the butterfly operations regardless of block they belong to. This is slow partly because it carries the overhead of having to load each time the corresponding *twiddle factor* ζ^k.
2. *coarse group NTT shuffling*: This variant overcomes the previous limitation. The idea is to shuffle the operations only within the same the block. Once a block is chosen, we execute all the butterflies in a shuffled order before moving to the next one. This way, we can get rid of the burden of loading the *twiddle factor* each time offering hence a speed-up.
3. *basic fine shuffling*: The butterflies execute in a predictable order. However, the order of storage and loading of the operands inside the butterfly operation is randomised. It is the fastest because it involves permuting only two

elements. It has a smaller space of permutations, albeit sufficient from an entropy point of view. This technique has already been used in elliptic curves in the previous works [12].

Algorithm 2 describes how *fine-shuffling* unfolds. The idea is to protect the `load` and `store` operations that involve manipulating $p[j]$ and $p[j + len]$ in Algorithm 2 by randomising the order at which they are loaded and stored to op_1 and op_2 and from out_1 and out_2 using a conditional swap. The decision to swap or not is based on random bit sampled at each execution. So, even if an attacker manages to recover op_1 or op_2 using a template attack for example, they don't know whether the recovered op_1 values corresponds to $p[j]$ or $p[j + len]$. The same reasoning applies to the storage using out_1 and out_2. However, this *basic* implementation suffers from an obvious flaw. Using m to decide whether to swap or not is substantially leaky because the difference of between `0` and `0xFFFF` is highly distinguishable even in very noisy environments [23].

Algorithm 2. Basic Fine Shuffling

Require: Array $p[0 \ldots 255]$
Ensure: p contains the NTT in bit-reversed order
$k \leftarrow 1$
for $len \leftarrow 128$ **downto** 2 **by** halving **do** ▷ NTT stages
  for $start \leftarrow 0$ **to** 255 **step** $2 \cdot len$ **do** ▷ Block loop
    $k \leftarrow k + 1$ ▷ Load twiddle factor
    for $j \leftarrow start$ **to** $start + len - 1$ **do** ▷ Butterflies inside block
      $r \xleftarrow{\$} \{0, 1\}$ ▷ $r \in \{0, 1\}$
      $m \leftarrow -r$ ▷ If $r = 0$, `m = 0x0000`, else `m = 0xFFFF`
      $op_1 \leftarrow p[j + r \cdot len]$ ▷ Secret-dependent memory access
      $op_2 \leftarrow p[j + (1 - r) \cdot len]$ ▷ Secret-dependent memory access
      $temp \leftarrow (op_1 \oplus op_2) \wedge m$
      $op_1 \leftarrow op_1 \oplus temp$
      $op_2 \leftarrow op_2 \oplus temp$
      $t \leftarrow \textsc{MontgomeryMul}(op_2, \zeta^k)$
      $out_1 \leftarrow op_1 + t$
      $out_2 \leftarrow op_1 - t$
      $r \xleftarrow{\$} \{0, 1\}$ ▷ $r \in \{0, 1\}$
      $m \leftarrow -r$ ▷ If $r = 0$, `m = 0x0000`, else `m = 0xFFFF`
      $temp \leftarrow (out_1 \oplus out_2) \wedge m$
      $out_1 \leftarrow out_1 \oplus temp$
      $out_2 \leftarrow out_2 \oplus temp$
      $p[j + r \cdot len] \leftarrow out_1$ ▷ Secret-dependent memory access
      $p[j + (1 - r) \cdot len] \leftarrow out_2$ ▷ Secret-dependent memory access
    end for
  end for
end for

---

3 Permutation Recovery of *bitwise Fine-Shuffling*

3.1 Description of the Bitwise Fine-Shuffling

To harden the implementation, Ravi introduced the *bitwise fine-shuffling*. The idea is to apply this mask m bit by bit instead as described in Algorithm 3. This suppresses the leakage coming from m because it is much more difficult to distinguish `0` from `1` than `0` from `0xFFFF`. However, this solution comes with an overhead of 59% over the entire algorithm. Furthemore, this implementation suffers from two major flaws: first, loading the operations involves handling secret-dependent memory accesses which can be exploited using the *mixing priors* technique mentioned by [11]. Another major flaw, is despite it being more difficult to distinguish `0` from `1` than `0` from `0xFFFF` on a single trace, the `AND` operation is repeated 16 times (32 in the case of ML-DSA), which means that an attacker can aggregate the leakage from all the leakage points and find the value of r with a very high level of confidence thus toppling the shuffling altogether.

3.2 Attack on Simulation

In this section, we explain how we can recover the permutation of the *bitwise fine shuffling*. We realised the attack first in simulation. The idea is to observe the moment when the control bit r is loaded before the `AND` operation in Line 11 is executed (cf. Algorithm 3). We assume as usual that the leakage follows the Hamming weight model for a variable x [17]:

$$l(x) = \omega(x) + N^{(t)}$$

This means that the leakage is composed of a deterministic part (the Hamming weight of the input x of the algorithm) and a random noise. We assume classically as well that the deterministic part and the noise are independent from one another, that the different noise sources are independent and that the noise follows a Gaussian distribution $N \leftarrow \mathcal{N}(0, \sigma^2)$.

Let L_i the random variable that tracks the leakage obtained at time i where r is manipulated and let R the random variable that tracks the value of the control bit r.

$$L_i = \omega(R) + N^{(i)}$$

Then,

$$L_i \mid (R = r) \leftarrow \mathcal{N}(\omega(r), \sigma^2)$$

Let $L = (L_1, \ldots, L_{16})$ the random variable that tracks the combined leakage. We use the maximum likelihood rule to guess the control bit.

$$r_{guess} = \arg\max_{r \in \{0,1\}} (P(R = r \mid L = l))$$

Using Bayes' theorem, we have:

$$P(R = r \mid L = l) = \frac{P(L = l \mid R = r)P(R = r)}{P(L)}$$

Algorithm 3. Bitwise fine-shuffling

Require: Array $p[0 \dots 255]$

Ensure: p contains the NTT in bit-reversed order

```
k ← 1
for len ← 128 downto 2 by halving do                         ▷ NTT stages
    for start ← 0 to 255 step 2 · len do                      ▷ Block loop
        k ← k + 1                                             ▷ Load twiddle factor
        for j ← start to start + len − 1 do                   ▷ Butterflies inside block
            r ←$ {0, 1}                                       ▷ r ∈ {0, 1}
            op1 ← p[j + r · len]
            op2 ← p[j + (1 − r) · len]
            temp ← (op1 ⊕ op2)
            for i ← 0 to 15 do
                temp ← temp ∧ (r ≪ i)                         ▷ r bitwise leaky iterations
            end for
            op1 ← op1 ⊕ temp
            op2 ← op2 ⊕ temp
            t ← MontgomeryMul(op2, ζ^k)
            out1 ← op1 + t
            out2 ← op1 − t
            r ←$ {0, 1}                                       ▷ r ∈ {0, 1}
            temp ← (out1 ⊕ out2)
            for i ← 0 to 15 do
                temp ← temp ∧ (r ≪ i)                         ▷ r bitwise leaky iterations
            end for
            out1 ← out1 ⊕ temp
            out2 ← out2 ⊕ temp
            p[j + r · len] ← out1
            p[j + (1 − r) · len] ← out2
        end for
    end for
end for
```

Since R follows the uniform distribution, $P(R = r) = \frac{1}{2}$.

$$P(R = r \mid L = l) = \frac{P(L = l \mid R = r)}{2P(L)}$$

Therefore, maximising $P(R = r \mid L = l)$ for r is equivalent to maximising $P(L = l \mid R = r)$ for r. We focus on maximising $P(L = l \mid R = r)$ instead because is it easier to compute. In fact,

$$P(L = (l_1, \dots, l_{16}) \mid R = r) = \prod_{i=1}^{16} P(L_i = l_i \mid R = r)$$

$$P(L \mid R = r) = \left(\frac{1}{\sqrt{2\pi\sigma^2}}\right)^{16} \exp\left(-\frac{1}{2\sigma^2} \sum_{i=1}^{16} (l_i - \omega(r))^2\right)$$

$$r_{guess} = \underset{r\in\{0,1\}}{\arg\max}(P(L \mid R = r))$$

To determine the success rate of the attack, we need to compare $P(L \mid R = 1)$ and $P(L \mid R = 0)$. Comparing $P(L \mid R = 1)$ and $P(L \mid R = 0)$ is equivalent to comparing $\sum_{i=1}^{16} (l_i - \omega(0))^2$ and $\sum_{i=1}^{16} (l_i - \omega(1))^2$.

$$P(L \mid R = 0) \geq P(L \mid R = 1) \iff \sum_{i=1}^{16} (l_i - 0)^2 \leq \sum_{i=1}^{16} (l_i - 1)^2$$

$$\iff \sum_{i=1}^{16} l_i^2 \leq \sum_{i=1}^{16} (l_i^2 - 2l_i + 1) \iff \frac{\sum_{i=1}^{16} l_i}{16} \leq \frac{1}{2}$$

Let's denote by $\bar{L} = \frac{\sum_{i=1}^{16} L_i}{16}$ the average of the leakage obtained from all the 16 leakage points in a single trace. So, we simply check the condition $\bar{L} \leq \frac{1}{2}$ and make a decision based on that.

Failure occurs when one of the two events happen:

$$\big((\bar{L} \geq \frac{1}{2}) \cap (R = 0)\big) \cup \big((\bar{L} \leq \frac{1}{2}) \cap (R = 1)\big)$$

This is equivalent to the rule:

$$r_{guess} = \underset{r\in\{0,1\}}{\arg\min} \mid \bar{l} - \omega(r) \mid$$

We have:

$$\bar{L} = \omega(R) + \frac{\sum_{i=1}^{16} N^{(i)}}{16}$$

The probability of failure is

$$P_{fail} = P\Big(\bar{L} > \frac{1}{2} \mid R = 0\Big) + P\Big(\bar{L} \leq \frac{1}{2} \mid R = 1\Big)$$

$$P_{fail} = P\Big(\frac{\sum_{i=1}^{16} N^{(i)}}{16} > \frac{1}{2}\Big) + P\Big(\frac{\sum_{i=1}^{16} N^{(i)}}{16} \leq -\frac{1}{2}\Big)$$

$$P_{fail} = 2 \cdot P\Big(\frac{\sum_{i=1}^{16} N^{(i)}}{16} \geq \frac{1}{2}\Big)$$

Since $N \leftarrow \mathcal{N}(0, \sigma^2)$ then, $\frac{\sum_{i=1}^{16} N^{(i)}}{16} \leftarrow \mathcal{N}\Big(0, \frac{\sigma^2}{16}\Big)$.

Hence,

$$P_{fail} = 8 \int_{\frac{1}{2}}^{+\infty} \frac{e^{\frac{-8x^2}{\sigma^2}}}{\sigma\sqrt{2\pi}} dx$$

Figure 2 shows the success rate for the attack. It stays above $p = 99.99\%$ for low noise values (up to $\sigma = 0.5$ for ML-KEM and $\sigma = 0.8$ for ML-DSA). In practice, this means that the chances to unscramble the entire NTT computation of all the 896 butterflies are $p^{896} = 91.43\%$.

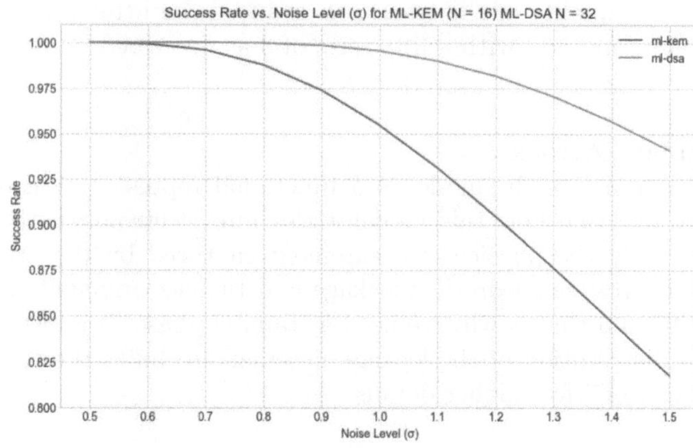

Fig. 2. Success rate of the attack as a function of noise-level for ML-KEM and ML-DSA.

Remark 1. While we have implemented the attack on ML-KEM, it also extends naturally to ML-DSA. We simply need to replace 16 by 32 in the formulas.

Remark 2. In ML-KEM, since $q = 3\ 329$, the elements have a length of 12 bits. Therefore, there is no need to iterate over 16 bits in the first place. This decreases the performance without providing any additional security. Similarly, in ML-DSA, the number of iterations can be brought down to 23 instead of 32 for the same reasons.

3.3 Attack on Real Implementation

3.3.1 Setup Description

In order to validate the result, we performed the attack on a `STM32F303` target. The setup is comprised of:

- `STM32F303` target equipped with `ARM-Cortex-M4` that runs at a frequency of 72 `MHZ`. (≈ 20$)
- `Chipwhisperer CW1173` that flashes the target. (≈ 300$)
- Oscilloscope `KeySight MSOX6004A` that captures the electromagnetic emanation from the target. (≈ 30,000$)
- Probe `YWBL-WH`to measure the ElectroMagnetic (EM) signal (10$).
- Sampling rate = $20Ga/s$.
- We put the `TRIGGER_HIGH` at the beginning of the portion of code executing the fine-shuffling and `TRIGGER_LOW` at the end of the fine shuffling (16 loop operation).
- The EM probe was positioned near the decoupling capacitor of the microcontroller. The optimal position was determined empirically by testing multiple spatial positions (x, y, z coordinates) until observing a repeating pattern corresponding to the 16 loop iterations of the *bitwise-fine-shuffling* (lines 10–12 of Algorithm 3).

- To increase the quality of the traces, we reduced the jitter using the *window average sliding* method with a filter size of 3 as described in [8].

3.3.2 Template Attack

While the Hamming weight model is a functional representation of the leakage, it fails to describe how this model scales into electromagnetic emanation which is concretely the physical measurement captured by the attacker. This correspondence between theoretical leakage and the electromagnetic emanation is board specific and that is why we need a training phase. It allows to estimate the statistical distribution of the leakage necessary to build the templates. We refer the reader to [7] for further details.

3.3.3 Attack Scenario

We performed the attack on the *bitwise-shuffling* implementations from [23][1]. The code has been compiled with the compiler `arm-none-eabi-gcc` with the compilation options `-O3 -Wall -mcpu=cortex-m4`. We suppose that the attacker has access to a clone device. For the training phase, we used 1000 traces per class. Using the *bitwise shuffling*, the input of MontgomeryMul is shuffled. The idea is to recover the permutation to realign the traces and perform a traditional attack on realigned traces as performed by Pessl *et al.* in [20]. A trace corresponds to an execution of the NTT function of ML-KEM where we target the control bit r during the 16 iterations of the `AND` operations (Lines 15 and 21 of Algorithm 3). Since the shuffling is unique per execution, the attack traces is comprised of a single-trace. In this experiment, we only show how to break the shuffling, we do not go to the extent of performing the full secret key recovery attack described by Pessl.

3.3.4 Traces Filtering

The jitter (slight timing misalignments between traces) is a very common phenomenon that degrades the quality of the traces in side-channel analysis. It is due to the imperfection in the measurements instruments or clock instability. To reduce its effect, we used *window average sliding* method described in [8] with a filter size of 3. Figure (a) shows a raw trace and (b) shows the same trace after applying the *sliding window method.* We can notice that the 16 peaks related to the activity are more visible. This is important to build clean templates for the training phase to increase the success rate (Fig. 3).

3.3.5 Points of Interest

In order to find the exact moments where the random bit leaks, we use the *sum of differences method* described in [24]. The idea is to compute the absolute value of the average trace of each class.

---

[1] code is available on https://github.com/PRASANNA-RAVI/Configurable_SCA_Countermeasures_for_NTT.

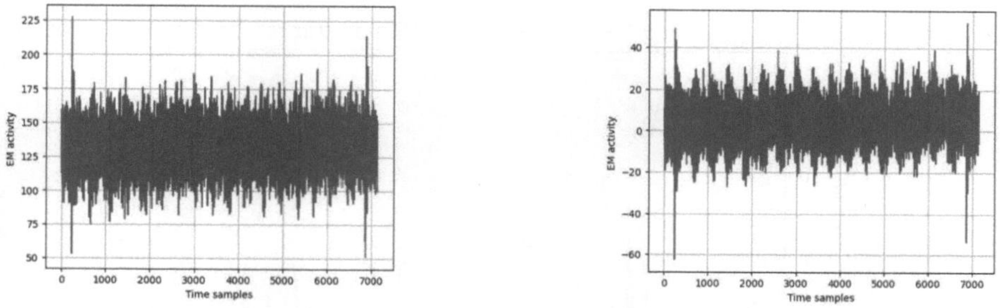

(a) raw trace

(b) filtered trace

Fig. 3. Jitter reduction.

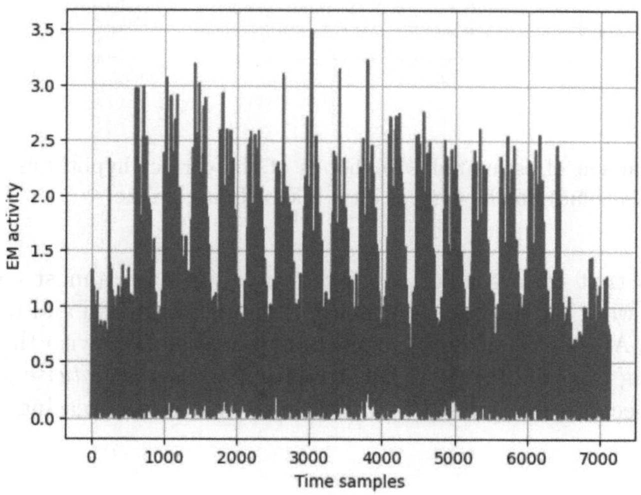

Fig. 4. Points of interests using the method of sums of differences

Figure 4 shows the points of interests. We can see that we observe 16 peaks which correspond to the loop. However, in practice, we take 16×3 points of interest. In theory, 16 should suffice. Nevertheless, although the variable is only manipulated once, the leakage is spread across multiple samples around the same timepoint.

3.3.6 Results

To determine the success rate of the attack, we generate a single execution with random value of r and we compute $P(L = l \mid R = r)$ for both hypothesis based on its corresponding trace. We repeat the experiment a 100 times and plot the results (cf. Fig. 5).

For all 100 experiments, the correct hypothesis achieves the highest likelihood, we can see that the correct hypothesis has always the highest likelihood,

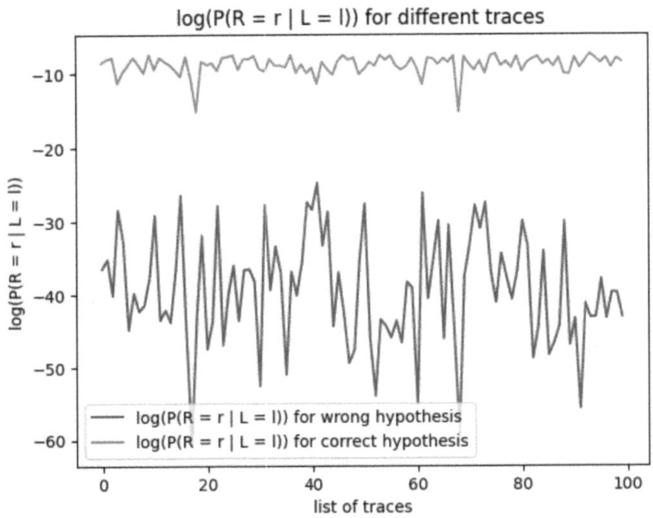

Fig. 5. Comparison of estimated Likelihoods of the correct hypothesis (orange) and false hypothesis (blue) on the control bit r (Color figure online)

which means that we are able to recover the swap with almost certainty. We did a similar work for the *basic-fine shuffling* implementation and we obtain the same results. Afterall, Both implementations were defeated with the same number of training traces. Therefore, it is irrelevant to use the *bitwise-fine shuffling* in practice because it incurs a high overhead without increasing the security significantly.

4 Masked Fine-Shuffling Implementation

4.1 Purpose of Masked Fine-Shuffling

To sum up, Sect. 3 and the works of [11] and [3] show that no variant of the shuffling is safe. Therefore, it is relevant to propose hardened/masked versions of these shuffling variants. The fine-shuffling is the lightweight variant compared with *coarse* and *coarse-in-group* as noted by Ravi [23]. In this section, we focus on masking that first variant, prove its security in the probing model and benchmark its performance against existing implementations.

4.2 Description of a New Masked Fine-Shuffling Implementation

We propose a masked implementation of the *fine-shuffling* that fixes the two vulnerabilities mentioned:

- The leakage of the secret dependent memory accesses exploited in [11].
- The leakage related to the bitwise application of the control bit r exploited in our attack.

4.2.1 Protecting r-Dependent Memory Accesses

To tackle the first vulnerability, we sample the control bit already in a masked way, by sampling each share $r_1^{(b)}$ and $r_2^{(b)}$ independently. The control bit $r = r_1^{(b)} \oplus r_2^{(b)}$ is never explicitly calculated. Then, we replace all the memory accesses manipulating the control bit r (cf. lines 8, 9, 21, 22 in Algorithm 2) with memory accesses manipulating only boolean shares of it instead (cf. lines 7, 8, 17–20 of Algorithm 5).

4.2.2 Protecting the Mask m Using `cswap`

To tackle the second vulnerability, we replace the lines 10–12 and lines 18–20 of Algorithm 2 corresponding to the application of the mask $m = -r$ by our `cswap` gadget. This gadget applies a boolean sharing/splitting to m and harnesses the well-known `B2A` gadget for masking conversion.

***B2A* gadget.** Cryptographic implementations mix in general linear and non-linear operations. We use arithmetic masking for linear operations and boolean masking for non-linear operations. Moving from one domain to the other thus requires either recomposing the shares to generate new shares corresponding to the new domain, but this is obviously not secure because it exposes the secret. The other solution is to securely convert the shares from arithmetic to boolean or the other way around. This is the purpose of the gadgets `A2B` and `B2A` designed by Goubin in [9].

`cswap` gadget.

The `cswap` allows to apply the mask m over boolean shares. The full description of the algorithm can be found in Algorithm 4.

The algorithm receives boolean sharings of r and converts them to arithmetic sharings using the `B2A` gadgets. Then, samples at random the first boolean share of m, labeled m_1. Then, blindly computes the second boolean share m_2 such that $m = m_1 \oplus m_2$ and $m = 0$ if $r = 0$ and $m = 2^{16} - 1$ otherwise. Then each share is applied individually as logical-`AND` mask to op_1 and op_2.

4.3 Correctness

To show the correctness of the implementation, we need to show the correctness at each of the following steps that depend on the bit control: loading step, `cswap` gadget and storage step.

Correctness of `cswap` Step.

First, we need to introduce the following lemma.

We use the usual two's complement representation to identify $\{0,1\}^n$ with $\mathbb{Z}/2^n\mathbb{Z}$ with the bijection

$$\varphi : \{0,1\}^n \longrightarrow \mathbb{Z}/2^n\mathbb{Z}$$

defined by

$$\varphi(x_{n-1}, \dots, x_0) = -x_{n-1} \cdot 2^{n-1} + \sum_{i=0}^{n-2} x_i \cdot 2^i \pmod{2^n}.$$

Algorithm 4. `cswap` gadget

Require: op_1, op_2, $r_1^{(b)}$, $r_2^{(b)}$ such that $r = r_1^{(b)} \oplus r_2^{(b)}$
Ensure: op_1 and op_2 are swapped iff $r = 1$
$(r_1^{(a)}, r_2^{(a)}) \leftarrow \texttt{B2A}(r_1^{(b)}, r_2^{(b)})$ ▷ $r_1^{(a)} + r_2^{(a)} = r \mod 2^{16}$
$m_1 \xleftarrow{\$} \mathbb{F}_{2^{16}}$
$temp \leftarrow 2^{16} - 1 - 2 \cdot m_1$
$m_2 \leftarrow temp \cdot r_1^{(a)} + m_1 + temp \cdot r_2^{(a)}$ ▷ $m_1 \oplus m_2 = 0$ if r = 0, -1 otherwise
$op1m1 \leftarrow op_1 \wedge m_1$
$op2m1 \leftarrow op_2 \wedge m_1$
$op1m2 \leftarrow op_1 \wedge m_2$
$op2m2 \leftarrow op_2 \wedge m_2$
$op12m1 \leftarrow op1m1 \oplus op2m1$
$op12m2 \leftarrow op1m2 \oplus op2m2$
$op_1 \leftarrow op_1 \oplus op12m1 \oplus op12m2$
$op_2 \leftarrow op_2 \oplus op12m1 \oplus op12m2$

In particular,

$$\varphi(1, \ldots, 1) = -1 = 2^n - 1 \pmod{2^n}.$$

Lemma.

$$\forall x, y \in \{0,1\}^n, x \oplus y = -1 \Leftrightarrow x + y = 2^n - 1 \pmod{2^n}.$$

Proof of Lemma. For all $x, y \in \{0,1\}^n$,

$$\begin{aligned} x \oplus y = -1 &\Leftrightarrow x \oplus x \oplus y = -1 \oplus x \\ &\Leftrightarrow (x \oplus x) \oplus y = \neg x \\ &\Leftrightarrow y = \neg x \\ &\Leftrightarrow x + y = \neg x + x \pmod{2^n} \\ &\Leftrightarrow x + y = 2^n - 1 \pmod{2^n}. \end{aligned}$$ □

Now let us prove the correctness of our `cswap` gadget.

- The last statements of `cswap`, consist in xor-ing

$$op12m1 \oplus op12m2 = (op_1 \oplus op_2) \wedge (m_1 \oplus m_2)$$

  to op_1 and op_2.
- With the lemma, we have $m_1 \oplus m_2 = 0$ if $r = 0$, and $m_1 \oplus m_2 = -1$ otherwise.
- If $r = 0$, $op12m1 \oplus op12m2 = 0$, so $op_1 \leftarrow op_1$ and $op_2 \leftarrow op_2$. No swap.
- If $r = 1$, $op12m1 \oplus op12m2 = op_1 \oplus op_2$, so $op_1 \leftarrow op_2$ and $op_2 \leftarrow op_1$. The elements are swapped.

Correctness of Loading Step.
The idea is that if $r = 0$, we `XOR` op_1 and op_2 with the same value, thus keeping it unchanged. Otherwise, we `XOR` with $p[j] \oplus p[j + len]$which has the effect of swapping the values inside op_1 and op_2.

Algorithm 5. first-order masking of shuffling operation in NTT

Require: Array $p[0 \ldots 255]$
Ensure: p contains the NTT in bit-reversed order

$k \leftarrow 1$
for $len \leftarrow 128$ **downto** 2 **by** halving **do** ▷ NTT stages
  for $start \leftarrow 0$ **to** 255 **step** $2 \cdot len$ **do** ▷ Block loop
    $k \leftarrow k + 1$ ▷ Load twiddle factor
    for $j \leftarrow start$ **to** $start + len - 1$ **do** ▷ Butterflies inside block
      $r_1^{(b)}, r_2^{(b)} \leftarrow \{0, 1\}$ ▷ $r_1^{(b)} \oplus r_2^{(b)} = r \in \{0, 1\}$
      $op_1 \leftarrow p[j + r_1^{(b)} \cdot len] \oplus p[j] \oplus p[j + r_2^{(b)} \cdot len]$
      $op_2 \leftarrow p[j + (1 - r_1^{(b)}) \cdot len] \oplus p[j + len] \oplus p[j + (1 - r_2^{(b)}) \cdot len]$
      $\texttt{cswap}(op_1, op_2, r_1^{(b)}, r_2^{(b)})$
      $t \leftarrow \textsc{MontgomeryMul}(\zeta^k, op_2)$
      $out_1 \leftarrow op_1 + t$
      $out_2 \leftarrow op_1 - t$
      $r_1^{(b)}, r_2^{(b)} \leftarrow \{0, 1\}$
      $\texttt{cswap}(out_1, out_2, r_1^{(b)}, r_2^{(b)})$
      $p[j] \leftarrow out_1$
      $p[j + len] \leftarrow out_2$
      $p[j + r_1^{(b)} \cdot len] \leftarrow p[j + r_1^{(b)} \cdot len] \oplus out_2$
      $p[j + (1 - r_1^{(b)}) \cdot len] \leftarrow p[j + (1 - r_1^{(b)}) \cdot len] \oplus out_1$
      $p[j + r_2^{(b)} \cdot len] \leftarrow p[j + r_2^{(b)} \cdot len] \oplus out_2$
      $p[j + (1 - r_2^{(b)}) \cdot len] \leftarrow p[j + (1 - r_2^{(b)}) \cdot len] \oplus out_1$
    end for
  end for
end for

– **Case** $r = 0$:

This implies that $r_1^{(b)} = r_2^{(b)}$ and $1 - r_1^{(b)} = 1 - r_2^{(b)}$, so $op_1 \leftarrow p[j]$ and $op_1 \leftarrow p[j + len]$. So the elements are loaded without swapping as expected.

– **Case** $r = 1$:

This implies that $r_1^{(b)} \neq r_2^{(b)}$ and $1 - r_1^{(b)} \neq 1 - r_2^{(b)}$. So, one element is $p[j]$ and the other one is $p[j + len]$. Without loss of generality, let's assume that $r_1^{(b)} = p[j]$ and $r_2^{(b)} = p[j + len]$. In that case, $op_1 \leftarrow p[j + len]$ and $op_2 \leftarrow p[j]$. Hence, the elements loaded swapped as expected.

Correctness of Storage Step.
In the storage step, if $r = 0$, *i.e.* $r_1 = r_2$, we XOR twice $p[j]$ and $p[j + len]$ by the same value either out_1 or out_2 which keeps the values of $p[j]$ and $p[j + len]$ unchanged. If $r = 1$, *i.e.* $r_1 = r_2$, we XOR $p[j]$ and $p[j + len]$ by $out_1 \oplus out_2$ which has the effect of swapping the values inside $p[j]$ and $p[j + len]$.

– **Case** $r_1^{(b)} = r_2^{(b)} = 0$:

$p[j] \leftarrow out_1$
$p[j + len] \leftarrow out_2$
$p[j] \leftarrow p[j] \oplus out_2 = out_1 \oplus out_2$
$p[j + len] \leftarrow p[j + len] \oplus out_1 = out_1 \oplus out_2$
$p[j] \leftarrow p[j] \oplus out_2 = out_1 \oplus out_2 \oplus out_2 = out_1$
$p[j + len] \leftarrow p[j + len] \oplus out_1 = out_1 \oplus out_2 \oplus out_1 = out_2$
So, no swap happens as expected.

- **Case** $r_1^{(b)} = r_2^{(b)} = 1$:

$p[j] \leftarrow out_1$
$p[j + len] \leftarrow out_2$
$p[j + len] \leftarrow p[j + len] \oplus out_2 = 0$
$p[j] \leftarrow p[j] \oplus out_1 = 0$
$p[j + len] \leftarrow p[j + len] \oplus out_2$
$p[j] \leftarrow p[j] \oplus out_1 = out_1$
So, no swap happens as expected.

- **Case** $r_1^{(b)} = 1, r_2^{(b)} = 0$:

$p[j] \leftarrow out_1$
$p[j + len] \leftarrow out_2$
$p[j + len] \leftarrow p[j + len] \oplus out_2 = 0$
$p[j] \leftarrow p[j] \oplus out_1 = 0$
$p[j] \leftarrow p[j] \oplus out_2 = out_2$
$p[j + len] \leftarrow p[j + len] \oplus out_1 = out_1$
So, the swap happens as expected.

- **Case** $r_1^{(b)} = 0, r_2^{(b)} = 1$:

$p[j] \leftarrow out_1$
$p[j + len] \leftarrow out_2$
$p[j] \leftarrow p[j] \oplus out_2 = out_1 \oplus out_2$
$p[j + len] \leftarrow p[j + len] \oplus out_1 = out_1 \oplus out_2$
$p[j + len] \leftarrow p[j + len] \oplus out_2 = out_1 \oplus out_2 \oplus out_2 = out_1$
$p[j] \leftarrow p[j] \oplus out_1 = out_1 \oplus out_2 \oplus out_1 = out_2$
So, the swap happens as expected. This concludes the correctness of the method.

4.4 Proof of Security in the Probing Model

We propose to prove the security under the probing model. In 2003, Ishai *et al.* introduce the probing model [13] to formalize the security of masking schemes against adversaries capable of observing a bounded number of internal wires/intermediate variables in an implementation. In this model, the attacker is able to observe at most t variables. An implementation is said to be t-probe secure if any set of at most t intermediate variables does not yield any information about the secret. In other words, to prove that an implementation is 1-probe secure, we have to show that for all intermediate variables V are independent of R. Notice that the control bit r is already generated in a masked way, is never recomposed and no intermediate variable depends on both shares of the bit control. This is what makes the implementation robust against first-order attacks.

$$P(R = r \mid V = v) = P(R = r)$$

or equivalently

$$P(V = v \mid R = r) = P(V = v)$$

4.4.1 `cswap` Gadget

The algorithm has been designed in such a way that no intermediate variable mixes the two shares of a (sensitive) variable that directly depends on r *i.e.* a function of $((r_1^{(b)}, r_2^{(b)})$ or $(r_1^{(a)}, r_2^{(a)})$ or $(m_1, m_2))$ without rerandomisation. Let V_i denote the set of all intermediate variables that appear at statement i of Algorithm 4.

- $V_1^{(1)} = r_1^{(b)}$, $V_1^{(2)} = r_2^{(b)}$, $V_1^{(3)} = r_1^{(a)}$, $V_1^{(4)} = r_2^{(a)}$, as well as all internal variables while executing gadget `B2A` are by design independent of R.
- $V_2 = m_1$ is picked uniformly at random, hence independent of R.
- $V_3 = 2^{16} - 1 - 2 \cdot V_2$ only depends on V_2, hence independent of R.
- Let $V_4^{(1)} = V_3.V_1^{(3)}$, $V_4^{(2)} = V_4^{(1)} + V_2$, $V_4^{(3)} = V_3.V_1^{(4)} = m_2$, $V_4^{(4)} = V_4^{(2)} + V_4^{(3)} = m_2$.

  V_3 is unrelated to r or its shares, and $V_1^{(3)}$ formally only depends on $r_1^{(b)}$ therefore independent of R, hence $V_4^{(1)}$ is independent of R.

  V_2 is unrelated to r or its shares, and $V_4^{(1)}$ is independent of R, hence $V_4^{(2)}$ is independent of R.

  V_3 is unrelated to r or its shares, and $V_1^{(4)}$ is independent of R, hence $V_4^{(3)}$ is independent of R.

  $V_4^{(4)} = m_2$ that is distributed as m_1 hence independent of R.
- V_5, V_6, V_7, V_8 are all in the form $op_i \wedge m_j$ with $i, j \in \{1, 2\}$; there are independent of R, as m_j was already proven independent of R, and the definition of op_i is independent of r or its shares.
- V_9, V_{10} are of the form $op_i \oplus m_j$, i.e. never recombine m_1 and m_2; as op_i does not formally depend on r or m, and m_j does not depend on R, V_9 and V_{10} also do not depend on R.
- (V_{11}, V_{12}) compute the output without ever recombining m_1 with m_2 before the very last addition, thus revealing nothing more than the information already contained in the output of the gadget.

Remark 3. If we want to use the `cswap` gadget in a more general setting, where op_1 and op_2 are jointly sensitive, we have to ensure that beyond the independence from r, no intermediate variable recombines op_1 and op_2. Our `cswap` gadget is purposely designed so that no such intermediate variable appears until the very last statements. The only update required to make our gadget definition completely free of any such combination consists in introducing an additional random value middle computation of $op12m1$ and $op12m2$ in statements 9, 10 acting as an intermediate mask as follows:

$$op12m1 \leftarrow op1m1 \oplus m_3 \oplus op2m1$$

$$op12m2 \leftarrow op1m2 \oplus m_3 \oplus op2m2$$

where m_3 is picked at random in $\mathbb{F}_{2^{16}}$. In so doing, no intermediate variable ever recombines op_1 and op_2. The m_3 masks simply cancel out in statements 11, 12 as $op12m1$ and $op12m2$ are added. Note however that this comes at the price of an additional random value, hence to be avoided if not necessary (as in our case of shuffling the NTT operation).

4.4.2 Masked Memory Access

Let V_i denote the set of all intermediate variables that appear at statement i of Algorithm 5.

- $V_6^{(1)} = r_1^{(b)}$, $V_6^{(2)} = r_2^{(b)}$ are generated independently at random, therefore, they are independent of R.
- $V_7^{(1)} = j + r_1^{(b)} \cdot len = j + V_6^{(1)} \cdot len$ only depend on $V_6^{(1)}$, hence independent of R. The same goes for $V_7^{(2)} = j + r_2^{(b)} \cdot len = j + V_6^{(2)} \cdot len$.
- $V_7^{(3)} = p[j + r_1^{(b)}]$ and $V_7^{(4)} = p[j + r_2^{(b)}]$ depend only respectively on $r_1^{(b)}$ and $r_2^{(b)}$, therefore they are independent of R.
- $V_7^{(5)} = p[j + r_1^{(b)} \cdot len] \oplus p[j]$ only depends on $r_1^{(b)}$ therefore is independent of R.
- $V_7^{(6)} = op_1 = p[j + r_1^{(b)} \cdot len] \oplus p[j] \oplus p[j + r_2^{(b)} \cdot len]$. $V_7^{(5)} = op_1$ takes values in $\mathbb{Z}_q$. Let $x \in \mathbb{Z}_q$.

$$P(op_1 = x \mid R = 0) = P(p[j] = x)$$

$$P(op_1 = x \mid R = 1) = P(p[j + len] = x)$$

$p[j]$ and $p[j+len]$ follow the same distribution law and whose value is unknown to the attacker. Therefore,

$$P(p[j] = x) = P(p[j + len] = x)$$

$$P(op_1 = x) = P(op_1 = x \mid R = 0) \cdot P(R = 0) + P(op_1 = x \mid R = 1) \cdot P(R = 1) = P(p[j] = x)$$

$$P(op_1 = x \mid R = r) = P(op_1 = x)$$

Hence, op_1 and R are independent.

- The proof is analogous for the $V_8^{(i)}$ for $i \in \{1, \ldots, 5\}$
- $V_9^{(1)} = op_1$ and $V_9^{(2)} = op_2$ are independent of R. Proof in the previous section.
- $V_{10} = t$ is independent of R because it only depends on op_2 that is independent of R.
- $V_{11} = op_1 + t$ takes values in $\mathbb{Z}_q$. Let $x \in \mathbb{Z}_q$.

$$P(op_1 + t = x \mid R = 0) = P(p[j] + p[j + len] \cdot \zeta^k = x)$$

$$P(op_1 + t = x \mid R = 1) = P(p[j + len] + p[j] \cdot \zeta^k = x)$$

$p[j]$ and $p[j+len]$ follow the same distribution law and whose value is unknown to the attacker. Therefore,

$$P(p[j] + p[j + len] \cdot \zeta^k = x) = P(p[j + len] + p[j] \cdot \zeta^k = x))$$

$$P(op_1 + t = x) = P(op_1 + t = x \mid R = 0) \cdot P(R = 0) + P(op_1 + t = x \mid R = 1) \cdot P(R = 1)$$

$$= P(p[j] + p[j + len] \cdot \zeta^k = x)$$

$$P(V_{11} = x \mid R = r) = P(V_{11} = x)$$

Hence, op_1 and R are independent.
- $V_{13}^{(1)} = out_1$ and $V_{13}^{(2)} = out_2$ are independent of R. Proof in the next section.
- The proof is analogous for $V_{12} = op_1 - t$.
- $V_{14} = p[j]$ is independent of R since out_1 is independent of R.
- $V_{15} = p[j + len]$ is independent of R since out_2 is independent of R.
- $V_{16}^{(1)} = p[j + r_1^{(b)} \cdot len] \cdot V_{15}$ is independent of R since it only dependents on $r_1^{(b)}$.
- $V_{16}^{(2)} = p[j + r_1^{(b)} \cdot len] \oplus out_2$ is independent of R because it only depends on $r_1^{(b)}$.
- $V_{17} = p[j + (1 - r_1^{(b)} \cdot len)]$, $V_{18} = p[j + r_2^{(b)} \cdot len]$, $V_{19} = p[j + (1 - r_2^{(b)}) \cdot len]$ can similarly be proven independent of R.

4.5 T-Test

To validate experimentally the implementation against first-order leakage, we perform the Test Vector Leakage Assessment (TVLA). The method is based on Welch's test. It measures whether two distinct distributions are statistically distinguishable. The idea is to collect two groups of traces:

- Group 0: traces where $r = 0$ with shares sampled at random.
- Group 1: traces where $r = 1$ with shares sampled at random.

For every sample t in the trace T, we compute Welch's test defined as follows:

$$T(t) = \frac{\mu_0(t) - \mu_1(t)}{\sqrt{\frac{\sigma_0^2(t)}{N_0} + \frac{\sigma_1^2(t)}{N_1}}}$$

where:

- $\mu_0(t)$ and $\mu_1(t)$ mean power at time t over all traces.
- $\sigma_0^2(t)$, $\sigma_1^2(t)$ the variances.
- N_0, N_1 number of traces of each class.

A t-value $|T(t)| > 4.5$ provides with a confidence level of 99.99% that there is a leakage at sample point t. The tests have been executed with 5,000 traces per group.

Figure 6 shows the first order leakage, as we can see, t-values remain well below the threshold. This means that no statistically significant leakage was detected.

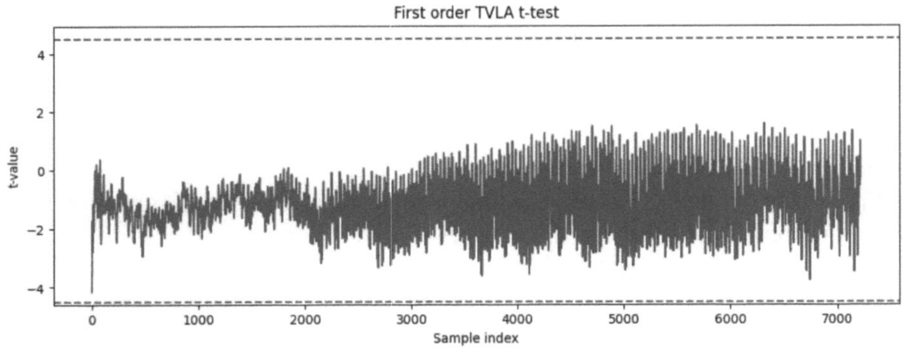

Fig. 6. First-order T-test

4.6 Benchmark

We perform a performance evaluation of the proposed countermeasure when integrated into the reference implementation of ML-KEM[2].

[2] The link of the implementation can be found in https://pq-crystals.org/kyber/resources.shtml.

4.6.1 Target Platform and Implementation Details

`STM32F303` does not support hardware accelerated Pseudo-Random Number Generator (PRNG). Hence, the benchmarks were run on the platform `TI CC2642R1-Q1` equipped with an `ARM Cortex-M4F` CPU running at a clock frequency of `48MHz` and a `SRAM` of 8 KB. For the randomness generation, we use a PRNG using AES hardware accelerator, initialised with a seed sampled by a True Random Number Generator (TRNG). The implementations were compiled using the compiler `TI ARM Clang` with the compilation flags `-O3 -mcpu=cortex-m4 -mfloat -abi=hard -mfpu=fpv4-sp-d16 -mlittle-endian -mthumb`. The AES hardware accelerator consumes 5 − 8 clock cycles per random byte generated according to the number of bytes requested to be generated. The performance of clock cycles per byte does not scale linearly when we increase the size of the input given. To amortise the cost of the PRNG, for both implementations, we made a single call to the AES-Deterministic Random Bit Generator (AES-DRBG) with the necessary number of random bytes to perform an entire single call of NTT/INTT operation and we store the random bytes in a buffer. This comes of course at a cost on the memory. Nevertheess, a trade-off can be found between the security and the memory size according to one's need. Since the buffer is accessed thousands of time during the NTT operations, we have forced the compiler to align the memory address of the buffer to a multiple of 4, and we read each time 32 or 64 bits of data from the buffer. This allows in one hand to reduce the number of memory accesses to the buffer and ensures that each access only costs 1 cycle instead of multiple clock cycles per access. The initial *bitwise-shuffling* implementation of Ravi used a slow hardware TRNG that consumes 54 cycles per byte. Therefore, we connected it to the AES-DRBG as well to provide a fair comparison with our implementation (we obtained an overhead of +281% compared with the original implementation incurred an overhead of +356%).

4.6.2 Performance Evaluation of Protected NTT/INTT Modules

Table 1 shows the performance of each implementation. We can see overall that our implementation is faster than the one proposed by [23] for both NTT and INTT despite our implementation being protected against first-order attacks. Moreover, we can further optimise the implementation by generating the asynchronously the random bytes thus, completely wipe out the overhead of random generation and reduce the memory impact. To measure the cycle count on `ARM-Cortex-M4` CPU, we read the register `DWT_CYCCNT`. We run the operation 10, 000 times and compute the average. Notice that the overhead of our countermeasure on the INTT (+60%) is significantly lower than the overhead incurred on NTT (+149%) because the cost of the countermeasure is in part diluted in the relatively higher cost of the INTT.

4.6.3 Performance Evaluation of ML-KEM768

Table 2 shows the overhead of the countermeasure over the entire decapsulation operation. As expected, we still do better than the bitwise implementation of

Table 1. Performance evaluation of NTT/INTT for the different implementations

variant	NTT		INTT	
	performance	overhead	performance	overhead
Reference implementation [2]	26, 266	_	44, 443	_
our *bitwise* implementation from [23]	100, 121	281%	111, 079	150%
Present work	65, 551	**149%**	71, 132	**60%**

Ravi. It is important to note that the decapsulation operation makes 6 calls to the NTT and 5 calls to INTT. Therefore, the overhead propagates significantly. However, it gets diluted in the entire execution of the algorithm. We end up with a 24% overhead.

Table 2. Performance evaluation of decapsulation for the different implementations

variant	ML-KEM implementation	
	performance	overhead
Reference implementation [2]	1,515,900	_
bitwise implementation [23]	2,293,518	51%
Present work	**1,885,946**	**24%**

5 Conclusion

This work addresses the security of the fine-shuffling in lattice-based cryptography with application to ML-KEM. We first defeated the *bitwise-fine-shuffling* variant proposed by Ravi *et al.* using a new angle of attack by aggregating the leakage from the 16 iterations of the bitwise masking loop. The attack has been performed in simulation and also on a real target STM32F303 with a very high success rate in practice in realistic noise scenarios. This practical demonstration confirms that the significant performance overhead of *bitwise-fine-shuffling* (+281%) for NTT does not provide security against first-order attacks. For that matter, we introduced an end-to-end masked fine-shuffling implementation. The implementation replaces the secret dependent memory accesses with ones depending only on its shares and uses a new `cswap` gadget to protect the mask for the swapping. Moreover, We have proved this implementation secure against first-order attacks. The implementation happens to be more secure and faster than the *bitwise-fine shuffling* incurring an overhead of only 24% over ML-KEM768.

Limitations and Future Work. While this study was applied to ML-KEM it can naturally be extended to ML-DSA, and more generally to other contexts such as fully homomorphic encryption and symmetric cryptography. Moreover, it is interesting to unravel how this countermeasure scales to higher-order levels. The proof in the probing model ensures security in the theoretical leakage model, but it does not address the micro-architectural leakage. Furthermore, it does not guarantee the same security level for composability with another gadget. Therefore, it is relevant to evaluate whether the gadget fullfills the composability and provide a hardened the implementation against microarchitectural leakage. Finally, it is important evaluate the overall cost of combining the first-order masking with our fine-shuffling implementation.

Acknowledgments. The authors would like to acknowledge the EU funding received under the FOCAL project (grant No. 101225859). This work was supported in part by French projects ANR-11-LABX-0020-01 "Centre Henri Lebesgue" and ANR-18-EURE-0004 "Cyberschool". We would like also to thank the reviewers for their relevant feedback that improved the quality of the paper.

Disclosure of Interests. The authors have no competing interests to declare that are relevant to the content of this article.

References

1. Agarwal, R.C., Burrus, C.S.: Number theoretic transforms to implement fast digital convolution. Proc. IEEE **63**(4), 550–560 (2005)
2. Alkim, E., et al.: Algorithm specifications and supporting documentation. Version **1**, 1–44
3. Backlund, L., Ngo, K., Gärtner, J., Dubrova, E.: Secret key recovery attack on masked and shuffled implementations of CRYSTALS-kyber and saber. In: In: Zhou, J., et al. (eds.) ACNS 2023. LNCS, vol. 13907, pp. 159–177. Springer, Cham (2023). https://doi.org/10.1007/978-3-031-41181-6_9
4. Bos, J.W., Gourjon, M.O., Renes, J., Schneider, T., Vredendaal, C.v.: Masking Kyber: first-and higher-order implementations. IACR Trans. Cryptographic Hardware Embedded Syst. **2021**(4), 173–214 (2021)
5. Brumley, D., Boneh, D.: Remote timing attacks are practical. Comput. Netw. **48**(5), 701–716 (2005)
6. Canteaut, A., Lauradoux, C., Seznec, A.: Understanding cache attacks. Ph.D. thesis, INRIA (2006)
7. Chari, S., Rao, J.R., Rohatgi, P.: Template attacks. In: Kaliski, B.S., Koç, K., Paar, C. (eds.) CHES 2002. LNCS, vol. 2523, pp. 13–28. Springer, Heidelberg (2003). https://doi.org/10.1007/3-540-36400-5_3
8. Fledel, D., Wool, A.: Sliding-window correlation attacks against encryption devices with an unstable clock. In: Cid, C., Jacobson Jr., M. (eds.) SAC 2018. LNCS, vol. 11349, pp. 193–215. Springer, Cham (2018). https://doi.org/10.1007/978-3-030-10970-7_9
9. Goubin, L.: A sound method for switching between Boolean and arithmetic masking. In: Koç, Ç.K., Naccache, D., Paar, C. (eds.) CHES 2001. LNCS, vol. 2162, pp. 3–15. Springer, Heidelberg (2001). https://doi.org/10.1007/3-540-44709-1_2
10. Goy, G., Maillard, J., Gaborit, P., Loiseau, A.: Single trace HQC shared key recovery with SASCA. IACR Trans. Cryptographic Hardware Embedded Syst. **2024**(2), 64–87 (2024)

11. Hermelink, J., Streit, S., Strieder, E., Thieme, K.: Adapting belief propagation to counter shuffling of NTTS. IACR Trans. Cryptographic Hardware and Embedded Syst. 60–88 (2023)
12. Hutter, M., Schwabe, P.: NaCl on 8-Bit AVR microcontrollers. In: Youssef, A., Nitaj, A., Hassanien, A.E. (eds.) AFRICACRYPT 2013. LNCS, vol. 7918, pp. 156–172. Springer, Heidelberg (2013). https://doi.org/10.1007/978-3-642-38553-7_9
13. Ishai, Y., Sahai, A., Wagner, D.: Private circuits: securing hardware against probing attacks. In: Boneh, D. (ed.) CRYPTO 2003. LNCS, vol. 2729, pp. 463–481. Springer, Heidelberg (2003). https://doi.org/10.1007/978-3-540-45146-4_27
14. Jendral, S., Ngo, K.,Wang, R., Dubrova, E.: A single-trace message recovery attack on a masked and shuffled implementation of CRYSTALS-kyber. Cryptology ePrint Archive (2023)
15. Kocher, P., Jaffe, J., Jun, B.: Differential power analysis. In: Wiener, M. (ed.) CRYPTO 1999. LNCS, vol. 1666, pp. 388–397. Springer, Heidelberg (1999). https://doi.org/10.1007/3-540-48405-1_25
16. Longo, J., De Mulder, E., Page, D., Tunstall, M.: SoC It to EM: ElectroMagnetic side-channel attacks on a complex system-on-chip. In: Güneysu, T., Handschuh, H. (eds.) CHES 2015. LNCS, vol. 9293, pp. 620–640. Springer, Heidelberg (2015). https://doi.org/10.1007/978-3-662-48324-4_31
17. Mangard, S., Oswald, E., Popp, T.: Power Analysis Attacks: Revealing the Secrets of Smart Cards, vol. 31. Springer, New York (2008). https://doi.org/10.1007/978-0-387-38162-6
18. Park, J.Y.: A Study of High-Performance, Low-Cost Software-Hardware Co-Design Implementation for Post Quantum Cryptographic Algorithms. Ph.D. thesis, kyushu University (2025)
19. Park, J.Y., Ju, J.W., Lee, W., Kang, B.G., Kachi, Y., Sakurai, K.: A statistical verification method of random permutations for hiding countermeasure against side-channel attacks. J. Inf. Secur. Appl. **84**, 103797 (2024)
20. Pessl, P., Primas, R.: More practical single-trace attacks on the number theoretic transform. In: Schwabe, P., Thériault, N. (eds.) LATINCRYPT 2019. LNCS, vol. 11774, pp. 130–149. Springer, Cham (2019). https://doi.org/10.1007/978-3-030-30530-7_7
21. Primas, R., Pessl, P., Mangard, S.: Single-trace side-channel attacks on masked lattice-based encryption. In: Fischer, W., Homma, N. (eds.) CHES 2017. LNCS, vol. 10529, pp. 513–533. Springer, Cham (2017). https://doi.org/10.1007/978-3-319-66787-4_25
22. Ravi, P., Chattopadhyay, A., D'Anvers, J.P., Baksi, A.: Side-channel and fault-injection attacks over lattice-based post-quantum schemes (Kyber, Dilithium): survey and new results. ACM Trans. Embedded Comput. Syst. **23**(2), 1–54 (2024)
23. Ravi, P., Poussier, R., Bhasin, S., Chattopadhyay, A.: On configurable SCA countermeasures against single trace attacks for the NTT. In: Batina, L., Picek, S., Mondal, M. (eds.) SPACE 2020. LNCS, vol. 12586, pp. 123–146. Springer, Cham (2020). https://doi.org/10.1007/978-3-030-66626-2_7
24. Remmerswaal, M.G., Wu, L., Tiran, S., Mentens, N.: Autopoi: automated points of interest selection for side-channel analysis. J. Cryptogr. Eng. **14**(3), 463–474 (2024)
25. Satriawan, A., Syafalni, I., Mareta, R., Anshori, I., Shalannanda, W., Barra, A.: Conceptual review on number theoretic transform and comprehensive review on its implementations. IEEE Access **11**, 70288–70316 (2023)

26. Xu, D., Wang, K., Tian, J.: A hardware-friendly shuffling countermeasure against side-channel attacks for Kyber. IEEE Trans. Circuits Syst. II: Express Briefs (2025)
27. Zijlstra, T., Bigou, K., Tisserand, A.: FPGA implementation and comparison of protections against SCAs for RLWE. In: Hao, F., Ruj, S., Sen Gupta, S. (eds.) INDOCRYPT 2019. LNCS, vol. 11898, pp. 535–555. Springer, Cham (2019). https://doi.org/10.1007/978-3-030-35423-7_27

Quantum and Post-qantum Attacks/Protocols

The Best of Both Worlds: Hybrid Authenticated Key Exchange for QKD(N) Without Signatures

Sebastian Clermont[1(✉)] and Johanna Henrich[2]

[1] Technical University of Darmstadt, Darmstadt, Germany
sebastian.clermont@tu-darmstadt.de
[2] Darmstadt University of Applied Sciences, Darmstadt, Germany
johanna.henrich@h-da.de

Abstract. Post-Quantum Cryptography (PQC) and Quantum Key Distribution (QKD) are both contenders for securing communication against quantum adversaries, but are at different stages of maturity. For hedging security risks, hybridization is the default approach. Unlike previous research on classical–post-quantum hybrids, we propose a QKD-PQC hybrid for Authenticated Key Exchange (AKE).

To minimize the attack surface, we completely remove the requirement for digital signature schemes and propose a Hybrid Authenticated Key Exchange (HAKE) that combines Post-Quantum (PQ) AKE and QKD key agreement, leveraging Key Encapsulation Mechanisms (KEMs) for both key exchange and authentication. Our fully modular security analysis, based on the recent multi-input Key Derivation Function (KDF) framework by Backendal et al. (Eurocrypt 2025), establishes AKE security in the CK01 model and yields a conditional information-theoretic security guarantee when the QKD component is uncompromised; a property not achieved by prior hybrid protocols. We demonstrate the protocol's practical feasibility with benchmarks using ML-KEM, FrodoKEM, and Classic McEliece.

Keywords: Hybrid Authenticated Key Exchange · Key Combiner · Quantum Key Distribution · Post-Quantum Cryptography · Key Encapsulation Mechanism · Provable Security · Benchmark

1 Introduction

Public-key cryptography encompasses mechanisms such as key exchange and digital signatures that enable secure communication. One such application is Authenticated Key Exchange (AKE), where two parties securely negotiate a shared secret. Such protocols often use two distinct public-key schemes for key establishment and entity authentication, with KEMs and digital signatures being the most common combination.

N. El Mrabet et al. (Eds.): AFRICACRYPT 2026, LNCS 16832, pp. 87–111, 2026.
https://doi.org/10.1007/978-3-032-31130-6_4

However, sufficiently powerful quantum computers (QCs), which may become available within the next few years [18], are capable of breaking classical asymmetric algorithms such as Elliptic-curve Diffie–Hellman (ECDH) and RSA in polynomial time [42]. Moreover, harvest-then-decrypt attacks [40] pose a threat to today's encrypted communication, thereby enabling the recording of data for later decryption.

Besides PQC [44], which is based on mathematical problems, QKD uses quantum effects to establish pairwise shared secrets in an information-theoretically secure way [33]. Due to the quantum phenomena used for key establishment, traditional attacks such as the aforementioned harvest-then-decrypt attacks are not applicable to QKD. Furthermore, QKD is the only current technology that enables the exchange of truly random keys and thus supports information-theoretic secure (ITS) communication. In addition to these advantages, QKD faces several challenges that must be overcome before it is ready for widespread adoption. Currently, there are no reliable, market-ready QKD modules that can bridge distances of more than 150 km [33]. Moreover, it is only possible to implement point-to-point connections and star topologies without additional measures. That is why QKD modules are often concatenated into QKD Network (QKDN) to distribute a key using hop-by-hop forwarding. This topology makes such a network vulnerable to insider attacks by compromised nodes. In addition, security vulnerabilities during implementation, such as insufficient authentication measures or side-channel leaks, must be given due consideration [18].

Hybridization can hedge security risks by combining the security guarantees of different schemes, ensuring that the security objectives are met as long as at least one of the schemes used has not been compromised [22]. Therefore, a HAKE based on both PQC and QKD can establish a secure channel that withstands an attacker, provided that at least one of these technologies remains secure. This approach aligns with the recommendations [20] of various European security organizations, including Federal Office for Information Security (BSI), French Cybersecurity Agency (ANSSI), and Netherlands National Communications Security Agency (NLNCSA). They conclude that QKD alone currently poses various risks from both theoretical and practical perspectives and should be used only as a supplementary security component.

1.1 Related Work

Entity authentication without signatures, e.g., via KEM-based authentication, is explored in several papers. Schwabe et al. describe a variant of TLS 1.3 that replaces the handshake's signature procedures with KEM-based authentication [41]. In addition, other AKE protocols with KEM-based authentication are discussed in the literature [21,25].

Boyd et al. provide modular building blocks to generate different AKE protocols that are suitable for instantiation with PQC [8]. In essence, this process provides various authentication options, both with and without signatures. The constructions are generic, allowing for instantiation with suitable primitives.

With respect to HAKE, Bindel et al. describe the general modeling of a HAKE using KEMs [7]. Dowling et al. describe the HAKE protocol Muckle [16], which combines classical schemes with PQC, QKD, and symmetric Pre-Shared Key (PSK). Authentication is done using a PSK, which is unfeasible for general deployments because preshared secrets must be established out of band and be available for each distinct pair of communicating parties. Bruckner et al. extend Muckle and call the result the Muckle+ protocol [9]. Muckle+ allows for PQC+QKD hybrid AKE using digital signatures. Using a Public Key Infrastructure (PKI) enables a hierarchical trust model, as is common practice. In a supplementary extension, Muckle# is also described, which provides KEM-based authentication [3]. However, as in Muckle+, it is assumed that QKD keys are synchronized internally and can be retrieved without specifying an identifier, whereas the industry standard [38] requires key retrieval via explicit key IDs. Moreover, Muckle# does not employ a formally analyzed key combiner and does not achieve the conditional information-theoretic security guarantee that our construction provides (cf. Theorem 2).

Ricci et al. describe a HAKE combining classical and PQC schemes with QKD using KEM-based authentication [39], but focus on benchmarking rather than formal security analysis of the key combiner.

Hövelmanns et al. propose a QKD + PQC hybrid protocol proven secure in a variant of the CK+ model [28] with modifications to accommodate QKD [24]. They identify misunderstandings on using key combiners in other designs but use an XOR-based combiner that introduces a dependent-key vulnerability, fixable by using a combiner that binds context information to the final key [1].

1.2 Our Contributions

We employ a combination of QKD and PQC to design a HAKE that operates entirely without digital signature schemes or symmetric PSKs during protocol execution, thereby reducing system complexity and overall attack surface. This choice eliminates the need to deploy a separate signature-key infrastructure and avoids the substantial communication and computational overhead of post-quantum digital signatures, which can inflate handshake sizes by several kilobytes per operation. Our construction integrates the KEM-based AKE of Boyd et al. [8] with a QKD key agreement and applies the multi-input KDF framework of Backendal et al. [1] to obtain security guarantees that neither component achieves alone. Its security is established in the well-known CK01 model [10], which we choose for compatibility with the underlying KEM-based AKE and because it already captures forward secrecy. More recent models such as eCK provide additional guarantees around ephemeral key leakage, but these are less relevant in the KEM-based setting where ephemeral secrets are not long-lived Diffie–Hellman exponents.

This yields a fully modular security analysis: the two component protocols are treated in isolation, and hybrid security follows from the combiner. If either component is replaced or improved, only the corresponding bound needs updating, without re-proving the entire protocol.

Crucially, this modular analysis yields a *conditional information-theoretic security* guarantee (Theorem 2): when the QKD system is uncompromised, the resulting session key is information-theoretically secure, even if all computational assumptions are broken. This property strictly exceeds what prior PQC–QKD hybrid protocols achieve. Prior constructions derive the combined key via hash-based key derivation, which yields computational rather than information-theoretic security even when one component provides unconditionally secure keys. This provides a graceful degradation guarantee: when QKD is secure, the resulting session key is information-theoretically secure; should QKD fail, the session key retains its full computational security under standard assumptions.

Finally, we have implemented the protocol with various KEMs and provide benchmarks on the real-world performance.

2 Preliminaries

2.1 Notation

This paper uses established notation for cryptographic papers. λ denotes the security parameter. $a \leftarrow b$ denotes deterministic assignment of the value b to variables a or assigning the output of the deterministic algorithm b to a. $c \leftarrow\!\$\ d$ denotes assigning the output of the probabilistic algorithm d to the variable c. $[\![\text{expr}]\!]$ denotes the boolean evaluation of the expression expr. $=$ denotes an equality check. The symbol $\perp$ indicates failure, $:=$ denotes a definition. $\|$ denotes the concatenation of values, $\Pr[event]$ the probability of some event and $|value|$ the absolute value. All $\mathsf{PPT}$and QPT adversaries are efficient adversaries, which means their runtime and memory are upper-bounded by some polynomial that is dependent on λ. For the advantage of adversaries, we write $\mathsf{Adv}^{\mathsf{property}}_{scheme,\mathcal{A}}(\lambda)$ for the advantage of an adversary $\mathcal{A}$ against the security property $\mathsf{property}$ of some cryptographic scheme *scheme*. $\mathsf{Exp}^{\mathsf{property}}_{scheme,\mathcal{A}}(\lambda)$ is used to define the corresponding experiment. Defining security of KDFs requires additional parameters; these advantage terms are introduced in Sect. 2.4.

For oracle definitions, we write "$\mathsf{O}_{\mathsf{Decaps}}(\mathsf{sk},\cdot)$ on input c" for an oracle called Decaps. The oracle takes a single input, as indicated by the single " $\cdot$ ", and we will call this input "c" in the algorithmic description of the oracle. We make sk explicit in the oracle description to highlight which secrets an adversary is given indirect access to.

2.2 Key Encapsulation Mechanisms

A KEM is an asymmetric primitive that can be used to establish a shared secret between two parties [13]. It consists of three algorithms.

$(\mathsf{pk},\mathsf{sk}) \leftarrow\!\$\ \mathsf{KGen}(1^\lambda)$**:** The probabilistic algorithm that, given the security parameter λ, generates a key pair $(\mathsf{pk},\mathsf{sk})$.

$(\mathsf{ct},\mathsf{k}) \leftarrow\!\$\ \mathsf{Encaps}(\mathsf{pk})$**:** Encaps is a probabilistic algorithm, taking the pk to compute a ciphertext ct encapsulating a shared secret and the shared secret k itself.

$\mathsf{k} \leftarrow \mathsf{Decaps}(\mathsf{sk}, \mathsf{ct})$: Decaps is a deterministic algorithm, using sk and ct to obtain the corresponding k.

We call a KEM ε-correct, iff for all $(\mathsf{sk}, \mathsf{pk}) \leftarrow_\$ \mathsf{KGen}(1^\lambda)$ it holds that if $(\mathsf{ct}, \mathsf{k}) \leftarrow_\$ \mathsf{Encaps}(\mathsf{pk})$ and $\mathsf{k}' \leftarrow \mathsf{Decaps}(\mathsf{sk}, \mathsf{ct})$, then $\mathsf{k}' = \mathsf{k}$ except with negligible probability.

$\mathsf{Exp}^{\text{IND-CPA}}_{\mathsf{KEM},\mathcal{A}}(\lambda)$:	$\mathsf{Exp}^{\text{IND-CCA}}_{\mathsf{KEM},\mathcal{A}}(\lambda)$:	$\mathsf{O}_{\mathsf{Decaps}}(\mathsf{sk}, \cdot)$ on input c:
$(\mathsf{pk}, \mathsf{sk}) \leftarrow_\$ \mathsf{KGen}(1^\lambda)$	$(\mathsf{pk}, \mathsf{sk}) \leftarrow_\$ \mathsf{KGen}(1^\lambda)$	**if** $[\![c = c^*]\!]$
$k_0 \leftarrow_\$ \mathcal{K}$	$k_0 \leftarrow_\$ \mathcal{K}$	**return** $\bot$
$(c^*, k_1) \leftarrow_\$ \mathsf{Encaps}(\mathsf{pk})$	$(c^*, k_1) \leftarrow_\$ \mathsf{Encaps}(\mathsf{pk})$	
$b \leftarrow_\$ \{0, 1\}$	$b \leftarrow_\$ \{0, 1\}$	**return** $\mathsf{Decaps}(\mathsf{sk}, c)$
$b' \leftarrow_\$ \mathcal{A}(\mathsf{pk}, c^*, k_b)$	$b' \leftarrow_\$ \mathcal{A}^{\mathsf{O}_{\mathsf{Decaps}}}(\mathsf{pk}, c^*, k_b)$	
return $[\![b' = b]\!]$	**return** $[\![b' = b]\!]$	

Fig. 1. Game definition for IND-ATK security of key encapsulation mechanisms with ATK $\in$ {CPA, CCA}.

Definition 1 (IND-ATKsecurity of KEM schemes). *Given the security game in Fig. 1, we define the advantage of an adversary against* IND-ATK *security of a key encapsulation scheme* KEM *for* ATK $\in$ {CPA, CCA}, *as*

$$\mathsf{Adv}^{\text{IND-ATK}}_{\mathsf{KEM},\mathcal{A}}(\lambda) := \left| \Pr\left[\mathsf{Exp}^{\text{IND-ATK}}_{\mathsf{KEM},\mathcal{A}}(\lambda) = 1\right] - \frac{1}{2} \right|.$$

2.3 Message Authentication Codes

A Message Authentication Code (MAC) is a symmetric scheme that can be used to ensure integrity and authenticity of messages. A MAC scheme comprises three algorithms.

1. $\mathsf{k} \leftarrow_\$ \mathsf{KGen}(\lambda)$: The probabilistic algorithm KGen takes the security parameter λ as input and generates a key k.
2. $\tau \leftarrow_\$ \mathsf{Tag}(\mathsf{k}, \mathsf{m})$: The probabilistic algorithm Tag maps a key k and a message $\mathsf{m} \in \{0, 1\}^*$ to a tag τ.
3. $d \leftarrow \mathsf{Vrfy}(\mathsf{k}, \mathsf{m}, \tau)$: The deterministic algorithm Vrfy takes a key k, a message m and a tag τ and outputs a decision $d \in \{\mathsf{true}, \mathsf{false}\}$, indicating if the tag is valid for given message and key.

The algorithms operate over key-, message-, and tag-spaces, which we refer to as $\mathcal{K}, \mathcal{M}, \mathcal{T}$, respectively.

We call a MAC scheme perfectly correct, iff

$$\mathsf{Vrfy}(\mathsf{k}, \mathsf{m}, \mathsf{Tag}(\mathsf{k}, \mathsf{m})) = \mathsf{true}$$

for any $\mathsf{k} \leftarrow_\$ \mathsf{KGen}(\lambda)$ and $m \in \mathcal{M}$.

$\mathsf{Exp}^{\text{EUF-CMA}}_{Mac,\mathcal{A}}(\lambda)$:

$\mathsf{k} \leftarrow\!\!\$\ \mathsf{KGen}(\lambda)$
$\mathcal{L}_m \leftarrow \emptyset$
$(m, \tau) \leftarrow\!\!\$\ \mathcal{A}^{\mathsf{O}_{\mathsf{Tag}}}$
return $[\![\mathsf{Vrfy}(\mathsf{k}, m, \tau) \wedge m \notin \mathcal{L}_m]\!]$

$\mathsf{O}_{\mathsf{Tag}}(\mathsf{k}, \cdot)$ on input m:

$\tau \leftarrow\!\!\$\ \mathsf{Tag}(\mathsf{k}, m)$
$\mathcal{L}_m \leftarrow \mathcal{L}_m \cup \{m\}$
return τ

Fig. 2. Game definition for EUF-CMA security of MAC schemes.

Definition 2 (EUF-CMA**security of MAC schemes).** *Given the security game in Fig. 2, we define the advantage of an adversary $\mathcal{A}$ against the* EUF-CMA *security of a MAC scheme* MAC *as:*

$$\mathsf{Adv}^{\text{EUF-CMA}}_{\mathsf{MAC},\mathcal{A}}(\lambda) := \Pr\left[\mathsf{Exp}^{\text{EUF-CMA}}_{\mathsf{MAC}}(\mathcal{A}) = 1\right].$$

2.4 Key Derivation Functions

For analyzing the security of multi-input KDFs (n-KDFs), as we use in the constructions we will introduce later, we use the newly established notion by Backendal et al. [1].

An n-KDF is a deterministic algorithm, which we also refer to as a *key combiner*, that takes up to n input pairs $(\sigma_1, c_1), \ldots, (\sigma_n, c_n)$, a protocol-specific label lbl, and a desired output length L, producing a combined key K:

$$K \leftarrow \mathsf{F}\big((\sigma_1, c_1), \ldots, (\sigma_n, c_n), \mathsf{lbl}, L\big).$$

The secret key material σ_i is the secret on which the n-KDF is evaluated, typically a shared secret established by a key exchange protocol. c_i denotes context information relevant to the creation of the key material input (e.g., in a Diffie–Hellman style key exchange, g^{xy} is the secret σ and a description of the underlying algebraic group together with the shares g^x, g^y is the context c). The label lbl is a fixed string that identifies the protocol and purpose of the derived key, providing domain separation and preventing cross-protocol attacks.

The inputs (σ_i, c_i) are sampled from so-called *key material sources*, denoted by Σ, which can be of different types. E.g., keys obtained from a KEM-style key agreement protocol are sampled from some source Σ_{KEM}, while keys obtained by a QKD system are sampled from Σ_{QKD}. The set of sources used by a KDF is denoted as the source collection $\mathbf{\Sigma}$. The mapping from key material sources to the input position of the KDF is fixed and encoded in a variable called Σ-map. The combiner function F used in the protocol presented in the next section expects a key (and associated context) from Σ_{KEM} as its first input, and Σ_{QKD} as its second input.

Security is defined using a real-or-random indistinguishability game that can be customized using a predicate *req*, which will be req_{Hybrid} throughout this paper. This predicate, as introduced by Backendal et al., intuitively requires that one of the sources of key material (i.e., either Σ_{KEM} or Σ_{QKD}) consistently outputs "good", i.e. keys that are not known by an adversary. In the indistinguishability game, an adversary has the ability to run the n-KDF honestly with arbitrary inputs and has access to a challenge oracle that evaluates either the real n-KDF or outputs a uniformly random key for new inputs. We write the advantage of an adversary against the KDF security of F with sources $\mathbf{\Sigma}$ and predicate *req* as $\mathsf{Adv}^{\mathsf{kdf}}_{\mathcal{A},\mathbf{\Sigma},req}(\lambda)$.

The security bounds demonstrated by Backendal et al. that are relevant for this work are based on the unpredictability of a key material source Σ. Intuitively, this means that, given all observable information, an adversary is unable to predict the keys obtained from this key exchange. This effectively reduces proving the security of the combiner to proving that the key exchange protocol generates random keys, a notion captured by the SK security discussed in Sect. 2.5. We write $\mathsf{Adv}^{\mathsf{up}}_{\mathcal{A},\Sigma}(\lambda)$ to denote the advantage of an adversary $\mathcal{A}$ against the unpredictability of source Σ. This unpredictability of the session keys is a weaker notion than the pseudorandomness obtained from key exchanges shown to be secure in the CK01 model [1, Lemma 23].

We choose this security model for our analysis because it explicitly allows leakage of some input secrets. This could be caused by a quantum computer breaking classical assumptions, or by a faulty implementation of Quantum Key Distribution, which is exactly the setting we are interested in.

The concrete instantiation chosen for our implementation and used during benchmarks is the "Random-Oracle-Based Construction" [1, Figure 4], instantiated with SHA-3-256 [17].

2.5 Authenticated Key Exchange

Since our work builds on the work by Boyd et al. [8], our results are in the same security model for authenticated key exchange, which, in turn, adopts the work by Canetti and Krawczyk [10], often referred to as the CK01-model. We adopt their notion of SK-secure AKE algorithms and call a protocol Π a secure authenticated key exchange, if it is SK-secure and provides PFS (formally defined in the PFS paragraph below). We will now formally introduce the required definitions.

The CK01 Setting: In the CK01 model, a key exchange is a message-driven protocol executed between two parties. Multiple instances of a protocol can be run in parallel between parties. We call each singular run a session and characterize it by the tuple $(P_i, P_j, s, \mathsf{role})$, where P_i intends to communicate with P_j in a session with the identifier s and P_i has the role $\mathsf{role} \in \{\mathsf{initiator}, \mathsf{responder}\}$. When a party completes its session, it computes its local output, which, most importantly, includes the session key.

Definition 3. *Matching Sessions We call two sessions matching, when for a session at P_i of the form $(P_i, P_j, s, \mathsf{initiator})$ a corresponding session at P_j of the form $(P_j, P_i, s', \mathsf{responder})$ exists and $s = s'$.*

Selecting adequate session identifiers is outside the scope of the model. We follow Krawczyk et al.'s assumption that there is some higher-level communication protocol ensuring the setup of unique session identifiers, e.g., by using a concatenation of random values generated by each party [10].

The model is initialized during a setup phase, where all participating parties generate their long-term keys without any influence from the adversary and make them available to all potential communication partners. Only after completing this initialization step can the adversary start interacting with the parties.

SK-secure *Key Exchange:* We now discuss what the CK01 model requires for AKE protocols to be secure, stating the adversary capabilities followed by the security definition. For the full formalization, we refer to [8,10].

In the CK01 model, an adversary has full control over all communication: it can withhold, fabricate, misdirect, or faithfully deliver messages, and can initiate protocol runs between parties. This complete control includes the ability to observe all messages sent as part of the protocol (which might be encrypted).

In addition to controlling the message flow, the adversary has access to oracles that reveal secrets, modeling partial corruptions in the system. Specifically, the adversary has access to three oracles

- Corrupt Oracle. This allows an adversary to learn a party's current internal state, including all its local secrets.
- Session-State Oracle. This allows an adversary to learn the internal state of a given session at a given party. The affected session must not have completed (i.e., derived the shared key) when the query is issued.
- Reveal Oracle. This allows an adversary to reveal the session key for a completed session.

Then, there is a Test Oracle. The adversary can query the Test oracle for any completed (i.e. calculated a session key) and fresh (i.e. the adversary cannot trivially obtain the session key) session (P_i, P_j, s). Depending on a bit b, the oracle will output either the actual session key or a uniform bitstring of the same length.

To model forward secrecy, a fifth oracle is added to the model.

- Expire-Session Oracle. This oracle expires a session, which deletes the derived session key at the respective parties.

Definition 4 (Freshness (informal)). *A session $(P_i, P_j, s, \mathsf{role})$ is fresh (and can thus be tested by an adversary), if the following conditions hold:*

1. *The session key has not been revealed.*
2. *The session state has not been revealed.*
3. *If it has been corrupted, it must have been expired first.*
4. *The same holds for the matching session $(P_j, P_i, s, \mathsf{role}')$.*

Observe that our definition of freshness includes forward secrecy.

Perfect Forward Secrecy. Perfect forward secrecy (PFS) guarantees that previously established session keys remain secure even if long-term keys are later compromised. We model PFS in the CK01 model using the Expire-Session Oracle. Namely, a session is still considered fresh (and can therefore be tested by the adversary), even if it has been corrupted before, as long as the session has been expired before the corruption.

Definition 5 (Key-indistinguishability security (informal)). *The security of an AKE protocol Π is defined using the key indistinguishability experiment* $\mathsf{Exp}^{\text{Key-IND}}_{\Pi,\mathcal{A}}(\lambda)$. *The adversary has the aforementioned capabilities and oracles with the objective of successfully identifying a real key from a random key without violating any freshness conditions. The advantage of $\mathcal{A}$ is defined as*

$$\mathsf{Adv}^{\text{Key-IND}}_{\Pi,\mathcal{A}}(\lambda) := \left|\Pr\left[\mathsf{Exp}^{\text{Key-IND}}_{\Pi,\mathcal{A}}(\lambda) = 1\right] - \frac{1}{2}\right|.$$

Definition 6 (SK-Security). *A key exchange protocol Π is* SK-secure*, if the following two conditions hold:*

(1) If two uncompromised parties complete matching sessions of the protocol Π, they obtain the same session key.
(2) Any efficient adversary $\mathcal{A}$ attacking key-indistinguishability of protocol Π has at most a negligible advantage over randomly guessing.

We extend this definition to the PQ setting by requiring indistinguishability from random for a quantum polynomial time (QPT) adversary. Since the parties performing the key exchange use classical hardware, we do not grant the adversary superposition access to any of the key exchange oracles. For the QKD protocol, the central entity is the detector that measures the incoming particles, which we also do not need to model with a quantum oracle.

To prevent trivial wins, Definition 6 requires the adversary to test a fresh session. Informally, a session is fresh if the adversary does not trivially know the session key, i.e. by corrupting both parties involved in a key exchange or revealing the secret of the tested session.

2.6 QKD as a Special Case of AKE

Quantum Key Distribution (QKD) is a key establishment protocol whose security relies on fundamental physical principles rather than computational hardness assumptions, dating back to the seminal work of Bennett and Brassard [4]. Despite a long research history, challenges remain for mainstream adoption, including limited range (roughly 150 km) and low key rates in the neighborhood of single-digit kbit/s. While acknowledging these limitations, European cybersecurity agencies agree that research must continue [20].

Due to the nature of QKD, functionality is provided by specialized hardware devices (QKD nodes) with physical connections to neighboring nodes. These nodes continuously negotiate key material, which is made available to clients via an interface standardized by the European Telecommunications Standards Institute (ETSI) in GS QKD 014 [38]. A Key Management System (KMS) is typically situated above the QKD node to manage keys and facilitate user access. Communication partners obtain a QKD key from their respective nodes using a *qkdKeyId*, assigned uniformly at random by the QKD node.

Definition 7 (QKD Interface). *Two parties connected to neighboring QKD nodes have the following functionality available to establish shared keys:*

- $(qkdKeyId, \mathsf{k}_{qkd}) \leftarrow\$ \mathsf{GetKey}$*: When the algorithm* GetKey *is called with no input, it selects an available QKD key and returns it along with the corresponding unique identifier.*
- $\mathsf{k}_{qkd}/\bot \leftarrow \mathsf{GetKeyById}(qkdKeyId)$*: The algorithm has to be executed at the partnered node, where the corresponding key will be retrieved, or an error will be indicated by outputting the dedicated failure symbol* $\bot$*.*

Each key can be output at most once; repeated queries to GetKeyById *with a previously used qkdKeyId return* $\bot$*.*

In order to establish a shared key using QKD, the initiating party retrieves a QKD key and an associated identifier *qkdKeyId* from its QKD node using GetKey. It then transmits *qkdKeyId* to the intended partner, who uses $\mathsf{GetKeyById}(qkdKeyId)$ to retrieve the same key from its own QKD node, thereby finalizing the key exchange. We call this protocol Π_{QKD}.

For this paper, we view QKD as a black box that delivers truly random keys as promised, including the classical communication over an authenticated channel. Established protocols include BB84 [4], Ekert91 [19], and BBM92 [5], which rely on two orthogonal quantum states, entanglement in combination with Bell inequalities, and entanglement with complementary bases, respectively.

Unlike other approaches such as [9,24] we do not model QKD with all its intricate details. This black-box abstraction is justified for two reasons. First, it preserves generality: modeling protocol-specific details (detector characteristics, authentication of the classical channel) would tie the analysis to a particular QKD implementation, whereas our construction is generic. Second, it is consistent with the established approach in the QKD security literature, where unconditional security proofs [32] yield a composable guarantee that the output is indistinguishable from ideal random keys, up to a failure probability. We collect all possible deviations from ideal behavior, including implementation vulnerabilities and side-channel leaks, under a single umbrella event QKD_fail. The concrete probability $\Pr[\mathsf{QKD\_fail}]$ can be instantiated from the security proof of the specific QKD protocol deployed, or set conservatively based on the risk tolerance of the deploying entity.

Lemma 1. Π_{QKD} *as described above is* SK-secure *(which in our definitions includes PFS) against any unbounded adversary* $\mathcal{A}$*. It holds that*

$$\mathsf{Adv}^{\mathsf{SK\text{-}secure}}_{\Pi_{\mathsf{QKD}},\mathcal{A}}(\lambda) \leq \Pr[\mathsf{QKD\_fail}], \tag{1}$$

where the event QKD_fail *indicates that the underlying QKD system failed in any way, e.g., by not returning identical keys for identical key identifiers, the output key not being uniformly random, or even just a constant value.*

This notion combines correctness (identical keys for identical identifiers) and security (here: SK security) into one convenient term.

Proof. While this claim has been analyzed with much greater formal rigor (but similar results) than here, e.g., in [32], this proof will show how to achieve the stated bound when assuming QKD to work as a black box.

First, we show that black-box QKD achieves key indistinguishability via a series of game hops.

$\mathsf{Game}_0(\lambda)$**:** We start with the regular key indistinguishability game $\mathsf{Exp}^{\text{Key-IND}}_{\Pi_{\mathsf{QKD}},\mathcal{A}}(\lambda)$

$\mathsf{Game}_1(\lambda)$**:** First, we modify the Corrupt Oracle to only return empty sets. This modification is undetectable by the adversary, as neither parties hold any state.

$\mathsf{Game}_2(\lambda)$**:** Now, we modify the Session-State Oracle to return empty sets. As with our first modification, this is undetectable, as the parties do not hold state.

$\mathsf{Game}_3(\lambda)$**:** Next, we modify the Reveal Oracle to always return truly random strings. This modification is undetectable by the adversary, as successful execution of the protocol yields a truly random session key. The exception to this is some failure in the QKD system, which results in non-uniform keys being output. This happens exactly with $\Pr[\mathsf{QKD\_fail}]$, which is exactly the success probability of a distinguisher $\mathcal{D}$ distinguishing Game 3 and Game 2.

$\mathsf{Game}_4(\lambda)$**:** Finally, we modify the Test Oracle to always return random keys. As with our previous modification to the Reveal Oracle, this is undetectable to the adversary because real keys are truly random.

Since the game's behavior is now completely independent of the secret bit b, the best strategy for the adversary is to guess. In particular, due to the modification of the Corrupt Oracle, forward secrecy is also achieved. As a result, Π_{QKD} achieves Key-IND up to $\Pr[\mathsf{QKD\_fail}]$.

The second requirement for a protocol to be SK-secure is that successfully completing the protocol must yield identical session keys for both parties. This is guaranteed by the underlying QKD system up to a likelihood of $\Pr[\mathsf{QKD\_fail}]$.

The requirement combination yields SK security up to the claimed bound. □

Remark 1. Lemma 1 gives a security bound for any unbounded adversary. We note that this directly implies security against the strictly weaker class of QPT adversaries, which we will use in Theorem 1.

We also note that due to the lack of classical long-term identity keys in QKD systems, they are, by definition, resistant to key compromise impersonation (KCI) attacks. Specifically, within our black-box model, the QKD sub-protocol does not expose an extractable long-term secret to the adversary.

2.7 Hybrid AKE

By Hybrid Authenticated Key Exchange (HAKE) we refer to utilizing multiple key exchange protocols simultaneously to achieve enhanced security even in the event that all except one of the component algorithms is compromised. We propose a direct construction for a hybrid authenticated key exchange based on KEMs and QKD, combining the resulting keys via a KDF following the paradigm proposed by BSI [18]. For our analysis, we adhere to the established CK01 model rather than the modified Bellare-Rogaway-style security model introduced by Dowling et al. [16].

3 The KEM-Based HAKE Protocol

A two-step approach is followed in the construction of the HAKE:

1. Execution of two different key exchanges. To achieve the desired hybridization properties, different hardness assumptions are used. (In this case QKD and regular cryptography.)
2. Key combination by means of a combiner function maintaining security as long as one of the component keys is secure, as described in Sect. 2.4.

These substeps can be carried out either sequentially or in parallel. In our construction, the QKD messages are sent in parallel with the PQ key exchange of [8], as illustrated in Fig. 3. Two preconditions must be taken into account:

1. Both, Alice and Bob must maintain a permanent key pair $(\mathsf{sk}_a, \mathsf{pk}_a)$ and $(\mathsf{sk}_b, \mathsf{pk}_b)$ that is tied to their respective identity. They also know the public key of the intended communication partner.
2. Both parties have to have access to QKD nodes that directly communicate with each other by means of an appropriate physical connection for executing the underlying QKD protocol. The keys are obtained via a well-defined interface, as previously outlined in Definition 7.

3.1 Protocol Flow

Figure 3 illustrates the full protocol flow for our newly proposed PQC-QKD HAKE protocol Π_{HAKE}. It consists of two independent key exchanges, with the bulk of the messages being attributed to the scheme originally proposed by Boyd et al. [8] which realizes the desired functionality using generic KEMs as its only building block. The QKD part of the protocol requires fewer messages, which are highlighted in the protocol.

From a high-level perspective, Alice and Bob first use their long-term public keys to authenticate each other. To achieve forward secrecy, Bob generates a new ephemeral KEM keypair rather than using his long-term key directly; otherwise, compromise of the static secret key would reveal all past session keys. In parallel, they use their QKD access to establish a second shared key. Initially, Alice

Alice		**Bob**
$\mathsf{pk}_a, \mathsf{sk}_a, \mathsf{pk}_b$		$\mathsf{pk}_b, \mathsf{sk}_b, \mathsf{pk}_a$
$\mathsf{k}_1, \mathsf{ct}_1 \leftarrow\!\!\$\ \mathsf{Encaps}(\mathsf{pk}_b)$		
	$\xrightarrow{\mathsf{ct}_1}$	
		$\mathsf{pk}_e, \mathsf{sk}_e \leftarrow\!\!\$\ \mathsf{KGen}(1^\lambda)$ $\mathsf{k}_1' \leftarrow \mathsf{Decaps}(\mathsf{sk}_b, \mathsf{ct}_1)$ $\mathsf{k}_2, \mathsf{ct}_2 \leftarrow\!\!\$\ \mathsf{Encaps}(\mathsf{pk}_a)$ $s \leftarrow \mathsf{ct}_1 \parallel \mathsf{ct}_2$ $\tau_1 \leftarrow\!\!\$\ \mathsf{Tag}(\mathsf{k}_1', \mathsf{pk}_e \Vert s \Vert A)$
	$\xleftarrow{\mathsf{pk}_e, \tau_1, \mathsf{ct}_2}$	
$s \leftarrow \mathsf{ct}_1 \parallel \mathsf{ct}_2$ **if** $\bot = \mathsf{Vrfy}(\mathsf{k}_1, \mathsf{pk}_e \Vert s \Vert A, \tau_1)$ **fail** $\mathsf{k}_2' \leftarrow \mathsf{Decaps}(\mathsf{sk}_a, \mathsf{ct}_2)$ $\mathsf{k}^*, \mathsf{ct}^* \leftarrow\!\!\$\ \mathsf{Encaps}(\mathsf{pk}_e)$ $\mathsf{k}_{qkd}, \mathit{qkdKeyId} \leftarrow\!\!\$\ \mathsf{GetKey}$ $\tau_2 \leftarrow\!\!\$\ \mathsf{Tag}(\mathsf{k}_2', \mathit{qkdKeyId} \parallel \mathsf{ct}^* \parallel s \parallel B)$		
	$\xrightarrow{\mathsf{ct}^*, \mathit{qkdKeyId}, \tau_2}$	
		if $\bot = \mathsf{Vrfy}(\mathsf{k}_2, \mathit{qkdKeyId} \Vert \mathsf{ct}^* \Vert s \Vert B, \tau_2)$ **fail** $\mathsf{k}^* \leftarrow \mathsf{Decaps}(\mathsf{sk}_e, \mathsf{ct}^*)$ $\mathsf{k}_{qkd} \leftarrow \mathsf{GetKeyById}(\mathit{qkdKeyId})$ **if** $\bot = \mathsf{k}_{qkd}$ **fail**

// Inputs defined in Section 3.1
 $\mathsf{k}_h \leftarrow \mathsf{F}(((\sigma_{\Pi_{\mathsf{KEM}}}, c_{\Pi_{\mathsf{KEM}}}), (\sigma_{\Pi_{\mathsf{QKD}}}, c_{\Pi_{\mathsf{QKD}}})),$ "KEM-QKD-Hybrid KEX", 512)
		// Bob performs same computation as Alice
		 $\mathsf{k}_h \leftarrow \mathsf{F}(\ldots)$
		 // Key is split into two equal halves
		 $\mathsf{k}_{1h} \Vert \mathsf{k}_{2h} \leftarrow \mathsf{k}_h$
		 // First half of key
		 // Used for key confirmation
		 $\tau_3 \leftarrow\!\!\$\ \mathsf{Tag}(\mathsf{k}_{1h}, \mathsf{k}_1 \Vert \mathit{qkdKeyId} \Vert \mathsf{pk}_e \Vert \tau_1 \Vert \mathsf{k}_2 \Vert \tau_2)$

	$\xleftarrow{\tau_3}$	
$\mathsf{k}_{1h} \Vert \mathsf{k}_{2h} \leftarrow \mathsf{k}_h$ **if** $\bot = \mathsf{Vrfy}(\mathsf{k}_{1h}, \mathsf{k}_1 \Vert \mathit{qkdKeyId} \Vert \mathsf{pk}_e \Vert \tau_1 \Vert \mathsf{k}_2 \Vert \tau_2, \tau_3)$ **fail**		

Fig. 3. Our proposed HAKE protocol Π_{HAKE} between Alice and Bob combining a KEM-based and a QKD key agreement. k_{2h} is the final 256-bit key shared between both parties. It is assumed that the parties own a public KEM key pk_a and pk_b, respectively, of each other. The QKD part of the protocol is composed of the highlighted actions. Note that the KEM and QKD sub-protocols operate independently (cf. Lemma 2); the second message from Alice to Bob batches transmissions from both sub-protocols to reduce round trips.

requests a fresh key from her KMS using GetKey and receives the key and its ID *qkdKeyId*. The ID is then transmitted to Bob, who uses it to retrieve the same key from his respective KMS. To reduce the number of messages, the ID is transmitted in parallel with a message from the KEM based AKE protocol. In general, the establishment of QKD keys necessitates a significantly greater investment of time and computing power than is required for KEM operations [9,30,33]. Furthermore, once a key has been requested at the QKD interface, it cannot be used a second time, as outlined in Definition 7. Consequently, the QKD key requests are executed in the latter phase of the protocol. In the event of an issue, such as a failure in the KEM-based authentication, no QKD key is wasted. Following the conclusion of both key exchanges, both parties run a key combiner in order to obtain the final hybrid key.

As explained in Sect. 2.4, our combiner design is based on the research by Backendal et al. and one of their proposed constructions based on SHA-3 [1, Theorem 8]. We will refer to the KDF as F. For evaluating (and later analyzing) the combiner-KDF in Backendal et al.'s security model, we need to define sources of key material (and the resulting secrets and contexts) as well as a label for the final execution of the combiner.

KEM-Based AKE: For the KEM-based AKE protocol Π_{KEM}, the secret $\sigma_{\Pi_{\mathsf{KEM}}}$ is the key resulting from the final decapsulation step and the context $c_{\Pi_{\mathsf{KEM}}}$ is composed of all public keys, the transcript of the KEM-based sub-protocol and the identities Alice (A) and Bob (B):

$$\begin{aligned}\sigma_{\Pi_{\mathsf{KEM}}} &:= \mathsf{k}^* \\ c_{\Pi_{\mathsf{KEM}}} &:= A \| \mathsf{pk}_a \| B \| \mathsf{pk}_b \| \mathsf{pk}_e \| \mathsf{k}_1 \| \mathsf{k}_2 \| \mathsf{k}^*\end{aligned}$$

QKD-Based AKE: Due to the characteristics of QKD, it is much simpler to identify secret key material and context for the QKD-based AKE (Π_{QKD}):

$$\begin{aligned}\sigma_{\Pi_{\mathsf{QKD}}} &:= \mathsf{k}_{qkd} \\ c_{\Pi_{\mathsf{QKD}}} &:= A \| B \| qkdKeyId\end{aligned}$$

The label lbl is a fixed, protocol-specific string that provides domain separation, ensuring that keys derived for different protocols or purposes cannot be confused; for our implementation, the string `KEM-QKD-Hybrid KEX` is used. The output length is chosen to be 512 bits, leaving both parties with 256 usable bits after the key confirmation step.

The aforementioned key confirmation step occurs after the key combiner is executed and ensures that both parties have derived identical keys. It is important not to use the final key for this step, as this might leak information related to this final key. Instead, the output of the combiner, k_h is split into two keys of equal length, k_{1h} and k_{2h}. k_{1h} will be used for key confirmation, while k_{2h} is the resulting key of the protocol. The key confirmation itself is carried out using a MAC that authenticates the entire transcript of the conversation. The tag is created by Bob and verified by Alice. Note that the key confirmation is one-directional (Bob to Alice). Full mutual confirmation would require an additional message, but cannot provide both parties with equal assurance due to the well-known impossibility result for coordinated agreement [10]. In practice, the first message Alice sends using the derived key k_{2h} serves as implicit confirmation to Bob. The long-term public keys assumed above can be distributed by direct pre-distribution in small networks, via a QKDN controller acting as a trusted third party, or via a PKI [3,9]; our "without signatures" property concerns the online protocol execution, so any such bootstrapping—which incurs signature operations only as a one-time setup cost—is fully compatible with our construction.

4 Security

We now give the formal security statements for the HAKE protocol introduced in the previous sections. Intuitively, the security of the protocol follows from the security of either the KEM-based AKE or the security of the QKD system, as long as one of the component keys remains secure.

The two component key exchanges based on KEMs and QKD are independent, so their security can be proven individually. The hybrid guarantee is then established via a key combiner that binds both transcripts to the final key. We start by establishing this independence, which is the foundation for the modular analysis.

Lemma 2 (Independence of sub-protocols). *Π_{HAKE} as proposed in Fig. 3 is composed of the KEM based AKE protocol Π_{KEM}, the QKD-based AKE protocol Π_{QKD} and a final combiner step using* F. *The two sub-protocols process their messages independently: neither sub-protocol's computation depends on secrets or intermediate values of the other.*

Proof. The messages of Π_{KEM} and Π_{QKD} are processed separately throughout the protocol. The only shared message is the second transmission from Alice to Bob, which batches messages from both sub-protocols into one network packet. This is a transport-level optimization that does not create a cryptographic dependency, as the message can equivalently be split into two separate transmissions without affecting the security reduction. □

Next, we establish the SK security of the two component protocols in the CK01 model.

Lemma 3 (sksecurity of the KEM based AKE). *Let $\mathcal{A}$ be an adversary against* SK *security. Observe that Π_{HAKE} as proposed in Fig. 3 without the gray boxes representing the QKD part and the combiner actions at the end is an instance of a KEM-based authenticated key exchange as proposed and proven secure by Boyd et al. [8, Figure 8]. Since these extra messages are handled independently, they do not affect the security of the key exchange, which is shown* *to be* SK-secure *by Boyd et al. [8, Theorem 2,3,4] with the following bound for efficient* QPT *adversaries* $\mathcal{B}, \mathcal{D}$, *and* $\mathcal{F}$:

$$\mathsf{Adv}^{\mathsf{SK\text{-}secure}}_{\Pi_{\mathsf{KEM}},\mathcal{A}}(\lambda) \leq \ell \cdot \left(\mathsf{Adv}^{\mathsf{CCA}}_{KEM,\mathcal{D}}(\lambda) + \mathsf{Adv}^{\mathsf{EUF-CMA}}_{MAC,\mathcal{F}}(\lambda)\right) + \ell \cdot \mathsf{Adv}^{\mathsf{CPA}}_{KEM,\mathcal{B}}(\lambda),$$

where $\ell := n^2 q$, n *denotes the number of parties, and* q *the number of challenge messages. The adversaries are as defined in [8].*

Proof Outline. The proof composes Theorems 2, 3, and 4 of [8]; we refer to the original work for full details and highlight the main steps here.

Following the approach of [10], the protocol is first proven secure in the authenticated links model, where adversaries cannot tamper with messages. Then, using a KEM-based authenticator, the protocol is lifted to the real-world setting of unauthenticated links. The resulting bound is additive, equal to the sum of the bounds for the protocol itself and the authenticator.

In the stated bound, the IND-CCA security of the KEM and EUF-CMA of the MAC scheme are due to the authenticator, while the IND-CPA security of the underlying KEM is required by the key exchange in the authenticated links model. Adversaries $\mathcal{B}, \mathcal{D}, \mathcal{F}$ are as defined in [8, Proof of Theorem 3,4]. The multiplicative factor ℓ accounts for the probability that the inner adversary in the reduction selects the target session in which the challenge is embedded. □

Theorem 1 (sksecurity of Π_{HAKE}). *Let* Π_{HAKE} *be the protocol introduced in Fig. 3. A* QPT *adversary* $\mathcal{A}$ *attacking the scheme has its success probability bound by the term*

$$\mathsf{Adv}^{\mathsf{SK\text{-}secure}}_{\Pi_{\mathsf{HAKE}},\mathcal{A}}(\lambda) \leq 2 \cdot \min\Big(\ell \cdot \left(\mathsf{Adv}^{\mathsf{CCA}}_{KEM,\mathcal{D}}(\lambda) + \mathsf{Adv}^{\mathsf{EUF-CMA}}_{MAC,\mathcal{F}}(\lambda)\right) + \ell \cdot \mathsf{Adv}^{\mathsf{CPA}}_{KEM,\mathcal{B}}(\lambda), \Pr\left[\mathsf{QKD\_fail}\right] \Big),$$

where $\ell := n^2 q$, n *denotes the number of parties and* q *the number of challenge queries and* $\mathcal{B}, \mathcal{D}, \mathcal{F}$ *are the* QPT *adversaries as defined in Lemma 3.*

Proof. The proof is composed of four components:

1. Independence of Π_{KEM} and Π_{QKD} (Lemma 2)
2. SK security of the KEM based AKE protocol (Lemma 3)
3. SK security of the QKD-based AKE protocol (Lemma 1)
4. Combiner Security of the KDF F (This proof and [1, Thm. 9])

In combination, the first three components, with the proofs stated in the associated lemmas above, allow us to focus on the security of the combiner function F for this proof. We have established that the two component-protocols are secure by themselves, it remains to prove that our combiner function F is a good combiner function that maintains SK security of the hybrid protocol Π_{HAKE} against QPT adversaries, as long as one of its components remains secure.

We show this result by following the work from Backendal et al. [1, Theorem 9]. Recall that our protocol uses the so-called $\mathsf{RO}-\mathsf{KDF}$, instantiated with SHA-3 with a fixed output length of 512 bits, as described in Sect. 2.4. SHA-3 is based on the Keccak sponge construction, which is indifferentiable from a random oracle [6], justifying the random oracle modeling used in Theorem 9 of [1]. Our instantiation is a 2-KDF with the source collection $\mathbf{\Sigma}$ containing the two sources Σ_{KEM} and Σ_{QKD}. The Σ-map maps Σ_{KEM} to the first input and Σ_{QKD} to the second input. Domain separation is achieved through the protocol-specific label lbl and the inclusion of both sub-protocol transcripts in the context, preventing cross-protocol attacks. Since we are building a QKD/PQ hybrid, we use the predicate req_{Hybrid} to determine which queries the adversary is allowed to make. SHA-3 is a non-extendable output function (i.e. queries with the same values, but different output lengths do not return values that are prefixes of each other), also called NOF. Therefore, the freshness predicate by Backendal et al. for this type of output behavior req_N also applies here.

This exact setup was analyzed by Backendal et al., allowing us to directly apply [1, Theorem 9], yielding the following bound for an adversary $\mathcal{G}$ attacking the combiner function F with QPT adversaries $\mathcal{C}$ and $\mathcal{E}$:

$$\begin{aligned}\mathsf{Adv}^{\mathsf{kdf}}_{\mathsf{F},\mathcal{A},\mathbf{\Sigma},req_N\wedge req_{\mathsf{Hybrid}}}(\lambda) \leq \\ 2\cdot min(\mathsf{Adv}^{\mathsf{up}}_{\mathsf{F},\mathcal{C},\Sigma_{\text{KEM}}}(\lambda), \mathsf{Adv}^{\mathsf{up}}_{\mathsf{F},\mathcal{E},\Sigma_{\text{QKD}}}(\lambda)).\end{aligned}$$

This establishes combiner security: F yields a secure key provided that either source is unpredictable.

It remains to connect this to AKE security of the full protocol Π_{HAKE}. The reduction proceeds as follows: SK security of Π_{KEM} (Lemma 3) and Π_{QKD} (Lemma 1) implies pseudorandomness of the respective session keys, which in turn implies unpredictability [1, Lemma 23]. Substituting the SK security bounds of the two component schemes into the above inequality yields the claimed bound for Π_{HAKE}. □

The *min* term in the final bound is exactly what we aim to achieve and gives us the desired property of the protocol being as secure as its best component.

While Theorem 1 establishes security in the well-established CK01 model, two advanced security properties might also be of interest. The first is security against unknown key-share (UKS) attacks, as first described in [15]. In Π_{HAKE}, both parties include the identity of their intended partner as part of the context information into the final key derivation step. Consequently any confusion about the communication partner would yield different keys for both partners, causing the key confirmation step to fail.

The second property is security against key compromise impersonation (KCI) attacks. Such attacks are possible if the final key depends only on the long-term key of one of the parties. However, running Π_{HAKE} includes calculating two MAC tags, one with a key resulting from an encapsulation under Alice's identity key and the other from encapsulating under Bob's identity key. An adversary who has compromised one party's long-term key can compute the corresponding MAC tag, but cannot forge the tag derived from the uncompromised party's key without breaking the IND-CCA security of the KEM. In combination with our earlier observation that the sub-protocol Π_{QKD} is also resistant against such attacks, we obtain security against KCI-style attacks for the resulting protocol Π_{HAKE}.

Conditional ITS Security. The $min()$ expression in the security bound of Theorem 1 reveals an interesting subtlety: if the QKD system is working as intended, the hybridization does not degrade security to be resistant "only" against QPT adversaries, but maintains security against unbounded adversaries. This covers both conditions of SK security (Definition 6): key agreement and key indistinguishability. Authentication of the classical channel is an integral part of the QKD protocol and is subsumed by our black-box model, so an uncompromised QKD sub-protocol independently provides both guarantees against unbounded adversaries. This improvement is obtained by using the modern framework for analyzing KDF security by Backendal et al. [1], which allows for a fine-grained analysis of KDFs with multiple inputs. That the resulting proof of Theorem 2 is short reflects the power of this modular decomposition: the technical work resides in establishing the min-bound of Theorem 1 and the QKD guarantee of Lemma 1, after which the ITS conclusion follows directly. The contribution is not a complex proof technique, but the identification that the combination of a suitable combiner framework with QKD yields a guarantee that no purely classical or PQC-only hybrid protocol can provide.

We note that this result relies on the random oracle assumption used in [1, Theorem 9], which our protocol instantiates with SHA-3. Precisely, Theorem 2 establishes information-theoretic security *in the random oracle model*: the only idealization is the hash function, while the bound itself holds for computationally unbounded adversaries. This is qualitatively different from computational security guarantees that rely on the hardness of lattice or code-based problems, since the random oracle models a single, fixed-length hash evaluation rather than an asymptotic hardness assumption. A combiner achieving the same guarantee without the random oracle exists [1, Theorem 17] but lacks a standardized implementation.

Theorem 2 (Information theoretic security of Π_{HAKE}). *Let Π_{HAKE} be the protocol introduced in Fig. 3. An unbounded adversary $\mathcal{A}$ attacking the scheme has its success probability bound by the term*

$$\mathsf{Adv}^{\mathsf{SK\text{-}secure}}_{\Pi_{\mathsf{HAKE}},\mathcal{A}}(\lambda) \leq 2 \cdot \Pr\left[\mathsf{QKD\_fail}\right].$$

This is a significant improvement over using the HKDF scheme as suggested by NIST [2], which also yields hybrid guarantees, but only in a computational setting [29, Theorem 4], since its security proof inherently relies on the pseudorandomness of HMAC.

Proof. By Theorem 1, the advantage of any adversary against Π_{HAKE} is bounded by $2 \cdot \min(\cdot, \Pr[\mathsf{QKD\_fail}])$. The first argument of the min depends on computational assumptions and is therefore only meaningful for QPT adversaries. However, the second argument, $\Pr[\mathsf{QKD\_fail}]$, is established in Lemma 1 without any computational assumption and holds for unbounded adversaries. Since the min is at most its smallest argument, the bound $2 \cdot \Pr[\mathsf{QKD\_fail}]$ applies regardless of the adversary's computational power, yielding the claimed result. □

In summary, Π_{HAKE} achieves a best-of-both-worlds guarantee: as long as the QKD component remains uncompromised, the protocol achieves full SK security against unbounded adversaries, even if all computational assumptions underlying the KEM-based AKE are broken. This strictly exceeds what classical–PQC hybrid protocols can offer and highlights the advantage of integrating QKD into a modular hybrid design. Conversely, if the QKD system is compromised, the KEM-based component ensures that the protocol remains secure against QPT adversaries under standard cryptographic assumptions, preserving the hybrid safety net.

5 Implementation and Evaluation

Based on the aforementioned protocol, a Hybridization Service (HS) was implemented. The source code is freely accessible and can be found at our Gitlab Repository[1]. HS has been written in the *Go* programming language and is run within a Docker container. It offers two interfaces, S_1 and S_2. S_1 is employed for the purposes of initial communication and control by a higher-level application. It facilitates the transmission of a hybridization request, encompassing the address data of the opposing HS, in addition to the QKD key to be hybridized and its id. HS is also capable of acquiring a specific QKD key via S_1 using the QKD key id. S_2 is employed to facilitate the exchange of a PQC key with another HS instance, based on an initially configured KEM. The implementation of the PQC schemes is achieved through the utilization of liboqs [35] and the liboqs Go wrapper [34]. The *Go* crypto package [43] provides functionality for the implementation of traditional cryptographic mechanisms. The transmission of data is facilitated by the use of Transmission Control Protocol (TCP).

5.1 Benchmarking Setup

The evaluation was conducted using a server configured with Ubuntu 24.04 LTS, 8 vCPUs (AMD EPYC Milan (DDR4-3200 ECC), 2.25 GHz), 16 GB RAM. Two Docker containers were executed, each containing an HS instance, designated HS Alice and HS Bob, respectively. Furthermore, two additional Docker containers each contain a KMS instance, designated KMS Alice and KMS Bob, respectively. HS Alice and HS Bob are assigned to their respective KMS and connected to them via S_1. In addition, the HS instances are connected to each other via S_2.

[1] https://code.fbi.h-da.de/hybridizekeyservice/gohybridizekeyservice.

The evaluation encompassed the entire protocol sequence, commencing from the hybridization request via S_1, culminating in the key receipt. The public and private keys necessary for KEM-based authentication were generated beforehand. Alice possesses its own key pair, (pk_a, sk_a), as well as Bob's pk_b, stored within its internal memory. In the case of Bob the situation is reversed. Furthermore, QKD keys have already been established. The hybridization process can only be started once KMS Alice has a QKD key to hybridize and an associated ID, meaning that cases where QKD key establishment has not yet taken place are disregarded and part of KMS key management. Consequently, it is not necessary to account for additional delays in the QKD key establishment process. The pertinent standards and recommendations [26,27,38] also propose the implementation of KMSs with designated storage for QKDN nodes, thereby ensuring the establishment of QKD keys in advance and their maintenance in a state of readiness, as described in [14]. An empty key storage is an undesirable special case. Any delay caused by this will have an accumulating effect on the total duration of the hybridization request.

Each experiment consisted of 1000 measurements per configuration. A total of three different KMSs were tested, each with security levels 1, 3, and 5. ML-KEM (*ML-KEM-512*, *ML-KEM-768*, *ML-KEM-1024*) that has been standardized by National Institute of Standards and Technology (NIST), as well as FrodoKEM (*FrodoKEM-640-AES*, *FrodoKEM-976-AES*, *FrodoKEM-1344-AES*) and Classic McEliece (*Classic-McEliece-348864f*, *Classic-McEliece-460896f*, *Classic-McEliece-6688128f*), which were recommended by other institutions, such as the German BSI [18,20]. MAC was implemented using Hash-based MAC (HMAC) and SHA-256. For the key combination, SHA3-512 was used.

5.2 Experimental Results

The results for the simple test configuration are presented in Fig. 4 in the form of a box plot diagram [36]. It is noteworthy that the ML-KEM variants exhibited an average time requirement of 11 to 13 ms with minimal dispersion. FrodoKEM is slightly slower, and the time penalties for the higher security levels are somewhat greater. In contrast, the variants of Classic McEliece are distinctly different. As demonstrated in Fig. 4, the median values range from approximately 50 ms for security level 1, to 113 ms for security level 3, and 150 ms for security level 5. Since no network delays were emulated in this initial setup, the results are dominated by the computational cost of the asymmetric schemes. ML-KEM is highly efficient, whereas Classic McEliece exhibits significant latency due to its key generation process (mceliece348864f 15–20 ms, mceliece6688128f up to 150 ms [12]). In the case of mceliece6688128f, this delay can reach up to 150 ms [11,12]. For each KEM, the minimum, 0.25 quantile, and median are close, indicating that most runs are near optimal.

In a subsequent series of tests, the delay between each message transmitted between the HS instances was incremented by 20 ms. On average, the duration increases by 100 ms with the same KEM scheme when latency is increased by 20 ms, as demonstrated in Table 1. The protocol requires five sequential

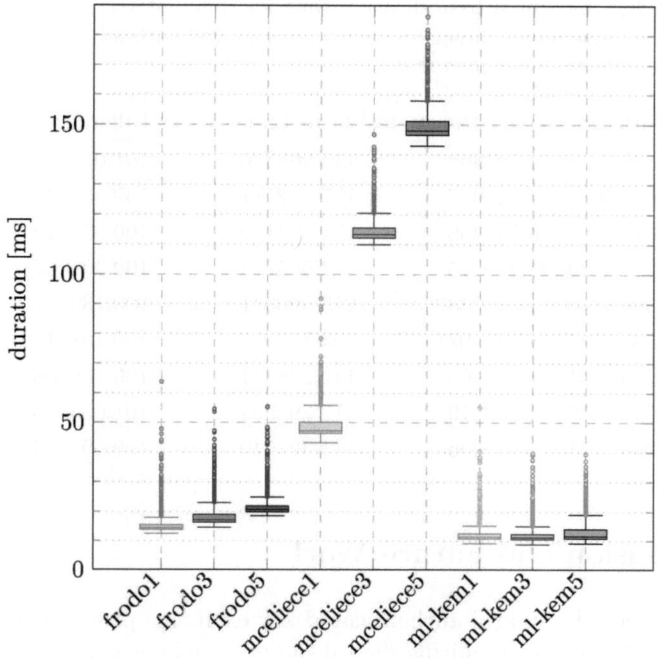

Fig. 4. Hybridization duration when using the PQC KEMs FrodoKEM (*FrodoKEM-640-AES*, *FrodoKEM-976-AES*, *FrodoKEM-1344-AES*), Classic McEliece (*Classic-McEliece-348864f*, *Classic-McEliece-460896f*, *Classic-McEliece-6688128f*), and ML-KEM (*ML-KEM-512*, *ML-KEM-768*, *ML-KEM-1024*). A total of 1,000 measurements were conducted for each of the three security levels (1, 3, and 5). Box plot diagram, which shows median, 0.25 quartile, 0.75 quartile, minimum, maximum, and outliers.

message transmissions (cf. Fig. 3), so the observed increase of approximately $5 \times 20\,\text{ms} = 100\,\text{ms}$ matches the expected behavior. However, the amount of data to be transmitted becomes a salient factor, given that large messages are divided into multiple packets and an additional sequential transmission introduces an extra delay. It is important to note that the experiments did not consider additional network constraints, such as diminished bandwidth, packet loss, or flow and congestion control under TCP. For a more comprehensive overview, please refer to the works of Paquin et al. [37] and Henrich et al. [23]. In particular, FrodoKEM and Classic McEliece possess significantly large key sizes, which would further reduce throughput under a limited TCP congestion window or constrained bandwidth.

Since QKD modules are limited to distances of 100–150 km, message delays beyond 20 ms are unlikely in typical deployments [31,45], and the evaluation thus covers the relevant use case. Even in the worst case (Classic McEliece at security level 5 with 20 ms latency), the total hybridization time remains below 250 ms, which is acceptable for applications where key establishment can be performed ahead of time.

Table 1. Median measured hybridization time for different KEM schemes. Columns illustrate measurements for direct connection (0 ms) and with added latency of 20 ms, as well as the difference between them.

Duration	0 ms Latency [ms]	20 ms Latency [ms]	Difference [ms]
Frodo1	14.503868	115.600346	101.096478
Frodo3	17.226027	117.882171	100.656144
Frodo5	20.746900	121.583129	100.836229
McEliece1	47.279915	147.685722	100.405807
McEliece3	113.400480	213.590071	100.189591
McEliece5	147.971071	248.159086	100.188015
ML-KEM1	11.472463	112.238871	100.766408
ML-KEM3	11.239579	112.292954	101.053375
ML-KEM5	11.630536	112.322540	100.692004

6 Conclusion and Future Work

We have presented a hybrid authenticated key exchange protocol that combines PQC and QKD without requiring digital signature schemes during protocol execution. By applying the multi-input KDF framework of Backendal et al. [1], we obtain a modular security proof in the CK01 model with a transparent min-bound (Theorem 1), and show that conditional information-theoretic security is achieved when the QKD component is uncompromised (Theorem 2). Our benchmarks confirm that the protocol is practical, with ML-KEM-based instantiations completing in under 15 ms and remaining well within acceptable latency bounds even under realistic network delays.

The elimination of signature schemes reduces the overall attack surface and system complexity, including the administrative burden of maintaining a crypto-inventory. However, the realization of these advantages is contingent on the specific cryptographic schemes employed and the fundamental requirements of the system in question.

Several directions for future work remain. The random oracle assumption underlying the ITS guarantee can be removed by adopting the non-RO combiner of [1, Theorem 17] once a standardized implementation becomes available. Extending the formal analysis to a composable security framework would allow reasoning about the protocol's use as a building block within larger systems. Finally, a more fine-grained integration of the QKD model, capturing aspects such as key synchronization and rate limitations, would further strengthen the practical relevance of the security guarantees.

References

1. Backendal, M., Clermont, S., Fischlin, M., Günther, F.: Key derivation functions without a grain of salt. In: Fehr, S., Fouque, P.A. (eds.) EUROCRYPT 2025, Part VIII. LNCS, vol. 15608, pp. 393–426. Springer, Cham, Switzerland, Madrid, Spain (2025). https://doi.org/10.1007/978-3-031-91101-9_14
2. Barker, E., Chen, L., (NIST), R.D.: Recommendation for key-derivation methods in key-establishment schemes. Tech. Rep. NIST Special Publication (SP) 800-56C-r2, National Institute of Standards an Technology (NIST), Gaithersburg, MD (2020). https://doi.org/10.6028/NIST.SP.800-56Cr2
3. Battarbee, C., Striecks, C., Perret, L., Ramacher, S., Verhaeghe, K.: Quantum-safe hybrid key exchanges with KEM-based authentication. EPJ Quantum Technol. **12**(1), 128 (2025). https://doi.org/10.1140/epjqt/s40507-025-00425-3, https://epjquantumtechnology.springeropen.com/articles/10.1140/epjqt/s40507-025-00425-3
4. Bennett, C.H., Brassard, G.: Quantum cryptography: public key distribution and coin tossing. Theoret. Comput. Sci. **560**, 7–11 (2014). https://doi.org/10.1016/j.tcs.2014.05.025
5. Bennett, C.H., Brassard, G., Mermin, N.D.: Quantum cryptography without bell's theorem. Phys. Rev. Lett. **68**, 557–559 (1992). https://doi.org/10.1103/PhysRevLett.68.557, https://link.aps.org/doi/10.1103/PhysRevLett.68.557
6. Bertoni, G., Daemen, J., Peeters, M., Van Assche, G.: On the indifferentiability of the Sponge construction. In: Smart, N.P. (ed.) EUROCRYPT 2008. LNCS, vol. 4965, pp. 181–197. Springer Berlin Heidelberg, Germany, Istanbul, Turkey (2008). https://doi.org/10.1007/978-3-540-78967-3_11
7. Bindel, N., Brendel, J., Fischlin, M., Goncalves, B., Stebila, D.: Hybrid key encapsulation mechanisms and authenticated key exchange. In: Ding, J., Steinwandt, R. (eds.) PQCrypto 2019: Post-Quantum Cryptography. Lecture Notes in Computer Science, vol. 11505, pp. 206–226. Springer, Berlin, Heidelberg, DE (2019). https://doi.org/10.1007/978-3-030-25510-7_12, veranstaltungstitel: 10th International Conference on Post-Quantum Cryptography
8. Boyd, C., de Kock, B., Millerjord, L.: Modular design of KEM-based authenticated key exchange. In: Simpson, L., Baee, M.A.R. (eds.) ACISP 23. LNCS, vol. 13915, pp. 553–579. Springer, Cham, Switzerland, Brisbane, QLD, Australia (2023). https://doi.org/10.1007/978-3-031-35486-1_24
9. Bruckner, S., Ramacher, S., Striecks, C.: Muckle+: end-to-end hybrid authenticated key exchanges. In: Johansson, T., Smith-Tone, D. (eds.) Post-Quantum Cryptography, pp. 601–633. Springer Nature Switzerland, Cham (2023)
10. Canetti, R., Krawczyk, H.: Analysis of key-exchange protocols and their use for building secure channels. In: Pfitzmann, B. (ed.) EUROCRYPT 2001. LNCS, vol. 2045, pp. 453–474. Springer Berlin Heidelberg, Germany, Innsbruck, Austria (2001). https://doi.org/10.1007/3-540-44987-6_28
11. Chen, M.S., Chou, T.: Classic McEliece on the ARM cortex-m4. Cryptology ePrint Archive, Paper 2021/492 (2021). https://eprint.iacr.org/2021/492
12. Chen, P.J., Chou, T., Deshpande, S., Lahr, N., Niederhagen, R., Szefer, J., Wang, W.: Complete and improved FPGA implementation of classic McEliece. IACR TCHES **2022**(3), 71–113 (2022). https://doi.org/10.46586/tches.v2022.i3.71-113
13. Cramer, R., Shoup, V.: Design and analysis of practical public-key encryption schemes secure against adaptive chosen ciphertext attack. SIAM J. Comput. **33**(1), 167–226 (2003)

14. Dervisevic, E., et al.: Quantum key distribution networks - key management: a survey. ACM Comput. Surv. **57**(10) (2025). https://doi.org/10.1145/3730575
15. Diffie, W., van Oorschot, P.C., Wiener, M.J.: Authentication and authenticated key exchanges. DCC **2**(2), 107–125 (1992). https://doi.org/10.1007/BF00124891
16. Dowling, B., Hansen, T.B., Paterson, K.G.: Many a mickle makes a muckle: a framework for provably quantum-secure hybrid key exchange. In: Ding, J., Tillich, J.P. (eds.) PQCrypto 2020, pp. 483–502. Springer, Cham, Switzerland, Paris, France (2020). https://doi.org/10.1007/978-3-030-44223-1_26
17. Dworkin, M.J.: Sha-3 standard: Permutation-based hash and extendable-output functions: (2015-07-01 04:07:00 2015). https://doi.org/10.6028/NIST.FIPS.202
18. Ehlen, S., et al.: Kryptografie quantensicher gestalten. Tech. Rep. BSI-Bro21/01, Bundesamt für Sicherheit in der Informationstechnik (BSI) (2021)
19. Ekert, A.K.: Quantum cryptography based on bell's theorem. Phys. Rev. Lett. **67**, 661–663 (1991). https://doi.org/10.1103/PhysRevLett.67.661, https://link.aps.org/doi/10.1103/PhysRevLett.67.661
20. French Cybersecurity Agency (ANSSI), Federal Office for Information Security (BSI), Netherlands National Communications Security Agency (NLNCSA), Swedish National Communications Security Authority: Position paper on quantum key distribution. Tech. Rep. 1.0, BSI (2024)
21. Fujioka, A., Suzuki, K., Xagawa, K., Yoneyama, K.: Strongly secure authenticated key exchange from factoring, codes, and lattices. In: Fischlin, M., Buchmann, J., Manulis, M. (eds.) PKC 2012. LNCS, vol. 7293, pp. 467–484. Springer, Heidelberg (2012). https://doi.org/10.1007/978-3-642-30057-8_28
22. Giron, A., et al.: Post-quantum hybrid key exchange: a systematic mapping study. J. Cryptographic Eng. **13**, 71–88 (2022)
23. Henrich, J., et al.: Performance impact of PQC KEMs on TLS 1.3 under varying network characteristics. In: Information Security: 26th International Conference (ISC), p. 267–287. Springer, Cham, Berlin, Heidelberg, DE (2023). https://doi.org/10.1007/978-3-031-49187-0_14
24. Hövelmanns, K., Planken, D., Schaffner, C., Verschoor, S.R.: QKD oracles for authenticated key exchange (2025). https://arxiv.org/abs/2509.12478
25. Hülsing, A., Ning, K.C., Schwabe, P., Weber, F.J., Zimmermann, P.R.: Post-quantum WireGuard. In: 2021 IEEE Symposium on Security and Privacy (SP), pp. 304–321. IEEE, Piscataway, NJ, US (2021). https://doi.org/10.1109/SP40001.2021.00030
26. International Telecommunication Union Telecommunication Standardization Sector: ITU-T Y.3802 Quantum key distribution networks - Functional architecture. Tech. rep., ITU-T (2020)
27. International Telecommunication Union Telecommunication Standardization Sector: ITU-T Y.3803 Quantum key distribution networks – Key management. Tech. rep., ITU-T (2020)
28. Krawczyk, H.: HMQV: A high-performance secure Diffie-Hellman protocol. In: Shoup, V. (ed.) CRYPTO 2005. LNCS, vol. 3621, pp. 546–566. Springer Berlin Heidelberg, Germany, Santa Barbara, CA, USA (2005). https://doi.org/10.1007/11535218_33
29. Krawczyk, H.: Cryptographic extraction and key derivation: The HKDF scheme. In: Rabin, T. (ed.) CRYPTO 2010. LNCS, vol. 6223, pp. 631–648. Springer Berlin Heidelberg, Germany, Santa Barbara, CA, USA (2010). https://doi.org/10.1007/978-3-642-14623-7_34

30. Li, J., et al.: Integration of quantum key distribution networks and classical networks: an evolution perspective. IEEE Network **39**(3), 180–187 (2025). https://doi.org/10.1109/MNET.2025.3537691
31. Martin, V., et al.: MadQCI: a heterogeneous and scalable SDN-QKD network deployed in production facilities. npj Quant. Inf. **10**(1), 80 (2024)
32. Mayers, D.: Unconditional security in quantum cryptography. J. ACM **48**(3), 351–406 (2001). https://doi.org/10.1145/382780.382781
33. Mehic, M., et al.: Quantum key distribution: a networking perspective. ACM Comput. Surv. **53**(5), 1–41 (2020). https://doi.org/10.1145/3402192
34. Open Quantum Safe Project: liboqs-go: Go bindings for the open quantum safe library. https://github.com/open-quantum-safe/liboqs-go (2024). version 0.14.0. Accessed 04 Feb 2026
35. Open Quantum Safe Project: liboqs: Open quantum safe cryptographic library. https://github.com/open-quantum-safe/liboqs (2024). version 0.14.0. Accessed 04 Feb 2026
36. Páez, A., Boisjoly, G.: Exploratory Data Analysis, pp. 25–64. Springer International Publishing, Cham (2022). https://doi.org/10.1007/978-3-031-20719-8_2
37. Paquin, C., Stebila, D., Tamvada, G.: Benchmarking post-quantum cryptography in TLS. In: Ding, J., Tillich, J.P. (eds.) Post-Quantum Cryptography, pp. 72–91. Springer International Publishing, Cham (2020)
38. (QKD), E.I.S.G.I.Q.K.D.: Quantum Key Distribution (QKD), Application Interface. etsi gs qkd 014 v1.1.1 (2019)
39. Ricci, S., Dobias, P., Malina, L., Hajny, J., Jedlicka, P.: Hybrid keys in practice: combining classical, quantum and post-quantum cryptography. IEEE Access **12**, 23206–23219 (2024). https://doi.org/10.1109/ACCESS.2024.3364520
40. Schanck, J., et al.: Criteria for selection of public-key cryptographic algorithms for quantum-safe hybrid cryptography. Tech. rep., IETF (2016). https://datatracker.ietf.org/doc/html/draft-whyte-select-pkc-qsh-02
41. Schwabe, P., Stebila, D., Wiggers, T.: Post-quantum TLS without handshake signatures. In: Proceedings of the 2020 ACM SIGSAC Conference on Computer and Communications Security, pp. 1461–1480. CCS '20, Association for Computing Machinery, New York, NY, USA (2020). https://doi.org/10.1145/3372297.3423350
42. Shor, P.W.: Polynomial-time algorithms for prime factorization and discrete logarithms on a quantum computer. SIAM J. Comput. **26**(5), 1484–1509 (1997). https://doi.org/10.1137/S0097539795293172
43. The Go Authors: Go standard library: crypto package. https://pkg.go.dev/crypto (2025). version go1.25.0. Accessed 04 Feb 2026
44. Xu, G., Mao, J., Sakk, E., Wang, S.P.: An overview of quantum-safe approaches: quantum key distribution and post-quantum cryptography. In: 2023 57th Annual Conference on Information Sciences and Systems (CISS), pp. 1–6. IEEE, Piscataway, NJ, US (2023). https://doi.org/10.1109/CISS56502.2023.10089619
45. Zhong, X., Chen, L., Li, Y., Jin, G.: Design and verification of TCP/IP offload engine in quantum key distribution system. Rev. Sci. Instrum. **90**(11), 115102 (2019). https://doi.org/10.1063/1.5117336, https://doi.org/10.1063/1.5117336

Quantum Polynomial-Time Key-Recovery Attacks on Generalized TWINE and LBlock

Hongyu Lu[1,2,3], Qingyuan Yu[4], Boyun Li[1,2,3], and Qun Liu[1,2,3](✉)

[1] School of Cyber Science and Technology, Shandong University, Qingdao, China
{hongyulu,boyunli}@mail.sdu.edu.cn, qunliu@sdu.edu.cn
[2] State Key Laboratory of Cryptography and Digital Economy Security, Shandong University, Qingdao, China
[3] Key Laboratory of Cryptologic Technology and Information Security, Ministry of Education, Shandong University, Jinan, China
[4] State Key Laboratory of Space Information System and Integrated Application, Beijing, China
yuqy@spacestar.com.cn

Abstract. Simon's algorithm is a fundamental quantum algorithm that finds the secret period of a periodic function in polynomial time. In symmetric cryptanalysis, polynomial-time quantum key-recovery attacks based on Simon's algorithm are important because they recover secret keys of reduced-round ciphers. Inspired by this, we consider generalized variants of TWINE and LBlock with n-bit branches and independent round keys, and we provide the first full quantum key-recovery attacks for 8-round generalized TWINE and 8-round generalized LBlock in this paper. By analyzing their multi-branch round transformations, we identify periodic functions and show how their round keys can be efficiently recovered under the quantum chosen-plaintext (qCPA) model. These attacks help clarify the qCPA security of these generalized variants in the quantum setting.

Keywords: Quantum cryptanalysis · Simon's algorithm · Key-recovery attack · TWINE · LBlock

1 Introduction

Quantum computing has introduced new challenges for classical cryptography, thereby increasing the attention devoted to understanding the security of cryptographic primitives in the presence of quantum adversaries. Shor's algorithm [23,24] shows that the integer factorization and discrete logarithm problems can be solved in polynomial time on a quantum computer, thereby threatening widely deployed public-key cryptosystems such as RSA and ECC. For symmetric primitives, Grover's algorithm [8] provides a generic quadratic speed-up for exhaustive key search; this has led to the common rule of thumb that

N. El Mrabet et al. (Eds.): AFRICACRYPT 2026, LNCS 16832, pp. 112–129, 2026.
https://doi.org/10.1007/978-3-032-31130-6_5

doubling the key length preserves the brute-force security level against Grover search. Other quantum attacks against symmetric primitives include quantum differential and linear cryptanalysis [14], quantum Demiric-Selçuk Meet-in-the-Middle attacks [11], and quantum linear key-recovery attacks [22].

Separately, Simon's algorithm [25] identifies hidden XOR periods using polynomially many quantum queries and gives a tool for structural cryptanalysis in the Q2 setting. In symmetric cryptanalysis, Kuwakado and Morii [15] initiated this direction in 2010 by giving a polynomial-time quantum distinguisher against the 3-round Feistel structure using Simon's algorithm [25]. Then, Kaplan et al. [13] extended Simon-based attacks to several symmetric constructions, including CBC-MAC, PMAC, GMAC, GCM, and OCB. Later, Leander and May [17] further proposed the Grover-meets-Simon algorithm and attacked the FX structure, while the offline Simon's algorithm was proposed in [1].

Subsequent Simon-based work includes the quantum key-recovery attacks of Dong et al. [6] on different rounds of Feistel structures using Grover's and Simon's algorithms. Quantum analyses of generalized Feistel schemes have also been studied; Dong et al. [5] gave quantum distinguishers for several Generalized Feistel Schemes, including Type-1 and Type-2 structures. Further improvements and more recent quantum attacks for Feistel structures and variants were provided in [4,7,9,10,12,16,18,21,26,31].

Many existing Simon-based attacks on Feistel-type structures require manually constructed periodic functions. To reduce this effort, several recent works have explored automated or semi-automated tools. Canale et al. [2] proposed a circuit-based automated search for quantum key-recovery attacks on MISTY and Feistel ciphers. Their method searches for periodic functions from a circuit representation; it was not directly applied to TWINE [27] or LBlock [29], whose permutation layers and larger number of branches make the setting different from the ciphers considered there. Xiang et al. [30] formally connected Simon-based quantum distinguishers to classical truncated differentials. This explains the relation between Simon-based distinguishers and truncated differentials, but the work focuses on interpreting existing distinguishers rather than developing new key-recovery attacks on lightweight designs. Wang et al. [28] adapted Simon's algorithm to the quantum chosen-ciphertext setting for the structures considered in their work. However, that work does not give key-recovery attacks on TWINE or LBlock. Liu et al. [19] and Lu et al. [20] developed automated tools for building quantum periodic distinguishers, reducing the cost of constructing periodic functions. Nevertheless, both tools focus on constructing distinguishers rather than quantum key-recovery attacks.

For TWINE [27], Chen et al. [3] presented an 8-round quantum periodic distinguisher, and Liu et al. [19] later gave 8- and 10-round distinguishers in the qCPA setting, but these results do not provide key-recovery attacks. The distinction between distinguishers and key-recovery attacks is important here: a distinguisher separates a reduced-round cipher from a random permutation, whereas our attacks recover all independent round keys of the 8-round generalized constructions.

The rationale of our attacks is to turn an 8-round periodic relation into a key-dependent function. For a target subkey k, we choose two input branches in the form $(x, S(x))$ so that, when x is replaced by $x \oplus k$, the active branch after the first round remains unchanged. The selected output branch after eight rounds then depends on the input only through this invariant active value and fixed constants, allowing Simon's algorithm to recover the subkey. Similar rotated input choices recover the remaining subkeys of the same round, and the recovered round keys are then used in local decryption to construct new periodic functions for later rounds. We do not claim that the number of rounds is optimal; the result is a full round-key recovery for the 8-round generalized constructions in the qCPA model.

1.1 Our Contributions

Despite recent progress in quantum cryptanalysis, specific lightweight block ciphers remain less studied. Lightweight block ciphers such as TWINE [27] and LBlock [29] are designed for resource-constrained environments such as IoT and embedded devices, where both efficiency and security are important. It is therefore useful to understand how such designs behave against quantum attacks. For symmetric primitives in the quantum setting, Zhandry [32] distinguishes between the Q1 and Q2 models: in the Q1 model, the adversary performs quantum computation but issues only classical oracle queries, whereas in the stronger Q2 model, the adversary is allowed quantum superposition queries. In this paper, we study generalized TWINE and LBlock in the Q2 model under the quantum chosen-plaintext (qCPA) setting. These variants use n-bit branches and independent round keys, which allows us to study the structural behavior of the round transformations without fixing a particular S-box size. The specific contributions are outlined as follows.

Quantum Key-Recovery Attack on Generalized TWINE. We present the first polynomial-time quantum key-recovery attack on 8-round generalized TWINE, recovering all independent round keys. We construct key-dependent periodic functions from its multi-branch round structure and apply Simon's algorithm in the qCPA model. Using rotational symmetries, we identify equivalent periodic functions so that Simon's algorithm can be applied in parallel to recover the subkeys of one round. We then update the periodic functions with the recovered keys to recover the remaining independent round keys in polynomial time.

Quantum Key-Recovery Attack on Generalized LBlock. For generalized LBlock, we give the first polynomial-time quantum key-recovery attack on the 8-round variant. Equivalent periodic functions allow Simon's algorithm to recover the first-round subkeys in parallel. Updating these functions round by round recovers the remaining independent round keys in polynomial time.

1.2 Organization

In Sect. 2, we introduce the notation and quantum algorithms. Sections 3 and 4 present our attacks on 8-round generalized TWINE and LBlock, respectively. Section 5 concludes the paper.

2 Preliminaries

2.1 Notation

We use the following notation throughout this paper. All algebraic operations are over the binary field $\mathbb{F}_2$. For a positive integer ℓ, let $\{0,1\}^\ell$ denote the set of all binary strings of length ℓ. We denote a block cipher with an N-bit plaintext and a κ-bit key by

$$E : \{0,1\}^N \times \{0,1\}^\kappa \rightarrow \{0,1\}^N.$$

The r-round encryption is denoted by E^r. In the later descriptions of generalized TWINE and LBlock, n is reserved for the branch size. For an n-bit function $f : \{0,1\}^n \rightarrow \{0,1\}^n$, we use U_f to denote the unitary transformation that acts on two registers

$$U_f : |x\rangle\,|y\rangle \mapsto |x\rangle\,|y \oplus f(x)\rangle\,.$$

When the second register is initialized to $|0^n\rangle$, we simply write $U_f\,|x\rangle\,|0^n\rangle = |x\rangle\,|f(x)\rangle$.

2.2 Simon's Algorithm

Consider a function $f : \{0,1\}^n \rightarrow \{0,1\}^n$ that satisfies $f(x) = f(x \oplus s)$ for all x. Here $s \neq 0$, and we use the standard Simon promise that $f(x) = f(x')$ holds iff $x' = x$ or $x' = x \oplus s$. Under this promise, Simon's algorithm recovers the hidden XOR-period s with $O(n)$ quantum queries. Classically, the corresponding query complexity is $O(2^{n/2})$. The procedure is as follows (Fig. 1):

1. Prepare two n-qubit registers initialized to the zero state $|0^n\rangle\,|0^n\rangle$. The Hadamard transform $H^{\otimes n}$ is then applied to the first register to generate a quantum superposition over all possible 2^n inputs:

$$|\psi_0\rangle = \frac{1}{\sqrt{2^n}} \sum_{x \in \{0,1\}^n} |x\rangle\,|0^n\rangle\,.$$

2. Apply the unitary operation U_f that maps $|x\rangle\,|0^n\rangle$ to $|x\rangle\,|f(x)\rangle$ to obtain the state:

$$|\psi_1\rangle = \frac{1}{\sqrt{2^n}} \sum_{x \in \{0,1\}^n} |x\rangle\,|f(x)\rangle\,.$$

3. Measuring the second register in the computational basis yields a value $f(z)$ and collapses the first register to the state:

$$|\psi_2\rangle = \frac{1}{\sqrt{2}} \left(|z\rangle + |z \oplus s\rangle\right).$$

4. Apply the Hadamard transform $H^{\otimes n}$ to the first register again to obtain:

$$|\psi_3\rangle = \frac{1}{\sqrt{2^{n+1}}} \sum_{y \in \{0,1\}^n} (-1)^{y \cdot z}(1 + (-1)^{y \cdot s}) |y\rangle .$$

5. If $y \cdot s = 1$, the amplitude of $|y\rangle$ is 0. Therefore, measuring the first register in the computational basis yields a random output value y satisfying $y \cdot s = 0$.

Repeating the procedure $O(n)$ times gives, with high probability, $n-1$ independent vectors orthogonal to s; solving the resulting linear system over $\mathbb{F}_2$ recovers s.

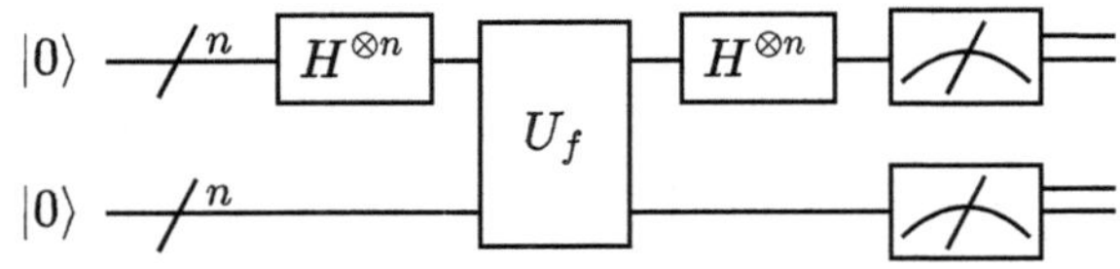

Fig. 1. Description of Simon's algorithm.

2.3 Quantum Polynomial-Time Key-Recovery Attacks on Feistel-FK in [2]

We recall the Feistel-FK example of Canale et al. [2], which illustrates how Simon-periodic functions can be identified from a circuit representation. Their observation is that a block-cipher circuit can define many candidate structural functions, and a suitable hidden XOR-period in such a function can lead to a Simon-based attack. The search for a Simon-based attack is then reduced to checking whether candidate functions obtained from the circuit have XOR periods. Canale et al. developed a circuit-based automated search model that enumerates candidate functions obtained from the cipher circuit. The model then constructs the corresponding unitary oracles and tests them for periodicity.

We next recall the Feistel-FK example used in [2].

The Feistel Structure. A Feistel network transforms round functions over $\{0,1\}^n$ into a permutation over $\{0,1\}^{2n}$. Let $F_0, F_1, \cdots, F_{r-1}$ be round functions with $F_i : \{0,1\}^n \rightarrow \{0,1\}^n$. For a $2n$-bit input (L_0, R_0), the r-round output (L_r, R_r) is computed by iterating

$$L_{i+1} = R_i, \quad R_{i+1} = F_i(R_i) \oplus L_i.$$

By replacing the round functions with a public permutation F and XORing round keys k_i into the output of F, one obtains the Feistel-FK structure shown in Fig. 2.

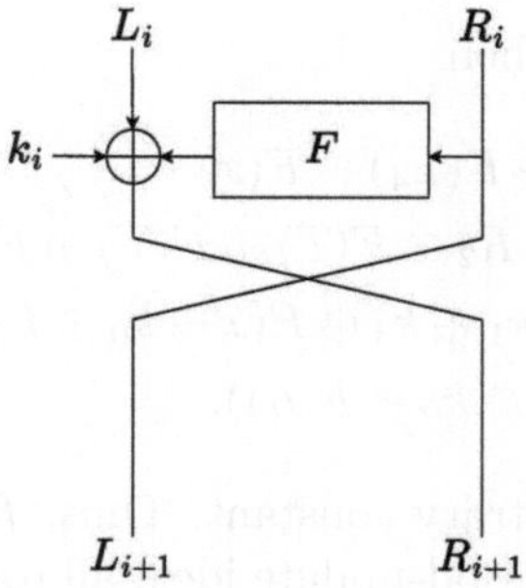

Fig. 2. Feistel-FK structure.

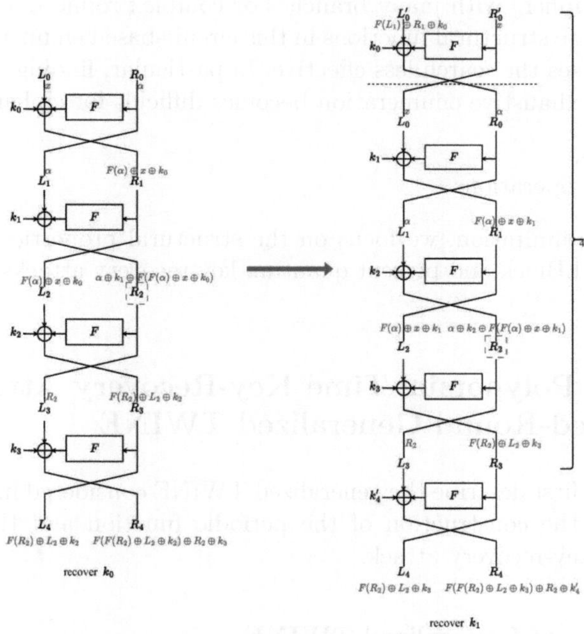

Fig. 3. Key-recovery attack on 4-round Feistel-FK.

Key-Recovery Attack on 4-Round Feistel-FK. Canale et al. [2] use the function

$$f_3(x) = E_R^4(x, \alpha) \oplus F(E_L^4(x, \alpha)) \oplus F(x).$$

For input $(L_0, R_0) = (x, \alpha)$, the intermediate values satisfy

$$\begin{aligned}
R_1 &= x \oplus k_0 \oplus F(\alpha), \\
R_2 &= \alpha \oplus k_1 \oplus F(x \oplus k_0 \oplus F(\alpha)), \\
R_3 &= L_4 = E_L^4(x, \alpha) = F(R_2) \oplus L_2 \oplus k_2, \\
R_4 &= E_R^4(x, \alpha) = k_3 \oplus R_2 \oplus F(F(R_2) \oplus L_2 \oplus k_2).
\end{aligned}$$

Let $T = F(R_2) \oplus L_2 \oplus k_2$. Then

$$\begin{aligned} f_3(x) &= R_4 \oplus F(L_4) \oplus F(x) \\ &= k_3 \oplus R_2 \oplus F(T) \oplus F(T) \oplus F(x) \\ &= \alpha \oplus k_1 \oplus k_3 \oplus F(x \oplus k_0 \oplus F(\alpha)) \oplus F(x) \\ &= f_3(x \oplus k_0 \oplus F(\alpha)), \end{aligned}$$

where $\alpha \in \{0,1\}^n$ is an arbitrary constant. Thus, f_3 has candidate period $s = k_0 \oplus F(\alpha)$. Using the same period-update idea, all round keys of 4-round Feistel-FK can be recovered; Fig. 3 illustrates the recovery of k_1. Canale et al. also gave a key-recovery attack on 5-round Feistel-FK; we refer to [2] for details.

However, for ciphers with many branches or complex round operations, the number of candidate structural functions in this circuit-based enumeration grows rapidly, which makes the search less effective. In particular, finding a valid periodic function by exhaustive enumeration becomes difficult for ciphers with:

- many branches,
- complex round operations.

Motivated by this limitation, we focus on the structural properties of generalized TWINE and LBlock and present quantum key-recovery attacks on them in Sect. 3 and Sect. 4.

3 Quantum Polynomial-Time Key-Recovery Attack on Reduced-Round Generalized TWINE

In this section, we first describe the generalized TWINE considered in this paper. We then present the construction of the periodic function and the resulting polynomial-time key-recovery attack.

3.1 Description of Generalized TWINE

TWINE [27] is a 36-round lightweight block cipher with a 64-bit block, represented as 16 4-bit sub-blocks $(X_0^i, X_1^i, \cdots, X_{15}^i)$. In this paper, we consider a generalized variant of TWINE in which each sub-block has size n bits, and the round keys are assumed to be independent. The round structure follows TWINE, with an n-bit nonlinear layer denoted by $S : \{0,1\}^n \to \{0,1\}^n$, as shown in Fig. 4. Note that the block shuffle operation is omitted in the last round.

3.2 Quantum Key-Recovery Attack on 8-Round Generalized TWINE

First-Round Key Recovery. For generalized TWINE, the i-th round key consists of eight n-bit subkeys, denoted by $RK^i = (k_0^i, k_1^i, \cdots, k_7^i)$, and we have the following theorem.

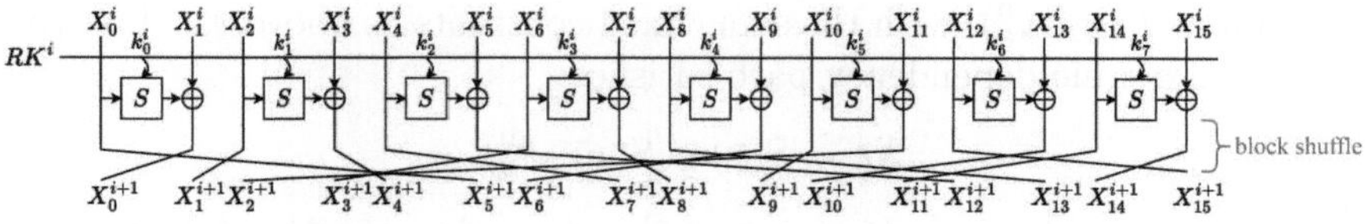

Fig. 4. Round function of generalized TWINE.

Theorem 1. *Given qCPA access to the 8-round encryption oracle* E^8*, there is a polynomial-time attack that recovers* k_0^0 *of the first round key by querying plaintexts of the form* $(x, S(x), c_2, \ldots, c_{15})$*, where* $c_2, \ldots, c_{15} \in \{0,1\}^n$ *are fixed constants.*

We prove Theorem 1 using the input pattern shown in Fig. 5.

Proof. Fix constants $c_2, \ldots, c_{15} \in \{0,1\}^n$ and let

$$P(x) = (x, S(x), c_2, \ldots, c_{15}).$$

Then

$$(X_0^8, X_1^8, \cdots, X_{15}^8) = E^8(P(x))$$

We use the selected output branch to define the function

$$g(x) = X_{15}^8.$$

It remains to prove that $g(x)$ has period k_0^0. The input pair is chosen so that replacing x by $x \oplus k_0^0$ gives the same active value after the first round. For the input $P(x)$, the first-round branch on the dependency path to the selected output satisfies

$$X_0^1 = S(x \oplus k_0^0) \oplus S(x),$$

The nonconstant intermediate states on this dependency path are as follows:

$$\begin{aligned}
&X_0^2 = S(X_0^1 \oplus k_0^1) \oplus X_1^1,\\
&X_5^2 = X_0^1,\\
&X_0^3 = S(S(X_0^1 \oplus k_0^1) \oplus X_1^1 \oplus k_0^2) \oplus X_1^2,\\
&X_{12}^3 = S(X_4^2 \oplus k_2^2) \oplus X_5^2,\\
&X_0^4 = S(S(S(X_0^1 \oplus k_0^1) \oplus X_1^1 \oplus k_0^2) \oplus X_1^2 \oplus k_0^3) \oplus X_1^3,\\
&X_{10}^4 = S(X_0^1 \oplus k_6^3) \oplus X_{13}^3,\\
&X_0^5 = S(S(S(S(X_0^1 \oplus k_0^1) \oplus X_1^1 \oplus k_0^2) \oplus X_1^2 \oplus k_0^3) \oplus X_1^3 \oplus k_0^4) \oplus X_1^4,\\
&X_2^5 = S(S(X_0^1 \oplus k_6^3) \oplus X_{13}^3 \oplus k_5^4) \oplus X_{11}^4,\\
&X_4^6 = S(S(S(X_0^1 \oplus k_6^3) \oplus X_{13}^3 \oplus k_5^4) \oplus X_{11}^4 \oplus k_1^5) \oplus X_3^5,\\
&X_5^6 = X_0^5,\\
&X_{12}^7 = S(X_4^6 \oplus k_2^6) \oplus X_5^6,\\
&X_{15}^8 = X_{12}^7.
\end{aligned}$$

For the input $P(x \oplus k_0^0)$, with the same fixed constants as above, the first-round branch on the same dependency path satisfies

$$X_0^1 = S(x) \oplus S(x \oplus k_0^0),$$

The nonconstant intermediate states on this dependency path are as follows:

$$\begin{aligned}
X_0^2 &= S(X_0^1 \oplus k_0^1) \oplus X_1^1,\\
X_5^2 &= X_0^1,\\
X_0^3 &= S(S(X_0^1 \oplus k_0^1) \oplus X_1^1 \oplus k_0^2) \oplus X_1^2,\\
X_{12}^3 &= S(X_4^2 \oplus k_2^2) \oplus X_5^2,\\
X_0^4 &= S(S(S(X_0^1 \oplus k_0^1) \oplus X_1^1 \oplus k_0^2) \oplus X_1^2 \oplus k_0^3) \oplus X_1^3,\\
X_{10}^4 &= S(X_0^1 \oplus k_6^3) \oplus X_{13}^3,\\
X_0^5 &= S(S(S(S(X_0^1 \oplus k_0^1) \oplus X_1^1 \oplus k_0^2) \oplus X_1^2 \oplus k_0^3) \oplus X_1^3 \oplus k_0^4) \oplus X_1^4,\\
X_2^5 &= S(S(X_0^1 \oplus k_6^3) \oplus X_{13}^3 \oplus k_5^4) \oplus X_{11}^4,\\
X_4^6 &= S(S(S(X_0^1 \oplus k_6^3) \oplus X_{13}^3 \oplus k_5^4) \oplus X_{11}^4 \oplus k_1^5) \oplus X_3^5,\\
X_5^6 &= X_0^5,\\
X_{12}^7 &= S(X_4^6 \oplus k_2^6) \oplus X_5^6,\\
X_{15}^8 &= X_{12}^7.
\end{aligned}$$

Let

$$A(x) = S(x) \oplus S(x \oplus k_0^0).$$

The two first-round derivations above show that $X_0^1 = A(x)$ for the input $P(x)$ and $X_0^1 = A(x \oplus k_0^0)$ for the input $P(x \oplus k_0^0)$. Since

$$A(x \oplus k_0^0) = S(x \oplus k_0^0) \oplus S(x) = A(x),$$

the active value entering the displayed nonconstant branches is the same for these two inputs. Branches outside this dependency path do not enter the selected output branch X_{15}^8 in the eight-round derivation. Therefore, there exists a deterministic function H, depending only on the fixed constants and the remaining round keys, such that the selected output branch can be written as

$$g(x) = X_{15}^8 = H(A(x)).$$

It follows that

$$g(x \oplus k_0^0) = H(A(x \oplus k_0^0)) = H(A(x)) = g(x).$$

Thus, $g(x)$ is a periodic function with period $s = k_0^0$, and Simon's algorithm recovers this subkey in polynomial time in the qCPA model.

Furthermore, rotating the input pattern in Fig. 5 gives seven additional equivalent periodic functions. Using these functions, the full first-round key can be recovered by applying Simon's algorithm in parallel. The fixed input branches are omitted from Table 1.

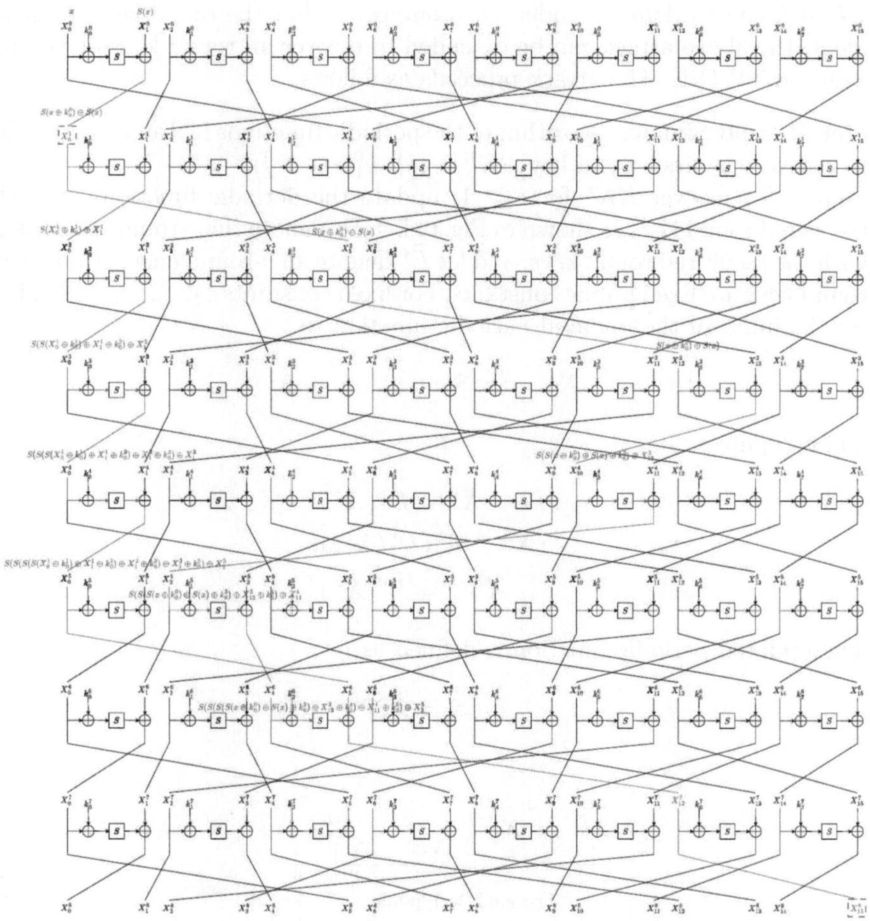

Fig. 5. Recovery of k_0^0 of the first round key.

Table 1. All periodic functions for recovering RK^0 of generalized TWINE.

Round	Input pattern	Periodic function	Period
8	$X_0^0 \to x, X_1^0 \to S(x)$	$g(x) = X_{15}^8$	k_0^0
8	$X_2^0 \to x, X_3^0 \to S(x)$	$g(x) = X_{13}^8$	k_1^0
8	$X_4^0 \to x, X_5^0 \to S(x)$	$g(x) = X_{11}^8$	k_2^0
8	$X_6^0 \to x, X_7^0 \to S(x)$	$g(x) = X_9^8$	k_3^0
8	$X_8^0 \to x, X_9^0 \to S(x)$	$g(x) = X_7^8$	k_4^0
8	$X_{10}^0 \to x, X_{11}^0 \to S(x)$	$g(x) = X_5^8$	k_5^0
8	$X_{12}^0 \to x, X_{13}^0 \to S(x)$	$g(x) = X_3^8$	k_6^0
8	$X_{14}^0 \to x, X_{15}^0 \to S(x)$	$g(x) = X_1^8$	k_7^0

Full Key-Recovery Attack. Under the assumption that the round keys are independent, the above attack can be extended to recover all round keys of 8-round generalized TWINE. The attack proceeds as follows:

- Step 1: Apply Simon's algorithm to the periodic functions in Table 1 in parallel to recover the first round key $RK^0 = (k_0^0, k_1^0, \cdots, k_7^0)$.
- Step 2: To recover RK^r for $r \geq 1$, update the periodic functions with the recovered round keys as shown in Fig. 6. Let D^r denote the r-round decryption with the recovered round keys, and let $\widetilde{E}^r$ denote an r-round encryption whose round keys are fixed public constants. For fixed constants $c_2, \ldots, c_{15} \in \{0,1\}^n$, set the input of the updated periodic function to

$$X^r = (x, S(x), c_2, \ldots, c_{15}),$$

and compute

$$X^0 = D^r(X^r),$$
$$X^8 = E^8(D^r(X^r)),$$
$$X^{8+r} = \widetilde{E}^r(X^8).$$

The updated periodic function is defined as

$$g_r(x) = X_{15}^{8+r}.$$

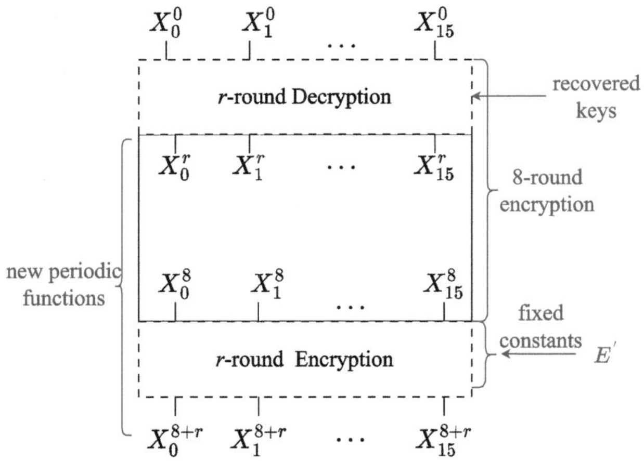

Fig. 6. Construction of updated periodic functions with recovered keys.

- Step 3: Applying the same argument as in Theorem 1 to the updated function $g_r(x)$ recovers the r-th round key $RK^r = (k_0^r, k_1^r, \cdots, k_7^r)$. As an example, we describe the recovery of $RK^1 = (k_0^1, k_1^1, \cdots, k_7^1)$ after RK^0 has been recovered. Set $X^1 = (x, S(x), c_2, \ldots, c_{15})$. For all $x \in \{0,1\}^n$, we have

$$X^0 = D^1(X^1) = D^1(x, S(x), c_2, \ldots, c_{15}),$$
$$X^8 = E^8(X^0),$$
$$X^9 = \widetilde{E}^1(X^8).$$

The updated periodic function is $g_1(x) = X_{15}^9$, and Simon's algorithm recovers k_0^1. Rotating the updated input pattern gives the remaining subkeys of RK^1. Repeating this update for $r = 1, 2, \ldots, 7$ recovers the remaining round keys of 8-round generalized TWINE.

4 Quantum Polynomial-Time Key-Recovery Attack on Reduced-Round Generalized LBlock

In this section, we first describe generalized LBlock and then present the key-recovery attack on its 8-round variant.

4.1 Description of Generalized LBlock

LBlock [29] is a 32-round lightweight block cipher with a 64-bit block, represented as 16 4-bit sub-blocks. Its round function uses eight S-boxes and applies a left circular shift to the right branch. We consider a generalized variant of LBlock in which each sub-block has size n bits, and the round keys are assumed to be independent. The round function is illustrated in Fig. 7, where the nonlinear layers are denoted by $S_i : \{0,1\}^n \to \{0,1\}^n$ for $0 \le i \le 7$.

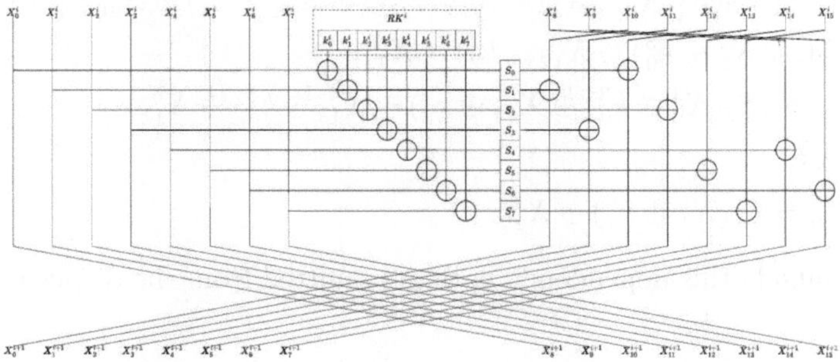

Fig. 7. Round function of generalized LBlock.

4.2 Quantum Key-Recovery Attack on 8-Round Generalized LBlock

First-Round Key Recovery. We first describe how to recover one subkey of the first round key.

Theorem 2. *Given qCPA access to the 8-round encryption oracle E^8, there is a polynomial-time attack that recovers k_0^0 of the first round key by querying plaintexts in which $X_0^0 = x$, $X_{12}^0 = S_0(x)$, and all other input branches are fixed constants.*

Figure 8 illustrates the recovery of k_0^0 with this input pattern, based on the periodic function

$$g(x) = X_8^8,$$

which has period $s = k_0^0$. We prove the periodicity below.

Proof. Fix constants $c_j \in \{0,1\}^n$ for all $j \neq 0, 12$. Let $P(x)$ be the plaintext satisfying $X_0^0 = x$, $X_{12}^0 = S_0(x)$, and $X_j^0 = c_j$ for all $j \neq 0, 12$. For input $P(x)$, the nonconstant intermediate states on the dependency path to the selected output are

$$\begin{aligned}
X_2^1 &= S_0(x \oplus k_0^0) \oplus S_0(x),\\
X_3^2 &= S_2(X_2^1 \oplus k_2^1) \oplus X_{13}^1,\\
X_{10}^2 &= X_2^1,\\
X_0^3 &= X_{10}^2 = X_2^1,\\
X_1^3 &= S_3(S_2(X_2^1 \oplus k_2^1) \oplus X_{13}^1 \oplus k_3^2) \oplus X_{11}^2,\\
X_0^4 &= S_1(S_3(S_2(X_2^1 \oplus k_2^1) \oplus X_{13}^1 \oplus k_3^2) \oplus X_{11}^2 \oplus k_1^3) \oplus X_{10}^3,\\
X_2^4 &= S_0(X_2^1 \oplus k_0^3) \oplus X_{12}^3,\\
X_2^5 &= S_0(S_1(S_3(S_2(X_2^1 \oplus k_2^1) \oplus X_{13}^1 \oplus k_3^2) \oplus X_{11}^2 \oplus k_1^3) \oplus X_{10}^3 \oplus k_0^4) \oplus X_{12}^4,\\
X_3^5 &= S_2(S_0(X_2^1 \oplus k_0^3) \oplus X_{12}^3 \oplus k_2^4) \oplus X_{13}^4,\\
X_1^6 &= S_3(S_2(S_0(X_2^1 \oplus k_0^3) \oplus X_{12}^3 \oplus k_2^4) \oplus X_{13}^4 \oplus k_3^5) \oplus X_{11}^5,\\
X_{10}^6 &= X_2^5,\\
X_8^8 &= X_0^7 = S_1(X_1^6 \oplus k_1^6) \oplus X_{10}^6.
\end{aligned}$$

Branches outside this dependency path are omitted from the displayed intermediate states.

Let

$$A_0(x) = S_0(x) \oplus S_0(x \oplus k_0^0).$$

For the input $P(x)$, the first-round active branch is $X_2^1 = A_0(x)$. For the shifted input $P(x \oplus k_0^0)$, the corresponding active branch is

$$A_0(x \oplus k_0^0) = S_0(x \oplus k_0^0) \oplus S_0(x) = A_0(x).$$

The displayed state relations show that every nonconstant branch on the dependency path to the selected output branch X_8^8 depends on the input only through X_2^1. Branches outside this path do not affect X_8^8 in the eight-round derivation. Therefore, for a deterministic function H determined by the public S-boxes, the fixed constants, and the remaining round keys, the selected output branch can be written as

$$g(x) = X_8^8 = H(A_0(x)).$$

It follows that

$$g(x \oplus k_0^0) = H(A_0(x \oplus k_0^0)) = H(A_0(x)) = g(x).$$

Thus, g is a periodic function with period $s = k_0^0$, and Simon's algorithm recovers this subkey in polynomial time in the qCPA model.

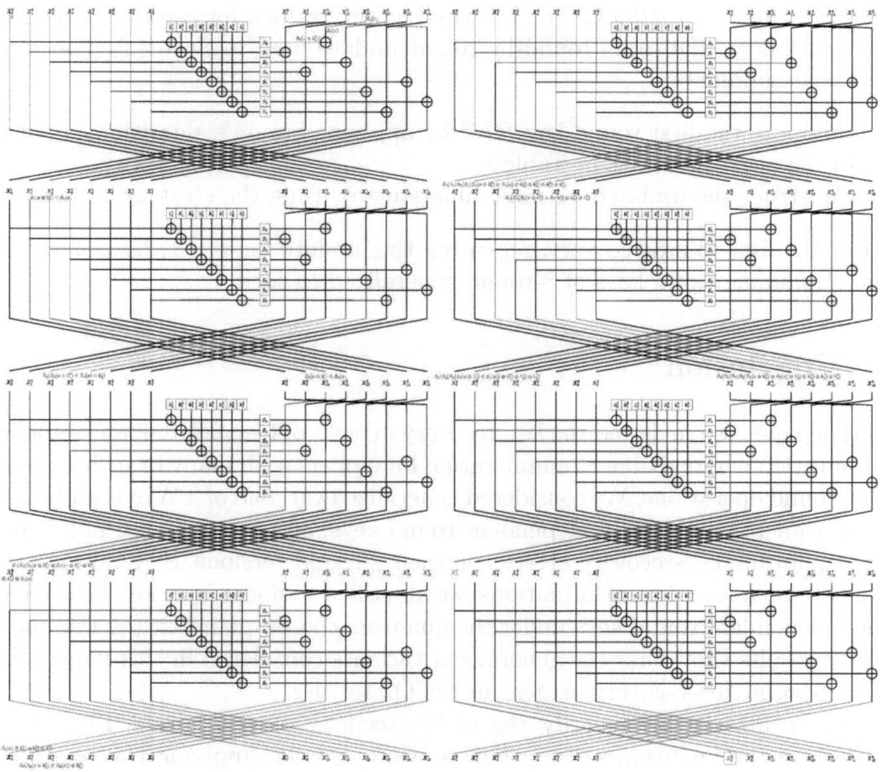

Fig. 8. Recovery of k_0^0 of the first round key.

Table 2 lists the equivalent periodic functions obtained by rotating the input pattern. The constant input sub-blocks are omitted in the following table. Applying Simon's algorithm to the periodic functions in Table 2 in parallel recovers $RK^0 = (k_0^0, k_1^0, \cdots, k_7^0)$.

Table 2. All periodic functions for recovering RK^0 of generalized LBlock.

Round	Input pattern	Periodic function	Period
8	$X_0^0 \to x, X_{12}^0 \to S_0(x)$	$g(x) = X_8^8$	k_0^0
8	$X_1^0 \to x, X_{10}^0 \to S_1(x)$	$g(x) = X_{14}^8$	k_1^0
8	$X_2^0 \to x, X_{13}^0 \to S_2(x)$	$g(x) = X_9^8$	k_2^0
8	$X_3^0 \to x, X_{11}^0 \to S_3(x)$	$g(x) = X_{15}^8$	k_3^0
8	$X_4^0 \to x, X_8^0 \to S_4(x)$	$g(x) = X_{12}^8$	k_4^0
8	$X_5^0 \to x, X_{14}^0 \to S_5(x)$	$g(x) = X_{10}^8$	k_5^0
8	$X_6^0 \to x, X_9^0 \to S_6(x)$	$g(x) = X_{13}^8$	k_6^0
8	$X_7^0 \to x, X_{15}^0 \to S_7(x)$	$g(x) = X_{11}^8$	k_7^0

Full Key-Recovery Attack. The full key-recovery attack for 8-round generalized LBlock follows the same round-by-round update used in Sect. 3.2. The attack proceeds as follows:

- Compute the first round key RK^0 by applying Simon's algorithm in parallel to the eight functions in Table 2.
- Construct the updated periodic functions by using the strategy in Fig. 6.

After the first-round recovery, repeating this update for $r = 1, 2, \dots, 7$ recovers the remaining round keys of 8-round generalized LBlock.

5 Conclusion

In this paper, we reviewed the key-recovery attacks of Canale et al. and explained a limitation of circuit-based enumeration for ciphers with many branches or complex round operations. We considered generalized variants of TWINE and LBlock with n-bit branches and independent round keys, and we presented polynomial-time quantum key-recovery attacks on their 8-round versions. By analyzing their multi-branch round transformations, we identified periodic functions that recover the independent round keys under the quantum chosen-plaintext (qCPA) model. These results show that the generalized variants considered in this paper admit Simon-based key-recovery attacks in the Q2 setting.

These attacks help clarify the qCPA security of generalized TWINE and LBlock in the quantum setting. Future work includes applying this analysis to other lightweight block-cipher structures.

Acknowledgements. The authors would like to thank the anonymous reviewers for their valuable comments and suggestions to improve the quality of the paper. This work was supported by the National Key R&D Program of China (Grant No. 2025YFA1017101), the National Natural Science Foundation of China (Grant No. 623B2067), the China Postdoctoral Science Foundation (Grant No. 2025M783119), and the Shandong Postdoctoral Science Foundation (Grant No. SDZZ-ZR-202501347).

We used generative AI tools (OpenAI's ChatGPT) for grammar checking and spell correction. All content was written and verified by the authors, who take full responsibility for the final text.

References

1. Bonnetain, X., Hosoyamada, A., Naya-Plasencia, M., Sasaki, Yu., Schrottenloher, A.: Quantum attacks without superposition queries: the offline Simon's algorithm. In: Galbraith, S.D., Moriai, S. (eds.) ASIACRYPT 2019. LNCS, vol. 11921, pp. 552–583. Springer, Cham (2019). https://doi.org/10.1007/978-3-030-34578-5_20
2. Canale, F., Leander, G., Stennes, L.: Simon's algorithm and symmetric crypto: generalizations and automatized applications. In: Dodis, Y., Shrimpton, T. (eds.) Advances in Cryptology - CRYPTO 2022, Part III. LNCS, vol. 13509, pp. 779–808. Springer, Cham (2022). https://doi.org/10.1007/978-3-031-15982-4_26
3. Chen, J., Liu, Q., Li, B., Qiao, J., Wang, J.: Simplified periodic distinguishers searching: application to GFS-4F/2F and TWINE. In: Lin, D., Wang, M., Yung, M. (eds.) Inscrypt 2024, Part II. LNCS, vol. 15544, pp. 425–443. Springer, Cham (2024). https://doi.org/10.1007/978-981-96-4734-7_21
4. Cid, C., Hosoyamada, A., Liu, Y., Sim, S.M.: Quantum cryptanalysis on contracting feistel structures and observation on related-key settings. In: Bhargavan, K., Oswald, E., Prabhakaran, M. (eds.) Progress in Cryptology - INDOCRYPT 2020. LNCS, vol. 12578, pp. 373–394. Springer, Cham (2020). https://doi.org/10.1007/978-3-030-65277-7_17
5. Dong, X., Li, Z., Wang, X.: Quantum cryptanalysis on some generalized feistel schemes. Sci. China Inf. Sci. **62**(2), 22501:1–22501:12 (2019). https://doi.org/10.1007/S11432-017-9436-7
6. Dong, X., Wang, X.: Quantum key-recovery attack on feistel structures. Sci. China Inf. Sci. **61**(10), 102501:1–102501:7 (2018). https://doi.org/10.1007/S11432-017-9468-Y
7. Feng, X., Wu, H., Zhang, K., Sun, H.: Quantum claw-finding attacks on 5-round feistel structure and generalized feistel schemes. Quantum Inf. Process. **24**(2), 52 (2025). https://doi.org/10.1007/S11128-025-04671-3
8. Grover, L.K.: A fast quantum mechanical algorithm for database search. In: Miller, G.L. (ed.) Proceedings of the Twenty-Eighth Annual ACM Symposium on the Theory of Computing, Philadelphia, Pennsylvania, USA, May 22-24, 1996. pp. 212–219. ACM (1996)
9. Hodžic, S., Knudsen, L.R.: A quantum distinguisher for 7/8-round SMS4 block cipher. Quantum Inf. Process. **19**(11), 411 (2020). https://doi.org/10.1007/S11128-020-02929-6
10. Hodžić, S., Knudsen Ramkilde, L., Brasen Kidmose, A.: On quantum distinguishers for type-3 generalized feistel network based on separability. In: Ding, J., Tillich, J.-P. (eds.) PQCrypto 2020. LNCS, vol. 12100, pp. 461–480. Springer, Cham (2020). https://doi.org/10.1007/978-3-030-44223-1_25
11. Hosoyamada, A., Sasaki, Y.: Quantum demiric-selçuk meet-in-the-middle attacks: applications to 6-round generic feistel constructions. In: Catalano, D., Prisco, R.D. (eds.) SCN 2018. LNCS, vol. 11035, pp. 386–403. Springer, Cham (2018). https://doi.org/10.1007/978-3-319-98113-0_21

12. Ito, G., Iwata, T.: Quantum distinguishing attacks against type-1 generalized feistel ciphers. IACR Cryptol. ePrint Arch. p. 327 (2019). https://eprint.iacr.org/2019/327
13. Kaplan, M., Leurent, G., Leverrier, A., Naya-Plasencia, M.: Breaking symmetric cryptosystems using quantum period finding. In: Robshaw, M., Katz, J. (eds.) CRYPTO 2016, Part II. LNCS, vol. 9815, pp. 207–237. Springer, Heidelberg (2016). https://doi.org/10.1007/978-3-662-53008-5_8
14. Kaplan, M., Leurent, G., Leverrier, A., Naya-Plasencia, M.: Quantum differential and linear cryptanalysis. IACR Trans. Symmetric Cryptol. **2016**(1), 71–94 (2016). https://doi.org/10.13154/TOSC.V2016.I1.71-94
15. Kuwakado, H., Morii, M.: Quantum distinguisher between the 3-round Feistel cipher and the random permutation. In: IEEE International Symposium on Information Theory, ISIT 2010, June 13–18, 2010, Austin, Texas, USA, Proceedings. pp. 2682–2685. IEEE (2010). https://doi.org/10.1109/ISIT.2010.5513654
16. Lan, Q., Zou, J., Wei, J.: New quantum attacks on some Feistel variants. Quantum Inf. Process. **24**(8), 233 (2025). https://doi.org/10.1007/S11128-025-04852-0
17. Leander, G., May, A.: Grover meets Simon – quantumly attacking the FX-construction. In: Takagi, T., Peyrin, T. (eds.) ASIACRYPT 2017. LNCS, vol. 10625, pp. 161–178. Springer, Cham (2017). https://doi.org/10.1007/978-3-319-70697-9_6
18. Li, B., Liu, Q.: Quantum cryptanalysis of generalized unbalanced Feistel structures: distinguisher and key recovery attack. In: Lin, D., Wang, M., Yung, M. (eds.) Inscrypt 2024, Part II. LNCS, vol. 15544, pp. 405–424. Springer, Cham (2024). https://doi.org/10.1007/978-981-96-4734-7_20
19. Liu, Q., Wang, H., Wang, J., Li, B., Wang, M.: Quantum periodic distinguisher construction: Symbolization method and automated tool. In: Hanaoka, G., Yang, B. (eds.) ASIACRYPT 2025, Part VIII. LNCS, vol. 16252, pp. 224–255. Springer, Cham (2025). https://doi.org/10.1007/978-981-95-5125-5_8
20. Lu, H., Liu, Q., Li, B., Qiao, J., Chen, J., Wang, M.: Automated periodic distinguisher search for AND-RX ciphers. In: Chen, R., Deng, R.H., Yung, M. (eds.) Inscrypt 2025, Part I. LNCS, vol. 16408, pp. 334–353. Springer, Cham (2025). https://doi.org/10.1007/978-981-95-6206-0_17
21. Mao, S., Guo, T., Wang, P., Hu, L.: Quantum attacks on lai-massey structure. In: Cheon, J.H., Johansson, T. (eds.) PQCrypto 2022. LNCS, vol. 13512, pp. 205–229. Springer, Cham (2022). https://doi.org/10.1007/978-3-031-17234-2_11
22. Schrottenloher, A.: Quantum linear key-recovery attacks using the QFT. In: Handschuh, H., Lysyanskaya, A. (eds.) CRYPTO 2023, Part V. LNCS, vol. 14085, pp. 258–291. Springer, Cham (2023). https://doi.org/10.1007/978-3-031-38554-4_9
23. Shor, P.W.: Algorithms for quantum computation: Discrete logarithms and factoring. In: 35th Annual Symposium on Foundations of Computer Science, Santa Fe, New Mexico, USA, 20–22 November 1994. pp. 124–134. IEEE Computer Society (1994)
24. Shor, P.W.: Polynomial-time algorithms for prime factorization and discrete logarithms on a quantum computer. SIAM J. Comput. **26**(5), 1484–1509 (1997)
25. Simon, D.R.: On the power of quantum computation. In: 35th Annual Symposium on Foundations of Computer Science, Santa Fe, New Mexico, USA, 20-22 November 1994. pp. 116–123. IEEE Computer Society (1994). https://doi.org/10.1109/SFCS.1994.365701
26. Sun, H., Cai, B., Qin, S., Wen, Q., Gao, F.: Quantum attacks on type-1 generalized feistel schemes. IACR Cryptol. ePrint Arch. p. 776 (2023). https://eprint.iacr.org/2023/776

27. Suzaki, T., Minematsu, K., Morioka, S., Kobayashi, E.: *TWINE*: a lightweight block cipher for multiple platforms. In: Knudsen, L.R., Wu, H. (eds.) SAC 2012. LNCS, vol. 7707, pp. 339–354. Springer, Heidelberg (2013). https://doi.org/10.1007/978-3-642-35999-6_22
28. Wang, X., Xiang, Z., Zhang, S., Chen, S., Zeng, X.: Quantum chosen-ciphertext attacks based on Simon's algorithm against unified structures. In: Patra, A. (ed.) Topics in Cryptology - CT-RSA 2025. LNCS, vol. 15598, pp. 99–122. Springer, Cham (2025). https://doi.org/10.1007/978-3-031-88661-4_5
29. Wu, W., Zhang, L.: LBlock: a lightweight block cipher. In: Lopez, J., Tsudik, G. (eds.) ACNS 2011. LNCS, vol. 6715, pp. 327–344. Springer, Heidelberg (2011). https://doi.org/10.1007/978-3-642-21554-4_19
30. Xiang, Z., et al.: Links between quantum distinguishers based on SIMON's algorithm and truncated differentials. IACR Trans. Symmetric Cryptol. **2024**(2), 296–321 (2024). https://doi.org/10.46586/TOSC.V2024.I2.296-321
31. Xu, Y., Du, X., Jia, M., Wang, X., Zou, J.: Quantum attacks on generalized Feistel networks based on the strong-weak separability. Quantum Inf. Process. **22**(10), 375 (2023). https://doi.org/10.1007/S11128-023-04135-6
32. Zhandry, M.: How to construct quantum random functions. In: 53rd Annual IEEE Symposium on Foundations of Computer Science, FOCS 2012, New Brunswick, NJ, USA, October 20-23, 2012, pp. 679–687. IEEE Computer Society (2012). https://doi.org/10.1109/FOCS.2012.37

Fully Homomorphic Encryption

Threshold (T)FHE Without Smudging by Means of Correct Threshold Additive HE

Antonina Bondarchuk(✉), Renaud Sirdey(✉), Aymen Boudguiga(✉), and Olive Chakraborty(✉)

Université Paris-Saclay, CEA, List, Palaiseau, France
antonina.bondarchuk@cea.fr, renaud.sirdey@cea.fr, aymen.boudguiga@cea.fr, olive.chakraborty@cea.fr

Abstract. Designing threshold lattice-based FHE schemes remains challenging due to the noise leakage that may occur during distributed decryption. The mainstream approach to avoid this consists of relying on noise flooding or smudging techniques. However, using these techniques comes at the cost of the much larger parameters required to ensure reliable decryption, and they are not easily applicable to schemes with smaller ciphertext moduli such as TFHE. In this paper, we demonstrate that smudging can be avoided for LWE-based FHE schemes, such as TFHE, by using a *correct* Linear Homomorphic Encryption (LHE) scheme, like Paillier, to encrypt the b-term of an LWE pair obtained *after* completing a homomorphic computation and sanitizing the resulting ciphertext. The key intuition is that, because the b-term of the LWE pair is *not* revealed to the decrypting parties, noise leakage is no longer an issue (with sanitization ensuring noise/message independence). We then instantiate this approach using TFHE as the baseline LWE scheme as well as the Tiresias threshold variant of Paillier. We prove the resulting construction, denoted thPLWE, is IND-CPA secure under static corruption and adaptive queries (Scor-Adp-IND-CPA) under the assumption that Tiresias achieves the same. We then provide experimental results to assess the practicality of the approach and compare it to other recent works.

1 Introduction

Threshold Fully Homomorphic Encryption (ThFHE) extends the capabilities of standard FHE by enabling function evaluation and threshold decryption among multiple parties. In this model, a subset of participants collaboratively generates a common public key, which they can then use to locally encrypt messages.

This work was supported by the France 2030 ANR Project ANR-22-PECY-003 SecureCompute and ANR-23-PECL-0009 TRUSTINCloudS as well as by the European Union under Grant Agreement No. 101167964. Views and opinions expressed are however those of the author(s) only and do not necessarily reflect those of the European Union or the European Cybersecurity Competence Centre. Neither the European Union nor the European Cybersecurity Competence Centre can be held responsible for them.

N. El Mrabet et al. (Eds.): AFRICACRYPT 2026, LNCS 16832, pp. 133–159, 2026.
https://doi.org/10.1007/978-3-032-31130-6_6

These ciphertexts serve as inputs to a target homomorphic computation, whose resulting output is a ciphertext shared among all participants. Finally, the parties must cooperate to decrypt this final result, ensuring that no single party can access the underlying data in isolation. Developing secure ThFHE schemes introduces several significant challenges, particularly regarding coordination and security against colluding parties.

To better understand challenges of constructing threshold encryption based on Learning With Errors (LWE), we first review how standard (non-threshold) LWE operates. We consider encrypting a plaintext $m \in \mathbb{Z}_t$ using a standard LWE ciphertext of the form $(\mathbf{a}, b)$ such that $\mathbf{a} \in \mathbb{Z}_q^n$, $b = \langle \mathbf{a}, \mathsf{sk} \rangle + \Delta m + e \in \mathbb{Z}_q$, where t and q are plaintext and ciphertext moduli respectively, $\mathsf{sk} \in \{0,1\}^n$ a secret key, $\Delta = \frac{q}{t}$ a scaling factor and e a Gaussian noise (i.e., the error term). To enable threshold LWE, the secret key sk is distributed among K parties P_i for $i \in [\![0, K-1]\!]$ using a linear secret sharing scheme with respect to a threshold $T < K$. We denote these shares as $(\mathsf{sk})_i$. From the ciphertext $(\mathbf{a}, b)$, P_i can produce a secret share of the *phase* $\varphi = \Delta m + e$ by computing $b - \langle \mathbf{a}, (\mathsf{sk})_i \rangle = (\varphi)_i$. Then by collaborating in opening the latter value, all the parties can perform rounding and obtain the value of m. However, this partial decryption discloses the value of e. When combined with the ciphertext $(\mathbf{a}, b)$ and the message m, the exposure of e reveals information about the secret key sk. Thus, ensuring security requires hiding the error term e during the decryption. This issue is addressed in two ways. A first approach, called *noise flooding* or *smudging*, consists in adding a significantly large noise to the shared values $(\varphi)_i$ before the opening to mask the original error. The second approach recovers the message m from the shared value $(\varphi)_i$ by running a generic MPC protocol to perform the rounding obliviously.

To perform smudging, the decrypting parties derive an additional secret shared noise E [1] that statistically masks the error e. The parties then open the value $\Delta m + e + E$. Choosing E too small leaks information about e, while choosing it excessively large prevents correct recovery of m after rounding [2]. Consequently, smudging naturally leads to significant overhead on the cryptosystem parameters. Indeed, to guarantee correct decryption after the addition of smudging noise, the ciphertext modulus q must be substantially increased, from $q > 2tB_e$ in the standard case to $q > 2^{\lambda+1}tB_e$ in the threshold setting, where B_e is the bound on the error for the evaluated function and λ is the security parameter. In RLWE-based homomorphic encryption schemes such as BGV [3], BFV [4,5] and CKKS [6], this problem is generally manageable because the ciphertext moduli are already very large, reaching several hundred bits, and provide enough margin to tolerate the additional inserted noise, while preserving decryption correctness. By contrast, schemes like FHEW [7] and TFHE [8,9] employ much smaller parameters (typically with 32 or 64-bit ciphertext modulus), making smudging integration more difficult. An alternative to smudging consists of running an MPC-protocol between decrypting parties to directly extract m [10,11]. That is, the MPC-protocol eliminates the noise entirely before any values are disclosed.

Summary of Contributions. In this paper, we propose a threshold LWE encryption scheme that eliminates the need for noise smudging. We introduce a novel threshold decryption technique inspired by [12], which combines threshold LWE-based encryption with a correct threshold Linear Homomorphic Encryption (LHE) scheme. Our core approach involves encrypting the LWE b-term and executing the linear part of the LWE decryption function under the LHE. This ensures that b remains inaccessible to the decrypting parties, thereby preventing secret key recovery attacks. We emphasize that our approach is simpler and more efficient than noise smudging, as it avoids the substantial parameter expansion typically required to accommodate smudging noise. Furthermore, for a large number of parties (20 or beyond), our construction offers a more efficient alternative compared to the threshold decryption approaches that use MPC-based message recovery, as it bypasses heavy MPC machinery and eliminates the need for a costly preprocessing phase. In essence, after homomorphic computation and sanitization (a technique which ensures circuit privacy and, perhaps more importantly, noise/message independence), a server encrypts the resulting b-term under the threshold LHE scheme thLHE, yielding $(\mathbf{a}, \mathsf{thLHE.Enc}(b))$. The parties P_i compute $\mathsf{thLHE.Enc}(b - \langle \mathbf{a}, (\mathsf{sk})_i \rangle) = \mathsf{thLHE.Enc}((\varphi)_i)$ and reconstruct the value $\mathsf{thLHE.Enc}(\varphi)$. Then, the parties jointly decrypt the LHE layer to retrieve the value $\varphi = \Delta m + e$. Note that the noise term e leaks no private information, as the LWE sample is sanitized before threshold decryption. Finally, the parties complete the LWE decryption by computing $\lfloor \frac{\varphi}{\Delta} \rceil$ to retrieve the message m. By following this algorithm, we avoid noise smudging while preventing an adversary from exploiting knowledge of e thanks to sanitization and the encryption of b under the LHE. We emphasize that our hybrid construction is generic and may be instantiated with any suitable threshold LWE and LHE schemes. However, for clarity, we first instantiate it using Tiresias, a threshold variant of Paillier. We adopt threshold Paillier as the primary building block because it is a standard, widely studied, and frequently deployed threshold LHE scheme. We then prove the security of our construction under the Static-corruption-Selective-query-IND-CPA model [13]. Subsequently, we propose concrete instantiations for both the LWE sanitization and the threshold LWE layer with TFHE. Our choice of threshold TFHE as the underlying scheme is motivated by its LWE-based structure and the fact that standard TFHE parameters provide an insufficient noise margin to accommodate smudging noise. Finally, we provide execution timings for our threshold decryption and discuss its overall efficiency.

Paper Organization. This paper is organized as follows: Sect. 2 briefly surveys existing literature on MPC-based message recovery, as well as threshold FHE and Paillier schemes. Section 3 provides the necessary background on threshold LWE and LHE, establishing notation used throughout our work. In Sect. 4, we introduce security notions for threshold FHE schemes. In Sect. 5, we detail our core construction; this Section also includes a formal security analysis of both the Tiresias scheme [14] and our proposed protocol. Section 6.1 suggests concrete instantiations for the LWE sanitization step and the threshold LWE layer, focusing on threshold TFHE, while Sect. 6.2 reports execution timings and performance benchmarks, and concludes the paper.

2 Related Works

Threshold LWE-Based FHE. In [15] Boneh et al. developed a general approach for adding threshold functionality to a large class of non-threshold schemes. They constructed a ThFHE scheme based on the LWE problem and introduced the concept of a *universal thresholdizer*. Since then, numerous (R)LWE-based constructions have been introduced [10, 16–20]. In most of these constructions, threshold decryption follows the noise flooding principle, which, as already highlighted, results in larger parameters for RLWE-based schemes such as BFV, BGV or CKKS and is difficult to adapt to TFHE due to the smaller moduli [21]. In a recent instantiation for TFHE [10], Bootland et al. presented mechanisms for robust threshold key generation and decryption for FHE schemes such as BGV, BFV and TFHE in the presence of malicious adversaries.

MPC Message Recovery. In [10], Bootland et al. perform threshold TFHE decryption via a generic MPC by applying *bit-extraction* techniques to extract the message m from the shares $(\varphi)_i$. In [11], Zyskind et al. propose a threshold FHE decryption protocol, where instead of masking the underlying ciphertext noise, the authors remove it via an MPC-based *rounding*.

Server-Aided Approach. Recently, Passelègue and Stehlé [22] introduced a server-aided approach for threshold FHE. In a nutshell, the syntax of ThFHE is extended by introducing an uncorrupted party, generally assumed to be a server that performs the homomorphic computation, that post-processes evaluated ciphertexts *before* the decrypting parties run the distributed decryption. This post-processing does not have to maintain any homomorphic properties. In exchange, it becomes possible in RLWE-based ThFHE to leverage this post-processing in order to optimize the amount of noise added during partial decryption [22]. Then, [23] adapts this approach to TFHE (by combining sanitization and small noise "flooding"). In some sense, the approach in this paper is a refinement of [23], where we completely remove the need for noise flooding.

Threshold Paillier. Motivated by applications in electronic voting, several threshold variants of the Paillier scheme were proposed [24–27], with all of them relying on a trusted dealer for the key setup. To address the need for a threshold Paillier with trustless distributed key generation and a robust proof system under standard assumptions, Friedman et al. introduced Tiresias [14]. Additionally, they establish that it is secure under the DCR assumption alone, the same assumption underlying standard Paillier CPA security.

3 Preliminaries

Let λ and τ respectively represent the computational and statistical security parameters. In the upcoming sections, we denote vectors by bold letters, so a vector $\mathbf{x}$ of n elements is $\mathbf{x} = (x_0, \ldots, x_{n-1})$. The inner product of two vectors $\mathbf{x}$ and $\mathbf{y}$ is $\langle \mathbf{x}, \mathbf{y} \rangle$. We write $[\![0, K-1]\!]$ for $\{0, 1, \ldots, K-1\}$ and let $\boxplus$ and $\boxtimes$ be homomorphic addition and multiplication.

3.1 Zero-Knowledge Protocol

In a zero-knowledge protocol, a prover convinces a verifier of some fact regarding a public statement without revealing any underlying information beyond the truth of this fact. It must meet three criteria: completeness ensures that valid proofs are always accepted by honest verifier; soundness guarantees that valid proofs cannot be produced for false claims to deceive the verifier; and zero-knowledge means that the verifier learns nothing about the instance except the truth of the fact. Additionally, Special Honest Verifier Zero-Knowledge (SHVZK) ensures that no private information is leaked if the verifier acts honestly. This property implies that a simulator can recreate a convincing transcript without knowing the witness. For the formal definitions, we refer the reader to [14].

3.2 Sanitization

The goal of sanitization is to remove all information conveyed by the ciphertext ct except for the message m. Following [28], a sanitization algorithm $\mathsf{Sanitize}$ is sanitizing if there exists a polynomial time simulator Sim such that for any $m \in \mathcal{M}$, any ciphertext ct that encrypts m, it holds that $(\mathsf{Sim}(1^\lambda, m, \mathsf{pk}), \mathsf{sk}) \approx_s (\mathsf{Sanitize}(\mathsf{pk}, \mathsf{ct}), \mathsf{sk})$ for an honestly sampled pk.

In [29], Ducas and Stehlé proposed a sanitization solution based on repeatedly applying the addition of moderately sized noise and performing bootstrapping. The idea is that through the successive injection of noise into two ciphertexts, their statistical distance decreases, and after a sufficient number of iterations, the ciphertexts become statistically indistinguishable. Then in [28], Bourse and Izabachène, and in [30], Kluczniak proposed a solution that addresses the overhead of repeated bootstrapping in [29] by randomizing the entire TFHE bootstrapping procedure to achieve sanitization with only a single execution of the bootstrapping. However, the added randomization overhead results in poorer practical performance than the strategy from [29], mainly due to the costly use of discrete Gaussian sampling. To address the aforementioned limitations, in [31] Hwang et al. construct a TFHE sanitization algorithm that requires only a single invocation of bootstrapping and introduces randomization only at the beginning and end of the bootstrapping, rather than randomizing the entire process.

3.3 Threshold Schemes

Let $\mathbb{A}_{T,K}$ denote a (T,K)-threshold access structure [13]. Let $\mathcal{M}$ and $\mathcal{C}$ denote plaintext and ciphertext spaces of a homomorphic scheme. In this paper, we partition $\mathcal{C}$ into two disjoint sets, $\mathcal{C} = \mathcal{C}_F \cup \mathcal{C}_E$, where $\mathcal{C}_F$ and $\mathcal{C}_E$ represent fresh and evaluated ciphertexts, respectively (for reasons that will become obvious, we will further always work under the assumption that $\mathcal{C}_F \cap \mathcal{C}_E = \emptyset$). Let SS be a linear secret sharing scheme, for example, Shamir Secret Sharing (SSS) introduced by [32]. In the following, we formally define the two core primitives used in this paper: a general threshold LWE-based FHE scheme (thLWE) and a general threshold LHE scheme (thLHE).

Definition 1 (Threshold LWE-based FHE). *A threshold T-out-of-K public-key LWE-based encryption scheme for an access structure $\mathbb{A}_{T,K}$ over K parties, with plaintext space $\mathcal{M}$ and ciphertext space $\mathcal{C}$, consists of the following PPT algorithms* $\mathsf{thLWE} = (\mathsf{DistKeyGen}, \mathsf{Enc}, \mathsf{Eval}, \mathsf{Sanitize}, \mathsf{DistDec})$*:*

- $\mathsf{DistKeyGen}(1^\lambda, \mathbb{A}_{T,K}; \mathcal{P}) \rightarrow (\mathsf{pk}, \{(\mathsf{sk})_i\}_{i\in\mathcal{K}})$: *the parties $\mathcal{P} = \{P_i\}_{i\in\mathcal{K}} \in \mathbb{A}_{T,K}$ execute a distributed key generation that returns a public key* pk *(containing $\{\rho_i\}_{i\in\mathcal{K}}$ and an evaluation key* evk*) and a set of K secret shares of the LWE secret key* sk*, denoted $\{(\mathsf{sk})_i\}_{i\in\mathcal{K}}$, where each party P_i receives only its corresponding share $(\mathsf{sk})_i$ generated via $\mathsf{SS.Share}_{T,K}(\mathsf{sk}; r) \rightarrow \{\rho_i, (\mathsf{sk})_i\}_{i\in\mathcal{K}}$ for randomness r.*
- $\mathsf{Enc}(\mathsf{pk}, m) \rightarrow \mathsf{ct} \in \mathcal{C}_F$: *using the public key, the encryption algorithm returns a ciphertext of the form $\mathsf{ct} = (\mathbf{a}, b = \langle \mathbf{a}, \mathsf{sk}\rangle + \Delta m + e)$, where e depends on the structure of the public key*[1]*, as a fresh LWE encryption of $m \in \mathcal{M}$, where $\mathbf{a} \in \mathbb{Z}_q^n$ and $b \in \mathbb{Z}_q$. Here, $\Delta = q/t$ is the scaling factor, q and t are the ciphertext and plaintext moduli, and n denotes the LWE dimension.*
- $\mathsf{Sanitize}(\mathsf{pk}, \mathsf{ct}) \rightarrow \mathsf{ct}' \in \mathcal{C}_E$: *the sanitization algorithm processes an LWE ciphertext* ct *to produce a sanitized ciphertext* ct'.
- $\mathsf{Eval}\left(\mathsf{pk}, f, \{\mathsf{ct}_i\}_{i\in[\![0,l]\!]}\right) \rightarrow \mathsf{ct}' \in \mathcal{C}_E$: *the evaluation algorithm computes a function f on ciphertexts $\{\mathsf{ct}_i\}_{i=0}^{l}$ producing $\mathsf{ct} = f(\mathsf{ct}_0, \ldots, \mathsf{ct}_l)$, and subsequently invokes the sanitization algorithm to return $\mathsf{ct}' \leftarrow \mathsf{Sanitize}(\mathsf{pk}, \mathsf{ct})$.*
- $\mathsf{DistDec}(\mathsf{pk}, \mathcal{T}, \{(\mathsf{sk})_i\}, \mathsf{ct}; \{P_i\}_{i\in\mathcal{T}}) \rightarrow \lfloor \frac{\varphi}{\Delta} \rceil \in \mathcal{M}$: *the parties $\{P_i\}_{i\in\mathcal{T}}$ where $\mathcal{T} \subseteq \mathcal{K}$ execute the distributed decryption on $\mathsf{ct} \in \mathcal{C}$ using three sub-algorithms to recover the plaintext:*
  - $\mathsf{ShareDec}((\mathsf{sk})_i, \mathsf{ct}; P_i) \rightarrow (\varphi)_i$: *each party P_i returns a partial decryption share of* ct *by computing $(\varphi)_i = b - \langle \mathbf{a}, (\mathsf{sk})_i\rangle = (\Delta m + e)_i$.*
  - $\mathsf{Comb}(\mathsf{pk}, \{(\varphi)_i\}_{i\in\mathcal{T}}; \{P_i\}_{i\in\mathcal{T}}) \rightarrow \varphi$: *the parties $\{P_i\}_{i\in\mathcal{T}}$ jointly reconstruct $\varphi = \Delta m + e$ by invoking the $\mathsf{SS.Recon}(\mathsf{pk}, \{(\varphi)_i\}_{i\in\mathcal{T}})$.*
  - $\mathsf{FinDec}(\mathsf{pk}, \varphi) \rightarrow m$: *this step finalizes the LWE decryption, returning some $m \in \mathcal{M}$ such that $m = \lfloor \frac{\varphi}{\Delta} \rceil$.*

[1] For example, when using the usual Regev-style public key made of $n \log_2 q$ encryptions of 0 (generated by means of the secret key), the noise e is the sum of the noises of the public-key element selected in the random subset used for encryption.

Definition 2 (Threshold LHE). *A threshold T-out-of-K LHE scheme for an access structure $\mathbb{A}_{T,K}$ on K parties, with plaintext space $\mathcal{M}$ and ciphertext space $\mathcal{C}$, consists of the following PPT algorithms* $\mathsf{thLHE} = (\mathsf{DistKeyGen}, \mathsf{Enc}, \mathsf{Eval}, \mathsf{DistDec})$*:*

- $\mathsf{DistKeyGen}(1^\lambda, \mathbb{A}_{T,K}; \mathcal{P}) \to (\mathsf{pk}, \{(\mathsf{sk})_i\}_{i\in\mathcal{K}})$*: the parties* $\mathcal{P} = \{P_i\}_{i\in\mathcal{K}} \in \mathbb{A}_{T,K}$ *execute a distributed key generation that returns an LHE public key* pk *together with evaluation points* $\{\rho_i\}_{i\in\mathcal{K}}$ *and a set of K secret shares of the LHE secret key* sk*, denoted* $\{(\mathsf{sk})_i\}_{i\in\mathcal{K}}$*, where each party P_i receives only its corresponding share* $(\mathsf{sk})_i$ *generated via* $\mathsf{SS.Share}_{T,K}(\mathsf{sk}; r) \to \{\rho_i, (\mathsf{sk})_i\}_{i\in\mathcal{K}}$ *for randomness r.*
- $\mathsf{Enc}(\mathsf{pk}, m) \to \mathsf{ct} \in \mathcal{C}_F$*: the encryption algorithm samples $r \in \mathcal{M}^*$ and returns* $\mathsf{ct} \in \mathcal{C}_F$ *as a fresh LHE encryption of $m \in \mathcal{M}$ using randomness r.*
- $\mathsf{Eval}\left(\mathsf{pk}, f, \{\mathsf{ct}_i\}_{i\in[\![0,l]\!]}\right) \to \mathsf{ct} \in \mathcal{C}_E$*: the evaluation algorithm computes an affine function f on ciphertexts* $\{\mathsf{ct}_i\}_{i=0}^{l}$ *producing* $\mathsf{ct} = f(\mathsf{ct}_0, \ldots, \mathsf{ct}_l)$ *by consequently applying*
  - $\mathsf{Add}(\mathsf{ct}_0, \mathsf{ct}_1) \to \mathsf{ct}' \in \mathcal{C}_E$*: it adds* $\mathsf{ct}_0, \mathsf{ct}_1 \in \mathcal{C}$ *returning* $\mathsf{ct}' = \mathsf{ct}_0 \boxplus \mathsf{ct}_1$.
  - $\mathsf{cAdd}(\mathsf{ct}, x) \to \mathsf{ct}' \in \mathcal{C}_E$*: it adds* $\mathsf{ct} \in \mathcal{C}$ *and $x \in \mathcal{M}$ returning* $\mathsf{ct}' = \mathsf{ct} \boxplus x$.
  - $\mathsf{cMult}(\mathsf{ct}, x) \to \mathsf{ct}' \in \mathcal{C}_E$*: it multiplies* $\mathsf{ct} \in \mathcal{C}$ *and $x \in \mathcal{M}$ returning* $\mathsf{ct}' = \mathsf{ct} \boxtimes x$.
- $\mathsf{DistDec}(\mathsf{pk}, \mathcal{T}, \{(\mathsf{sk})_i\}, \mathsf{ct}; \{P_i\}_{i\in\mathcal{T}}) \to m \in \mathcal{M}$*: the parties* $\{P_i\}_{i\in\mathcal{T}}$ *where* $\mathcal{T} \subseteq \mathcal{K}$ *execute the distributed decryption on* $\mathsf{ct} \in \mathcal{C}$ *using three sub-algorithms to recover the plaintext:*
  - $\mathsf{ShareDec}((\mathsf{sk})_i, \mathsf{ct}; P_i) \to (\mathsf{pd})_i$*: each party P_i returns a partial decryption share* $(\mathsf{pd})_i$ *of* ct.
  - $\mathsf{Comb}(\mathsf{pk}, \{(\mathsf{pd})_i\}; \{P_i\}_{i\in\mathcal{T}}) \to \mathsf{c}$*: the parties* $\{P_i\}_{i\in\mathcal{T}}$ *jointly reconstruct* c *by invoking the* $\mathsf{SS.Recon}(\mathsf{pk}, \{(\mathsf{pd})_i\})$.
  - $\mathsf{FinDec}(\mathsf{pk}, \mathsf{c}) \to m$*: this step finalizes the decryption by returning some $m \in \mathcal{M}$ from the reconstructed value* c.

In this paper, we require thLHE *schemes to be perfectly correct, i.e., for any* $\mathbb{A}_{T,K}$*, sets* $\mathcal{P} = \{P_i\}_{i\in\mathcal{K}} \in \mathbb{A}_{T,K}$ *and* $\{P_i\}_{i\in\mathcal{T}} \in \mathbb{A}_{T,K}$ *where* $\mathcal{T} \subseteq \mathcal{K}$*,* $m_0, \ldots, m_l \in \mathcal{M}$ *and* $(\mathsf{pk}, \{(\mathsf{sk})_i\}_{i\in\mathcal{K}}) \in \mathsf{DistKeyGen}(1^\lambda, T, K; \mathcal{P})$*, it satisfies*

$$\Pr\left[m' = f(m_0, \ldots, m_l) \;\middle|\; \begin{array}{l} \mathsf{ct}_j \leftarrow \mathsf{Enc}(\mathsf{pk}, m_j) \text{ for } j \in [\![0,l]\!] \\ \mathsf{ct} \leftarrow \mathsf{Eval}\left(\mathsf{pk}, f, \{\mathsf{ct}_j\}_{j\in[\![0,l]\!]}\right) \\ m' \leftarrow \mathsf{DistDec}(\mathsf{pk}, \mathcal{T}, \{(\mathsf{sk})_i\}, \mathsf{ct}; \{P_i\}_{i\in\mathcal{T}}) \end{array} \right] = 1,$$

with the probability taken encryption randomness.

4 Security Notions

In this paper, we assume the asynchronous setting, where any authorized subset of T parties can decrypt without knowing in advance which T decryptors will contribute. This is in contrast with the synchronous setting, where the subset of

T parties is known at the outset. ThFHE security in the synchronous setting as recently been addressed in [33].

In the standard CPA game, the adversary A is only granted access to encryption and challenge oracles, while in the threshold setting, A additionally obtains the secret key shares of corrupted parties and naturally sees the associated partial decryptions. This is modeled by providing A with a partial decryption oracle, which answers two types of partial decryption queries: (I) queries on non-challenge ciphertexts (i.e., those not depending on the challenge bit); (II) queries on challenge ciphertexts (i.e., whose underlying plaintexts depend on the challenge bit). Still, even in the CPA setting, corruptions and query timing must be considered. Corruption timing determines whether an adversary is restricted to static corruption (Scor), where the corrupted set is fixed upfront, or can adaptively corrupt (AdpCor) parties during execution up to a maximal threshold $T + 1$ (MaxCor). Similarly, query timing defines whether the adversary must selectively declare (Sel) its game requests before the protocol begins or can issue them adaptively (Adp) based on the ongoing interaction. Also, we highlight that *LWE-based FHE presently offers no practical alternative for achieving CCA1 (or beyond) in the single-key setting, even based on heuristics.* Although some theoretical works indicate that this may be possible, to the best of our knowledge, all present LWE-based CCA-secure FHE constructions (e.g., [34]) are only of theoretical interest.

In the following, we adapt the recent definitions for IND-CPA and SIM-CPA security notions for Threshold Public Key Encryption (TPKE) schemes proposed in [13, Sect. 2.1] to cope with FHE schemes. Our adaptation essentially consists in providing the adversary with an evaluation oracle (over well-formed ciphertexts) such that it can also ask for partial decryption of well-formed evaluated ciphertexts and not only fresh ones. In spirit, the security games below are generalizations of the CPA^D games (for both the IND and SIM notions) introduced by Li&Micciancio [35] to the threshold setting. In particular, as in [35], we make explicit the challenger game state and how it is handled. Note that, as in CPA^D [35, Def. 2], the encryption oracle is necessary in both the private and public-key setting in order to fill the challenger state with well-formed ciphertexts.

Our game model assumes a multi-challenge setting with adaptive (Adp) queries (including Type II partial decryption queries) and considers the adversary A that statically corrupts (Scor) a subset of parties. We permit adaptive queries because selective security is considered too weak to be a reasonable target notion, as it requires the adversary to declare its queries upfront. In contrast, allowing adaptive queries ensures the model captures more realistic adversarial behaviours, where A's strategy can evolve based on previously observed oracles' responses. Furthermore, we allow Type II queries; security models that exclude these are inherently weaker for TPKE applications, where the adversary may observe partial decryptions related to the challenge ciphertext. Eventually, we adopt a static corruption model because, as demonstrated in [13, Thm. 3.6], simulation security with adaptive corruption is not achievable, assuming adaptive partial decryption queries. This choice is further motivated by Sect. 5.2, where we establish the security of our construction through a reduction to the simulation-based security of the threshold Paillier scheme.

Definition 3 (Scor-Adp-IND-CPA for ThFHE). *Given a threshold FHE scheme* $\mathsf{thFHE} = (\mathsf{DistKeyGen}, \mathsf{Enc}, \mathsf{Eval}, \mathsf{DistDec})$ *with plaintext space* $\mathcal{M}$ *and ciphertext space* $\mathcal{C}$*, we define a security game for an adversary* A *and a security parameter* λ*. The game is parameterized by a bit* $\gamma \leftarrow\!\$\, \{0,1\}$*, unknown to* A*, and an initially empty state* Ω *consisting of message-message-ciphertext-index* $(m_0, m_1, \mathsf{ct}, \mathsf{ind})$ *quadruples. At the beginning of the game,* A *statically corrupts a set of parties* $\mathcal{S} = \{P_i\}_{i\in\mathcal{T}}$ *for some* $\mathcal{T} \subset \mathcal{K}$*:*

- *Key generation: given* $\mathcal{P} = \{P_i\}_{i\in\mathcal{K}}$*, check* $(\mathcal{S} \subset \mathcal{P}) \wedge (\mathcal{S} \notin \mathbb{A}_{T,K})$*. If* True*, run* $(\mathsf{pk}, \{(\mathsf{sk})_i\}_{i\in\mathcal{K}}) \leftarrow \mathsf{thFHE.DistKeyGen}(1^\lambda, \mathbb{A}_{T,K})$ *and return to* A *a public key* pk *and a set* $\{(\mathsf{sk})_i\}_{i\in\mathcal{T}}$*.*
- *Encryption request: when* A *queries* $(\mathsf{plaintext}, m)$*, where* $m \in \mathcal{M}$*, compute* $\mathsf{ct} \leftarrow \mathsf{thFHE.Enc}(\mathsf{pk}, m)$*, return* ct *to* A *and do* $\Omega := [\Omega; (m, m, \mathsf{ct}, \{\emptyset\})]$*.*
- *Challenge request: when* A *queries* $(\mathsf{test}, m_0, m_1)$*, where* $m_0, m_1 \in \mathcal{M}$*,* $m_0 \neq m_1$*, get* $\mathsf{ct} \leftarrow \mathsf{thFHE.Enc}(\mathsf{pk}, m_\gamma)$ *and return* ct *to* A *after updating* $\Omega := [\Omega; (m_0, m_1, \mathsf{ct}, \{\emptyset\})]$*.*
- *Evaluation request: when* A *queries* $(\mathsf{eval}, f, \ell_0, \dots, \ell_v)$*,* $\forall i$*:* $\ell_i \in [\![0, |\Omega|-1]\!]$*, set* $m'_0 = f(\Omega[\ell_0].m_0, \dots, \Omega[\ell_v].m_0)$*,* $m'_1 = f(\Omega[\ell_0].m_1, \dots, \Omega[\ell_v].m_1)$ *and* $\mathsf{ct}' \leftarrow \mathsf{thFHE.Eval}(\mathsf{pk}, f, \Omega[\ell_0].\mathsf{ct}, \dots, \Omega[\ell_v].\mathsf{ct})$*, then return* ct' *to* A *after updating* $\Omega := [\Omega; (m'_0, m'_1, \mathsf{ct}', \{\emptyset\})]$*.*
- *Partial decryption request: when* A *queries* $(\mathsf{ciphertext}, \ell, j)$*,* $\ell \in [\![0, |\Omega|-1]\!]$*,* $j \in \mathcal{K}$*, if* $\Omega[\ell].m_0 = \Omega[\ell].m_1$*,* $(\mathsf{pd})_j \leftarrow \mathsf{thFHE.ShareDec}((\mathsf{sk})_j, \Omega[\ell].\mathsf{ct})$*, and return* $(\mathsf{pd})_j$ *to* A*. If* $\Omega[\ell].m_0 \neq \Omega[\ell].m_1$*, do* $\Omega[\ell].\mathsf{ind} := [\Omega[\ell].\mathsf{ind}; \{j\}]$ *and check* $(\{P_i\}_{i\in\Omega[\ell].\mathsf{ind}} \cup \mathcal{S}) \notin \mathbb{A}_{T,K}$*; if* True*, compute* $(\mathsf{pd})_j$ *and return it to* A*.*
- *Guessing stage (after polynomially many interleaved encryption, challenge, evaluation and partial decryption requests): when* A *outputs* $(\mathsf{guess}, \gamma')$*, if* $\gamma' = \gamma$ *then* A *wins the game. Otherwise,* A *loses the game.*

In addition, we give a definition of the associated (strictly stronger [13, Prop. 3.2]) simulation-based notion that we also use later in the paper.

Definition 4 (Scor-Adp-SIM-CPA for ThFHE). *Given a threshold FHE scheme* $\mathsf{thFHE} = (\mathsf{DistKeyGen}, \mathsf{Enc}, \mathsf{Eval}, \mathsf{DistDec})$ *with plaintext space* $\mathcal{M}$ *and ciphertext space* $\mathcal{C}$*, we define a security game for an adversary* A *and a security parameter* λ*. Let* Sim *be a PPT (stateful) simulator, which maintains its own state* ω*. The game is parameterized by a bit* $\gamma \leftarrow\!\$\, \{0,1\}$*, unknown to* A*, and an initially empty state* Ω *consisting of message-message-ciphertext-index* $(m_0, m_1, \mathsf{ct}, \mathsf{ind})$ *quadruples. At the beginning of the game,* A *statically corrupts a set of parties* $\mathcal{S} = \{P_i\}_{i\in\mathcal{T}}$ *for some* $\mathcal{T} \subset \mathcal{K}$*:*

- *Key generation: given* $\mathcal{P} = \{P_i\}_{i\in\mathcal{K}}$*, check* $(\mathcal{S} \subset \mathcal{P}) \wedge (\mathcal{S} \notin \mathbb{A}_{T,K})$*. If* True*, then proceed as*
  - *if* $\gamma = 0$*, run* $(\mathsf{pk}, \{(\mathsf{sk})_i\}_{i\in\mathcal{K}}) \leftarrow \mathsf{thFHE.DistKeyGen}(1^\lambda, \mathbb{A}_{T,K})$*,*
  - *if* $\gamma = 1$*, run* $(\mathsf{pk}, \{(\mathsf{sk})_i\}_{i\in\mathcal{T}}, \omega) \leftarrow \mathsf{Sim}(1^\lambda, \mathbb{A}_{T,K}, \mathcal{S})$*,*

return to A *a public key* pk *and a set* $\{(\mathsf{sk})_i\}_{i\in\mathcal{T}}$.

- *Encryption request: when* A *queries* $(\mathsf{plaintext}, m)$, *where* $m \in \mathcal{M}$,
  - *if* $\gamma = 0$, *compute* $\mathsf{ct} \leftarrow \mathsf{thFHE.Enc}(\mathsf{pk}, m)$,
  - *if* $\gamma = 1$, *compute* $\mathsf{ct} \leftarrow \mathsf{Sim}(m, \omega)$,

  return ct *to* A *and update* $\Omega := [\Omega; (m, m, \mathsf{ct}, \{\emptyset\})]$.
- *Challenge request: when* A *queries* (test, m), *where* $m \in \mathcal{M}$,
  - *if* $\gamma = 0$, *compute* $\mathsf{ct} \leftarrow \mathsf{thFHE.Enc}(\mathsf{pk}, m)$,
  - *if* $\gamma = 1$, *compute* $\mathsf{ct} \leftarrow \mathsf{Sim}(\omega)$,

  pick a random $m' \in \mathcal{M}$, *return* ct *to* A *after updating* $\Omega := [\Omega; (m, m', \mathsf{ct}, \{\emptyset\})]$.
- *Evaluation request: when* A *queries* $(\mathsf{eval}, f, \ell_0, \ldots, \ell_v)$, $\forall i$: $\ell_i \in [\![0, |\Omega| - 1]\!]$, *set* $m'_0 = f(\Omega[\ell_0].m_0, \ldots, \Omega[\ell_v].m_0)$, $m'_1 = f(\Omega[\ell_0].m_1, \ldots, \Omega[\ell_v].m_1)$ *and compute* $\mathsf{ct}' \leftarrow \mathsf{thFHE.Eval}(\mathsf{pk}, f, \Omega[\ell_0].\mathsf{ct}, \ldots, \Omega[\ell_v].\mathsf{ct})$, *then return* ct' *to* A *after updating* $\Omega := [\Omega; (m'_0, m'_1, \mathsf{ct}', \{\emptyset\})]$.
- *Partial decryption request: when* A *queries* $(\mathsf{ciphertext}, \ell, j)$, $\ell \in [\![0, |\Omega| - 1]\!]$, $j \in \mathcal{K}$,
  - *if* $\gamma = 0$, *compute* $(\mathsf{pd})_j \leftarrow \mathsf{thFHE.ShareDec}((\mathsf{sk})_j, \Omega[\ell].\mathsf{ct})$,
  - *if* $\gamma = 1$, *update* $\Omega[\ell].\mathsf{ind} := [\Omega[\ell].\mathsf{ind}; \{j\}]$ *and check* $(\Omega[\ell].m_0 \neq \Omega[\ell].m_1) \wedge \big((\{P_i\}_{i\in\Omega[\ell].\mathsf{ind}} \cup \mathcal{S}) \in \mathbb{A}_{T,K}\big)$; *if True,* $(\mathsf{pd})_j \leftarrow \mathsf{Sim}(\Omega[\ell].\mathsf{ct}, \Omega[\ell].m_0, j, \omega)$; *else,* $(\mathsf{pd})_j \leftarrow \mathsf{Sim}(\Omega[\ell].\mathsf{ct}, j, \omega)$,

  then return $(\mathsf{pd})_j$ *to* A.
- *Guessing stage (after polynomially many interleaved encryption, challenge, evaluation and partial decryption requests): when* A *outputs* $(\mathsf{guess}, \gamma')$, *if* $\gamma' = \gamma$, *then* A *wins the game. Otherwise,* A *loses the game.*

5 Threshold LWE Without Smudging

In this paper, we leverage the *server-aided* framework of Passelègue and Stehlé [22] (Sect. 2) that extends the definition of ThFHE by introducing an uncorrupted party (modelled as a server) that post-processes evaluated LWE ciphertexts before the decryption parties participate. Consequently, the parties execute the threshold decryption algorithm on the post-processed LWE ciphertext provided by the server, following homomorphic evaluation.

We now present our LWE without smudging construction, employing instantiations of threshold LWE and LHE layers. Let $\mathsf{thLWE} = (\mathsf{DistKeyGen}, \mathsf{Enc}, \mathsf{Eval}, \mathsf{Sanitize}, \mathsf{DistDec})$ and $\mathsf{thLHE} = (\mathsf{DistKeyGen}, \mathsf{Enc}, \mathsf{Eval}, \mathsf{DistDec})$ denote generic T_{L}-out-of-K threshold LWE-based FHE (Definition 1) and T_{P}-out-of-K threshold LHE[2] (taking threshold Paillier as a concrete instance, we follow the construction in Definition 2). We define the plaintext/ciphertext moduli as (t, q) for thLWE and (μ, μ^2) for thLHE, where μ is an RSA-style composite modulus. Our core strategy is to shield the LWE b-term from the decryption parties by keeping it encrypted under thLHE throughout the distributed decryption. After sanitizing

[2] We note that any other LHE scheme, which satisfies Definition 2, can be used as well.

an LWE sample $(\mathbf{a}, b)$, the server S computes $(\mathbf{a}, \mathsf{thLHE.Enc}(b))$ and distributes it to the parties. Each party P_i homomorphically computes a partial decryption share $\mathsf{thLHE.Enc}(b - \langle \mathbf{a}, (\mathbf{s})_i \rangle) = \mathsf{thLHE.Enc}((\varphi)_i)$. Then the parties jointly reconstruct φ under thLHE, getting $\mathsf{thLHE.Enc}(\varphi)$, and decrypt the thLHE layer to recover the value φ. Finally, they retrieve the message by computing $\lfloor \varphi / \Delta \rceil$. Although φ may allow the parties to obtain the ciphertext noise, the prior sanitization of the LWE sample ensures circuit privacy.

Let $\mathcal{P} = \{P_i\}_{i \in \mathcal{K}}$ be the set of participating parties and S the associated server. We define the access structures as $\mathbb{A}_{T,K} = (\mathbb{A}_{\mathcal{T}_\mathsf{L},K}, \mathbb{A}_{\mathcal{T}_\mathsf{P},K})$, where $\mathcal{T}_\mathsf{L}, \mathcal{T}_\mathsf{P} \subseteq \mathcal{K}$ denote the respective index sets of parties participating in the partial decryptions of thLWE and thLHE. Our construction $\mathsf{thPLWE} = (\mathsf{DistKeyGen}, \mathsf{Enc}, \mathsf{Eval}, \mathsf{PartDec}, \mathsf{DistDec})$ is formally defined as follows:

- $\mathsf{DistKeyGen}(1^\lambda, \mathbb{A}_{T,K}; \mathcal{P}) \rightarrow (\mathsf{thLWE}.(\mathsf{pk}, \{(\mathsf{sk})_i\}), \mathsf{thLHE}.(\mathsf{pk}, \{(\mathsf{sk})_i\}))$: The algorithm, run by $\mathcal{P}$ executes

$$(\mathsf{thLWE.pk}, \{(\mathsf{thLWE.sk})_i\}) \leftarrow \mathsf{thLWE.DistKeyGen}(1^\lambda, \mathbb{A}_{\mathcal{T}_\mathsf{L},K}; \mathcal{P}),$$
$$(\mathsf{thLHE.pk}, \{(\mathsf{thLHE.sk})_i\}) \leftarrow \mathsf{thLHE.DistKeyGen}(1^\lambda, \mathbb{A}_{\mathcal{T}_\mathsf{P},K}; \mathcal{P}),$$

  returning thLWE, thLHE public keys $\mathsf{thLWE.pk}$, $\mathsf{thLHE.pk}$, and two tuples of K secret shares of $\mathsf{thLWE.sk}$, $\mathsf{thLHE.sk}$, i.e. $\{(\mathsf{thLWE.sk})_i\}$, $\{(\mathsf{thLHE.sk})_i\}$.
- $\mathsf{Enc}(\mathsf{thLWE.pk}, m) \rightarrow \mathsf{ct}$: encrypts $m \in \mathbb{Z}_t$ as $\mathsf{ct} = (\mathbf{a}, b = \langle \mathbf{a}, \mathsf{thLWE.sk} \rangle + \Delta m + e) \leftarrow \mathsf{thLWE.Enc}(\mathsf{thLWE.pk}, m)$, where $\mathbf{a} \in \mathbb{Z}_q^n$, $b \in \mathbb{Z}_q$ and $\Delta = \frac{q}{t}$.
- $\mathsf{Eval}(\mathsf{thLWE.pk}, f, \mathsf{ct}_0, \dots, \mathsf{ct}_l; \mathsf{S})$: evaluates a function f on $\{\mathsf{ct}_i\}_{i \in [\![0,l]\!]}$. It computes $\mathsf{ct} \leftarrow \mathsf{thLWE.Eval}(\mathsf{thLWE.pk}, f, \mathsf{ct}_0, \dots, \mathsf{ct}_l)$ and sanitizes ct as $\mathsf{ct}' = (\mathbf{a}', b') \leftarrow \mathsf{thLWE.Sanitize}(\mathsf{thLWE.pk}, \mathsf{ct})$. It finally does $p \leftarrow \mathsf{thLHE.Enc}(\mathsf{thLHE.pk}, b')$ and outputs $\mathsf{ct}'' = (\mathbf{a}', p)$.
- $\mathsf{PartDec}(\mathsf{thLWE.pk}, \{(\mathsf{thLWE.sk})_i\}, \mathsf{ct}''; \{P_i\}_{i \in \mathcal{T}_\mathsf{L}}) \rightarrow \mathsf{thLHE.Enc}(\varphi)$: each party P_i for $i \in \mathcal{T}_\mathsf{L}$ homomorphically computes $\varphi = b - \langle \mathbf{a}, \mathsf{sk} \rangle = \Delta m + e$ on ct'' under thLHE returning $\mathsf{thLHE.Enc}((\varphi)_i) = \mathsf{thLHE.cAdd}(p, [\langle -\mathbf{a}', (\mathsf{thLWE.sk})_i \rangle]_q)$. Then the parties $\{P_i\}_{i \in \mathcal{T}_\mathsf{L}}$ execute $\mathsf{thLWE.Comb}$ on $\mathsf{thLHE.Enc}((\varphi)_i)$ by homomorphically running $\mathsf{SS.Recon}(\mathsf{thLWE.pk}, \{(\varphi)_i\}_{i \in \mathcal{T}_\mathsf{L}})$ under thLHE. They compute the Lagrange coefficients $\lambda_i \in \mathbb{Z}_q$ and return[3]

$$\mathsf{thLHE.Enc}(\varphi) = \bigoplus_{i=0}^{|\mathcal{T}_\mathsf{L}|-1} \left(\mathsf{thLHE.cMult}\left(\mathsf{thLHE.Enc}((\varphi)_i), \lambda_i\right)\right),$$

  where $\oplus$ defines $\mathsf{thLHE.Add}$.
- $\mathsf{DistDec}(\mathsf{thLHE.pk}, \{(\mathsf{thLHE.sk})_i\}, \mathsf{thLHE.Enc}(\varphi); \{P_i\}_{i \in \mathcal{T}_\mathsf{P}}) \rightarrow m$: the parties $\{P_i\}_{i \in \mathcal{T}_\mathsf{P}}$ compute $(\mathsf{pd})_i \leftarrow \mathsf{thLHE.ShareDec}((\mathsf{thLHE.sk})_i, \mathsf{thLHE.Enc}(\varphi))$. By

[3] Note that the correctness of φ reconstruction under thLHE is preserved. The operation is linear and $q \ll \mu$ (with $\log_2 q = 32$ and $\log_2 \mu = 2048$ as typical values), meaning no modulo μ reduction occurs under thLHE. By ensuring that the evaluation points are chosen from an Exceptional Set in $\mathbb{Z}_q$ [10], it is guaranteed that $\lambda_i \in \mathbb{Z}_q$. Thus, in the worst case, it requires $\lceil \log_2(2q-1) \rceil$ bits to store $(\varphi)_i$ and $\lceil \log_2(|\mathcal{T}_\mathsf{L}|) + 2\log_2(q) + 1 \rceil$ bits to store $\mathsf{thLHE.Enc}(\varphi)$.

combining $T_{\mathsf{P}}+1$ valid partial decryption shares $(\mathsf{pd})_i$, a designated party obtains $\mathsf{c} \leftarrow \mathsf{thLHE.Comb}(\mathsf{thLHE.pk}, \{(\mathsf{pd})_i\})$. The decryption is finalized by $\varphi = \Delta m{+}e \leftarrow \mathsf{thLHE.FinDec}(\mathsf{thLHE.pk}, \mathsf{c}), m \leftarrow \mathsf{thLWE.FinDec}(\mathsf{thLWE.pk}, \varphi)$.

Remark that fresh ciphertexts can also be decrypted, as long as they are also post-processed by the server. In this case, there is no need for sanitization, as the fresh ciphertext noise is inherently independent of the message. Also, the above construction uses the schemes in Definitions 1 and 2 as building blocks and is not an instantiation of any of them. Thus, it can adopt a modified syntax: during $\mathsf{thPLWE.PartDec}$, the decrypting parties homomorphically compute $\mathsf{thLHE.Enc}((\varphi)_i)$ and jointly reconstruct φ under thLHE. Then, by running $\mathsf{thPLWE.DistDec}$, they remove the thLHE layer to recover φ and retrieve the message.

5.1 Tiresias Threshold Simulation-Based Security (Scor-Adp-SIM-CPA)

In this section, we prove the Scor-Adp-SIM-CPA security of Tiresias (App. A). This will later allow us to assume that Tiresias is Scor-Adp-IND-CPA secure (since the former implies the latter from [13, Prop. 3.2]); however, the proof is more easily done in the simulation-based setting. We recall that if the zero-knowledge property (Sect. 3.1) does not hold, the verifier learns information about the witness beyond what is available from the statement and proof. This implies the verifier can distinguish real proofs from simulated ones with a non-negligible advantage. Moving forward, we assume the existence of two PPT simulators for the Tiresias scheme: $\mathsf{Sim}_{\text{DKG}}$ for distributed key generation [14, Sect. F.5] and $\mathsf{Sim}_{\text{ZKP}}$ for the zero-knowledge proofs [14, Sect. 4.3].

Proposition 5. *Tiresias is Scor-Adp-SIM-CPA secure (static corruption, Scor, adaptive queries, Adp, and simulation chosen plaintext) under the zero-knowledge property of Tiresias ZKP.*

Proof. The simulation game is parameterized by a secret bit $\gamma \leftarrow \$ \{0,1\}$, unknown to A, and an initially empty state Ω of message-message-ciphertext-index $(m_0, m_1, \mathsf{ct}, \mathsf{ind})$ quadruples managed by the challenger C.

Game 0. This is the original Scor-Adp-SIM-CPA game against Tiresias where encryption, challenge, evaluation and partial decryption requests are processed as in Definition 4. As a reminder, the key generation is handled as follows:

– The adversary A selects a set of corrupted parties $\mathcal{S}$ and communicates it to the challenger C on the Scor-Adp-SIM-CPA of Tiresias. After verifying that $\mathcal{S} \subset \mathcal{P}$ and $\mathcal{S} \notin \mathbb{A}_{T,K}$, C chooses a numbering for the corrupted parties by $\mathcal{T} \subset \mathcal{K}$ and performs key generation
  · if $\gamma = 0$, it runs $(\mathsf{pk}, \mathsf{vk}, \{(\mathsf{sk})_i\}_{i\in\mathcal{K}}) \leftarrow \mathsf{Tir.DistKeyGen}(1^\lambda, \mathbb{A}_{T,K})$;
  · if $\gamma = 1$, it runs $(\mathsf{pk}, \mathsf{vk}, \{(\mathsf{sk})_i\}_{i\in\mathcal{T}}) \leftarrow \mathsf{Sim}_{\text{DKG}}(1^\lambda, \mathbb{A}_{T,K}, \mathcal{S})$.
  Finally, C returns $(\mathsf{pk}, \mathsf{vk}, \{(\mathsf{sk})_i\}_{i\in\mathcal{T}})$ to A.

Game 1. This game is the same as Game 0, except for the way C handles key generation. The adversary A selects a set of corrupted parties $\mathcal{S}$ and communicates it to C. After verifying that $\mathcal{S} \subset \mathcal{P}$ and $\mathcal{S} \notin \mathbb{A}_{T,K}$, C runs $(\mathsf{pk}, \mathsf{vk}, \{(\mathsf{sk})_i\}_{i\in\mathcal{K}}) \leftarrow \mathsf{Tir.DistKeyGen}(1^\lambda, \mathbb{A}_{T,K})$ and returns $(\mathsf{pk}, \mathsf{vk}, \{(\mathsf{sk})_i\}_{i\in\mathcal{T}})$ to A.
Game 0 and Game 1 are indistinguishable, which follows directly from the simulation indistinguishability of Tir keys. Hence, $|\mathsf{Adv}^{G_1}_{\mathsf{Tir}}(\mathsf{A}) - \mathsf{Adv}^{G_0}_{\mathsf{Tir}}(\mathsf{A})| \leq \mathsf{neg}(\lambda)$.

Game 2. This game is the same as Game 1 except for the way C returns simulated encryptions:

- Encryption request: when A queries $(\mathsf{plaintext}, m)$, where $m \in \mathcal{M}$, return $\mathsf{ct} \leftarrow \mathsf{Tir.Enc}(\mathsf{pk}, m)$ to A after updating $\Omega := [\Omega; (m, m, \mathsf{ct}, \{\emptyset\})]$.
- Challenge request: when A queries (test, m), where $m \in \mathcal{M}$, return $\mathsf{ct} \leftarrow \mathsf{Tir.Enc}(\mathsf{pk}, m)$ to A, pick a random $m' \in \mathcal{M}$ and do $\Omega := [\Omega; (m, m', \mathsf{ct}, \{\emptyset\})]$.

Game 1 and Game 2 are computationally indistinguishable, which follows directly from the DCR assumption. Hence, $|\mathsf{Adv}^{G_2}_{\mathsf{Tir}}(\mathsf{A}) - \mathsf{Adv}^{G_1}_{\mathsf{Tir}}(\mathsf{A})| \leq \mathsf{neg}(\lambda)$. By transitivity, Game 0 is computationally indistinguishable from Game 2: $|\mathsf{Adv}^{G_2}_{\mathsf{Tir}}(\mathsf{A}) - \mathsf{Adv}^{G_0}_{\mathsf{Tir}}(\mathsf{A})| \leq \mathsf{neg}(\lambda)$.

Final Reduction. We now prove that, from an adversary A against Game 2 we can build an adversary B against the zero-knowledge property of Tiresias ZKP, which uses A as a subroutine while achieving the same advantage as A.

- Key generation: the adversary A selects a set of corrupted parties $\mathcal{S}$ and communicates it to B, which forwards it to the challenger C against the zero-knowledge property of Tiresias ZKP. After verifying that $\mathcal{S} \subset \mathcal{P}$ and $\mathcal{S} \notin \mathbb{A}_{T,K}$, C runs $(\mathsf{pk}, \mathsf{vk}, \{(\mathsf{sk})_i\}_{i\in\mathcal{K}}) \leftarrow \mathsf{Tir.DistKeyGen}(1^\lambda, \mathbb{A}_{T,K})$ and returns $(\mathsf{pk}, \mathsf{vk}, \{(\mathsf{sk})_i\}_{i\in\mathcal{T}})$ to B, which provides them to A.
- When A issues an encryption request over $m \in \mathcal{M}$, B sends $\mathsf{ct} \leftarrow \mathsf{Tir.Enc}(\mathsf{pk}, m)$ to A after updating $\Omega := [\Omega; (m, m, \mathsf{ct}, \{\emptyset\})]$.
- When A issues a challenge request over $m \in \mathcal{M}$, B sends $\mathsf{ct} \leftarrow \mathsf{Tir.Enc}(\mathsf{pk}, m)$ to A. Then B picks a random $m' \in \mathcal{M}$ and updates $\Omega := [\Omega; (m, m', \mathsf{ct}, \{\emptyset\})]$.
- When A issues an evaluation request over $(f, \ell_0, \ldots, \ell_v)$, $\forall i$: $\ell_i \in [\![0, |\Omega| - 1]\!]$, B sets $m_0' = [f(\Omega[\ell_0].m_0, \ldots, \Omega[\ell_v].m_0)]_\mu$, $m_1' = [f(\Omega[\ell_0].m_1, \ldots, \Omega[\ell_v].m_1)]_\mu$ and computes $\mathsf{ct}' \leftarrow \mathsf{Tir.Eval}(\mathsf{pk}, f, \Omega[\ell_0].\mathsf{ct}, \ldots, \Omega[\ell_v].\mathsf{ct})$. B returns ct' to A after updating $\Omega := [\Omega; (m_0', m_1', \mathsf{ct}', \{\emptyset\})]$.
- When A issues a partial decryption request over $\ell \in [\![0, |\Omega| - 1]\!]$, $i \in \mathcal{K}$, B sends $(\Omega[\ell].\mathsf{ct}, i)$ to C. Then
  · if $\gamma = 0$, C computes $((\mathsf{pd})_i, \nu_i) \leftarrow \mathsf{Tir.ShareDec}((\mathsf{sk})_i, \mathsf{ct})$,
  · if $\gamma = 1$, C computes $(\mathsf{pd})_i = \mathsf{ct}^{(\mathsf{sk})_i}$ and $\nu_i \leftarrow \mathsf{Sim}_{\text{ZKP}}(\mathsf{ct}, i)$.

  C returns $((\mathsf{pd})_i, \nu_i)$ to B, which sends it to A.

Hence, if A breaks the Scor-Adp-SIM-CPA security of Tir with a non-negligible advantage, then B breaks the zero-knowledge property of Tir ZKP with the same advantage. □

5.2 Security of Our Construction

We now construct the LHE layer of thPLWE with the Tiresias scheme (Sect. A). We prove the security of thPLWE via a reduction to the CPA security of Tiresias from Sect. 5.1. We note that as Tiresias is secure under Scor-Adp-SIM-CPA, then it implies that it is also secure under Scor-Adp-IND-CPA [13, Prop. 3.2]. Below we consider a sequence of hybrid games starting from the original Scor-Adp-IND-CPA game for thPLWE. In a nutshell, we end up with a new challenger that also stores left and right values for the b-terms in its internal state. This allows it to duplicate homomorphic calculations in order to delay the Tir part of post-evaluation challenge ciphertexts generation after the effective homomorphic evaluation is done. This mechanic will then allow a reduction towards a challenger on the Scor-Adp-IND-CPA security of Tiresias to simulate evaluation requests on ciphertexts depending on the challenge bit.

Proposition 6. thPLWE *is Scor-Adp-IND-CPA secure under the assumption that* Tir *achieves the same.*

Proof. The proof first performs a number of game hops in which we gradually modify the Scor-Adp-IND-CPA challenger for thPLWE in order to allow for a final reduction towards the Scor-Adp-IND-CPA security of Tir.

Game 0. This is the original Scor-Adp-IND-CPA game against thPLWE, where, as a reminder, encryption, challenge and evaluation requests are processed as follows by the challenger:

- When A issues an encryption request over $m \in \mathbb{Z}_t$, B computes $(\mathbf{a}, b) = \mathsf{thLWE.Enc}(\mathsf{thLWE.pk}, m)$ and returns $\mathsf{ct} = (\mathbf{a}, b)$ to A after updating its internal state $\Omega := [\Omega; (m, m, (\mathbf{a}, b), \{\emptyset, \emptyset\})]$.
- When A issues a challenge request over $m_0, m_1 \in \mathbb{Z}_t^2$, $m_0 \neq m_1$ the challenger C against Scor-Adp-IND-CPA security of thPLWE returns $\mathsf{ct} = (\mathbf{a}, b) \leftarrow \mathsf{thLWE.Enc}(\mathsf{thLWE.pk}, m_\gamma)$ to A after doing $\Omega := [\Omega; (m_0, m_1, (\mathbf{a}, b), \{\emptyset, \emptyset\})]$.
- When A issues an evaluation request over $(f, \ell_0, \ldots, \ell_v)$, $\forall i$: $\ell_i \in [\![0, |\Omega|-1]\!]$, C sets $m_0' = [f(\Omega[\ell_0].m_0, \ldots, \Omega[\ell_v].m_0)]_t$, $m_1' = [f(\Omega[\ell_0].m_1, \ldots, \Omega[\ell_v].m_1)]_t$, $(\mathbf{a}', b') \leftarrow \mathsf{thLWE.Eval}(\mathsf{thLWE.pk}, f, \Omega[\ell_0].(\mathbf{a}, b), \ldots, \Omega[\ell_v].(\mathbf{a}, b))$, $(\mathbf{a}'', b'') \leftarrow \mathsf{thLWE.Sanitize}(\mathsf{thLWE.pk}, (\mathbf{a}', b'))$, $p \leftarrow \mathsf{Tir.Enc}(\mathsf{Tir.pk}, b'')$ and return $\mathsf{ct} = (\mathbf{a}'', p)$ to A after updating $\Omega := [\Omega; (m_0', m_1', (\mathbf{a}'', p), \{\emptyset, \emptyset\})]$.

For conciseness, we do not remind how partial decryptions are handled, as we do not modify it in our sequence of game hops (please refer to Definition 3).

Game 1. This game is the same as Game 0 except that we modify the way the challenger handles challenge requests:

- When A issues a challenge request over $m_0, m_1 \in \mathbb{Z}_t^2$, $m_0 \neq m_1$, C computes $(\mathbf{a}, b) \leftarrow \mathsf{thLWE.Enc}(\mathsf{thLWE.pk}, 0)$, sets $b_0 = [b + \Delta m_0]_q$, $b_1 = [b + \Delta m_1]_q$ and returns $\mathsf{ct} = (\mathbf{a}, b_\gamma)$ to A after updating $\Omega := [\Omega; (m_0, m_1, (\mathbf{a}, b_\gamma), \{\emptyset, \emptyset\})]$.

Game 0 and Game 1 are identical from A's view. In Game 1, C just modifies the way it computes the challenge ciphertext: it first computes $(\mathbf{a}, b_0)$ and $(\mathbf{a}, b_1)$, embeds the messages via an encryption of zero, and then selects b_γ. Either way the same challenge ciphertext is returned to A. Hence, $|\mathsf{Adv}^{G_1}_{\mathsf{thPLWE}}(\mathsf{A}) - \mathsf{Adv}^{G_0}_{\mathsf{thPLWE}}(\mathsf{A})| = 0$.

Game 2. This game is the same as Game 1 except the following changes in the handling of encryption, challenge and evaluation requests:

- When A issues an encryption request over $m \in \mathbb{Z}_t$, B computes $(\mathbf{a}, b) = \mathsf{thLWE.Enc}(\mathsf{thLWE.pk}, m)$ and returns $\mathsf{ct} = (\mathbf{a}, b)$ to A after updating its internal state $\Omega := [\Omega; (m, m, (\mathbf{a}, b, b, \bot), \{\emptyset, \emptyset\})]$.
- When A issues a challenge request over $m_0, m_1 \in \mathbb{Z}_t^2$, $m_0 \neq m_1$, C computes $(\mathbf{a}, b) \leftarrow \mathsf{thLWE.Enc}(\mathsf{thLWE.pk}, 0)$, sets $b_0 = [b + \Delta m_0]_q$, $b_1 = [b + \Delta m_1]_q$ and returns $\mathsf{ct} = (\mathbf{a}, b_\gamma)$ to A after doing $\Omega := [\Omega; (m_0, m_1, (\mathbf{a}, b_0, b_1, \bot), \{\emptyset, \emptyset\})]$.
- When A issues an evaluation request over $(f, \ell_0, \ldots, \ell_v)$, $\forall i$: $\ell_i \in [\![0, |\Omega| - 1]\!]$, C sets $m_0' = [f(\Omega[\ell_0].m_0, \ldots, \Omega[\ell_v].m_0)]_t$, $m_1' = [f(\Omega[\ell_0].m_1, \ldots, \Omega[\ell_v].m_1)]_t$ and computes

$$
\begin{aligned}
(\mathbf{a}', b_0') &\leftarrow \mathsf{thLWE.Eval}(\mathsf{thLWE.pk}, f, \Omega[\ell_0].(\mathbf{a}, b_0), \ldots, \Omega[\ell_v].(\mathbf{a}, b_0)),\\
(\mathbf{a}', b_1') &\leftarrow \mathsf{thLWE.Eval}(\mathsf{thLWE.pk}, f, \Omega[\ell_0].(\mathbf{a}, b_1), \ldots, \Omega[\ell_v].(\mathbf{a}, b_1)),\\
(\mathbf{a}'', b_0'') &\leftarrow \mathsf{thLWE.Sanitize}(\mathsf{thLWE.pk}, (\mathbf{a}', b_0')),\\
(\mathbf{a}'', b_1'') &\leftarrow \begin{cases} (\mathbf{a}'', b_0'' + \Delta(m_1' - m_0')), & \text{if } b_0' \neq b_1',\\ (\mathbf{a}'', b_0''), & \text{otherwise,} \end{cases}\\
p &\leftarrow \mathsf{Tir.Enc}(\mathsf{Tir.pk}, b_\gamma'').
\end{aligned}
$$

  C sends $\mathsf{ct} = (\mathbf{a}'', p)$ to A after setting $\Omega := [\Omega; (m_0', m_1', (\mathbf{a}'', \bot, \bot, p), \{\emptyset, \emptyset\})]$.

In a nutshell, C now also stores left and right values for the b-terms and duplicate homomorphic calculations to allow delaying the Tir part of post-evaluation challenge ciphertexts generation after the effective homomorphic evaluation is done. Game 1 and Game 2 are identical. In Game 2, C only changes its internal bookkeeping for the state Ω and the evaluation output:

- For an evaluation request that does not depend on the challenge bit γ (i.e., which does not involve any ciphertext obtained by means of a challenge request), we have $m_0' = m_1', b_0' = b_1'$ as well as, $b_0'' = b_1''$ so both game proceed identically.
- For an evaluation request that depends on the challenge bit γ, although m_0' may be equal to m_1', we have $b_0' \neq b_1'$ (with overwhelming probability), and hence $b_0'' \neq b_1''$. In Game 1, we proceed only with the evaluation yielding b_γ' (and b_γ''). In Game 2, the challenger proceeds with both candidate evaluations with either $b_\gamma' = b_0'$ (and $b_\gamma'' = b_0''$) or $b_\gamma' = b_1'$ (and $b_\gamma'' = b_1''$), so the same ciphertext is eventually returned to A, and both games also proceed identically in this case.

Hence, these changes do not alter the view of A and the advantage remains the same: $|\mathsf{Adv}^{G_2}_{\mathsf{thPLWE}}(\mathsf{A}) - \mathsf{Adv}^{G_1}_{\mathsf{thPLWE}}(\mathsf{A})| = 0$.

Game 3. This game is the same as Game 2 except that we further modify challenge request handling as follows:

- When A issues a challenge request over $m_0, m_1 \in \mathbb{Z}_t^2$, $m_0 \neq m_1$, C computes $(\mathbf{a}, b) \leftarrow \mathsf{thLWE.Enc}(\mathsf{thLWE.pk}, 0)$, sets $b_0 = [b + \Delta m_0]_q$, $b_1 = [b + \Delta m_1]_q$ and returns $\mathsf{ct} = (\mathbf{a}, b_0)$ to A after doing $\Omega := [\Omega; (m_0, m_1, (\mathbf{a}, b_0, b_1, \perp), \{\emptyset, \emptyset\})]$.

Game 2 and Game 3 are computationally indistinguishable, which follows directly from the LWE assumption, i.e., the computational indistinguishability of $(\mathbf{a}, b_0), (\mathbf{a}, b_1)$ LWE encryptions. Hence, $|\mathsf{Adv}^{G_3}_{\mathsf{thPLWE}}(\mathsf{A}) - \mathsf{Adv}^{G_2}_{\mathsf{thPLWE}}(\mathsf{A})| \leq \mathsf{neg}(\lambda)$. By transitivity, Game 0 is computationally indistinguishable from Game 3: $|\mathsf{Adv}^{G_3}_{\mathsf{thPLWE}}(\mathsf{A}) - \mathsf{Adv}^{G_0}_{\mathsf{thPLWE}}(\mathsf{A})| \leq \mathsf{neg}(\lambda)$.

Final Reduction. We now prove that from an adversary A against Game 3, we can build an adversary B against the Scor-Adp-IND-CPA security of Tir, which uses A as a subroutine while achieving the same advantage as A. First, A chooses two sets of corrupted parties $\mathcal{S}_\mathsf{L}$ and $\mathcal{S}_\mathsf{P}$ for thLWE and Tir, respectively, indexed by sets $\mathcal{T}_\mathsf{L}' \subset \mathcal{T}_\mathsf{L}$ and $\mathcal{T}_\mathsf{P}' \subset \mathcal{T}_\mathsf{P}$, and sends them to the reduction B, which then proceeds as follows. First, B checks $(\mathcal{S}_\mathsf{L} \subset \mathcal{P}) \wedge (\mathcal{S}_\mathsf{L} \notin \mathbb{A}_{\mathcal{T}_\mathsf{L},K})$; if True, it runs $(\mathsf{thLWE.pk}, \{(\mathsf{thLWE.sk})_i\}_{i \in \mathcal{K}}) \leftarrow \mathsf{thLWE.DistKeyGen}(1^\lambda, \mathbb{A}_{\mathcal{T}_\mathsf{L},K})$. B sends $\mathcal{S}_\mathsf{P}$ to C, who checks $(\mathcal{S}_\mathsf{P} \subset \mathcal{P}) \wedge (\mathcal{S}_\mathsf{P} \notin \mathbb{A}_{\mathcal{T}_\mathsf{P},K})$; if True, runs $(\mathsf{Tir.pk}, \mathsf{Tir.vk}, \{(\mathsf{Tir.sk})_i\}_{i \in \mathcal{K}}) \leftarrow \mathsf{Tir.DistKeyGen}(1^\lambda, \mathbb{A}_{\mathcal{T}_\mathsf{P},K})$ and returns to B a set $(\mathsf{Tir.pk}, \mathsf{Tir.vk}, \{(\mathsf{Tir.sk})_i\}_{i \in \mathcal{T}_\mathsf{P}'})$, which forwards it to A together with $(\mathsf{thLWE.pk}, \{(\mathsf{thLWE.sk})_i\}_{i \in \mathcal{T}_\mathsf{L}'})$. Lastly, B maintains an initially empty state Ω containing message-message-ciphertext-index $(m_0, m_1, \mathsf{ct}, \mathsf{ind})$ quadruples and handles A's request by doing:

- When A issues an encryption request over $m \in \mathbb{Z}_t$, B computes $(\mathbf{a}, b) = \mathsf{thLWE.Enc}(\mathsf{thLWE.pk}, m)$ and returns $\mathsf{ct} = (\mathbf{a}, b)$ to A after updating its internal state $\Omega := [\Omega; (m, m, (\mathbf{a}, b, b, \perp), \{\emptyset, \emptyset\})]$.
- When A issues a challenge request over $m_0, m_1 \in \mathbb{Z}_t^2$, $m_0 \neq m_1$, B does $(\mathbf{a}, b) \leftarrow \mathsf{thLWE.Enc}(\mathsf{thLWE.pk}, 0)$, sets $b_0 = [b + \Delta m_0]_q$, $b_1 = [b + \Delta m_1]_q$ and returns $\mathsf{ct} = (\mathbf{a}, b_0)$ to A after setting $\Omega := [\Omega; (m_0, m_1, (\mathbf{a}, b_0, b_1, \perp), \{\emptyset, \emptyset\})]$.
- When A issues an evaluation request over $(f, \ell_0, \ldots, \ell_v)$, $\forall i$: $\ell_i \in [\![0, |\Omega| - 1]\!]$, B sets $m_0' = [f(\Omega[\ell_0].m_0, \ldots, \Omega[\ell_v].m_0)]_t$, $m_1' = [f(\Omega[\ell_0].m_1, \ldots, \Omega[\ell_v].m_1)]_t$ and computes

$$
\begin{aligned}
(\mathbf{a}', b_0') &\leftarrow \mathsf{thLWE.Eval}(\mathsf{thLWE.pk}, f, \Omega[\ell_0].(\mathbf{a}, b_0), \ldots, \Omega[\ell_v].(\mathbf{a}, b_0)), \\
(\mathbf{a}', b_1') &\leftarrow \mathsf{thLWE.Eval}(\mathsf{thLWE.pk}, f, \Omega[\ell_0].(\mathbf{a}, b_1), \ldots, \Omega[\ell_v].(\mathbf{a}, b_1)), \\
(\mathbf{a}'', b_0'') &\leftarrow \mathsf{thLWE.Sanitize}(\mathsf{thLWE.pk}, (\mathbf{a}', b_0')), \\
(\mathbf{a}'', b_1'') &\leftarrow \begin{cases} (\mathbf{a}'', b_0'' + \Delta(m_1' - m_0')) & \text{if } b_0' \neq b_1', \\ (\mathbf{a}'', b_0''), & \text{otherwise,} \end{cases}
\end{aligned}
$$

obtaining two samples $(\mathbf{a}'', b_0'')$ and $(\mathbf{a}'', b_1'')$. B then forwards (b_0'', b_1'') to C as the challenge request to get $p \leftarrow \mathsf{Tir.Enc}(\mathsf{Tir.pk}, b_\gamma'')$ and returns $\mathsf{ct} = (\mathbf{a}'', p)$ to A after updating $\Omega := [\Omega; (m_0', m_1', (\mathbf{a}'', \perp, \perp, p), \{\emptyset, \emptyset\})]$.

- When A issues a decryption request over $\ell \in [\![0, |\Omega|-1]\!]$, $i, j \in \mathcal{K}$, if $\Omega[\ell].p \neq \perp$, B proceeds as
  - if $\Omega[\ell].m_0 = \Omega[\ell].m_1$, B computes

$$p_i \leftarrow \mathsf{Tir.cAdd}(\Omega[\ell].p, [-\langle \Omega[\ell].\mathsf{a}, (\mathsf{thLWE.sk})_i \rangle]_q)$$

  and sends (p_i, j) to C to get $(\mathsf{pd}_{i,j}, \nu_{i,j}) \leftarrow \mathsf{Tir.ShareDec}((\mathsf{Tir.sk})_j, p_i)$ and return it to A.
  - if $\Omega[\ell].m_0 \neq \Omega[\ell].m_1$, B updates the index state $\Omega[\ell].\mathsf{ind} := [\Omega[\ell].\mathsf{ind}; \{i, j\}]$ and checks $(\{P_i\}_{i \in \Omega[\ell].\mathsf{ind}[0]} \cup \mathcal{S}_\mathsf{L}) \notin \mathbb{A}_{T_\mathsf{L},K}$; if True, B computes p_i. Then B checks $(\{P_i\}_{i \in \Omega[\ell].\mathsf{ind}[1]} \cup \mathcal{S}_\mathsf{P}) \notin \mathbb{A}_{T_\mathsf{P},K}$; if True, B sends (p_i, j) to C to get $(\mathsf{pd}_{i,j}, \nu_{i,j})$ and returns it to A; if False, B returns p_i to A.

It follows that if A breaks the Scor-Adp-IND-CPA security of thPLWE with a non-negligible advantage, then B breaks the Scor-Adp-IND-CPA security of Tir with the same advantage. □

6 Concrete Construction and Experimental Results

The thPLWE, introduced in Sect. 5, combines threshold LWE and threshold LHE layers, i.e. it is generic in nature. However, as previously noted, we construct thPLWE threshold LHE layer with Tiresias ([14] and App. A). Further, as an example, we consider in this section a concrete construction that reuses the distributed key generation from the threshold TFHE variant in [10]. In our concrete instantiation, we also use the LWE sanitization from [31]. Hence, to illustrate the practicality of thPLWE, we only provide timings for these underlying algorithms *based on the experimental results reported in* [10,31] *and* [14]. Finally, we also assess the efficiency of our threshold decryption by providing benchmarks in Table 2 and compare its performance against threshold decryption with smudging as well as MPC-based threshold decryption. *Since we compare timings that have not been consistently obtained on a single machine, we provide orders of magnitude.*

6.1 Construction

Threshold TFHE Key Generation. More specifically, we propose constructing $\mathsf{thLWE.DistKeyGen}$ using the threshold key generation described in [10, Sect. 7.5.4.1, Fig. 81]. This algorithm is a thresholdized version of the classical TFHE key generation. It maintains correctness and security as long as it is executed over a robust MPC protocol. The online phase of the algorithm requires 3 rounds of MPC communication, while the full DKG is completed in 5 rounds. We provide the expected computational and communication complexities in Table 1 for three (t, q, n) TFHE parameter sets, with a fixed threshold $T = \frac{K}{4}$ and varying numbers of parties $K \in \{10, 100, 1000\}$. For a detailed security analysis and an evaluation of the analytic complexity, we refer the reader to [10, Sect. 8.5.4.1, Sect. 9.6.5].

Table 1: Expected communication (bits) and computational (operations) complexities computed following [10, Sect. 9.6.13] for the TFHE DKG for three TFHE parameter sets. We obtain the first two TFHE parameter sets (detailed in [12]) following the methodology in [36]. The third parameter set is taken from [11] and is a standard choice in TFHE implementations like [9]. The parameter sets achieve 128-bit security according to the lattice-estimator [37].

$(t,q,n)=(2,2^{32},550)$				$(t,q,n)=(16,2^{32},750)$				$(t,q,n)=(2,2^{64},1024)$			
K	$T+1$	Comm.	Comp.	K	$T+1$	Comm.	Comp.	K	$T+1$	Comm.	Comp.
10	3	2^{44}	2^{46}	10	3	2^{46}	2^{48}	10	3	2^{49}	2^{51}
100	26	2^{51}	2^{54}	100	26	2^{54}	2^{56}	100	26	2^{56}	2^{59}
1000	251	2^{58}	2^{62}	1000	251	2^{61}	2^{64}	1000	251	2^{63}	2^{67}

LWE Sanitization. The sanitization from [31] limits randomization to the steps before key-switching and after blind rotation, which reduces computational overhead. We recall that blind rotation homomorphically computes $\mathrm{tv}\cdot X^{b-\sum_{i=0}^{n-1} a_i \mathsf{sk}_i}$, where tv is a public polynomial and $\mathsf{ct}=(\mathbf{a},b)$ is a scaled LWE ciphertext. The process begins by multiplying tv by X^b, followed by a sequence of multiplications by $X^{a_i \mathsf{sk}_i}$ for each $i \in [\![0, n-1]\!]$ using the blind rotation keys. While prior works [28,30] randomize the entire blind rotation to preserve privacy, [31] reduces this overhead by reordering the evaluation. First, $\mathbf{a}$ is randomized by adding an encryption of zero. The evaluation order is then modified to defer the private term b until the end: the algorithm computes $\mathrm{tv}\cdot X^{\sum a_i \mathsf{sk}_i}$ first. The final multiplication by X^b is performed using the randomized linear evaluation from [38], which enables circuit-private multiplication of ring elements with ciphertexts. Therefore, sanitization requires randomization only at the beginning and at the end of the blind rotation, keeping the core algorithm intact. Experimental results demonstrate that [31] reduces sanitization latency to just 42.17ms, significantly lower than the 7500ms in [28] or 1330ms in [30]. Their sanitization algorithm adds only 0.81ms of overhead to standard TFHE bootstrapping. For detailed benchmark results, see [31, Sect. 6.2].

6.2 Threshold Decryption Efficiency Evaluation

thPLWE Decryption Efficiency. Recall that to eliminate the need for smudging or the MPC noise removal, we sanitize an LWE ciphertext and hide the resulting b-term by encrypting it under Tir, $p = \mathsf{Tir.Enc}(\mathsf{Tir.pk}, b)$, before proceeding to the threshold decryption. Note that thPLWE threshold decryption consists of two steps, PartDec and DistDec, which may involve different sets of participating parties and different thresholds. The core idea of thPLWE.PartDec is to let LWE decryption parties $\{P_i\}_{i\in\mathcal{T}_\mathsf{L}}$ compute the partial decryption of φ under Tir as

$$\mathsf{Tir.Enc}((\varphi)_i) = \mathsf{Tir.cAdd}(p, [\langle -\mathbf{a}, (\mathsf{thLWE.sk})_i\rangle]_q), \tag{1}$$

and jointly reconstruct $\mathsf{Tir.Enc}(\varphi) = \mathsf{Tir.Enc}(\Delta m + e)$ such that

$$\mathsf{Tir.Enc}(\varphi) = \bigoplus_{i=0}^{|\mathcal{T}_\mathsf{L}|-1} \left(\mathsf{Tir.cMult}\left(\mathsf{Tir.Enc}((\varphi)_i), \lambda_i\right)\right), \tag{2}$$

where $\oplus$ defines $\mathsf{Tir.Add}$. Note that, by getting rid of smudging, we naturally solve the problem of error growth during secret share reconstruction, as we avoid the scaling of smudging noise by Lagrange coefficients. This allows us to resolve the same issue addressed in [33] without restricting ourselves to the synchronous model. Finally, the decryption is completed by $\mathsf{thPLWE.DistDec}$, which consists of the $\mathsf{Tir.DistDec}$ algorithm (run by $\{P_i\}_{i\in\mathcal{T}_\mathsf{P}}$ to output φ) followed by the message recovery $\lceil \frac{\varphi}{\Delta} \rfloor$.

Below, we analyze the computational complexity of our decryption approach and present experimental results comparing it with state-of-the-art threshold decryption techniques to demonstrate its efficiency. In the Paillier cryptosystem, ciphertext-ciphertext addition involves a single modular multiplication in $\mathbb{Z}^*_{\mu^2}$. This requires $\mathcal{O}(M(\kappa))$ bit operations, where $M(\kappa)$ denotes the cost of multiplying two κ-bit integers. Plaintext-ciphertext addition, $[\mathsf{ct} \cdot g^m]_{\mu^2}$, where $g^m = [1 + m\mu]_{\mu^2}$ for $g = 1 + \mu$, requires one modular multiplication.

Finally, plaintext-ciphertext multiplication requires a modular exponentiation, ct^m. This is typically implemented via the square-and-multiply algorithm, requiring $\mathcal{O}(\ell)$ modular multiplications where $\ell = \lceil \log_2 m \rceil$. Consequently, plaintext-ciphertext multiplication incurs $\mathcal{O}(\ell \cdot M(\kappa))$ bit operations.

Computing (1) requires a dot product for vectors of size n, along with one Paillier plaintext-ciphertext addition. This results in a computational complexity of $\mathcal{O}(n + M(\kappa))$. Let $T + 1 = |\mathcal{T}_\mathsf{L}|$. Computing (2) involves $T+1$ Paillier plaintext-ciphertext multiplications and T ciphertext-ciphertext additions[4]. Therefore, the computational complexity of (2) is given by $\mathcal{O}(T \cdot \log q \cdot M(\kappa))$.

To highlight the efficiency of our threshold LWE decryption, we implemented (1) and (2) in C using GMP and libpaillier [40] libraries. Benchmarks were performed on a 12th Gen Intel Core i7-12700H processor. Table 2 reports timings for a 2048-bit modulus μ, the three (t, q, n) TFHE parameter sets, and varying numbers of parties $K \in \{10, 100, 1000\}$. We evaluate threshold values $T \in \{\frac{K}{4}, \frac{2K}{3}\}$, assuming that $T + 1$ parties participate in $\mathsf{thPLWE.PartDec}$.

[4] This sequence constitutes a multi-exponentiation, where the cost of modular squarings is amortized across all shares. Employing [39] yields a smaller complexity.

Table 2: Performance comparison (ms) for PartDec ((1) and (2)) for a 2048-bit modulus μ. All timings are reported as the mean of 10 single-core executions.

$(t,q,n) = (2, 2^{32}, 550)$				$(t,q,n) = (16, 2^{32}, 750)$				$(t,q,n) = (2, 2^{64}, 1024)$			
K	$T+1$	(1)	(2)	K	$T+1$	(1)	(2)	K	$T+1$	(1)	(2)
10	3	0.158	0.237	10	3	0.168	0.235	10	3	0.544	0.970
	7	0.156	0.678		7	0.169	0.708		7	0.501	2.931
100	26	0.142	2.644	100	26	0.158	2.618	100	26	0.540	11.505
	67	0.161	7.296		67	0.187	7.392		67	0.561	32.210
1000	251	0.173	27.396	1000	251	0.173	27.472	1000	251	0.553	125.998
	667	0.172	73.358		667	0.165	74.671		667	0.557	324.616

It is important to note that the overall efficiency of thPLWE threshold decryption is highly dependent on the performance of the underlying LHE distributed decryption (Tir.DistDec in this case). We highlight that Tiresias adapts batching techniques by [41], which allows a party to generate a ZKP for the correctness of multiple decryption shares instead of one proof per ciphertext. Batching is highly effective for scalability, as it significantly reduces the amortized cost per decryption. Table 3 illustrates the efficiency of Tir.DistDec using benchmarks from [14]. These timings consider a 2048-bit μ, $K \in \{10, 100, 1000\}$ parties, $B \in \{1, 100, 1000\}$ ciphertexts and a threshold $T = \frac{2K}{3}$ for the participating $\{P_i\}_{i \in \mathcal{T}_P}$.

Table 3: Performance comparison (ms) for Tir.DistDec. Third columns report timings for a single party to produce B decryption shares (where B is a batch size) and ZKPs of equality for K parties. Fourth columns report timings for ZKP verification and decryption share combination.

K	B	Comp.	Comb.	K	B	Comp.	Comb.	K	B	Comp.	Comb.
10	1	151.93	89.517	100	1	193.28	262.53	1000	1	790.67	9722.5
	100	873.98	763.5		100	959.41	1559.8		100	2138.8	35058.0
	1000	7424.6	6746.1		1000	7909.8	12362.0		1000	14558.0	266640.0

For example, for decryption share computation (3rd columns, Table 3) with $K \in \{10, 100, 1000\}$, a prover requires $\{151, 193, 790\}$ms to generate a share for a single ciphertext. However, when batching $B = 1000$ ciphertexts, the cost drops to only $\{7, 7, 14\}$ms per share, representing an improvement of approximately $\{21\times, 27\times, 56\times\}$, respectively. This efficiency gain extends to the decryption share combination and the proof verification (4th columns, Table 3).

To assess the practical performance of our threshold decryption, we combine the costs of the PartDec with the underlying Tir.DistDec across various batch sizes. Since each of the B ciphertexts requires an individual PartDec execution to produce the corresponding Tir ciphertexts, the PartDec-related costs scale linearly with the batch size. Table 4 summarizes the total estimated execution time for both thPLWE decryption steps (excluding communication overhead) using the parameters described above with thresholds $T = \frac{2K}{3}$, where $T+1 = |\mathcal{T}_\mathsf{L}| = |\mathcal{T}_\mathsf{P}|$.

Finally, Table 5 confirms that thPLWE.DistDec remains quite scalable. By batching $B = 1000$ ciphertexts, the average latency per decryption for $K = 1000$ parties is reduced from over 10 seconds to between 354ms and 606ms, depending on the TFHE parameter set.

Table 4: Total estimated timings (ms) for the thPLWE threshold decryption. The timings reflect the total latency to process a batch of size B, running B individual PartDec and the subsequent Tir.DistDec.

$(t,q,n) = (2, 2^{32}, 550)$				$(t,q,n) = (16, 2^{32}, 750)$				$(t,q,n) = (2, 2^{64}, 1024)$			
K	$T+1$	B	Total (ms)	K	$T+1$	B	Total (ms)	K	$T+1$	B	Total (ms)
10	7	1	242.281	10	7	1	242.324	10	7	1	244.879
		100	1720.880			100	1725.180			100	1980.680
		1000	15004.700			1000	15047.700			1000	17602.700
100	67	1	463.267	100	67	1	463.389	100	67	1	488.581
		100	3264.910			100	3277.110			100	5796.310
		1000	27728.800			1000	27850.800			1000	53042.800
1000	667	1	10586.700	1000	667	1	10588.006	1000	667	1	10838.343
		100	44549.800			100	44680.400			100	69714.100
		1000	354728.000			1000	356034.000			1000	606371.000

Comparison with the State-of-the-Art. As a starting point, we analyze the performance of [21] threshold TFHE with smudging. In the Noah's Ark, decryption employs the offline phase when $\binom{K}{T} > 100$.[5] It utilizes a generic MPC protocol to generate random bit shares, which are then used to produce two uniformly random 128-bit smudging terms. Hence, the parties must collectively generate 256 shared random bits per decryption to obtain the necessary masks. To accommodate the smudging noise, Noah's Ark requires a significant parameter size increase: the LWE parameters $(q,n) = (2^{64}, 777)$ are increased to $(2^{128}, 4096)$, which significantly expands the ciphertext size. The authors report that the non-interactive part of the decryption takes between 241 and 316ms. In contrast, the interactive distributed decryption requires approximately 2ms when

[5] It holds for $K = 10$, $T \in [\![3, 7]\!]$; $K = 100$, $T \in [\![2, 98]\!]$; $K = 1000$, $T \in [\![1, 999]\!]$.

Table 5: Total amortized estimated timings (ms) for the thPLWE threshold decryption. Each entry represents the average latency to process a single ciphertext within a batch of size B. The values are obtained by summing the time for one PartDec with the amortized timing of the Tir.DistDec.

$(t,q,n)=(2,2^{32},550)$				$(t,q,n)=(16,2^{32},750)$				$(t,q,n)=(2,2^{64},1024)$			
K	$T+1$	B	Amort.	K	$T+1$	B	Amort.	K	$T+1$	B	Amort.
10	7	1	242.281	10	7	1	242.324	10	7	1	244.879
		100	17.209			100	17.252			100	19.807
		1000	15.005			1000	15.048			1000	17.603
100	67	1	463.267	100	67	1	463.389	100	67	1	488.581
		100	32.649			100	32.771			100	57.963
		1000	27.729			1000	27.851			1000	53.043
1000	667	1	10586.700	1000	667	1	10588.006	1000	667	1	10838.343
		100	445.498			100	446.804			100	697.141
		1000	354.728			1000	356.034			1000	606.371

$(K,T)=(4,1)$, 3ms when $(K,T)=(10,3)$, and 19ms when $(K,T)=(40,13)$. *With respect to Noah's Ark, the key takeaway is that our approach offers comparable unitary costs and latencies for decrypting one ciphertext but* without *increasing the size of the TFHE parameters (i.e., without incurring a significant decrease in the performances of the homomorphic computations) and with an additional potential for amortization that is not offered by the former.*

By employing MPC-based rounding, Zyskind et al. [11] avoid smudging and the consequent modulus expansion seen in [21], so, *as we do*, they keep standard parameters, however, at the cost of a heavier offline phase. While online decryption [11] is efficient, it relies on a computationally and memory-intensive (offline) preprocessing to generate Beaver triples and shared random bits. Each threshold decryption call consumes approximately 64 shared random bits and requires 2478 multiplications. Since each multiplication utilizes one Beaver triple, the offline communication cost (using [42] triple generation at 14.9kbit per triple) amounts to roughly 4.5MB per decryption and approximately 36ms of transfer time. For [11] online phase, the online preprocessing for 1000 runs of the decryption requires 1.35sec and 79MB of communication per party (excluding offline triple and random-bit generation costs). Finally, Zyskind et al. report $\{8.48, 10.08, 24.23\}$ms needed for $K \in \{4,8,16\}$ parties to run a single online decryption, i.e., 8.48ms for $K=4$ compared to approximately 315.62ms of [21]. However, as the number of parties increases, the online latency demonstrates non-linear growth, rising to 24ms at $K=16$. Extrapolating it to 100 or 1000 parties suggests that it would likely push the latter latencies from milliseconds into the range of several seconds or even minutes. *In contrast, our approach has* *no offline phase beyond key generation. Although it is less efficient for small K, it offers much better scaling when the number of parties increases.*

In [10], a threshold TFHE decryption is implemented via MPC bit extraction. Because the authors do not provide concrete execution timings, we cannot perform a direct empirical comparison. Instead, [10, Sect. 9.6.13] evaluates the protocol via round, communication and computational complexities. For concrete parameters with $q = 2^{64}$ and $T = \frac{K}{4}$, the protocol requires 16 rounds of communication. While the number of rounds remains constant, the overhead scales with K: for $K = 10$, it requires 2^{25} bits of communication/storage and 2^{27} computational operations; for $K = 100$, these rise to 2^{36} and 2^{104}; and for $K = 1000$, they reach 2^{46} and 2^{837}. While the $K = 10$ case is practical, the $K = 100$ and $K = 1000$ cases are strictly theoretical. *In contrast, our solution requires only 4 rounds and scales linearly with the number of parties* (Table 6).

Table 6: Comparison of threshold decryption (Sect. 6.2) for a single LWE. Note that we excluded key generation since [10,11,21] do not report any timings for this (offline) step and, as already stated, our intent is to reuse the one from [10] in a black-box fashion.

	[21]	[11]	[10]	Our Work
(q, n, K)	$(2^{128}, 4096, 10)$	$(2^{64}, 1024, 16)$	$(2^{64}, 1024, 10)$	$(2^{32}, 750, 10)$
Preprocessing	$\approx$ 5 ms	$\approx$ 36 ms	$\approx$ 32 ms	–
Preproc. bandwidth	$\approx$ 1 KB	$\approx$ 4.5 MB	$\approx$ 4 MB	–
Local computation	$\approx$ 241-316 ms	$\approx$ 36 ms	2^{27} ops	$\approx$ 152.10 ms
Online latency	$\approx$ 3 ms	$\approx$ 24.23 ms	not reported	$\approx$ 92.23 ms
Comm. rounds	1	multi-round	16	4
Bandwidth ($B = 1$)	$\approx$ 1.31 MB	$\approx$ 4.5 MB	$\approx$ 4.2 MB	$\approx$ 70 KB

Concluding Remarks. Our approach has the desirable property of not impacting TFHE parameters, thus leaving unchanged TFHE ciphertext size as well as the performances of the homomorphic operators. We emphasize that thPLWE decryption requires only a single additional execution of the LHE distributed key generation (performed via MPC) as an offline preprocessing step. Our decryption algorithm requires just 4 communication rounds, compared to 16 in [10]: 2 to compute PartDec (Eqs. 1 and 2) and 2 to run DistDec (Tir.ShareDec and Tir.Comb). While [10,11] MPC message recovery is more efficient for a small number of parties, $K < 20$, our approach becomes advantageous as the number of parties grows. Furthermore, by avoiding the need for MPC machinery during threshold decryption, our approach scales efficiently up to $K = 1000$ participating parties. By keeping $(q, n) = (2^{32}, 550)$, we require just 350ms (amortized) per decryption for $K = 1000$. We also highlight that the cost of our solution is dominated by Tiresias, which we have used as a black-box. Hence, any other (possibly more efficient) correct linearly homomorphic threshold PKE can be plugged into our construction. Lastly, we emphasize that, at the conceptual level, our construction is quite simple.

A Tiresias Scheme

Let $\mathsf{Tir} = (\mathsf{DistKeyGen}, \mathsf{Enc}, \mathsf{Eval}, \mathsf{DistDec})$ be a T-out-of-K Tiresias scheme:

- $\mathsf{DistKeyGen}(1^\lambda, \mathbb{A}_{T,K}; \mathcal{P}) \rightarrow (\mathsf{pk}, \mathsf{vk}, \{(\mathsf{sk})_i\}_{i \in \mathcal{K}})$: $\mathcal{P} = \{P_i\}_{i \in \mathcal{K}}$ run Setup_1 to get μ and shares of its factors p', q': $(\mu; \{(p')_i, (q')_i\}_{i \in \mathcal{K}}) \leftarrow \mathsf{Setup}_1(K, 1^\lambda, 1^\tau)$. Then, they run Setup_2 to generate shares of $\mathsf{sk} = d$, using SSS over the Integers ($\mathsf{SS}^{\mathbb{Z}}$) [14, Sect. 2.1], and verification keys $(\{(\mathsf{sk})_i, (\mathsf{vk})_i\}_{i \in \mathcal{K}}) \leftarrow \mathsf{Setup}_2(K, \mu, 1^\lambda, 1^\tau; \{(p')_i, (q')_i\}_{i \in \mathcal{K}})$. The algorithm outputs $\mathsf{pk} = \mu$ and $\mathsf{vk} = \{(\mathsf{vk})_i\}_{i \in \mathcal{K}}$, where each $(\mathsf{vk})_i = \mathbf{g}^{(\mathsf{sk})_i}$ for a base $\mathbf{g} = \prod g_i$ sampled by the parties, and the secret $(\mathsf{sk})_i = (d)_i$ owned by each P_i.
- $\mathsf{Enc}(\mathsf{pk}, m)$, $\mathsf{Eval}\left(\mathsf{pk}, f, \{\mathsf{ct}_i\}_{i \in [\![0,l]\!]}\right)$ are identical to classical Paillier [43].
- $\mathsf{DistDec}\left(\mathsf{vk}, \mathcal{T}, \{(\mathsf{sk})_i\}, \mathsf{ct}; \{P_i\}_{i \in \mathcal{T}}\right) \rightarrow (m \in \mathbb{Z}_\mu) \cup \bot$: the parties $\{P_i\}_{i \in \mathcal{T}}$ execute a distributed decryption on $\mathsf{ct} \in \mathbb{Z}_{\mu^2}$, consisting of three sub-algorithms:
  - $\mathsf{ShareDec}((\mathsf{sk})_i, \mathsf{ct}; P_i) \rightarrow ((\mathsf{pd})_i, \nu_i)$: each party P_i outputs $(\mathsf{pd})_i = \mathsf{ct}^{(\mathsf{sk})_i}$ and a ZKP ν_i, which proofs that $\log_{\mathsf{ct}}(\mathsf{pd})_i = \log_{\mathbf{g}}(\mathsf{vk})_i = (\mathsf{sk})_i$. It ensures that P_i used its correct secret share $(\mathsf{sk})_i$ as the witness.
  - $\mathsf{Comb}(\mathsf{pk}, \{(\mathsf{pd})_i, \nu_i\}_{i \in \mathcal{T}}; \{P_i\}_{i \in \mathcal{T}}) \rightarrow \mathsf{c} \cup \bot$: if $\geq T+1$ shares have valid proofs, return $\mathsf{c} = \mathsf{ct}^{4\Delta_K^3 d} \leftarrow \mathsf{SS}^{\mathbb{Z}}.\mathsf{Recon}(\{(\mathsf{pd})_i, (\mathsf{sk})_i\}_{i \in \mathcal{T}})$, where $\Delta_K = K!$;[6] otherwise, return $\bot$.
  - $\mathsf{FinDec}(\mathsf{pk}, \mathsf{c}) \rightarrow m$: the final step retrieves $m = \left[\left(\frac{\mathsf{c}-1}{\mu}\right)(4\Delta_K^3)^{-1}\right]_\mu$.

References

1. Asharov, G., Jain, A., López-Alt, A., Tromer, E., Vaikuntanathan, V., Wichs, D.: Multiparty computation with low communication, computation and interaction via threshold FHE. In: Pointcheval, D., Johansson, T. (eds.) EUROCRYPT 2012. LNCS, vol. 7237, pp. 483–501. Springer, Heidelberg (2012). https://doi.org/10.1007/978-3-642-29011-4_29
2. Checri, M., Sirdey, R., Boudguiga, A., Bultel, J.P.: On the practical CPAD security of "exact" and threshold FHE schemes and libraries. In: Reyzin, L., Stebila, D. (eds.) Advances in Cryptology – CRYPTO 2024. CRYPTO 2024. Lecture Notes in Computer Science, vol. 14922, pp. 3–33. Springer, Cham (2024). https://doi.org/10.1007/978-3-031-68382-4_1
3. Brakerski, Z., et al.: Fully homomorphic encryption without bootstrapping. In: ITCS'12, pp. 309–325 (2011)

[6] Multiplication by Δ_K clears denominators in the Lagrange coefficients, ensuring that every exponent used in reconstruction is in $\mathbb{Z}$. The factor $4\Delta_K^3$ arises from combining several scaling sources. For further details, see [14, Sect. 2.1, D].

4. Brakerski, Z.: Fully homomorphic encryption without modulus switching from classical GapSVP. In: Safavi-Naini, R., Canetti, R. (eds.) CRYPTO 2012. LNCS, vol. 7417, pp. 868–886. Springer, Heidelberg (2012). https://doi.org/10.1007/978-3-642-32009-5_50
5. Fan, J., Vercauteren, F.: Somewhat practical fully homomorphic encryption. Cryptology ePrint Archive, Paper 2012/144 (2012)
6. Cheon, J.H., Kim, A., Kim, M., Song, Y.: Homomorphic encryption for arithmetic of approximate numbers. In: Takagi, T., Peyrin, T. (eds.) ASIACRYPT 2017. LNCS, vol. 10624, pp. 409–437. Springer, Cham (2017). https://doi.org/10.1007/978-3-319-70694-8_15
7. Ducas, L., Micciancio, D.: FHEW: bootstrapping homomorphic encryption in less than a second. In: Oswald, E., Fischlin, M. (eds.) EUROCRYPT 2015. LNCS, vol. 9056, pp. 617–640. Springer, Heidelberg (2015). https://doi.org/10.1007/978-3-662-46800-5_24
8. Chillotti, I., Gama, N., Georgieva, M., Izabachène, M.: TFHE: fast fully homomorphic encryption over the torus. J. Cryptol. **33**(1), 34–91 (2019). https://doi.org/10.1007/s00145-019-09319-x
9. Zama: TFHE-rs (2022). https://github.com/zama-ai/tfhe-rs
10. Bootland, C., et al.: Threshold (fully) homomorphic encryption. Cryptology ePrint Archive, Paper 2025/699 (2025)
11. Zyskind, G., et al.: High-throughput universally composable threshold FHE decryption. In: ACM SIGSAC, CCS 2025, pp. 2339–2353 (2025)
12. Bondarchuk, A., et al.: Downlink (T)FHE ciphertexts compression. In: Boura, C., Mashatan, A., Miri, A. (eds.) Selected Areas in Cryptography – SAC 2025. SAC 2025. Lecture Notes in Computer Science, vol. 16207, pp. 647–678. Springer, Cham (2025). https://doi.org/10.1007/978-3-032-10536-3_24
13. Brzuska, C., Klooß, M., Woo, I.K.Y.: Threshold public-key encryption: definitions, relations, and CPA-to-CCA transforms. In: Bai, S., Persichetti, E. (eds.) Public-Key Cryptography – PKC 2026. PKC 2026. Lecture Notes in Computer Science, vol. 16554. Springer, Cham (2026). https://doi.org/10.1007/978-3-032-26740-5_6
14. Friedman, O., Marmor, A., Mutzari, D., Scaly, Y.C., Spiizer, Y., Yanai, A.: Tiresias: large scale, UC-secure threshold Paillier. In: Chung, KM., Sasaki, Y. (eds.) Advances in Cryptology – ASIACRYPT 2024. ASIACRYPT 2024. Lecture Notes in Computer Science, vol. 15486, pp. 141–173. Springer, Singapore (2024). https://doi.org/10.1007/978-981-96-0891-1_5
15. Boneh, D., et al.: Threshold cryptosystems from threshold fully homomorphic encryption. In: Shacham, H., Boldyreva, A. (eds.) CRYPTO 2018. LNCS, vol. 10991, pp. 565–596. Springer, Cham (2018). https://doi.org/10.1007/978-3-319-96884-1_19
16. Brakerski, Z., et al.: Threshold FHE with efficient asynchronous decryption. Cryptology ePrint Archive, Paper 2025/712 (2025)
17. Mouchet, C., et al.: Multiparty homomorphic encryption from ring-learning-with-errors. Proc. Priv. Enh. Techn. **4**, 291–311 (2021)
18. Mouchet, C., Bertrand, E., Hubaux, J.P.: An efficient threshold access-structure for RLWE-based multiparty homomorphic encryption. J. Cryptology **36**(2) (2023). https://doi.org/10.1007/s00145-023-09452-8
19. Urban, A., Rambaud, M.: Robust multiparty computation from threshold encryption based on RLWE. In: Mouha, N., Nikiforakis, N. (eds.) Information Security. ISC 2024. Lecture Notes in Computer Science, vol. 15257, pp. 294–314. Springer, Cham (2024). https://doi.org/10.1007/978-3-031-75757-0_15

20. Chang, Y., Li, S.: Arbitrary-threshold fully homomorphic encryption with lower complexity. In: SEC'25 (2025)
21. Dahl, M.: Noah's ark: efficient threshold-FHE using noise flooding. In: WAHC CCS 2023, pp. 35–46. ACM (2023)
22. Passelègue, A., Stehlé, D.: Low communication threshold fully homomorphic encryption. In: Chung, KM., Sasaki, Y. (eds.) Advances in Cryptology – ASIACRYPT 2024. ASIACRYPT 2024. Lecture Notes in Computer Science, vol. 15484, pp. 297–329. Springer, Singapore (2024). https://doi.org/10.1007/978-981-96-0875-1_10
23. Smart, N.P., Walter, M.: Error-simulatable sanitization for TFHE and applications. Cryptology ePrint Archive, Paper 2025/275 (2025)
24. Fouque, P.-A., Poupard, G., Stern, J.: Sharing decryption in the context of voting or lotteries. In: Frankel, Y. (ed.) FC 2000. LNCS, vol. 1962, pp. 90–104. Springer, Heidelberg (2001). https://doi.org/10.1007/3-540-45472-1_7
25. Baudron, O., et al.: Practical multi-candidate election system. In: ACM, PODC 2001, pp. 274–283 (2001)
26. Damgård, I., Jurik, M.: A generalisation, a simplification and some applications of Paillier's probabilistic public-key system. In: Kim, K. (ed.) PKC 2001. LNCS, vol. 1992, pp. 119–136. Springer, Heidelberg (2001). https://doi.org/10.1007/3-540-44586-2_9
27. Dåmgard, I.: A generalization of Paillier's public-key system with applications to electronic voting. Int. J. of Inf. Secur. 371–385 (2010)
28. Bourse, F., Izabachène, M.: Plug-and-play sanitization for TFHE. Cryptology ePrint Archive, Paper 2022/1438 (2022)
29. Ducas, L., Stehlé, D.: Sanitization of FHE ciphertexts. In: Fischlin, M., Coron, J.-S. (eds.) EUROCRYPT 2016. LNCS, vol. 9665, pp. 294–310. Springer, Heidelberg (2016). https://doi.org/10.1007/978-3-662-49890-3_12
30. Kluczniak, K.: Circuit privacy for FHEW/TFHE-style fully homomorphic encryption in practice. IACR Commun. Cryptol. (2024)
31. Hwang, I., et al.: Practical TFHE ciphertext sanitization for oblivious circuit evaluation. In: SIGSAC, CCS 2025, pp. 4064–4078 (2025)
32. Shamir, A.: How to share a secret. Commun. ACM 612–613 (1979)
33. de Verdière, F.C., et al.: On threshold fully homomorphic encryption with synchronized decryptors. Cryptology ePrint Archive, Paper 2026/031 (2026)
34. Yang, R., et al.: Fully homomorphic encryption with chosen-ciphertext security from LWE. In: Tauman Kalai, Y., Kamara, S.F. (eds.) Advances in Cryptology – CRYPTO 2025. CRYPTO 2025. Lecture Notes in Computer Science, vol. 16002, pp. 371–405. Springer, Cham (2025). https://doi.org/10.1007/978-3-032-01881-6_12
35. Li, B., Micciancio, D.: On the security of homomorphic encryption on approximate numbers. In: Canteaut, A., Standaert, F.-X. (eds.) EUROCRYPT 2021. LNCS, vol. 12696, pp. 648–677. Springer, Cham (2021). https://doi.org/10.1007/978-3-030-77870-5_23
36. Clet, P.-E., et al.: ComBo: a novel functional bootstrapping method for efficient evaluation of nonlinear functions in the encrypted domain. In: El Mrabet, N., De Feo, L., Duquesne, S. (eds.) Progress in Cryptology – AFRICACRYPT 2023. AFRICACRYPT 2023. Lecture Notes in Computer Science, vol. 14064, pp. 317–343. Springer, Cham (2023). https://doi.org/10.1007/978-3-031-37679-5_14
37. Albrecht, M.R., et al.: On the concrete hardness of learning with errors. J. Math. Cryptol. 169–203 (2015)

38. de Castro, L., et al.: More efficient lattice-based OLE from circuit-private linear HE with polynomial overhead. ePrint Archive, Paper 2024/1534 (2024)
39. Pippenger, N.: On the evaluation of powers and related problems. In: SFCS'76, pp. 258–263 (1976)
40. Bethencourt, J.: libpaillier. https://github.com/mortendahl/libpaillier
41. Aditya, R., Peng, K., Boyd, C., Dawson, E., Lee, B.: Batch verification for equality of discrete logarithms and threshold decryptions. In: Jakobsson, M., Yung, M., Zhou, J. (eds.) ACNS 2004. LNCS, vol. 3089, pp. 494–508. Springer, Heidelberg (2004). https://doi.org/10.1007/978-3-540-24852-1_36
42. Hasler, S., et al.: Multipars: reduced-communication MPC over Z2k. Proc. Priv. Enhancing Technol. 5–28 (2024)
43. Paillier, P.: Public-key cryptosystems based on composite degree residuosity classes. In: Stern, J. (ed.) EUROCRYPT 1999. LNCS, vol. 1592, pp. 223–238. Springer, Heidelberg (1999). https://doi.org/10.1007/3-540-48910-X_16

Minimizing Noise in TFHE Bootstrapping

Anas Boudi and Louis Goubin(✉)

Université Paris-Saclay, UVSQ, CNRS, Laboratoire de mathématiques de Versailles, 78000 Versailles, France
{anas.boudi2,louis.goubin}@uvsq.fr

Abstract. Lattice-based homomorphic encryption schemes use noisy ciphertexts to encrypt messages, which limits the depth of circuits that can be evaluated correctly. To address this issue, Fully Homomorphic Encryption schemes implement a bootstrapping procedure that produces a new ciphertext encrypting the original plaintext with reduced noise. In this work, we homomorphically modify the distribution of encryption keys to reduce the noise produced during bootstrapping in the Torus Fully Homomorphic Encryption scheme. We show that this approach reduces the variance of the rounding noise in a bootstrapped ciphertext by 50% compared to the previous state of the art, at the cost of a slight computational overhead. In practice, this enables up to 1.6× more homomorphic operations. We also investigate an alternative approach based on modifying the blind rotation equation using lower-variance keys. We show, however, that this method leads to higher output noise.

Keywords: Homomorphic encryption · Blind rotation · Noise

1 Introduction

Homomorphic Encryption (HE) schemes are encryption algorithms that allow computations to be performed on plaintexts by operating on ciphertexts. Currently, the most efficient HE schemes are lattice-based and their security depends on some random noise added to ciphertexts. However, computing homomorphic operations may increase this noise, eventually corrupting the message and preventing correct decryption. To address this limitation, a procedure called bootstrapping takes a ciphertext as input and homomorphically produces a new ciphertext encrypting the same plaintext with reduced noise. HE schemes that implement a bootstrapping procedure are referred to as Fully Homomorphic Encryption (FHE) schemes. However, existing bootstrapping algorithms remain computationally expensive, making their improvement crucial for enhancing the efficiency of FHE schemes.

Among FHE schemes, Torus Fully Homomorphic Encryption [5] (TFHE) relies on both Learning With Errors (LWE) and Ring Learning With Errors (RLWE) ciphertexts. In particular, the efficiency of its bootstrapping algorithm

N. El Mrabet et al. (Eds.): AFRICACRYPT 2026, LNCS 16832, pp. 160–184, 2026.
https://doi.org/10.1007/978-3-032-31130-6_7

heavily depends on the noise in LWE ciphertexts after key switching and modulus switching, while the blind rotation applied to RLWE ciphertexts determines the noise in the output ciphertext. Recent works [4,8] specifically aim to reduce the noise generated by these operations and show significant performance improvements. In particular, [8] shows how to reduce the noise introduced by key switching and modulus switching with negligible computational overhead by using a technique called *mean compensation*. However, mean compensation slows down blind rotation, introducing an overhead of around 30% time complexity compared to the original algorithm. Since the noise in a bootstrapped ciphertext is determined by blind rotation, reducing the noise output of this algorithm would enable more homomorphic operations and reduce the number of calls to the expensive bootstrapping procedure.

Contributions. The goal of this work is to reduce as much as possible the noise in a bootstrapped ciphertext.

With TFHE, ciphertexts are usually encrypted under binary secret keys uniformly sampled over $\{0,1\}^n$. By homomorphically computing on these keys, we modify their distribution to *centered binary keys* i.e., keys uniformly sampled over $\{\frac{-1}{2}, \frac{1}{2}\}^n$. This transformation reduces the variance of the noise introduced by key switching, modulus switching and blind rotation to the same extent as the mean compensation technique described in [8]. Specifically, we show that for blind rotation, our algorithm is significantly more efficient than mean compensation and only incurs a 2.7% computational overhead in the worst case. In practice, this improvement enables up to 1.6× more homomorphic operations on bootstrapped ciphertexts.

In an attempt to further reduce the noise output of blind rotation, we show that, contrary to the claim in [8], it is possible to perform blind rotation with blind rotation keys encrypting coefficients in $\{\frac{-1}{2}, \frac{1}{2}\}$. We propose an algorithm satisfying this requirement and demonstrate that, although this variant benefits from a key distribution centered around zero, it still produces more noise than the standard algorithm.

2 Preliminaries

2.1 Notations

For $a \in \mathbb{R}$, we note $\lceil a \rfloor$ the closest integer to a. Let q be an integer, we denote $\mathbb{Z}_q = \mathbb{Z}/q\mathbb{Z}$ the ring of integers modulo q. We denote $R_N = \mathbb{Z}[X]/(X^N+1)$ the polynomial ring of integers modulo (X^N+1), where N is a power of two. This polynomial ring modulo an integer q is noted $R_{N,q} = \mathbb{Z}_q[X]/(X^N+1)$. We use boldface to denote polynomials or vectors, and for a polynomial/vector $\mathbf{a}$, we denote $\mathbf{a_i}$ (or a_i) its i-th coefficient (in bold only if it is a polynomial or a vector). An integer a modulo q may be denoted $[a]_q$, similarly a polynomial $\mathbf{a}$ modulo q may be written $[\mathbf{a}]_q$. For a polynomial/vector $\mathbf{a} \in R_{N,q}$, we denote $\|\mathbf{a}\|_\infty$ its ℓ_∞-norm. We write $x \leftarrow \chi(E)$ the sampling of an element x from a distribution χ over the set E. In particular, $\mathcal{U}(E)$ denotes the uniform distribution over E and

$\chi(\mu, \sigma^2)$ the discrete Gaussian distribution of mean μ and standard deviation σ. We denote $\mathrm{msb}(a)$ the most significant bit of an integer a. For a variable x, we may denote by σ_x^2 or $\sigma^2(x)$ its variance and by μ_x or $\mu(x)$ its expected value. By extension, for a polynomial/vector $\mathbf{a}$ we denote by $\sigma_{\mathbf{a}}^2$ (resp. $\mu_{\mathbf{a}}$) the variance (resp. the expected value) of its coefficients.

2.2 Lattice-Based Encryption

LWE Ciphertext. Let $n, k, p, q \in \mathbb{N}^*$ and let N be a power of two.

Definition 1 (LWE ciphertext). *Let* $\mathbf{s} \leftarrow \chi(\mathbb{Z}_q^n)$. *An* LWE *encryption of a plaintext* $m \in \mathbb{Z}_p$, *encrypted under* $\mathbf{s}$, *is defined as:*

$$\mathrm{LWE}_{\mathbf{s}}(m) = (\mathbf{a}, b) \in \mathbb{Z}_q^{n+1},$$

where $\mathbf{a} \leftarrow \mathcal{U}(\mathbb{Z}_q^n)$, $b = -\mathbf{a} \cdot \mathbf{s} + m + e \mod q$ *and* $e \leftarrow \chi'\left(\mathbb{Z}_q^n\right)$.

Definition 2 (Modulus switching). *Let* $\mathrm{LWE}_{\mathbf{s}}(m) = (\mathbf{a}, b) \in \mathbb{Z}_q^{n+1}$ *and let* $q' \in \mathbb{Z}^*$ *such that* $q' \leq q$. *A modulus switching operation is defined as:*

$$\mathbf{ModSwitch}(\mathrm{LWE}_{\mathbf{s}}(m)) = \left(\left\lceil \frac{q' \cdot \mathbf{a}}{q} \right\rfloor \mod q', \left\lceil \frac{q' \cdot b}{q} \right\rfloor \mod q'\right).$$

It can be verified that the output ciphertext is an encryption of the plaintext $\frac{q'}{q} \cdot m$ modulo q':

$$\begin{aligned} \left\lceil \frac{q' \cdot b}{q} \right\rfloor + \left\lceil \frac{q' \cdot \mathbf{a}}{q} \right\rfloor \cdot \mathbf{s} &= \frac{q' \cdot b}{q} + \epsilon_b + \left(\frac{q' \cdot \mathbf{a}}{q} + \epsilon_{\mathbf{a}}\right) \cdot \mathbf{s} \\ &= \frac{q'}{q}(b + \mathbf{a} \cdot \mathbf{s}) + \epsilon_b + \epsilon_{\mathbf{a}} \cdot \mathbf{s} \\ &= \frac{q'}{q}(m + e) + \epsilon_b + \epsilon_{\mathbf{a}} \cdot \mathbf{s} + kq', \end{aligned}$$

where $\epsilon_{\mathbf{a}}, \epsilon_b$ respectively represent the errors due to the rounding of $\mathbf{a}$ and b.

Let $a \in \mathbb{Z}_q$. This integer can be decomposed in a basis $(\beta_1, \ldots, \beta_r) \in \mathbb{Z}_q^r$ such that:

$$a = \sum_{i=1}^{r} a_i \beta_i \mod q.$$

Decomposing a into smaller components $(a_1, \ldots, a_r)$ before performing multiplications is a technique commonly used in HE schemes to control noise growth.

Definition 3 (Integer gadget decomposition). *Let* $\mathbf{g} = (\beta_1, \ldots, \beta_r) \in \mathbb{Z}_q^r$. *A function* $h : \mathbb{Z}_q \to \mathbb{Z}_q^r$ *is called a gadget decomposition with respect to* $\mathbf{g}$, *if there exists a real number* $B > 0$ *such that for any* $a \in \mathbb{Z}_q$, *we have:*

$$\sum_{i=1}^{r} h(a)_i \beta_i = a \mod q \text{ and } \|\mathbf{h}(\mathbf{a})\|_\infty < B.$$

Definition 4 (LWE' ciphertext). *Let* $\mathbf{g} = (\beta_1, \ldots, \beta_r) \in \mathbb{Z}_q^r$ *and* $\mathbf{s} \leftarrow \chi(\mathbb{Z}_q^r)$. *A gadget* LWE *ciphertext with respect to* $\mathbf{g}$*, encrypting a plaintext* $m \in \mathbb{Z}_p$ *under a secret key* $\mathbf{s}$*, is defined as:*

$$\mathrm{LWE'}_{\mathbf{s}}(m) = (\mathrm{LWE}_{\mathbf{s}}(m \cdot \beta_1), \ldots, \mathrm{LWE}_{\mathbf{s}}(m \cdot \beta_r)).$$

For a vector $\mathbf{a} \in \mathbb{Z}_q^n$, we denote $\odot$ the scalar product between $\mathbf{a}$ and $\mathrm{LWE'}_{\mathbf{s}}(m)$:

$$\mathbf{a} \odot \mathrm{LWE'}_{\mathbf{s}}(m) = \sum_{i=1}^{n} a_i \cdot \mathrm{LWE}_{\mathbf{s}}(m \cdot \beta_i).$$

Definition 5 (LWE key switching). *Let* $\mathbf{s} \leftarrow \chi_1(\mathbb{Z}_q^n)$ *and* $\hat{\mathbf{s}} \leftarrow \chi_2(\mathbb{Z}_q^{n'})$. *Let* $\mathbf{g} = (\beta_1, \ldots, \beta_k) \in \mathbb{Z}_q^r$ *and* h *be its associated gadget decomposition. A Key Switching Key* $\mathrm{KSK}_{\mathbf{s}\to\hat{\mathbf{s}}}$ *is defined as:*

$$\mathrm{KSK}_{\mathbf{s}\to\hat{\mathbf{s}}} = (\mathrm{LWE'}_{\hat{\mathbf{s}}}(s_1), \ldots, \mathrm{LWE'}_{\hat{\mathbf{s}}}(s_n)).$$

For a ciphertext $\mathrm{LWE}_{\mathbf{s}}(m) = (\mathbf{a}, b)$*, the key switching operation is defined as:*

$$\begin{aligned}
\mathbf{KeySwitch}(\mathrm{LWE}_{\mathbf{s}}(m), \mathrm{KSK}_{\mathbf{s}\to\hat{\mathbf{s}}}) &= (0, b) + \sum_{i=1}^{n} \mathbf{h}(\mathbf{a_i}) \odot \mathrm{LWE'}_{\hat{\mathbf{s}}}(s_i) \\
&= (0, b) + \sum_{i=1}^{n}\sum_{j=1}^{r} h(a_i)_j \cdot \mathrm{LWE}_{\hat{\mathbf{s}}}(s_i \cdot \beta_j) \\
&\simeq (0, b) + \sum_{i=1}^{n} \mathrm{LWE}_{\hat{\mathbf{s}}}(a_i \cdot s_i) \\
&= \mathrm{LWE}_{\hat{\mathbf{s}}}(b + \mathbf{a} \cdot \mathbf{s}) \\
&= \mathrm{LWE}_{\hat{\mathbf{s}}}(m + e) \\
&\simeq \mathrm{LWE}_{\hat{\mathbf{s}}}(m).
\end{aligned}$$

Next, we define the ring variant of an LWE ciphertext, namely an RLWE ciphertext.

RLWE Ciphertext. In the case of RLWE ciphertexts, the symbol $\cdot$ will denote polynomial multiplications.

Definition 6 (RLWE ciphertext). *Let* $\mathbf{s} \leftarrow \chi(R_{N,q}^k)$ *be* k *secret polynomials. An* RLWE *ciphertext of a plaintext* $\mathbf{m} \in R_{N,p}$*, encrypted under* $\mathbf{s}$*, is defined as:*

$$\mathrm{RLWE}_{\mathbf{s}}(\mathbf{m}) = (\mathbf{a}, \mathbf{b}) = (\mathbf{a_1}, \ldots, \mathbf{a_k}, \mathbf{b}) \in R_{N,q}^{k+1},$$

where $\mathbf{a} \leftarrow \mathcal{U}(R_{N,q}^k)$, $\mathbf{b} = -\sum_{i=1}^{k} \mathbf{a_i} \cdot \mathbf{s_i} + \mathbf{m} + \mathbf{e} \mod q$ *and* $\mathbf{e} \leftarrow \chi'(R_{N,q})$.

Definition 7 (Polynomial gadget decomposition). *Let* $\mathbf{g} = (\beta_1, \ldots, \beta_\ell) \in \mathbb{Z}_q^\ell$. *A function* $h : R_{N,q} \longrightarrow R_{N,q}^\ell$ *is called a gadget decomposition with respect to* $\mathbf{g}$, *if there exists a real number* $B > 0$ *such that for any* $\mathbf{a} \in R_{N,q}$, *we have:*

$$\sum_{i=0}^{\ell} \mathbf{h}(\mathbf{a})_\mathbf{i} \cdot \beta_i = \mathbf{a} \mod q \text{ and } \|\mathbf{h}(\mathbf{a})\|_\infty < B.$$

Definition 8 (RLWE'). *Let* $\mathbf{g} = (\beta_1, \ldots, \beta_\ell) \in \mathbb{Z}_q^\ell$ *and* $\mathbf{s} \leftarrow \chi(R_{N,q}^k)$. *A gadget* $\mathrm{RLWE}_\mathbf{s}$ *ciphertext with respect to* $\mathbf{g}$, *encrypting a plaintext* $\mathbf{m} \in R_{N,p}$ *under a secret key* $\mathbf{s}$, *is defined as:*

$$\mathrm{RLWE'}_\mathbf{s}(\mathbf{m}) = (\mathrm{RLWE}_\mathbf{s}(\mathbf{m} \cdot \beta_1), \ldots, \mathrm{RLWE}_\mathbf{s}(\mathbf{m} \cdot \beta_\ell)).$$

For a vector of polynomials $\mathbf{a} = (\mathbf{a_i})_{i \in [\![1,k]\!]}$, we denote $\odot$ the scalar multiplication between $\mathbf{a}$ and $\mathrm{RLWE'}_\mathbf{s}(\mathbf{m})$:

$$\mathbf{a} \odot \mathrm{RLWE'}_\mathbf{s}(\mathbf{m}) = \sum_{i=1}^{k} \mathbf{a_i} \cdot \mathrm{RLWE}_\mathbf{s}(\mathbf{m} \cdot \beta_i).$$

Here, with a slight abuse of notation, we write $\mathbf{a_i} \cdot \mathrm{RLWE}_\mathbf{s}(\mathbf{m} \cdot \beta_i)$ to mean that each polynomial in $\mathrm{RLWE}_\mathbf{s}(\mathbf{m} \cdot \beta_i)$ is multiplied by $\mathbf{a_i}$.

Definition 9 (RGSW). *Let* $\mathbf{g} = (\beta_1, \ldots, \beta_\ell) \in \mathbb{Z}_q^\ell$, $\mathbf{s} \leftarrow \chi_1(R_{N,q}^k)$ *and* $\hat{\mathbf{s}} \leftarrow \chi_2(R_{N,q}^{k'})$. *An* $\mathrm{RGSW}_{\mathbf{s}\to\hat{\mathbf{s}}}$ *ciphertext with respect to a basis* $\mathbf{g}$ *and a secret key* $\mathbf{s}$, *encrypting a plaintext* $\mathbf{m} \in R_{N,p}$ *under a secret key* $\hat{\mathbf{s}}$, *is defined as:*

$$\mathrm{RGSW}_{\mathbf{s}\to\hat{\mathbf{s}}}(\mathbf{m}) = (\mathrm{RLWE'}_{\hat{\mathbf{s}}}(\mathbf{s_1} \cdot \mathbf{m}), \ldots, \mathrm{RLWE'}_{\hat{\mathbf{s}}}(\mathbf{s_k} \cdot \mathbf{m}), \mathrm{RLWE'}_{\hat{\mathbf{s}}}(\mathbf{m})).$$

We simply denote it $\mathrm{RGSW}_\mathbf{s}(\mathbf{m})$ *if* $\mathbf{s} = \hat{\mathbf{s}}$.

Definition 10 (External product). *Let* $\mathbf{s} \leftarrow \chi_1(R_{N,q}^k)$ *and* $\hat{\mathbf{s}} \leftarrow \chi_2(R_{N,q}^{k'})$. *Let* $\mathbf{g} = (\beta_1, \ldots, \beta_\ell) \in \mathbb{Z}_q^\ell$ *and* h *be its associated gadget decomposition. An external product* $\boxdot$ *between* $\mathrm{RLWE}_\mathbf{s}(\mathbf{m}) = (\mathbf{a}, \mathbf{b})$ *and* $\mathrm{RGSW}_{\mathbf{s}\to\hat{\mathbf{s}}}(\mathbf{m'})$ *is defined as:*

$$\begin{aligned}
\mathrm{RLWE}_\mathbf{s}(\mathbf{m}) \boxdot \mathrm{RGSW}_{\mathbf{s}\to\hat{\mathbf{s}}}(\mathbf{m'}) &= \sum_{j=1}^{k} \mathbf{h}(\mathbf{a_j}) \odot \mathrm{RLWE'}_{\hat{\mathbf{s}}}(\mathbf{s_j} \cdot \mathbf{m'}) + \mathbf{h}(\mathbf{b}) \odot \mathrm{RLWE'}_{\hat{\mathbf{s}}}(\mathbf{m'}) \\
&= \sum_{j=1}^{k} \sum_{i=1}^{\ell} \mathbf{h}(\mathbf{a_j})_\mathbf{i} \cdot \mathrm{RLWE}_{\hat{\mathbf{s}}}(\mathbf{s_j} \cdot \mathbf{m'} \cdot \beta_i) \\
&+ \sum_{i'=1}^{\ell} \mathbf{h}(\mathbf{b})_{\mathbf{i'}} \cdot \mathrm{RLWE}_{\hat{\mathbf{s}}}(\mathbf{m'} \cdot \beta_{i'}) \\
&= \sum_{j=1}^{k} \mathrm{RLWE}_{\hat{\mathbf{s}}}(\mathbf{a_j} \cdot \mathbf{s_j} \cdot \mathbf{m'}) + \mathrm{RLWE}_{\hat{\mathbf{s}}}(\mathbf{b} \cdot \mathbf{m'}) \\
&= \mathrm{RLWE}_{\hat{\mathbf{s}}}(\mathbf{m'} \cdot (\mathbf{b} + \mathbf{a} \cdot \mathbf{s})) \\
&= \mathrm{RLWE}_{\hat{\mathbf{s}}}(\mathbf{m'} \cdot (\mathbf{m} + \mathbf{e})) \\
&\simeq \mathrm{RLWE}_{\hat{\mathbf{s}}}(\mathbf{m'} \cdot \mathbf{m}).
\end{aligned}$$

2.3 Torus Fully Homomorphic Encryption

In this work, we only consider Torus Fully Homomorphic Encryption (TFHE) for binary secrets. For a more diverse secret sampling, we refer the reader to [7].

Encryption. Let $\mathbf{s} \leftarrow \mathcal{U}(\{0,1\}^n)$. Let $p < q$ be two integers such that $\mathbb{Z}_p$ is the plaintext space and $\mathbb{Z}_q$ the ciphertext space. In TFHE, an LWE encryption of a message $m \in \mathbb{Z}_p$ under the secret key $\mathbf{s}$ is defined as:

$$\text{LWE}_{\mathbf{s}}\left(\left\lceil \frac{q}{p} \cdot m \right\rfloor\right) = (\mathbf{a}, b).$$

The error term e is sampled from a discrete Gaussian centered around 0 and of standard deviation σ, i.e., $e \leftarrow \chi\left(0, \sigma^2\right)$.

Decryption. Decryption is performed as follows:

$$\begin{aligned} \left\lceil \frac{p}{q} \cdot (b + \mathbf{a} \cdot \mathbf{s}) \right\rfloor &= \left\lceil \frac{p}{q} \cdot \left(\frac{q}{p} \cdot m + e + kq \right) \right\rfloor \\ &= \left\lceil m + \frac{p}{q} \cdot e + kp \right\rfloor \\ &= m + \left\lceil \frac{p}{q} \cdot e \right\rfloor \quad \text{mod } p. \end{aligned}$$

If the error e verifies $|e| < \frac{p}{2q}$, the message is correctly decrypted.

Addition. For two ciphertexts:

$$\begin{aligned} \text{LWE}_{\mathbf{s}}(m_1) &= (\mathbf{a}, b), \\ \text{LWE}_{\mathbf{s}}(m_2) &= (\hat{\mathbf{a}}, \hat{b}), \end{aligned}$$

an element-wise addition yields:

$$(a_1 + \hat{a}_1, \ldots, a_n + \hat{a}_n, b + \hat{b}) = \text{LWE}_{\mathbf{s}}(m_1 + m_2).$$

Analogously, subtractions and scalar multiplications are straightforward operations. In the following, we slightly abuse notation '+', '−' to denote the addition and subtraction of ciphertexts, and '·' to denote the scalar multiplication of a ciphertext. After several homomorphic operations, the noise in a ciphertext may need to be reduced to prevent the message from being corrupted. This is done by homomorphically computing a new ciphertext that encrypts the original message with less noise, this technique is called **bootstrapping**. In the case of TFHE, it is possible to evaluate any function on the encrypted input at the same time, this algorithm is called **Programmable Bootstrapping** (PBS).

Let $\hat{\mathbf{s}} \leftarrow \mathcal{U}\left(\{0,1\}^{kN}\right)$ and $\left(\bar{\mathbf{a}}, \bar{b}\right) = \text{LWE}_{\hat{\mathbf{s}}}\left(\left\lceil \frac{q}{p} \cdot m \right\rfloor\right)$ with $m \in \mathbb{Z}_p$. Let $p' \in \mathbb{N}^*$ and $f : \mathbb{Z}_p \to \mathbb{Z}_{p'}$ be a function. The PBS is composed of four steps: key switching, modulus switching, blind rotation, and sample extraction.

Key Switching. Perform a key switching from the original key $\hat{\mathbf{s}}$ to a key $\mathbf{s} \leftarrow \mathcal{U}(\{0,1\}^n$ with $n < kN$. This reduces the computation time of blind rotation, which is the most time-consuming operation of bootstrapping. This step also reduces the errors introduced by modulus switching and blind rotation.

Modulus Switching. Perform a modulus switching from q to $2N$ to obtain a ciphertext $(\mathbf{a}, b) = \text{LWE}_{\mathbf{s}}\left(\left\lceil \frac{2N}{p} \cdot m \right\rfloor\right)$. This step introduces a noise term sometimes called **drift**.

Blind Rotation. Define an accumulator $\text{ACC}_0 = (\mathbf{0}, \mathbf{v}(X) \cdot X^{-b})$, which is an RLWE encryption of the polynomial:

$$\mathbf{v}(X) = X^{-\Delta_p/2}\Delta_{p'} \cdot \sum_{i=0}^{p-1} X^{i \cdot \Delta_p} \cdot \left(\sum_{j=0}^{\Delta_p - 1} f(i) \cdot X^j\right),$$

with $\Delta_p = \frac{N}{p}$ and $\Delta_{p'} = \frac{q}{p'}$. This is a look-up table where every possible output is repeated Δ_p times. Note that it is the definition for an even integer p and that the message has to verify $0 \leq m < \frac{p}{2}$. This is due to the *negacyclicity problem* which is discussed at more length in [2,6].

The idea is to homomorphically multiply the accumulator by $X^{-(b+\mathbf{a} \cdot \mathbf{s})} = X^{-\Delta_p m - e}$. Then, the constant term of the encrypted polynomial is $f(m)$ if $|e| < \Delta_p/2$. Performing this rotation requires a Blind Rotation Key BRK $= (\text{RGSW}_{\hat{\mathbf{s}}}(s_i))_{i \in [\![1,n]\!]}$ to sequentially compute CMUX [5] operations:

$$\text{ACC}_i \longleftarrow \left(\text{ACC}_{i-1} \cdot X^{-a_i} - \text{ACC}_{i-1}\right) \boxdot \text{RGSW}_{\hat{\mathbf{s}}}(s_i) + \text{ACC}_{i-1},$$

for $i \in [\![1,n]\!]$. Observe that

$$s_i \cdot (\alpha X^{-a_i} - 1) + \alpha = \alpha X^{-a_i s_i},$$

therefore if ACC_{i-1} encrypts $\mathbf{v}(X) \cdot X^{-b-\sum_{j<i} a_j s_j}$, then ACC_i encrypts $\mathbf{v}(X) \cdot X^{-b-\sum_{j \leq i} a_j s_j}$. This step is the most computationally expensive of bootstrapping.

Sample Extraction. Retrieve the constant term of the encrypted polynomial as an LWE ciphertext; this ciphertext encrypts the message $f(m)$. In more details, for a ciphertext $\text{RLWE}_{\hat{\mathbf{s}}}(\mathbf{m}) = (\mathbf{a_1}, \ldots, \mathbf{a_k}, \mathbf{b}) \in R_{N,q}^{k+1}$, the constant coefficient b_0 of $\mathbf{b}$ encrypts m_0 with an error e_0 and satisfies:

$$b_0 = \sum_{i=1}^{k} \left(a_{i,0}\hat{s}_{i,0} - \sum_{j=1}^{N-1} a_{i,j}\hat{s}_{i,N-j}\right) + \Delta_p m_0 + e_0 \mod q.$$

Therefore,

$$\left((a_{i,0}, -a_{i,1}, \ldots, -a_{i,N-1})_{i \in [\![1,k]\!]}, b_0\right)$$

is an LWE encryption of m_0 under the secret key $\left((\hat{s}_{i,0}, \hat{s}_{i,1}, \ldots, \hat{s}_{i,N-1})_{i \in [\![1,k]\!]}\right)$.

3 Computing on Secret Keys

Homomorphic encryption is employed to compute on plaintexts. However, it is also possible to homomorphically evaluate linear operations on secret keys. In this section, we show how this is done, and as a consequence we derive the security of keys uniformly sampled over $\left\{\frac{-1}{2}, \frac{1}{2}\right\}^n$.

3.1 Homomorphic Operations

Let $\mathrm{LWE}_{\mathbf{s}}(m) = (\mathbf{a}, b) \in \mathbb{Z}_q^{n+1}$ be an LWE ciphertext encrypted under a secret key $\mathbf{s} \leftarrow \mathcal{U}(\{0,1\}^n)$. We remind that:

$$b = -\mathbf{a} \cdot \mathbf{s} + m + e \mod q.$$

Homomorphically computing operations on secret keys is done by modifying the mask or the body of the ciphertext.

Real Addition. Let $\mathbf{w} \in \mathbb{R}^n$. Adding $\mathbf{w}$ to $\mathbf{s}$ is done as follows:

$$b - \mathbf{w} \cdot \mathbf{a} = -\mathbf{a} \cdot (\mathbf{s} + \mathbf{w}) + m + e \mod q.$$

Then, the ciphertext $(a, b - \mathbf{w} \cdot \mathbf{a})$ is a correct encryption of m under the secret key $\mathbf{s}+\mathbf{w}$. Note however that rounding $\mathbf{w}\cdot\mathbf{a}$ introduces a noise term that depends on the fractional part of the coefficients of $\mathbf{w}$.

Integer Multiplication. Let $u \in \mathbb{Z}$. Multiplying a secret key by u is done by dividing the mask by u:

$$b = -\frac{\mathbf{a}}{u} \cdot (u \cdot \mathbf{s}) + m + e \mod q.$$

Then, the ciphertext $\left(\left\lceil \frac{\mathbf{a}}{u} \right\rfloor, b\right)$ is a correct encryption of m under the secret key $u \cdot \mathbf{s}$. Note however that rounding adds a noise $u \cdot \epsilon \cdot \mathbf{s}$ with $\epsilon \leftarrow \mathcal{U}\left(\left\{\frac{i}{q}, i \in \left[\!\left[\frac{-q}{2u}, \frac{q}{2u}\right]\!\right]\right\}^n\right)$.

Considering the operations that can be homomorphically performed on secret keys, it is possible to transform a secret key $\mathbf{s}$ into $u \cdot \mathbf{s} + \mathbf{v}$, with $u \in \mathbb{Z}, \mathbf{v} \in \mathbb{R}^n$. Similarly, the same transformations can be applied on the secret key of an RLWE ciphertext, we do not go through the details again for the sake of succinctness.

3.2 Security of Centered Binary Keys

Binary secret keys uniformly sampled over $\{0,1\}^n$ are commonly used in TFHE. Here, we prove that encrypting with **centered binary keys**, i.e., secret keys uniformly sampled over $\{\frac{-1}{2}, \frac{1}{2}\}^n$, is as secure as encrypting using keys uniformly sampled over $\{0,1\}^n$.

Theorem 1. *Let* $\mathbf{s} \leftarrow \mathcal{U}(\{0,1\}^n)$ *and* $m \in \mathbb{Z}_p$. *From a ciphertext* $\mathrm{LWE}_{\mathbf{s}}(m)$, *it is possible to derive another ciphertext* $\mathrm{LWE}_{\mathbf{s}'}(m)$ *encrypted under a secret key* $\mathbf{s}' \leftarrow \mathcal{U}(\{-\frac{1}{2},\frac{1}{2}\}^n)$, *while adding a noise term* e_r *that satisfies* $e_r \leftarrow \mathcal{U}(\{-\frac{1}{2},0,\frac{1}{2}\})$.

Proof. Let

$$\mathrm{LWE}_{\mathbf{s}}(m) = (\mathbf{a}, b) = (a_1, \ldots, a_n, b).$$

We define b' as:

$$\begin{aligned} b' = b + \left\lceil \frac{\sum_{i=1}^n a_i}{2} \right\rfloor &= -\sum_{i=1}^n a_i \cdot s_i + \sum_{i'=1}^n \frac{a_{i'}}{2} + e_r + m + e \mod q \\ &= -\sum_{i=1}^n a_i \cdot \left(s_i - \frac{1}{2}\right) + m + e_r + e \mod q. \end{aligned}$$

Then, $\mathbf{s}' = \left(s_i - \frac{1}{2}\right)_{i \in [\![1,n]\!]}$ is uniformly sampled over $\{-\frac{1}{2},\frac{1}{2}\}^n$. Since e_r is the rounding error after a division by two, and $\forall i \in [\![1,n]\!], a_i \in [\![-\frac{q}{2},\frac{q}{2}[\![$, it verifies $e_r \leftarrow \mathcal{U}(\{-\frac{1}{2},0,\frac{1}{2}\})$. □

Conversely, a key $\mathbf{s}' \leftarrow \mathcal{U}(\{\frac{-1}{2},\frac{1}{2}\}^n)$ can be transformed into a key $\mathbf{s} \leftarrow \mathcal{U}(\{0,1\}^n)$.

Corollary 1. *Let* $\mathbf{s}' \leftarrow \mathcal{U}(\{\frac{-1}{2},\frac{1}{2}\}^n)$ *and* $m \in \mathbb{Z}_p$. *From a ciphertext* $\mathrm{LWE}_{\mathbf{s}'}(m)$, *it is possible to derive another ciphertext* $\mathrm{LWE}_{\mathbf{s}}(m)$ *encrypted under a secret key* $\mathbf{s} \leftarrow \mathcal{U}(\{0,1\}^n)$, *while adding a noise term* e_r *that satisfies* $e_r \leftarrow \mathcal{U}(\{-\frac{1}{2},0,\frac{1}{2}\})$.

Proof. Let

$$\mathrm{LWE}_{\mathbf{s}'}(m) = (\mathbf{a}, b) = (a_1, \ldots, a_n, b).$$

The demonstration is similar to Theorem 1, except that we define $b' = b - \left\lceil \frac{\sum_{i=1}^n a_i}{2} \right\rfloor$ instead. □

An analogous proof can be given for an RLWE ciphertext encrypted under a uniformly sampled binary key.

Theorem 2. *Let* $\mathbf{s} = (\mathbf{s_1}, \ldots, \mathbf{s_k}) \leftarrow \mathcal{U}(\{0,1\}^{kN})$ *and* $\mathbf{m} \in R_{N,p}$. *From a ciphertext* $\mathrm{RLWE}_{\mathbf{s}}(\mathbf{m})$, *it is possible to derive another ciphertext* $\mathrm{RLWE}_{\mathbf{s}'}(\mathbf{m})$ *encrypting* $\mathbf{m}$ *under a secret key* $\mathbf{s}' \leftarrow \mathcal{U}(\{-\frac{1}{2},\frac{1}{2}\}^{kN})$, *while adding a noise term* $\mathbf{e_r} = e_r \cdot (1 + X + \cdots + X^{N-1})$ *that satisfies* $e_r \leftarrow \mathcal{U}(\{-\frac{1}{2},0,\frac{1}{2}\})$.

Proof. Let

$$\mathrm{RLWE}_{\mathbf{s}}(m) = (\mathbf{a_1}, \ldots, \mathbf{a_k}, \mathbf{b}).$$

We define $\mathbf{b}'$ as:

$$\begin{aligned}\mathbf{b}' &= \mathbf{b} + \left\lceil \sum_{i=1}^{k} \frac{\mathbf{a_i}}{2} \cdot (1 + X + \cdots + X^{N-1}) \right\rfloor \\ &= -\mathbf{a} \cdot \mathbf{s} + \sum_{i=1}^{k} \frac{\mathbf{a_i}}{2} \cdot (1 + X + \cdots + X^{N-1}) + \mathbf{e_r} + \mathbf{m} + \mathbf{e} \mod q, X^N + 1 \\ &= -\sum_{i=1}^{k} \mathbf{a_i} \cdot \left(\mathbf{s_i} - \frac{1 + X + \cdots + X^{N-1}}{2} \right) + \mathbf{m} + \mathbf{e_r} + \mathbf{e} \mod q, X^N + 1.\end{aligned}$$

Then, the key $\mathbf{s}' = \left(\mathbf{s_i} - \frac{1+X+\cdots+X^{N-1}}{2} \right)_{i \in [\![1,k]\!]}$ is uniformly sampled over $\{-\frac{1}{2}, \frac{1}{2}\}^{kN}$, and since e_r is the rounding error after a division by two, it verifies $e_r \leftarrow \mathcal{U}(\{-\frac{1}{2}, 0, \frac{1}{2}\})$. □

Corollary 2. *Let* $\mathbf{s}' \leftarrow \mathcal{U}(\{\frac{-1}{2}, \frac{1}{2}\}^{kN})$ *and* $\mathbf{m} \in R_{N,p}$. *From an* RLWE *ciphertext* $\mathrm{RLWE}_{\mathbf{s}'}(\mathbf{m})$, *it is possible to derive another ciphertext* $\mathrm{RLWE}_{\mathbf{s}}(\mathbf{m})$ *encrypted under a secret key* $\mathbf{s} \leftarrow \mathcal{U}(\{0,1\}^n)$, *while adding a noise term* $\mathbf{e_r} = e_r \cdot (1 + X + \cdots + X^{N-1})$ *that satisfies* $e_r \leftarrow \mathcal{U}(\{-\frac{1}{2}, 0, \frac{1}{2}\})$.

The previous theorems and corollaries demonstrate that encrypting LWE or RLWE ciphertexts using centered binary keys adds a negligible noise term to the ciphertexts. Therefore, it is possible to encrypt messages using such keys with the same parameters as the ones used for secret keys uniformly sampled over $\{0,1\}^n$, without any security loss. In the next section, we show how this is useful in practice.

4 Centered Binary Keys in TFHE Bootstrapping

To determine how many homomorphic operations can be performed on a ciphertext before the message gets corrupted by the noise, it is possible to monitor the mean and the variance of the noise. In [8], the authors notice that for some homomorphic operations, the mean of the coefficients of the secret key adds a term to the variance of the noise produced. They define an operation to remove this variance term, called *mean compensation*, which reduces the noise introduced by key switching and modulus switching. The technique also reduces the noise introduced by blind rotation, but at the cost of a significant time-complexity overhead, leading the authors to discard its use for this operation.

In the next section, we briefly review the work in [8] and propose an alternative approach to obtain a similar result. In particular, we show that for blind rotation, our method achieves the same noise reduction at a significantly lower computational cost.

4.1 Noise and Mean Compensation

To determine the distribution of the noise, we consider that all random variables are independent. We also remind the properties of variances σ^2 for independent variables x and y:

$$\sigma_{xy}^2 = \sigma_x^2 \cdot (\sigma_y^2 + \mu_y^2) + \sigma_y^2 \mu_x^2,$$

and

$$\sigma_{x+y}^2 = \sigma_x^2 + \sigma_y^2,$$

with μ_x, μ_y the expected values of x and y.

Rounding Noise for Modulus Switching. The operations of modulus switching and gadget decomposition (needed for key switching and blind rotation), introduce rounding errors that depend on the mean of the coefficients of the secret key. For a ciphertext $(\mathbf{a}', b') = \mathrm{LWE}_{\mathbf{s}}\left(\left\lceil \frac{q}{p} \cdot m \right\rfloor\right)$ encrypted under a secret key $\mathbf{s} \leftarrow \mathcal{U}(\{0,1\}^n)$, modulus switching yields:

$$\mathbf{ModSwitch}(\mathbf{a}', b') = \left(\left\lceil \frac{2N \cdot \mathbf{a}'}{q} \right\rfloor \mod 2N, \left\lceil \frac{2N \cdot b'}{q} \right\rfloor \mod 2N\right) = (\mathbf{a}, b).$$

From Definition 2, we obtain:

$$\left\lceil \frac{2N \cdot b}{q} \right\rfloor + \left\lceil \frac{2N \cdot \mathbf{a}}{q} \right\rfloor \cdot \mathbf{s} = \frac{2N}{q}(m + e) + \epsilon_b + \epsilon_{\mathbf{a}} \cdot \mathbf{s} \mod 2N.$$

The noise term $\epsilon_b + \epsilon_{\mathbf{a}} \cdot \mathbf{s} = \epsilon_b + \sum_{i=0}^{n} \epsilon_i s_i$ represents the rounding noise and its variance σ_{ms}^2 is equal to:

$$\sigma_{\mathrm{ms}}^2 = \sigma_\epsilon^2 \cdot (n \cdot (\sigma_{\mathbf{s}}^2 + \mu_{\mathbf{s}}^2) + 1),$$

where σ_ϵ^2 is the variance of the rounding error for one integer, $\sigma_{\mathbf{s}}^2$ is the variance of the coefficients of the secret key, and $\mu_{\mathbf{s}}$ is the mean of the secret key. Since with TFHE, the secret keys of LWE ciphertexts are uniformly sampled over $\{0,1\}^n$, $\sigma_{\mathbf{s}}^2 = \mu_{\mathbf{s}}^2 = \frac{1}{4}$.

Previous Work: Mean Compensation Technique. In [8], the authors notice that it is possible to eliminate the mean term $\mu_{\mathbf{s}}$. Their idea is that since $\sum_{i=1}^{n} \epsilon_i$ is publicly known as well as the mean of the coefficients of the secret key, removing $\mu_{\mathbf{s}} \cdot \sum_{i=1}^{n} \epsilon_i$ from the body yields:

$$\hat{b} = b - \mu_{\mathbf{s}} \cdot \sum_{i=1}^{n} \epsilon_i,$$

and the decryption outputs:

$$\hat{b} + \mathbf{a} \cdot \mathbf{s} = \frac{2N}{q}(m + e) + \epsilon_b + \sum_{i=1}^{n} \epsilon_i (s_i - \mu_{\mathbf{s}}) \mod 2N.$$

Then, the noise variance is reduced to:

$$\hat{\sigma}_{\text{ms}}^2 = \sigma_\epsilon^2 \cdot (n \cdot \sigma_{\mathbf{s}}^2 + 1).$$

Since the mean of $(s_i - \mu_{\mathbf{s}})_{i \in [\![1,n]\!]}$ is zero, the noise variance has been halved. Note that this a very desirable outcome since bootstrapping heavily depends on the amount of noise in the ciphertext after modulus switching. In fact, the larger the noise is, the larger the quotient polynomial $(X^N + 1)$ must be, and the more computations blind rotation requires. Since the polynomial degree N is necessarily a power of two, the computational cost of blind rotation is growing exponentially with the amount of noise inside the modulus-switched ciphertext.

Our Work: Centered Binary Keys. We propose to choose the secret key $\mathbf{s}$ sampled uniformly at random in $\{-\frac{1}{2}, \frac{1}{2}\}^n$. Then, $\mu_{\mathbf{s}} = 0$ natively and we obtain the same result:

$$\sigma_{\text{ms}}^2 = \sigma_\epsilon^2 \cdot (n \cdot \sigma_{\mathbf{s}}^2 + 1).$$

Rounding Noise for Key Switching. For key switching, a common technique is to decompose only the most significant bits of the mask $\mathbf{a}'$ of the ciphertext $(\mathbf{a}', b') = \text{LWE}_{\mathbf{s}}\left(\left\lceil \frac{q}{p} \cdot m \right\rfloor\right)$, as the message is encoded in the most significant bits. This is equivalent to decompose the mask in a basis $(\beta_1, \dots, \beta_\ell)$ after performing a modulus switching from q to $\beta = \prod_{i=1}^{\ell} \beta_i < q$. Therefore, the variance of the rounding error σ_{ks}^2 is similar to the rounding error of modulus switching, except that the body is not rounded this time:

$$\sigma_{\text{ks}}^2 = \left(\frac{q}{\beta}\right)^2 \cdot \sigma_\epsilon^2 \cdot n \cdot (\sigma_{\mathbf{s}}^2 + \mu_{\mathbf{s}}^2).$$

Previous Work: Mean Compensation. Similarly to modulus switching, mean compensation reduces the error variance to:

$$\sigma_{\text{ks}}^2 = \left(\frac{q}{\beta}\right)^2 \cdot \sigma_\epsilon^2 \cdot n \cdot \sigma_{\mathbf{s}}^2.$$

Our Work: Centered Binary Keys. Again, we obtain the same result by choosing a secret key $\mathbf{s}$ sampled uniformly at random in $\{-\frac{1}{2}, \frac{1}{2}\}^n$.

Rounding Noise for Blind Rotation. A blind rotation step is defined as:

$$\text{ACC}_i \longleftarrow (\text{ACC}_{i-1} \cdot X^{-a_i} - \text{ACC}_{i-1}) \boxdot \text{RGSW}_{\mathbf{s}_{\mathbf{rlwe}}}(s_i) + \text{ACC}_{i-1}.$$

The external product needed at every step of blind rotation requires the gadget decomposition of the accumulator. As for key switching, using the approximate decomposition introduces a rounding error:

$$\begin{aligned}\sigma^2_{\text{round}(1)} &= \left(\frac{q}{\beta}\right)^2 \cdot \sigma^2(e_{ms} \cdot s_i)\\ &= \left(\frac{q}{\beta}\right)^2 \cdot \sigma^2(e_{ms}) \cdot (\sigma^2_{\mathbf{s}} + \mu^2_{\mathbf{s}}) + \sigma^2(\mathbf{s}) \cdot \mu(e_{ms})^2\\ &= \left(\frac{q}{\beta}\right)^2 \cdot \sigma^2_\epsilon \cdot (kN \cdot (\sigma^2_{\mathbf{s_{rlwe}}} + \mu^2_{\mathbf{s_{rlwe}}}) + 1) \cdot (\sigma^2_{\mathbf{s}} + \mu^2_{\mathbf{s}}),\end{aligned}$$

where e_{ms} is the noise introduced by modulus switching the RLWE ciphertext, σ^2_ϵ is the variance of the rounding error and $\sigma^2_{\text{round}(1)}$ is the variance of the rounding noise added in the first blind rotation step. The variance follows an arithmetic progression, thus we obtain $\sigma^2_{\text{round}(n)}$ the total rounding noise variance after blind rotation:

$$\sigma^2_{\text{round}(n)} = \left(\frac{q}{\beta}\right)^2 \cdot \sigma^2_\epsilon \cdot (kN \cdot (\sigma^2_{\mathbf{s_{rlwe}}} + \mu^2_{\mathbf{s_{rlwe}}}) + 1) \cdot (\sigma^2_{\mathbf{s}} + \mu^2_{\mathbf{s}}) \cdot n.$$

Previous Work: Mean Compensation. In this case, it is more difficult to apply mean compensation because it requires computing polynomial products modulo $(X^N + 1)$ instead of integer products. Indeed, the compensated body is defined as:

$$\hat{\mathbf{b}} = \mathbf{b} - \frac{1}{2}\left(1 + X + ... + X^{N-1}\right) \cdot \epsilon,$$

with ϵ the rounding error. Then, the variance of the rounding noise introduced by a blind rotation step is:

$$\sigma^2_{\text{round}(1)} = \left(\frac{q}{\beta}\right)^2 \cdot \sigma^2_\epsilon \cdot (N \cdot \sigma^2_{\mathbf{s_{rlwe}}} + 1) \cdot (\sigma^2_{\mathbf{s}} + \mu^2_{\mathbf{s}}),$$

and for the whole blind rotation algorithm:

$$\sigma^2_{\text{round}(n)} = \left(\frac{q}{\beta}\right)^2 \cdot \sigma^2_\epsilon \cdot (N \cdot \sigma^2_{\mathbf{s_{rlwe}}} + 1) \cdot (\sigma^2_{\mathbf{s}} + \mu^2_{\mathbf{s}}) \cdot n.$$

However, the cost of mean compensation is n polynomial multiplications which is computationally expensive, and although the authors find some trick to reduce its cost, they finally give up on its use because of the significant overhead it incurs in practice.

Our Work: Centered Binary Keys. By choosing centered binary keys, the mean $\mu^2_{\mathbf{s_{rlwe}}}$ is set to zero. Therefore, we obtain the same result as mean compensation but with a negligible computational overhead. We show how to achieve this result in the next section.

4.2 Comparing Centered Binary Keys with Mean Compensation for Blind Rotation

In [8], the authors propose to use mean compensation to reduce the noise introduced by blind rotation. However, in their implementation the authors observe that using mean compensation introduces an increase of 30% time complexity against the standard blind rotation algorithm. Since it represents a prohibitively high overhead for a 50% decrease in noise variance, they discard the use of the technique for blind rotation.

Complexity of Mean Compensation for Blind Rotation. Mean compensation for blind rotation consists in computing for each step the compensated body:

$$\hat{\mathbf{b}} = \mathbf{b} - \frac{1}{2}\sum_{i=1}^{k}\left(\sum_{j=0}^{N-1} X^j\right)\cdot \epsilon_{\mathbf{i}},$$

with $\epsilon_{\mathbf{i}} = \sum_{j=0}^{N-1} \epsilon_{i,j} X^j$ the rounding error. Since an additional multiplication in each blind rotation step significantly increases time complexity, the authors propose another way of computing this multiplication more efficiently. Let $\mathbf{r}$ be a polynomial defined as:

$$\mathbf{r} = \sum_{i=1}^{k}\left(\sum_{j=0}^{N-1} X^j\right)\left(\sum_{j'=0}^{N-1} \epsilon_{i,j'} X^{j'}\right) = \sum_{i=1}^{k}\sum_{i=0}^{N-1} r_i X^i,$$

then computing the coefficient r_{N-1} requires kN additions. Knowing r_{N-1}, the coefficient r_{N-2} can be computed as:

$$r_{N-2} = r_{N-1} - 2\cdot \sum_{i=1}^{k} \epsilon_{i,N-1},$$

and in general:

$$\forall j \in [\![1, N-1]\!],\ r_{j-1} = r_j - 2\cdot \sum_{i=1}^{k} \epsilon_{i,j}.$$

With this method, the authors count $(2k + 3)\cdot N$ additions or subtractions to perform these polynomial multiplications. In the following, we theoretically determine the complexity of mean compensation for blind rotation on the set of parameters used in [8] (see Table 1).

Table 1. Parameters set used in [8].

Parameters	Set
n	834
N	2^{11}
k	1
q	2^{64}
ℓ	1

The integer ℓ is the number of levels of decomposition of any RGSW ciphertext in the blind rotation key. The RLWE ciphertexts are defined in $R_{N,q}^{k+1}$ and the Fast Fourier Transform (FFT) and Inverse Fast Fourier Transform (IFFT) are used to compute polynomial multiplications. We denote C_{FFT} (resp. C_{IFFT}) the computational cost of the FFT (resp. IFFT). Then, the complexity of the standard blind rotation step is:

- $\ell(k+1)$ polynomial multiplications for the external product in roughly:

  $$\ell(k+1)(C_{\mathrm{FFT}}+C_{\mathrm{IFFT}}+2N) \simeq \ell(k+1)(2N\log(N)+2N\log(N)) = 4\ell(k+1)N\log(N)$$

  additions (we suppose here that one subtraction costs as much as an addition and we make the optimistic approximation that a multiplication costs 2 additions),
- $(\ell(k+1)-1)N$ additions for the external product,
- $(k+1)N$ additions to sum the accumulators,

and in total the complexity of one step is around

$$4\ell(k+1)N\log(N) + ((\ell+1)(k+1)-1)N$$

additions. Therefore, the evolution of the complexities between the method without mean compensation C_{nmc} and the complexity with mean compensation C_{mc} for the set of parameters defined above is:

$$\begin{aligned} V = \frac{C_{\mathrm{mc}} - C_{\mathrm{nmc}}}{C_{\mathrm{nmc}}} &= \frac{(2k+3)\cdot N}{4\ell(k+1)N\log(N) + ((\ell+1)(k+1)-1)N} \\ &= \frac{5}{4\cdot 2\cdot 11 + 2\cdot 2 - 1} \simeq 5,5\%. \end{aligned}$$

It is a moderate overhead compared to the 30% increase reported in [8]. The discrepancy between theoretical and practical complexities is due to the lack of parallelism of their method. Indeed, the operations in the FFT and IFFT are parallelizable to a certain extent while computing the mean noise is purely sequential. We show next how homomorphically computing on secret keys allows decreasing the noise introduced by blind rotation more efficiently.

Computing on Centered Binary Key RLWE Ciphertexts. Using centered binary keys reduces the noise of blind rotation as much as mean compensation but it raises the issue of computing operations on ciphertexts. Indeed, linear operations on ciphertexts encrypted under keys including non-integer coefficients is not homomorphically correct. For two ciphertexts:

$$\mathrm{RLWE}_{\mathbf{s}}(\mathbf{m}) = (\mathbf{a}, \mathbf{b}) \in R_{N,q}^{k+1},$$
$$\mathrm{RLWE}_{\mathbf{s}}(\hat{\mathbf{m}}) = (\hat{\mathbf{a}}, \hat{\mathbf{b}}) \in R_{N,q}^{k+1},$$

with $\mathbf{s} \leftarrow \mathcal{U}\left(\{\frac{-1}{2}, \frac{1}{2}\}^{kN}\right)$, a homomorphic addition yields:

$$\left([\mathbf{a}+\hat{\mathbf{a}}]_q, [\mathbf{b}+\hat{\mathbf{b}}]_q\right),$$

with

$$\begin{aligned}\mathbf{b}+\hat{\mathbf{b}} &= \mathbf{a}\cdot\mathbf{s}+\hat{\mathbf{a}}\cdot\mathbf{s}+\Delta\mathbf{m}+\Delta\hat{\mathbf{m}}+\mathbf{e}+\hat{\mathbf{e}} \mod q\\ &= (\mathbf{a}+\hat{\mathbf{a}})\cdot\mathbf{s}+\Delta(\mathbf{m}+\hat{\mathbf{m}})+\mathbf{e}+\hat{\mathbf{e}} \mod q.\end{aligned}$$

However, reducing the coefficients of the mask modulo q discards its most significant bits, which are still required for correct decryption (because $\forall i \in [\![1,k]\!], \forall j \in [\![1,N]\!], |s_{i,j}| = \frac{1}{2}$). Therefore, computing a modular reduction without losing correctness is no longer straightforward. Let $(\mathbf{a_1},\ldots,\mathbf{a_k},\mathbf{b})$ be an RLWE ciphertext encrypted under a key $\mathbf{s} \leftarrow \{\frac{-1}{2},\frac{1}{2}\}^{kN}$, which is the result of an external product, and that has not been reduced modulo q yet. It is known that:

$$\mathbf{b} = -\sum_{i=1}^{k}\mathbf{a_i}\cdot\mathbf{s_i}+\mathbf{m}+\mathbf{e} \mod q = -\sum_{i=1}^{k}\left(\sum_{j=0}^{N-1}a_{i,j}X^j\right)\left(\sum_{j'=0}^{N-1}s_{j'}X^{j'}\right)+\mathbf{m}+\mathbf{e} \mod q.$$

To reduce the ciphertext modulo q, it is possible to transform it into a ciphertext encrypted under a standard binary key, then compute the modular reduction, and transform this ciphertext back into a ciphertext encrypted under a centered binary key.

1. Computing

$$\begin{aligned}\tilde{\mathbf{b}} &= \mathbf{b}-\frac{1}{2}\sum_{i=1}^{k}\left(\sum_{j=0}^{N-1}a_{i,j}X^j\right)\left(\sum_{j'=0}^{N-1}X^{j'}\right)\\ &= \sum_{i=1}^{k}\left(\sum_{j=0}^{N-1}a_{i,j}X^j\right)\left(\sum_{j'=0}^{N-1}\left(s_{i,j'}+\frac{1}{2}\right)\cdot X^{j'}\right)+\mathbf{m}+\mathbf{e} \mod q\end{aligned}$$

   yields an encryption of the same plaintext but under a key sampled over $\{0,1\}^{kN}$. Since this key is now sampled over integer coefficients, the modular reduction is a correct homomorphic operation, and it returns $([\mathbf{a_1}]_q,\ldots,[\mathbf{a_k}]_q,\tilde{\mathbf{b}})$.
2. Computing

$$\begin{aligned}\hat{\mathbf{b}} &= \tilde{\mathbf{b}}+\frac{1}{2}\sum_{i=1}^{k}\left(\sum_{j=0}^{N-1}[a_{i,j}]_q\cdot X^j\right)\left(\sum_{j'=0}^{N-1}X^{j'}\right)\\ &= -\sum_{i=1}^{k}\left(\sum_{j=0}^{N-1}[a_{i,j}]_q\cdot X^j\right)\left(\sum_{j'=0}^{N-1}s_{i,j'}\cdot X^{j'}\right)+\mathbf{m}+\mathbf{e} \mod q\end{aligned}$$

   yields a ciphertext encrypting the same plaintext but encrypted under a centered binary key.

Therefore, computing the modular reduction costs $2k$ polynomial multiplications and $2kN$ additions. In fact, it is possible to merge the two steps together to reduce the overall cost. The resulting ciphertext $(\hat{\mathbf{a}},\hat{\mathbf{b}})$ is defined as:

$$\hat{\mathbf{a}} = \mathbf{a} \mod q,$$

and

$$\hat{\mathbf{b}} = \mathbf{b} - \frac{1}{2}\sum_{i=1}^{k}\left(\sum_{j=0}^{N-1} a_{i,j}X^j\right)\left(\sum_{j'=0}^{N-1} X^{j'}\right) + \frac{1}{2}\sum_{i=1}^{k}\left(\sum_{j=0}^{N-1} [a_{i,j}]_q \cdot X^j\right)\left(\sum_{j'=0}^{N-1} X^{j'}\right)$$
$$= \mathbf{b} - \frac{1}{2}\sum_{i=1}^{k}\left(\sum_{j=0}^{N-1} (a_{i,j} - [a_{i,j}]_q) \cdot X^j\right)\left(\sum_{j'=0}^{N-1} X^{j'}\right) \mod q,$$

which is $\mathbf{b}$ with its most significant bits XORed with a sum of binary polynomial multiplications. Let $\mathbf{r}$ be defined as:

$$\mathbf{r} = \sum_{i=1}^{k}\left(\sum_{j=0}^{N-1} \mathrm{msb}\left(\left[\frac{a_{i,j}}{2}\right]_q\right) \cdot X^j\right)\left(\sum_{j'=0}^{N-1} X^{j'}\right) \mod q.$$

To compute this multiplication faster, it is possible to use the technique from [8] and described previously: computing r_{N-1} with kN additions and $\forall i \in [\![1, N-1]\!]$, $r_{i-1} = r_i - 2 \cdot \sum_{i=1}^{k} \frac{q}{2} \cdot \mathrm{msb}([\frac{a_{i,j}}{2}]_q)$. However, observe that in our case, additions and subtractions represent XOR operations. This means that r_{N-1} is computed using kN XOR operations, and since the computation is performed modulo q,

$$\forall i \in [\![0, N-2]\!],\ r_i = r_{N-1}.$$

Therefore, depending on the value of r_{N-1}, we may flip or not the most significant bits of $\mathbf{b}$; this costs at most N XOR operations which can be performed in parallel. Overall, this method only requires $(k+1)N$ operations compared to the $(2k+3)N$ operations necessary for mean compensation. Also, our technique is almost fully parallelizable, which makes it very efficient in comparison.

Algorithm 1: Centered binary key RLWE modular reduction (**CenModRed**)

Data: $\mathrm{RLWE}_{\mathbf{s}}(\mathbf{m}) = (\mathbf{a}_1, \ldots, \mathbf{a}_k, \mathbf{b}) \in R_N^{k+1}$ with $\mathbf{s} \leftarrow \mathcal{U}(\{\frac{-1}{2}, \frac{1}{2}\}^{kN})$, $\mathbf{m} \in R_{N,p}$, resulting from an external product.
Result: $\mathrm{RLWE}_{\mathbf{s}}(\mathbf{m}) = (\hat{\mathbf{a}}_1, \ldots, \hat{\mathbf{a}}_k, \hat{\mathbf{b}}) \in R_{N,q}^{k+1}$.

```
r = 0;
for i = 1, i ≤ k, i ← i + 1 do
    for j = 0, j < N, j ← j + 1 do
        r ← r ⊕ msb(a_{i,j}/2 mod q);
        a_{i,j} ← a_{i,j} mod q
    end
end
for i = 0, i < N, i ← i + 1 do
    b_i ← b_i ⊕ q/2 · r;
end
```

5 Bootstrapping with Reduced Noise

In [8], the authors observe that performing blind rotation while encrypting a centered binary key would remove the term $\mu_{\mathbf{s}}^2$ from the output noise variance. However, they claim that it is not possible to perform such a blind rotation, and as a proof they design an incorrect blind rotation step defined as:

$$\begin{aligned} \mathrm{ACC}_i \longleftarrow \mathrm{RGSW}_{\mathbf{s_{rlwe}}}\left(s_i - \frac{1}{2}\right) \boxdot (\mathrm{ACC}_{i-1}X^{-a_i} - \mathrm{ACC}_{i-1}) \\ + (\mathrm{ACC}_{i-1}X^{-a_i} + \mathrm{ACC}_{i-1})/2. \end{aligned}$$

In this case, the blind rotation key elements encrypt centered values $(s_i - \frac{1}{2}) \in \{-\frac{1}{2}, \frac{1}{2}\}$. However, this blind rotation step outputs an incorrect result because it is not possible to divide a ciphertext by two without losing correctness on the most significant bit. More precisely, let $(\mathbf{a}, \mathbf{b}) = \mathrm{RLWE}_{\mathbf{s}}(\mathbf{m}) \in R_{N,q}^{k+1}$. We have:

$$\mathbf{b} = \mathbf{a} \cdot \mathbf{s} + \mathbf{m} + \mathbf{e} + q\mathbf{I},$$

and dividing by two yields:

$$\begin{aligned} \frac{\mathbf{b}}{2} &= \frac{\mathbf{a} \cdot \mathbf{s}}{2} + \frac{\mathbf{m}}{2} + \frac{\mathbf{e}}{2} + \frac{q}{2}\mathbf{I} \\ &= \frac{\mathbf{a} \cdot \mathbf{s}}{2} + \frac{\mathbf{m}}{2} + \frac{\mathbf{e}}{2} + \frac{q}{2}\mathbf{e}' + q\mathbf{I}'. \end{aligned}$$

The term $\frac{q}{2}\mathbf{e}'$ corrupts the plaintext, thus the division by two is not a correct homomorphic operation, and this blind rotation step outputs an incorrect result in general.

5.1 New Blind Rotation Step

We challenge this statement and show that it is in fact possible to build a blind rotation algorithm encrypting a centered binary key. For a secret key $\mathbf{s} \leftarrow \mathcal{U}(\{0,1\}^n)$, the new blind rotation equation is defined as:

$$\mathrm{ACC}_i \longleftarrow \left(\mathrm{RGSW}_{\mathbf{s_{rlwe}}}\left(s_i - \frac{1}{2}\right) \boxdot \mathrm{ACC}_{i-1}\right) \cdot (X^{-a_i} - 1) + \frac{\mathrm{ACC}_{i-1}}{2} \cdot (X^{-a_i} + 1).$$

In our case, dividing by two is a correct operation, this is captured by Theorem 3. The intuition is that dividing an RLWE ciphertext by two only introduces an error term on the most significant bit of the plaintext. After computing this blind rotation step, the error and the message are multiplied by two by the property:

$$s \cdot \alpha \cdot (x - y) + \frac{\alpha}{2} \cdot (x + y) = \begin{cases} \alpha x \text{ if } s = \frac{1}{2} \\ \alpha y \text{ if } s = \frac{-1}{2}, \end{cases}$$

and the modular reduction discards the corrupted most significant bit.

Theorem 3. *Let* $\text{ACC}_{i-1} = \text{RLWE}_{\mathbf{s_{rlwe}}}(\mathbf{m})$, $\mathbf{s_{rlwe}} \leftarrow \chi(R^k_{N,q})$, *and* $\mathbf{s} \leftarrow \mathcal{U}(\{0,1\}^n)$. *Then,* ACC_i *defined by the equation:*

$$\text{ACC}_i = \left(\text{RGSW}_{\mathbf{s_{rlwe}}}\left(s_i - \frac{1}{2}\right) \boxdot \text{ACC}_{i-1}\right) \cdot (X^{-a_i} - 1) + \frac{\text{ACC}_{i-1}}{2} \cdot (X^{-a_i} + 1)$$

is a correct encryption of $X^{-a_i s_i}\mathbf{m}$.

Showing that its computational complexity does not differ much from the original algorithm is straightforward.

Rounding Noise. As before, determining the rounding noise of this blind rotation yields:

$$\sigma^2_{\text{round}(n)} = 2 \cdot \sigma^2_\epsilon \cdot (kN \cdot \sigma^2_{\mathbf{s_{rlwe}}} + 1) \cdot \sigma^2_{\mathbf{s}} \cdot n,$$

which is equal to the rounding noise introduced by the standard algorithm. In fact, contrarily to what was anticipated, using a blind rotation key encrypting a centered binary key does not reduce the rounding noise introduced by the algorithm, even though the variance of the key has been divided by two. To determine if there is any benefit in using this equation, it is necessary to further analyze its effects on noise growth.

5.2 Noise Due to the Keys

While computing an external product, the noise originally in the RGSW ciphertext is multiplied by the polynomials from the decomposition of the RLWE ciphertext. These noise terms are then summed. Here, we determine the variance of this noise.

Since the gadget decomposition used in the external product is built with respect to a vector $\mathbf{g} = (\beta, \ldots, \beta) \in \mathbb{Z}^\ell_q$ and the elements of an RLWE ciphertext are uniformly random, the coefficients of the polynomials of the gadget decomposition are uniformly sampled over $[\![\frac{-\beta}{2}, \frac{\beta}{2}]\!]$. Then, a coefficient $a_{i,j}$ of any polynomial $\mathbf{a_i}$ of the decomposition satisfies $\mu_{a_{i,j}} = 0$ and $\sigma^2(a_{i,j}) = \frac{(\beta+2)(\beta+1)}{12} \simeq \frac{\beta^2}{12}$.

Let $\hat{\mathbf{a}}$ be a polynomial from the gadget decomposition, and $\text{RLWE}_{\mathbf{s_{rlwe}}}(\mathbf{m}) = (\mathbf{a}, \mathbf{b})$ a ciphertext from the blind rotation key. Then, a polynomial multiplication also multiplies the noise term:

$$\hat{\mathbf{a}} \cdot (\mathbf{b} + \mathbf{a} \cdot \mathbf{s_{rlwe}}) = \hat{\mathbf{a}} \cdot \mathbf{m} + \hat{\mathbf{a}} \cdot \mathbf{e}.$$

Let $\mathbf{r}$ represent an error term after a polynomial multiplication, it satisfies:

$$\mathbf{r} = \hat{\mathbf{a}} \cdot \mathbf{e} = \sum_{j=0}^{2N-1} \sum_{i=0}^{j} \hat{a}_i e_{j-i} X^j \mod X^N + 1 = \sum_{i=0}^{N-1} r_i X^i.$$

Each r_u, $u \in [\![0, N-1]\!]$ is the sum or subtraction of N integer multiplications, therefore:

$$\mu(r_u) = N \cdot \mu(\hat{a}_s e_t) = N \cdot \mu(\hat{a}_s) \cdot \mu(e_t) = 0,$$

where a_s is a coefficient of $\hat{\mathbf{a}}$ and e_t is a coefficient of $\mathbf{e}$. Its variance is:

$$\begin{aligned}\sigma^2(r_u) &= N \cdot \sigma^2(\hat{a}_s e_t) = N \cdot \left(\sigma^2(\hat{a}_s) \cdot \sigma^2(e_t) + \sigma^2(\hat{a}_s) \cdot \mu(e_t)^2 + \sigma^2(e_t) \cdot \mu(\hat{a}_s)^2\right) \\ &= N \cdot \sigma^2(e_t) \cdot \sigma^2(\hat{a}_s).\end{aligned}$$

Since the variance σ_e^2 of e_t is given in parameter, the total noise due to the polynomial multiplication is:

$$\sigma^2(r_u) = N \cdot \sigma_e^2 \cdot \frac{\beta^2}{12}.$$

In an external product algorithm, there are $\ell(k+1)$ such multiplications. Now we can determine the variance of the noise introduced by blind rotation due to the polynomial multiplications with the blind rotation keys.

Standard Blind Rotation Algorithm. We denote $\sigma^2_{\text{keys}(i)}$ the variance of the noise introduced by the blind rotation keys after the multiplications and sums required by the external products. We remind that the standard blind rotation step is defined as:

$$\text{ACC}_i \longleftarrow (\text{ACC}_{i-1} \cdot X^{-a_i} - \text{ACC}_{i-1}) \boxdot \text{RGSW}_{\mathbf{s}_{\mathbf{rlwe}}}(s_i) + \text{ACC}_{i-1}.$$

Then, at each step of blind rotation the variance is updated as:

$$\sigma^2_{\text{keys}(i+1)} \leftarrow \ell \cdot (k+1) \cdot \sigma^2(r_u) + \sigma^2_{\text{keys}(i)} = \ell \cdot (k+1) \cdot N \cdot \sigma_e^2 \cdot \frac{\beta^2}{12} + \sigma^2_{\text{keys}(i)}.$$

This sequence follows an arithmetic progression with $\sigma^2_{\text{keys}(0)} = 0$, thus:

$$\sigma^2_{\text{keys}(n)} = n \cdot \ell \cdot (k+1) \cdot N \cdot \sigma_e^2 \cdot \frac{\beta^2}{12}.$$

New Blind Rotation Algorithm. With the new equation defined as:

$$\text{ACC}_i \longleftarrow \left(\text{RGSW}_{\mathbf{s}_{\mathbf{rlwe}}}\left(s_i - \frac{1}{2}\right) \boxdot \text{ACC}_{i-1}\right) \cdot (X^{-a_i} - 1) + \frac{\text{ACC}_{i-1}}{2} \cdot (X^{-a_i} + 1),$$

the variance of the noise introduced by the keys is updated as:

$$\hat{\sigma}^2_{\text{keys}(i+1)} \leftarrow 2\ell \cdot (k+1) \cdot \sigma^2(r_u) + \sigma^2_{1/2} + \sigma^2_{\text{keys}(i)},$$

where $\sigma^2_{1/2} \simeq \frac{kN}{4} \cdot \sigma^2_{\mathbf{s}_{\mathbf{rlwe}}} = \frac{kN}{16}$ is the error variance after a division by 2. Then:

$$\hat{\sigma}^2_{\text{keys}(n)} \simeq 2n \cdot \ell \cdot (k+1)N \cdot \sigma_e^2 \cdot \frac{\beta^2}{12},$$

which is twice the noise variance introduced by the standard blind rotation. This means that the best blind rotation algorithm with respect to noise growth is the standard algorithm, but with the blind rotation keys encrypted under a centered binary secret key.

5.3 Algorithms and Complexity

By taking into account the previous sections, we define a bootstrapping algorithm with reduced noise output.

Key Switching. The key switching key is still encrypted under a standard binary key $\mathbf{s}$, however it encrypts the centered binary key $\hat{\mathbf{s}}$:

$$\mathrm{KSK}_{\hat{\mathbf{s}}\to\mathbf{s}} = \left(\mathrm{LWE'}_{\mathbf{s}}\left(\hat{s}_1\right), \ldots, \mathrm{LWE'}_{\mathbf{s}}\left(\hat{s}_{kN}\right)\right).$$

Then, performing the standard key switching operation on an LWE ciphertext encrypted under the secret key $\hat{\mathbf{s}}$ outputs a ciphertext $\mathrm{LWE}_{\mathbf{s}}(m) \in \mathbb{Z}_q^{n+1}$ encrypted under $\mathbf{s} \leftarrow \mathcal{U}(\{0,1\}^n)$. Alternatively, one can use mean compensation, which produces the same amount of noise.

Modulus Switching. We modify the distribution of the encryption key $\mathbf{s}$ to obtain a centered key, perform modulus switching, then transform the ciphertext back into one encrypted under a standard binary key. This is equivalent to modulus switching with mean compensation.

Blind Rotation. For blind rotation (see Algorithm 2), we use the standard equation with the blind rotation key encrypted under a centered key. We use the **CenModRed** (see Algorithm 1) to reduce an RLWE ciphertext modulo q efficiently. The complexity of the new algorithm relatively to the standard blind

---

Algorithm 2: Centered binary key blind rotation

Data: $\mathrm{LWE}_{\mathbf{s}}(m) = (\mathbf{a}, b) \in \mathbb{Z}_{2N}^{n+1}$ an LWE encryption of a message $m \in \mathbb{Z}_p$ encrypted under $\mathbf{s} \leftarrow \mathcal{U}(\{0,1\}^n)$, $\mathrm{ACC} = \mathrm{RLWE}_{\mathbf{s_{rlwe}}}(\mathbf{lut})$ with $\mathbf{lut}$ a look-up table, $\mathrm{BRK} = (\mathrm{RGSW}_{\mathbf{s_{rlwe}}}(\mathbf{s_i}))_{i\in[\![1,n]\!]}$ a blind rotation key encrypted under $\mathbf{s_{rlwe}} \leftarrow \mathcal{U}(\{\frac{-1}{2}, \frac{1}{2}\}^{kN})$.

Result: $\mathrm{RLWE}_{\mathbf{s_{rlwe}}}(\mathbf{lut} \cdot X^{-(b+\mathbf{a}\cdot\mathbf{s})})$.

$\mathrm{ACC} \leftarrow \mathrm{ACC} \cdot X^{-b}$;

for $i = 0, i < N, i \leftarrow i+1$ **do**

  $\mathrm{ACC} \leftarrow \mathrm{RGSW}_{\mathbf{s_{rlwe}}}(s_i) \boxdot (\mathrm{ACC} \cdot (X^{-a_i} - 1)) + \mathrm{ACC}$;

  $\mathrm{ACC} \leftarrow$ **CenModRed**(ACC);

end

---

rotation is defined as:

$$V = \frac{(k+1)}{4\ell(k+1)\log(N) + ((\ell+1)(k+1) - 1)}.$$

Generally, $\log(N) \geq 9$ and in the worst case $k = \ell = 1$ yields:

$$V = \frac{2}{75} \simeq 2,7\%.$$

Therefore, the complexity analysis shows that this bootstrapping algorithm incurs at most a 2.7% computational overhead.

Sample Extraction. This algorithm remains unchanged.

In the next section, we illustrate the effect of using centered binary keys on the noise of bootstrapped ciphertexts using realistic parameters sets.

6 Evaluation of Centered Binary Keys in Practice

6.1 Standard Blind Rotation

The total noise variance of a bootstrapped ciphertext is:

$$\sigma^2_{\text{br}(n)} = \sigma^2_{\text{round}(n)} + \sigma^2_{\text{keys}(n)} \simeq \left(\frac{q}{\beta\ell}\right)^2 \cdot \sigma^2_\epsilon \cdot \frac{kN \cdot n}{4} + n \cdot \ell \cdot (k+1)N \cdot \sigma^2_e \cdot \frac{\beta^2}{12},$$

where the constants k, N, n, q, σ_e are all determined by security requirements. Also, σ_ϵ is a fixed constant as it is determined by rounding. Since $\epsilon \leftarrow \mathcal{U}\left(\left\{\frac{\beta}{q} \cdot i, i \in [\![\frac{-q}{2\beta}, \frac{q}{2\beta}]\!]\right\}^N\right)$, we have $\sigma^2_\epsilon \simeq \left(\frac{\beta}{q}\right)^2 \cdot \frac{\left(\frac{q}{2\beta}\right)^2}{3} = \frac{1}{12}$ and $\mu_\epsilon = 0$. Then, the noise variance reaches its minimum when $\beta = \left(\frac{c_1}{c_2}\right)^{\frac{1}{2\ell+2}}$ with $\frac{c_1}{c_2} = \frac{q^2 \cdot k}{8 \cdot \sigma^2_e \cdot (k+1)}$.

Using centered keys, the output noise variance is $\hat{\sigma}^2_{\text{br}(n)} = \frac{\sigma^2_{\text{round}(n)}}{2} + \sigma^2_{\text{keys}(n)}$ and similarly it is possible to determine its minimum. The results are compared in Table 2 with the parameters sets defined in [1], which are the most recent optimized parameters we could find.

Table 2. Comparison of the output noise from the previous state-of-the-art method and our method for three sets of parameters defined in [1].

Parameters	Set 1	Set 2	Set 3
n	750	797	796
N	2^9	2^{10}	2^{11}
k	3	1	1
q	2^{64}	2^{64}	2^{64}
p	2^2	2^3	2^4
β_{br}	2^{17}	2^{23}	2^{23}
ℓ_{br}	1	1	1
σ_{rlwe}	$2^{28.38}$	$2^{15.66}$	$2^{15.66}$
σ^2_{br}	$2^{109.20}$	$2^{97.36}$	$2^{97.44}$
(New) $\hat{\sigma}^2_{\text{br}}$	$\mathbf{2^{108.65}}$	$\mathbf{2^{96.61}}$	$\mathbf{2^{96.74}}$
$\frac{\hat{\sigma}^2_{\text{br}}}{\sigma^2_{\text{br}}}$	**0.68**	**0.59**	**0.62**

Table 2 shows that our method reduces the output noise variance of blind rotation by 32% to 41%. Since variances are additive, this noise reduction enables up to 1.6× more additions or subtractions before a new bootstrapping is required.

6.2 Blind Rotation with Key Unfolding

Blind Rotation with Key Unfolding (BRKU) [3,9] is a variant of the standard blind rotation algorithm that reduces by a factor 2 the number of external products required for blind rotation, at the expense of increasing the blind rotation key size by a factor $\frac{3}{2}$. This technique introduces a trade-off between memory usage and computational cost, and has been claimed in [3] to reduce the rounding noise by a factor of two. We revisit this claim and provide a more precise analysis of the noise behavior.

In BRKU, the blind rotation step is defined as:

$$\begin{aligned}\mathrm{ACC}_{i+1} \leftarrow \mathrm{ACC}_{i-1} \boxdot ((X^{-a_{i+1}-a_i} - 1) \cdot \mathrm{RGSW}_{\mathbf{s_{rlwe}}}(s_i s_{i+1}) \\ + (X^{-a_i} - 1) \cdot \mathrm{RGSW}_{\mathbf{s_{rlwe}}}(s_i(1 - s_{i+1})) \\ + (X^{-a_{i+1}} - 1) \cdot \mathrm{RGSW}_{\mathbf{s_{rlwe}}}(s_{i+1}(1 - s_i))) + \mathrm{ACC}_{i-1}.\end{aligned}$$

At each step, there are two cases that determine whether a rounding noise is added.

- If $s_i = s_{i+1} = 0$, then $s_i s_{i+1} = s_i(1-s_{i+1}) = s_{i+1}(1-s_i) = 0$ and no rounding error is added.
- If $s_i = 1$ or $s_{i+1} = 1$, then only one of the coefficients $s_i s_{i+1}, s(1 - s_{i+1})$ or $s_{i+1}(1 - s_i)$ is equal to 1 and the others are equal to 0. In this case, a single rounding error is added.

To analyze the rounding error, we introduce a random variable X that indicates whether a rounding error is added during a given step. Since $s \leftarrow \mathcal{U}(\{0,1\}^n)$, the random variable X satisfies: $P(X = 0) = \frac{1}{4}$, and $P(X = 1) = \frac{3}{4}$. Then, $\mu_X = \frac{3}{4}$ and $\sigma_X^2 = \frac{3}{16}$, and the variance of the rounding noise introduced by BRKU is:

$$\begin{aligned}\sigma^2_{\mathrm{round}(n/2)} &= \sigma_\epsilon^2 \cdot (N \cdot (\sigma^2_{\mathbf{s_{rlwe}}} + \mu^2_{\mathbf{s_{rlwe}}}) + 1) \cdot (\mu_X^2 + \sigma_X^2) \cdot \frac{n}{2} \\ &= \sigma_\epsilon^2 \cdot (N \cdot (\sigma^2_{\mathbf{s_{rlwe}}} + \mu^2_{\mathbf{s_{rlwe}}}) + 1) \cdot \frac{3}{4} \cdot \frac{n}{2}.\end{aligned}$$

Therefore, the variance is scaled by a factor $\frac{3}{4}$ rather than $\frac{1}{2}$ as claimed in [3]; consequently the rounding noise reduction is smaller than expected. Similarly to the analysis provided in the previous section, it is straightforward to show that the variance of the noise introduced by the keys is multiplied by a factor 3 compared to the standard blind rotation.

Table 3 summarizes the resulting noise levels for several parameters sets. The results show that using BRKU indeed increases the noise output of blind rotation compared to the values reported in Table 2. However, using centered binary keys may completely compensate this increase. This is due to the fact that the rounding noise often dominates the total noise value in realistic parameters regimes. Therefore, the smaller reduction of rounding noise due to centering the keys can outweigh the increase in key noise from using BRKU.

Table 3. Comparison of the noise introduced by BRKU with and without centered binary keys for three sets of parameters.

Parameters	Set 1	Set 2	Set 3
n	750	797	796
N	2^9	2^{10}	2^{11}
k	3	1	1
q	2^{64}	2^{64}	2^{64}
p	2^2	2^3	2^4
β_{br}	2^{17}	2^{23}	2^{23}
ℓ_{br}	1	1	1
σ_{rlwe}	$2^{28.38}$	$2^{15.66}$	$2^{15.66}$
σ^2_{br}	$2^{109.84}$	$2^{97.59}$	$2^{97.80}$
(New) $\boldsymbol{\beta_{\mathbf{br}}}$	$\mathbf{2^{16}}$	2^{23}	2^{22}
(New) $\hat{\sigma}^2_{\mathbf{br}}$	$\mathbf{2^{109.49}}$	$\mathbf{2^{97.16}}$	$\mathbf{2^{97.44}}$
$\frac{\hat{\sigma}^2_{\mathbf{br}}}{\sigma^2_{\mathbf{br}}}$	**0.78**	**0.74**	**0.77**

7 Conclusion

In this work, we have shown that computing the blind rotation of TFHE with RLWE ciphertexts encrypted under centered binary keys halves the variance of the rounding noise introduced by the algorithm. In practice, this yields a 32% to 41% reduction in noise variance and enables up to 1.6× more homomorphic operations, at the cost of a slight overhead of at most 2.7% compared to the original algorithm. We have also demonstrated that, contrary to the claim in [8], blind rotation can be performed using keys that encrypt centered key bits, although this approach results in higher noise than the standard algorithm.

We then reassessed the noise in the output of BRKU and showed that, although the technique increases the noise introduced by the keys, this can be compensated by using centered keys. In fact, if the two noise sources were perfectly balanced, key unfolding would always increase the noise in a bootstrapped ciphertext, but this does not necessarily happen in practice. Similarly, under this balanced assumption, halving the rounding noise would yield only a 25% reduction in the output noise. With practical parameters, however, centering the keys leads to varying outcomes depending on the dominant noise source: when the key noise dominates, the reduction can be as low as 23%, whereas when the rounding noise dominates, it can reach up to 41%.

These results suggest practical benefits in settings with high plaintext precision, where only a limited number of linear operations is permissible, or in circuits involving many linear operations. For example, the evaluation of neural networks considered in [3] requires the homomorphic computation of several weighted sums. In this case, reducing the noise in a bootstrapped ciphertext could enable the use of a wider range of weights or a larger number of neurons per layer without increasing the parameters sizes, which would otherwise reduce efficiency.

Disclosure of Interests. The authors have no competing interests to declare that are relevant to the content of this article.

References

1. Bergerat, L., Orfila, J.B., Roux-Langlois, A., Tap, S.: Accelerating TFHE with sorted bootstrapping techniques. In: Hanaoka, G., Yang, BY. (eds.) International Conference on the Theory and Application of Cryptology and Information Security, pp. 68–100. Springer, Singapore (2025). https://doi.org/10.1007/978-981-95-5122-4_3
2. Bon, N., Pointcheval, D., Rivain, M.: Optimized homomorphic evaluation of boolean functions. IACR Trans. Cryptogr. Hardw. Embed. Syst. **2024**(3), 302–341 (2024). https://doi.org/10.46586/TCHES.V2024.I3.302-341
3. Bourse, F., Minelli, M., Minihold, M., Paillier, P.: Fast homomorphic evaluation of deep discretized neural networks. Cryptology ePrint Archive, Paper 2017/1114 (2017). https://eprint.iacr.org/2017/1114
4. Chartier, P., Koskas, M., Lemou, M., Méhats, F.: Fully homomorphic encryption on large integers. Cryptology ePrint Archive, Paper 2024/155 (2024). https://eprint.iacr.org/2024/155
5. Chillotti, I., Gama, N., Georgieva, M., Izabachène, M.: TFHE: fast fully homomorphic encryption over the torus. J. Cryptol. **33**(1), 34–91 (2020). https://doi.org/10.1007/S00145-019-09319-X
6. Hwang, I., Lee, S., Min, S., Song, Y.: Efficient full domain functional bootstrapping from recursive LUT decomposition. In: Boura, C., Mashatan, A., Miri, A. (eds.) International Conference on Selected Areas in Cryptography, pp. 679–699. Springer, Cham (2025). https://doi.org/10.1007/978-3-032-10536-3_25
7. Micciancio, D., Polyakov, Y.: Bootstrapping in FHEW-like cryptosystems. In: WAHC '21: Proceedings of the 9th on Workshop on Encrypted Computing & Applied Homomorphic Cryptography, Virtual Event, Korea, 15 November 2021, pp. 17–28. WAHC@ACM (2021). https://doi.org/10.1145/3474366.3486924
8. de Ruijter, T., D'Anvers, J., Verbauwhede, I.: Don't be mean: reducing approximation noise in TFHE through mean compensation. IACR Cryptol. ePrint Arch, p. 809 (2025). https://eprint.iacr.org/2025/809
9. Zhou, T., Yang, X., Liu, L., Zhang, W., Ding, Y.: Faster bootstrapping with multiple addends. Cryptology ePrint Archive, Paper 2017/735 (2017). https://eprint.iacr.org/2017/735

Symmetric Cryptography and Implementation Security

Ciphertext-Only Attack on HALFLOOP-24

Marcus Dansarie[1,2], Gregor Leander[3], Shahram Rasoolzadeh[3], Lukas Stennes[4(✉)], and Cihangir Tezcan[5]

[1] Swedish Defence University, Stockholm, Sweden
marcus.Dansarie@fhs.se
[2] University of Skövde, Skövde, Sweden
[3] Ruhr University Bochum, Bochum, Germany
{gregor.leander,shahram.rasoolzadeh}@rub.de
[4] cryptosolutions GmbH, Essen, Germany
lukas@cryptosolutions.de
[5] Middle East Technical University, Ankara, Turkey
cihangir@metu.edu.tr

Abstract. We present a full key-recovery ciphertext-only attack on the tweakable block cipher HALFLOOP-24 which is standardized by the US military and NATO for use in the Automatic Link Establishment protocol for high-frequency radio. Our attack is based on the observation that the probability-one differential, which was used for known- and chosen-plaintext attacks in prior works, can be viewed as a probability-p differential when the plaintexts are unknown, where p is the network-dependent probability that plaintext differences line up with tweak differences. Further, due to the fact that the tweak is publicly known, the specific values of the plaintexts are not necessary to identify the correct key. Our attack has a theoretical complexity of roughly 2^{65} encryptions, given a favorable ALE network setup that allows us to collect enough suitable ciphertexts. To give a hardware-grounded estimate of the cost of the whole attack, we provide optimized CPU and GPU implementations.

Keywords: HF Radio · ALE · HALFLOOP-24 · Differential Cryptanalysis

1 Introduction

The HALFLOOP family of tweakable block ciphers is used in the Automatic Link Establishment (ALE) protocol in high-frequency (HF) radio. HF radio provides long-range, beyond-line-of-sight communication via ionospheric propagation, which is useful when satellite or terrestrial infrastructure is unavailable or degraded. ALE automatically selects the best HF channel to set up and maintain a reliable link. Although HF radio allows for communication across large distances, it has the disadvantage of having a rather small bandwidth. Due to this small bandwidth, the ALE protocols use short messages, as short as 24 bits.

N. El Mrabet et al. (Eds.): AFRICACRYPT 2026, LNCS 16832, pp. 187–209, 2026.
https://doi.org/10.1007/978-3-032-31130-6_8

HALFLOOP, standardized in [4], is a tweakable block cipher family used to secure ALE linking messages in modern HF systems, including in military contexts. All HALFLOOP ciphers use a state-of-the-art key length of 128 bits, a 64-bit tweak, and are essentially scaled-down versions of the AES-128. More concretely, there are HALFLOOP-24, HALFLOOP-48, and HALFLOOP-96 that act on 24-, 48-, and 96-bit blocks, respectively. However, as recent works have shown, HALFLOOP-24 is insecure in several relevant settings.

The first attacks against HALFLOOP-24 were introduced in [3]. However, their data complexity was too high to be considered practical. This was changed by the attacks in [6] which showed that, in fact, two hours of intercepted communication (plaintexts and ciphertexts) are enough to find the secret key. The ciphertext-only attack against HALFLOOP-24 presented here was first outlined in [10], the PhD thesis of one of the authors of this work.

From a cryptographic perspective, these attacks are already devastating. However, in a real-world scenario, the requirement of roughly two hours of intercepted communication with known plaintext may be difficult to meet under typical conditions. Although the long range of HF radio makes it easy to capture ciphertext at scale, obtaining the corresponding plaintext generally requires more targeted access and may therefore be less threatening in practice.

As we show in this work, HALFLOOP-24 is insecure even in a *ciphertext-only* setting under the ALE traffic assumptions considered here.

Our Contribution. We present a ciphertext-only attack against HALFLOOP-24 as used in ALE. Given roughly 8 h worth of intercepted ciphertext in a high-traffic scenario, our attack recovers the complete secret key in a time of about 2^{65} encryptions using 20 MiB of memory.

For this, we make use of the differential used in the previous work. Our cryptanalytic contribution is viewing this as a probabilistic differential over unknown plaintexts. The second contribution is implementing and benchmarking the attack on CPUs and GPUs in a lab setting.

Based on the CPU results, we argue that a supercomputer could run the attack within a year. This cost appears within reach of well-resourced adversaries, such as state-level attackers, under the assumed traffic model.

Moreover, we optimized the attack for GPUs. With our optimized implementation, 102 RTX 4090 GPUs can perform this attack in a year, if the attacker is willing to accept a 50% probability of success. We elaborate below on the exact details of the potential tradeoffs of time vs success probability. Table 1 gives an overview of our new attacks on HALFLOOP-24 and the prior art.

We emphasize that ciphertext-only attacks are rare in modern cryptography. Indeed, most practical ciphertext-only attacks reduce to brute force searches against ciphers with short keys. For example, the practical brute force attacks of [12] on A5/3, SPECK, and TEA3 exploit key sizes of 64, 72, or 80 bits. In contrast, brute forcing HALFLOOP-24 is infeasible even for an adversary with effectively unbounded monetary resources, as it uses 128-bit keys. Unlike these examples, our ciphertext-only attacks recover 80 bits of the secret key using a

Table 1. Overview of the attacks on HALFLOOP-24.

Setting	Time	Data	Memory	Reference
COA-ALE	2^{65} Enc.	8 h	20 MiB	Sect. 3
COA-ALE	2^{87} Enc.	1000 years	2^{63}	[3]
KPA-ALE	2^{56} Enc.	541 years	2 MiB	[3]
KPA-ALE	2^{48} Enc.	2 h	5 GiB	[6]
CCA*	2^{10} Enc.	2^{10}	negligible	[3]
CPA	2^{56} Enc.	6	5 GiB	[6]
CPA	2^{48} Enc. + 2^{48} LUT	8	5 GiB	[6]

CCA: Chosen-Ciphertext Attack, COA: Ciphertext-Only Attack,
CPA: Chosen-Plaintext Attack, KPA: Known-Plaintext Attack,
*: The CCA attack in [3] restores only the first 24-bit round key.

probability-p differential. The remaining 48 bits are then found by brute force at negligible cost.

Impact on the Standard. In May 2025, the standard was updated [5]. In addition to some editorial changes, this update changed the number of rounds. Before, it said [4, p. 354]:

```
The HALFLOOP algorithm uses ten rounds: Nr = 10.
```

Now, the updated standard states [5, p. 361]:

```
Nr rounds, where Nr = 10 for HALFLOOP-96, Nr = 20 for HALFLOOP-48,
and Nr = 40 for HALFLOOP-24.
```

That is, the change *quadrupled* the number of rounds for HALFLOOP-24. Although not explicitly stated, it seems likely that this is due to the results published in [3,6].

While revising a standard can be done relatively quickly on paper, actually rolling out the change requires updating and redeploying cryptographic implementations across a large, heterogeneous installed base of devices, often a far slower, operationally constrained process. If deployment follows typical slow upgrade cycles for heterogeneous radio equipment, vulnerable implementations may persist for some time. Thus, beyond its interest as a rare ciphertext-only attack, our results are likely to be of practical relevance. Furthermore, the increased number of rounds does *not* protect against the generic attack discussed in [3,6] due to the fact that the tweak is still simply XORed to the master key.

Related Works. Beyond the cryptanalysis of HALFLOOP-24, several works have investigated the security of the larger versions HALFLOOP-48 and HALFLOOP-96, in particular in the related-key model. In addition, [6] presents reduced-round Demirci-Selçuk meet-in-the-middle attacks in the single-key setting, further illustrating structural weaknesses of the design even without related-key assumptions. Lin and Sun [7], Liu and Sun [8], and Shi *et al.* [9] analyze the structural properties arising from the keytweak combination and derive related-key distinguishers and key-recovery attacks under various assumptions. These results indicate that the security margin of the HALFLOOP design is sensitive not only to the reduced block size, but also to the specific way the tweak is injected into the key schedule.

In a broader design context, the weaknesses of SODARK, the predecessor of HALFLOOP, were identified by Dansarie [2]. Since SODARK employs the same tweak format and combines key and tweak by simple XOR, these findings highlight inherent structural issues that persist in the design lineage. Taken together, the existing literature suggests that the interaction between key schedule and tweak handling constitutes a recurring attack surface within these ciphers.

Structure of the Paper. We explain our notation and the inner workings of HALFLOOP-24 in Sect. 2. In Sect. 3, we first recap the attack from [6] and then show how it can be turned into a ciphertext-only attack. To ease the understanding of our attack, we start with a naive and non-optimal version, which we then improve. We discuss the implementation of our attack in Sect. 4.

2 Preliminaries

In this paper, we follow the notation established in [6]. We denote the finite field with two elements $\{0, 1\}$ by $\mathbb{F}_2$, and write $\mathbb{F}_{2^n}$ for the finite field with 2^n elements and $\mathbb{F}_2^n$ for the vector space of dimension $n \in \mathbb{N}$ over $\mathbb{F}_2$. We write $\oplus$ for the component-wise addition in $\mathbb{F}_2^n$ which we call *XOR*. For two vectors $x, x' \in \mathbb{F}_2^n$, Δx is the *difference* $x \oplus x'$. The concatenation of two vectors a and b is denoted as $a \,\|\, b$.

In line with [6], we refer to a tuple of plaintext, tweak, and ciphertext (p, t, c) as *plaintext-tweak-ciphertext tuple* and call a pair of such tuples $((p, t, c), (p', t', c'))$, related by a fixed XOR-difference, a *differential pair*.

Recall the basic differential properties of the AES S-box $S\colon \mathbb{F}_2^8 \to \mathbb{F}_2^8$, also stated in [6]: For a non-zero input difference $\delta \in \mathbb{F}_2^8$ there are 127 possible output differences γ. For 126 of those, the equation $S(x) \oplus S(x \oplus \delta) = \gamma$ has two solutions in x. For each δ, there is one and only one γ such that the equation has four solutions in x. We denote a possible transition of δ to γ through S by $\delta \xrightarrow{S} \gamma$, i.e.,

$$\delta \xrightarrow{S} \gamma \quad \Leftrightarrow \quad \exists\; x \text{ such that } S(x) \oplus S(x \oplus \delta) = \gamma.$$

When we apply S in parallel to a vector $x \in \mathbb{F}_2^{k \cdot 8}$, we write $\mathtt{SB}(x)$.

2.1 Description of HALFLOOP-24 and Related Notation

The family of HALFLOOP tweakable block ciphers, HALFLOOP-24, HALFLOOP-48 and HALFLOOP-96, is specified in the US military standard 188–141 [4]. In this paper, we are only concerned with HALFLOOP-24. For the sake of self-completeness, we give a brief description of it based on the description in [6].

HALFLOOP-24 uses a 128-bit key k and a 64-bit tweak t. It originally consisted of 10 rounds which we are analyzing in this work. However, as discussed in the introduction, an updated version of the standard mandates 40 rounds [5]. Each round is built up of four steps: AddRoundKey, SubBytes, RotateRows and MixColumns. These components are very similar to the building blocks of AES and are explained in detail in the following. In the last round there is no MixColumns operation. Instead, there is an extra round key addition.

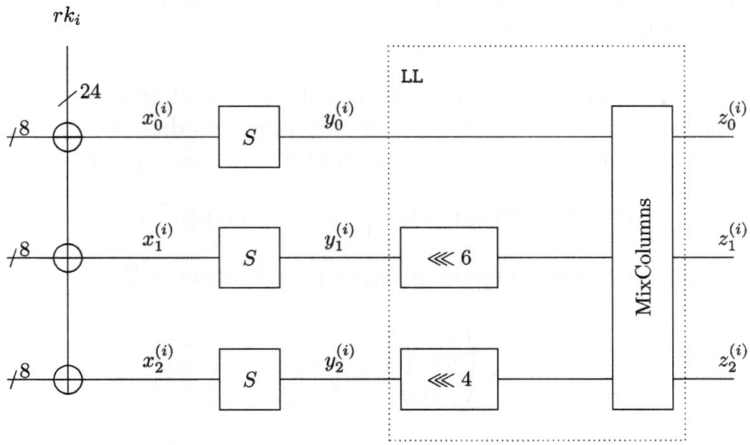

Fig. 1. HALFLOOP-24 round function.

State. Similar to AES, the state of HALFLOOP-24 is represented as a matrix of 8-bit cells. That is, the 24-bit state is represented as a 3×1 matrix, i.e., a single column containing 3 bytes.

For convenience, throughout the paper, we denote the state immediately after the addition of the round key with the letter x, the state after the S-boxes by y and the state after the linear layer by z. Moreover, in the partial decryption phase of our key-recovery attack, we conceptually interchange the MixColumns operation of the i-th round with the AddRoundKey operation using $rk^{(i+1)}$ from the subsequent round. Since MixColumns is linear, this reordering is equivalent to applying a modified round key. In this context, we denote by $v^{(i)}$ the state obtained after the addition of the modified round key but before the application of MixColumns.

Furthermore, we use the superscript to illustrate the round, e.g., $x^{(0)}$ denotes the XOR of the plaintext p and the very first round key $rk^{(0)}$ and $x^{(10)}$ corresponds to the ciphertext. At times, we are only interested in some bytes of a state or a round key. Then, we use the subscript to denote the corresponding cell. Thus, we denote the state x of HALFLOOP-24 with (x_0, x_1, x_2).

AddRoundKey. The round keys are represented in the same way as the state and the key addition is simply the bitwise XOR of state and key.

SubBytes. We apply the 8-bit AES S-box S to each cell of the state.

RotateRows. It corresponds to ShiftRows in AES. In contrast to ShiftRows, the rotation does not take place at the cell level but at the bit level. The first byte of the state is not changed. The second byte is rotated to the left by 6 bit positions and the third by 4 bit positions. Conceptually, this could also be merged into having three different S-boxes.

MixColumns. For this operation, each column is treated as a polynomial over $\mathbb{F}_{2^8}$. We multiply with $c(\alpha) = \alpha^2 + 2\alpha + 9$ and reduce modulo $\alpha^3 + 1$. This linear mapping is MDS. More concretely, for a state $x = (x_0, x_1, x_2)$, we compute

$$(\alpha^2 + 2\alpha + 9) \cdot (x_0\alpha^2 + x_1\alpha + x_2) \bmod (\alpha^3 + 1)$$

which corresponds to the following matrix multiplication in $\mathbb{F}_{2^8}$:

$$\begin{pmatrix} 9 & 1 & 2 \\ 2 & 9 & 1 \\ 1 & 2 & 9 \end{pmatrix} \times \begin{pmatrix} x_0 \\ x_1 \\ x_2 \end{pmatrix} \tag{1}$$

The linear layer of the round functions (excluding the last round) is the composition of the RotateRows and MixColumns operations. For the description of our attacks, we call the combined linear layer LL.

Key Schedule. First, the 64-bit tweak t is added to the most significant 64 bits of the key k. For ease of use, we split the 128-bit key k into two parts: k' the most significant half and k'' the least significant, i.e., $k = (k' \parallel k'')$ and the tweak is XORed to k'. Then, the same Feistel network as in the AES-128 key schedule is used to derive the round keys. That is, we start with $(k' \oplus t \parallel k'')$ for the first 128 bits of the round keys. Then, we apply one round of the AES-128 key schedule to derive the next 128 bits and so forth. However, since the round keys are only of size 24 bits, we do *not* need the full AES-128 key expansion. More concretely, for 10-round HALFLOOP-24, we only need 264 round key bits. This means that the tweak has only linear influence on the round keys except for the very last byte, which was already observed in [3].

Round Key Normalization. As usual in attacks on block ciphers, in our attacks, we are guessing parts of the round keys to then obtain information about other parts of the key. For HALFLOOP, those round keys depend on the tweak which is time-dependent. This means that the round keys are different for each considered ciphertext, even when the secret key is fixed.

However, as shown in [3], the influence of the tweak on the round keys is (mostly) linear. Hence, we can easily guess a round key and then adapt it based on the tweak for partial decryption. Once we obtain information about another part of the key, we undo this adaptation there, i.e., we *normalize* the round key before, for example, incrementing a counter for the key. A small exception is the very last byte of the last round key $rk^{(10)}$. Here, the influence of the tweak also depends on $rk^{(9)}$. This is not a problem as we always guess $rk^{(10)}$ and $rk^{(9)}$ at the same time.

Throughout the rest of the paper, we will deliberately omit the round key normalization as it significantly and unnecessarily complicates the presentation of our attacks. The round key normalization must be (and, of course, is) incorporated in the implementation of our attacks.

2.2 ALE Network Model

We adapt the same ALE network attack scenario as used in [3,6]. We describe it briefly here, but refer to those two papers for details about the ALE message format and how the attacks are adapted to it. While ALE radios can exchange many types of messages, we only consider link establishment calls, the most common type of message sent in ALE networks, in our analysis. One such message frame has three 24-bit words that each consist of a 3-bit type field followed by a callsign in the form of three 7-bit characters. The first two of these words are always identical. A requirement for the attacks presented in this paper as well as in [3,6] is that the two plaintexts in each pair differ only in the last byte, and that the tweaks differ only in the sixth byte with the same difference. As shown in [3,6], since not all 7-bit characters are allowed by the protocol, if the callsigns are assigned uniformly at random, we expect two callsigns to differ only in the last byte with probability $2^{-17.30}$. In [3], an online source [1] was used to show that the distribution of callsigns in unencrypted ALE networks is often non-random. In one Swedish ALE network, the probability that two randomly selected pairs of callsigns will differ only in the least significant byte is $2^{-10.22}$.

Tweaks in HALFLOOP are generated from the current time, word number in the frame, and transmission frequency. Those values can be directly observed by any attacker that is able to collect the ciphertexts. Due to the tweak format, two frames sent on the same frequency in a 16-minute window on the same second modulo 4 will have tweaks that differ only in the sixth byte, as required for our attack. In a 16-minute window with n three-word frames, there will be approximately $\left\lfloor \frac{n^2}{8} - \frac{n}{2} \right\rfloor$ words with the required tweak difference [3].

We adopt the favorable, but real-world setting of [3,6]. That is, we work with probability $2^{-10.22}$ for the suitable difference and adopt the same traffic rate as in previous papers, with one ALE call every 10 s. This means that each 16-minute time window contains 96 calls and is expected to yield, on average, $\frac{96^2}{8} - \frac{96}{2} = 1104$ pairs with the required tweak difference.

3 The Ciphertext-Only Attack

To ease the understanding of our new ciphertext-only attack, we first recap the (naive version of the) chosen-plaintext attack from [6]. We then show how this can be turned into a ciphertext-only attack. After this, we make improvements to enhance its efficiency.

3.1 Recap of the Naive Chosen-Plaintext Attack From [6]

As it was already observed in [3], for a differential pair of plaintexts and tweaks $((p, t), (p', t'))$ and a non-zero difference $\delta \in \mathbb{F}_2^8$ with

$$\Delta p = (0, 0, \delta) \quad and \quad \Delta t = (0, 0, \delta, 0, 0, 0, 0, 0),$$

it holds that the state difference after six rounds is $\Delta x^{(6)} = (\delta, 0, 0)$. In other words, there is a probability-one differential over six rounds of HALFLOOP-24. The reason for this lies in the key schedule of HALFLOOP-24 that we depict in Fig. 2. The tweak is simply added to the master key, making the tweak and plaintext differences cancel each other when the round key $rk^{(0)}$ is added to the plaintext. Hence, there is no state difference until $rk^{(6)}$ is added.

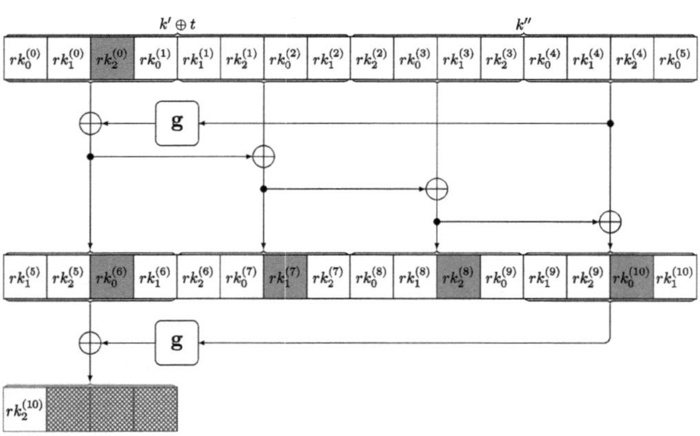

Fig. 2. Key schedule of HALFLOOP-24 together with the effect of tweak difference $(0, 0, \delta, 0, 0, 0, 0, 0)$ adapted from [3]. The orange blocks depict the round key bytes that will be affected by the tweak difference. Note that the induced difference in each of these bytes are the same as δ. Taken from [6].

This allows for a straightforward differential attack. Given differential pairs as above, we guess 80 bits of key material, namely $rk^{(10)}, rk^{(9)}, rk^{(8)}$ and the first byte of $\mathtt{LL}^{-1}(rk^{(7)})$. This is sufficient to check $\Delta x^{(6)} \stackrel{?}{=} (\delta, 0, 0)$ to filter the key guesses. As discussed in [6], three differential pairs are sufficient to narrow the search space down to, on average, 256 80-bit candidates. After this, we can apply the same final brute force step as in [3] to find the master key.

Of course, the run time of this, which is dominated by the 2^{80} partial decryptions, is far from optimal and greatly improved in [6]. We do not go into the details of the improvements here, but instead present the observations that allow us to make this attack ciphertext-only.

3.2 Naive Ciphertext-Only Attack

A *theoretical* ciphertext-only attack was already presented in [3]. The fundamental insight for this, as well as our new and more efficient attack, is that we do not have to rely on the specific values of the plaintexts. For the first phase of our attacks, which resembles differential cryptanalysis, we rely solely on the differences of the plaintexts. As the plaintexts are small and not distributed uniformly, it is sufficient to wait for the specific differences to occur by chance. For our analysis, analogously to [3,6], we use the probability $2^{-10.22}$ that was observed for the (unencrypted) Swedish ALE network. For the second phase, i.e., the brute force of the remaining key bits, we can rely on the same fact. That is, we can discard wrong key guesses based solely on the *structure* of the plaintexts.

To make the attack described above ciphertext-only, we essentially only need one crucial observation: Instead of using the probability-one differential starting with the plaintext difference $\Delta p = (0, 0, \delta)$, when we do not know the plaintexts, we can consider it as a differential with probability $\Pr[\Delta p = (0, 0, \delta)] = 2^{-10.22}$. Here, as before, we only consider the data with $\Delta t = (0, 0, \delta, 0, 0, 0, 0, 0)$ where $\delta \in \mathbb{F}_2^8 \setminus \{0\}$. We assume that we have d such pairs $((t, c), (t', c'))$. We determine the specific value of d in our analysis below.

Conceptually, our attack resembles a plain differential attack. First, we initialize a list of counters $C \in \mathbb{N}^{2^{80}}$ to zero. Then, for all

$$\tilde{k} = (rk^{(10)}, rk^{(9)}, rk^{(8)}, \mathtt{LL}^{-1}(rk^{(7)})_0) \in \mathbb{F}_2^{80}$$

and all d pairs, we compute the state difference $\Delta x^{(6)}$. If $\Delta x^{(6)} = (\delta, 0, 0)$, we increase the counter $C[\tilde{k}]$. After this, we take the guesses with the highest counters as candidates for the correct partial key and continue our attack the same way as in [6].

Complexity Analysis. In terms of data complexity, we argue that less than 2 h of traffic is sufficient. This data requirement is, non-coincidentally, the same as in [6]. Intuitively speaking, the increased demand for data triggered by the lower probability of the differential is countered by the fact that we now consider *all* pairs with a good tweak difference and not only the ones with a good plaintext difference. More precisely, the expected counter value for the correct guess is

$$d \cdot (2^{-10.22} \cdot 1 + (1 - 2^{-10.22}) \cdot 2^{-24}) \approx d \cdot 2^{-10.22}.$$

Here, $2^{-10.22}$ is the probability that Δp is of the correct form, and 2^{-24} is the assumed probability that $\Delta x^{(6)} = (\delta, 0, 0)$ occurs by chance for any other input difference.

We expect a counter value of $d \cdot 2^{-10.22}$ when guessing the right key value, while for wrong guesses, the average value will be $d \cdot 2^{-24}$. That means that the signal-to-noise ratio of our attack is extremely high: $2^{24} \cdot 2^{-10.22} = 2^{13.78}$.

Moreover, assuming that the counters follow independent binomial distributions, we estimate the expected number of incorrect guesses whose counter reaches at least τ as

$$2^{80} \cdot \left(1 - \sum_{j=0}^{\tau-1} \binom{d}{j} 2^{-24j} \left(1 - 2^{-24}\right)^{d-j}\right).$$

We will discard those by brute forcing the remaining 48 key bits for all 80-bit candidates with a counter value of at least τ. The attack succeeds if the counter value for the correct key reaches τ. The probability of this is

$$1 - \sum_{j=0}^{\tau-1} \sum_{k=0}^{j} \frac{d!}{k!\,(j-k)!\,(d-j)!} \cdot 2^{-17k} \cdot 2^{-10.22 \cdot (j-k)} \cdot \left(1 - 2^{-17} - 2^{-10.22}\right)^{d-j},$$

as each pair yields either a *wrong-pair hit* with probability $128 \cdot 2^{-24} = 2^{-17}$, a *right-pair hit* with probability $2^{-10.22}$, or no hit otherwise. For fixed j total hits and k wrong-pair hits, the multinomial coefficient counts the number of ways to place these outcomes among d trials. The sum gives the probability of having less than τ hits, and we then take the complement.

Like in [3,6], we assume a high-traffic scenario where each 16-minute traffic bin contains 96 ALE calls, one every ten seconds. Thus, we expect each such bin to yield about 1104 differential pairs with a suitable tweak difference. When we collect data for $16 \cdot s$ minutes, it is then expected that the number of differential pairs is equal to $d = s \cdot 1104$.

Choosing, for example, $s = 7$ and $\tau = 6$, we get a valid attack with a success probability of roughly 64%. Then, the run time is dominated by the 2^{80} partial decryptions and the memory is dominated by the 2^{80} counters. Of course, this is far from practical. However, as indicated, the above description is only *conceptual*. We improve the attack analogously to [6] in the following section and then also refine the analysis.

3.3 Improvement with Heavy Precomputation

As an intermediate step, we improve the attack using a similar precomputation technique presented in [6]. Then, it suffices to guess $(rk^{(10)}, rk^{(9)}) \in \mathbb{F}_2^{48}$. For each of the d differential pairs, this guess will then suggest a list of roughly 2^8 candidates for $(rk^{(8)}, \mathtt{LL}^{-1}(rk^{(7)})_0) \in \mathbb{F}_2^{32}$. Therefore, only a list of $C \in \mathbb{N}^{2^{32}}$ counters is sufficient.

Algorithm 1. Recover $(rk^{(10)}, rk^{(9)}, rk^{(8)}, \mathtt{LL}^{-1}(rk^{(7)})_0)$ (with precomputation).

Input d differential pairs $((t_i, c_i), (t'_i, c'_i))$ with tweak differences $\Delta t_i = (0, 0, \delta_i, 0, 0, 0, 0, 0)$

Output a list of candidates for $(rk^{(10)}, rk^{(9)}, rk^{(8)}, \mathtt{LL}^{-1}(rk^{(7)})_0)$

Initialize empty table T ▷ precomputation, cf. Eq. (2)

for each $\delta \in \mathbb{F}_2^8 \setminus \{0\}$ **and each** $y_6 \in \mathbb{F}_2^{24}$ **do**

  Compute $y'^{(6)} = \mathtt{SB}\left(\mathtt{SB}^{-1}(y^{(6)}) \oplus (\delta, 0, 0)\right)$.

  for each $\kappa \in \mathbb{F}_2^8$ **do** ▷ $\kappa = \mathtt{LL}^{-1}(rk^{(7)})_0$

    Compute $z^{(7)} = \mathtt{LL} \circ \mathtt{SB} \circ \mathtt{LL}(y^{(6)} \oplus (\kappa, 0, 0))$.

    Compute $z'^{(7)} = \mathtt{LL} \circ \mathtt{SB}(\mathtt{LL}(y'^{(6)} \oplus (\kappa, 0, 0)) \oplus (0, \delta, 0))$.

    if $z^{(7)} < z'^{(7)}$ **then** ▷ compress T

      Add $(z^{(7)}, \kappa)$ to $T_\delta[z^{(7)} \oplus z'^{(7)}]$.

$K \leftarrow \{\}$ ▷ the list of key candidates

for each $rk^{(10)} \in \mathbb{F}_2^{24}$ **and each** $rk^{(9)} \in \mathbb{F}_2^{24}$ **do**

  $C \leftarrow (0, \ldots, 0) \in \mathbb{N}^{2^{32}}$ ▷ initializing the counters

  for each data pair (t_i, c_i) and (t'_i, c'_i) **do**

    Compute the corresponding $x^{(8)}$ and $x'^{(8)}$.

    for each $(z^{(7)}, \kappa)$ in $T_{\delta_i}[x^{(8)} \oplus x'^{(8)}]$ **do**

      Increase $C[z^{(7)} \oplus x^{(8)}, \kappa]$ and $C[z^{(7)} \oplus x'^{(8)}, \kappa]$.

  for each $rk^{(8)} \in \mathbb{F}_2^{24}$ **and each** $\kappa \in \mathbb{F}_2^8$ **do.**

    if $C[rk^{(8)}, \kappa] \geq \tau$ **then**

      Add $(rk^{(10)}, rk^{(9)}, rk^{(8)}, \kappa)$ to K.

return K

More precisely, for every non-zero $\delta \in \mathbb{F}_2^8$ (the difference in active byte of plaintext and tweak) we precompute a table

$$T_\delta[\Delta x^{(8)}] := \left\{ (z^{(7)}, \kappa) \;\middle|\; \begin{array}{l} \Delta x^{(8)} = z^{(7)} \oplus z'^{(7)} \text{ where} \\ y^{(6)} = \mathtt{LL}^{-1} \circ \mathtt{SB}^{-1} \circ \mathtt{LL}^{-1}(z^{(7)}) \oplus (\kappa, 0, 0), \\ y'^{(6)} = \mathtt{SB}\left(\mathtt{SB}^{-1}(y^{(6)}) \oplus (\delta, 0, 0)\right), \\ z'^{(7)} = \mathtt{LL} \circ \mathtt{SB}(\mathtt{LL}(y'^{(6)} \oplus (\kappa, 0, 0)) \oplus (0, \delta, 0)) \end{array} \right\} \quad (2)$$

which contains all the combinations of $z^{(7)}$ and the first byte of $\mathtt{LL}^{-1}(rk^{(7)})$, denoted by κ, for which we might obtain $\Delta x^{(8)}$. Clearly, if $(z^{(7)}, \kappa)$ is in $T_\delta[\Delta x^{(8)}]$, then $(z^{(7)} \oplus \Delta x^{(8)}, \kappa)$ is as well. Hence, we can compress T by only storing the element with the smaller first entry. As stated above, the expected size $|T_\delta[\Delta x^{(8)}]|$ (without considering removing trivial duplicate solutions) is roughly 2^8 which follows from the analysis in [6]. Other than that, the attack is basically the same as in the previous section. So, in a nutshell, we guess $(rk^{(10)}, rk^{(9)}) \in \mathbb{F}_2^{48}$ and use it to precompute $\Delta x^{(8)}$. We then do a look-up in the table T and increase the corresponding counters. Partial keys with counters higher than a given threshold are kept as candidates. We give the complete attack in Algorithm 1.

The correctness of the attack is not affected by the time-memory trade-off. This also means that the analysis for the number of differential pairs d and the threshold τ is essentially the same as before. Regarding the complexity of attack, we need to compute $d \cdot 2^{48}$ times two-round pair decryptions and look-ups into a table of approximate size

$$(2^8 - 1) \cdot 2^{24} \cdot 2^7 \cdot 32 \text{ bits} \approx 2.2 \text{ TB}.$$

Furthermore, we need 2^{32} bytes for the counters. In practice, the look-ups would be the bottleneck, especially for a parallelized implementation. We refrain from a more thorough analysis, because we present the precomputation solely as an intermediate step towards our memoryless version of the improved attack.

3.4 Improvement Without Heavy Precomputation

To eliminate heavy precomputation, we can again follow the lines of [6]. In short, we guess $rk^{(10)}$ and $rk^{(9)}$ to compute backward as before. Instead of using the large table T to find candidates for $rk^{(8)}$ and one byte of $rk^{(7)}$, we use small tables to determine all possible input differences of the S-boxes in Round 8, i.e., candidates for $\Delta x^{(7)}$. With this, we have both the input and output differences and can determine candidates for $y^{(7)}$ which in turn implies candidates for $rk^{(8)}$ for which we increase the corresponding counters. We give a graphical overview of the attack in Fig. 3, the complete attack in Algorithm 2, and more details below.

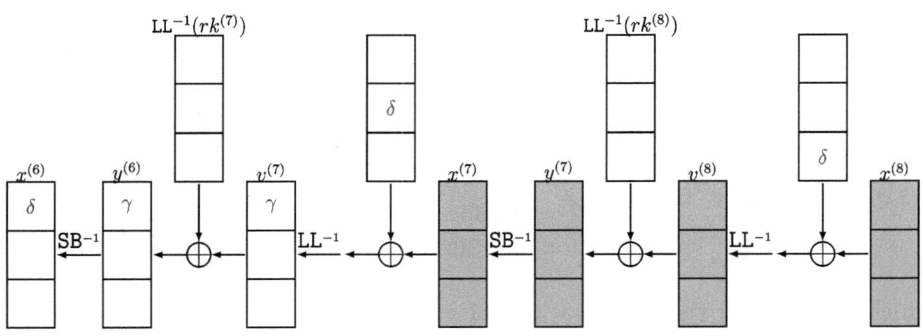

Fig. 3. Overview of the attack after guessing (rk_{10}, rk_9) and partially decrypting the last two rounds. Taken from [6].

To find candidates for $\Delta x^{(7)}$, we use the fact that, given δ, the four values $\Delta y_0^{(6)}, \Delta x_0^{(7)}, \Delta x_1^{(7)}$ and $\Delta x_2^{(7)}$ are pairwise in a one-to-one correspondence because $\Delta y_1^{(6)} = \Delta y_2^{(6)} = 0$. Hence, we can precompute look-up tables for the following process for $i \in \{0, 1, 2\}$: Given $\Delta y_i^{(7)}$, determine all possible input differences $\Delta x_i^{(7)}$. Use this and δ to compute $\gamma := \Delta y_0^{(6)}$ by partially reverting the

Algorithm 2. Recover $(rk^{(10)}, rk^{(9)}, rk^{(8)}, \mathtt{LL}^{-1}(rk^{(7)})_0)$ (with less memory).

Input d differential pairs $((t_i, c_i), (t'_i, c'_i))$ with tweak differences $\Delta t = (0, 0, \delta_i, 0, 0, 0, 0, 0)$
Output a list of candidates for $(rk^{(10)}, rk^{(9)}, rk^{(8)}, \mathtt{LL}^{-1}(rk^{(7)})_0)$

Precompute D, L_0, L_1, L_2. ▷ see Eqs. (3) and (5)

function ValidateRk8$(rk^{(10)}, rk^{(9)}, rk^{(8)})$
    $C' \leftarrow (0, \ldots, 0) \in \mathbb{N}^{2^8}$
    for each data pair (t_i, c_i) and (t'_i, c'_i) **do**
        Compute $v^{(7)}$ and $v'^{(7)}$.
        if $\Delta v_0^{(7)} \neq 0$ and $\Delta v_1^{(7)} = 0$ and $\Delta v_2^{(7)} = 0$ **then**
            for each $\kappa \in \mathbb{F}_2^8$ **do**
                if $S^{-1}[v_0^{(7)} \oplus \kappa] \oplus S^{-1}[v_0'^{(7)} \oplus \kappa] = \delta$ **then**
                    Increment $C'[rk_0^{(7)}]$.
    return $\arg\max(C'), \max(C')$

$K \leftarrow \{\}$ ▷ the list of key candidates
for each $rk^{(10)} \in \mathbb{F}_2^{24}$ **and each** $rk^{(9)} \in \mathbb{F}_2^{24}$ **do**
    $C \leftarrow (0, \ldots, 0) \in \mathbb{N}^{2^{24}}$ ▷ initializing the counters
    $K' \leftarrow \{\}$
    for each data pair (t_i, c_i) and (t'_i, c'_i) **do**
        Compute $v^{(8)}$ and $v'^{(8)}$.
        $\Delta y^{(7)} \leftarrow \Delta v^{(8)}$
        $\Delta X_2^{(7)} \leftarrow L_0[\Delta y_0^{(7)}] \cap L_1[\Delta y_1^{(7)}, \delta] \cap L_2[\Delta y_2^{(7)}]$
        for each $\Delta x_2^{(7)} \in \Delta X_2^{(7)}$ **do**
            $\Delta x_0^{(7)} \leftarrow 9 \cdot \Delta x_2^{(7)}$ ▷ see Eq. 4
            $\Delta x_1^{(7)} \leftarrow 2 \cdot \Delta x_2^{(7)} \oplus \delta$
            $Y^{(7)} \leftarrow D[\Delta x_0^{(7)}, \Delta y_0^{(7)}] \times D[\Delta x_1^{(7)}, \Delta y_1^{(7)}] \times D[\Delta x_2^{(7)}, \Delta y_2^{(7)}]$
            for each $y^{(7)} \in Y^{(7)}$ **do**
                $rk^{(8)} \leftarrow y^{(7)} \oplus v^{(8)}$
                Increment $C[rk^{(8)}]$.
                if $C[rk^{(8)}] = \tau_1$ **then**
                    Add $rk^{(8)}$ to K'.
    for each $rk^{(8)} \in K'$ **do**
        $\mathtt{LL}^{-1}(rk_0^{(7)}), v \leftarrow$ ValidateRk8$(rk^{(10)}, rk^{(9)}, rk^{(8)})$
        if $v \geq \tau_2$ **then**
            Add $(rk^{(10)}, rk^{(9)}, rk^{(8)}, \mathtt{LL}^{-1}(rk^{(7)})_0)$ to K.
return K

linear layer. If $\delta \rightarrow \gamma$ is a possible transition through the S-box, apply the linear layer partially to obtain $\Delta x_2^{(7)}$.

As we are going to intersect the candidates for $\Delta x_2^{(7)}$, we can actually skip the $\delta \rightarrow \gamma$ check for $i \in \{0, 2\}$ which simplifies the corresponding look-up tables as they are then independent of δ. Recall the definition of the MixColumns matrix in Eq. (1) to see that the look-up tables are as follows:

$$
\begin{aligned}
L_0[\Delta y_0^{(7)}] &:= \left\{ \Delta x_2^{(7)} \;\middle|\; 9 \cdot \Delta x_2^{(7)} \to \Delta y_0^{(7)} \right\} \\
L_1[\Delta y_1^{(7)}, \delta] &:= \left\{ \Delta x_2^{(7)} \;\middle|\; \delta \to \Delta x_2^{(7)} \text{ and } 2 \cdot \Delta x_2^{(7)} \oplus \delta \to \Delta y_1^{(7)} \right\} \\
L_2[\Delta y_2^{(7)}] &:= \left\{ \Delta x_2^{(7)} \;\middle|\; \Delta x_2^{(7)} \to \Delta y_2^{(7)} \right\}
\end{aligned} \tag{3}
$$

For efficiency, we can store these as indicator sets. Next, we need to compute $\Delta x_0^{(7)}$ and $\Delta x_1^{(7)}$ given $\Delta x_2^{(7)}$. For this, we simply have the following.

$$
\begin{aligned}
\Delta x_0^{(7)} &= 9 \cdot \Delta x_2^{(7)} , \\
\Delta x_1^{(7)} &= 2 \cdot \Delta x_2^{(7)} \oplus \delta ,
\end{aligned} \tag{4}
$$

from the definition of the MixColumns operation in Eq. (1).

Finally, we need a table that stores all possible outputs of the AES S-box S, given its input and output difference.

$$D[\alpha, \beta] := \{ S(x) \mid S(x) \oplus S(x \oplus \alpha) = \beta \} \tag{5}$$

That is, D is similar to the DDT but we store the actual values instead of the cardinality. Note that D is called $\widetilde{DDT}$ in [6]. With this, we have all the ingredients of the attack.

Analysis. Again, the underlying idea of the attack is the same as for our naive attack in Sect. 3.2. That is, we are still computing the counters for each key guess, only in a more efficient way. In contrast to Algorithm 1, Algorithm 2 only considers 72-bit partial keys in the first step, since it does not involve $rk^{(7)}$. This also means that our filter is reduced to roughly 17 bits as we are not checking $\Delta x_0^{(6)} \stackrel{?}{=} \delta$ but only $\delta \stackrel{?}{\to} \gamma$. We adapted the formulas from Sect. 3.2 accordingly and evaluated them for a few values of s (the number of 16-minute bins) and the threshold value τ (denoted by τ_1 in Algorithm 2 and Algorithm 3). The results are given in Table 2. Here, the main takeaway is that $d \approx 2^{15}$ is a sufficient data complexity which corresponds to roughly 8 h of intercepted radio traffic.

Table 2. The data complexity d, the expected counter value c for the correct key, the success probability of the attack (in %), and the ratio of false positives for different threshold values τ and number of 16-minute bins s, for recovering the 72 key bits of $(rk^{(10)}, rk^{(9)}, rk^{(8)})$.

s	26	27	28	29	30	31	32
d	$2^{14.81}$	$2^{14.86}$	$2^{14.92}$	$2^{14.97}$	$2^{15.02}$	$2^{15.06}$	$2^{15.11}$
c	24.29	25.22	26.15	27.09	28.02	28.96	29.89
$\tau = 18$	92.14	94.44	96.14	97.36	98.23	98.83	99.24
$\tau = 19$	88.32	91.48	93.90	95.71	97.03	97.98	98.65
$\tau = 20$	83.43	87.54	90.81	93.35	95.26	96.69	97.72
$\tau = 21$	77.49	82.58	86.78	90.15	92.79	94.81	96.33
$\tau = 22$	70.62	76.61	81.75	86.02	89.48	92.23	94.35
$\tau = 18$	$2^{-20.25}$	$2^{-19.28}$	$2^{-18.35}$	$2^{-17.45}$	$2^{-16.58}$	$2^{-15.74}$	$2^{-14.93}$
$\tau = 19$	$2^{-26.69}$	$2^{-25.67}$	$2^{-24.68}$	$2^{-23.73}$	$2^{-22.82}$	$2^{-21.93}$	$2^{-21.07}$
$\tau = 20$	$2^{-33.21}$	$2^{-32.13}$	$2^{-31.09}$	$2^{-30.09}$	$2^{-29.12}$	$2^{-28.19}$	$2^{-27.28}$
$\tau = 21$	$2^{-39.79}$	$2^{-38.66}$	$2^{-37.57}$	$2^{-36.52}$	$2^{-35.50}$	$2^{-34.52}$	$2^{-33.57}$
$\tau = 22$	$2^{-46.45}$	$2^{-45.26}$	$2^{-44.12}$	$2^{-43.01}$	$2^{-41.95}$	$2^{-40.92}$	$2^{-39.92}$

In terms of run time, in Algorithm 2, we need to perform $d \cdot 2^{48}$ two-round pair decryptions and find the intersection of the results for look-ups in each of the L_0, L_1 and L_2 tables. In the most common case, occurring with probability $\left(\frac{255}{256}\right)^3$, look-up tables L_0 and L_2 will provide 127 possible input differences each, while table L_1 will provide an average of 63 input differences. Since only the input differences that are given by all three tables are actually possible, we expect

$$256 \cdot \left(\frac{127}{256}\right)^4 \approx 15.51$$

candidate input differences to continue with. For each of these candidates and each S-box, there are either 2 or 4 values in the table D. The corresponding probabilities are $126/127$ and $1/127$. Therefore, on average, we expect

$$|Y^{(7)}| = 8 \cdot \frac{126^3}{127^3} + 16 \cdot 3 \cdot \frac{126^2}{127^3} + 32 \cdot 3 \cdot \frac{126}{127^3} + 64 \cdot \frac{1}{127^3} \approx 8.19\,.$$

When $\Delta y_1^{(7)} = 0$, which occurs with probability $(1/256) \cdot (255/256)^2$, a single input difference will exist with probability $(127/256)^3$. In this case, we expect

$$|Y^{(7)}| = 256 \cdot \left(4 \cdot \frac{126^2}{127^2} + 8 \cdot 2 \cdot \frac{126}{127^2} + 16 \cdot \frac{1}{127^2}\right) \approx 1040\,.$$

Finally, if either $\Delta y_0^{(7)} = 0$ or $\Delta y_2^{(7)} = 0$, which occurs with probability $1 - (255/256)^2$, there are no possible input differences.

This means that, for a fixed $(rk^{(10)}, rk^{(9)})$, we expect to do about 126 increments per differential pair. Incrementing the key counter C dominates the run time. For $d \approx 2^{15}$, we obtain a run time equivalent to roughly 2^{70} increments. In comparison, the run time of a brute force attack will be dominated by the 30 S-box look-ups per encryption or decryption. Assuming that the key counter increment and S-box look-up operations have similar execution times, our attack has an expected run time equivalent to about 2^{65} encryptions.

In terms of memory consumption, assume that each counter is stored as a single byte. Then the counters require

$$2^{24} \cdot 1 \text{ Byte} = 16 \text{ MiB}.$$

In addition, the tables L_0, L_1, and L_2, stored as indicator sets, require

$$2 \cdot 256 \cdot 256 \text{ Bit} + 256^2 \cdot 256 \text{ Bit} \approx 2 \text{ MiB},$$

while the table D, also represented as an indicator set, requires

$$256^2 \cdot 256 \text{ Bit} = 2 \text{ MiB}.$$

Altogether, this amounts to roughly 20 MiB of memory.

However, note that for a parallel implementation, the memory for the counters must be allocated separately for each execution unit. To avoid memory-access bottlenecks, the lookup tables should likewise be replicated locally rather than shared across threads or devices.

The Full Attack. The first part of Algorithm 2 only recovers candidates for the 72 key bits $(rk^{(10)}, rk^{(9)}, rk^{(8)})$. However, given the list of candidates for these, we can quickly validate them and restore one byte of information about $rk^{(7)}$. This is done by the function VALIDATERK8, which partially decrypts the ciphertexts with the key candidates. For the good pairs, i.e., the pairs where $\Delta v^{(7)}$ is of the form $(\gamma, 0, 0)$, it then checks which values of $\mathrm{LL}^{-1}(rk^{(7)})_0$ fulfill $\delta \to \gamma$. The computational cost for this is negligible since $|K|$ is small.

After this, we brute force the remaining 48 key bits. This step is similar to that in the prior works [3,6]. The difference here is that we do not have access to any plaintexts to compare to. Instead, we leverage the fact that the first and second 24-bit words transmitted in a standard 2G ALE call are identical, and their tweaks differ only in a single bit. By using at least two such pairs for the trial decryptions, we can expect to uniquely identify the remaining 48 bits of the key. Since the tweaks for the first round are identical in this case, the trial decryptions only need to cover five of the ten rounds. Thus, the complexity of this step is equivalent to approximately 2^{48} decryptions of HALFLOOP-24. Again, this is negligible to the complexity of the search for the other 80 bits of the key.

4 Implementation of the Attack

In this section, we discuss the practical realization of our attack and the engineering considerations required to obtain competitive performance on modern hardware. In particular, we describe a cache-aware modification of Algorithm 2, present CPU benchmarks, and then detail our optimized GPU implementations. The source code for our implementations is available at https://doi.org/10.5281/zenodo.20088257.

4.1 Cache-Efficient CPU Implementation

While Algorithm 2 can be directly implemented on modern computers and GPUs, the size of the counter array (16 MiB) makes it too big to fit into the L1 cache. This means that the speed of the L2 cache becomes a major bottleneck. To rectify this problem, we modified Algorithm 2 to ensure all critical tables fit inside the L1 cache on modern processors.

Here, we restore $rk^{(8)}$ in two steps, by first searching only for two of the three bytes of the round key. The third byte is then only restored for the partial keys that exceed the threshold τ_1. Thereby, we only need $2^{16} + 2^8$ instead of 2^{24} counters at a time. This reduces the memory requirement for the critical tables to 579 KiB, making them fit in the 704 KiB L1 data cache of our target computer. We give the modification in Algorithm 3.

We implemented Algorithm 3 to benchmark our attack. For the benchmark, we simulated 8 h of traffic in our high-traffic scenario using callsigns from the Swedish ALE network observed in [1]. This yielded 16,566 viable ciphertext pairs. Using that data, we benchmarked our implementation on a single Intel Core Ultra 7 core. We selected $\tau_1 = 30$ and $\tau_2 = 8$, which represents a success probability of about 51%. Under those conditions, our implementation can check about 377 choices for $(rk^{(10)}, rk^{(9)})$ per second, meaning that the full attack would take approximately 23,700 years to run on a single core. However, (massively) parallelizing the attack is rather trivial as different machines can tackle different ranges for $(rk^{(10)}, rk^{(9)})$, meaning that 23,700 cores could be expected to complete the attack in a year. The majority of the supercomputers on the TOP500 list have core counts that exceed this. Although their individual cores are slower, we nevertheless estimate that most of them could complete the attack within one year. Based on the spot prices for cloud computing instances, a conservative estimate of the cost of an attack using cloud infrastructure is about four million US dollars. Since the speed of the implementation is strongly dependent on the selection of parameters τ_1, τ_2 and the number of differential pairs d, and therefore on success probability, an attack with a higher success probability will require significantly more time. For example, selecting $\tau_1 = 29$ and $\tau_2 = 8$ gives a success probability of 57.8% and a single-core attack time of about 29,800 years.

4.2 Practical Implementations on GPU

The most common techniques for implementing symmetric encryption algorithms for CPUs, GPUs, and FPGAs are straightforward, table-based, and bitsliced. On modern GPUs, a straightforward implementation provides significant speed-ups compared to CPUs due to the large number of available cores. The

Algorithm 3. Recover $(rk^{(10)}, rk^{(9)}, rk^{(8)}, \mathtt{LL}^{-1}(rk^{(7)})_0)$ (cache-friendly).

Input d differential pairs $((t_i, c_i), (t'_i, c'_i))$ with tweak differences $\Delta t = (0, 0, \delta_i, 0, 0, 0, 0, 0)$
Output a list of candidates for $(rk^{(10)}, rk^{(9)}, rk^{(8)}, \mathtt{LL}^{-1}(rk^{(7)})_0)$

Precompute D, L_0, L_1, L_2 . ▷ see Eqs. (3) and (5)

$K \leftarrow \{\}$ ▷ the list of key candidates
for each $rk^{(10)} \in \mathbb{F}_2^{24}$ **and each** $rk^{(9)} \in \mathbb{F}_2^{24}$ **do**
  $C \leftarrow (0, \ldots, 0) \in \mathbb{N}^{2^{16}}$ ▷ initializing the counters
  $K' \leftarrow \{\}$
  for each data pair (t_i, c_i) and (t'_i, c'_i) **do**
    Compute $v^{(8)}$ and $v'^{(8)}$.
    $\Delta y^{(7)} \leftarrow \Delta v^{(8)}$
    $\Delta X_2^{(7)} \leftarrow L_0[\Delta y_0^{(7)}] \cap L_1[\Delta y_1^{(7)}, \delta] \cap L_2[\Delta y_2^{(7)}]$
    for each $\Delta x_2^{(7)} \in \Delta X_2^{(7)}$ **do**
      $\Delta x_0^{(7)} \leftarrow 9 \cdot \Delta x_2^{(7)}$ ▷ see Eq. (4)
      $Y^{(7)} \leftarrow D[\Delta x_0^{(7)}, \Delta y_0^{(7)}] \times D[\Delta x_2^{(7)}, \Delta y_2^{(7)}]$
      for each $(y_2^{(7)}, y_0^{(7)}) \in Y^{(7)}$ **do**
        $rk_0^{(8)} \leftarrow y_0^{(7)} \oplus v_0^{(8)}$
        $rk_2^{(8)} \leftarrow y_2^{(7)} \oplus v_2^{(8)}$
        Increment $C[(rk_0^{(8)}, rk_2^{(8)})]$.
        if $C[(rk_0^{(8)}, rk_2^{(8)})] = \tau_1$ **then**
          Add $(rk^{(10)}, rk^{(9)}, rk_0^{(8)}, rk_2^{(8)})$ to K'.
  for each $(rk^{(10)}, rk^{(9)}, rk_0^{(8)}, rk_2^{(8)}) \in K'$ **do**
    $C' \leftarrow (0, \ldots, 0) \in \mathbb{N}^{2^8}$
    $K'' \leftarrow \{\}$
    for each data pair (t_i, c_i) and (t'_i, c'_i) **do**
      Compute $v_0^{(7)}$, $v_2^{(7)}$, $v_0'^{(7)}$ and $v_2'^{(7)}$.
      if $\Delta v_0^{(7)} = 9 \cdot \Delta v_2^{(7)}$ **then** ▷ see Eq. (4)
        $\Delta x_1^{(7)} \leftarrow 2 \cdot \Delta v_2^{(7)} \oplus \delta$
        for each $y_1^{(7)} \in D[\Delta x_1^{(7)}, \Delta y_1^{(7)}]$ **do**
          $rk_1^{(8)} \leftarrow y_1^{(7)} \oplus v_1^{(8)}$
          Increment $C'[rk_1^{(8)}]$.
          if $C'[rk_1^{(8)}] = \tau_2$ **then**
            Add $rk_1^{(8)}$ to K''.
    for each $rk_1^{(8)} \in K''$ **do**
      $\mathtt{LL}^{-1}(rk_0^{(7)}), v \leftarrow \textsc{ValidateRk8}(rk^{(10)}, rk^{(9)}, rk^{(8)})$ ▷ see Algorithm 2
      if $v \geq \tau_2$ **then**
        Add $(rk^{(10)}, rk^{(9)}, rk^{(8)}, \mathtt{LL}^{-1}(rk^{(7)})_0)$ to K.
return K

---

bottleneck in the straightforward implementation is the number of operations. This bottleneck can be overcome by using table-based implementations, whereby intermediate layers of some ciphers can be partitioned into disjoint subspaces.

That way, the output for each possible input of these subspaces can be precomputed and stored in a table. Thus, the computation of those layers can be reduced to table look-up operations for the inputs of these subspaces and combining the values obtained from the tables. Such tables are generally too large to be stored in GPU registers. Storing them in GPU global memory causes significant latency, due to the relatively low memory speed. The best performance is normally provided by storing the tables in GPU shared memory. However, the amount of on-chip shared memory is generally very limited, placing limitations on the size of the look-up tables. Shared memory bank conflicts are generally the main bottleneck in this approach.

For instance, the best GPU optimization of AES is obtained in [11] in which the shared bank memory conflicts were removed by duplicating one table 32 times and obtaining other tables by byte rotations. Since HALFLOOP has a similar design to AES, it can also benefit from the table-based implementation technique. However, the small block size of HALFLOOP-24 makes it suitable also for the bitsliced implementation technique. In the bitsliced technique, each bit of the state or key is stored in different variables. Letting each bit in the variables represent data from different encryptions creates single-instruction-multiple-data (SIMD)-level parallelism. The bottleneck in this technique is the number of registers used per thread.

When a GPU kernel is launched, threads are organized into blocks, and the total number of threads often exceeds the number of physical cores by a large margin. A high number of threads per block makes it possible to interleave the execution of many threads, thereby hiding latencies. As a result, the kernel launch configuration, namely the number of blocks and threads per block, has a significant effect on performance. We refer to these numbers as *blocks* and *threads*, respectively. For instance, blocks of 1024 threads can be called on modern GPUs when the number of registers per thread is less than or equal to 64. Thus, the number of required registers per thread for a GPU kernel determines the maximum number of threads per block.

Table 3. Estimated time required for completing the full attack using a single GPU.

GPU model	Estimated time
Nvidia MX250	3302 years
Nvidia GTX 860M	3242 years
Nvidia GTX 970	891 years
Nvidia GTX 1070	457 years
Nvidia RTX 2070 Super	338 years
Nvidia GTX 1080 Ti	296 years
Nvidia L40S	111 years
Nvidia RTX 4090	102 years

We successfully optimized our C implementation Algorithm 3 for GPUs using the CUDA language. Like in the CPU implementation, the size of the counter array was the largest bottleneck. In fact, the 2^{16} 8-bit counters are too large for some GPUs where the shared memory is limited to 49,152 bytes. To overcome this limitation, we used 5-bit counters on those platforms, fitting 6 counters into each 32-bit word. This limited the maximum τ_1 value to 31, which was sufficient for our purposes. Additionally, we applied best-practice optimizations to ensure maximum occupancy and execution efficiency throughout our CUDA implementation.

For our benchmarks, we used the same data as for the test of the CPU implementation, i.e. 16,566 viable ciphertext pairs. We selected $\tau_1 = 30$ and $\tau_2 = 13$ to get a theoretical success probability of 51%. The results of our benchmarks on different GPU models are shown in Table 3. For example, on an RTX 4090 GPU, the full attack would take 102 years, or conversely, 102 such GPUs would be able to complete the attack within one year. Under ideal linear scaling, this corresponds to roughly 37,230 RTX 4090-GPU-days.

The performance of the attack is heavily dependent on the selected success probability. This is because each candidate partial key that reaches τ_1 counts in Algorithm 3 causes an entirely new search through all data pairs. In fact, the relationship between success probability and attack time appears to be super-exponential, as illustrated in Fig. 4. The attack time can be reduced at higher probabilities by using more ciphertexts to increase the signal-to-noise ratio. However, this is limited by the counter sizes, which are dictated by the amount of available shared memory.

The speed of Algorithm 2 is significantly less dependent on the selected success probability. Despite this, it is still slower than Algorithm 3 even for high probabilities. To test this, we developed a highly optimized GPU implementation of Algorithm 2. As expected, this variant performed significantly worse despite careful tuning. This is due to the much higher latency of the GPU global memory, compared to the shared memory used by Algorithm 3.

The search for the final 48 bits of key is performed by a bitslice implementation that uses the optimizations described at the end of Sect. 3.

Our optimized implementation of the attack uses two CUDA kernels: `ct_attack3()` and `bitslice_kernel()`. We use the kernel attributes `__launch_bounds__(1024,2)` and `__launch_bounds__(128,5)`, respectively to specify the number of maximum threads per block and maximum blocks per multiprocessor for these two kernels. Although we make this choice to obtain the best performance, our choice of these kernel attributes also enforces usage of at most 32 and 96 registers per thread for these kernels, respectively. It should be noted that the number of required registers per thread might change depending on the used CUDA SDK and compiled compute capability. For instance, we observed that when we compiled our code for CUDA compute capability 7.5 or 8.9, the number of registers per thread exceeds 32 for the `ct_attack3()` kernel. Such implementations require 140 RTX 4090 GPUs to perform the attack in one year. Thus, simply compiling the same code for compute capability 6.1 or 5.2

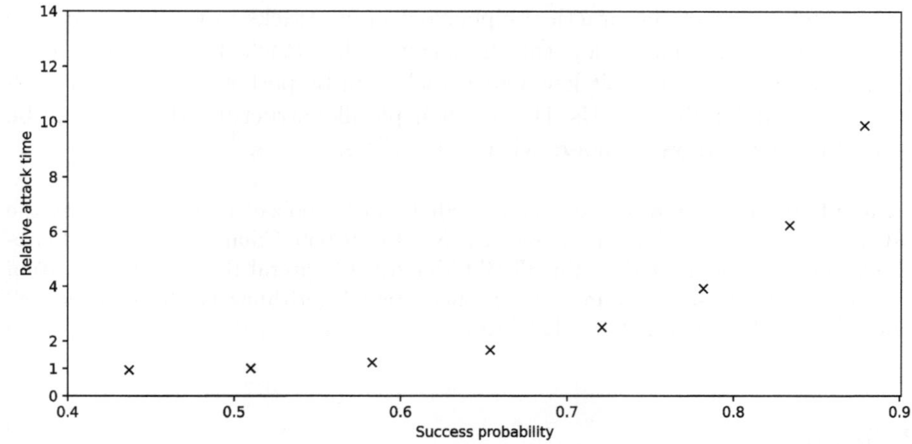

Fig. 4. Plot of the time required for a complete attack using Algorithm 3 at different success probabilities obtained with τ_1 values between 24 and 31 for our generated benchmark data. The attack times in the plot are relative to the benchmark test with $\tau_1 = 30$ with a success probability of 0.51.

(deprecated in CUDA SDK 13.x) provides significant speed-up and reduces the required number of GPUs to 102.

Cost of the Attack. Energy requirements place a lower bound on the cost of the attack. Based on the energy use in our experiments, we estimate the energy required for the full attack using our GPU implementation to be about 340 megawatt-hours. At an assumed cost of \$0.15 per kilowatt-hour, electricity for the full attack with 51% probability of success would cost \$51,000. Coefficients from Fig. 4 can be used to derive the cost of attacks with higher success probabilities. We estimate that the necessary hardware for performing the attack in a year, i.e. computers with 102 Nvidia RTX 4090 GPUs, can be bought for around \$300,000. For a one-off attack, an attacker can rent GPU power. The average price to rent an Nvidia RTX 4090 GPU for an hour ranges between \$0.20 and \$0.60, meaning the full attack costs between \$178,200 and \$535,600 in the 51% case. When renting GPUs, the attack time is primarily dependent on the number of GPUs that are available for the attacker to rent. Thus, the attack may potentially be completed in just a few hours.

5 Conclusion

HALFLOOP is a standard tweakable block cipher family used to secure ALE linking messages in modern HF systems used in the US military and NATO contexts. We presented, to our knowledge, the first ciphertext-only key-recovery attack on 10-round HALFLOOP-24 with experimentally benchmarked costs that are within reach of well-resourced adversaries under favorable traffic assumptions.

Although most of the practical ciphertext-only attacks in the literature are brute-force attacks that exploit the short key of the attacked cipher, our target HALFLOOP-24 uses a 128-bit key. Our attacks can be performed in a year with only about one hundred GPUs. Due to their parallel structure, the time can be reduced to weeks, days, or hours with more GPUs.

Acknowledgments. Gregor Leander and Shahram Rasoolzadeh were funded by the ERC project SYMTRUST, grant agreement No. 101097056. Cihangir Tezcan and Gregor Leander were supported by the TÜBİTAKDAAD Bilateral Research Cooperation Project "Cryptanalysis of Symmetric Key Encryption Algorithms: Theory vs. Practice" under TÜBİTAK 2531 grant No. 123N546.

References

1. List of automatic link establishment agencies and frequencies (2023). http://www.ominous-valve.com/ale-list.txt
2. Dansarie, M.: Cryptanalysis of the SoDark cipher for HF radio automatic link establishment. IACR Trans. Symmetric Cryptol. **2021**(3), 36–53 (2021). https://doi.org/10.46586/TOSC.V2021.I3.36-53
3. Dansarie, M., Derbez, P., Leander, G., Stennes, L.: Breaking HALFLOOP-24. IACR Trans. Symmetric Cryptol. **2022**(3), 217–238 (2022). https://doi.org/10.46586/TOSC.V2022.I3.217-238
4. Interoperability and performance standards for medium and high frequency radio systems. United States Department of Defense Interface Standard MIL-STD-188-141D (2017). https://quicksearch.dla.mil/qsDocDetails.aspx?ident_number=67563
5. Interoperability and performance standards for medium and high frequency radio systems. United States Department of Defense Interface Standard MIL-STD-188-141D Change 1 (2025). https://quicksearch.dla.mil/qsDocDetails.aspx?ident_number=67563
6. Leander, G., Rasoolzadeh, S., Stennes, L.: Cryptanalysis of HALFLOOP block ciphers. IACR Trans. Symmetric Cryptol. **2023**(4), 58–82 (2023). https://doi.org/10.46586/TOSC.V2023.I4.58-82
7. Lin, Y., Sun, L.: Related-tweak and related-key differential attacks on HALFLOOP-48. In: Pöpper, C., Batina, L. (eds.) Applied Cryptography and Network Security - 22nd International Conference, ACNS 2024, Abu Dhabi, United Arab Emirates, 5–8 March 2024, Proceedings, Part III. Lecture Notes in Computer Science, vol. 14585, pp. 355–377. Springer, Heidelberg (2024). https://doi.org/10.1007/978-3-031-54776-8_14
8. Liu, J., Sun, L.: Distinguisher and related-key attack on HALFLOOP-96. In: Seo, H., Kim, S. (eds.) Information Security and Cryptology - ICISC 2023 - 26th International Conference on Information Security and Cryptology, ICISC 2023, Seoul, South Korea, 29 November–1 December 2023, Revised Selected Papers, Part I. Lecture Notes in Computer Science, vol. 14561, pp. 19–40. Springer, Heidelberg (2023). https://doi.org/10.1007/978-981-97-1235-9_2
9. Shi, K., Ren, J., Chen, S.: Related-key boomerang attacks on two larger variants of HALFLOOP. Frontiers Comput. Sci. **20**(4), 2004801 (2026). https://doi.org/10.1007/S11704-025-40755-0

10. Stennes, L.: Symmetric Cryptography in the Real World. Phd thesis, Ruhr University Bochum, Bochum, Germany (2025). https://doi.org/10.13154/294-13081
11. Tezcan, C.: Optimization of advanced encryption standard on graphics processing units. IEEE Access **9**, 67315–67326 (2021). https://doi.org/10.1109/ACCESS.2021.3077551
12. Tezcan, C., Leander, G.: GPU assisted brute force cryptanalysis of GPRS, GSM, RFID, and TETRA. IACR Trans. Symmetric Cryptol. **2025**(1), 309–327 (2025). https://doi.org/10.46586/TOSC.V2025.I1.309-327

Can We Tolerate Small Side-Channel Leakages: The Role of Registers in Glitch-Stopping Circuits

Artemii Ovchinnikov[1(✉)], Jelle Biesmans[1], Kris Myny[1], Ventzislav Nikov[2], and Svetla Nikova[1]

[1] COSIC, KU Leuven, Leuven, Belgium
{artemii.ovchinnikov,jelle.biesmans, kris.myny,svetla.nikova}@esat.kuleuven.be
[2] KU Leuven, Leuven, Belgium
venci.nikov@gmail.com

Abstract. Research on cryptographic algorithms implemented in hardware and protected against side-channel attacks has advanced rapidly in recent years. Generalized masking schemes, such as Threshold Implementations (TI) and Domain-Oriented Masking (DOM), currently provide a solid theoretical security foundation. Security models, including the probing model and its various extensions, enable formal verification of these guarantees. In addition, established guidelines for designing securely composable gadgets, along with tools for the automatic generation of masked designs, have further advanced the field. Experimental security assessment approaches, such as the Test Vector Leakage Assessment (TVLA) complement these efforts. Consequently, the primary focus of the research community has shifted toward optimizing existing techniques and bridging the gap between theoretical and practical security models.

In this work, we demonstrate a case in which side-channel leakage, caused by glitches, can be concealed during experimental assessment in a setup that is theoretically not robustly secure. This effect arises due to specific patterns of glitch propagation. We investigate whether a particular layout of the complete logic chain can further contribute to a design's resistance to side-channel attacks, potentially reducing latency and area by relaxing glitch-mitigation requirements, such as reducing the number of pipeline registers. To this end, we introduce new adversarial model which further relaxes the model of Müller and Moradi, introduced at CHES 2024. To illustrate the practical relevance of our proposal, we provide experimental evidence by modifying a well-known, provably secure AES S-box design by De Cnudde, rendering it insecure under the robust probing model. We conduct TVLA of power consumption for both FPGA-based (physical) and ASIC-like (simulation) implementations of our netlists, demonstrating the absence of detectable leakage, similar to the originally robustly secure version of the algorithm.

Keywords: Masking · Side-Channel Analysis · Probing Models · Glitches · FPGA · ASIC · Spectre · AES

N. El Mrabet et al. (Eds.): AFRICACRYPT 2026, LNCS 16832, pp. 210–235, 2026.
https://doi.org/10.1007/978-3-032-31130-6_9

1 Introduction

For over a quarter of a century, both research and industrial communities working on cryptographic hardware implementations have been dealing with a major threat introduced by Kocher *et al.* [22], known as differential power analysis (DPA). Such side-channel attacks (SCA) allow adversaries to retrieve secret data processed by an embedded system. They exploit the relationship between data-dependent switching activity in logic gates and the device's power consumption, allowing statistical attacks [5] without breaking theoretically secure algorithms. Other examples of SCA include electromagnetic emission [15,33] and timing attacks [23].

Numerous approaches have been proposed to eliminate the above-mentioned dependency, which are commonly categorized into *hiding* and *masking*. *Hiding* aims to obscure the leakage by inserting dummy operations, adding random delays, and employing other obfuscation techniques [26]. These methods increase noise: signal components that are unrelated to the processed secret data but contribute to the overall power consumption of the device, thereby reducing its correlation with the secret.

Masking, in contrast, aims to make the processed data appear uniformly distributed. This is one of the most extensively studied solutions based on secret sharing schemes, which allow to correctly process the data that is statistically independent of the unmasked values. The latter is achieved by introducing sufficient randomness and ensuring that the leakages of the shared functions are independent [8,16]. One of the most widely adopted masking techniques is Boolean masking, in which the shares can be recombined to recover the original value using the bitwise XOR operation. This scheme has gained popularity in cryptographic hardware implementations due to its simplicity when applied to affine and linear functions, which constitute a large part of symmetric-key algorithms for a proper diffusion. Specifically, each such operation can be instantiated multiple times, equal to the number of shares, and applied to each share individually. However, symmetric-key cryptography also relies on non-linear functions for substitution layers (S-boxes), which poses challenges, as Boolean masking cannot be straightforwardly applied to them.

To address this issue, different approaches were proposed, either aiming to mask non-linear AND operations [35] or to design frameworks that transform SCA-insecure circuits into masked ones [19]. However, despite their value to the research community, early works either did not consider or underestimated the impact of unintentional gate switching activity, known as *glitches*, which can leak more information through side channels than assumed by existing frameworks [27]. Later techniques, such as Threshold Implementations (TI) [31] and Domain-Oriented Masking (DOM) [17], account for these physical effects, leading to more robust designs.

Despite the algorithmic complexity of implementing masking countermeasures, they have attracted significant attention from the research community, as their security can be theoretically proven. To provide general guidelines for the design of SCA-secure cryptographic circuits, Ishai *et al.* [19] introduced one of the first theoretical models of an adversary with physical access to a device, commonly referred to as the d-probing adversary. In this model, d denotes the number of wires observed by the adversary within a given time period, typically a single clock cycle in hardware implementations. If the information observed by probes placed arbitrarily within the masked design remains independent of the secret, the circuit is considered SCA-secure. To account for the effects of glitches, the d-probing model was later extended to the *robust probing model* [14], which is widely considered the strongest adversary model to date. Crucially, a design that is secure in this model is also considered secure in the noisy leakage [32] and the bounded moment leakage model, as shown by Barthe et al. [2]. The latter model restricts the adversary to analyzing up to the d-th statistical moment of the leakage distribution, thereby establishing a connection with practical leakage assessment techniques, such as TVLA [3], which are widely used to evaluate the DPA resistance of masked implementations.

Those findings contributed to the development of robust, secure designs and composable security notions [1,7], the latter allowing the automatic generation of masking [20,21]. Despite the availability of strong theoretical security guarantees, these models and design recommendations can be overly conservative. Auto-generated, composable designs tend to incur high area and randomness requirements, often underperforming hand-crafted designs. As a result, recent efforts have focused on optimizing the proposed countermeasures, studying different techniques to overcome the effect of glitches [36,37] or relaxing existing models. The latter includes the introduction of *Robust but Relaxed probing (RR-probing) model* [30], which represents a step toward bridging the gap between strong theoretical security guarantees and practical attacker models. This model implies a more realistic probe information collected from the glitch propagation mechanism, as it accounts for the functions implemented by the gates encountered along the probe's propagation and is data dependent. Using this model, it has become possible to demonstrate the security of certain masked glitch-immune circuits, such as LUT-based Masked Dual-Rail with Pre-charge Logic (LMDPL) [25]. These circuits do not propagate glitches by design, making the application of the robust probing model to them over-conservative, unrealistic, and incorrect. Even with this relaxation in place, there remains a gap between theoretical security guarantees and the practical observation of leakage.

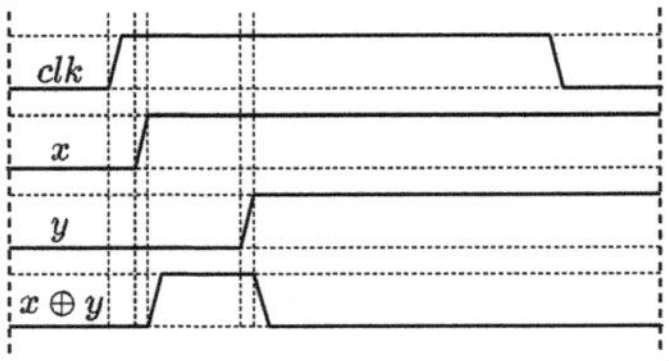

Fig. 1. Illustration of a glitch in a combinational gate. The output briefly spikes due to asynchronous input changes.

Contributions. Our goal is to investigate the discrepancy between the magnitude of leakage caused by glitches in silicon and that predicted by theoretical probing models. We revisit several axioms for secure glitch-stopping circuits introduced over 20 years ago with TI, such as the use of registers to prevent leakage. We study a range of examples in the robust probing model [14], the relaxed probing model [30], and a variant of the RR-probing model, which we term the ***highly relaxed probing (HR-probing) model***. We further examine the role of registers and glitch-induced leakage in the presence of noise (FPGA measurements) as well as in noiseless settings (Spectre power simulations). Our work builds on recent studies that aim to simultaneously mitigate specific glitches and optimize existing implementations [24], while also taking into account known security flaws in these designs [29]. In our study, we investigate a modified AES design, originally introduced by De Cnudde *et al.* [12]. Our implementation omits a register stage between the final two stages of the AES S-box from the original work. This is considered insecure in the robust and RR-probing models but practical FPGA experiments and Spectre simulations do not exhibit first-order leakage. We argue that leakage detection is avoided due to the circuit's complexity and the fact that the glitch behavior can be shaped by careful engineering of the combined stage. We reason that in the HR-probing model the resulting glitch behavior of the investigated circuit does not consistently reveal sufficient information about the masked secrets.

2 Preliminaries

We begin this section with an introduction to the notation used throughout the paper. We then introduce Threshold Implementations (TI) [31], a variant of masking that is provably secure in the presence of glitches. We finalize the section with a description of existing adversary models.

2.1 Notation

We denote stochastic variables by capital letters in italic, e.g., X, and deterministic Boolean variables by lowercase letters, e.g., x. Field elements are represented in bold $\mathbf{x} = (x^{n-1}, \ldots, x^1, x^0)$, where $\mathbf{x} \in \mathbb{GF}(2^n)$, with coordinates indexed by lowercase superscripts. For operations in $\mathbb{GF}(2^n)$, we use $\oplus$ for XOR, and $\odot$ for multiplication. Bitwise operations follow the same convention, with the multiplication symbol $\odot$ omitted when it is clear from the context. To model masking, we use vector spaces and denote their components as subscripts for share indices, e.g., $\overline{x} = (x_0, x_1, \ldots, x_{s-1}) \in \mathbb{F}_2^s$, with the total number of shares denoted by s. The bit values from two consecutive clock cycles are written as $x[clk], x[clk-1]$, and are subsequently referred to as x, x', respectively, for brevity. In addition to the mathematical notation, we adopt the following definitions describing the behavior of digital signals.

Definition 1 (Switch and Glitch of a Signal).

- **Switch**—*a transition of a signal between logical levels;*
- **Glitch**—*a sequence of two consecutive switches.*

That said, the glitch illustrated in Fig. 1 for the $x \oplus y$ signal consists of two switches ($0 \rightarrow 1$ and $1 \rightarrow 0$).

2.2 Threshold Implementations

To design countermeasures against side-channel attacks, we employ Boolean masking [8,16]. In this technique, a secret bit $x \in \mathbb{F}_2$ is split into s shares $\overline{x} = (x_0, x_1, \ldots, x_{s-1}) \in \mathbb{F}_2^s$, such that $\bigoplus_{i=0}^{s-1} x_i = x$. Each share should be statistically independent of the original secret. To achieve this, the first $s-1$ shares are drawn uniformly at random $r_0, \ldots, r_{s-2} \overset{\$}{\leftarrow} \mathbb{F}_2$ and the last share is computed as $x_{s-1} = x \oplus r_0 \oplus r_1 \oplus \cdots \oplus r_{s-2}$. Such a sharing is called *uniform* if all possible maskings of the secret are equally likely.

Masking a single variable is theoretically simple, but issues arise when those masked values must be processed by functions while preserving correctness and uniformity of the result. To address this, Nikova *et al.* [31] proposed Threshold Implementations (TI), a technique that enables secure masking of functions by satisfying three properties, namely *correctness, non-completeness, uniformity.*

Definition 2 (Threshold Implementations [31]**).** *Let $F : \mathbb{F}_2^n \to \mathbb{F}_2^m$ be a function, and let $\overline{F} : \mathbb{F}_2^{ns_x} \to \mathbb{F}_2^{ms_y}$ be a masking of F. The masking $\overline{F}$ is said to be:*

1. correct *if, for all $x_0, \ldots, x_{s_x-1} \in \mathbb{F}_2^n$,*

$$\bigoplus_{i=0}^{s_y-1} F_i(x_0, \ldots, x_{s_x-1}) = F\left(\bigoplus_{i=0}^{s_x-1} x_i\right);$$

2. non-complete *if any share function F_i depends on at most $s_x - 1$ input shares;*
3. uniform *if $\overline{F}$ maps a uniform random masking of any $x \in \mathbb{F}_2^n$ to a uniform random masking of $F(x) \in \mathbb{F}_2^m$.*

Later, the intuition that TIs are secure in the presence of glitches has been formally demonstrated by Dhooghe *et al.* [13]. To make the underlying notion of security precise, we introduce the adversary models on which it is based.

2.3 Probing Models

When discussing probing models, we typically represent a masked algorithm under evaluation as a circuit, or equivalently as a directed acyclic graph. Wires carrying digital values (bits) correspond to edges, and binary operations (logic gates) correspond to vertices. Such a circuit can be augmented with special *random gates* with fan-in 0, which produce random bits that may be used for refreshing. To store specific execution states of the algorithm for synchronization or glitch-stopping purposes, we introduce *memory gates*, which output the previously stored value whenever the circuit is active and store the value present at their input. In practice, random gates can be realized using pseudo-random number generators (PRNG), whereas memory gates can be implemented as registers (based on flip-flops and synchronized by a clock signal in ASICs and FPGAs).

We illustrate this abstraction using an example circuit, namely one half of a DOM AND gate [17] with $d+1 = 2$ shares (Fig. 2), in order to further highlight the capabilities of the considered adversary models. Tn this example, x_0 denotes a share of variable x, y_0, y_1 denote shares of y, and r is a fresh random bit. The share x_1 is absent; consequently, only a joint observation of both y_0 and y_1 can reveal information about the secret. We analyze this example under different probing models.

ISW Probing Model. In the foundational model by Ishai *et al.* [19], the adversary is granted the capability of observing (probing) up to d intermediate wires in a circuit, designed according to the principles described above, during its execution. The probes may be reallocated every clock cycle, but their placement remains fixed within a cycle. If the joint distribution of any d observed signals is independent of any function of the secret input of the entire algorithm, which includes plaintext and key information in cryptographic context, then the circuit is considered secure. We note that, despite providing a foundation for theoretical description of a side-channel adversary, circuits that are secure in ISW probing model are not necessarily secure in more realistic scenarios where dynamic hazards, such as glitches and transitions, contribute to the overall information leakage [27].

To illustrate this, we refer to Fig. 2(a), which models a first-order adversary with $d = 1$. The probe may be placed on any wire of the combinational circuit between two registers. However, placing the probe on the outputs of the leftmost register reveals no more information than a single bit. Similarly, placing a probe after AND gates or after the lower XOR gate does not reveal more information than a single share of the secret. Consequently, the most advantageous location to place a probe for the adversary is at the input of the second, rightmost register. According to the definition of ISW probing adversary, this probe reveals information of the stable signal carried by this wire. Although the wire carries information about the secret $y = y_0 \oplus y_1$, the presence of the fresh random bit r renders the resulting distribution uniform. As a result, probing any single wire of the circuit depicted in Fig. 2(a) does not allow the adversary to distinguish the secret.

Robust Probing Model. In practice, signal propagation delays between logic and memory gates may differ, which can lead to short time intervals during which a probe observes a signal combining multiple shares before it is re-masked. This may provide the adversary with an opportunity to mount statistical attacks [22] or, in some cases, to recover the secret value from a single measurement [26]. To eliminate this issue, an extension of ISW probing model was introduced by Faust *et al.* [14], known as the *robust probing model.* This model is the most comprehensive probing model proposed to date. It accounts for three types of physical effects that may arise in ASIC and FPGA implementations, namely:

- Glitches - unintended signal transitions in combinational circuits [27,31];
- Transitions - state transition leakage in memory cells (registers) [9];
- Couplings - crosstalk effects between adjacent wires caused by parasitic capacitance [11].

In the robust probing model, a single ISW-type probe is extended according to the rules of a chosen set of physical effects. We illustrate the impact of these effects using the same circuit employed to depict the ISW probing case. In corresponding figures, the solid probe symbol indicates the originally placed probe, whereas dashed probes represent the additional probe positions induced by the considered physical effects.

Figure 2(b) illustrates the case of a *glitch-extended* probe. Since the probe, placed at the input of the leftmost register, remains fixed there for an entire clock cycle and signals require time to stabilize, it observes all intermediate signal variations occurring before the cycle's idle phase. These transient glitches can leak information about the inputs of the preceding gate. For example, in the case of an XOR gate, observing a glitch on its output implies that either at least one input had a glitch, or both inputs switched with a delay. Since glitches can arise at any combinational gate in a circuit, their effects were first taken into account in Consolidating Masking Schemes (CMS) [34], where a probe is assumed to be extendable backwards either to the primary inputs of the circuit or to the outputs of the preceding register stage. This intuition was later formalized by Faust *et al.* [14] in the robust glitch-extended probing model. Registers, being synchronized with the clock, stabilize the state and do not propagate glitches. Thus, a probe considered safe under the standard ISW probing adversary model effectively extends throughout the entire combinational logic, granting the adversary access to all intermediate wires. Consequently, this enables statistical distinguishability of secret y, because the adversary observes both of its shares y_0, y_1. In the glitch-extended probing model, the optimal probe placement is therefore at the input of the next register stage, as it covers all inputs influencing the probed wire's signal.

Figure 2(c) illustrates the effect of a *transition-extended* probe. This type of leakage relates to the transitions between consecutive values stored in a register. Specifically, when a register switches its state at the beginning of a clock cycle, an adversary can briefly observe both the previous and current register outputs. In theory, a set of d probes can be expanded to $2d$ probes, placed on the register outputs and observing two consecutive clock cycles. As shown in Fig. 2(c), such an extension is generally safe, unless there exists a correlation between the input and the output of the register through the following combinational logic. For this reason, transitional leakage is never assessed as a standalone extension; it is always combined with the glitch-extended probe. This combination extends the probe placed in Fig. 2(b) to the values: $\{y_0[clk]; y_0[clk-1]; y_1[clk]; y_1[clk-1]; x_0[clk]; x_0[clk-1]; r[clk]; r[clk-1]\}$, yielding theoretically the most powerful *glitch-transition-extended* probing adversary.

We also consider the *coupling-extended* probe, although this effect only arises during the placement and routing steps of hardware design and does not contribute to the theoretical security guarantees defined by the robust probing model. As mentioned above, it results from crosstalk between adjacent wires, which occurs only if the wires are physically neighboring in the circuit layout. Figure 2(d) illustrates an example in which the outputs of AND gates are neigh-

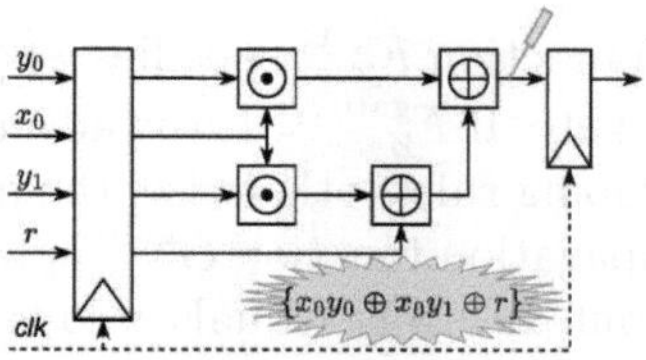

(a) ISW probing model

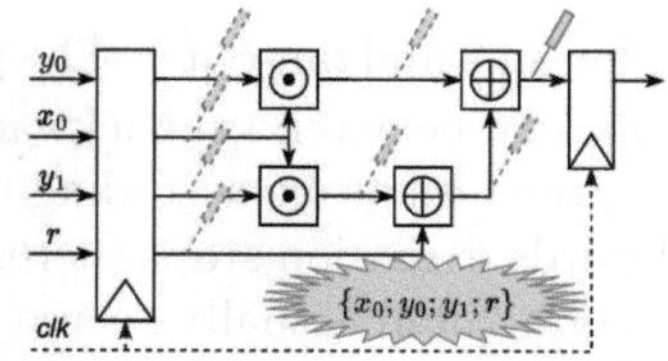

(b) Glitch-extended probing model

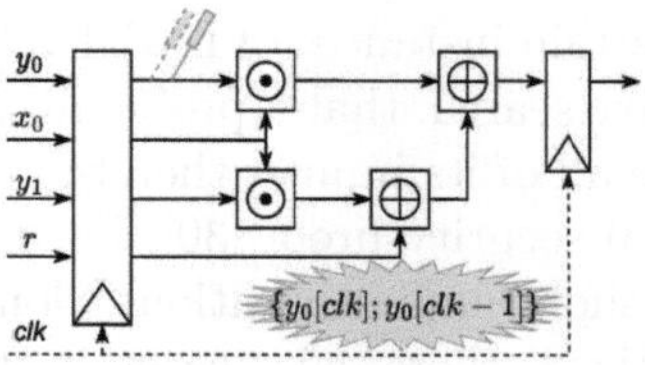

(c) Transition-extended probing model

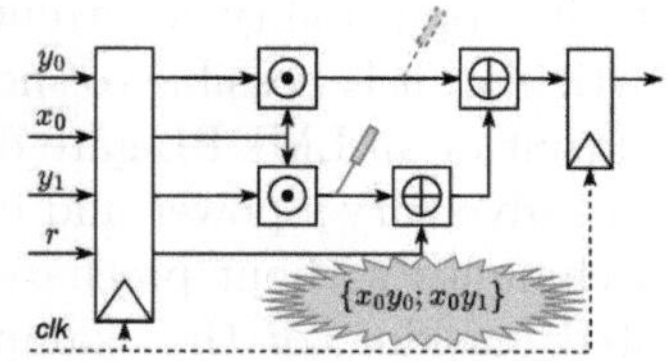

(d) Coupling-extended probing model

Fig. 2. Probing rules for ISW [19] and the robust probing [14] models

boring wires, potentially leaking some information about the secret. However, coupling effects are generally much weaker in statistical tests, like TVLA, than glitches and transitions [11] and cannot be accounted for at the RTL design stage.

Overall, the robust glitch-transition-extended probing model grants the probing adversary maximal capabilities among the known models. A design that is secure under this model is expected to exhibit no leakage in practical assessments. However, the model can be over-conservative, potentially classifying some designs as insecure even if they are safe in practice.

Robust but Relaxed Probing Model. To account for more realistic glitch behavior, Müller and Moradi introduced an extension of the robust probing model, referred to as the *Robust but Relaxed Probing Model* (RR-probing) [30]. The main intuition behind this work is that glitch patterns do not occur uniformly and differ across combinational gates; therefore, a probe does not always need to be extended to the inputs of the preceding gate. For example, consider an AND gate with at least one stable input equal to 0. In this case, the adversary always observes 0 at the output, regardless of the value of the other input. Consequently, the probe reveals no information about either input of the gate, since the adversary cannot determine which input is stable, which one is switching, or whether both inputs are stable. As a result, glitches originating from preceding combinational gates do not propagate further. A similar intuition applies to XOR gates, which do not reveal additional information about their inputs if both inputs are stable. In their work, Müller and Moradi introduced two new notions: *probe-extension* and *glitch-propagation* functions, defined for each basic logic gate with fan-in 2 and fan-out 1. The probe-extension function F_Z^{gate} specifies whether a probe can be extended backwards through the gate. If $F_Z^{\text{gate}} = 1$, the adversary may extend its probe according to the robust probing rules; otherwise, the probe backwards extension stops there. The glitch-propagation function G_Z^{gate} specifies whether a glitch actually occurs at the gate output. It always equals zero for the wires representing register outputs or initial inputs of the circuit.

Evidently, the RR-probing model is data-dependent. Although it bridges the gap between the robust probing model and practical side-channel leakage assessments, its applicability is currently limited to certain instances of LMDPL logic. In particular, it is possible to show, via exhaustive search, that a probe placed at the output of an LMDPL gate does not observe all of its inputs, thereby reducing the adversary's power and enabling a formal security proof [30]. For masking techniques without precharge, such as threshold implementations, domain-oriented masking, or the examples shown in Fig. 2, there exist cases in which an RR-probe expands into a robust glitch-transition probe. However, this is not always the case and depends strongly on the input data and the circuit type.

3 Highly Relaxed Probing Model

In this paper, we demonstrate that the RR-probing model can be further adapted to more practical scenarios. To this end, we revisit several information-leakage assumptions introduced in [30] and propose an additional relaxation, which we will call the *Highly Relaxed Probing Model* (HR-probing). We emphasize that, unlike its predecessors, this model is not robust, as it relies on assumptions about the physical layout of the evaluated circuit.

We begin by modeling the adversary's capabilities. To formalize the HR adversary model, we first provide a visualization of the considered probing scenarios. This differs from the RR-probing model, where an adversary may observe either two consecutive outputs of a gate or two consecutive values on each input wire of a basic logic gate (XOR, XNOR, OR, NOR, AND, NAND), that is, $\{z', z\}$ or $\{x', x, y', y\}$, respectively. The observable extensions, in RR probing, depend on the gate type and the preceding signal switches. Without loss of generality, it suffices to consider one balanced gate (XOR) and one unbalanced gate (AND), as these cases cover all relevant switch and glitch behaviors up to symmetry. Tables 1a and 6a of the original RR-probing work [30] enumerate possible patterns of output switches based on two consecutive values of the inputs X and Y for the AND and XOR gates, respectively. As noted by the authors, the tables are simplified and do not account for propagation delays. Subsequent work by Moradi [29] partially addresses this limitation by analyzing glitch patterns of differently masked AND gates (ISW, E-ISW, and DOM). In particular, Moradi demonstrated that it is possible to distinguish based only on the output switches, the input (secret) values of y when analyzing a single domain that forms one half of the ISW and E-ISW gadgets. He argued that for those two gadgets ensuring controlled delays and prioritizing randomness propagation does not provide security against the RR-probing adversary, whereas the DOM-gadget guarantees security by making y indistinguishable regardless of the observed glitch patterns by and RR adversary. However, the examined glitch patterns in [29] remain incomplete since they do not explicitly capture the cases in which glitchy inputs are provided, even though such effects are supposedly covered by the formal RR definitions.

Our next aim is to extend these examples to incorporate switch propagation. In addition, we argue that observing switching activity does not necessarily imply that a probe is extendable in practice. In particular, in the HR-probing model the adversary can observe all switching events and their timings at the probe location and, only in certain cases (in contrast to RR-probing), can extend a probe backward along the signal path. It generally occurs when the adversary can control (or has knowledge of) one of the inputs while attempting to infer the other. However, such expansion scenarios are considerably less likely than what is assumed in the RR-probing model. Consequently, the HR adversary is weaker than RR and non-robust, yet also more realistic. A single HR-probe observes the complete set of switches occurring on a wire *within a single clock cycle*. However, HR attacker is not necessarily able to align these observed switches with their originating signals and can therefore draw conclusions about the input data only in a probabilistic manner. Importantly, such conclusions depend entirely on the physical layout of the probed circuit, which may or may not be known to the attacker. As a result, one may either prove security against this adversary under specific layout assumptions or quantify the resulting information leakage.

3.1 XOR Gate Probing

We begin investigating switch patterns with the XOR gate, as featured in Table 6a of the original RR-probing work [30]. Consider a circuit similar to that in Fig. 2, but consisting solely of XOR gates, as shown in Fig. 3. As previously observed, placing a probe at any position other than wire ① does not reveal sufficient information to determine the secret variable y. When the probe is placed at position ①, an ISW probe observes the stable value $y_0 \oplus y_1 \oplus r$, which is secure due to masking by a fresh random bit r. A glitch-extended probe, in contrast, observes all circuit inputs and therefore leaks information about y.

We now examine what is observed by an RR probe. According to the RR-probing definitions, any switch of XOR gate output leaks information about both of its inputs. Consider the case in which x_0 switches while all other signals remain stable. Since x_0 contributes to all XOR gates in the circuit, wires ②, ③, and ④ each experience one transition, while wire ① may glitch due to unequal propagation delays. Under the RR-probing abstraction, the probe therefore reconstructs the secret y by observing

$$\mathcal{P}_{RR}^{①} = \{x_0, y_0, y_1, r\} \tag{1}$$

However, this abstraction does not accurately reflect practical behavior, which we will illustrate below.

We model the leakage behavior precisely for both $y = 0$, where $(y_0, y_1) \in \{(0,0), (1,1)\}$, and $y = 1$, where $(y_0, y_1) \in \{(0,1), (1,0)\}$. As illustrated in Fig. 4, the glitch patterns observed on wire ① are identical for the stable cases $y = 0$ and $y = 1$. The symmetric case $x_0 : 1 \rightarrow 0$ is omitted for brevity. Consequently, the example used to justify the robustness of the RR probe does not hold in practice for this circuit, as the secret variable y remains indistinguishable; in particular, it cannot be determined whether it is equal to 0 or 1. We emphasize that this does not invalidate the RR-probing model, which intentionally captures worst-case, data-dependent scenarios. Rather, it highlights that, with a single probe and a single trace, recovering y may be impossible, even under relaxed assumptions, leaving room for further refinement of the model.

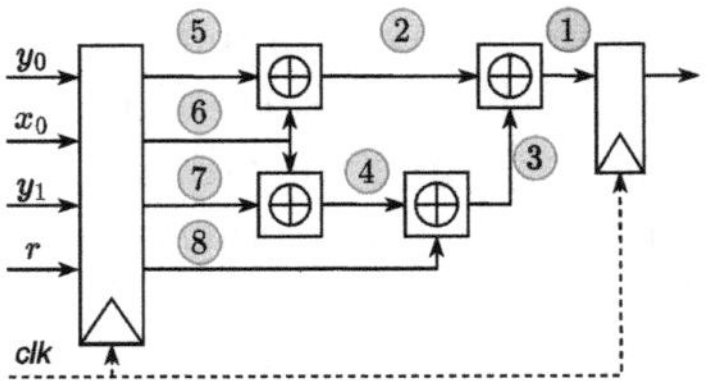

Fig. 3. XOR chain, operating on a secret y, share x_0, and a fresh random bit r.

We continue with the circuit of Fig. 3 to identify which practical switch scenarios enable our adversary to extract information about y, and, in particular, whether such information reveals the actual value of y or merely allows distinguishing between observations corresponding to different values of y. The latter distinction is important, because a violation of indistinguishability leads to potentially detectable leakage in practical statistical tests such as TVLA–where different sets of side-channel measurements are compared. We count the number of switches induced on wire ① by each input transition and argue that both the number and the timing of these switches determine the leakage. It leads to the following general conclusion:

Lemma 1 (XOR gate switching). *Let the two inputs of an XOR gate exhibit k_1 and k_2 switches, respectively, with $k_1 \geq k_2$. Then the output exhibits k_1+k_2-2i switches for some $i \in \{0, \dots, k_2\}$. Equivalently, the number of output switches lies between $k_1 - k_2$ and $k_1 + k_2$.*

Proof. Each switch on an input of an XOR gate induces a potential output transition. If switches on the two inputs occur at distinct times, their effects propagate independently and contribute additively to the number of output switches. However, when a switch on one input coincides in time with a switches on the other input, the two transitions cancel at the output of the XOR gate and produce no output switches.

At most k_2 such cancellations can occur, since the second input has only k_2 switches. Each cancellation removes two potential output switches. Therefore, starting from the maximal case of $k_1 + k_2$ output switches, the number of output switches can be reduced by $2i$ for any $i \in \{0, \dots, k_2\}$, yielding the stated range. □

The Lemma 1 allows a straightforward composition throughout a circuit consisting of XOR gates. We now recall our initial example in Fig. 3. To capture

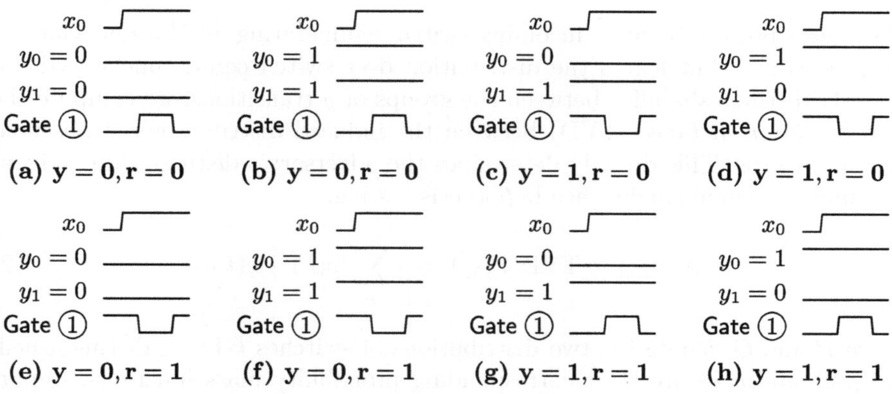

Fig. 4. Signal switches and glitch behavior in the XOR gate chain, illustrating indistinguishability between $y = 0$ and $y = 1$.

the worst-case scenario, we assume that each switch is associated with a distinct propagation time. Then, each input may induce the following number of switches:

- r causes 0 or 1 switches further noted as $\{0, 1\}$ switches;
- x_0 causes $\{0, 2\}$ switches, as it affects two XOR gates;
- y_0 causes $\{0, 1\}$ switches;
- y_1 causes $\{0, 1\}$ switches;
- $\{y_0; y_1\}$ jointly cause $\{0, 1, 2\}$ switches, with an important distinction:
  - if y remains constant across two consecutive clock cycles, it causes $\{0, 2\}$ switches;
  - if y transitions as $0 \to 1$ or $1 \to 0$, it always causes exactly $\{1\}$ switch.

Combining the cases above, the signal on wire ① may exhibit between 0 and 5 switches. Therefore, we analyze the distinguishability of the four transitions of the secret bit y, namely $y : \{0 \to 0,\ 0 \to 1,\ 1 \to 0,\ 1 \to 1\}$. As noted above, these transitions fall into two groups: the set $\{0, 1, 2, 3, 4, 5\}$ of possible switch counts for $y : \{0 \to 0,\ 1 \to 1\}$, and the set $\{1, 2, 3, 4\}$ for $y : \{0 \to 1,\ 1 \to 0\}$. However, the probabilities of individual switch counts differ: observing 0 or 5 switches requires, respectively, that all inputs remain unchanged or that all of them toggle, whereas, for example, observing 2 switches can arise from several distinct input patterns. To cover all possibilities in the circuit of Fig. 3, we consider the $2^4 = 16$ input-transition cases per input wire and, in principle, all $5! = 120$ permutations of arrival orders for the resulting switches (accounting for the fact that the wire carrying x_0 may incur different delays after the split). In practice, the synthesized layout restricts the number of realizable propagation delay orderings: while many permutations are theoretically possible, only a limited subset can occur on an actual device (after FPGA placement or ASIC tape-out), depending on the routing choices, the physical distances between gates and the cell types. Moreover, for an XOR-only circuit, permutations of arrival times do not affect the count of switches. As we consider the worst-case scenario, where

XOR gates propagate every incoming switch, enumerating all 5! orders changes only the timing but leaves the distribution over switch counts unchanged. To quantify distinguishability between the groups of y transitions, we compute the *total variation distance* (TVD) between the induced distributions of observed switch patterns. This directly determines the adversary's distinguishing advantage under optimal single-trace hypothesis testing.

$$\mathrm{Adv}_{HR} = \mathrm{TVD}(P, Q) = \frac{1}{2}\sum_{k} |p(k) - q(k)| \tag{2}$$

where P and Q denote the two distributions of switches k being distinguished, and $p(k)$ and $q(k)$ are their corresponding probability mass functions. Importantly, this metric does not reveal the actual value of y; instead, it only indicates how y changed between two consecutive inputs. For the circuit in Fig. 3, we define the distributions P corresponding to $y = \{0 \to 0,\ 1 \to 1\}$, and Q corresponding to $y = \{0 \to 1,\ 1 \to 0\}$.

$$\begin{aligned} P(k) &= \mathbf{Pr}[K = k | y \in \{0 \to 0,\ 1 \to 1\}] \\ Q(k) &= \mathbf{Pr}[K = k | y \in \{0 \to 1,\ 1 \to 0\}] \\ &\qquad\qquad \text{for } k \in \{0, 1, 2, 3, 4, 5\} \end{aligned}$$

k	0	1	2	3	4	5
$P(k)$	1/8	1/8	2/8	2/8	1/8	1/8
$Q(k)$	0	2/8	2/8	2/8	2/8	0

We then obtain the following calculations:

$$\mathrm{TVD}(P, Q) = \frac{1}{2}\sum_{k=0}^{5} |P(k) - Q(k)| = 0.25 = \mathrm{Adv}_{HR}$$

The adversary's distinguishing advantage is normalized between 0 and 1, where 0 corresponds to performance no better than random guessing, and 1 corresponds to always identifying the correct hypothesis. In terms of advantage over the random guesser, the adversary has 12.5% better chances of distinguishing between the two groups in our case. Designs that are secure under the robust probing model yield zero advantage to our HR-probing adversary.

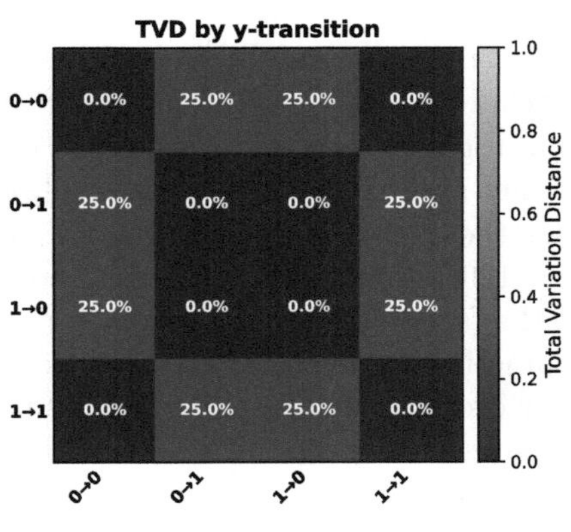

Fig. 5. Total variation distances between all pairs of y transitions (XOR chain).

To conclude the analysis, we provide a pair-wise comparison of all sets of y switching, depicted in Fig. 5. It further corroborates the adversary's distinguishing advantage of 0.25 and, moreover, confirms the indistinguishability within the pairs $y : 0 \to 0$ versus $y : 1 \to 1$ and $y : 0 \to 1$ versus $y : 1 \to 0$.

As stated at the beginning of this section, the HR-probing adversary observes all switches and their timings at the probe location. In practice, however, hardware delays are not perfectly stable. Even if delays follow a nominal pattern due to careful circuit design, their timings cannot be assumed to be precise and constant across executions. Consequently, the adversary cannot align the observed switches with the specific inputs that generated them, unless the circuit is deliberately engineered to enforce particular delay constraints, causing specific switches to occur at similar times. Moreover, some switches may cancel when multiple input transitions arrive at an XOR gate simultaneously.

The adversary therefore observes the following sequence at the probe location:

$$\mathcal{P}_{HR}^{①} = \{x'_0 \oplus y'_0 \oplus x'_0 \oplus y'_1 \oplus r', x_0 \oplus y_0 \oplus x_0 \oplus y_1 \oplus r; \mathcal{SW}\} = \{z', z; \mathcal{SW}\} \quad (3)$$

where $\mathcal{SW}$ denotes the sequence of switches.

3.2 AND Gate Probing

The case of the AND gate is more intricate, as its output switching behavior depends on joint switching patterns of the inputs rather than on their individual transitions alone. Specifically, an output switch occurs if and only if one input is stable at 1 while a switch occurs on the other input. Consequently, even if multiple glitches arrive at the inputs, they may follow one another in such a way that no switches propagate to the output.

Lemma 2 (AND gate switching). *If the two inputs of an AND gate carry k_1 and k_2 switches then the output has between 0 and $(k_1 + k_2)$ switches.*

Proof. Each switch on an input of an AND gate can produce at most one output switch, since the output is a Boolean signal. Therefore the output can exhibit no more than $k_1 + k_2$ switches in total. That said, to prove our claim, it is sufficient to demonstrate the test-cases for both extremal cases. We provide a visual example to facilitate the claim of the Lemma in Fig. 6. It demonstrates cases with 0 and with $k_1 + k_2$ number of switches, confirming our initial claim. □

Corollary 1. *If the propagation delays of all input switches are distinct, then the total number of output switches of an AND gate $a \odot b$ with k_1 switches on a and k_2 switches on b can be expressed in terms of the event sequence $\mathcal{SW} = \langle e_1, \ldots, e_K \rangle$, where $e_j \in \{A, B\}$ indicates whether the j-th event is a switch on a or b, and $K = k_1 + k_2$. $\mathbf{1}[\cdot]$ is the indicator function. Let*

$$\alpha_j = \big(\#\{\, i < j : e_i = A \,\}\big) \bmod 2, \qquad \beta_j = \big(\#\{\, i < j : e_i = B \,\}\big) \bmod 2.$$

Then the number of output switches equals

$$K_{\text{AND}}(a', b'; \mathcal{SW}) = \sum_{j=1}^{K} \Big(\mathbf{1}[e_j = A]\,(b' \oplus \beta_j) + \mathbf{1}[e_j = B]\,(a' \oplus \alpha_j) \Big), \quad (4)$$

Proof. Consider first the case where both inputs originate from register outputs, so that $k_1, k_2 \in \{0, 1\}$ and $\mathcal{SW} = \langle e_1, e_2 \rangle$. Since no two switches arrive simultaneously, the AND output can toggle at most once per event. If $e_1 = A$ and $e_2 = B$, the output toggles first iff $b' = 1$, and then iff $a' \oplus 1 = 1$ at the second event, yielding $K_{\text{AND}} = (b') + (a' \oplus 1)$. Similarly, if $e_1 = B$ and $e_2 = A$, we obtain $K_{\text{AND}} = (a') + (b' \oplus 1)$. These two cases correspond exactly to the two terms in Eq. 4. For general $k_1, k_2 \in \mathbb{N}$, each event toggles exactly one input, and the output toggles at event j iff the non-switching input is 1 immediately prior to that event. The parities α_j and β_j track the instantaneous input values, and summing these per-event toggle conditions over all K events yields Eq. 4. □

In contrast to the XOR gate, the AND gate's switching behavior may in some cases reveal the exact values of its inputs, but only when those inputs are equal to 1. Another important difference is that, for an AND gate, the order in which input switches arrive matters, as follows from Corollary 1. The same is also illustrated in Table 1 of the RR-probing model work [30]. Since the RR adversary is robust, it observes a glitch in both cases S_6 and S_9. This is possible because real hardware delays are not stable and may vary across clock cycles.

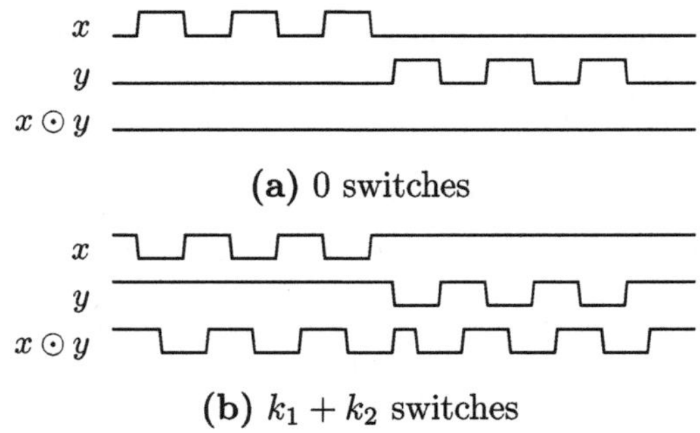

Fig. 6. Signal switches behavior in the AND gate as a proof for Lemma 2.

We illustrate the difference between the pure XOR-chain case from Sect. 3.1 and a combined design beginning with AND gates using the example in Fig. 2. Unlike in the XOR case, we must now consider all orderings of the switches produced by x_0, y_0, y_1 and by the second branch of x_0 (to account for the rare case where a split wire induces slightly different delays). Moreover, the two AND gates cannot be analyzed independently, as both depend on the same transition pattern of x_0. As a result, we must consider $4! = 24$ possible delay-ordering permutations of the four relevant input transitions. We omit r, as it affects only the XOR sub-chain, which is composable regardless of ordering. In addition, we complement the cases with $4^4 = 256$ (4 per input wire) input-transition patterns, since the transition pattern itself influences the behavior of the AND gates. We omit the detailed calculations here. Instead, we implemented a program that enumerates all scenarios and produces $4! = 24$ heatmaps, one for each possible delay-ordering. Among these 24 cases, only three distinct heatmaps appear, shown in Fig. 7. These heatmaps fall into three groups: (i) twelve cases where the shares of y arrive in a different order than the corresponding branches of x_0; (ii) six cases where the y shares always arrive later; and (iii) six cases where the y shares always arrive earlier. This observation suggests that the analysis can be further optimized by exploiting this structural grouping. Namely, for secret-dependent behavior, only the relative ordering of the secret's shares matters, which reduces the analysis from factorial to exponential complexity. Introducing additional structural assumptions can reduce the computational complexity even further. Based on the input-arrival ordering, we can now compute the corresponding advantage of the HR-probing adversary for the circuit in Fig. 2:

$$\mathrm{Adv}_{HR} \in [0.219, 0.281].$$

This aligns with our earlier claim that the adversary effectively observes the initial and final states of the probed wire, together with all intermediate switches, which collectively determine its ability to distinguish between different sets of secret transitions. However, the adversary does not necessarily know the order in which these switches were induced by the input signals. Furthermore, estimating the adversary's advantage becomes more complex when AND gates are preceded by XOR operations, as this increases the number of possible switch-propagation patterns affecting the AND gates.

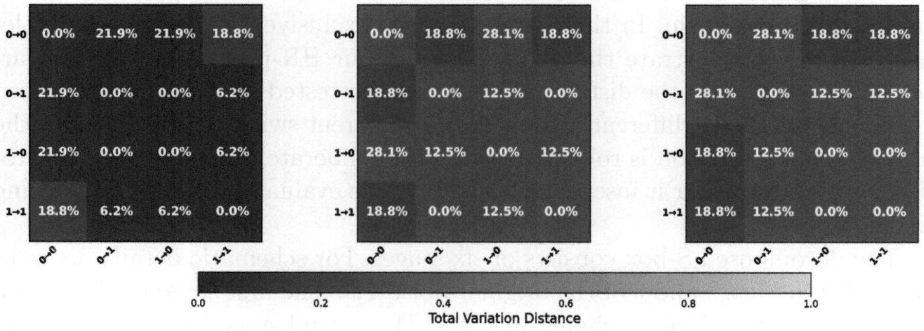

Fig. 7. Heatmaps, case of Sect. 3.2.

Finally, the adversary's advantage depends on the specific pattern of delay propagation, which may vary even across logically equivalent implementations produced by different synthesis outcomes, and which, under perfect synchronization, may eliminate certain switches in the XOR chain. Consequently, the advantage values we compute represent a maximal adversarial advantage; certain implementations—-especially those with long XOR chains combined with wide and balanced layers of AND operations—-may exhibit significantly lower advantages and thus may not leak under distinguishability-based tests, such as TVLA.

Definition 3 (HR-probing adversary). *An HR-probing adversary observes, on a probed wire w and for each clock cycle, the pair of logic values $(v_{\text{prev}}(w), v_{\text{curr}}(w))$ together with the full, time-ordered sequence of switching events $\mathcal{SW}(w)$. Given two secret-behavior hypotheses, the HR advantage equals* TVD *between the induced distributions of the observation. Feasible switch counts and schedules are constrained by Lemma 1, Lemma 2, and Eq. 4.*

4 Case Study: AES S-Box

We examine a masked implementation of the AES S-box to illustrate our research idea in practice. AES is a block cipher standardized by NIST [10], operating on a 128-bit state and key, each arranged as 16 bytes in a square structure. The cipher consists of 10 rounds, with each round applying the S-box to each byte, followed by ShiftRows and a matrix multiplication on the state's columns. The AES S-box is the only nonlinear layer of the cipher, operating on 8-bit values. Masking linear operations is straightforward, as each operation can be replicated for every masking share. By contrast, designing a securely masked AES S-box is challenging due to the complexity of finite field operations.

We re-implemented a design similar to that proposed by De Cnudde *et al.* [12], which employs the Canright decomposition technique [6] to enable masking of only low-degree functions. That implementation uses $d + 1 = 2$ shares, providing security against a first-order SCA adversary. This minimal number of shares was chosen to facilitate the implementation of the linear operations across the full AES algorithm. In this work, we focus exclusively on the S-box implementation to demonstrate the applicability of our HR-probing model. In particular, we show that the distinguishability of the tested secret bits depends on the circuit layout, as different layouts induce different switch patterns. Since the original implementation is robustly secure, we deliberately remove one synchronization step to render it insecure and thus enable evaluation of our HR-probing model.

The decomposed S-box consists of six stages. For schematic details, we refer the reader to Figs. 2 and 3 of the original work [12]. The first stage implements a linear map that performs a change of basis. The second stage implements a nonlinear multiplication in $\mathbb{GF}(2^4)$, followed by a square-scaling operation in $\mathbb{GF}(2^4)$, which is affine. At this stage, the data bus is divided into two 4-bit halves. Remasking is applied to the outputs of these operations to restore uniformity. The third stage is analogous to the second and implements similar operations in the smaller field $\mathbb{GF}(2^2)$. The outputs are again re-shared to maintain uniformity. The fourth stage motivates the preceding decompositions. In this stage, inversion in $\mathbb{GF}(2^2)$ is linear and is implemented by bit swapping. This layer is followed by two additional multipliers, whose outputs are concatenated to form four 4-bit shares. In addition to these operations, the registers following stages 2, 3, and 4 each store 4 bits derived from the originally split 8-bit input, with each bit represented by two shares. We highlight these buses because they are used in the subsequent fifth stage, which we investigate in more details with sixth stage.

4.1 Fifth and Sixth Stage Combination

Stage 5 has multiple inputs, which can be divided into three groups. The first two groups consist of the signals propagated from Stage 2 after the split following the linear-map stage. Each group comprises 4-bit buses divided into two shares. We denote these buses as Top_1, Top_2 and Bot_1, Bot_2, corresponding to the upper and lower groups, respectively. The third group consists of four buses of so-called middle shares, each also four bits wide. These shares are re-masked in the preceding stage and stored in the register before Stage 5, as they are compressed in Stage 5 into two middle shares, denoted Mid_1 and Mid_2. Combining corresponding shares, such as Top_1 with Top_2, Bot_1 with Bot_2, or Mid_1 with Mid_2, would directly reveal secret information. Therefore, Stage 5 combines only statistically independent variables using $\mathbb{GF}(2^4)$ multiplication blocks. As a result, the following products are computed:

$$Bot_1Mid_1 = Bot_1 \odot Mid_1, \qquad Top_1Mid_1 = Top_1 \odot Mid_1, \tag{5}$$
$$Bot_1Mid_2 = Bot_1 \odot Mid_2, \qquad Top_1Mid_2 = Top_1 \odot Mid_2, \tag{6}$$
$$Bot_2Mid_1 = Bot_2 \odot Mid_1, \qquad Top_2Mid_1 = Top_2 \odot Mid_1, \tag{7}$$
$$Bot_2Mid_2 = Bot_2 \odot Mid_2, \qquad Top_2Mid_2 = Top_2 \odot Mid_2. \tag{8}$$

We present the equations in this form because the corresponding multiplication results are concatenated, producing the output of Stage 5 as four 8-bit shares, with the $BotMid$ values forming the most significant nibble. In the original implementation, this block is considered secure because it does not fully recombine any of the shares, thereby preserving non-completeness. The subsequent refreshing step restores uniformity of the output masking and enables a further compression in Stage 6, as the introduction of fresh randomness maintains the non-completeness of the compressed terms as well. It is worth noting that the aforementioned uniformity issue arises only in the special case where the middle share equals the zero nibble, i.e., $(Mid^3, \ldots, Mid^0) = (0, 0, 0, 0)$. Stage 6 of the original design applies inverse linear maps to each of the two remaining shares after compression:

$$Out_1 = ILM(Bot_1Mid_1\_Top_1Mid_1 \oplus Bot_1Mid_2\_Top_1Mid_2), \tag{9}$$
$$Out_2 = ILM(Bot_2Mid_1\_Top_2Mid_1 \oplus Bot_2Mid_2\_Top_2Mid_2). \tag{10}$$

Clearly, if the register between Stages 5 and 6 is removed, a robust probing adversary gains the opportunity to observe both shares of the secret nibble Mid. The RR-probing adversary, while depending on the input data, still provides robustness and can therefore be extended to cover all input bits. However, we view this design as a particularly suitable example for evaluation under the HR-probing model. This intuition stems from the fact that a $\mathbb{GF}(2^4)$ multiplication can be represented as a long chain of XOR gates due to its internal structure. As discussed in Sect. 3.1, XOR chains propagate switches. In the case of $\mathbb{GF}(2^4)$ multiplication, each output bit may switch up to 1822 times, depending on the configuration of the corresponding AND gates. To increase the number of switches and further obscure their patterns, we swap the positions of the compression and ILM layers. As a result, this modification requires twice as many ILM instances. However, the resulting overhead amounts to only 116 gate equivalents (GE)[1], whereas removing the register between Stages 5 and 6 saves more than 140 GE.

4.2 Unbalanced Tree Version of the Design

We implement the combination of the fifth and sixth stages in two different ways, while keeping the remainder of the S-box identical to the original design of De Cnudde *et al.* For both approaches, we aimed to prevent the preceding $\mathbb{GF}(2^4)$ and ILM layers from being optimized by the netlist synthesizer. To this end, we enforced the absence of optimizations across module boundaries in our Verilog RTL using synthesis constraints, such as `keep_hierarchy` in Xilinx ISE and `set_dont_touch` together with `compile -exact_map` in Synopsys Design Compiler.

For the first design, we ensured that each gate in the combined stage is instantiated as a standalone submodule. In addition, XOR chain following AND-gate layer is implemented in an unbalanced manner, a portion of which, amounting to at least 1/4 of the entire compression chain, is shown in Fig. 8(a)[2]. To estimate the TVD for a probe placed at the compression step, we optimize our code to operate on probabilistic switch propagation rather than enumerating all exact switch patterns. We further assume that the switching order observed after compression is stable, because the chain is unbalanced and the signals Top_i^j and Bot_i^j propagate faster, originating directly from registers. Under these realistic conditions, we obtain $Adv_{HR} \in [1.704e^{-3}, 2.991e^{-3}]$. This version fails the TVLA evaluation both on the FPGA (Sect. 5.1) and in the Spectre simulations (Sect. 5.2), exhibiting noticeable–though not severe–leakage. This behavior can be attributed to the unbalanced structure of the tree, which resembles the example discussed in Sect. 3.2.

4.3 Balanced Tree Version of the Design

To mitigate the likelihood of leakage, we redesign the combined stages such that the corresponding operation tree is balanced (Fig. 8(b)). In addition, we allow the synthesizer to optimize the logic within each $\mathbb{GF}(2^4)$ multiplication block. In this way, security is preserved up to the compression step, while increasing the likelihood of unpredictable switching behavior. Balancing the tree reduces the stability of switching patterns, as the timing delays observed by an HR-probe become more closely aligned. Consequently, it becomes difficult to attribute a particular observed switch to a specific input signal. Focusing

[1] Evaluated using the NANGATE 45 nm open cell library.

[2] To save space, we omit the full layout for a single S-box output bit, as it comprises more than 80 gates. The complete layout description can be found at https://github.com/KULeuven-COSIC/HR_probing_model.

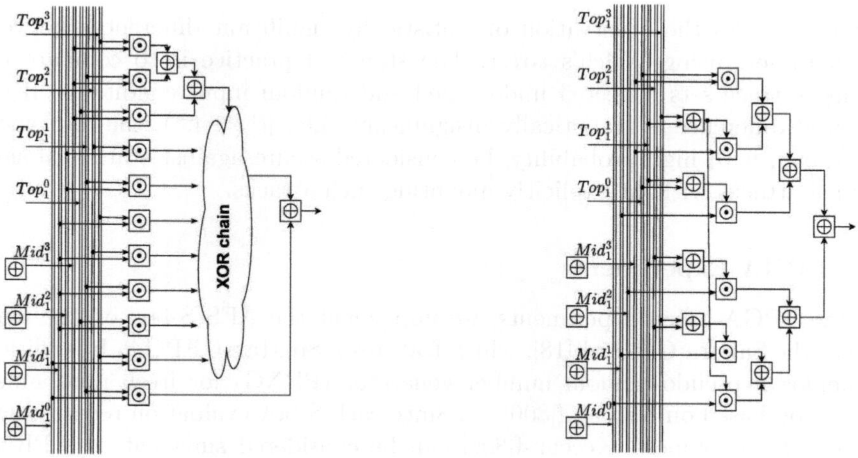

(a) Unbalanced tree **(b)** Balanced tree

Fig. 8. Two versions of the five-stage AES S-Box layout.

on a timing pattern analogous to the unbalanced-tree case–although potentially obscured by other delay permutations–yields an approximate estimate of $Adv_{HR} \in [1.2577e^{-4}, 2.4613e^{-4}]$. We evaluate this version using Spectre simulations and observe that it passes the TVLA test (Sect. 5.2).

5 Experimental Analysis

Our contribution to the experimental analysis is twofold. First, we evaluate the security of the AES S-box implemented on an FPGA. We begin with the six-stage implementation in order to reproduce and confirm the results of De Cnudde *et al.* [12], which report the absence of leakage. We then investigate two variants of specially configured five-stage implementations described in Sects. 4.2 and 4.3. The goal of the latter experiments is to demonstrate how different combinational logic layouts can affect the leakage assessment. One should note that the results of FPGA-based tests may be influenced by several factors that can obscure leakage. These include, but are not limited to, platform-induced noise, noise generated by a PRNG located on the same evaluation board, placement and routing optimizations.

To mitigate the influence of these factors, we complement our FPGA experiments with a second contribution: Spectre simulations for the test cases described above. It allows to retrieve noiseless power simulations, since we only simulate the netlists of our AES S-boxes. Further details on Spectre and the methodology of these tests are provided in Sect. 5.2.

For the traces generated by both methods, we employ TVLA [3] to analyze the result and determine whether the designs exhibit leakage. This assessment method enables the observation of statistically significant differences between two data sets using Welch's t-test. The standard practice is to compare the means of trace sets collected under fixed and random input conditions. If the observed difference is statistically insignificant (i.e., $|t| < 4.5$), the implementation can, with high probability, be considered secure against statistical side-channel attacks without explicitly mounting such attacks.

5.1 FPGA Experiments

For the FPGA-based experiments, we implement the AES S-box on the main chip of the Sakura-G board [18], which features a Spartan-6 FPGA. In addition, we deploy a pseudo-random number generator (PRNG) for fresh randomness generation based on Keccak-f[800] [4]. Since each S-box evaluation requires only 64 bits of randomness, Keccak-f[800] can be considered sufficient as a PRNG for up to 12 clock cycles. To ensure adequate entropy, we run Keccak-f[800] for approximately 24 clock cycles after providing the initial seed. The setup operates at a stable clock frequency of 6.144 MHz. The masked inputs are generated on the control board of the Sakura-G and therefore do not contribute to the measured power consumption of the S-box. We collect power consumption traces by monitoring the voltage drop across a 1 Ω shunt resistor placed on the VDD path of the target FPGA, using a digital oscilloscope with a sampling rate of 500 MS/s. This configuration allows us to capture approximately 80 sample points per clock cycle.

We begin by testing the original $d + 1 = 2$ shared, first-order secure S-box, re-implemented based on the description by De Cnudde *et al.* [12], as a sanity check of our experimental setup. The results are shown in Fig. 9(c), confirming the absence of leakage after collecting 100 million traces. We then consider the case described in Sect. 4.2 depicted in Fig. 10(a). The first-order TVLA results exhibit clearly observable leakage, with the statistic growing to $|t| \approx 10$. The leakage is observed at every clock cycle, as we start supplying masked inputs during initialization stage prior catching the trace image, so the full pipeline is busy, meaning that there is an input reached stage 5 at the moment of the first clock cycle. Even though the leakage is observable, it is not considered extremely large for 100 million runs. We conclude our tests running the second version of five-stage implementation, implementing $\mathbb{GF}(2^4)$ blocks in the balanced way, described in Sect. 4.3. This TVLA result indicates no first-order leakage with 250 million traces collected, confirming our initial assumption. We proceed with simulation-based experiments to verify our model assumptions in a noiseless setting.

5.2 Spectre Experiments

Spectre is a transistor-level circuit simulator provided by Cadence Design Systems, capable of accurately simulating the currents and voltages in an integrated circuit. It is based on the SPICE simulation methodology and enables accurate, time-resolved analysis of switching activity for side-channel evaluation. Spectre requires only a netlist of the design and the corresponding cell library to run the

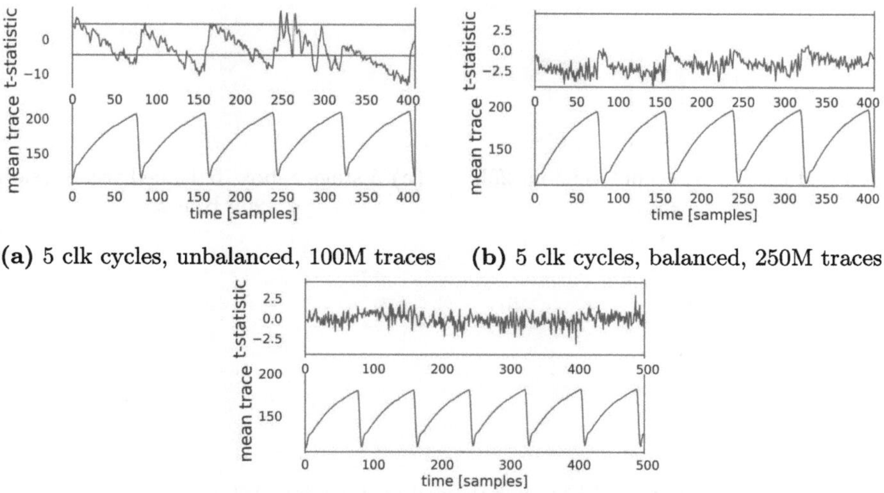

(a) 5 clk cycles, unbalanced, 100M traces **(b)** 5 clk cycles, balanced, 250M traces

(c) 6 clk cycles, secure, 100M traces

Fig. 9. TVLA results for the AES S-boxes implemented on FPGA.

simulations. For our experiments, we use the open-source FreePDK45 transistor models together with the NANGATE 45 nm cell library, and we synthesize the netlists using Synopsys Design Compiler. The synthesis tool is configured to prevent cross-module optimizations, ensuring that the individual RTL modules remain structurally distinct. Moreover, Spectre allows us to evaluate a standalone AES S-box without interference from the PRNG, as fresh random bits can be pre-generated and supplied directly as simulation inputs. Since no physical platform is involved, the results are free from platform-induced noise.

In contrast to FPGA-based measurements, Spectre does not use a fixed sampling rate; instead, it records voltage changes only at the time points where switching activity occurs in the simulated netlist. Although SPICE-based simulations have historically been considered complex and slow, taking between 4 and 26 h to evaluate a masked DOM gate with an additional XOR operation, and potentially unreliable due to false positives introduced by Analysis Time-Step (ATS) optimizations [28], Spectre provides high temporal resolution precisely where it is needed most. To reduce false positives in our experiments, we use *Spectre X* configured in the most accurate *CX* preset. For the initial part of a clock cycle, where most glitches occur, new samples are generated with sub-picosecond precision (less than 0.1 ps), while during idle portions of the clock cycle, the sampling rate is reduced to 0.1 ns. This approach substantially improves simulation efficiency: we were able to evaluate our fully masked AES S-box implementations within 35 days, even when simulating twice the number of clock cycles required for proper initialization. In our experiments, we record the output signals as well as selected intermediate signals to verify the correctness of our tests, which increases the data volume and, consequently, the simulation time.

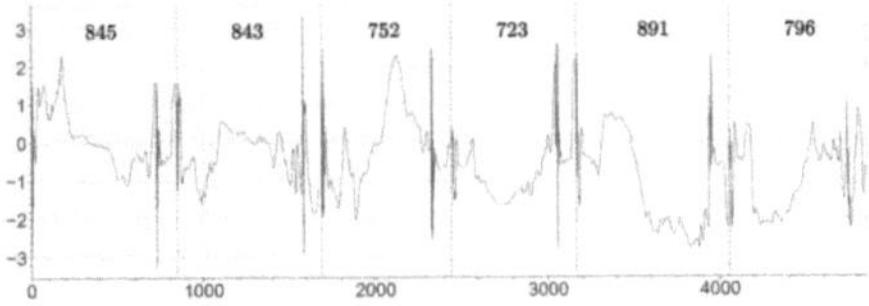

(a) 6 stage S-box, secure version, 20k traces.

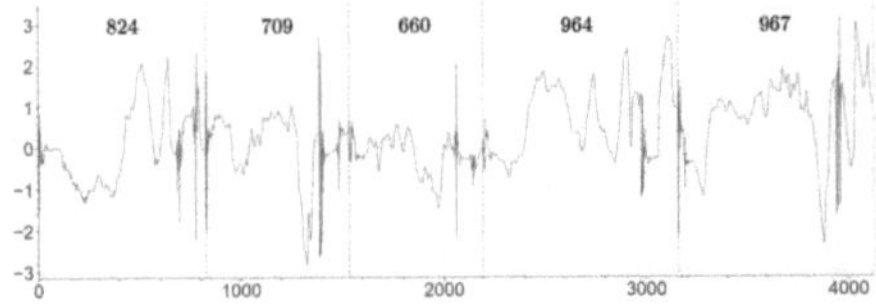

(c) 5 stage S-box, balanced tree version, 20k traces.

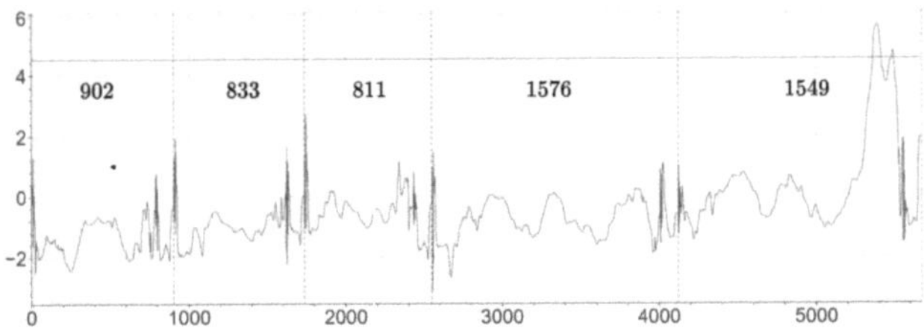

(b) 5 stage S-box, unbalanced tree version, 10k traces.

Fig. 10. TVLA results for the AES S-box simulated in Spectre.

As mentioned above, Spectre uses a dynamic sampling rate, which is illustrated in Fig. 10. As a result, TVLA cannot be applied directly, because each trace contains a variable number of switching events in the combinational logic. To address this issue, we apply linear interpolation on a per-cycle basis as follows. First, we scan all traces to identify the clock edges (the stimulation frequency is fixed at 100 MHz, so each clock cycle has a constant duration). Second, for each cycle, we determine the trace that contains the largest number of samples. Finally, we interpolate all remaining traces to match this maximal sample count, ensuring uniform sampling across experiments.

We perform the same set of experiments previously carried out on the FPGA. For additional noise reduction, we supply only a single input value to the S-box. Furthermore, we allow several clock cycles to elapse to ensure that the pipeline is fully initialized and not affected by transient input noise. Because Spectre simulations are significantly more time-consuming and inherently noise-free, we collect a reduced number of traces. As a sanity check, we first evaluate the original De Cnudde design over 20,000 traces, again confirming the absence of leakage (Fig. 10(a)).

Next, we evaluate the reduced-latency design from Sect. 4.2. As shown in Fig. 10(b), this version exhibits leakage, particularly in the penultimate stage, when the actual data is replaced by zeros. These observations confirm our intuition that an unbalanced tree is a suboptimal choice in settings with minimal noise.

Finally, we evaluate the second variant of our implementation described in Sect. 4.3. The balanced structure increases the indistinguishability of the timing of switches, and the subsequent recombination of inputs further reinforces this effect. As shown in Fig. 10(c), this design exhibits no observable leakage.

6 Conclusion

In this work, we demonstrated that conventional probing models, including the robust and RR-probing models, can be overly conservative for complex circuits where glitches interact in non-trivial ways. By introducing the HR-probing model, we provided a framework that captures data-dependent glitch propagation more accurately and reflects the practical limits of leakage observability. Using this model, we showed that the modified S-box implementation is secure against first-order attacks in both noiseless simulations and FPGA measurements, despite being theoretically vulnerable under standard robust probing assumptions.

However, the HR-probing model is not yet fully formalized, and its applicability to general circuits remains limited, as the success probability of an HR-probing adversary depends strongly on the specific layout of the implementation. Future work should focus on generalizing the model to arbitrary designs and integrating it with standard cell libraries to enable automated leakage analysis of practical layouts.

Acknowledgments. This work was supported by the Flemish Government through the Cybersecurity Research Program with grant number: VOEWICS02. In addition, this work was partially supported by the Flemish Government through FWO Project "MatSec": G0ABK25N.

Disclosure of Interests. The authors have no competing interests to declare that are relevant to the content of this article.

References

1. Barthe, G., et al.: Strong non-interference and type-directed higher-order masking. In: Proceedings of the 2016 ACM SIGSAC Conference on Computer and Communications Security, pp. 116–129. CCS 2016. Association for Computing Machinery (2016)
2. Barthe, G., Dupressoir, F., Faust, S., Grégoire, B., Standaert, F.-X., Strub, P.-Y.: Parallel implementations of masking schemes and the bounded moment leakage model. In: Coron, J.-S., Nielsen, J.B. (eds.) EUROCRYPT 2017. LNCS, vol. 10210, pp. 535–566. Springer, Cham (2017). https://doi.org/10.1007/978-3-319-56620-7_19
3. Becker, G., et al.: Test vector leakage assessment (tvla) methodology in practice. In: International Cryptographic Module Conference, vol. 1001, p. 13. sn (2013)
4. Bertoni, G., Daemen, J., Peeters, M., Van Assche, G.: Keccak. In: Johansson, T., Nguyen, P.Q. (eds.) EUROCRYPT 2013. LNCS, vol. 7881, pp. 313–314. Springer, Heidelberg (2013). https://doi.org/10.1007/978-3-642-38348-9_19
5. Brier, E., Clavier, C., Olivier, F.: Correlation power analysis with a leakage model. In: Joye, M., Quisquater, J.-J. (eds.) CHES 2004. LNCS, vol. 3156, pp. 16–29. Springer, Heidelberg (2004). https://doi.org/10.1007/978-3-540-28632-5_2
6. Canright, D.: A very compact S-Box for AES. In: Rao, J.R., Sunar, B. (eds.) CHES 2005. LNCS, vol. 3659, pp. 441–455. Springer, Heidelberg (2005). https://doi.org/10.1007/11545262_32

7. Cassiers, G., Standaert, F.: Trivially and efficiently composing masked gadgets with probe isolating non-interference. IEEE Trans. Inf. For. Sec. **15**, 2542–2555 (2020)
8. Chari, S., Jutla, C.S., Rao, J.R., Rohatgi, P.: Towards sound approaches to counteract power-analysis attacks. In: Wiener, M. (ed.) Advances in Cryptology – CRYPTO' 99, pp. 398–412. Springer, Heidelberg (1999)
9. Coron, J.S., Giraud, C., Prouff, E., Renner, S., Rivain, M., Vadnala, P.K.: Conversion of security proofs from one leakage model to another: a new issue. In: Schindler, W., Huss, S.A. (eds.) Constructive Side-Channel Analysis and Secure Design, pp. 69–81. Springer, Heidelberg (2012)
10. Daemen, J., Rijmen, V.: Advanced Encryption Standard (AES). National Institute of Standards and Technology (NIST), FIPS PUB 197, November 2001
11. De Cnudde, T., Bilgin, B., Gierlichs, B., Nikov, V., Nikova, S., Rijmen, V.: Does coupling affect the security of masked implementations? In: Guilley, S. (ed.) Constr. Side-Channel Anal. and Sec. Design, pp. 1–18. Springer Internn. Publ. (2017)
12. De Cnudde, T., Reparaz, O., Bilgin, B., Nikova, S., Nikov, V., Rijmen, V.: Masking aes with d+1 shares in hardware. In: Gierlichs, B., Poschmann, A.Y. (eds.) Cryptogr. Hardw. and Emb. Systems – CHES 2016, pp. 194–212. Springer, Heidelberg (2016)
13. Dhooghe, S., Nikova, S., Rijmen, V.: Threshold implementations in the robust probing model. In: Proceedings of ACM Workshop on Theory of Implementation Security Workshop, pp. 30–37. TIS'19. Association for Computing Machinery (2019)
14. Faust, S., Grosso, V., Pozo, S.M.D., Paglialonga, C., Standaert, F.: Composable masking schemes in the presence of physical defaults & the robust probing model. IACR Trans. Cryptogr. Hardw. Embed. Syst. **2018**(3), 89–120 (2018)
15. Gandolfi, K., Mourtel, C., Olivier, F.: Electromagnetic analysis: concrete results. In: Koç, Ç.K., Naccache, D., Paar, C. (eds.) CHES 2001. LNCS, vol. 2162, pp. 251–261. Springer, Heidelberg (2001). https://doi.org/10.1007/3-540-44709-1_21
16. Goubin, L., Patarin, J.: Des and differential power analysis the "duplication" method. In: Koç, Ç.K., Paar, C. (eds.) Cryptographic Hardware and Embedded Systems, pp. 158–172. Springer, Heidelberg (1999)
17. Gross, H., Mangard, S., Korak, T.: Domain-oriented masking: Compact masked hardware implementations with arbitrary protection order. In: Proceedings of the 2016 ACM Workshop on Theory of Implementation Security, p. 3. Association for Computing Machinery (2016)
18. Guntur, H., Ishii, J., Satoh, A.: Side-channel attack user reference architecture board SAKURA-G. In: IEEE 3rd Global Conference on Consumer Electronics, GCCE 2014, pp. 271–274. IEEE (2014)
19. Ishai, Y., Sahai, A., Wagner, D.: Private circuits: securing hardware against probing attacks. In: Boneh, D. (ed.) CRYPTO 2003. LNCS, vol. 2729, pp. 463–481. Springer, Heidelberg (2003). https://doi.org/10.1007/978-3-540-45146-4_27
20. Knichel, D., Moradi, A.: Low-latency hardware private circuits. In: Proceedings of the 2022 ACM SIGSAC Conference on Computer and Communications Security, pp. 1799–1812. CCS '22, Association for Computing Machinery (2022)
21. Knichel, D., Moradi, A., Müller, N., Sasdrich, P.: Automated generation of masked hardware. IACR Trans. Cryptogr. Hardw. Embed. Syst. **1**, 589–629 (2022)
22. Kocher, P., Jaffe, J., Jun, B.: Differential power analysis. In: Wiener, M. (ed.) Advances in Cryptology – CRYPTO' 99, pp. 388–397. Springer, Heidelberg (1999)

23. Kocher, P.C.: Timing attacks on implementations of diffie-hellman, rsa, dss, and other systems. In: Koblitz, N. (ed.) Advances in Cryptology – CRYPTO '96, pp. 104–113. Springer, Heidelberg (1996)
24. Kumar, S.V.D., Balasch, J., Gierlichs, B., Verbauwhede, I.: Low-cost first-order secure boolean masking in glitchy hardware. IEEE Trans. Inf. For. Sec. **20**, 2437–2449 (2025)
25. Leiserson, A.J., Marson, M.E., Wachs, M.A.: Gate-level masking under a path-based leakage metric. In: Batina, L., Robshaw, M. (eds.) CHES 2014. LNCS, vol. 8731, pp. 580–597. Springer, Heidelberg (2014). https://doi.org/10.1007/978-3-662-44709-3_32
26. Mangard, S., Oswald, E., Popp, T.: Power analysis attacks -revealing the secrets of smart cards. Springer (2007)
27. Mangard, S., Pramstaller, N., Oswald, E.: Successfully attacking masked AES hardware implementations. In: Rao, J.R., Sunar, B. (eds.) CHES 2005. LNCS, vol. 3659, pp. 157–171. Springer, Heidelberg (2005). https://doi.org/10.1007/11545262_12
28. Monta, K., Nagata, M., Balasch, J., Verbauwhede, I.: On the unpredictability of SPICE simulations for side-channel leakage verification of masked cryptographic circuits. In: 60th ACM/IEEE Design Automation Conference, DAC 2023, pp. 1–6. IEEE (2023)
29. Moradi, A.: Postponing the glitches is not enough - A critical analysis of the DATE 2024 E-ISW masking scheme (2025). https://eprint.iacr.org/2025/2084
30. Müller, N., Moradi, A.: Robust but relaxed probing model. IACR Trans. Cryptogr. Hardw. Embed. Syst. **2024**(4), 451–482 (2024)
31. Nikova, S., Rechberger, C., Rijmen, V.: Threshold implementations against side-channel attacks and glitches. In: Ning, P., Qing, S., Li, N. (eds.) Information and Communications Security, pp. 529–545. Springer, Heidelberg (2006)
32. Prouff, E., Rivain, M.: Masking against side-channel attacks: a formal security proof. In: Johansson, T., Nguyen, P.Q. (eds.) EUROCRYPT 2013. LNCS, vol. 7881, pp. 142–159. Springer, Heidelberg (2013). https://doi.org/10.1007/978-3-642-38348-9_9
33. Quisquater, J.J., Samyde, D.: Electromagnetic analysis (ema): Measures and counter-measures for smart cards. In: Attali, I., Jensen, T. (eds.) Smart Card Programming and Security, pp. 200–210. Springer, Heidelberg (2001)
34. Reparaz, O., Bilgin, B., Nikova, S., Gierlichs, B., Verbauwhede, I.: Consolidating masking schemes. In: Gennaro, R., Robshaw, M. (eds.) CRYPTO 2015. LNCS, vol. 9215, pp. 764–783. Springer, Heidelberg (2015). https://doi.org/10.1007/978-3-662-47989-6_37
35. Trichina, E.: Combinational logic design for AES subbyte transformation on masked data. IACR Cryptol. ePrint Arch. p. 236 (2003). http://eprint.iacr.org/2003/236
36. V., D.K.S., Dhooghe, S., Balasch, J., Gierlichs, B., Verbauwhede, I.: Time sharing - A novel approach to low-latency masking. IACR Trans. Cryptogr. Hardw. Embed. Syst. **2024**(3), 249–272 (2024)
37. Zhang, Z., Petkova-Nikova, S., Nikov, V.: Glitch-stopping circuits: Hardware secure masking without registers. In: Proceedings of the 2024 on ACM SIGSAC Conference on Computer and Communications Security, pp. 3406–3420. CCS '24. Association for Computing Machinery (2024)

MATSE: Amortized Threshold Symmetric-Key Encryption for Matrices

Rittwik Hajra[1,2], Subha Kar[2(✉)], and Pratyay Mukherjee[2,3]

[1] AlgoBengal Research Labs, New Town, India
[2] Indian Statistical Institute, Kolkata, India
subhakar9732@gmail.com
[3] Hashgraph, Kolkata, India

Abstract. Threshold Symmetric-key Encryption (TSE) was introduced by Agrawal et al. [CCS 2018], in that a client needs to interact for every encryption and decryption. Later, Christodorescu et al.. [CCS 2021] proposed an amortization technique where a large block of data can be encrypted with a single interaction by a possibly more privileged encryptor, whereas a decryptor (who is possibly less privileged) must interact for decryption of each individual ciphertext. Even more recently, Dey et al. [CiC 2025] proposed a hierarchical TSE scheme, in that decryption for a contiguous data set (of size n_c) can be performed with $\log(n_c)$ interactions, but with an additional logarithmic overhead in the encryption.

In this work, we consider amortized TSE for data that is structured in a tabular (or matrix) form. We specifically consider the setting where data can be encrypted row-wise and decrypted column-wise (or vice versa) – this pattern emerges for any time-series data where encryption takes place, say hour-wise for each day, and decryption may request to decrypt data for a particular time slot of all days of the week.

Our main technique uses the same building block as Christodorescu et al. [CCS 2021], namely flexible threshold key derivation, but used in a different way – this leads to a TSE scheme where a single interaction suffices for decryption of a column. Furthermore, instead of group commitments (aka Merkle trees) of each message, our construction uses simple commitments for rows and columns – this way we can also improve the additional storage overhead (beyond the ciphertexts) from $O(mn)$ to $O(m+n)$ for a table consisting of m rows and n columns.

Keywords: Threshold Symmetric-key Encryption · Flexible Threshold Key-Derivation · Commitment

1 Introduction

Many important applications, such as healthcare systems, financial services, and government records, deal with *sensitive data* that is often stored in a *tabular format* consisting of rows and columns. Consider, for example, *time-series data* such as credit card transaction logs collected by a bank. Such data naturally

N. El Mrabet et al. (Eds.): AFRICACRYPT 2026, LNCS 16832, pp. 236–260, 2026.
https://doi.org/10.1007/978-3-032-31130-6_10

forms a table or matrix: each row represents all the transactions for a particular day, while each column corresponds to a specific time window across multiple days. For instance, data from 12:00 PM to 1:00 PM for each day of a week would form a column. A bank may wish to encrypt data row-wise for storage efficiency and privacy–for example, encrypting each day's transactions as a single unit. Later, however, an analyst might need to retrieve and decrypt only the transactions that occurred between 12:00 PM and 1:00 PM across all days, which corresponds to decrypting data column-wise. This scenario highlights a common challenge in tabular datasets: encryption and decryption are often performed along different dimensions, requiring a scheme that can efficiently support both.

Threshold symmetric encryption (TSE) addresses the core problem of key compromise by splitting a master key into multiple parts, or *shares*, which are distributed among n servers. To perform any cryptographic operation, at least t out of the n servers must work together. This ensures that no single server can misuse or reveal the secret key, significantly reducing the risk of key compromise.

The TSE framework was formally introduced by Agrawal et al. in their DiSE model [AMMR18]. In this model, encryption and decryption are achieved through interactive protocols with the servers holding the key shares. For example, to encrypt a message, a server must engage with $t-1$ other servers to generate a valid ciphertext. Similarly, to decrypt, one need to interact with $t-1$ or more servers to recover the original plaintext. As long as there are fewer than t malicious corruptions, this (informally) guarantees:

- **Correctness:** the adversary cannot make the decryption go wrong,
- **Confidentiality:** the adversary cannot learn anything about the data,
- **Authenticity/Integrity:** the adversary cannot forge valid ciphertexts.

Later, Christodorescu et al. introduced *Amortized TSE (ATSE)* [CGMS21], which improves efficiency by allowing many records to be encrypted together in a single threshold operation by a more privileged encryptor. This bulk encryption significantly reduces the time and communication needed for very large datasets. However, the decryption, potentially performed by a less privileged decryptor (who may perform certain data analytics on specific data and thus may not need to access the entire set), still happens individually, requiring one interaction per operation.

More recently, a hierarchical extension called *HiSE* was proposed by Dey et al. [DMSS24]. HiSE supports both bulk encryption and bulk decryption (of a subset) in a hierarchical fashion, enabling efficient handling of structured datasets. However, its strengths are best realized when decrypting *contiguous blocks* of data, such as consecutive rows or consecutive time intervals. When the access pattern is highly scattered or selective, such as same time across different days, HiSE provides limited benefits. Moreover, to enable its hierarchical decryption features, HiSE incurs additional overheads: its encryption process is slower by a multiplicative factor of $\log N$, where N is the total number of encrypted items (for our case $N = \mathsf{mn}$ denotes the total number of elements in the matrix/table of m rows and n columns).

Despite these advances, existing TSE and ATSE schemes struggle to scale when applied directly to large tabular datasets. So we ask the following question:

Can we design a TSE scheme amortized for matrices/tabular data?

In this paper, we resolve this by proposing the notion of MATSE, or *amortized TSE for matrices*, and then providing a provably secure construction that satisfies all requirements as laid out above.

Our Approach. Basically, our approach is to encrypt a matrix M of dimension (say) $\mathsf{m} \times \mathsf{n}$ row-wise. Each row M_k is committed and subsequently sent to the servers to get the row-specific key. An element M_k^ℓ in the cell which is at the k-th row and ℓ-th column is then locally encrypted using a unique key specific to that (k, ℓ)-th cell – this key is derived locally using the derived row-wise key, and the column information. Our decryption is column-wise, in that the derived key is column-specific, and the computation of the cell-specific key is done locally using row information. To enable ciphertext integrity, we also use a Merkle-tree commitment on top of the column-wise commitments – so the total number of commitments still stays $O(\mathsf{m}+\mathsf{n})$. We stress that it is possible to allow encryption and decryption column-wise and row-wise, respectively, or even both row and column-wise in the same scheme.[1] However, for notational simplicity, we give up on the generality and focus on a specific case where encryption is always row-wise and decryption is always column-wise.

1.1 Our Contribution

Our contribution can be summarized as follows:

- We introduce the formal notion of *Amortized TSE for Matrices* (MATSE). We provide rigorous definitions for *correctness*, *message privacy*, and *ciphertext integrity*. While our framework broadly follows earlier works on TSE, it diverges by explicitly modeling the common structure underlying these protocols – namely: local commitment, a request-response phase, and a final local encryption. This structural specification simplifies the analysis and enables a more precise definition of ciphertext integrity, avoiding the "one-more" style formulation adopted by almost all prior TSE definitions.[2]

[1] We note that, to enable decryption along any dimension, we need to incorporate a Merkle tree on top of the individual commitments. For example, if there are n many columns, and therefore n many commitments, the Merkle tree will have $2\mathsf{n}$ many elements.

[2] Prior works [AMMR18, CGMS21, DMSS24] refer to this property as *authenticity*. To avoid confusion, we use the term ciphertext integrity. Although intuitively stronger than authenticity, the two properties appear formally incomparable due to syntactic differences.

- We propose a concrete MATSE construction, built generically on the same underlying primitive used by ATSE [CGMS21], namely *flexible threshold key-derivation* (FTKD). Similar to ATSE, our construction relies on a special type of FTKD called *simple FTKD*. We introduce a notation, aligned with our MATSE definition, that explicitly captures the structure of simple FTKD. Unlike [CGMS21], which uses Merkle-tree-based group commitments, we employ lightweight commitments to individual rows and columns. However, to achieve ciphertext integrity, we add a layer of Merkle commitments over the column-wise commitments, so that decrypted plaintexts can be verified correctly. This design keeps the total number of commitments bounded by $O(\mathsf{m}+\mathsf{n})$.[3]
- We provide a formal proof showing that our construction satisfies the MATSE security definition. The proof relies on generic FTKD properties such as pseudorandomness. Correctness and integrity are ensured by the binding properties of both the base commitments and the Merkle commitments.

2 Technical Overview

Recall FTKD. Our construction builds generically on any simple FTKD scheme. Recall from [CGMS21] that an FTKD (which builds on the notion of left/right constrained PRFs [BW13]) allows a party to derive keys at different granularities: a *whole-key* bound to the entire input (x, y), or a *partial-key* bound to one component (x or y). A partial key can later be locally combined with the other component to reconstruct the whole key. The long-term key sk is secret-shared among n parties, such that any subset of t parties can jointly derive either partial keys $(k_{x\|\star}, k_{\star\|y})$ or the full output $w = \mathsf{PRF}_k(x, y)$. Security requires w to remain pseudorandom given arbitrary inputs or constrained keys, unless enough information is present to trivially recover it.[4]

Working Principle of DiSE. Now, to set the stage, first recall the DiSE TSE scheme, which is built from a distributed PRF (DPRF). An encryptor with identity j first generates a standard commitment γ of a message m using randomness r. Next, the encryptor and the servers interactively evaluate the DPRF on the pair $(j\|\gamma)$, producing a pseudorandom, message-specific key $w = \mathsf{DPRF}(j\|\gamma)$. This key is then used to deterministically encrypt $(m\|r)$ as $e = \mathsf{PRG}(w) \oplus (m\|r)$. The resulting ciphertext is (j, γ, e). Decryption proceeds by re-evaluating the DPRF to recover w, using it to decrypt e, and finally verifying that the opening (m, r) matches the original commitment γ.

[3] Additionally, since we do not follow one-more type definitions for ciphertext integrity, we do not need to use the so-called cardinality binding property associated with Merkle trees, which was essential in the ATSE construction.

[4] The instantiation follows from bilinear pairing, and is included (cf. Fig. A.1) for completeness. For a detailed analysis we refer to [CGMS21].

Revisiting ATSE Construction. To enable bulk encryption, the ATSE construction mirrors this basic flow but replaces the standard commitment with a *Merkle-tree commitment*, which supports fine-grained openings. Specifically, a sequence of messages $(m_1, \ldots, m_N)$ is committed with a single short root γ, while preserving the ability to later reveal any specific message m_i without exposing the others. To ensure privacy of unrevealed messages, the leaf nodes are randomized using independent salts $(r_1, \ldots, r_N)$. Each message m_i has a unique root-to-leaf opening path q_i of size $O(\log(N))$. To encrypt in bulk, the encryptor first commits to the entire message tuple $(m_1, \ldots, m_N)$ to obtain the Merkle root γ. It then runs FTKD on the partial input $(j\|\gamma)$ – corresponding to the shared group context – deriving a *group key* $K_{(j\|\gamma)\|\star}$. For each individual message m_i, the encryptor locally derives a message-specific key $K_{j\|\gamma\|q_i}$ from the derived key $K_{(j\|\gamma)\|\star}$ and the unique message-specific Merkle opening path q_i and encrypts it deterministically:

$$e_i = \mathsf{PRG}(K_{j\|\gamma\|q_i}) \oplus (m_i\|r_i).$$

The ciphertext for m_i is (j, γ, q_i, e_i). To decrypt, a user directly invokes FTKD on the full input $(j\|\gamma\|q_i)$ to obtain $K_{j\|\gamma\|q_i}$, uses it to recover (m_i, r_i) from e_i, and finally verifies that this pair is consistent with the root commitment γ via the path q_i.

Our MATSE Construction. Our construction uses FTKD as well, but the message-specific key now has a different form. For a matrix M of dimensions $\mathsf{m} \times \mathsf{n}$, the encryptor first chooses a randomness matrix R of the same dimension, and then executes the following steps:

- For each row M_k ($k \in [\mathsf{m}]$) generate plain commitment α_k using corresponding row R_k from the randomness matrix. Then deterministically commit (e.g. simply using a hash function) $\boldsymbol{\alpha} = (\alpha_1, \ldots, \alpha_{\mathsf{m}})$ to obtain γ_α.
- For each column M^ℓ ($\ell \in [\mathsf{n}]$) generate plain commitment β_ℓ using corresponding column R^ℓ from the randomness matrix.
- Compute deterministically a Merkle tree root γ_β from $(\beta_1, \ldots, \beta_{\mathsf{n}})$, where the unique column-specific opening paths are denoted by ϕ_ℓ.

Then, for each row k it uses the FTKD on partial input $(j\|\gamma\|\alpha_k)$ to derive the partial row key $K_{(j\|\gamma\|\alpha_k)\|\star}$, where $\gamma = (\gamma_\alpha\|\gamma_\beta)$. Then, for each message M_k^ℓ it locally derives a message-specific key $K_{(j\|\gamma\|\alpha_k)\|(\beta_\ell\|\phi_\ell)}$. The rest of the procedure is similar to DiSE and ATSE, as the full ciphertext is $(j, \gamma, \alpha_k, \beta_\ell, \phi_\ell, E_k^\ell)$ where:

$$E_k^\ell = \mathsf{PRG}(K_{(j\|\gamma\|\alpha_k)\|(\beta_\ell\|\phi_\ell)}) \oplus (M_k^\ell\|R_k^\ell).$$

Now, let us elaborate how decryption works. A decryptor, who has the ℓ-th ciphertext column $(j, \gamma, \boldsymbol{\alpha}, \beta_\ell, \phi_\ell, E^\ell)$, first makes a partial FTKD call to obtain the column key $K_{\star\|(\beta_\ell\|\phi_\ell)}$. Then, for the k-th element of the column, the decryptor locally derives the key $K_{(j\|\gamma\|\alpha_k)\|(\beta_\ell\|\phi_\ell)}$ by combining the partial key with $(j\|\gamma\|\alpha_k)$. Then, the plaintext is recovered as $(M_k^\ell\|R_k^\ell)$. Once the entire column $(M^\ell\|R^\ell)$ is recovered, then for integrity, the following verification must be done:

- parse γ as $\gamma_\alpha \| \gamma_\beta$;
- check if γ_α is a correct commitment of $\boldsymbol{\alpha}$;
- check if β_ℓ correctly opens as the ℓ-th element with respect to Merkle root γ_β and path opening ϕ_ℓ;
- finally if β_ℓ is the correct commitment of $(M^\ell \| R^\ell)$.

Some Intuitions. Now, let us provide some intuitions on why this construction works. Firstly, due to the consistency properties of FTKD, the correctness follows easily. Message privacy relies on the pseudorandomness of the message-specific FTKD whole key, even when up to $t-1$ parties are corrupt. To break ciphertext integrity, a party must compute one of the partial keys, which is impossible, as that would either break the pseudorandomness of FTKD or the binding of the commitments. Note that, our ciphertext integrity definition requires one to produce a new ciphertext column $(j^*, \gamma^*, \boldsymbol{\alpha}^*, \beta_\ell^*, \phi_\ell^*, E^\ell)$ such that neither of the components $(j^* \| \gamma^*)$ or $(\boldsymbol{\alpha}^*, \beta_\ell^*, \phi_\ell^*)$ were queried before. Assuming that the commitments are binding, this basically makes the ciphertext unique given the message, randomnesses and the FTKD secret key. So, in order to break integrity, one must be able to compute $K_{(j\|\gamma\|\alpha_k)\|(\beta_\ell\|\phi_\ell)}$ without explicitly querying the FTKD servers – this would contradict the pseudorandomness.

Comparison with ATSE. We note that the main difference from ATSE is that, instead of using a Merkle commitment on all $N = \mathsf{mn}$ messages, we use plain commitments for each row and column. Though we use a Merkle tree on top of the column commitments, the overall number of commitment strings (each may be of length 128 bits or any other security parameter) remains $O(\mathsf{m} + \mathsf{n})$, whereas for ATSE this becomes $O(\mathsf{mn})$. Since the encrypted values are supposed to be stored in a data server, this accounts for substantial savings in additional storage (beyond ciphertexts). The rest of the parameters are almost same as ATSE. In particular, as compared to HiSE [DMSS24], this is beneficial because HiSE incurs an additional $\log(\mathsf{mn})$ factor in the encryption time.

2.1 Extensions

Encryption/Decryption Across Other Dimensions. While we focus on only a specific setting where the encryption is always row-wise and decryption is always column-wise, it is possible to easily adapt the idea to column-wise encryption and row-wise decryption. To enable this, the only change needed is to use the Merkle commitment on the row commitments instead of the column commitments – this is because, the ciphertext integrity must ensure that the decrypted row is consistent with commitment. Since the information for other rows are not available at this point, it is important that the root, in this case γ_α, should be verified with the Merkle path and only α_k. In fact, one can further extend to encryption or decryption across both columns – this would require having Merkle commitments for both γ_α and γ_β.

Strong Construction. Similar to prior works, DiSE, ATSE or HiSE, we can also augment our construction to support a stronger definition using specific efficient non-interactive zero-knowledge proofs. However, for simplicity we refrain from describing that in details.

3 Related Works

Threshold Cryptography. Threshold cryptography, where cryptographic operations require cooperation among t out of n participants, was established through Shamir's foundational secret sharing scheme [Sha79] and Blakley's geometric approach [Bla79], later extended to threshold cryptographic primitives by Desmedt and Frankel [DF90]. The field advanced significantly with robust threshold signature schemes, including Gennaro et al.'s threshold DSA [GJKR96], Shoup's practical threshold RSA [Sho00], and more recently Gennaro and Goldfeder's fast threshold ECDSA [GG18]. Modern applications have focused on blockchain integration, with Boneh et al.'s threshold BLS signatures [BLS01] for consensus mechanisms, practical cryptocurrency wallet security by Gennaro and Goldfeder [GG20], and connections to secure multiparty computation as surveyed by Lindell [Lin22].

More Threshold Schemes, PRFs, Key-Management, etc. More relevant to our work are the threshold PRFs [MS95,NPR99,Nie02,Dod03,DY05,DYY06, BLMR13]. Naor et al. [NPR99] introduced a design for encrypting messages using their DPRF construction, though it does not provide any integrity. Beyond symmetric-key primitives, the area of *threshold public-key encryption* has also been extensively studied [Fra90,DF90,DDFY94,SG98,CG99,NPR99,DP08]. In such schemes, similar to our symmetric-key setting, the decryption key is distributed among a group of servers using secret sharing, and a minimum threshold of servers must cooperate to decrypt a ciphertext. Jarecki et al. [JKR19] proposed a *threshold, updatable, and oblivious key management* system built on oblivious pseudo-random functions and public-key encryption. However, their public-key systems have the inherent property that *any* party, including potentially untrusted entities, can encrypt a message and generate a ciphertext without any interaction. This makes them unsuitable for our setting, where ciphertext integrity is crucial. Related works such as PASTA [AMMM18], BETA [ABM+21], and PESTO [BFH+20] provide frameworks for threshold authentication, without any privacy.

Threshold Symmetric-Key Encryption (TSE). The concept of threshold symmetric-key encryption (TSE) was first formalized in the DiSE framework, which utilizes a distributed pseudorandom function (DPRF) to ensure that each encryption or decryption operation requires collaboration of t out of n key-sharing servers [AMMR18]. DiSE provides both privacy and authenticity; however, its design incurs significant per-message interaction, limiting throughput to a few hundred operations per second.

Table 1. Comparison of threshold symmetric encryption schemes for an $m \times n$ dataset.

Scheme	Enc Int.	Dec Int.	Storage	Use Case
DiSE [AMMR18]	mn	mn	$O(mn)$	Small data
ATSE [CGMS21]	1	mn	$O(mn)$	Bulk enc.
HiSE [DMSS24]	1	$O(\log(mn))$	$O(mn)$	Ranges
MATSE(Our)	m	n	$O(m+n)$	Tabular

Amortized Threshold Encryption. To alleviate DiSE's per-message overhead, the ATSE scheme introduces an amortized approach whereby a client performs a single threshold key-derivation (FTKD) to obtain a group key for a large batch of messages [CGMS21]. This design reduces encryption latency by up to 40 and increases bulk throughput by approximately 30 compared to DiSE, though decryption still requires one server interaction per ciphertext, and hence is not suitable for tabular data. However, in the same paper [CGMS21], the authors briefly mentioned how FTKD can be used for tabular data, without providing any specifics. In this work, we expand on that by combining with adequate commitment schemes, which yields a substantial savings in the storage overhead.

Hierarchical (Threshold) Symmetric-Key Encryption. HiSE extends ATSE by employing a hierarchical (Merkle) access structure enabling sub-linear decryption cost: decrypting any contiguous subsequence of length N_s requires $O(\log N_s)$ interactions rather than $O(N_s)$ [DMSS24]. However, this comes for $O(\log N)$ encryption overhead. Even more importantly, their techniques are most beneficial for the decryption of contiguous data, and hence is not suitable for matrices or tabular data.

Other TSE Schemes. Apart from the above works, [Muk20] construct a scheme which is secure against adaptive adversaries, whereas [ADL+22] worked with a unified definition with enhanced security. In this paper, we stick to static adversaries and work with new definitions that follow the past frameworks starting from DiSE, but with some significant differences (Table 1).

Connections to Constrained PRFs and ABE/HIBE. The FTKD core in ATSE and in our work can be viewed as a threshold instantiation of left/right constrained PRFs (Boneh–Waters) [BW13]. HiSE's hierarchical decryption structure draws on binary-tree encryption techniques from the HIBE/ABE literature [CHK03,BMS22], suitably tailored to symmetric-key settings with built-in authenticity guarantees.

4 Preliminaries

4.1 Notation

We use $\mathbb{N}$ to denote the set of positive integers, and for any $n \in \mathbb{N}$ we write $[n] = \{1, 2, \ldots, n\}$. The security parameter is denoted by κ. Unless otherwise specified, we assume that every algorithm implicitly takes κ as input, and all definitions are understood to hold for sufficiently large choices of $\kappa \in \mathbb{N}$. For brevity, we typically omit explicit mention of the security parameter. Throughout the paper, we use the symbol $\perp$ to denote invalidity; in particular, if an algorithm outputs $\perp$, it indicates that the algorithm has either failed or detected an error during execution. For a matrix A, we denote the i-th column as A^i, and the j-th row as A_j and the (i, j)-th cell by A_i^j. Vectors or tuples of the form $(v_1, \ldots, v_n)$ are denoted as $\boldsymbol{v}$. The i-th element of $\boldsymbol{v}$ is denoted by v_i.

4.2 Commitments

We need plain commitments and Merkle tree commitments.

Plain Commitments. We use notation CMT for plain commitments. We assume that the scheme takes arbitrary-length inputs and produces strings of length κ. In general, we assume CMT to be a deterministic algorithm that has the *binding property* – it is computationally infeasible to produce two inputs, such that both map to the same output string. For hiding, we additionally use a randomness of length equal to the message in the input. The entire input serves as an opening. Such commitments are instantiated by any collision-resistant hash function.

Merkle Tree Commitments. We also need Merkle tree commitments, which consist of three deterministic algorithms:

- $\mathsf{MKT.Com}(v_1, \ldots, v_\mathsf{n})$ takes a vector of length n as input, and output a Merkle root γ of size κ.
- $\mathsf{MKT.Open}(\boldsymbol{v}, i)$ takes the entire vector, and a position i, and outputs a Merkle opening path ϕ_i unique to v_i. ϕ_i consists of $\log(\mathsf{n})$ elements each of size κ.
- $\mathsf{MKT.Ver}(\gamma, v, \phi, i)$ verifies whether the value v is indeed the i-th element of the vector which yields the root γ using the opening ϕ. It outputs 1 if the verification succeeds, and 0 otherwise.

Merkle tree has a well-known instantiation using collision-resistant hash, which takes 2κ bit input and produces κ-bit output. We omit the detailed description.

4.3 Simple Flexible Threshold Key-Derivation (Simple FTKD)

Our construction is generically based on an FTKD scheme [CGMS21], precisely a simple FTKD scheme, in that the key-derivation protocol has a specific request-response (or one full round trip) structure. Here we provide the simple FTKD syntax, which is consistent with our notations.

Definition 1 ***(Simple Flexible Threshold Key-Derivation (Simple FTKD)).*** *A* flexible threshold key-derivation *FTKD for a threshold access structure* (t, n) *tuple of algorithms/protocols* $(\mathsf{FT.Setup}, \mathsf{FT.}\Pi_{\mathsf{KDF}}, \mathsf{FT.Combine}, \mathsf{FT.WKGen})$ *with the following syntax:*

- $\mathsf{FT.Setup}(1^\kappa, n, t)$. FT.Setup *is a one-time setup that takes the total number of participants* n *and a threshold* $t(\leq n)$ *as input, along with the security parameters, and outputs the secret share* sk_i *of the key* sk *and public parameters* pp. *All algorithms/protocols below obtain* pp *as implicit input.*
- $\mathsf{FT}.\Pi_{\mathsf{KDF}}(i, S, (v, \mathtt{f.mode}))$*: This is a one-round trip requestresponse protocol initiated by a party-*i*, who sends a message of the form* $(v, \mathtt{f.mode})$ *to the parties belonging to some set* S *where* $|S| \geq t-1$*. Upon receiving the request, each party* $j \in S$ *responds directly to party* i *with a reply* $\mathtt{resp}_j$*. Importantly, the parties within set* S *do not communicate among themselves. The variable* f.mode *specifies the type of request and can take values from the set* $\{\mathtt{left}, \mathtt{right}\}$.
- $\mathsf{FT.Combine}(\mathsf{sk}_i, \{\mathtt{resp}_j\}_{j \in S\setminus\{i\}})$. *A deterministic local combining function initiated by party-*i *to combine responses* $\mathtt{resp}_j$ *from a set* $S \setminus \{i\}$ *of size* $t-1$ *with the party's own secret to derive the* key.
- $\mathsf{FT.WKGen}(\mathsf{key}, x, \mathtt{f.mode})$. *A deterministic algorithm that computes the whole-key* wk *on input a derived key* key*, an input* x *and a* $\mathtt{f.mode} \in \{\mathtt{left}, \mathtt{right}\}$.

For any $n, t, \kappa \in \mathbb{N}$ *such that* $t \leq n$ *and any* $(\{\mathsf{sk}_i\}_{i\in[n]}, \mathsf{pp})$ *output by* $\mathsf{FT.Setup}(1^\kappa, n, t)$*, the FTKD scheme must satisfy the following properties:*

Key Consistency*: For any set* $S \subseteq [n]$ *with* $|S| \geq t$*, any party* $j \in S$*, any input* $x \in \{(\gamma, \alpha_k), (\gamma, \beta_\ell, \phi_\ell)\}$*, and any* $\mathtt{f.mode} \in \{\mathtt{left}, \mathtt{right}\}$*, if all parties act honestly, then the following probability is at most* $\mathsf{negl}(\kappa)$*:*

$$\Pr\left[\mathsf{FT.WKGen}(\mathsf{key}, x', \mathtt{f.mode}') \neq \mathsf{wk} \;\middle|\; \begin{array}{c} \{\mathtt{resp}_j\}_{j\in S\setminus\{i\}} \leftarrow \mathsf{FT}.\Pi_{\mathsf{KDF}}(i, S, (x, \mathtt{f.mode})); \\ \mathsf{key} \leftarrow \mathsf{FT.Combine}(\mathsf{sk}_i, \{\mathtt{resp}_j\}_{j\in S\setminus\{i\}}); \\ \mathsf{wk} \leftarrow \mathsf{FT.WKGen}(\mathsf{key}, x, \mathtt{f.mode}) \end{array}\right]$$

Where $x' \neq x \in \{(\gamma, \alpha_k), (\gamma, \beta_\ell, \phi_\ell)\}$ *and* $\mathtt{f.mode}' \in \{\mathtt{left}, \mathtt{right}\}$.

Threshold Consistency*: For any two sets* $S, S' \subseteq [n]$ *such that* $|S|, |S'| \geq t$ *any input* x,$\mathtt{f.mode} \in \{\mathtt{left}, \mathtt{right}\}$*, and any two parties* i *and* i' *if all parties act honestly, then the following probability is at most* $1 - \mathsf{negl}(\kappa)$*:*

$$\Pr\left[\mathsf{key} \leftarrow \mathsf{FT.Combine}(\mathsf{sk}_i, \{\mathtt{resp}_j\}_{j\in S\setminus\{i\}}) \;\middle|\; \begin{array}{c} \mathsf{key} \leftarrow \mathsf{FT.Combine}(\mathsf{sk}_{i'}, \{\mathtt{resp}_j\}_{j\in S'\setminus\{i'\}}); \\ \{\mathtt{resp}_j\}_{j\in S\setminus\{i\}} \leftarrow \mathsf{FT}.\Pi_{\mathsf{KDF}}(i, S, (x, \mathtt{f.mode})); \\ \{\mathtt{resp}_j\}_{j\in S'\setminus\{i'\}} \leftarrow \mathsf{FT}.\Pi_{\mathsf{KDF}}(i', S', (x, \mathtt{f.mode})) \end{array}\right]$$

Pseudorandomness*: The* pseudorandomness *property guarantees that the keys derived by the Flexible Threshold Key Derivation (FTKD) scheme are computationally indistinguishable from uniformly random values, even in the presence of an active adversary. Intuitively, an adversary may corrupt up to* $t-1$ *servers and obtain their secret shares, interact with honest servers in multiple executions of the key-derivation protocol, and adaptively request keys in different modes. Nevertheless, the adversary should not be able to distinguish* *any honestly derived whole-key from a truly random string. We say that the scheme satisfies* pseudorandomness *if no probabilistic polynomial-time* (PPT) *adversary* A*, corrupting at most* $t-1$ *parties, can distinguish between honestly derived whole-keys and uniformly random strings with more than negligible advantage in* κ*.*

This is formalised via the following game:

- **Setup.**
  - *Run* $(\{\mathsf{sk}_i\}_{i\in[n]}, \mathsf{pp}) \leftarrow \mathsf{FT.Setup}(1^\kappa, n, t)$*. Give* pp *to the adversary* A*.*
  - *After* A *outputs a set* $C \subseteq [n]$ *of corrupted parties, give* $\{\mathsf{sk}_i\}_{i\in C}$ *to* A*.*
  - *Initialize lists* L_{msg} *with empty set and* $L_{\mathtt{left}}, L_{\mathtt{right}}$ *with 0.*
- **Oracle Access.** *The adversary* A *is given access to the following oracles:*
  - **KDF Oracle Queries:** *On query* $(i, S, (x, \mathtt{f.mode}))$ *such that* $i \in S$
    * *Run* $\{\mathtt{resp}_j\}_{j\in S} \leftarrow \mathsf{FT}.\Pi_{\mathsf{KDF}}(i, S, (x, \mathtt{f.mode}))$*, and compute* $\mathsf{key} \leftarrow \mathsf{FT.Combine}(\mathsf{sk}_i, \{\mathtt{resp}_j\}_{j\in S\setminus\{i\}})$
    * *If* $i \notin C$*, return* key *to* A
    * *If* $i \in C$*, set* $L_{\mathtt{f.mode}} = L_{\mathtt{f.mode}} + |S\setminus C|$ *for* $\mathtt{f.mode} \in \{\mathtt{left}, \mathtt{right}\}$*. When* $L_{\mathtt{f.mode}} \geq t - |C|$ *and* $x = x^*$*, abort. Otherwise when* $x \neq x^*$*, append* x *to* L_{msg}*.*
- **Challenge Oracle.**
  - *At any point* A *outputs a challenge query* $(i^*, S^*, (x^*, \mathtt{f.mode}^*))$*, such that* $i^* \in S^* \setminus C$ *and* $|S^*| \geq t$*.*
  - *If* $x^* \in L_{\mathsf{msg}}$ *then output* $\perp$*.*
  - *Else:*
    * *Run* $\{\mathtt{resp}_j\}_{j\in S^*} \leftarrow \mathsf{FT}.\Pi_{\mathsf{KDF}}(i^*, S^*, (x^*, \mathtt{f.mode}^*))$*.*
    * *Compute* $\mathsf{key}^* \leftarrow \mathsf{FT.Combine}(\mathsf{sk}_i^*, \{\mathtt{resp}_j^*\}_{j\in S^*\setminus\{i^*\}})$
    * *The challenger samples a random bit* $b \xleftarrow{R} \{0,1\}$ *and:*
    * *If* $b = 0$*, compute* $\mathsf{wk}^* \leftarrow \mathsf{FT.WKGen}(\mathsf{key}^*, x, \mathtt{f.mode})$*.*
    * *If* $b = 1$*, sample* $\mathsf{wk}^* \leftarrow \{0,1\}^{|\mathsf{wk}|}$ *uniformly at random.*

  Return wk^* *to* A*. Then the adversary outputs a bit* b'*.*

The adversary's advantage is defined as

$$\mathsf{Adv}_{\mathsf{A}}^{\mathsf{PR}}(\kappa) \;=\; \left|\Pr[b' = b] - \tfrac{1}{2}\right|.$$

The FTKD scheme is pseudorandom *if for all PPT adversaries* A*,*

$$\mathsf{Adv}_{\mathsf{A}}^{\mathsf{PR}}(\kappa) \;\leq\; \mathsf{negl}(\kappa).$$

Instantiating Simple FTKD. We use the same construction as [CGMS21]. For completeness we provide it in Appendix Subsect. A.1. Briefly, it is built over cyclic groups $(\mathbb{G}_0, \mathbb{G}_1, \mathbb{G})$ of prime order q, with hash functions H_1 and H_2 modeled as random oracles and a bilinear pairing $\mathbf{e} : \mathbb{G}_0 \times \mathbb{G}_1 \rightarrow \mathbb{G}$. A secret is shared among n parties using Shamir's (t, n) secret sharing. To derive a key, a party initiates a one-round requestresponse protocol with a subset S of servers, where each server returns a response based on its secret share and the input value v under the chosen mode $\{\texttt{left}, \texttt{right}\}$. Given t valid responses, the initiator combines them using Lagrange interpolation to reconstruct a partial key key, which is then mapped via pairings with the hash of v to obtain the final whole key wk. This design ensures threshold security, consistency across honest servers, and pseudorandomness of derived keys.

5 Our MATSE Definition

Definition 2 (MATSE). *An amortized TSE scheme for tabular data (MATSE) scheme, defined for a t-out-of-n threshold access structure, consists of the following interactive protocols and algorithms:*

- $\mathsf{Setup}(1^\kappa, 1^n, 1^t)$ *. The setup algorithm outputs a t out of n Shamir share of a secret key* sk *and public parameters* pp*. Each party receives its private share* sk_i*. The setup is a one-time procedure and can be executed in a distributed manner using a distributed key generation protocol.*[5] *For simplicity, in this paper, we assume a centralized setup. All subsequent algorithms/protocols take* pp *as input.*
- $\mathsf{Commit}(M, R)$. *The commit procedure takes a matrix plaintext M of dimension* $\mathsf{m} \times \mathsf{n}$ *along with a randomness matrix R of the same dimension to produce a pair of commitment vectors* $(\boldsymbol{\alpha}, \boldsymbol{\beta})$ *of dimensions* m *and* n *respectively plus whole commitments* $\gamma = (\gamma_\alpha, \gamma_\beta)$ *and Merkle opening vector* $\boldsymbol{\phi}$.
- $\Pi_{\mathsf{REQ}}(i, S, (\texttt{req}, \texttt{mode}))$. *The one round trip request-response protocol is initiated by any party-i by sending messages of the form* $(\texttt{req}, \texttt{mode})$ *to at least* $(t-1)$ *other parties in some set S. Based on* $\texttt{mode}$ *each party j ($j \in S$) replies with a response* $\texttt{resp}_j$ *only to party i. Parties in set S do not interact among themselves. The variable* $\texttt{mode}$ *can take values from* $\{\texttt{row}, \texttt{col}\}$.
- $\mathsf{RowEnc}(M_k, R_k, \alpha_k, \boldsymbol{\beta}, \gamma, \boldsymbol{\phi}, \mathsf{sk}_i, \{\texttt{resp}_j\}_{j\in S})$. *The row-encryption algorithm take a plaintext row of dimension* n*, a randomness row R_k of the same dimension, the corresponding row-commitment value α_k, entire column-commitment vector $\boldsymbol{\beta}$ of dimension* n*, matrix commitment γ, a secret key share* sk_i*, and at least $(t-1)$ responses to compute a ciphertext-row E_k of dimension* n.
- $\mathsf{ColDec}(E^\ell, \boldsymbol{\alpha}, \beta_\ell, \phi_\ell, \gamma, \mathsf{sk}_i, \{\texttt{resp}_j\}_{j\in S})$. *The column-decryption algorithm takes a ciphertext column E^ℓ of dimension* m*, the entire row-commitment vector $\boldsymbol{\alpha}$ of dimension* m*, a single column commitment β_ℓ, a matrix commitment γ along with a secret key share* sk_i *and at least $(t-1)$ responses to compute a plaintext column vector M^ℓ of dimension* m *or* $\perp$.

We require the above algorithms/protocols to satisfy **consistency** *for basic correctness. Informally, consistency guarantees that running a decryption of a ciphertext generated by running an encryption honestly (without the presence of any corrupt parties) would ensure that the original message is obtained after decryption. Formally, for a sufficiently large κ and any $n, t \in \mathbb{N}$ ($n \geq t$) let*

[5] For example, by running any standard DKG [Kat24].

$\mathsf{Setup}(1^\kappa, 1^n, 1^t)$ *is run among parties in* $[n]$*; then for any matrix* M *of dimensions* $\mathsf{m} \times \mathsf{n}$*, uniformly sampled randomness* R *of the same dimension and any two subsets* $S, S' \subseteq [n]$ *both of size at least* t*, and any two parties* $j \in S$ *and* $j' \in S$ *do:*

- *randomly sample* R *of the same dimension;*
- *compute* $(\boldsymbol{\alpha}, \boldsymbol{\beta}, \gamma, \boldsymbol{\phi}) := \mathsf{Commit}(M, R)$*;*
- *for each* $k \in [\mathsf{m}]$ *run the protocol* $\Pi_{\mathsf{REQ}}(j, S, ((\gamma, \alpha_k, \phi_\ell), \mathtt{row}))$*, in that party-*$j$ *gets back responses* $\mathtt{resp}_j$ *and then run* $E_k \xleftarrow{R} \mathsf{RowEnc}(M_k, R_k, \alpha_k, \boldsymbol{\beta}, \gamma, \boldsymbol{\phi}, \mathsf{sk}_i, \{\mathtt{resp}_j\}_{j\in S})$.
- *for each* $\ell \in [\mathsf{n}]$ *run the protocol* $\Pi_{\mathsf{REQ}}(j', S', ((\gamma, \beta_\ell, \phi_\ell), \mathtt{col}))$ *where party* j' *gets back responses* $\mathtt{resp}_j$ *and then locally run* $M'^{\ell} := \mathsf{ColDec}(E^\ell, \boldsymbol{\alpha}, \beta_\ell, \phi_\ell, \gamma, \mathsf{sk}_i, \{\mathtt{resp}_j\}_{j\in S})$.

We say that consistency holds if $M = M'$.

The **execution flow** is described in Sect. 2.

For security, we require our MATSE scheme to satisfy **correctness**, **message privacy** and **authenticity**.

Definition 3 (Correctness). *Correctness intuitively guarantees that, an encrypted plaintext, if decrypted, must return either the original plaintext or* $\perp$ *irrespective of the parties involved in the interaction. Formally, for a sufficiently large* κ *and any* $n, t \in \mathbb{N}$ $(n \geq t)$*, the probability that the following game outputs* 1 *is negligible in* κ*:*

- *Run* $\mathsf{Setup}(1^\kappa, 1^n, 1^t)$ *to obtain* sk_i*s and* pp*. Return* pp *to* A*. Once* A *returns a corrupt set* $C \subseteq [n]$*, return shares* $\{\mathsf{sk}_i\}_{i\in C}$ *to* A.
- *Upon receiving an encryption query* $(\mathtt{Encrypt}, j, M, S)$ *from* A *for an honest party* $j \in S \setminus C$*:*
  - *Sample uniform random* R *of dimension same as* M.
  - *Generate commitments* $(\boldsymbol{\alpha}, \boldsymbol{\beta}, \gamma, \boldsymbol{\phi}) \leftarrow \mathsf{Commit}(M, R)$*. Then for* $k \in [\mathsf{m}]$ *execute the following steps:*
    * *Run* $\Pi_{\mathsf{REQ}}(j, S, ((\gamma, \alpha_k), \mathtt{row}))$ *by sending messages from party-*j *to the adversary. Once adversary responds with* $\{\mathtt{resp}_i\}_{i\in C}$*, generate* $\{\mathtt{resp}_i\}_{i\in S\setminus C}$ *honestly.*
    * *Run* $\mathsf{RowEnc}(M_k, R_k, \alpha_k, \boldsymbol{\beta}, \boldsymbol{\phi}, \gamma, \mathsf{sk}_i, \{\mathtt{resp}_i\}_{i\in S})$ *to obtain an encrypted row* E_k.
  - *Return* $(E, \boldsymbol{\alpha}, \boldsymbol{\beta}, \gamma, \boldsymbol{\phi})$ *to* A.
- *Upon receiving a decryption query* $(\mathtt{Decrypt}, j', S')$ *from* A *for an honest* $j' \in S' \setminus C$*:*
  - *For each column* $\ell \in [\mathsf{n}]$ *execute the following steps:*
    * *Run* $\Pi_{\mathsf{REQ}}(j', S', ((\gamma, \beta_\ell, \boldsymbol{\phi}), \mathtt{col}))$ *by sending messages from party-*j' *to the adversary. Once adversary responds with* $\{\mathtt{resp}_i\}_{i\in C}$*, generate* $\{\mathtt{resp}_i\}_{i\in S'\setminus C}$ *honestly.*

  * *Run* $\mathsf{ColDec}(E^\ell, \boldsymbol{\alpha}, \beta_\ell, \phi_\ell, \gamma, \mathsf{sk}_i, \{\mathtt{resp}_i\}_{i\in S})$ *to obtain a value* temp_ℓ*. If* $\mathsf{temp}_\ell \notin \{M^\ell, \perp\}$ *then output* 1 *and stop.*
- *If the loop exits, then output* 0*.*

Definition 4 (Message Privacy). *Message privacy ensures that if adversary does not corrupt at least t parties, the transcript does not reveal any information about the message even if the adversary takes part in encryption/decryption sessions and can behave arbitrarily. Formally, for a sufficiently large* κ *and any* $n, t \in \mathbb{N}$ $(n \geq t)$*, the probability that the following game outputs* 1 *is* $\leq 1/2 - \mathsf{negl}(\kappa)$*:*

- *Run* $\mathsf{Setup}(1^\kappa, 1^n, 1^t)$ *to obtain* $\mathsf{sk}_i s$ *and* pp*. Return* pp *to* A*. Once* A *returns a corrupt set* $C \subseteq [n]$*, return shares* $\{\mathsf{sk}_i\}_{i\in C}$ *to* A*.*
- *Give* A *access to four oracles:*
  - **Honest Encryption:** *On query* $(\mathtt{Hon-Enc}, j, M, S)$ *such that* $j \in S \setminus C$ *from* A*:*
    * *Sample uniform random* R *of dimension same as* M*.*
    * *Generate commitments* $(\boldsymbol{\alpha}, \boldsymbol{\beta}, \gamma, \boldsymbol{\phi}) \leftarrow \mathsf{Commit}(M, R)$*. Then for* $k \in [\mathsf{m}]$ *execute the following steps:*
      - *Run* $\Pi_{\mathsf{REQ}}(j, S, ((\gamma, \alpha_k), \mathtt{row}))$ *by sending messages* $((\alpha_k, \gamma), \mathtt{row})$ *from party-j to the adversary. Once adversary responds with* $\{\mathtt{resp}_i\}_{i\in C}$*, generate* $\{\mathtt{resp}_i\}_{i\in S\setminus C}$ *honestly.*
      - *Run* $\mathsf{RowEnc}(M_k, R_k, \alpha_k, \boldsymbol{\beta}, \boldsymbol{\phi}, \gamma, \mathsf{sk}_i, \{\mathtt{resp}_i\}_{i\in S})$ *to obtain an encrypted row* E_k*.*
    * *Return* $(E, \boldsymbol{\alpha}, \boldsymbol{\beta})$ *to* A*.*
  - **Honest Column Decryption:** *On query* $(\mathtt{Hon-Col-Dec}, j, E^\ell, \boldsymbol{\alpha}, \beta_\ell, S)$ *such that* $j \in S \setminus C$ *from* A*:*
    * *For each column* $\ell \in [\mathsf{n}]$ *execute the following steps:*
      - *Send messages* $((\gamma, \beta_\ell, \phi_\ell), \mathtt{col})$*, generated as per* Π_{REQ} *from party-j to the adversary.*

  - **Adversarial Queries:** *On query* $(\mathtt{req}, j, S)$ *such that* $j \in S \cap C$ *from* A*, produce* $\mathtt{resp}_i$ *for each honest* $i \in S \setminus C$ *according to the specification of* Π_{REQ} *and send them back to* A*.*
- *At any point* A *outputs two matrices* (M_0, M_1) *of dimensions* $\mathsf{m} \times \mathsf{n}$*. Choose a random bit* b *and then execute:*
  - *Sample uniform random* R_b *of dimension same as* M_b*.*
  - *Generate commitments* $(\boldsymbol{\alpha}, \boldsymbol{\beta}, \gamma, \boldsymbol{\phi}) \leftarrow \mathsf{Commit}(M_b, R_b)$*. Then for* $k \in [\mathsf{m}]$ *execute the following steps:*
    * *Run* $\Pi_{\mathsf{REQ}}(j, S, ((\gamma, \alpha_k), \mathtt{row}))$ *by sending messages* $((\gamma, \alpha_k), \mathtt{row})$ *from party-j to the adversary. Once adversary responds with* $\{\mathtt{resp}_i\}_{i\in C}$*, generate* $\{\mathtt{resp}_i\}_{i\in S\setminus C}$ *honestly.*
    * *Run* $\mathsf{RowEnc}(M_k, R_k, \alpha_k, \boldsymbol{\beta}, \gamma, \boldsymbol{\phi}, \mathsf{sk}_i, \{\mathtt{resp}_i\}_{i\in S})$ *to obtain an encrypted row* E_k*.*
  - *Return* $(E, \boldsymbol{\alpha}, \boldsymbol{\beta}, \gamma)$ *to* A*.*
- *Eventually A outputs* b'*, output* 1 *if and only if* $b = b'$*.*

Definition 5 (Ciphertext Integrity). *Ciphertext Integrity intuitively guarantees that an adversary that actively corrupts up to $t-1$ parties can not produce a ciphertext on its own without explicitly querying the honest parties. Formally, for a sufficiently large κ and any $n, t \in \mathbb{N}$ ($n \geq t$), the probability that the following game outputs 1 is $\leq \mathsf{negl}(\kappa)$:*

- *Run* $\mathsf{Setup}(1^\kappa, 1^n, 1^t)$ *to obtain* $\mathsf{sk}_i s$ *and* pp. *Return* pp *to* A. *Once* A *returns a corrupt set* $C \subseteq [n]$, *return shares* $\{\mathsf{sk}_i\}_{i \in C}$ *to* A.
- *Initialize two lists* $L_{\mathsf{hon}}, L_{\mathsf{cor}}$ *with empty sets and a counter* $\mathsf{ct} := 0$.
- *Give* A *access to following oracles:*
  - **Honest Encryption:** *On query* $(\mathtt{Hon-Enc}, j, M, S)$ *such that* $j \in S \setminus C$ *from* A*:*
    * *Sample uniform random* R *of dimension same as* M.
    * *Generate commitments* $(\boldsymbol{\alpha}, \boldsymbol{\beta}, \gamma, \boldsymbol{\phi}) \leftarrow \mathsf{Commit}(M, R)$. *Then for* $k \in [\mathsf{m}]$ *execute the following steps:*
      - *Run* $\Pi_{\mathsf{REQ}}(j, S, ((\gamma, \alpha_k), \mathtt{row}))$ *by sending messages* $((\gamma, \alpha_k), \mathtt{row})$ *from party-j to the adversary. Once adversary responds with* $\{\mathtt{resp}_i\}_{i \in C}$, *generate* $\{\mathtt{resp}_i\}_{i \in S \setminus C}$ *honestly.*
      - *Run* $\mathsf{RowEnc}(M_k, R_k, \alpha_k, \boldsymbol{\beta}, \gamma, \boldsymbol{\phi}, \mathsf{sk}_i, \{\mathtt{resp}_i\}_{i \in S})$ *to obtain an encrypted row* E_k.
    * *Increase* ct *by 1. Append* $(\mathsf{ct}, E, (\boldsymbol{\alpha}, \boldsymbol{\beta}, \gamma, \boldsymbol{\phi}))$ *to* L_{hon} *and return* ct *to* A.
  - **Honest Targeted Decryption:** *On query* $(\mathtt{Hon-Tar-Dec}, \tau, j, S)$ *such that* $j \in S \setminus C$ *from* A, *retrieve* $(\tau, E, (\boldsymbol{\alpha}, \boldsymbol{\beta}, \gamma, \boldsymbol{\phi}))$ *from* L_{hon} *and execute:*
    * *For each column* $\ell \in [\mathsf{n}]$ *execute the following steps:*
      - *Send messages* $((\gamma, \beta_\ell, \phi_\ell), \mathtt{col})$, *generated as per* Π_{REQ} *from party-j to the adversary.*

  - **Adversarial Queries:** *On query* $(\mathtt{req}, j, S)$ *such that* $j \in S \cap C$ *from* A, *produce* $\mathtt{resp}_i$ *for each honest* $i \in S \setminus C$ *according to the specification of* Π_{REQ} *and send them back to* A. *Additionally, append* $\mathtt{req}$ *to* L_{cor}. *While appending, split entries of the form* $(\boldsymbol{\alpha}, \gamma)$ *(resp.* $(\boldsymbol{\beta}, \gamma, \phi)$ *) into* m *(resp.* n*) many entries* $(\alpha_1, \gamma), \ldots, (\alpha_{\mathsf{m}}, \gamma)$ *(resp.* $(\beta_1, \gamma, \phi_1), \ldots, (\beta_{\mathsf{n}}, \gamma, \phi_{\mathsf{n}})$*).*
  - **Forgery:** *Eventually* A *outputs a forgery* $(\mathbf{e}, \boldsymbol{\alpha}, \beta, \gamma, \phi)$. *Output 1 if and only if all of the following holds, otherwise output 0:*
    1. *There does not exist any entry in* L_{cor} *of the form either* (α_k, γ) *for any* $k \in [\mathsf{m}]$ *or* (β, γ, ϕ).
    2. *Running the code of* Π_{REQ} *honestly for all parties locally first for any set* S *of size* t *to generate* $\{\mathtt{resp}_i\}_{i \in S}$ *and then running* $\mathsf{ColDec}(\mathbf{e}, \boldsymbol{\alpha}, \beta, \phi, \gamma, \{\mathtt{resp}_i\}_{i \in S})$ *does not yield* $\perp$.

Remark on Ciphertext Integrity. Our notion of ciphertext integrity departs significantly from prior works [AMMR18, CGMS21, DMSS24, Muk20], which predominantly adopt a *one-more style definition* that may not fully capture the practical realities of the setting. In those earlier definitions, the honest servers are essentially limited to tracking the count of plausible valid ciphertexts and nothing beyond that. Moreover, these definitions have an inherent shortcoming: the adversary can potentially generate a valid ciphertext indirectly through its decryption queries, thereby weakening the intended security guarantees. In contrast, our property is cleaner and more natural, aligning closely with the traditional notion of ciphertext integrity for symmetric schemes, where the adversary must explicitly produce a valid forgery. We achieve this improvement by giving up on generality, although our specialized setting still encompasses all known TSE schemes, as far as we know. It is worth noting that, because our construction uses plain commitments for rows and columns, it cannot satisfy the so-called "cardinality-binding" notion of ATSE [CGMS21]. Thus, while our definitions conceptually feel closer to real-world behavior, they appear formally incomparable to the existing ones.

Limitation: Lack of Cell Decryption. Unlike ATSE [CGMS21], our construction does not support decryption at the level of individual cells. This limitation arises because, from a single cell alone, the associated commitments cannot be verified – the entire row or column is needed. To enable cell-level decryption, one would need to employ a Merkle tree commitment for each individual cell. However, this approach would revert the storage overhead back to $O(\mathsf{m} \cdot \mathsf{n})$, as opposed to the much more efficient $O(\mathsf{m} + \mathsf{n})$ overhead that our current scheme achieves. We believe this is a reasonable trade-off to gain the significant efficiency benefits our construction currently supports. Nevertheless, if cell-level decryption is required for a specific application, one can incorporate Merkle-based commitments, albeit at the cost of increased storage overhead.

6 Our Construction

Below we present our MATSE construction.

<u>Ingredients</u>

- A *simple* FTKD scheme $(\mathsf{FT.Setup}, \mathsf{FT.\Pi_{KDF}}, \mathsf{FT.Combine}, , \mathsf{FT.WKGen})$.
- A Merkle Commitment MKT.
- A commitment scheme CMT.
- A PRG PRG with polynomial stretch.

<u>Construction</u>

$\mathsf{Setup}(1^\kappa, 1^n, 1^t)$. Run $\mathsf{FT.Setup}(1^\kappa, 1^n, 1^t)$ to generate a (t, n) Shamir share of FTKD secret key sk_i and public parameters pp. Each party-i holds sk_i, and everyone also gets pp.

$\mathsf{Commit}(M, R)$. Execute the following:

- Compute $\{\alpha_k := \mathsf{CMT}(M_k, R_k)\}_{k \in [\mathsf{m}]}$ and then $\gamma_\alpha := \mathsf{CMT}(\boldsymbol{\alpha})$.
- Compute $\{\beta_\ell := \mathsf{CMT}(M^\ell, R^\ell)\}_{\ell \in [\mathsf{n}]}$ and then the Merkle tree root $\gamma_\beta := \mathsf{MKT.Com}(\boldsymbol{\beta})$, and openings $\{\phi_\ell := \mathsf{MKT.Open}(\boldsymbol{\beta}, \ell)\}_{\ell \in [\mathsf{n}]}$.

- Define $\boldsymbol{\phi} := (\phi_1, \ldots, \phi_\mathsf{n})$ and $\gamma := (\gamma_\alpha, \gamma_\beta)$.

Output $(\boldsymbol{\alpha}, \boldsymbol{\beta}, \gamma, \boldsymbol{\phi})$.

$\Pi_{\mathsf{REQ}}(i, S, (\mathtt{req}, \mathtt{mode}))$. Party-$i$ parses $(\mathtt{req}, \mathtt{mode})$ and runs an instance of $\mathsf{FT}.\Pi_{\mathsf{KDF}}(i, S, (v, \mathtt{f.mode}))$ protocol with other parties in a set S to obtain the responses $\{\mathtt{resp}_j\}_{j \in S \setminus \{i\}}$ as private output where:

- If $(\mathtt{req}, \mathtt{mode}) = ((\gamma, \alpha_k), \mathtt{row})$ then $v := (\gamma, \alpha_k)$ and $\mathtt{f.mode} := \mathtt{left}$.
- If $(\mathtt{req}, \mathtt{mode}) = ((\gamma, \beta_\ell, \phi_\ell), \mathtt{col})$ then $v := (\gamma, \beta_\ell, \phi_\ell)$ and $\mathtt{f.mode} := \mathtt{right}$.

No other party gets anything.

$\mathsf{RowEnc}(M_k, R_k, \alpha_k, \boldsymbol{\beta}, \gamma, \boldsymbol{\phi}, \mathsf{sk}_i, \{\mathtt{resp}_j\}_{j \in S \setminus \{i\}})$.
Compute $\mathsf{key} := \mathsf{FT.Combine}(\mathsf{sk}_i, \{\mathtt{resp}_j\}_{j \in S \setminus \{i\}})$. Then for each $\ell \in [\mathsf{n}]$:

- $ek_{k,\ell} := \mathsf{FT.WKGen}(\mathsf{key}, (\gamma, \alpha_k), \mathtt{left})$.
- $E_k^\ell := \mathsf{PRG}(ek_{k,\ell}) \oplus (M_k^\ell \| R_k^\ell)$.

Output E_k.

$\mathsf{ColDec}(E^\ell, \boldsymbol{\alpha}, \beta_\ell, \phi_\ell, \gamma, \mathsf{sk}_i, \{\mathtt{resp}_j\}_{j \in S})$.
Compute $\mathsf{key} := \mathsf{FT.Combine}(\mathsf{sk}_i, \{\mathtt{resp}_j\}_{j \in S \setminus \{i\}})$. Then for each $k \in [\mathsf{m}]$:

- $ek_{k,\ell} := \mathsf{FT.WKGen}(\mathsf{key}, (\gamma, \beta_\ell, \phi_\ell), \mathtt{right})$.
- $(M_k^\ell \| R_k^\ell) := \mathsf{PRG}(ek_{k,\ell}) \oplus E_k^\ell$.

Verify:

- $(\beta_\ell = \mathsf{CMT}(M^\ell, R^\ell))$.
- $(\gamma_\alpha = \mathsf{CMT}(\boldsymbol{\alpha}))$, where $(\gamma_\alpha, \gamma_\beta) := \gamma$.
- $\mathsf{MKT.Ver}(\gamma_\beta, \beta_\ell, \phi_\ell, \ell)$.

If all of them succeed, then output M^ℓ, else output $\perp$.

We establish that our construction satisfies consistency, correctness, privacy and integrity via the following theorem:

Theorem 1. *The above construction is a secure MATSE scheme, satisfying* consistency, correctness, message privacy *and* ciphertext integrity.

To write a concrete proof of theorem 1, we need to show that the security of the MATSE depends on the security of the underlying FTKD and commitment schemes. Counting on the pseudorandomness of the FTKD and the hiding property of the underlying commitment scheme, we first show that the MATSE achieves message privacy. Then we show that the key consistency of the FTKD yields correctness of the MATSE. Finally, we conclude the security analysis by proving that MATSE achieves ciphertext integrity assuming the key consistency, threshold consistency, and pseudorandomness of the FTKD, along with the binding property of the underlying commitments. So we prove Theorem 1 by proving the following lemmas.

Lemma 1 (Message Privacy). *If the underlying FTKD is pseudorandom and the commitment is hiding, then MATSE has message privacy.*

Lemma 2 (Correctness). *Key consistent FTKD implies the correctness of MATSE.*

Lemma 3 (Ciphertext Integrity). *Assuming the FTKD scheme is secure(*Key Consistency,Threshold Consistency, *and* Pseudorandomness*) and both the commitment schemes are binding, then MATSE achieves the* Ciphertext Integrity *property.*

The detailed proofs of the above lemma are written in A.2.

7 Conclusion

We presented MATSE, an amortized threshold encryption scheme tailored to tabular data, achieving efficiency and strong integrity with only $O(\mathsf{m} + \mathsf{n})$ commitments. While our design provides rigorous security and practical utility for row-wise encryption and column-wise decryption, several extensions remain open. Future work includes enabling cell-level decryption without losing efficiency, supporting more flexible access patterns beyond strict rows and columns, and integrating non-interactive zero-knowledge proofs for verifiable correctness. Exploring applications to higher-dimensional or differently structured datasets and combining MATSE with techniques like differential privacy could further broaden its impact in real-world secure data management.

A Additional Building Blocks

A.1 Simple FTKD Construction

Below, we present the Simple FTKD instantiation from [CGMS21] for completeness.

<u>TOOLS</u>

- Let $\mathbb{G}_0 = \langle g_0 \rangle$, $\mathbb{G}_1 = \langle g_1 \rangle$, $\mathbb{G} = \langle g \rangle$ be cyclic groups of prime order q, with bilinear pairing $\mathbf{e} : \mathbb{G}_0 \times \mathbb{G}_1 \rightarrow \mathbb{G}$.
- Let $\mathsf{H}_1 : \{0,1\}^* \rightarrow \mathbb{G}_0$ and $\mathsf{H}_2 : \{0,1\}^* \rightarrow \mathbb{G}_1$ be two hash function model as random oracles.
- $\mathsf{SSS}(\mathsf{sk}, 1^n, 1^t) \rightarrow (\{\mathsf{sk}_i\}_{i\in[n]}, \mathsf{pp})$ is Shamir's (t, n) secret sharing.

<u>SCHEME</u>

- $\mathsf{FT.Setup}(1^\kappa, 1^n, 1^t) \rightarrow (\{\mathsf{sk}_i\}_{i\in[n]}, \mathsf{pp})$: Generate a (t, n) Shamir share of secret key sk_i and public parameters pp. Each party-i holds sk_i, and everyone also gets pp.
- $\mathsf{FT.\Pi_{KDF}}(i, S, (\mathtt{req}, \mathtt{f.mode}))$: This is one round trip request-response protocol initiated by the party-i described as follows:
  Request: Party-i sends a message $(i, S, (v, \mathtt{f.mode}))$ to each party $j \in S$, where $\mathtt{f.mode} \in \{\mathtt{left}, \mathtt{right}\}$ and $|S| > t$.

Response: Each party-$j \in S$ respond with $\texttt{resp}_j$ only to the party i, where

$$\texttt{resp}_j := \begin{cases} \mathsf{H}_1(\alpha)^{\mathsf{sk}_j} & \text{if } \texttt{f.mode} = \texttt{left}), \& v := (\gamma, \alpha) \\ \mathsf{H}_2(\beta)^{\mathsf{sk}_j} & \text{if } \texttt{f.mode} = \texttt{right}), \& v := (\gamma, \beta, \phi_)), \end{cases}$$

where sk_j is the secret key share of party-$j \in S$

- $\mathsf{FT.Combine}(\mathsf{sk}_i, \{\texttt{resp}_j\}_{j \in S \setminus \{i\}}) \rightarrow \mathsf{key}$: If $|S| \geq t-1$ valid $\texttt{resp}_j$, compute:

$$\mathsf{key} := \prod_{j \in S'} \texttt{resp}_j^{\lambda_{0,j,S'}}, \quad \text{where } S' \subseteq S \cup \{i\} \text{ and } |S'| = t.$$

Where $\lambda_{0,j,S'}$ be the Lagrange's coefficient.
Otherwise, output $\perp$.

- $\mathsf{FT.WKGen}(\mathsf{key}, v, \texttt{f.mode}) \rightarrow \mathsf{wk}$: Compute

$$\mathsf{wk} := \begin{cases} \mathsf{e}(\mathsf{key}, \mathsf{H}_2(\alpha)) & \text{if } \texttt{f.mode} = \texttt{left} \wedge v := (\gamma, \alpha) \\ \mathsf{e}(H_1(\beta), \mathsf{key}) & \text{if } \texttt{f.mode} = \texttt{right} \wedge v := (\gamma, \beta, \phi_)), \end{cases}$$

A.2 Proof of Theorem 1

The proof is established by proving the lemmas one by one described in 1.

Proof of Lemma 1.

Proof (Message privacy of MATSE scheme). Message privacy of the *MATSE* scheme fundamentally relies on the pseudorandomness of the FTKD and PRG, and the hiding property of the commitment. For any PPT adversary $\mathcal{A}$ outputting (j^*, M_0, M_1, S^*), we establish the computational indistinguishability between the ciphertext E_b^*. Our proof proceeds by initiating from the ciphertext E_0^* and progressively transitioning through a carefully designed sequence of hybrid experiments, ultimately arriving at E_1^*. Let us start by describing the hybrid experiments

- $\mathsf{Hyb}_{1,i,j}$: For any output (j^*, M_0, M_1, S^*) of $\mathcal{A}$, for all $k \in [i]$ and $\ell \in [j]$ the $k\ell$-th cell of E_0^* is generated as follows:
  - Compute the commitments locally by

  $$\boldsymbol{\alpha} = (\alpha_k = \mathsf{CMT}(M_k, R_k))_{k \in [\mathsf{m}]} \quad \text{and} \quad \boldsymbol{\beta} = (\beta^\ell = \mathsf{CMT}(M^\ell, R^\ell))_{\ell \in [\mathsf{n}]}$$

  $$\gamma = \{\mathsf{CMT}(\boldsymbol{\alpha}), \mathsf{MKT.Com}(\boldsymbol{\beta})\} \quad \text{and} \quad \phi = \{\phi_\ell = \mathsf{MKT.Open}(\boldsymbol{\beta}, \ell)\}_{\ell \in [\mathsf{n}]}$$

  where R is a matrix of random elements of dimension $\mathsf{m} \times \mathsf{n}$.
  - Choose $e_{k,\ell}$ randomly for $k \in [i]$ and $\ell \in [j]$. Otherwise compute $e_{k,\ell}$ correctly.

- For $k \in [\mathsf{m}]$ and $\ell \in [\mathsf{n}]$ compute the ciphers by $E_k^\ell = \mathsf{PRG}(e_{k,\ell}) \oplus M_k^\ell$.

Clearly $\mathsf{Hyb}_{1,0,0}$ is equivalent to experiment 0. The difference between $\mathsf{Hyb}_{1,i-1,j}$ and $\mathsf{Hyb}_{1,i,j}$ for $i \in [\mathsf{m}]$ and $j \in [\mathsf{n}]$, is that the first j many plaintexts in the ith row in $\mathsf{Hyb}_{1,i,j}$ is masked by the outputs of the PRG with random inputs instead of the outputs when original $e_{k,\ell}$ are given as inputs. Similarly the difference between $\mathsf{Hyb}_{1,i,j-1}$ and $\mathsf{Hyb}_{1,i,j}$ follows. Thus if there exists an adversary $\mathcal{A}$ distinguishing between $\mathsf{Hyb}_{1,i-1,j}$ and $\mathsf{Hyb}_{1,i,j}$ (or $\mathsf{Hyb}_{1,i,j-1}$ and $\mathsf{Hyb}_{1,i,j}$), we can construct a PPT adversary $\mathcal{B}^{\mathcal{A}}$ that can break security of the FTKD. Thus the advantage of the experiment 0 i.e. $\mathsf{Adv\text{-}MsgPriv}(0) \approx_c \mathsf{Hyb}_{1,\mathsf{m},\mathsf{n}}$. Now we describe the second hybrid experiment, which works as follows:

- $\mathsf{Hyb}_{2,i,j}$: This experiment is same as $\mathsf{Hyb}_{1,\mathsf{m},\mathsf{n}}$ except for the following steps:
  - Compute the commitments locally by
$$\boldsymbol{\alpha} = (\alpha_k = \mathsf{CMT}(M_k, R_k))_{k\in[\mathsf{m}]} \quad \text{and} \quad \boldsymbol{\beta} = \left(\beta^\ell = \mathsf{CMT}(M^\ell, R^\ell)\right)_{\ell\in[\mathsf{n}]}$$
$$\gamma = \{\mathsf{CMT}(\boldsymbol{\alpha}), \mathsf{MKT.Com}(\boldsymbol{\beta})\} \quad \text{and} \quad \phi = \{\phi_\ell = \mathsf{MKT.Open}(\boldsymbol{\beta}, \ell)\}_{\ell\in[\mathsf{n}]}$$
    where R is a matrix of random elements of dimension $\mathsf{m} \times \mathsf{n}$.
  - For $k \in [\mathsf{m}]$ and $\ell \in [\mathsf{n}]$, sample $e_{k,\ell}$ randomly.
  - For $k \in [i]$ and $\ell \in [j]$ generate the ciphertexts $E_k^\ell = r_k^\ell \oplus M_k^\ell$, where r_k^ℓ is randomly chosen. Otherwise set the ciphertexts to be $E_k^\ell = \mathsf{PRG}(e_{k,\ell}) \oplus M_K^\ell$.

Clearly $\mathsf{Hyb}_{2,0,0}$ is same as $\mathsf{Hyb}_{1,\mathsf{m},\mathsf{n}}$. Furthermore, we can argue that due to the pseudorandomness of the PRG, $\mathsf{Hyb}_{2,i-1,j} \approx_c \mathsf{Hyb}_{2,i,j}$ for all $i \in [\mathsf{m}]$ and $j \in [\mathsf{n}]$. Finally we get $\mathsf{Hyb}_{2,\mathsf{m},\mathsf{n}} \approx_c \mathsf{Hyb}_{1,\mathsf{m},\mathsf{n}}$.

The third set of hybrid experiments is described as follows :

- $\mathsf{Hyb}_{3,i,j}$: This hybrid is same as $\mathsf{Hyb}_{2,\mathsf{m},\mathsf{n}}$ except for the following steps :
  - Compute the commitments locally by
$$\boldsymbol{\alpha} = (\alpha_k = \mathsf{CMT}(M_k, R_k))_{k\in[\mathsf{m}]} \quad \text{and} \quad \boldsymbol{\beta} = \left(\beta^\ell = \mathsf{CMT}(M^\ell, R^\ell)\right)_{\ell\in[\mathsf{n}]}$$
$$\gamma = \{\mathsf{CMT}(\boldsymbol{\alpha}), \mathsf{MKT.Com}(\boldsymbol{\beta})\} \quad \text{and} \quad \phi = \{\phi_\ell = \mathsf{MKT.Open}(\boldsymbol{\beta}, \ell)\}_{\ell\in[\mathsf{n}]}$$
    where R is a matrix of random elements of dimension $\mathsf{m} \times \mathsf{n}$.
  - For $k \in [\mathsf{m}]$ and $\ell \in [\mathsf{n}]$, sample $e_{k,\ell}$ randomly.
  - For $k \in [\mathsf{m}]$ and $\ell \in [\mathsf{n}]$ set the ciphertexts to be $E_k^\ell = s_k^\ell$, where s_k^ℓ are randomly sampled. Otherwise, compute the ciphertexts as $E_k^\ell = r_k^\ell \oplus M_K^\ell$, for randomly sampled r_k^ℓ.

Note that $\mathsf{Hyb}_{3,0,0}$ is identical to $\mathsf{Hyb}_{2,\mathsf{m},\mathsf{n}}$. Also $\mathsf{Hyb}_{3,i-1,j}$ and $\mathsf{Hyb}_{3,i,j}$ are statistically close for all $i \in [\mathsf{m}]$ and $j \in [\mathsf{n}]$. Thus we have $\mathsf{Hyb}_{2,\mathsf{m},\mathsf{n}} \approx_s \mathsf{Hyb}_{3,\mathsf{m},\mathsf{n}}$.

Finally, the last hybrid experiment goes as follows :

- $\mathsf{Hyb}_{4,i,j}$: This hybrid is same as $\mathsf{Hyb}_{3,\mathsf{m},\mathsf{n}}$ except for the following steps

- For $k \in [i]$ and $\ell \in [j]$ randomly sample U_k^ℓ and set $\mathcal{M} = (\mathsf{M}_k^\ell)_{\mathsf{m}\times\mathsf{n}}$, where $\mathsf{M}_k^\ell = U_k^\ell$ for $k \in [i]$, $\ell \in [j]$ and $\mathsf{M}_k^\ell = M_k^\ell$ otherwise. Then locally compute the commitments by

$$\boldsymbol{\alpha} = (\alpha_k = \mathsf{CMT}(\mathcal{M}_k, R_k))_{k\in[\mathsf{m}]} \quad \text{and} \quad \boldsymbol{\beta} = \left(\beta^\ell = \mathsf{CMT}(\mathcal{M}^\ell, R^\ell)\right)_{\ell\in[\mathsf{n}]}$$

$$\gamma = \{\mathsf{CMT}(\boldsymbol{\alpha}), \mathsf{MKT.Com}(\boldsymbol{\beta})\} \quad \text{and} \quad \phi = \{\phi_\ell = \mathsf{MKT.Open}(\boldsymbol{\beta}, \ell)\}_{\ell\in[\mathsf{n}]}$$

where R is a matrix of random elements of dimension $\mathsf{m} \times \mathsf{n}$.
- For $k \in [\mathsf{m}]$ and $\ell \in [\mathsf{n}]$, sample $e_{k,\ell}$ randomly.
- For $k \in [\mathsf{m}]$ and $\ell \in [\mathsf{n}]$, set the ciphertexts $E_k^\ell = t_k^\ell$, where t_k^ℓ are randomly sampled.

Again it is evident that $\mathsf{Hyb}_{4,0,0}$ is identical to $\mathsf{Hyb}_{3,\mathsf{m},\mathsf{n}}$. For any $i \in [\mathsf{m}]$ and $j \in [\mathsf{n}]$ the hybrids $\mathsf{Hyb}_{4,i-1,j}$ and $\mathsf{Hyb}_{4,i,j}$ are computationally indistinguishable due to the hiding property of the commitment scheme. One can construct a simulator such that the challenge query (M_0, M_1) by the adversary to the **Honest Encryption** oracle passes through the simulator. Thus, the simulator can return satisfiable private openings for the random commitments of the challenge. Thus we can conclude that $\mathsf{Hyb}_{3,\mathsf{m},\mathsf{n}} \approx_c \mathsf{Hyb}_{4,\mathsf{m},\mathsf{n}}$.

Also note that the final hybrid $\mathsf{Hyb}_{4,\mathsf{m},\mathsf{n}}$ is independent of the challenge bit b. Since the commitment is binding, other adversarial queries, including the post-challenge decryption queries, would not help, as different plaintext rows/columns would lead to different keys. Thus, we can conclude that the adversary can guess the bit b with probability at most 1/2. Also, we can start from experiment 1 i.e. for E_1^* and reach $\mathsf{Hyb}_{4,\mathsf{m},\mathsf{n}}$ using the same type of transitions, which concludes the proof.

Proof of Lemma 2.

Proof. The required condition for correctness of the MATSE is, if any honest party i initiating RowEnc with input $(M_k, R_k, \alpha_k, \boldsymbol{\beta}, \gamma, \phi, \mathsf{sk}_i, \{\mathtt{resp}_j\}_{j\in S\setminus\{i\}})$ for $k \in [\mathsf{m}]$ to encrypt a matrix $M_{\mathsf{m}\times\mathsf{n}}$ and for any PPT adversary corrupting at most $(t-1)$ many parties, then any other honest party j' while decrypting the ciphertext matrix $E_{\mathsf{m}\times\mathsf{n}}$, the outcome must be $M_{\mathsf{m}\times\mathsf{n}}$ or $\perp$.

For any PPT adversary $\mathcal{A}$ corrupting at most $t-1$ parties, getting j' to decrypt any cipher E_k^ℓ to $m' \neq M_k^\ell$ is not feasible as it would imply binding failure of the underlying commitment scheme. More concretely, if any cipher E_k^ℓ decrypts to two different plaintexts m' and M_k^ℓ, then both the plaintexts would open to the same commitment, which contradicts the binding property of the commitment scheme.

Moreover, the key consistency of the underlying FTKD guarantees that if the honest run of $\mathsf{FT.WKGen}(\mathsf{key}, x, \mathtt{f.mode}) \rightarrow \mathsf{wk}$, then another honest run of $\mathsf{FT.WKGen}$ with inputs $(x', \mathtt{f.mode}')$ and the same key must yield to wk except for some negligible probability, where $x' \neq x$ and $\mathtt{f.mode}' \in \{\mathtt{left}, \mathtt{right}\}$. Therefore, we can say that honest n many column-wise decryptions would lead to the correct $M_{\mathsf{m}\times\mathsf{n}}$ due to the argument of FTKD's key consistency. Thus, we can conclude that the Key consistency of FTKD implies a strongly correct MATSE.

Proof of Lemma 3.

Proof. Let A be any PPT adversary corrupting at most $t-1$ servers that plays the Ciphertext-Integrity game as in 5, where the challenger runs Setup returns the public parameters pp, gives A up to $t-1$ shares, answers Honest Encryption/Honest Targeted Decryption/Adversarial Queries and finally A outputs a forgery $(\boldsymbol{e}, \boldsymbol{\alpha}, \beta, \gamma, \phi)$. We will prove this by contradiction. Assume that A wins with non-negligible probability $\epsilon(\kappa)$. We show that this contradicts the FTKD *pseudorandomness*. For that, we construct a PPT adversary B that uses A as a subroutine to break the *pseudorandomness* of the underlying FTKD scheme with a non-negligible advantage.

Here B is an adversary to the FTKD *pseudorandomness* game, which works as follows:

- After receiving public parameters pp from its challenger. It forwards these to adversary A.
- A output a set of corrupt parties C, then B forwards C to its challenger and receives the corresponding secret shares $\{\mathsf{sk}_i\}_{i\in C}$.
- B initializes the lists $L_{\mathsf{hon}}, L_{\mathsf{cor}}$ with empty sets and a counter $\mathsf{ct} := 0$ as specified in the Ciphertext Integrity game.

B simulates the oracles for A by interacting with its own FTKD challenger's oracles.

- When A makes query **Honest Encryption Oracle** with a message $(\mathtt{Hon}-\mathtt{Enc}, j, M, S)$ then B honestly executes $(\boldsymbol{\alpha}, \boldsymbol{\beta}, \gamma, \boldsymbol{\phi}) \leftarrow \mathsf{Commit}(M, R)$ with randomly sampled R. Now for each row in $[\mathsf{m}]$, B needs the row-specific key so it will form a FTKD request $\mathtt{req} := ((\gamma, \alpha_k), \mathtt{row})$ which corresponds to $(x, \mathtt{f.mode})$ with $x = (\gamma, \alpha_k)$ and $\mathtt{f.mode} = \mathtt{left}$. B sends a **(Key Derivation Function) query** for $(j, s, (x, \mathtt{left}))$ to its challenger. The challenger returns a response from an honest server. B uses this to complete the RowEnc, generate the ciphertext E adds it to L_{hon} and returns ct to A.
- When A queries the **Adversarial Queries Oracle** with $(\mathtt{req}, j, S)$ with $j \in S \cap C$, B first appends the request to its internal list L_{cor}. Let the request be $(x, \mathtt{f.mode})$, then B sends a **(Key Derivation Function) query** $(j, S, (x, \mathtt{f.mode}))$ to its challenger. The challenger returns the responses from the parties in S to B. Then B sends responses according to $(x, \mathtt{f.mode})$.

Eventually, A outputs a forgery $(\boldsymbol{E}^*, \boldsymbol{\alpha}^*, \beta^*, \gamma^*, \boldsymbol{\phi}^*)$. Since A wins with probability $\epsilon(\kappa)$, this forgery satisfies the winning conditions with at least the same probability as the following event: For every row $k \in [\mathsf{m}]$, the request (α_k^*, γ^*) does not appear in L_{cor}, and honest decryption of the forgery succeeds and does not return $\perp$. Now B uses this forgery to break the FTKD pseudorandomness:

- B sends a *challenge query* $(j^*, S^*, (x, \mathtt{f.mode}))$ to its challenger, where $j^* \in S^* \setminus C$ and $x = (\gamma^*, \beta_\ell^*, \phi_\ell^*)$ and $\mathtt{f.mode} = \mathtt{right}$.
- The challenger returns wk^*.

- Using wk^*, B decrypts E^ℓ, the ℓ-th column of E^* and obtains some $(M_k^\ell \| R_k^\ell) := \mathsf{PRG}(\mathsf{wk}^*) \oplus E_k^\ell$ for all $k \in [\mathsf{m}]$. Then B checks $\beta^\ell \stackrel{?}{=} \mathsf{CMT}(M^\ell, R^\ell)$ and $\mathsf{MKT.Ver}(\gamma_\beta, \beta_\ell, \phi_\ell, \ell) \stackrel{?}{=} 1$. If both the checks pass, B outputs $b' := 0$, otherwise $b' := 1$.

Let's analyse the probability of B being correct:

Case 1: $b = 0$, The challenger provides the real whole key, wk^* is the correct column-specific key. Since A wins with probability $\epsilon(\kappa)$, its forgery is valid, meaning an honest decryption must succeed. A successful decryption implies all verification checks. Therefore, if $b = 0$, B outputs $b' = 0$ with probability at least $\epsilon(\kappa)$ i.e. $\Pr[b' = 0 \mid b = 0] \geq \epsilon(\kappa)$.

Case 2: $b = 1$ The challenger provides a uniformly random string for wk^*. The decrypted plaintext $(M_k^\ell \| R_k^\ell)$ will be uniformly random garbage. The probability that this random string, when re-committed, happens to match the specific commitment value β_ℓ is negligible, due to the binding property of the commitment scheme, i.e. $\Pr[b' = 0 \mid b = 1] \leq \mathsf{negl}(\kappa)$. The advantage of B in the FTKD pseudorandomness game is

$$
\begin{aligned}
\mathsf{Adv}_{\mathsf{B}}(\kappa) &= \left| \Pr[b' = b] - \tfrac{1}{2} \right| \\
&= \tfrac{1}{2} \left| \Pr[b' = 0 \mid b = 0] + \Pr[b' = 1 \mid b = 1] - 1 \right| \\
&= \tfrac{1}{2} \left| \Pr[b' = 0 \mid b = 0] - \Pr[b' = 0 \mid b = 1] \right| \\
&\geq \tfrac{1}{2} \left(\epsilon(\kappa) - \mathsf{negl}(\kappa) \right).
\end{aligned}
$$

References

[ABM+21] Agrawal, S., Badrinarayanan, S., Mohassel, P., Mukherjee, P., Patranabis, S.: BETA: Biometric-enabled threshold authentication, pp. 290–318 (2021)

[ADL+22] Agrawal, S., Dai, W., Luykx, A., Mukherjee, P., Rindal, P.: ParaDiSE: efficient threshold authenticated encryption in fully malicious model, pp. 26–51 (2022)

[AMMM18] Agrawal, S., Miao, P., Mohassel, P., Mukherjee, P.: PASTA: PASsword-based threshold authentication, pp. 2042–2059 (2018)

[AMMR18] Agrawal, S., Mohassel, P., Mukherjee, P., Rindal, P.: DiSE: distributed symmetric-key encryption, pp. 1993–2010 (2018)

[BFH+20] Baum, C., Frederiksen, T., Hesse, J., Lehmann, A., Yanai, A.: PESTO: proactively secure distributed single sign-on, or how to trust a hacked server. In: 2020 IEEE European Symposium on Security and Privacy (EuroS&P), pp. 587–606. IEEE (2020)

[Bla79] Blakley, G.R.: Safeguarding cryptographic keys. In: Proceedings of the 1979 AFIPS National Computer Conference, pp. 313–317 (1979)

[BLMR13] Boneh, D., Lewi, K., Montgomery, H.W., Raghunathan, A.: Key homomorphic PRFs and their applications, pp. 410–428 (2013)

[BLS01] Boneh, D., Lynn, B., Shacham, H.: Short signatures from the Weil pairing, pp. 514–532 (2001)

[BMS22] Baird, L., Mukherjee, P., Sinha, R.: I-TiRE: incremental timed-release encryption or how to use timed-release encryption on blockchains? pp. 235–248 (2022)

[BW13] Boneh, D., Waters, B.: Constrained pseudorandom functions and their applications, pp. 280–300 (2013)

[CG99] Canetti, R., Goldwasser, S.: An efficient threshold public key cryptosystem secure against adaptive chosen ciphertext attack, pp. 90–106 (1999)

[CGMS21] Christodorescu, M., Gaddam, S., Mukherjee, P., Sinha, R.: Amortized threshold symmetric-key encryption, pp. 2758–2779 (2021)

[CHK03] Canetti, R., Halevi, S., Katz, J.: A forward-secure public-key encryption scheme, pp. 255–271 (2003)

[DDFY94] De Santis, A., Desmedt, Y., Frankel, Y., Yung, M.: How to share a function securely, pp. 522–533 (1994)

[DF90] Desmedt, Y., Frankel, Y.: Threshold cryptosystems, pp. 307–315 (1990)

[DMSS24] Dey, P., Mukherjee, P., Sasmal, S., Sinha, R.: HiSE: Hierarchical (threshold) symmetric-key encryption. Cryptology ePrint Archive . Paper 2024/158 (2024)

[Dod03] Dodis, Y.: Efficient construction of (distributed) verifiable random functions, pp. 1–17 (2003)

[DP08] Delerablée, C., Pointcheval, D.: Dynamic threshold public-key encryption, pp. 317–334 (2008)

[DY05] Dodis, Y., Yampolskiy, A.: A verifiable random function with short proofs and keys, pp. 416–431 (2005)

[DYY06] Dodis, Y., Yampolskiy, A., Yung, M.: Threshold and proactive pseudo-random permutations, pp. 542–560 (2006)

[Fra90] Frankel, Y.: A practical protocol for large group oriented networks, pp. 56–61 (1990)

[GG18] Gennaro, R., Goldfeder, S.: Fast multiparty threshold ECDSA with fast trustless setup, pp. 1179–1194 (2018)

[GG20] Gennaro, R., Goldfeder, S.: One round threshold ECDSA with identifiable abort. Cryptology ePrint Archive, Report 2020/540 (2020)

[GJKR96] Gennaro, R., Jarecki, S., Krawczyk, H., Rabin, T.: Robust threshold DSS signatures, pp. 354–371 (1996)

[JKR19] Jarecki, S., Krawczyk, H., Resch, J.K.: Updatable oblivious key management for storage systems, pp. 379–393 (2019)

[Kat24] Katz, J.: Round-optimal, fully secure distributed key generation, pp. 285–316 (2024)

[Lin22] Lindell, Y.: Secure multiparty computation. Commun. ACM **65**(1), 86–96 (2022)

[MS95] Micali, S., Sidney, R.: A simple method for generating and sharing pseudo-random functions, with applications to clipper-like escrow systems, pp. 185–196 (1995)

[Muk20] Mukherjee, P.: Adaptively secure threshold symmetric-key encryption, pp. 465–487 (2020)

[Nie02] Nielsen, J.B.: A threshold pseudorandom function construction and its applications, pp. 401–416 (2002)

[NPR99] Naor, M., Pinkas, B., Reingold, O.: Distributed pseudo-random functions and KDCs, pp. 327–346 (1999)

[SG98] Shoup, V., Gennaro, R.: Securing threshold cryptosystems against chosen ciphertext attack, pp. 1–16 (1998)

[Sha79] Shamir, A.: How to share a secret. Commun. ACM **22**(11), 612–613 (1979)

[Sho00] Shoup, V.: Practical threshold signatures. In: Advances in Cryptology – EUROCRYPT 2000, pp. 207–220. Springer (2000). https://doi.org/10.1007/3-540-45539-6_15

ECC, Pairings, and RSA

On the Complexity Reduction of Final Exponentiation for BLS12 and BLS24 Curves

Siradji Sadikou Gaya[1(✉)], Senegue Gomez Nyamsi[2(✉)], Emmanuel Fouotsa[3(✉)], and Morou Amidou[4(✉)]

[1] Department of Mathematics, University Abdou Moumouni of Niamey, P.O. Box 10662 Niamey, Niger
sadikougayasiradji@gmail.com

[2] Department of Mathematics and Computer Science, University of Dschang, P.O. Box 67 Dschang, Cameroon
nyamsigomez@gmail.com

[3] Centre for Cybersecurity and Mathematical Cryptology, University of Bamenda, P.O. Box 39 Bambili, Cameroon
emmanuelfouotsa@yahoo.fr

[4] IREM, Abdou Moumouni University, P.O. Box 10662 Niamey, Niger
morou.amidou@uam.edu.ne

Abstract. The overall efficiency of pairing-based cryptographic schemes is intrinsically linked to the performance of the final exponentiation step. This study introduces a series of algorithmic enhancements designed to streamline the "hard part" of the exponentiation process, with a primary focus on the BLS12 and BLS24 elliptic curve families. Our methodology combines optimized addition chain synthesis with specialized cyclotomic and compressed squaring techniques to reduce the total number of field multiplications. Experimental results indicate that our refinements achieve significant latency reductions, specifically 18.32% using cyclotomic squaring, 10.16% using compressed squaring for BLS12 at the 128-bit security level and 26.46% for BLS24 at the 256-bit level. Additionally, at 192-bit security, the integration of compressed squaring improves the efficiency of BLS24 by 7.3%. The proposed mathematical frameworks are formally verified through rigorous implementations using the Magma computational algebra system.

Keywords: pairing-based cryptography · final exponentiation · addition chain

1 Introduction

Since the foundational breakthroughs nearly a quarter-century ago [4,5,28], pairing-based primitives have evolved into a cornerstone of contemporary cryptographic architectures. Their versatility is evidenced by their integration into a broad spectrum of protocols, ranging from identity-based encryption and signature schemes [2,35,38] to advanced privacy-preserving tools such as zkSNARKs

N. El Mrabet et al. (Eds.): AFRICACRYPT 2026, LNCS 16832, pp. 263–287, 2026.
https://doi.org/10.1007/978-3-032-31130-6_11

[24], polynomial commitments [30], and anonymous credential frameworks [3,9,10]. Mathematically, a Cryptography pairing is defined as a non-degenerate bilinear map:

$$e : \mathbb{G}_1 \times \mathbb{G}_2 \longrightarrow \mathbb{G}_T$$

where $\mathbb{G}_1, \mathbb{G}_2$ are cyclic subgroups of order r and the target group $\mathbb{G}_T$ resides within a multiplicative subgroup of the extension field $\mathbb{F}_{p^k}$ [8].

The landscape of pairing-friendly curves [19] underwent a significant shift following the emergence of Special Tower Number Field Sieve (STNFS) vulnerabilities [29]. These cryptanalytic advancements forced a recalibration of security parameters, positioning the Barreto-Lynn-Scott (BLS) family [6] as a preferred standard due to its optimal balance between embedding degree k and computational throughput. Specifically, within the BD model framework [36]. Incidentally, in the context of cryptography, BLS can refer to the BLS curves or to BLS signatures. The BLS curve has been identified as the most competitive candidates after exhaustive evaluations of both the Miller loop and the final exponentiation phase.

While substantial efforts by Guillevic et al. [25], Aranha et al. [12], Senegue Gomez et al. [33] and others [23,32], have successfully optimized the Miller loop, the final exponentiation remains a formidable computational hurdle. Prior attempts to mitigate this bottleneck involved diverse methodologies, including lattice-based approaches [15], vector addition-subtraction chains [21,37], cyclotomic polynomial-based reductions [42], Hayashida et al. [14], Walid Haddaji et al. [41]and Ghammam et al. [31]. Although techniques tailored for BLS at the 128, 192, 256-bit level [22], various taxonomic studies [7] and Aranha et al. [1] have advanced the state-of-the-art, there remains a critical need for more streamlined arithmetic procedures.

Our Contribution. This work presents a new approach to cyclotomic family parameterization by isolating powers of 2 within the curve seeds. This structural modification enables a radical simplification of the "hard part" of the final exponentiation. By substituting intricate vector addition chains with a linear sequence of power-of-2 additions, we minimize arithmetic overhead. We validate the efficient of this method on BLS12 and BLS24 curves, providing comparative benchmarks against the results of Ghammam and Fouotsa [22], Razvan et al. [7] and Aranha et al. [1] to demonstrate superior performance and implementational simplicity.

Roadmap. The remainder of this article is organized as follows: Sect. 2 provides the necessary background on addition chains and the properties of pairing-friendly curves. Section 3 details the updated security parameters established for the BLS12 and BLS24 families. Our proposed methodologies for optimizing the final exponentiation are developed and evaluated in Sect. 4. A comprehensive synthesis of the computational costs and performance benchmarks is presented in Sect. 5. Finally, Sect. 6 offers concluding remarks and perspectives for future research.

2 Preliminaries

Let E be an elliptic curve defined over a prime field $\mathbb{F}_p$. We denote by r a large prime factor of the curve order $\#E(\mathbb{F}_p)$ such that $\gcd(r, p) = 1$. The embedding degree k is the minimal positive integer for which r divides $p^k - 1$ while r^2 does not divide the same term. The subgroups $\mathbb{G}_1$ and $\mathbb{G}_2$ involved in the Optimal Ate pairing [40] are characterized via the r-torsion subgroup $E[r]$ and the Frobenius map π_p as:

$$\mathbb{G}_1 = E[r] \cap \ker(\pi_p - [1]), \quad \mathbb{G}_2 = E[r] \cap \ker(\pi_p - [p]).$$

For any elements $P \in \mathbb{G}_1$ and $Q \in \mathbb{G}_2$, the computation of this pairing consists of two steps: Miller loop and final exponentiation.

The Ate pairing is defined by

$$a_T(Q, P) = (f_{T,Q}(P))^{\frac{p^k-1}{r}},$$

where $T = t - 1$, with t denoting the trace of the Frobenius endomorphism. The function $f_{T,Q}$ is a rational function whose divisor is given by

$$\mathrm{div}(f_{T,Q}) = T(Q) - ([T]Q) - (T-1)(\mathcal{O}).$$

The first step, the Miller loop, computes the value $f' = f_{T,Q}(P) \in \mathbb{F}_{p^k}^*$. The second step, known as the final exponentiation, raises this value to the power $e = (p^k - 1)/r$ to ensure a unique result in the group of r-th roots of unity μ_r. According to [37], the exponent e is typically decomposed as:

$$e = \frac{p^k - 1}{\Phi_k(p)} \cdot \frac{\Phi_k(p)}{r}$$

This calculation is divided into two phases: an "easy part" and a "hard part". The first stage maps f to the cyclotomic subgroup $\mathbb{G}_{\Phi_k(p)}$ through the exponent $(p^k - 1)/\Phi_k(p)$. This step is computationally efficient, involving only a few multiplications, inversions, and Frobenius operations. The hard part requires raising the result to the power $d = \Phi_k(p)/r$, which represents the primary arithmetic cost. In the case of pairing-friendly curves, this exponentiation is optimized by leveraging the polynomial representation of parameters and using vectorial addition chains [15,21,37]. In the following of this section, we define a pairing-friendly elliptic curve [19] and an addition chain [34]

2.1 Family of Pairing-Friendly Elliptic Curves

Let $p(x)$, $t(x)$, and $r(x)$ be non-zero polynomials. A triplet of polynomials $(p(x), t(x), r(x))$ is said to parameterize a family of pairing-friendly ordinary elliptic curves with embedding degree k and Complex Multiplication (CM) discriminant D if it satisfies the following properties [19]:

1. $p(x) = q(x)^n$ for some $n \geq 1$, where $q(x)$ is prime for some value of x.

2. $r(x) = c \times r'(x)$ with $c \geq 1$, where $r'(x)$ is prime for some value of x.
3. $p(x) + 1 - t(x) \equiv 0 \pmod{r(x)}$.
4. $\Phi_k(t(x) - 1) \equiv 0 \pmod{r(x)}$, where Φ_k is the k-th cyclotomic polynomial.
5. The equation $D(y(x))^2 = 4p(x) - (t(x))^2$ has an infinite number of integer solutions.

The ρ-value of a polynomial family $(p(x), t(x), r(x))$ is defined as $\rho(p, t, r) = \frac{\deg p}{\deg r}$. Let $f(x) = 4p(x) - t(x)^2 \in \mathbb{Q}[x]$ be the CM polynomial of the form $f(x) = g(x)y(x)^2$ with $y(x), g(x) \in \mathbb{Q}[x]$ and $\deg g \leq 2$. If $\deg g = 0$, the family $(p(x), t(x), r(x))$ is complete where The term 'complete' signifies that the family can represent elliptic curves for any given discriminant D, as the CM equation is satisfied by the polynomial structure itself rather than being restricted to specific values of x and thus $f(x) = Dy(x)^2$, for some square-free $D > 0$. If $\deg g = 1$, the family is complete with variable discriminant and finally, if $\deg g = 2$, with $g(x)$ not a perfect square and $lc(g) > 0$, the family is sparse.

2.2 Addition Chain

The efficiency of exponentiation within group structures is heavily dependent on the use of addition chains [34,37], a process that remains a fundamental requirement for executing the Tate pairing on elliptic curves.

Definition 1. *(Basic Concept) An addition chain for a positive integer n is defined as an ordered sequence of positive integers $\{e_0, e_1, e_2, \ldots, e_s\}$ that fulfills the following criteria:*

- *The sequence begins with $e_0 = 1, e_1 = 2$ and terminates with $e_s = n$.*
- *For every index i in the range $1 < i < s$, there exist prior indices j and k (where $j, k < i$) such that the relation $e_i = e_j + e_k$ is satisfied.*

Definition 2. *(Generalized Sequence) A generalized addition chain of length l for a set of positive integers $\{n_1, n_2, \ldots, n_s\}$ is a sequence $\{e_0, e_1, e_2, \ldots, e_l\}$ that encompasses all values within the target set $\{n_1, n_2, \ldots, n_s\}$. This construction requires:*

- *Starting values $e_0 = 1, e_1 = 2$ and a final value $e_l = n_s$.*
- *For each i $(1 < i < l)$, the existence of indices $0 \leq k \leq j < i$ such that $e_i = e_j + e_k$.*

Such chains define the necessary sequence of multiplications and squarings for field exponentiation. According to Olivos' theorem [34], operations using a chain of length l can be completed in $l + s - 1$ group operations. However, finding the absolute minimal length for such a sequence remains an NP-hard problem.

3 New Secure Parameters for BLS Curves

In this section, we review the original parameters $(T(x), p(x), r(x))$ introduced by Barreto et al. [6] for the BLS12 and BLS24 curve families. Furthermore, we describe a methodological approach to derive a new set of secure parameters $(T(t), p(t), r(t))$ for these specific curves.

The fundamental parameters governing the BLS12 curve are defined by the following polynomials:

$$\begin{aligned} T(x) &= x + 1 \\ r(x) &= x^4 - x^2 + 1 \\ p(x) &= \frac{1}{3}(x-1)^2 r(x) + x \end{aligned}$$

For a specific seed value $x = -2^{77} + 2^{50} + 2^{33}$, Razvan et al. [7] demonstrated that $p(x)$ and $r(x)$ result in prime numbers of approximately 460 bits and 307 bits, respectively. This configuration provides a security level of 128 bits, for which they developed an optimized final exponentiation procedure.

To enhance implementation efficiency, let us consider the substitution $x = 2^{33}t$, where $t = -2^{44} + 2^{17} + 1$. By applying this transformation to the original parameter set, we derive the following updated security parameters:

$$\begin{aligned} T(t) &= 2^{33}t + 1 \\ r(t) &= 2^{132}t^4 - 2^{66}t^2 + 1 \\ p(t) &= \frac{1}{3}(2^{33}t - 1)^2 r(t) + 2^{33}t \end{aligned}$$

Using the seed $t = -2^{44} + 2^{17} + 1$, the resulting values for $p(t)$ and $r(t)$ remain prime with bit lengths of 460 and 307, respectively, thereby maintaining the 128-bit security threshold.

In a similar fashion, we utilize the substitution $x = 2^{26}t$ and the new parameters for the BLS24 192-bit security level are

$$\begin{aligned} T(t) &= 2^{26}t + 1 \\ r(t) &= 2^{208}t^8 - 2^{104}t^4 + 1 \\ p(t) &= \frac{1}{3}(2^{26}t - 1)^2 r(t) + 2^{26}t. \end{aligned}$$

For $t = 2^{22} - 2^4 + 1$, p and r are primes of lengths 479 bits and 384 bits, respectively.

Furthermore, for the 256-bit security level we utilize the substitution $x = 2^{50}t$ and the new parameters are

$$\begin{aligned} T(t) &= 2^{50}t + 1 \\ r(t) &= 2^{400}t^8 - 2^{200}t^4 + 1 \\ p(t) &= \frac{1}{3}(2^{50}t - 1)^2 r(t) + 2^{50}t \end{aligned}$$

For $t = -2^{53} - 2^{51} + 2^{18} + 1$, p and r are primes of lengths 1032 bits and 827 bits, respectively.

3.1 Arithmetic in $\mathbb{F}_{p^{12}}$ and $\mathbb{F}_{p^{24}}$

This section details the computational costs associated with arithmetic in the extension fields $\mathbb{F}_{p^{12}}$ and $\mathbb{F}_{p^{24}}$. To achieve efficient field arithmetic, we utilize a tower of extensions. For $\mathbb{F}_{p^{12}}$, the construction begins with a quadratic extension $\mathbb{F}_{p^2} = \mathbb{F}_p[\alpha]/(\alpha^2+1)$, followed by a cubic extension $\mathbb{F}_{p^6} = \mathbb{F}_{p^2}[\beta]/(\beta^3-(\alpha+1))$, and finally a quadratic extension $\mathbb{F}_{p^{12}} = \mathbb{F}_{p^6}[\gamma]/(\gamma^2-\beta)$. Similarly, the $\mathbb{F}_{p^{24}}$ field is established by extending the $\mathbb{F}_{p^{12}}$ structure through the relation $\mathbb{F}_{p^{24}} = \mathbb{F}_{p^{12}}[\theta]/(\theta^2-\gamma)$, where the intermediate $\mathbb{F}_{p^6}$ layer is defined as $\mathbb{F}_{p^2}[\beta]/(\beta^3-(\alpha+2))$.

We denote M, S, and I as the costs for multiplication, squaring, and inversion in the base field $\mathbb{F}_p$. In the extension field $\mathbb{F}_{p^k}$, the costs for multiplication, squaring, cyclotomic squaring, and inversion are represented by M_k, S_k, S_c, and I_k, respectively. Additionally, f_k^i signifies the p-th Frobenius map operation. The comparative costs for these operations, based on the findings in [12], are summarized in Table 1. According to [25], the cost of the Frobenius operation for even values of k is approximately $(k-2)M$ and $I = 25M$.

Table 1. Arithmetic costs in $\mathbb{F}_{p^{12}}$ and $\mathbb{F}_{p^{24}}$ [12]

Operation	Cost in $\mathbb{F}_{p^{12}}$	Cost in $\mathbb{F}_{p^{24}}$
Multiplication	$54M$	$162M$
Squaring (S_k)	$36M$	$108M$
Cyclotomic squaring (S_c)	$18M$	$54M$
Inversion	$120M$	$275M + I$
Frobenius	$10M$	$22M$
Compressed Squaring (cS_k)	$12M$	$36M$
Simult. Decomp. (n elements)	$(24n-5)M + I$	$27(2n-1)M + 18nM + 14M + I$

The efficiency of the final exponentiation, as summarized in Table 1, relies on the specific arithmetic properties of the cyclotomic subgroup $\mathbb{G}_{\Phi_k(p)} \subset \mathbb{F}_{p^k}^*$. In this subgroup, elements satisfy the condition $\alpha^{\Phi_k(p)} = 1$. This structure allows for significant optimizations. Cyclotomic Squarings (S_c) : In the cyclotomic subgroup, an elevation to the square can be computed more efficiently than a regular squaring in $\mathbb{F}_{p^k}$. For instance, for $k = 12$ (BLS12) or $k = 24$ (BLS24), the cyclotomic squaring uses the formulas from [12], which reduce the number of base field multiplications by exploiting the fact that the result must remain in $\mathbb{G}_{\Phi_k(p)}$.

Compressed Squarings (cS_k): This technique further improves performance by representing elements of the cyclotomic subgroup in a compressed form (using only d coordinates instead of k, where $d = \phi(k)$). The compressed squaring, often associated with the Karabina's method [12], allows for even faster iterations during the Miller loop and the hard part of the final exponentiation, though it requires a final decompression step.

4 Final Exponentiation

To optimize the computation of the final exponentiation, we adopt the methodology proposed by Scott et al. [37], leveraging specialized addition chains. Assuming an even embedding degree k, the target exponent is defined as:

$$d(t) = \frac{p(t)^k - 1}{r(t)}$$

This expression can be strategically decomposed into two distinct components:

$$\frac{p(t)^k - 1}{r(t)} = \frac{p(t)^k - 1}{\Phi_k(p(t))} \cdot \frac{\Phi_k(p(t))}{r(t)}$$

Given that k is even, we can utilize the factorization $p(t)^k - 1 = (p(t)^{k/2} - 1)(p(t)^{k/2} + 1)$. This leads to the following structural breakdown:

$$\frac{p(t)^k - 1}{r(t)} = \underbrace{(p(t)^{k/2} - 1) \cdot \frac{p(t)^{k/2} + 1}{\Phi_k(p(t))}}_{\text{easy part}} \cdot \underbrace{\frac{\Phi_k(p(t))}{r(t)}}_{\text{hard part}}$$

The first segment, known as the *easy part*, is computationally inexpensive as it mainly involves the Frobenius automorphism and field inversions. In contrast, the second segment the *hard part* represents the most demanding phase of the pairing, requiring sophisticated addition chains to handle the specific exponentiation efficiently.

4.1 Evaluation for the BLS12 Family

For the BLS12 curve, we utilize the updated parameters $p(t)$ and $r(t)$ as defined in Sect. 3. To facilitate the computation, we consider the modified exponent $d'(t) = 3 \times d(t)$. The core challenge lies in the hard part, which the exponent can be expressed as:

$$3 \times \left(\frac{\Phi_{12}(p(t))}{r(t)} \right) = \sum_{i=0}^{3} m_i(t) p^i(t) \qquad (1)$$

where

$$\begin{aligned}
m_0(t) &= 2^{165}t^5 - 2^{133}t^4 + 2^{67}t^2 - 2^{33}t + 3 \\
m_1(t) &= 2^{122}t^4 - 2^{100}t^3 + 2^{34}t - 1 \\
m_2(t) &= 2^{99}t^3 - 2^{67}t^2 + 2^{33}t \\
m_3(t) &= 2^{66}t^2 - 2^{34}t + 1
\end{aligned}$$

From these expressions, we isolate the absolute values of each coefficient. Let A denote the set containing these coefficients expressed as powers. This set consists of 11 distinct elements, which serve as the foundation for constructing our optimized addition chain.

$$A = [1, 3, 2^{33}, 2^{34}, 2^{66}, 2^{67}, 2^{99}, 2^{100}, 2^{132}, 2^{133}, 2^{165}]$$

Using the following equalities:

$$2^n + 2^{n+1} = 2^n \times 3, \quad 2^n + 2^n \times 3 = 2^{n+2}, \quad 2^n + 2^n = 2^{n+1} \quad \text{and} \quad 2^{2n} = (2^n)^2.$$

We construct an addition 2-pseudo-chain of length 30 elements which is:

$$B = [1, \underline{2}, 3, \underline{2^2}, 2^4, 2^8, \underline{2^9}, \underline{2^{10}}, \underline{2^{11}}, \underline{2^{12}}, 2^{16}, 2^{20}, 2^{24}, 2^{32}, \underline{2^{33}}, \underline{2^{34}}, 2^{40}, \underline{2^{41}}, 2^{48}, \underline{2^{49}}, \\ 2^{66}, \underline{2^{67}}, 2^{82}, 2^{98}, \underline{2^{99}}, \underline{2^{100}}, 2^{132}, \underline{2^{133}}, 2^{164}, \underline{2^{165}}].$$

For an element $f \in \mathbb{G}_{\Phi_{12}(p)}$, the computation of f^{t^i} for $1 \leq i \leq 5$ requires $5(44S_c + 2M_{12}) = 4500M$, given that $t = -2^{44} + 2^{17} + 1$ with $\log_2(t) = 44$ and a Hamming weight $HW(t) = 3$. Alternatively, by employing compressed squaring (cS_k), this cost is reduced to $5(44 \times cS_{12} + 2M_{12}) = 3180M$. To this, we must add the decompression cost for 3 elements, which is calculated as $(24n - 5)M + I = 67M + I$. In the next step, the Frobenius operator is utilized to determine the required factors of the form $(f^{t^i})^{p^j}$. Although there are 18 possible factors for $0 \leq i \leq 5$ and $1 \leq j \leq 3$, Eq. (1) only necessitates 10 of them, resulting in a total cost of $10 \times 10 = 100M$.

Analysis of Eq. (1) reveals that specific coefficients recur across different terms; for instance, the coefficient 1 appears in both $m_1(t)$ and $m_3(t)$, while 2^{33} is a factor in $m_2(t)$. To minimize the number of required multiplications in the final exponentiation, we can precompute shared components by grouping terms with common exponents. We can optimize the computation by grouping these coefficients as products of the factors $(f^{t^i})^{p^j}$. To facilitate this, variables y_0, y_1, and y_2 are introduced to aggregate the terms associated with the coefficients 1 and 2^{33} as follows :

$$y_0 = \frac{1}{f^p} \cdot f^{p^3}, \quad y_1 = (f^t)^{p^2}$$

By extending this logic, we define a total of 11 coefficients y_k for $k = 0, \ldots, 10$, transforming the original expression into a multi-exponentiation problem:

$$f^{d'} = \prod_{k=0}^{10} y_k^{A[k]}$$

where $A[k]$ represents the values from the set of coefficients A.

Extracting all y_k coefficients from Eq. (1) costs 4 multiplications plus a few negligible field inversions. These inversions are efficiently performed via simple conjugation, leveraging the fact that the BLS12 curve has an even embedding degree [17]. Finally, to resolve the multi-exponentiation, we develop an addition chain based on the absolute values of the distinct coefficients found in $m_i(t)$. According to Olivo's theorem, the number of group operations where operations refer to multiplications and squarings in the cyclotomic subgroup $\mathbb{G}_{\Phi_k(p)}$ is $l + s - 1 = 30 + 11 - 1 = 40$, which consists of 15 cyclotomic squarings and 25 multiplications in $\mathbb{F}_{p^{12}}$. This yields a cost of $25M_{12} + 15S_c + 4M_{12} = 1836M$. When including the easy part calculation cost $2M_{12} + I_{12} + 2f_{12}^{i} = 248$. the total final exponentiation costs are:

- Using Cyclotomic Squaring $(S_c) : 4500M + 100M + 1836M + 248M = 6659M + I$.
- Using Compressed Squaring $(cS_k) : 3180M + 67 + I + 100M + 1836M + 248M = 5431M + I$.

Algorithm 1. Final Exponentiation of BLS12 (128 bits of security) : compute of $f^{\frac{p^{12}-1}{r}}$

Require: $f \in \mathbb{G}_{\Phi_{12}(p)}$, m_0, m_1, m_2, m_3, $t \leftarrow -2^{44} + 2^{17} + 1$
Ensure: F
$E \leftarrow ((p^6 - 1) \cdot (p^2 + 1))$;
$H \leftarrow (m_3 \cdot p^3 + m_2 \cdot p^2 + m_1 \cdot p + m_0)$;
$g_0 \leftarrow f$; $g_1 \leftarrow f^{t}$; $g_2 \leftarrow f^{t^2}$; $g_3 \leftarrow f^{t^3}$; $g_4 \leftarrow f^{t^4}$; $g_5 \leftarrow f^{t^5}$;
$y_0 := g_0^{-p} \cdot g_0^{p^3}$; $y_1 := g_0$; $y_2 := g_1^{-1} \cdot g_1^{p^2}$; $y_3 := g_1^{p} \cdot g_1^{-p^3}$; $y_4 := g_2^{p^3}$; $y_5 := g_2 \cdot g_2^{-p^2}$; $y_6 := g_3^{p^2}$;
$y_7 := g_3^{-p}$; $y_8 := g_4^{p}$; $y_9 := g_4^{-1}$; $y_{10} := g_5$;
$A := [1, 3, 2^{33}, 2^{34}, 2^{66}, 2^{67}, 2^{99}, 2^{100}, 2^{132}, 2^{133}, 2^{165}]$;
$Y \leftarrow [y_0, y_1, y_2, y_3, y_4, y_5, y_6, y_7, y_8, y_9, y_{10}]$;
for $k = 1$ **to** 11 **do**
    $G \leftarrow Y[k]^{A[k]}$
end for
$F \leftarrow G^{E}$;
return F

4.2 Evaluation for the BLS24 Curve (192-Bit Security)

In this section, we apply the same methodology to this curve as was previously used for the BLS12 family. The updated parameters $p(t)$ and $r(t)$ for the BLS24 curve are those defined in Sect. 3.

By setting $d'(t) = 3 \times d(t)$, the following relationship is established:

$$3 \times \left(\frac{\Phi_{24}(p(t))}{r(t)} \right) = \sum_{i=0}^{7} m_i(t) p^i(t) \tag{2}$$

where

$$
\begin{aligned}
m_0(t) &= 2^{234}t^9 - 2^{209}t^8 + 2^{182}t^7 - 2^{130}t^5 + 2^{105}t^4 - 2^{78}t^3 + 3 \\
m_1(t) &= 2^{208}t^8 - 2^{183}t^7 + 2^{156}t^6 - 2^{104}t^4 + 2^{79}t^3 - 2^{52}t^2 \\
m_2(t) &= 2^{182}t^7 - 2^{157}t^6 + 2^{130}t^5 - 2^{78}t^3 + 2^{53}t^2 - 2^{26}t \\
m_3(t) &= 2^{156}t^6 - 2^{131}t^5 + 2^{104}t^4 - 2^{52}t^2 + 2^{27}t - 1 \\
m_4(t) &= 2^{130}t^5 - 2^{105}t^4 + 2^{78}t^3 \\
m_5(t) &= 2^{104}t^4 - 2^{79}t^3 + 2^{52}t^2 \\
m_6(t) &= 2^{78}t^3 - 2^{53}t^2 + 2^{26}t \\
m_7(t) &= 2^{52}t^2 - 2^{27}t + 1
\end{aligned}
$$

Upon isolating the absolute values of the distinct coefficients from the polynomials $m_i(t)$, we identify a collection of 19 elements. These coefficients, represented as powers, form the following set:

$$
\begin{aligned}
C = [&1, 3, 2^{26}, 2^{27}, 2^{52}, 2^{53}, 2^{78}, 2^{79}, 2^{104}, 2^{105}, 2^{130}, 2^{131}, 2^{156}, 2^{157}, 2^{182}, 2^{183}, \\
&2^{208}, 2^{209}, 2^{234}].
\end{aligned}
$$

Using the following equalities:

$$2^n + 2^{n+1} = 2^n \times 3, \quad 2^n + 2^n \times 3 = 2^{n+2}, \quad 2^n + 2^n = 2^{n+1} \quad \text{and} \quad 2^{2n} = (2^n)^2.$$

We construct an addition 2-pseudo-chain of 51 elements:

$$
\begin{aligned}
D = [&1, \underline{2}, 3, \underline{2^2}, \underline{2^3}, \underline{2^4}, \underline{2^5}, \underline{2^6}, \underline{2^7}, \underline{2^8}, \underline{2^9}, \underline{2^{10}}, \underline{2^{11}}, \underline{2^{12}}, \underline{2^{13}}, \underline{2^{14}}, \underline{2^{15}}, \underline{2^{16}}, 2^{19}, 2^{22}, \\
&2^{26}, \underline{2^{27}}, \underline{2^{28}}, \underline{2^{29}}, 2^{32}, 2^{38}, \underline{2^{39}}, 2^{44}, \underline{2^{45}}, 2^{52}, \underline{2^{53}}, 2^{58}, 2^{64}, \underline{2^{65}}, 2^{78}, \underline{2^{79}}, 2^{90}, \\
&\underline{2^{91}}, 2^{104}, \underline{2^{105}}, 2^{116}, \underline{2^{117}}, 2^{130}, \underline{2^{131}}, 2^{156}, \underline{2^{157}}, 2^{182}, \underline{2^{183}}, 2^{208}, \underline{2^{209}}, 2^{234}].
\end{aligned}
$$

The final exponentiation derived from Eq. (1) is expressed as:

$$f^{3\times\left(\frac{\Phi_{24}(p(t))}{r(t)}\right)} = f^{\sum_{i=0}^{7} m_i(t)p^i(t)} = f^{\sum_{i=0}^{7}(\sum_{j=0}^{9} a_{ij}t^j)p^i} = f^{\sum_{j=0}^{9}\sum_{i=0}^{7}(a_{ij}t^j)p^i}.$$

For an element $f \in \mathbb{G}_{\phi_{24}(p)}$, the computation of f^{t^j} for $1 \leq j \leq 9$ requires:

$$9(22cS_k + 2M_{24}) = 9(22 \times 36 + 2 \times 162) = 10044M$$

This evaluation assumes $t = 2^{22} - 2^4 + 1$, where $\log_2(t) = 22$ and $HW(t) = 3$. Additionally, the compression of three elements incurs a cost of $(27(2n-1) + 18n + 14)M + I = 203M + I$.

The Frobenius operator is subsequently applied to determine specific factors of the form $(f^{t^j})^{p^i}$ for $0 \leq j \leq 9$ and $1 \leq i \leq 7$. Although 70 such factors exist, only 30 are required by Eq. (2), costing:

$$30 \times 22 = 660M.$$

In Eq. (2), we observe that the coefficient 1 appears twice (in $m_3(t)$ and $m_7(t)$), and similarly, 2^{26} appears twice (in $m_2(t)$ and $m_6(t)$). These can be efficiently grouped as products of the $(f^{t^i})^{p^j}$ factors. We introduce variables y_0, y_1, and y_2 to aggregate these coefficients:

$$y_0 = \frac{1}{f^{p^3}} \cdot f^{p^7}, \quad y_1 = (f^t)^{p^6} \frac{1}{(f^t)^{p^2}}$$

Following this procedure for all terms, we define 18 coefficients y_k (for $k = 0, \ldots, 18$), transforming the process into a multi-exponentiation problem:

$$f^d = \prod_{k=0}^{18} y_k^{C[k]}$$

where the values $C[k]$ are drawn from the set C.

The extraction of all y_k coefficients from Eq. (2) requires 18 multiplications. The necessary field inversions are negligible and can be computed via conjugation, as the BLS24 curve possesses an even embedding degree [17]. To resolve the multi-exponentiation, an addition chain is constructed from the absolute values of the distinct coefficients in the m_i expressions. According to Olivo's theorem, the number of group operations is $l + s - 1 = 51 + 19 - 1 = 69$, comprising 31 doublings and 38 multiplications in $\mathbb{F}_{p^{24}}$. This results in:

$$38M_{24} + 31S_c + 18M_{24} = 10746M$$

Including the cost of the easy part $2M_{24} + 1I_{24} + 2f_{24}^i = 643 + IM$, the total final exponentiation cost is:

$$10044M + 660M + 203M + I + 10746M + 643M + I = 22296M + 2I.$$

Algorithm 2. final exponentiation of BLS24 (192 bits of security) : compute of $f^{\frac{p^{24}-1}{r}}$

Require: $f \in \mathbb{G}_{\Phi_{24}(p)}$, $m_0, m_1, m_2, m_3, m_4, m_5, m_6, m_7$, $t \leftarrow 2^{22} - 2^4 + 1$
Ensure: F

$E \leftarrow ((p^{12}-1) \cdot (p^4+1));$
$H \leftarrow (m_7 \cdot p^7 + m_6 \cdot p^6 + m_5 \cdot p^5 + m_4 \cdot p^4 + m_3 \cdot p^3 + m_2 \cdot p^2 + m_1 \cdot p + m_0);$
$g_0 \leftarrow f; g_1 \leftarrow f^t; g_2 \leftarrow f^{t^2}; g_3 \leftarrow f^{t^3}; g_4 \leftarrow f^{t^4};$
$g_5 \leftarrow f^{t^5}; g_6 \leftarrow f^{t^6}; g_7 \leftarrow f^{t^7}; g_8 \leftarrow f^{t^8}; g_9 \leftarrow f^{t^9};$
$y_0 \leftarrow g_0^{-p^3} \cdot g_0^{p^7}$ $y_1 := g_0$; $y_2 \leftarrow g_1^{p^6} \cdot g_1^{-p^2}$; $y_3 \leftarrow g_1^{p^3} \cdot g_1^{-p^7}$; $y_4 \leftarrow g_2^{-p} \cdot g_2^{-p^3} \cdot g_2^{p^5} \cdot g_2^{p^7}$;
$y_5 \leftarrow g_2^{p^2} \cdot g_2^{-p^6}$;
$y_6 \leftarrow g_3 \cdot g_3^{-p^2} \cdot g_3^{p^4} \cdot g_3^{p^6}$; $y_7 \leftarrow g_3^{p} \cdot g_3^{-p^5}$; $y_8 \leftarrow g_4^{-p} \cdot g_4^{p^3} \cdot g_4^{p^5}$; $y_9 \leftarrow g_4 \cdot g_4^{-p^4}$;
$y_{10} \leftarrow g_5 \cdot g_5^{p^2} \cdot g_5^{p^4}$;
$y_{11} \leftarrow g_5^{-p^3}$; $y_{12} \leftarrow g_6^{p} \cdot g_6^{p^3}$; $y_{13} \leftarrow g_6^{-p^2}$; $y_{14} \leftarrow g_7 \cdot g_7^{p^2}$; $y_{15} \leftarrow g_7^{-p}$; $y_{16} \leftarrow g_8^{p}$;
$y_{17} \leftarrow g_8^{-1}$;
$y_{18} \leftarrow g_9;$
$C \leftarrow [1, 3, 2^{26}, 2^{27}, 2^{52}, 2^{53}, 2^{78}, 2^{79}, 2^{104}, 2^{105}, 2^{130}, 2^{131}, 2^{156}, 2^{157}, 2^{182}, 2^{183}, 2^{208}, 2^{209}, 2^{234}];$
$Y \leftarrow [y_0, y_1, y_2, y_3, y_4, y_5, y_6, y_7, y_8, y_9, y_{10}, y_{11}, y_{12}, y_{13}, y_{14}, y_{15}, y_{16}, y_{17}, y_{18}];$
for $k = 1$ **to** 19 **do**
    $G \leftarrow Y[k]^{C[k]}$
end for
$F \leftarrow G^E;$
return F

4.3 Evaluation for the BLS24 Family (256-Bit Security)

This subsection extends our analysis to the BLS24 curve at the 256-bit security level, employing a procedure identical to that used for the previous curve families. We utilize the updated parameters $p(t)$ and $r(t)$ as established in Sect. 3.

By defining the modified exponent as $d'(t) = 3d(t)$, the core of the final exponentiation can be expressed through the following polynomial decomposition:

$$3 \cdot \frac{\Phi_{24}(p(t))}{r(t)} = \sum_{i=0}^{7} m_i(t)\, p^i(t), \tag{3}$$

where

$$\begin{aligned}
m_0(t) &= 2^{450}t^9 - 2^{401}t^8 + 2^{350}t^7 - 2^{250}t^5 + 2^{201}t^4 - 2^{150}t^3 + 3 \\
m_1(t) &= 2^{400}t^8 - 2^{351}t^7 + 2^{300}t^6 - 2^{200}t^4 + 2^{151}t^3 - 2^{100}t^2 \\
m_2(t) &= 2^{350}t^7 - 2^{301}t^6 + 2^{250}t^5 - 2^{150}t^3 + 2^{101}t^2 - 2^{50}t \\
m_3(t) &= 2^{300}t^6 - 2^{251}t^5 + 2^{200}t^4 - 2^{100}t^2 + 2^{51}t - 1 \\
m_4(t) &= 2^{250}t^5 - 2^{201}t^4 + 2^{150}t^3 \\
m_5(t) &= 2^{200}t^4 - 2^{151}t^3 + 2^{100}t^2 \\
m_6(t) &= 2^{150}t^3 - 2^{101}t^2 + 2^{50}t \\
m_7(t) &= 2^{100}t^2 - 2^{51}t + 1
\end{aligned}$$

Taking the absolute values of all distinct coefficients appearing in the polynomials $m_i(t)$ yields the following set of 19 elements:

$$\begin{aligned}
E = [&1,\ 3,\ 2^{50},\ 2^{51},\ 2^{100},\ 2^{101},\ 2^{150},\ 2^{151},\ 2^{200},\ 2^{201},\ 2^{250}, \\
&2^{251},\ 2^{300},\ 2^{301},\ 2^{350},\ 2^{351},\ 2^{400},\ 2^{401},\ 2^{450}].
\end{aligned}$$

Using the identities

$$2^n + 2^{n+1} = 3 \cdot 2^n, \qquad 2^n + 3 \cdot 2^n = 2^{n+2}, \qquad 2^n + 2^n = 2^{n+1}, \qquad 2^{2n} = (2^n)^2,$$

we construct an addition 2-pseudo-chain of length 57.

$$\begin{aligned}
F = [&1, \underline{2}, 3, \underline{2^2}, 2^3, \underline{2^4}, \underline{2^5}, \underline{2^6}, \underline{2^7}, \underline{2^8}, \underline{2^9}, \underline{2^{10}}, 2^{12}, 2^{14}, \underline{2^{15}}, 2^{18}, 2^{20}, \underline{2^{21}}, 2^{24}, \underline{2^{25}}, 2^{28}, \\
&2^{30}, \underline{2^{31}}, 2^{36}, \underline{2^{37}}, 2^{42}, \underline{2^{43}}, 2^{50}, 2^{52}, 2^{56}, 2^{62}, 2^{74}, \underline{2^{75}}, 2^{86}, \underline{2^{87}}, 2^{100}, \underline{2^{101}}, 2^{112}, \\
&2^{124}, \underline{2^{125}}, 2^{150}, \underline{2^{151}}, 2^{174}, \underline{2^{175}}, 2^{200}, \underline{2^{201}}, 2^{224}, \underline{2^{225}}, 2^{250}, \underline{2^{251}}, 2^{300}, \underline{2^{301}}, \\
&2^{350}, 2^{352}, 2^{400}, \underline{2^{401}}, 2^{450}].
\end{aligned}$$

The exponentiation presented in Eq. (1) can be expressed as:

$$f^{3 \cdot \frac{\Phi_{24}(p(t))}{r(t)}} = f^{\sum_{i=0}^{7} m_i(t) p^i(t)} = f^{\sum_{j=0}^{9} \sum_{i=0}^{7} a_{ij} t^j p^i}.$$

For an element $f \in \mathbb{G}_{\Phi_{24}(p)}$. In the first stage, we determine f^{t^j} for $1 \leq j \leq 9$. This computation costs:

$$9(53S_c + 3M_{24}) = 9(53 \cdot 54 + 3 \cdot 162) = 30132M,$$

given that $t = -2^{53} - 2^{51} + 2^{18} + 1$, which implies $\log_2(t) = 53$ and $\mathrm{HW}(t) = 4$. By applying compressed squaring (cS_k), the required operations become:

$$9(53cS_k + 3M_{24}) = 9(53 \times 36M + 3 \times 162M) = 21546M$$

To this, we add the cost of decompressing 4 elements, calculated as $(27(2n - 1) + 18n + 14)M + I = 275M + I$.

Subsequently, the Frobenius endomorphism is utilized to generate terms of the form $(f^{t^j})^{p^i}$ for $0 \leq j \leq 9$ and $1 \leq i \leq 7$. Out of the 70 potential factors, only 30 are necessary for Eq. (3), resulting in a cost of:

$$30 \times 22 = 660M.$$

Within Eq. (3), the coefficient 1 is present twice (in $m_3(t)$ and $m_7(t)$), while the coefficient 2^{50} appears in both $m_2(t)$ and $m_6(t)$. These elements are grouped using the following variables:

$$y_0 = f^{p^7} \cdot \frac{1}{f^{p^3}}, \qquad y_1 = (f^t)^{p^6} \cdot \frac{1}{(f^t)^{p^2}}.$$

Using this same strategy, we define a total of 19 distinct elements y_k (for $k = 0, \ldots, 18$), which transforms the task into a multi-exponentiation problem:

$$f^d = \prod_{k=0}^{18} y_k^{E[k]},$$

where the values $E[k]$ are selected from the list E. Extracting these y_k coefficients requires 18 multiplications in $\mathbb{F}_{p^{24}}$. The inversion costs are considered negligible as they are performed via conjugation, a property of the even embedding degree of the BLS24 curve [17]. According to Olivo's theorem, this multi-exponentiation involves $l + s - 1 = 75$ group operations, consisting of 26 squarings and 49 multiplications in $\mathbb{F}_{p^{24}}$. Thus, the cost is:

$$49M_{24} + 26S_c + 18M_{24} = 49 \cdot 162 + 26 \cdot 54 + 18 \cdot 162 = 12258M.$$

The easy part of the final exponentiation contributes a cost of:

$$2M_{24} + 1I_{24} + 2f_{24}^i = 2 \cdot 162 + 275 + I + 2 \cdot 22 = 643M + I.$$

As a result, the cumulative cost for the final exponentiation is:

- Using Cyclotomic squaring (S_c): $30132M + 660M + 12258M + 643M + I = 43693M + I$.
- Using compressed squaring (cS_k): $21546M + 275M + I + 660M + 12258M + 643M + I = 35382M + 2I$.

Algorithm 3. Final exponentiation BLS24 (256 bits of security) : compute of $f^{\frac{p^{24}-1}{r}}$

Require: $f \in \mathbb{G}_{\Phi_{24}(p)}, m_0, m_1, m_2, m_3, m_4, m_5, m_6, m_7, t \leftarrow -2^{53} - 2^{51} + 2^{18} + 1$
Ensure: Z
$L \leftarrow ((p^{12} - 1) \cdot (p^4 + 1));$
$H \leftarrow (m_7 \cdot p^7 + m_6 \cdot p^6 + m_5 \cdot p^5 + m_4 \cdot p^4 + m_3 \cdot p^3 + m_2 \cdot p^2 + m_1 \cdot p + m_0);$
$g_0 \leftarrow f; g_1 \leftarrow f^t; g_2 \leftarrow f^{t^2}; g_3 \leftarrow f^{t^3}; g_4 \leftarrow f^{t^4};$
$g_5 \leftarrow f^{t^5}; g_6 \leftarrow f^{t^6}; g_7 \leftarrow f^{t^7}; g_8 \leftarrow f^{t^8}; g_9 \leftarrow f^{t^9};$
$y_0 \leftarrow g_0^{-p^3} \cdot g_0^{p^7}$ $y_1 := g_0; y_2 \leftarrow g_1^{p^6} \cdot g_1^{-p^2}; y_3 \leftarrow g_1^{p^3} \cdot g_1^{-p^7}; y_4 \leftarrow g_2^{-p} \cdot g_2^{-p^3} \cdot g_2^{p^5} \cdot g_2^{p^7};$
  $y_5 \leftarrow g_2^{p^2} \cdot g_2^{-p^6};$
$y_6 \leftarrow g_3 \cdot g_3^{-p^2} \cdot g_3^{p^4} \cdot g_3^{p^6}; y_7 \leftarrow g_3^{p} \cdot g_3^{-p^5}; y_8 \leftarrow g_4^{-p} \cdot g_4^{p^3} \cdot g_4^{p^5}; y_9 \leftarrow g_4 \cdot g_4^{-p^4};$
  $y_{10} \leftarrow g_5 \cdot g_5^{p^2} \cdot g_5^{p^4};$
$y_{11} \leftarrow g_5^{-p^3}; y_{12} \leftarrow g_6^{p} \cdot g_6^{p^3}; y_{13} \leftarrow g_6^{-p^2}; y_{14} \leftarrow g_7 \cdot g_7^{p^2}; y_{15} \leftarrow g_7^{-p}; y_{16} \leftarrow g_8^{p};$
  $y_{17} \leftarrow g_8^{-1};$
$y_{18} \leftarrow g_9;$
$E \leftarrow [1, 3, 2^{50}, 2^{51}, 2^{100}, 2^{101}, 2^{150}, 2^{151}, 2^{200}, 2^{201}, 2^{250}, 2^{251}, 2^{300}, 2^{301}, 2^{350}, 2^{351}, 2^{400},$
  $2^{401}, 2^{450}]$
$Y \leftarrow [y_0, y_1, y_2, y_3, y_4, y_5, y_6, y_7, y_8, y_9, y_{10}, y_{11}, y_{12}, y_{13}, y_{14}, y_{15}, y_{16}, y_{17}, y_{18}];$
for $k = 1$ **to** 19 **do**
  $G \leftarrow Y[k]^{E[k]}$
end for
$Z \leftarrow G^L;$
return Z

5 Comparison and Discussion

The analysis in Tables 2 and 3 provides a comparative study of the theoretical computational costs for the final exponentiation and the complete optimal ate pairing for BLS12 and BLS24 curves.

Table 2. Comparison of the final exponentiation (F.E.) costs for BLS12 and BLS24 curves.

Curve	Security	Method	Miller loop	**F.E. (S_c)**	F.E. (cS_k)
BLS12	128 bits	[7]	-	8151M + I	6018M+6I
		This work	-	**6659M + I**	**5406M + 6I**
BLS24	192 bits	[22]	-	23864M + 10 I	-
		This work	-	-	**22096M + 10 I**
BLS24	256 bits	[1]	-	59415M + I	43213M + 10I
		This work	-	**43693M + I**	**35182M + 10I**

This work preserves the Miller loop cost across all curves while significantly improving the final exponentiation efficiency. For BLS12 at the 128-bit security level, the final exponentiation cost is reduced by $1493M$ (18.32%) using cyclotomic squaring and 10.16% using compressed squaring. For BLS24 at the 256-bit security level, the reduction reaches $15726M$, representing a 26.46% improvement with S_c and 18.6% with cS_k. Regarding the BLS24 curve at 192-bit security, we observe a 7.4% gain over the results in [22].

Table 3. Comparison of optimal ate pairing costs using Cyclotomic (S_c) and Compressed (cS_k) Squaring.

Curve	Security	Method	Using S_c	Using cS_k
BLS12	128 bits	[7]	$15589M + I$	$13626M + 6I$
		This work	**14097M + I**	**12844M+6I**
BLS24	192 bits	[22]	$38438M + 10I$	–
		This work	-	**36870M+2I**
BLS24	256 bits	[1]	$96541M + I$	$80339M + 8I$
		This work	**80819M + I**	**72358M+8I**

As shown in Table 3, our approach consistently minimizes multiplications. For BLS12 (128-bit), the total cost decreases by 9.6% (S_c) and 5.73% (cS_k). For BLS24 (256-bit), we achieve gains of 16.3% and 10% respectively. Finally, for the 192-bit BLS24 curve, using compressed squaring provides a 4% reduction in total computational overhead.

6 Conclusion

In this paper, we presented an optimized approach for the final exponentiation in pairing-based cryptography, with a particular focus on the BLS12 and BLS24 curve families. By constructing efficient addition chains for the hard part of the exponentiation, we reduced the number of required field multiplications while preserving the targeted security levels.

At the 128-bit security level for the BLS12 curve, the proposed method reduces the cost of the final exponentiation by 18.32% compared to the reference implementation. For the BLS24 curve at the 256-bit security level, the reduction reaches 26.46%, confirming that the proposed optimization becomes increasingly effective as the security level rises. For BLS24 at the 192-bit security level, our results using compressed squaring provide a 7.4% improvement over the cyclotomic squaring costs reported in [22].

When considering the total cost of the optimal Ate pairing, including both the Miller loop and the final exponentiation, the proposed method provides a reduction of 9.58% for BLS12 at 128-bit security. For BLS24 curves, the total cost is reduced by 4.10% at the 192-bit security level and by 16.29% at the 256-bit security level. These results demonstrate that the proposed approach leads to consistent and scalable efficiency gains, particularly for high-security pairing-based cryptographic settings. Future work could explore the application of these addition chain techniques to other pairing-friendly curve families.

Declarations

Acknowledgements. The first author would like to thank the **Centre for Cybersecurity and Mathematical Cryptology (CCMC)** at the **University of Bamenda.** I am sincerely grateful to the members of the Centre for their hospitality and for providing such a productive atmosphere during the preparation of this work. I sincerely thank **Afrimath** and the **European Mathematical Society (EMS)** for their financial support, which was crucial to my time in Cameroon. Additionally, we would like to thank **Marie-Françoise Roy** from the University of Renne, France. Her unwavering dedication to bridging mathematical networks and her unwavering personal support were crucial to this collaboration's success. The Third author acknowledges funding from the ARES PRD PFS 2022–2027 Programme on Cybersecurity and Cryptology at The University of Bamenda in Cameroon.

Author contributions. The theoretical framework and the core methodology of this research were collaboratively developed by all authors. Sadikou Gaya Siradji and Nyamsi Senegue Gomez were responsible for the primary drafting of the manuscript and the technical refinement of the results and all authors reviewed the manuscript. Every contributor provided critical insights during the revision process. The final version of this work has been thoroughly reviewed and unanimously approved by all authors for publication.

Funding Information. This research was conducted as an independent study. The authors confirm that no specific financial support, grants, or sponsorship were received from any public, private, or non-profit funding agencies for this work.

Data Availability Statement. The findings presented in this article are based on theoretical mathematical derivations. Consequently, no external datasets were generated or analyzed, and data sharing is not applicable to this study.

Competing Interests. The authors declare that they have no known competing financial interests or personal relationships that could have influenced the objectivity or the results reported in this manuscript.

Ethical Standards. This research is purely mathematical and did not involve any studies with human participants or animal subjects conducted by any of the authors.

Consent for Publication. Not applicable, as the study does not contain any individual person's data in any form.

A Magma Code for Final Exponentiation Decomposition

```
//////////////////Final Exponentiation Decomposition Verification on BLS12 with the new parameters (p1,r1,T1) (that is 3*(p1^12-1)/r1 = E*H)////////////////
t:=Integers()!(- 2^44 + 2^17 + 1);
T1 := Integers()!(2^33*t + 1);
r1 := Integers()!(2^132*t^4 - 2^66*t^2 + 1);
p1 := Integers()!(1/3*(2^33*t-1)^2*r1 + 2^33*t);
/////Construction of finite fields
Fp:=FiniteField(p1);
Fp2<a>:=ExtensionField<Fp,a|a^2+1>;
Fp6<b>:=ExtensionField<Fp2,b|b^3-(a+1)>;
Fp12<c>:=ExtensionField<Fp6,c|c^2-b>;
//////////We choose randomly f in F_12^{*}//////////////
repeat
f := Random(Fp12);
until f ne Fp12!0;
/////we define the polynomials m0, m1, m2, m3////////////
m0 := Integers()!(2^165*t^5 - 2^133*t^4 + 2^67*t^2 - 2^33*t + 3);
m1 :=Integers()!( 2^122*t^4 - 2^100*t^3 + 2^34*t - 1);
m2 :=Integers()!( 2^99*t^3 - 2^67*t^2 + 2^33*t);
m3 := Integers()!(2^66*t^2 - 2^34*t + 1);
E:= Integers()!((p1^6-1)*(p1^2+1)); //// here is the easy part////
H:= Integers()!(m3*p1^3+m2*p1^2+m1*p1+m0); /// here is the hard part////
//////Addition Chain process for the expression of H///////////
g0 := f;
g1 := f^t;
g2 := f^(t^2);
g3 := f^(t^3);
g4 := f^(t^4);
g5 := f^(t^5);
y0  := g0^(-p1) * g0^(p1^3);
y1  := g0;
y2  := g1^(-1)*g1^(p1^2);
y3  := g1^(p1)*g1^(-p1^3);
y4  := g2^(p1^3);
y5  := g2*g2^(-p1^2);
y6  := g3^(p1^2);
y7  := g3^(-p1);
y8  := g4^(p1);
```

```
y9  := g4^(-1);
y10 := g5;
A := [1, 3, 2^33, 2^34, 2^66, 2^67, 2^99, 2^100, 2^132, 2^133, 2^165];
Y :=[y0,y1,y2,y3,y4,y5,y6,y7,y8,y9,y10];
G := &*[Y[k]^A[k]:k in [1..11]];
F := G^(Integers()!(E));
//// The Verification of the final exponenetiation on BLS12 ///////

f^(3*(p1^12-1) div r1)-F;
```

Listing 1.1. Verification on BLS12 with parameters (p_1, r_1, T_1)

```
////////////////////Final Exponentiation Decomposition Verification on BLS24 with the new parameters (p1,r1,T1) (that is 3*(p1^24-1)/r1 = E*H)////////////////

t := Integers()!(2^22-2^4+1);
T1 := Integers()!(2^26*t+1);
r1 := Integers()!(2^208*t^8-2^104*t^4+1);
p1 := Integers()!(1/3*(2^26*t-1)^2*r1+2^26*t);

/////Construction of finite fields
Fp := FiniteField(p1);
P1<x> := PolynomialRing(Fp);

Fp2<a> := ext< Fp | x^2 + 1 >;
P2<y> := PolynomialRing(Fp2);

Fp6<b> := ext< Fp2 | y^3 - (a+2) >;
P6<z> := PolynomialRing(Fp6);

// --- Construction of Fp12 ---
xi12 := b;
while IsSquare(xi12) do
xi12 := xi12 + 1;
end while;

// we use ext< Base | Poly >
Fp12<c> := ext< Fp6 | z^2 - xi12 >;
P12<w> := PolynomialRing(Fp12);

// --- Construction of Fp24 ---
xi24 := c;
while IsSquare(xi24) do
xi24 := xi24 + 1;
end while;

```

```
Fp24<d> := ext< Fp12 | w^2 - xi24 >;
//////////We choose randomly f in F_12^{*}//////////////
repeat f := Random(Fp24); until f ne Fp24!0;
/////we define the polynomials mi ////////////
m0 := 2^234*t^9 - 2^209*t^8 + 2^182*t^7 - 2^130*t^5 + 2^105*t^4 - 2^78*t^3 + 3;
m1 := 2^208*t^8 - 2^183*t^7 + 2^156*t^6 - 2^104*t^4 + 2^79*t^3 - 2^52*t^2;
m2 := 2^182*t^7 - 2^157*t^6 + 2^130*t^5 - 2^78*t^3 + 2^53*t^2 - 2^26*t;
m3 := 2^156*t^6 - 2^131*t^5 + 2^104*t^4 - 2^52*t^2 + 2^27*t - 1;
m4 := 2^130*t^5 - 2^105*t^4 + 2^78*t^3;
m5 := 2^104*t^4 - 2^79*t^3 + 2^52*t^2;
m6 := 2^78*t^3 - 2^53*t^2 + 2^26*t;
m7 := 2^52*t^2 - 2^27*t + 1;
E := Integers()!((p1^12-1)*(p1^4+1));//// here is the easy part////
H := Integers()!(m7*p1^7+m6*p1^6+m5*p1^5+m4*p1^4+m3*p1^3+m2*p1^2+m1*p1+m0);/// here is the hard part////
//////Addition Chain process for the expression of H///////////
g0 := f; g1 := f^t; g2 := f^(t^2); g3 := f^(t^3); g4 := f^(t^4);
g5 := f^(t^5); g6 := f^(t^6); g7 := f^(t^7); g8 := f^(t^8); g9 := f^(t^9);
y0  := g0^(-p1^3) * g0^(p1^7);
y1  := g0;
y2  := g1^(p1^6) * g1^(-p1^2);
y3  := g1^(p1^3) * g1^(-p1^7);
y4  := g2^(-p1^1) * g2^(-p1^3) * g2^(p1^5) * g2^(p1^7);
y5  := g2^(p1^2) * g2^(-p1^6);
```

```
y6  := g3^(-p1^0) * g3^(-p1^2) * g3^(p1^4) * g3^(p1^6);
y7  := g3^(p1^1) * g3^(-p1^5);
y8  := g4^(-p1^1) * g4^(p1^3) * g4^(p1^5);
y9  := g4^(p1^0) * g4^(-p1^4);
y10 := g5^(-p1^0) * g5^(p1^2) * g5^(p1^4);
y11 := g5^(-p1^3);
y12 := g6^(p1^1) * g6^(p1^3);
y13 := g6^(-p1^2);
y14 := g7^(p1^0) * g7^(p1^2);
y15 := g7^(-p1^1);
y16 := g8^(p1^1);
y17 := g8^(-p1^0);
y18 := g9;

C := [1, 3, 2^26, 2^27, 2^52, 2^53, 2^78, 2^79, 2^104, 2^105, 2^130, 2^131, 2^156, 2^157, 2^182, 2^183, 2^208, 2^209, 2^234];
Y := [y0, y1, y2, y3, y4, y5, y6, y7, y8, y9, y10, y11, y12, y13, y14, y15, y16, y17, y18];

G := &*[Y[k]^C[k] : k in [1..#Y]];
F := G^(Integers()!(E));

//// The Verification of the final exponenetiation on BLS24 ///////
f^(3*(p1^24-1) div r1) - F;
```

Listing 1.2. Verification on BLS24 at (192 bits of security) with parameters (p_1, r_1, T_1)

```

///////////////////Final Exponentiation Decomposition Verification on BLS24 with the new parameters (p1,r1,T1) (that is 3*(p1^24-1)/r1 = L*H)////////////////

t := Integers()!(-2^53 - 2^51 + 2^18 + 1);
T1 := Integers()!(2^50*t + 1);
r1 := Integers()!(2^400*t^8 - 2^200*t^4 + 1);
p1 := Integers()!(((2^50*t - 1)^2*r1 + 3*2^50*t) div 3);

/////Construction of finite fields
Fp:=GF(p1);
Fp2<w2>:=ext<Fp|2>;
Fp4<w4>:=ext<Fp2|2>;
Fp8<w8>:=ext<Fp4|2>;
Fp24<w24>:=ext<Fp8|3>;


```

```
///////////We choose randomly f in F_24^{*}//////////////

repeat f := Random(Fp24); until f ne Fp24!0;
m0 := 2^450*t^9 - 2^401*t^8 + 2^350*t^7 - 2^250*t^5 + 2^201*t^4 - 2^150*t^3 + 3;

m1 := 2^400*t^8 - 2^351*t^7 + 2^300*t^6 - 2^200*t^4 + 2^151*t^3 - 2^100*t^2;

m2 := 2^350*t^7 - 2^301*t^6 + 2^250*t^5 - 2^150*t^3 + 2^101*t^2 - 2^50*t;

m3 := 2^300*t^6 - 2^251*t^5 + 2^200*t^4 - 2^100*t^2 + 2^51*t - 1;

m4 := 2^250*t^5 - 2^201*t^4 + 2^150*t^3;

m5 := 2^200*t^4 - 2^151*t^3 + 2^100*t^2;

m6 := 2^150*t^3 - 2^101*t^2 + 2^50*t;

m7 := 2^100*t^2 - 2^51*t + 1;

L := Integers()!((p1^12-1)*(p1^4+1));//// here is the easy part////

H := Integers()!(m7*p1^7+m6*p1^6+m5*p1^5+m4*p1^4+m3*p1^3+m2*p1^2+m1*p1+m0);/// here is the hard part////

//////Addition Chain process for the expression of H///////////

g0 := f; g1 := f^t; g2 := f^(t^2); g3 := f^(t^3); g4 := f^(t^4);
g5 := f^(t^5); g6 := f^(t^6); g7 := f^(t^7); g8 := f^(t^8); g9 := f^(t^9);

///// Frobenius(gi,j):=gi^(p^j) and  Frobenius(gi, -j):= 1/Frobenius(gi, j)
y0  := Frobenius(g0, -3) * Frobenius(g0, 7);
y0  := (1/Frobenius(g0, 3))  * Frobenius(g0, 7);
y1  := g0;
y2  := Frobenius(g1, 6) * (1/Frobenius(g1, 2));
y3  := Frobenius(g1, 3) * (1/Frobenius(g1, 7));
y4  := (1/Frobenius(g2, 1)) * (1/Frobenius(g2, 3)) * Frobenius(g2, 5) * Frobenius(g2, 7);
y5  := Frobenius(g2, 2) * (1/Frobenius(g2, 6));
```

```
y6  := (1/g3) * (1/Frobenius(g3, 2)) * Frobenius(g3
    , 4) * Frobenius(g3, 6);
y7  := Frobenius(g3, 1) * (1/Frobenius(g3, 5));
y8  := (1/Frobenius(g4, 1)) * Frobenius(g4, 3) *
    Frobenius(g4, 5);
y9  := g4 * (1/Frobenius(g4, 4));
y10 := (1/g5) * Frobenius(g5, 2) * Frobenius(g5, 4)
    ;
y11 := 1/Frobenius(g5, 3);
y12 := Frobenius(g6, 1) * Frobenius(g6, 3);
y13 := 1/Frobenius(g6, 2);
y14 := g7 * Frobenius(g7, 2);
y15 := 1/Frobenius(g7, 1);
y16 := Frobenius(g8, 1);
y17 := 1/g8;
y18 := g9;
E := [1,3, 2^50, 2^51, 2^100, 2^101, 2^150,
    2^151,2^200,2^201,2^250,2^251,2^300,2^301,
    2^350, 2^351, 2^400,2^401, 2^450];
Y := [y0, y1, y2, y3, y4, y5, y6, y7, y8, y9, y10,
    y11, y12, y13, y14, y15, y16, y17, y18];

G := &*[Y[k]^E[k] : k in [1..#Y]];
F := G^(Integers()!(L));

//// The Verification of the final exponenetiation
    on BLS24 ///////
f^(3*(p1^24-1) div r1) - F;
```

Listing 1.3. Verification on BLS24 at (256 bits of security) with parameters (p_1, r_1, T_1)

References

1. Aranha, D.F., Fotiadis, G., Guillevic, A.: A short-list of pairing-friendly curves resistant to the special TNFS algorithm at the 192-bit security level. IACR Commun. Cryptol. (CIC) **1**(3), 44 (2024)
2. Boneh, D., Boyen, X.: Short signatures without random Oracles. In: Cachin, C., Camenisch, J.L. (eds.) EUROCRYPT 2004. LNCS, vol. 3027, pp. 56–73. Springer, Heidelberg (2004). https://doi.org/10.1007/978-3-540-24676-3_4
3. Brickell, E., Chen, L., Li, J.: A new direct anonymous attestation scheme from bilinear maps. In: Lipp, P., Sadeghi, A.-R., Koch, K.-M. (eds.) Trust 2008. LNCS, vol. 4968, pp. 166–178. Springer, Heidelberg (2008). https://doi.org/10.1007/978-3-540-68979-9_13
4. Boneh, D., Franklin, M.: Identity-based encryption from the weil pairing. In: Kilian, J. (ed.) CRYPTO 2001. LNCS, vol. 2139, pp. 213–229. Springer, Heidelberg (2001). https://doi.org/10.1007/3-540-44647-8_13
5. Boneh, D., Lynn, B., Shacham, H.: Short signatures from the Weil pairing. In: Boyd, C. (ed.) ASIACRYPT 2001. LNCS, vol. 2248, pp. 514–532. Springer, Heidelberg (2001). https://doi.org/10.1007/3-540-45682-1_30

6. Barreto, P., Lynn, B., Scott, M.: Constructing elliptic curves with prescribed embedding degrees. In: SCN 2002. Springer, LNCS vol. 2576, pp. 257–267 (2002)
7. Barbulescu, R., El Mrabet, N., and Ghammam, L.: A taxonomy of pairings, their security, their complexity. Cryptology ePrint Archive, Report 2019/485 (2019)
8. Blake, I.F., Seroussi, G., Smart, N.P.: Advances in Elliptic Curve Cryptography. Cambridge University Press (2005)
9. Camenisch, J., Lysyanskaya, A.: Signature schemes and anonymous credentials from bilinear maps. In: Franklin, M. (ed.) CRYPTO 2004. LNCS, vol. 3152, pp. 56–72. Springer, Heidelberg (2004). https://doi.org/10.1007/978-3-540-28628-8_4
10. Chen, L., Morrissey, P., Smart, N.P.: Pairings in trusted computing. In: Galbraith, S.D., Paterson, K.G. (eds.) Pairing 2008. LNCS, vol. 5209, pp. 1–17. Springer, Heidelberg (2008). https://doi.org/10.1007/978-3-540-85538-5_1
11. Cai, S., Hu, Z., Zhao, C.: Faster final exponentiation on the KSS18 curve. IEICE Trans. Fundament. **E105.A**(8), 1162–1164 (2022)
12. Aranha, D.F., et al.: Implementing pairings at the 192-bit security level. LNCS, Springer **7708**, 177–195 (2013)
13. Duquesne, S., El Mrabet, N., Fouotsa, E.: Efficient computation of pairings on Jacobi quartic elliptic curves. J. Math. Cryptol. **8**(4), 331–362 (2014)
14. Hayashida, D., Hayasaka, K., Teruya, T.: Efficient final exponentiation via cyclotomic structure for pairings over families of elliptic curves. topics in cryptology - CT-RSA 2020. LNCS **12006**, 424–444 (2020)
15. Fuentes-Castañeda, L., Knapp, E., Rodríguez-Henríquez, F.: Faster hashing to G2. Selected Areas in Cryptography, pp. 412–430. Springer (2012)
16. Fotiadis, G., Konstantinou, E.: TNFS resistant families of pairing-friendly elliptic curves. J. Theor. Comput. Sci.(TCS) **800**, 73–89 (2019)
17. Fotiadis, G., Martindale, C.: Optimal tnfs-secure pairings on elliptic curves with composite embedding degree. IACR Cryptol. ePrint Arch, p. 555. (2019)
18. Feng, Q.Y., et al.: Super-optimal pairings. Mech. Eng., Mater. Energy II, Trans. Tech. Public. Ltd. **281**, 127–133 (2013)
19. Freeman, D., Scott, M., Teske, E.: A taxonomy of pairing-friendly elliptic curves. J. Cryptol. **23**(2), 224–280 (2010)
20. Fouotsa, E., Guimagang, L.A., Ayissi, R.: X-superoptimal pairings on elliptic curves with odd prime embedding degrees. AAECC **1–19**,(2023). https://doi.org/10.1007/s00200-023-00596-5
21. Guzmán-Trampe, J.E., et al.: Low-cost addition-subtraction sequences for the final exponentiation in pairings. Finite Fields Appl. **29**, 1–17 (2014)
22. Ghammam, L. and Fouotsa, E.: On the computation of the optimal ate pairing at the 192-bit security level. Cryptology ePrint Archive, Report 2016/130 (2016)
23. Ghammam, L., Fouotsa, E.: Improving the computation of the optimal ate pairing for a high security level. J. Appl. Math. Comput. **59**, 21–36 (2019)
24. Groth, J.: On the size of pairing-based non-interactive arguments. In: Fischlin, M., Coron, J.-S. (eds.) EUROCRYPT 2016. LNCS, vol. 9666, pp. 305–326. Springer, Heidelberg (2016). https://doi.org/10.1007/978-3-662-49896-5_11
25. Guillevic, A., Masson, S., Thomé, E.: Cocks-Pinch curves of embedding degrees five to eight and optimal ate pairing computation. Des. Codes Crypt. **88**(6), 1047–1081 (2020)
26. Guillevic, A.: A short-list of pairing-friendly curves resistant to special TNFS at the 128-bit security level. In: Kiayias, A., Kohlweiss, M., Wallden, P., Zikas, V. (eds.) PKC 2020. LNCS, vol. 12111, pp. 535–564. Springer, Cham (2020). https://doi.org/10.1007/978-3-030-45388-6_19

27. Iida, T., et al.: Improvement of optimal-ate pairing on cocks-pinch curve with embedding degree 6 in affine coordinates. In: CANDAR, pp. 309–315 (2022)
28. Joux, A.: A one round protocol for tripartite Diffie-Hellman. J. Cryptol. (JOC) **17**(4), 263–276 (2004)
29. Kim, T., Barbulescu, R.: Extended tower number field sieve: a new complexity for the medium prime case. In: Robshaw, M., Katz, J. (eds.) CRYPTO 2016. LNCS, vol. 9814, pp. 543–571. Springer, Heidelberg (2016). https://doi.org/10.1007/978-3-662-53018-4_20
30. Kate, A., Zaverucha, G.M., Goldberg, I.: Constant-size commitments to polynomials and their applications. In: Abe, M. (ed.) ASIACRYPT 2010. LNCS, vol. 6477, pp. 177–194. Springer, Heidelberg (2010). https://doi.org/10.1007/978-3-642-17373-8_11
31. Ghammam, L.: Optimizing Final Exponentiation for Pairing-Friendly Elliptic Curves. Cryptology ePrint Archive (2025). Paper 2025/384
32. Mbiang, N.B., Aranha, D.D.F., Fouotsa, E.: Computing the optimal ate pairing over elliptic curves with embedding degrees 54 and 48. Int. J. Appl. Cryptograph. **4**(1), 45–59 (2020)
33. Nyamsi, S.G., Fouotsa, E., Tcheka, C.: Faster optimal ate pairings for cyclotomic sparse families of curves. Discr. Math., Algorithms Appl. **16**(5), 2350054 (2024)
34. Olivos, J.: On vectorial addition chains. J. Algorithms **2**(1), 13–21 (1981)
35. Pointcheval, D., Sanders, O.: Short randomizable signatures. In: Sako, K. (ed.) CT-RSA 2016. LNCS, vol. 9610, pp. 111–126. Springer, Cham (2016). https://doi.org/10.1007/978-3-319-29485-8_7
36. Barbulescu, R., Duquesne, S.: Updating key size estimations for pairings. J. Cryptol. (JOC) **32**(4), 1298–1336 (2019)
37. Scott, M., Benger, N., Charlemagne, M., Dominguez Perez, L.J., Kachisa, E.J.: On the final exponentiation for calculating pairings on ordinary elliptic curves. In: Shacham, H., Waters, B. (eds.) Pairing 2009. LNCS, vol. 5671, pp. 78–88. Springer, Heidelberg (2009). https://doi.org/10.1007/978-3-642-03298-1_6
38. Tessaro, S., Zhu, C.: Revisiting BBS signatures. Adv. Cryptol. (EUROCRYPT). Springer, LNCS **14008**, 691–721 (2023)
39. Nyamsi, S.G., Azebaze Guimagang, L., Fouotsa, E.: Accelerating pairings on BW10 and BW14 curves. Cryptologia, **49**(5), 486–504 (2025). https://doi.org/10.1080/01611194.2024.2439496
40. Vercauteren, F.: Optimal pairings. IEEE Trans. Inf. Theory **56**(1), 455–461 (2010)
41. Haddaji, W.: Efficient Pairings Final Exponentiation Using Cyclotomic Cubing. Cryptology ePrint Archive (2025). Paper 2025/958
42. Zhang, X., Lin, D.: Analysis of optimum pairing products at high security levels. In: Galbraith, S., Nandi, M. (eds.) INDOCRYPT 2012. LNCS, vol. 7668, pp. 412–430. Springer, Heidelberg (2012). https://doi.org/10.1007/978-3-642-34931-7_24

Batch Subgroup Membership Testing on Pairing-Friendly Curves

Dimitri Koshelev[1], Youssef El Housni[2], and Georgios Fotiadis[3](✉)

[1] Department of Mathematics, University of Lleida, Catalonia, Spain
dmitrii.koshelev@udl.cat
[2] Consensys, Linea, New York, USA
youssef.elhousni@consensys.net
[3] Digital Security and Trusted Computing Group, Ubitech Ltd., Athens, Greece
gfotiadis@ubitech.eu

Abstract. A major challenge in elliptic curve cryptosystems consists in efficiently mitigating the small-subgroup attack. This paper explores batch subgroup membership testing (SMT) on pairing-friendly curves, particularly for the Barreto–Lynn–Scott family of embedding degree 12 (BLS12) due to its critical role in modern pairing-based cryptography. Our research introduces a novel two-step procedure for batch SMT to rapidly verify multiple points at once, cleverly combining the already existing tests based on the Tate pairing and a non-trivial curve endomorphism. We clarify why the invented technique is significantly faster (despite a negligible error probability) than testing each point individually. Moreover, it is applicable to prominent curves like BLS12-381 and BLS12-377 being frequently employed in zero-knowledge applications. Nonetheless, to further enhance the speed (or reduce the error probability) of the proposed batch point validation, we have generated two new BLS12 curves that are specifically optimized for this purpose. We also provide an open-source high-speed software implementation in Go, showcasing significant performance improvements achieved by our work.

Keywords: multi-scalar multiplication · pairing-friendly curves · power residue symbols · subgroup membership testing · Tate pairing

1 Introduction

Pairing-based cryptography is a well-known type of ECC (elliptic curve cryptography), which is widely used in a variety of security mechanisms, starting with Boneh–Franklin's identity-based encryption scheme [12] and Joux's one-round tripartite key exchange [45]. All three researchers were awarded the Gödel Prize in 2013 for such a constructive view on pairings. In recent years, pairings have also become an important tool in achieving scalability and privacy of blockchain technology by enabling key functionalities such as digital signature aggregation (e.g., for Boneh-Lynn-Shacham signatures [14]) and ZK-SNARKs

N. El Mrabet et al. (Eds.): AFRICACRYPT 2026, LNCS 16832, pp. 288–315, 2026.
https://doi.org/10.1007/978-3-032-31130-6_12

(zero knowledge - succinct non-interactive argument of knowledge). Despite the potential threat posed by large-scale quantum computers, the given area of pre-quantum cryptography remains an integral part of the modern cryptographic landscape, since post-quantum analogs are mostly less performant by the ratio speed/compactness. NIST also examined pairings (see report [57]) before ultimately deciding not to standardize quantum-vulnerable cryptographic solutions.

1.1 Problem Statement

We consider a pairing-friendly elliptic curve $E/\mathbb{F}_q$ with a subgroup $\mathbb{G}_1$ of prime order r and cofactor $h_1 \neq 1$. Given N points $P_i \in E(\mathbb{F}_q)$, we seek a batch subgroup membership test that outputs 1 if all $P_i \in \mathbb{G}_1$ and otherwise outputs 0 with error probability at most $1/2^{\mu}$ for some admissible value μ, while minimizing the total verification cost (whenever N is considerable). In this paper, the focus is on the subgroup $\mathbb{G}_1$ of BLS12 curves, but extensions to remaining pairing groups $\mathbb{G}_2$ and $\mathbb{G}_T$ (for other curve families) are straightforward mutatis mutandis.

1.2 Background

Throughout the paper, $E : y^2 = x^3 + ax + b$ will denote a pairing-friendly elliptic curve over a finite (usually prime) field $\mathbb{F}_q$ of large characteristic. For simplicity, let the infinity point $\mathcal{O} := (0 : 1 : 0)$ be the identity for the group law on E. By definition, the curve has two subgroups $\mathbb{G}_1, \mathbb{G}_2 \subset E(\mathbb{F}_{q^k})$ and a bilinear map $\mathbb{G}_1 \times \mathbb{G}_2 \to \mathbb{G}_T \subset \mathbb{F}_{q^k}^*$, where k is a moderate extension degree (so-called *embedding degree*). As always, k is taken minimal such that $\mathbb{G}_T \subset \mathbb{F}_{q^k}^*$ or, equivalently, $\#\mathbb{G}_T \mid \Phi_k(q)$, where Φ_k is the k-th cyclotomic polynomial. For our purposes, it is sufficient to assume that the pairing is of type III, the most popular choice in practice. This means in particular that all groups $\mathbb{G}_1, \mathbb{G}_2, \mathbb{G}_T$ are of prime order r. Besides, $\mathbb{G}_1 \subset E(\mathbb{F}_q)$ and $\mathbb{G}_2 \hookrightarrow E_2(\mathbb{F}_{q^d})$, where E_2 is a twist of E (of degree k/d) over a subfield $\mathbb{F}_{q^d} \subset \mathbb{F}_{q^k}$. For convenience, put $\mathbb{H}_1 := E(\mathbb{F}_q)$, $\mathbb{H}_2 := E_2(\mathbb{F}_{q^d})$ and $\mathbb{H}_T := \mu_{\Phi_k(q)}$, the group of all $\Phi_k(q)$-roots of unity. Finally, $h_i := \#\mathbb{H}_i/r$ will stand for the cofactor of $\mathbb{G}_i \subset \mathbb{H}_i$ with $i \in \{1, 2, T\}$.

For a long time, it was believed that the most suitable curves for pairings for the classical 128-bit security level λ are *BN (Barreto–Naehrig) curves* [7] of j-invariant 0 (i.e., the coefficient $a = 0$) with $k = 12$ and $d = 2$. Among them, BN-254 [79] is probably the most famous within the blockchain community. The main feature of BN curves is the primality of $E(\mathbb{F}_q)$, that is, $h_1 = 1$. However, after remarkable improvements (initiated by Kim and Barbulescu [48]) of the number field sieve (NFS) in $\mathbb{F}_{q^k}^*$, BN curves lost several tens of security bits and now offer roughly 100-bit security. A naive countermeasure fixing this problem consists in increasing essentially the field $\mathbb{F}_q$ (and so $\mathbb{F}_{q^k}$), most often to $\approx 384 = 6 \cdot 64$ bits. Such a magnitude yields λ being just a little smaller than 128, albeit its true value (also as λ for $\log_2(q) \approx 256$) is a subject of ongoing debate in the community such as [17,33,38,43]. Nonetheless, the given trade-off is commonly recognized to be satisfactory, as for the classical security level, one needs the non-linearly greater length $\log_2(q) \approx 448 = 7 \cdot 64$.

For fixed field sizes, the cost of pairing computation scales roughly with $\log_2(r)$. When q varies, the cost of field arithmetic also grows with $\log_2(q)$ and dominates. That is why even a modest growth of $\mathbb{F}_q$ noticeably slows down pairings on BN curves for which $\log_2(r) \approx \log_2(q)$. As a consequence, these curves were principally replaced in the real world by *BLS12 (Barreto–Lynn–Scott) curves* [6]. They have the identical parameters $j = 0$, $k = 12$, $d = 2$ and $\log_2(q) \approx 384$, but the subgroup order is of the optimal length $\log_2(r) \approx 256$ bits, that is, $\log_2(h_1) \approx \log_2(r)/2 \approx 128$ bits (the other cofactors h_2, h_T also grow accordingly). In other words, BN curves have the value $\rho := \lceil \log_2(q) \rceil / \lceil \log_2(r) \rceil$ equal to 1, whereas BLS12 ones enjoy $\rho \approx 1.5$. A subtle, rigorous and relatively recent analysis of NFS-type attacks on the BN and BLS12 families is contained in [37, Section 7.2, Tables 8, 10].

1.3 Subgroup Membership Testing Context

At the same time, the non-triviality of h_1 (as well as of h_2, h_T) is a big drawback of BLS12 curves in comparison with BN ones. Indeed, the question arises of how to successfully combat the *small-subgroup attack* [54], one of fault attacks that regularly bothers developers of cryptosystems (see justifications in [3,66, 72,73,76]). In a nutshell, the given roguery is nothing but sending to an honest receiver a point from $\mathbb{H}_i \setminus \mathbb{G}_i$. As a rule, *subgroup membership testing* (SMT for laconicity) is not a very cheap primitive, i.e., each of its calls takes some non-negligible time. The situation is worsened by the fact that it is often necessary to check membership to $\mathbb{G}_i$ for thousands or even millions of points from $\mathbb{H}_i$ at a time. Concrete examples include Ethereum batch verification of BLS consensus signatures, verification of N elliptic curve based SNARK proofs (e.g. PLONK or Groth16) in rollup infrastructure, and server-side transfer or validation of SNARK proving keys, where large structured collections of curve points must be validated before further processing. In the literature there are several ways of SMT to process each input point separately. But surprisingly, there has been until now no (detailed) discussion of *batch subgroup checks*, except for a few too short Internet posts [34,77] without clarifications. Moreover, some of them are even skeptical about the usefulness of SMT.

It is emphasized that some BN curves are still maintained for the sake of compatibility with older software. So, testing membership to their subgroups $\mathbb{G}_2$, $\mathbb{G}_T$ partially remains an adequate task. It should also be noted (see, e.g., [28, Remark 2]) that the cost of $\mathbb{G}_2$ membership testing may be almost free if it is allowed to be executed during pairing computation. Nonetheless, let's continue with the BLS12 family to be definite. As an illustration, we proceed only with the subgroup $\mathbb{G}_1$, although the below theory is readily extended mutatis mutandis to $\mathbb{G}_2$, $\mathbb{G}_T$. Moreover, $\log_2(h_2)$, $\log_2(h_T) \gtrsim \log_2(r)$ and the polynomials defining h_2, h_T in the BN and BLS12 constructions are irreducible over $\mathbb{Q}$. Therefore, it is feasible to generate (or borrow from [4,5,69,70]) *subgroup-secure curves* also known as $\mathbb{G}_2$ and/or $\mathbb{G}_T$*-strong curves*. Here, strength means that h_2 and/or h_T do not have divisors smaller than r, which prevents the small-subgroup attack even if a receiver deals with fraudulent input points. However, the absence of subgroup checks in advanced cryptographic protocols may lead at least to the loss of security proofs or to specific vulnerabilities [75]. Thus, it seems wrong to count subgroup-secure curves absolutely trustworthy.

1.4 Existing Subgroup Tests

It is worth remembering that for the BLS12 family, the cofactor $h_1 = 3e_1^2$ (with $e_1 \in \mathbb{N}$) and $E[e_1] \subset E(\mathbb{F}_q)$. Furthermore, $e := 3e_1$ divides $q-1$. Among other things, there is always in $\mathbb{F}_q^*$ a primitive cubic root ω of unity. In combination with the primality of q, this is equivalent to the fact that BLS12 curves (as well as BN ones) are ordinary, i.e., non-supersingular. Unless $E[r] \subset E(\mathbb{F}_q)$ and so $k = 1$, there exists a universal (but quite slow) SMT that consists in comparing $rP_i = \mathcal{O}$ given N points $P_i \in E(\mathbb{F}_q)$. We have at our disposal two commonly used methods of subgroup checks, which are fundamentally different from each other[1]. The first (with a straightforward modification for $\mathbb{G}_2$) is grounded on a shorter scalar multiplication in $E(\mathbb{F}_q)$ due to the non-trivial $\mathbb{F}_q$-automorphism $[\omega] : (x, y) \mapsto (\omega x, y)$. Meanwhile, the second (not existing de facto for $\mathbb{G}_2$) leverages the reduced *Tate pairing* $t_e : E(\mathbb{F}_q)[e] \times E(\mathbb{F}_q) \to \mu_e \subset \mathbb{F}_q^*$, because SMT in a finite field is easier than on an elliptic curve of the same magnitude.

The pairing-free test was initially suggested by Bowe [18] for a concrete BLS12 curve (namely BLS12-381 [16]) and then discussed by Scott [71] for the whole BLS12 family. An extension of this technique to other pairing-friendly families is carried out in [28,30]. In turn, the test via the Tate pairing was proposed by Koshelev [49,50] originally for many non-pairing-friendly curves with small cofactors $\leqslant 16$. The point is that the *power residue symbol* $(\frac{x}{q})_i := x^{(q-1)/i}$ for $x \in \mathbb{F}_q^*$ enjoys fast *Euclidean-type algorithms* [21,22,46] when $i \leqslant 16$ (and $i \mid q-1$ of course). In the follow-up paper [27], Koshelev et al. demonstrated the advantage of the given approach for a series of pairing-friendly curves (two of which are from [26]). They have the smaller value $\rho < 1.5$ than BLS12 curves at the price of the larger embedding degree $k > 12$ to respect a desired security level. For the BLS12 family, the two mentioned tests are comparable in speed: $\rho \approx 1.5$ is a kind of the borderline between them.

In this article, we keep the main exposition centered on the Bowe–Scott subgroup check because it is already widely deployed in cryptographic libraries and hence allows us to compare directly batch and non-batch SMT on concrete implementations. This choice should not be interpreted as essential to the batching idea itself: for BLS12 curves, the Koshelev(-type) and Bowe–Scott(-type) checks serve the same purpose in the second stage and have comparable cost. The key extra ingredient is rather the Tate-pairing-based prefilter, which removes the

[1] The Pornin method [63] via sequential point halvings in $E(\mathbb{F}_q)$ should be put into a separate category. But among real-world curves, it wins exclusively (to the authors' knowledge) in the case of Curve25519 [24, Section 3.2.2.1]. This effect occurs, because neither of the two other SMT is applicable to this curve (cf. [50, Problem 1]). For other practical curves, the Pornin method is much more expensive than the Bowe–Scott(-type) or Koshelev(-type) ones.

small divisors of the cofactor that would otherwise force too many batching rounds. Finally, it is worth bearing in mind that the (non-reduced) Tate pairing may be potentially computed even faster via a novel technique under the name *cubical arithmetic* [55,61,65], at least if E admits the Montgomery $\mathbb{F}_q$-form. All this is a promising subject of further research.

1.5 Batch Verification Background

The batching idea is well known from *batch signature verification.* It was invented and thoroughly analyzed already in the previous century [8,20,41,58] in the context of classical signatures RSA and DSA. Batching is also inherent to more modern pairing-based signatures such as the mainstream BLS (Boneh–Lynn–Shacham) one [10,11,13,14].

1.6 Why Cofactor Clearing Is Insufficient

Another naive countermeasure against the small-subgroup attack is just the multiplication by h_1 (or less costly by e). It is especially tempting when the cofactor is modest, as for small-cofactor curves. However, this is not a panacea. First, the given trick often nullifies security proofs of complicated cryptographic schemes or directly leads to unambiguous bugs. Even for more elementary protocols for which clearing h_1 seems harmless, regulators (including NIST [24, Appendix D.1]) explicitly ask to fairly validate input points P_i. Second, the resulting points $h_1 P_i \neq P_i$ (except for $P_i \in E[h_1 - 1]$), hence all the parties of a protocol need to take into account such a modification. This can increase total overhead, since some of the additional work may fall on senders as well as receivers. Third, the cofactor multiplication cannot always be seamlessly incorporated into a cryptosystem at any stage of its functioning and by any party independently of others. So, implementing a more optimized explicit SMT is actually the best solution in all respects.

1.7 Contributions and Organization

Our principal contributions are:

1. a two-step batch SMT in which a Tate-pairing-based Koshelev prefilter removes the small-divisor obstruction before the batched main subgroup check,
2. a soundness analysis and parameter selection guidance,
3. two new BLS12 curves whose cofactors make batch SMT especially efficient,
4. a high-speed Go implementation with benchmarks on existing and new curves. The source code is available in [52].

Section 2 presents the batch SMT algorithm as well as its soundness and cost model. Section 3 covers curve selection and parameter choices. Section 4 reports implementation details and benchmarks. Section 5 briefly discusses a limitation of batch SMT. Finally, Sect. 6 concludes the article. Besides, a consolidated notation table is provided in Appendix C.

2 Batch Subgroup Membership Testing

It is reasonable to diminish somehow the number of SMT calls by treating simultaneously N received points $P_i \in E(\mathbb{F}_q)$. In a nutshell, aggregating P_i into the n sums $S_j := \sum_{i=1}^{N} c_{i,j} P_i$ with random numerical coefficients $c_{i,j}$ underlies the article's results. Afterwards, it is suggested to launch the subgroup checks $S_j \in_? \mathbb{G}_1$, rejecting all the points P_i (corresponding to $c_{i,j} \neq 0$) as soon as any sum $S_j \notin \mathbb{G}_1$. Whenever $n \ll N$, one can expect that the given approach is much more performant than the separate checks $P_i \in_? \mathbb{G}_1$, although the authors do not pretend at all to the originality of this insight. The non-trivial point is that on elliptic curves this strategy is often ineffective as-is, because the soundness is governed by the smallest prime divisor of the cofactor. The purpose of the first phase below is precisely to remove these small divisors before batching.

2.1 Soundness and Parameter Choices

Note that $\gcd(r, e) = 1$ and $E(\mathbb{F}_q) = \mathbb{G}_1 \times E(\mathbb{F}_q)[e]$, hence the points P_i are uniquely decomposed into the components $Q_i := (e^{-1} \bmod r) e P_i$ and $R_i := P_i - Q_i$ lying in $\mathbb{G}_1$ and $E(\mathbb{F}_q)[e]$, respectively. Inter alia, $P_i \in \mathbb{G}_1$ if and only if $P_i = Q_i$ or, equivalently, $R_i = \mathcal{O}$. Obviously, if all the points P_i belong to $\mathbb{G}_1$, then all the sums S_j also do. The converse statement is not true, because the components R_i may annihilate each other, that is, the equalities $S_j = \sum_{i=1}^{N} c_{i,j} Q_i$ imply nothing from the mathematical point of view. In our soundness model, an adversary chooses the points P_i first, possibly correlating the components R_i adversarially, and afterwards an honest receiver samples the coefficients $c_{i,j}$ independently and uniformly. Since a malicious sender of P_i is able to prepare the small-subgroup attack at his discretion, he can try increasing the probability $\mathbb{P}$ of acceptance by an honest receiver of at least one poisoned point P_i. It is natural to assume that $0 \leqslant c_{i,j} < m \leqslant e$ for a certain $m \in \mathbb{N}$. Temporarily, put $n = 1$ and denote by p (not the field characteristic) the smallest prime divisor of e, i.e., just 2 if e is even and 3 otherwise. The probability $\mathbb{P}$ evidently grows when all R_i lie in the same order-p subgroup (and some $R_i \neq \mathcal{O}$ of course). It is readily seen (cf. [8, Lemma 3.1], [34]) that $\mathbb{P} \leqslant 1/\min\{m, p\}$ and this upper bound does not seem to be (significantly) improvable. In particular, there is not any sense for the receiver to slow down computation of S_j by picking $m > p$.

The bound $\mathbb{P} \leqslant 1/3$ (not mention to $\mathbb{P} \leqslant 1/2$) is too big to rely on such an ingenuous batch SMT. Fortunately, one can mitigate this analogously as in the paper [49]. Let $\pi := 2^4 \cdot 3^2 \cdot 5 \cdot 7 \cdot 11 \cdot 13$ and $\pi' := \gcd(\pi, e)$. It is always possible to first employ the Koshelev test via the Tate pairing $t_{\pi'}$ with respect to the subgroup $\mathbb{G}_1' := E(\mathbb{F}_q)[re']$, where $e' := e/\pi'$. Since the symbol $(\frac{\cdot}{q})_{\pi'}$ is "Euclidean-friendly", the bit complexity of each intermediate check $P_i \in_? \mathbb{G}_1'$ is only quadratic in $\log_2(q)$. Consequently, this step is asymptotically faster than the other operations involved in (batch) SMT, although its cost may still be noticeable in practice. More importantly, it removes the small prime divisors of e that would otherwise make the batched second phase ineffective. We can efficiently (although separately) detect the fraudulent points $P_i \notin \mathbb{G}_1' \supset \mathbb{G}_1$. For the remaining ones, let's redefine the value p, making it often (much) greater than 3. It now becomes reasonable to augment the coefficients $c_{i,j}$. By abuse of notation, let p be the minimal prime divisor of e'. Since $\log_2(\pi) \approx 19.5$, we can in practice exclude the scenario when p is not correctly defined, i.e., $e' = 1$. Indeed, this happens only if $e \mid \pi$, but $\log_2(e) \approx 64$ for the quasi-classical λ.

To provide a desired level μ of the error probability $\mathbb{P}$, that is, to guarantee the bound $\mathbb{P} \leqslant 1/2^\mu$, there is an alternative way workable even if $p = 2$. It is enough to repeat n times the described batch SMT. Since the coefficients $c_{i,j}$ are assumed to be independent for different j (and $m \leqslant p$ as we understood), $\mathbb{P} \leqslant 1/m^n$ and hence the probability rapidly converges to zero as $n \to \infty$. Specifically, $n = \lceil \mu/\log_2(m) \rceil$ rounds allow to satisfy the inequality $1/m^n \leqslant 1/2^\mu$. For instance, $n = \lceil \mu \rceil$ with $m = 2$, whereas $n = 1$ with $\mu \leqslant \log_2(m)$. The first extreme case inevitably occurs when $p = 2$, i.e., the number e is highly 2-adic, which means for us that the 2-adic valuation $\nu_2(e) \geqslant 5$. It is well known that this frequently takes place in the ZK realm, e.g., for the curve BLS12-377 [78] with $\nu_2(e) = 46$ or for Guillevic–Masson's ones [36, Section 4.4] with $\nu_2(e) \geqslant 25$. Thereby, the high 2-adicity of e is a downside in the context of batch SMT. Meanwhile, the second extreme case is optimal in n and it is achieved on $m = \lceil 2^\mu \rceil$. Note that $\log_2(m) \leqslant \log_2(p) \leqslant \log_2(e_1) \approx 62.5$. When $n = 1$, the latter is consequently the maximal possible value of μ. It is not said anywhere (including the seminal sources on batch signature verification) that μ must be $\approx \lambda$. If desired, the given equilibrium can be nevertheless obtained with $n = 2$.

It is shown that the number of rounds n is reduced (with the same parameter μ) when the prime p becomes larger. Unfortunately, the latter is tightly attached to each BLS12 curve. Today's real-world ones were generated in the past without regard to simultaneous subgroup checks and hence to the size of p. It therefore seems impractical to change curves that underlie already running multi-user cryptosystems. Thus, a by-product of the current paper is to motivate further study of efficient implementations of higher power residue symbols $(\frac{\cdot}{q})_i$, especially for $i \leqslant 16$. Lately, there has been significant progress [2,40,62] in speeding up the Legendre symbol $(\frac{\cdot}{q})_2$, fueled primarily by its utilization in hashing to elliptic curves and point decompression. The present work also includes an efficient Euclidean-type implementation of the cubic symbol $(\frac{\cdot}{q})_3$, which is a key ingredient of batch SMT on BLS12 curves due to the structure of the cofactor $h_1 = 3e_1^2$. More generally, the cubic analog of the Legendre symbol often occurs in various cryptographic primitives on curves of j-invariant 0. Higher residue symbols with $i > 3$, however, remain outside the attention of most developers, since existing cryptographic libraries support them less frequently.

2.2 Algorithm and Cost Model

The batch SMT for the subgroup $\mathbb{G}_1$ of BLS12 curves is formalized in Algorithm 1. As before, we are given N points $P_i \in E(\mathbb{F}_q)$ and hence their n sums $S_j = \sum_{i:=1}^N c_{i,j} P_i$ with random uniform coefficients $c_{i,j} \in \mathbb{Z}/m$. Step 1 is the Tate-pairing-based Koshelev prefilter and Step 2 is the batched main check on random

Algorithm 1: Batch subgroup membership testing

Data: BLS12 curve $E/\mathbb{F}_q$, its subgroup $\mathbb{G}_1$ with order r and cofactor $h_1 = 3e_1^2$;
the intermediate subgroup $\mathbb{G}_1' = E(\mathbb{F}_q)[re']$;
the number $m \leqslant p$, the level μ, and the number of rounds $n = \lceil \mu / \log_2(m) \rceil$;
N points $P_i \in E(\mathbb{F}_q)$.
Result: if all $P_i \in \mathbb{G}_1$, then 1; otherwise, 0 with error probability $\mathbb{P} \leqslant 1/2^\mu$.

```
begin
    for i := 1 to N do
        if P_i ∉ G'_1 then
            return 0.
        end
    end
    for j := 1 to n do
        c_{i,j} := Random(Z/m);
        S_j := Σ_{i:=1}^{N} c_{i,j} P_i;
        if S_j ∉ G_1 then
            return 0.
        end
    end
    return 1.
end
```

linear combinations. For BLS12 curves, the latter can be instantiated either with the Bowe–Scott test or with the Koshelev test again; in this paper we benchmark the former due to wider adoption in current libraries. Instead of the maximal allowable $m = p$, it is more convenient in practice to take $m = 2^{\lfloor \log_2(p) \rfloor}$. Fortunately, this choice should not affect μ and n once p is at least moderate.

The process of computing S_j is called *MSM (multi-scalar multiplication)*. It can often be carried out substantially faster than computing each scalar multiplication $c_{i,j}P_i$ individually and then summing them. The literature on MSM is vast, with recent important works including [25,32,39,44,51,64,81]. A new stage of research interest in accelerating MSM is again related to ZK proofs, where the given primitive is typically a bottleneck. On one hand, $\log_2(c_{i,j}) \leqslant \log_2(m) \lesssim 62.5$. On the other hand, the Bowe–Scott subgroup check for $\mathbb{G}_1$ requires two sequential scalar multiplications by the seed $z := 1 \pm e$. Thus, the total length is about $2 \cdot \log_2(e) \approx 128$ bits. In practice, the Hamming weight (of the non-adjacent form) of z is not far from zero. But even if the coefficients $c_{i,j}$ are weighted considerably, (the shortest) addition chains for them are still not longer than those for z^2. Therefore, individual tests $P_i \in_? \mathbb{G}_1$ at best have a similar cost as the scalar multiplications $c_{i,j}P_i$. Hence, batch SMT should be noticeably more efficient than its non-batch analog and it actually is as we will see later.

Whenever N is small, the *Straus algorithm* [74] should be the best for finding S_j. In turn, we will resort to the *Pippenger (bucket) algorithm* for the large N. It is asymptotically optimal (see, e.g., [42, Section 1]) and its various optimizations have occurred in recent years. Since for the modest N conventional non-batch tests are competitive with (or even better if $n \geqslant N$ than) their batch versions, we are (only) interested in the truly multi-dimensional setting. Besides, note that the coefficients $c_{i,j}$ are zero with probability $1/m$. Consequently, the sums S_j consist on average of $N' := N(m-1)/m$ terms. This is a useful remark in the case of the small m, since it permits to reduce (extremely for $m = 2$) the running time of an MSM algorithm.

The symbols $\mathcal{A}$, $\mathcal{D}$ will stand for the general addition and doubling operations in $E(\mathbb{F}_q)$, respectively. Let's fix a window size $c \in \mathbb{N}$ not exceeding $\log_2(m)$. Recall that the Pippenger algorithm costs

$$\approx \mathcal{P} := \frac{\log_2(m)}{c}(N' + 2^{c+1} - 3)\cdot\mathcal{A} + \big(\log_2(m) - c\big)\cdot\mathcal{D}$$

according to [25, Section 2.3] for example. In particular, if we deal with the scenario $m = 2$, then necessarily $c = 1$ and the algorithm boils down to computing a sum with approximately $N' = N/2$ terms, that is, $\mathcal{P} \approx N'\cdot\mathcal{A}$. Meanwhile, the Bowe–Scott subgroup check requires

$$\approx \mathcal{BS} := 2w\cdot\mathcal{A} + \frac{\log_2(r)}{2}\cdot\mathcal{D}$$

if the scalar multiplication by z^2 is carried out via the standard double-add-subtract method. This is reasonable, because the weight w is chosen to be as minimal as possible and hence there are no substantially shorter addition-subtraction chains. Furthermore, it is understandable that the Pippenger and Bowe–Scott algorithms are not amenable to precomputation, as the curve points are variables. As a result, the overall overhead of performing the batch SMT at worst amounts to $\approx n(\mathcal{P} + \mathcal{BS})$ versus N separate group checks, i.e., $\approx N\cdot\mathcal{BS}$.

Asymptotically, there is no difference (subject to the same N and μ) between computing n sums S_j with shorter coefficients $c_{i,j}$ and finding one sum with longer $c_{i,j}$. Indeed, the corresponding complexity is equal to

$$\Theta\left(\frac{nN\log_2(m)}{\log_2\big(nN\log_2(m)\big)}\right) = \Theta\left(\frac{\mu N}{\log_2(\mu N)}\right)$$

curve additions/doublings (cf. the formula of $\mathcal{P}$) by virtue of [42, Section 1] and by the definition of n. Consequently, the given quantity is independent of n and $\log_2(m)$ and hence it is difficult to see why (and if) the growth of the parameter m is really a winning strategy (at least for moderate N). The fundamental reason lies in the fact that n is the number of calls of the Bowe–Scott test. Nevertheless, the benchmarks of Sect. 4 are helpful to dispel doubts in this regard.

3 Curve Selection and Parameters

All formulas and tables of this section are verified by means of the code [52] in the computer algebra system Magma. For the sake of completeness, let's recall the polynomial expressions in $z \in \mathbb{Z}$ of the main parameters of the BLS12 family:

$$\begin{aligned}
&e_1 = |z-1|/3, \qquad h_1 = 3e_1^2, \qquad r = z^4 - z^2 + 1, \qquad q = h_1 r + z,\\
&h_2 = (z^8 - 4z^7 + 5z^6 - 4z^4 + 6z^3 - 4z^2 - 4z + 13)/9,\\
&h_T = (z^{20} - 8z^{19} + 25z^{18} - 32z^{17} - 8z^{16} + 76z^{15} - 93z^{14} + 36z^{13} + 51z^{12}\\
&\quad - 112z^{11} + 86z^{10} - 16z^9 - 24z^8 + 84z^7 - 90z^6 + 28z^5 - 14z^4 - 38z^3\\
&\quad + 70z^2 - 14z + 73)/81.
\end{aligned}$$

The formulas of the first line are widespread in the literature. In turn, the formula for h_2 is contained in [23, Section 3.1] and that for h_T is immediately established, because $\Phi_{12}(q) = q^4 - q^2 + 1$.

It is common in the literature to use the length $\log_2(|z|) \approx 64$. To be more precise, $\log_2(q) \approx 382.5$ in this case rather than ≈ 384. As always, the symbol $\approx$ does not have a strict sense. For concrete BLS12 curves, it would be fairer to say a more exact value of $\log_2(|z|)$, because even a minimal discrepancy leads to a larger one in the derived parameters. For instance, the curves BLS12-377 and BLS12-381 have as $\log_2(q)$ slightly smaller values than 382.5, because $\log_2(|z|) \approx$ 63 and ≈ 63.5, respectively. Nevertheless, 64 is a round number, hence it is taken in our abstract reasoning as the main approximation.

It is worth emphasizing that the inverse operation on elliptic curves (point negation) is essentially free in practice, since it only negates a field element, hence it is reasonable to consider the NAF (non-adjacent form) instead of the conventional binary form of the seed z. Hereafter, w will stand for the Hamming weight of this NAF. It should be as small as possible, because the (optimal) Ate pairing $\mathbb{G}_1 \times \mathbb{G}_2 \to \mathbb{G}_T$ on BLS12 curves forces to evaluate at $P \in \mathbb{G}_1$ the Miller function $f_{|z|,Q}$, where $Q \in \mathbb{G}_2$. At the same time, the bottleneck of the Bowe–Scott subgroup check is the scalar multiplication by z^2, i.e., twice by z. In this connection, minimizing w is compatible with versatile acceleration of a pairing-based cryptosystem.

Table 1 exhibits several BLS12 curves from existing cryptographic sources and their indicators primary for us. Some of these curves are even deployed in the real world, whereas the others are rather of theoretical interest. The symbol p_ℓ signifies a certain prime with bit length ℓ. The number of rounds n is meant with respect to the level $\mu = 60$ and $m = p$. This choice for μ, made also in [8, Section 2.1], [20, Section 4.1], will be clear in Sect. 3.2. For instance, $p = p_{14} = 10177$ if we are talking about the curve BLS12-381. Curiously, the gap between 11 and p_{14} is essential. Without the fast implementation (from [46]) of the symbol $(\frac{\cdot}{q})_{11}$, we get $n = 18$ and thereby the more expensive batch SMT. Last but not least, the row starting with BLS12-(377–383) is dedicated to a set of curves (such that $377 \lesssim \log_2(q) \lesssim 383$) for which there are universal answers in all the entries.

Table 1. Notable BLS12 curves

<table>
<tr><th>Curve</th><th>Reference</th><th>w</th><th>$e_1 = e/3$</th><th>$\pi'/3$</th><th>p</th><th>n</th><th>$\mathbb{G}_2$-strong</th><th>$\mathbb{G}_T$-strong</th></tr>
<tr><td>BLS12-377</td><td>[78]</td><td>7</td><td>$2^{46}{\cdot}7{\cdot}13{\cdot}p_9$</td><td>$2^4{\cdot}7{\cdot}13$</td><td>2</td><td>60</td><td rowspan="5">no</td><td rowspan="3">no</td></tr>
<tr><td>BLS12-380</td><td>[68, Section 6]</td><td>20</td><td>$5{\cdot}7{\cdot}23{\cdot}p_{22}{\cdot}p_{31}$</td><td>$5{\cdot}7$</td><td>23</td><td>14</td></tr>
<tr><td>BLS12-381</td><td>[16]</td><td>6</td><td>$11{\cdot}p_{14}{\cdot}p_{20}{\cdot}p_{26}$</td><td>11</td><td>$p_{14}$</td><td>5</td></tr>
<tr><td>BLS12-383</td><td>[70, Section 2]</td><td>5</td><td>$89{\cdot}p_9{\cdot}p_{48}$</td><td>1</td><td>89</td><td>10</td><td>yes</td></tr>
<tr><td>BLS12-(377–383)</td><td>[36, Section 4.4]</td><td>$\leqslant 7$</td><td>highly 2-adic</td><td>$0 \bmod 2^4$</td><td>2</td><td>60</td><td>no</td></tr>
<tr><td>BLS12-461</td><td>[4, Section 7.5]</td><td>7</td><td>$3{\cdot}5^4{\cdot}7{\cdot}p_{62}$</td><td>$3{\cdot}5{\cdot}7$</td><td>5</td><td>26</td><td colspan="2">yes</td></tr>
</table>

3.1 High 2-Adicity and Embedded Curves

For the sake of completeness, it was decided to include in the paper Table 2 of embedded curves $E_e/\mathbb{F}_r$ for some BLS12 ones from Table 1. In today's ZK protocols, such elliptic curves are not required to be pairing-friendly, although they still possess subgroups of large prime order r'. Therefore, they unchangeably have a modest cofactor h (including the trivial one $h = 1$) and so the batch SMT (or even SMT itself) for them is useless. Indeed, $r - 1$ is (mostly) highly 2-adic to benefit from the FFT (fast Fourier transform), whereas h is a small power of 2 (typically, $h \leqslant 8$) to enjoy cheaper elliptic curve forms. As a result, the Koshelev subgroup check is an ideal solution in the situation under consideration. Table 2 is thus secondary for the current investigation, but it transparently demonstrates that pairing-friendly curves come into play together with their plain counterparts. Inter alia, this circumstance should be accounted for during generation of new BLS12 curves. Otherwise, they will have very restricted applications in the modern cryptographic landscape.

Table 2. Notable embedded curves for the ZK-oriented BLS12 ones from Table 1

<table>
<tr><th>BLS12 curve</th><th>Embedded curve</th><th>Reference</th><th>$\nu_2^*(q)$</th><th>$\nu_2^*(r)$</th><th>$\nu_2^*(r')$</th><th>h</th><th>$-D$</th></tr>
<tr><td>BLS12-377</td><td rowspan="2">no name</td><td>[1]</td><td>46</td><td>47</td><td rowspan="3">1</td><td>4</td><td>$\approx 2^{252}$</td></tr>
<tr><td>BLS12-380</td><td>[68, Section 6]</td><td rowspan="4">1</td><td>38</td><td>1</td><td>3</td></tr>
<tr><td rowspan="3">BLS12-381</td><td>Jubjub</td><td>[31]</td><td rowspan="3">32</td><td>8</td><td>$\approx 2^{255}$</td></tr>
<tr><td>Bandersnatch</td><td>[56]</td><td>5</td><td>4</td><td>8</td></tr>
<tr><td rowspan="2">no name</td><td>[36, Section 3.3.1]</td><td>2</td><td>1</td><td>6673027</td></tr>
<tr><td>BLS12-(377–383)</td><td>[36, Section 4.4]</td><td colspan="3">$25 \leqslant$</td><td>1, 4</td><td>3</td></tr>
</table>

In order to save the table space, put $\nu_2^*(u) := \nu_2(u-1)$ for an arbitrary $u \in \mathbb{Z}$. Besides, $D < 0$ stands for the CM (complex multiplication) discriminant of an elliptic curve. The $\mathbb{G}_T$-strong curves BLS12-383 and BLS12-461 were proposed without regard to ZK proofs, hence apparently nobody has never tried to produce for them appropriate embedded curves. We also do not elaborate on this minor problem. If necessary, E_e of huge D can be found with an overwhelming probability by iterating the curve coefficients over $\mathbb{F}_r$ as was done for BLS12-377 and BLS12-381. Since embedded curves are plain, their efficiency does not suffer from the absence of higher-degree twists (when $D < -4$).

In addition, Koshelev–Sanso's fresh result [53] generalizes the famous GLV (Gallant–Lambert–Vanstone) decomposition for accelerating (multi-)scalar multiplication to a much wider class of CM discriminants than previously believed. Nonetheless, the GLV technique continues to be the most impressive on curves of $j = 0$ (along with even-order ones of $j = 1728$). Besides, it is better when E_e is of the prime order r', i.e., $h = 1$. In this scenario, there is one more elliptic curve $E'_e/\mathbb{F}_{r'}$ with which E_e constitutes a 2-cycle, that is, $\#E_e(\mathbb{F}_r) = r'$ and dually $\#E'_e(\mathbb{F}_{r'}) = r$. Otherwise, we can only count on non-closed (2-)chains and hence infinite recursive ZK-SNARKs starting with E_e are impossible. Sought embedded curves of moderate D are derived (if any) with the help of [56, Algorithm 1] or of more optimized [36, Algorithm 1]. As reflected in Table 2, such a search has already been accomplished for BLS12-381. Most likely, the cited algorithms yield positive outcomes similarly for BLS12-377.

Recall that $t = z + 1$ is the Frobenius trace for the BLS12 family. The valuation $\nu_2^*(r)$ is not low for all the table curves without exception. This phenomenon is explicable thanks to the simple decomposition $r - 1 = z^2 \cdot e \cdot |t|$. First, $\nu_2^*(r) = 2 \cdot \nu_2(z)$ provided that z is even. And the 2-adicity of z is easily controlled (as for the seeds of BLS12-380 and BLS12-381). An alternative way to make the higher $\nu_2^*(r)$ consists in increasing $\nu_2^*(z) = \nu_2(e_1) = \nu_2(e)$, which is the case for BLS12-377 and BLS12-(377–383). Moreover, this approach equally augments $\nu_2^*(q)$, which is sometimes no less useful, for example in Zexe [19]. This construction leverages a pairing-friendly curve (such as in [29]) over a new base field and equipped with a subgroup of order q. It is readily verified that

$$q - 1 = e_1 \cdot |z^5 - z^4 - z^3 + z^2 + z + 2|.$$

The second factor is irreducible over $\mathbb{Z}$, so the growth of $\nu_2(e)$ is the unique visible way for that of $\nu_2^*(q)$. However, the high 2-adicity of e radically affects the speed of the batch SMT as already noted in the introduction.

According to [68, Section 5.3], the embedded curves of j-invariant 0 for BLS12 ones admit the prime order r' only if it is parametrized in z by one of the formulas

$$r'_1 := z^4 - 3z^2 + 3, \qquad r'_2 := z^4 + 3, \qquad r'_3 := z^4 - 2z^2 + 4.$$

We have the factorizations

$$r'_1 - 1 = (z^2 - 2) \cdot e \cdot |t|, \qquad r'_2 - 1 = z^4 + 2, \qquad r'_3 - 1 = z^4 - 2z^2 + 3.$$

The last two polynomials are irreducible over $\mathbb{Z}$, hence we focus on the first one. Whenever the seed z is even, $\nu_2^*(r'_1) = \nu_2^*(r'_2) = 1$ and r'_3 is not even prime. As a consequence, one cannot construct in this case an embedded 2-cycle of $j = 0$ curves over highly 2-adic fields. In turn, $\nu_2^*(r'_1) = \nu_2(e) + 1$ and $\nu_2^*(r'_1) = \nu_2(t) + 1$ once $\nu_2(e) > 1$ and $\nu_2(t) > 1$, respectively. In other words, $\nu_2^*(r)$, $\nu_2^*(r')$ both grow in parallel with $\nu_2(e)$ or $\nu_2(t)$. Fortunately, the highly 2-adic t (unlike e) does not slow down the batch SMT, hence such a trace is preferable.

3.2 New Elliptic Curves

To sum up, we want $z \in \mathbb{Z}$ such that

1. The bit length $\log_2(|z|) \approx 64$;
2. The orders q, r and $r' = r'_1$ are primes;
3. The cofactors h_2, h_T are strong, i.e., do not have divisors less than r;
4. The prime p is as large as possible;
5. The Frobenius trace t is highly 2-adic: Let's say, $\nu_2(t)$ is close to 32;
6. The Hamming weight w is as small as possible.

In fact, the binary logarithms of the orders q, r and r' should not exceed in the strict sense the bounds 384, 256 and 256, respectively. Otherwise, the finite field arithmetic becomes slower in vain if hardware operates with long machine words, particularly with 64-bit ones. It is thereby desirable for $\log_2(|z|)$ to be closer to 63 than to 64, which is assumed hereafter.

Since $\nu_2(e) = 1$, at best $p = e_1/2 = e/6$ and so $\pi' = 6$. This means that $\log_2(p) \approx 60.5$ does not achieve $\log_2(e_1) \approx 61.5$. Thus, the one-round batch SMT ensures the level $\mu \approx 60.5$ instead of 61.5 (not to mention 62.5 as initially supposed in the introduction). For simplicity and unambiguity, put $\mu = 60$. Formally, n must be doubled, albeit the coefficients $c_{i,2}$ in the second sum S_2 are allowed to be just binary. However, it is not worthwhile, as the difference is in only one bit. On the other hand, the evenness of e implies that $E[2] \subset E(\mathbb{F}_q)$, that is, the curve E is isomorphic or 2-isogenous over $\mathbb{F}_q$ to a Montgomery/twisted Edwards curve (see, e.g., [35, Theorem 9.12.11]). In the authors' opinion, the high-speed arithmetic on these forms more than compensates for the one-bit loss in estimating the error probability $\mathbb{P}$ and for the necessity of determining the two Legendre symbols (in addition to the cubic one) per point $P_i \in E(\mathbb{F}_q)$.

Recall that $\nu_2^*(r) = \nu_2^*(r') = \nu_2(t) + 1$. In order to obtain the fields $\mathbb{F}_r$, $\mathbb{F}_{r'}$ of the same high 2-adicity v, it is sufficient to sequentially iterate an auxiliary seed z' of length $\approx 63 - v$, putting $z := 2^v z' - 1$, until a desired BLS12 curve is met. For transparency, z' must start with a canonical value such as $\pm 2^{63-v}$. Two new curves BLS12-376 and BLS12-377 were produced in this way. Their parameters (along with the generation Sage script) can be found in [52] or in Table 3. By construction, the curves are well suited for ZK applications (see Table 4 as a confirmation). Furthermore, both of them have $e_1 = 2p$ and the prime cofactor h_2. The cofactor h_T is also prime for BLS12-377, but at least $73 \mid h_T$ for BLS12-376. Therefore, one of the curves satisfies all the properties imposed above. However, this happens at the price of skewed values of v, w. In turn, the second curve possesses more balanced values of these parameters. The appendix shows that the two new curves remain close to BLS12-381 on common operations, except for pairings where the very low Hamming weight of the BLS12-381 seed is especially favorable. To be honest, the (quasi-)primality of h_T is much less important than that of e_1, h_2, as in the majority[2] of pairing-based protocols, entities usually do not receive from a communication channel field elements unlike curve points.

[2] A quite exotic exception is the scheme [67] proposed by the Ethereum Foundation research team before it has been recently decided to carry over the ecosystem to post-

Table 3. New BLS12 curves

<table>
<tr><th>Curve</th><th>z</th><th>w</th><th>$e_1 = e/3$</th><th>$\pi'/3$</th><th>p</th><th>n</th><th>$\mathbb{G}_2$-strong</th><th>$\mathbb{G}_T$-strong</th></tr>
<tr><td>BLS12-376</td><td>$-1008476051 \cdot 2^{33} - 1$</td><td>10</td><td rowspan="2">$2 \cdot p_{61}$</td><td rowspan="2">2</td><td rowspan="2">p_{61}</td><td rowspan="2">1</td><td rowspan="2">yes</td><td>no</td></tr>
<tr><td>BLS12-377</td><td>$-555684677407 \cdot 2^{24} - 1$</td><td>15</td><td>yes</td></tr>
</table>

Table 4. New embedded curves for the ZK-oriented BLS12 ones from Table 3

<table>
<tr><th>BLS12 curve</th><th>$\nu_2^*(q)$</th><th>$\nu_2^*(r)$</th><th>$\nu_2^*(r')$</th><th>h</th><th>$-D$</th></tr>
<tr><td>BLS12-376</td><td rowspan="2">1</td><td colspan="2">34</td><td rowspan="2">1</td><td rowspan="2">3</td></tr>
<tr><td>BLS12-377</td><td colspan="2">25</td></tr>
</table>

4 Implementation and Benchmarks

In this section we provide an open-source high-speed software implementation in Golang, using the `gnark-crypto` library [15]. We chose to implement Algorithm 1 for BLS12-381 and BLS12-377, two pairing-friendly elliptic curves widely used in production. We also fully implemented in `gnark-crypto` the two new BLS12 curves presented in Sect. 3.2, alongside the new batch SMT for them. The source code is available in [52]:

https://github.com/yelhousni/batch-subgroup-membership-testing.

We benchmarked the new batch SMT algorithm against the naive separate checks, namely the Bowe–Scott membership test. All benchmarks reported in this section and in Appendix A were run on an AWS `c7a.8xlarge` machine (AMD EPYC 9R14) in a single-threaded setup. Although we also explored code parallelism using Goroutines, with the corresponding implementation accessible in [52], our primary focus remains on the sequential execution. This decision facilitates a more straightforward analysis within the scope of this paper and avoids confounding factors introduced by diverse parallelism strategies.

The BLS12-381 Case: This $\mathbb{F}_q$-curve of equation $E : y^2 = x^3 + 4$ has seed $z =$ `-0xd201000000010000` and thus $\pi' = 3 \cdot 11$ and $e' = 10177 \cdot 859267 \cdot 52437899$. Given N points $P_i \in E(\mathbb{F}_q)$ purported in $\mathbb{G}_1$, Algorithm 1 is a two-step procedure:

- *Step 1*: We check that $P_i \in \mathbb{G}_1' = E[re'] \supset \mathbb{G}_1$ via the Koshelev test. For this, we need to compute the N Tate pairings $t_3(Q_3, P_i)$ together with the $2N$ Tate pairings $t_{11}(Q_{11}, P_i)$ and $t_{11}(Q_{11}', P_i)$. We then check that they are all equal to 1. Here, the point $Q_3 := (0, 2)$ is of order 3 and hence the Miller function $f_{3,Q_3} = y - 2$ is elementary. We evaluate the cubic residue symbol by means of the Euclidean-type algorithm implemented in [52]. In turn, the

quantum cryptography. In addition, testing membership to $\mathbb{G}_T$ is indispensable in the scope of pairing delegation (see, e.g., the fresh paper [47]), although the authors are not sure about the spread of such a mechanism in the real world.

points Q_{11} and Q'_{11} constitute a basis of $E[11]$ (see Appendix B). The Miller function for Q_{11} is of the form

$$f_{11,Q_{11}} = \frac{\ell_{1,1}^4 \cdot (\ell_{4,1} \cdot \ell_{2,2})^2 \cdot \ell_{5,5}}{v_2^4 \cdot (v_5 \cdot v_4)^2},$$

where $v_i := x - x_{[i]Q_{11}}$, $\ell_{i,j} := (y - y_{[i]Q_{11}}) - \lambda_{i,j} \cdot v_i$ and

$$\lambda_{i,j} := \begin{cases} \dfrac{y_{[i]Q_{11}} - y_{[j]Q_{11}}}{x_{[i]Q_{11}} - x_{[j]Q_{11}}} & \text{if} \quad i \neq j, \\ \dfrac{3 \cdot x_{[i]Q_{11}}^2}{2 \cdot y_{[i]Q_{11}}} & \text{otherwise.} \end{cases}$$

Since Q_{11} is fixed, we precompute all the 7 lines $\ell_{i,j}$, v_i and only evaluate them at P_i during the Tate pairing computation. Instead of inverting the denominator $v_2^4 \cdot (v_5 \cdot v_4)^2$, we raise it to the power 10, since $(\frac{1/x}{q})_i = (\frac{x^{i-1}}{q})_i$ for arbitrary $i \mid q-1$ and $x \in \mathbb{F}_q^*$. The same applies to computing $f_{11,Q'_{11}}$. Finally, we exponentiate by $(q-1)/11$, using a short addition chain of 372 squarings and 77 multiplications.

- *Step 2*: After detecting some fraudulent points $P_i \notin \mathbb{G}'_1$, we compute the n MSMs $S_j = \sum_{i=1}^{N} c_{i,j} P_i$ with random coefficients $c_{i,j} \in \mathbb{Z}/m$ (of course, $c_{i,j} = 0$ when $P_i \notin \mathbb{G}'_1$). We then check that $S_j \in \mathbb{G}_1$, using the Bowe–Scott test. For BLS12-381, $p = 10177$ is the smallest prime divisor of e'. Consequently, for the error probability $\mathbb{P} \leqslant 1/2^{60}$, we chose $m = 2^{13} < p < 2^{14}$ and the number of rounds $n = \lceil 60/\log_2(m) \rceil = 5$ (as well as in Table 1 when m is replaced by p).

Figure 1 reports the execution times of the new batch SMT compared to the collection of the naive separate checks. The benchmarks were run on a set of $N \in \{2^{3+2j}\}_{j=1}^{9}$ random points $P_i \in \mathbb{G}_1$, albeit correctness of the batch strategy was verified for non-restricted $P_i \in E(\mathbb{F}_q)$. Since Step 2 becomes even more efficient when a part of P_i are outside the subgroup $\mathbb{G}'_1$, the graph in reality showcases the worst-case running time of Algorithm 1. In other words, its average running time essentially matches the worst case unless incorrect points appear, in which case an early exit can occur. On BLS12-381 the full two-step method remains slower than the naive method on valid inputs, because the first-stage Tate/residue checks still dominate the total cost. By contrast, if the cost of Step 1 is disregarded, Step 2 alone is between 9.59× and 47.02× faster than the naive collection of separate subgroup checks.

The BLS12-377 Case: This $\mathbb{F}_q$-curve of equation $E\colon y^2 = x^3 + 1$ has the seed $z =$ `0x8508c00000000001` and thus $\pi' = 2^4 \cdot 3 \cdot 7 \cdot 13$ and $e' = 2^{42} \cdot 499$. The latter number is highly 2-adic and thereby the first step of the batch SMT is useless ($p = 2$). We proceed directly to the second step as follows:

- *Step 2*: We compute the n MSMs S_j with random coefficients $c_{i,j} \in \{0, 1\}$. We implement this, using mixed additions of the points P_i in affine coordinates

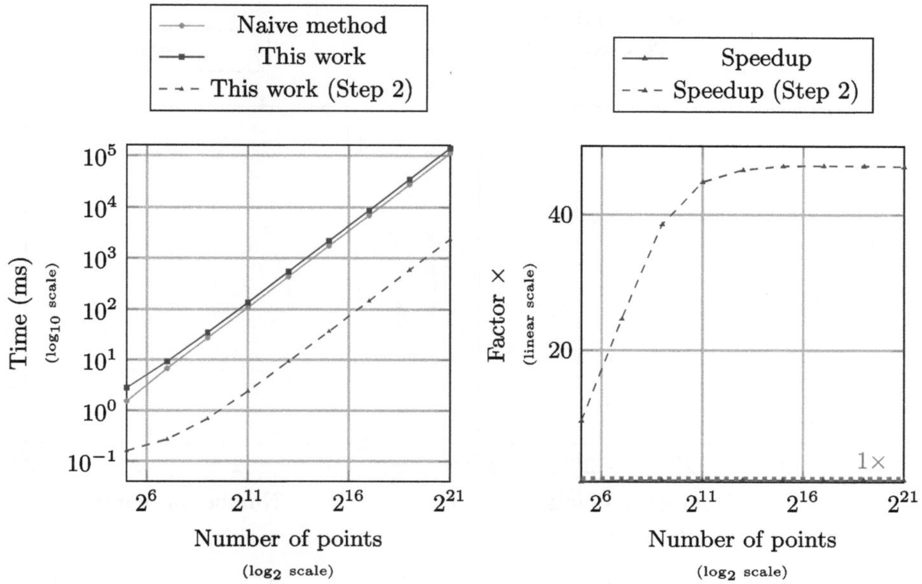

Fig. 1. Comparison of execution time and speedup between the naive method and this work for $\mathbb{P} \leqslant 1/2^{60}$ in the case of the curve BLS12-381.

and the running sum in extended Jacobian coordinates. We then check that $S_j \in \mathbb{G}_1$ through the Bowe–Scott test. For the error probability $\mathbb{P} \leqslant 1/2^{60}$, we obviously need $n = 60$ sums.

Figure 2 exhibits the results for the BLS12-377 curve. It is again normal that the new method is slower for $N = 32$, since we compare 32 Bowe–Scott tests to 60 ones and 60 sums. For the larger N, the new method is between 1.37× and 4.33× faster than the naive one. The performance gain is more pronounced for greater values of N, since we only keep the running sum in memory contrary to the general Pippenger algorithm, which is more memory-heavy. We also note that for the large N we might speed up the approach by using affine additions and implementing Montgomery's batch inversion technique to invert all the denominators at the cost of a single inversion.

The new BLS12-377 Case: This $\mathbb{F}_q$-curve of equation $E : y^2 = x^3 + 1$ has the seed $z =$ `-0x816163471f000001` and thus $\pi' = 2 \cdot 3$ and $e' = p =$ 1553806976791259819. Following Algorithm 1, we proceed as follows:

- *Step 1*: We verify the belongingness $P_i \in \mathbb{G}'_1$ by checking that $t_3(Q_3, P_i) = 1$ and $t_2(Q_2, P_i) = t_2(Q'_2, P_i) = 1$. Here, the point $Q_3 := (0, 1)$ is of order 3 and hence $f_{3,Q_3} = y - 1$. We evaluate the cubic residue symbol by means of the Euclidean-type algorithm implemented in [52]. In turn, the points $Q_2 := (-1, 0)$ and $Q'_2 := (-\omega, 0)$, with $\omega = z^5 - 3z^4 + 3z^3 - z + 1 \pmod q$ being a cubic root of unity in $\mathbb{F}_q^*$, are of order 2 and hence $f_{2,Q_2} = x + 1$ and $f_{2,Q'_2} = x + \omega$. To evaluate the Legendre symbol, we do not exponentiate

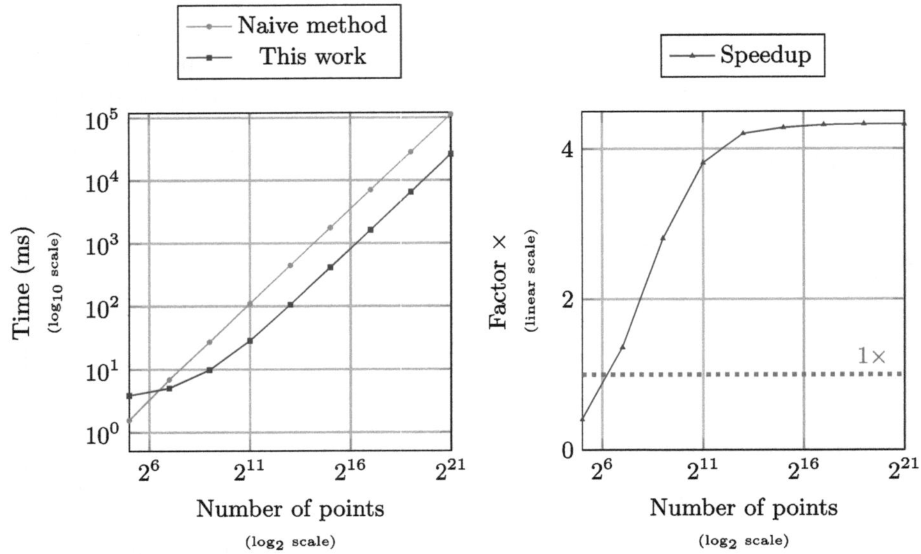

Fig. 2. Comparison of execution time and speedup between the naive method and this work for $\mathbb{P} \leqslant 1/2^{60}$ in the case of the curve BLS12-377.

banally by $(q-1)/2$, using instead Pornin's variant [62] of the binary GCD and quadratic reciprocity. This is significantly faster than the exponentiation even with the shortest addition chains.

- *Step 2*: We compute the single MSM $S_1 = \sum_{i=1}^{N} c_{i,1} P_i$ with random scalars $c_{i,1} \leq 2^{60} < p < 2^{61}$ and test if $S_1 \in_? \mathbb{G}_1$, with error probability $\mathbb{P} \leqslant 1/2^{60}$.

Figure 3 shows that the new method is already slightly faster for $N = 32$. For larger values of N, it achieves speedup ranging from $1.10\times$ to $1.47\times$.

The new BLS12-376 Case: This $\mathbb{F}_q$-curve of equation $E\colon y^2 = x^3 + 1$ has seed $z =$ `-0x78383f2600000001`, thus $\pi' = 2 \cdot 3$ and $e' = p = 14437905526147426 99$. We proceed as in the case of the new BLS12-377 curve, in particular evaluating the cubic residue symbol with the same Euclidean-type strategy. Similar results can be seen in Fig. 4, with speedup of $1.18\times$ to $1.54\times$. Since we propose the two new curves as batch-SMT-friendly replacements to BLS12-381, we also benchmark and compare common operations on these three curves (Appendix A).

Note 1. The benchmarks indicate that Step 1 on BLS12-381 is still the main obstacle to end-to-end gains. The Euclidean-type implementation of $(\frac{\cdot}{q})_3$ is efficient in practice, so the most natural remaining engineering targets inside Step 1 are the 11-th residue symbol and lower-level implementation details such as parallelism and memory behavior.

Note 2. For moderate number N of points, maximizing the MSM coefficients size and minimizing the number n of rounds always yields the best performance, while for large N, minimizing the MSM coefficients to $\{0, 1\}$ and maximizing n to 60 is conversely better. This is because point additions scale better than the

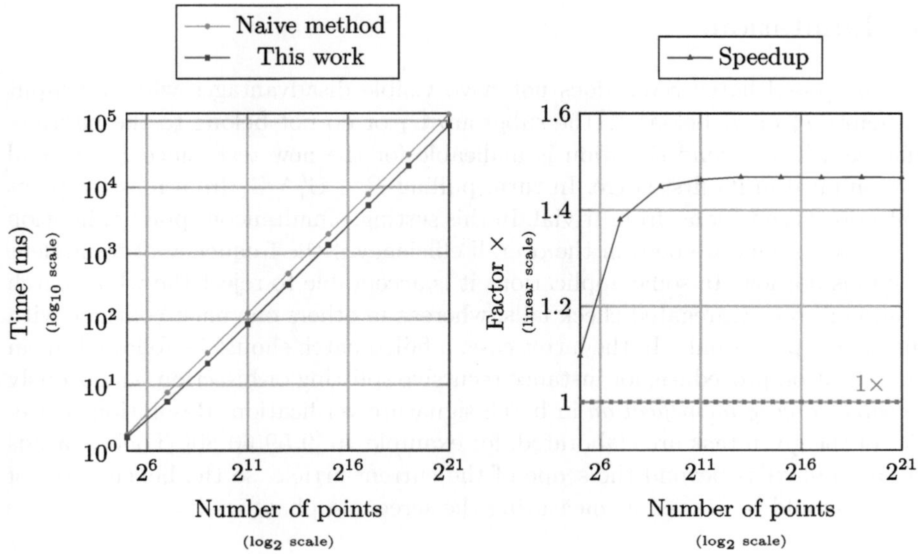

Fig. 3. Comparison of execution time and speedup between the naive method and this work for $\mathbb{P} \leqslant 1/2^{60}$ in the case of the new curve BLS12-377.

Pippenger algorithm memory-wise. However, all the speedup figures plateau as N increases. This is likely because for the large N, the dominant factor becomes iterating through extensive in-memory point arrays. We believe that a tailored parallelism strategy could alleviate this behavior.

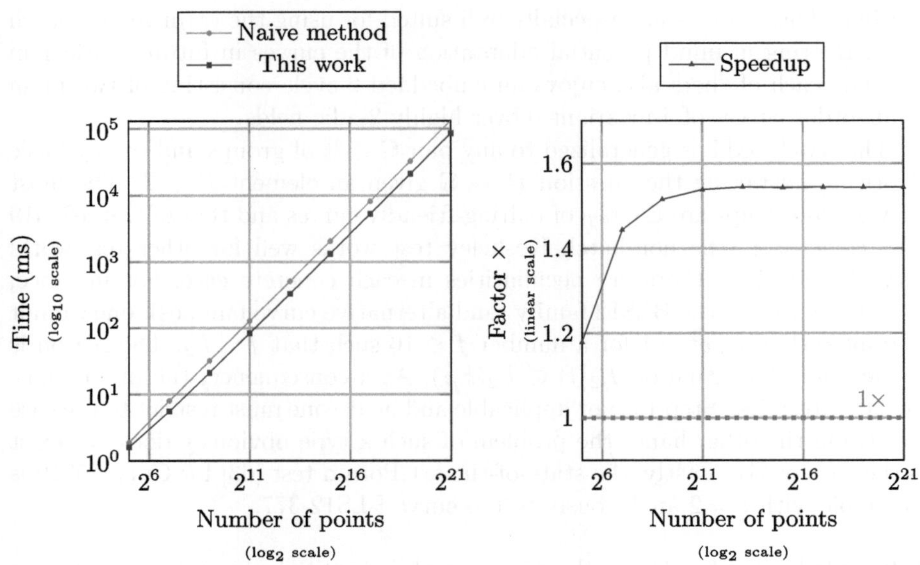

Fig. 4. Comparison of execution time and speedup between the naive method and this work for $\mathbb{P} \leqslant 1/2^{60}$ in the case of the new curve BLS12-376.

5 Limitation

The proposed batch SMT does not have visible disadvantages when all input $\mathbb{F}_q$-points P_i on E belong to the subgroup $\mathbb{G}_1$ or do not belong to the intermediate $\mathbb{G}_1'$. The second situation is malleable for the new test, since P_i are still not summed in its first stage. In turn, pulling $P_i \in \mathbb{G}_1' \setminus \mathbb{G}_1$ from massive point collections is a task far from trivial. In this setting, simultaneous point validation may lose to separate ones in the overall efficiency if the frequency of fraudulent points is not low. In some applications it is acceptable to reject the whole batch as soon as one aggregated check fails, whereas in others one must continue with the honest points only. In the latter case, a failed batch should be followed by an identification procedure, for instance recursive splitting or bisection, analogously to *batch forgery identification* in batch signature verification. Resolution strategies of the given task are elaborated, for example, in [9,59,60,80]. Their analysis in our context is beyond the scope of the current article, so the benchmarks of Sect. 4 should be viewed as measuring the screening phase itself.

6 Conclusion

The present paper analyzed batch SMT with emphasis on the subgroup $\mathbb{G}_1$ of a BLS12 curve $E/\mathbb{F}_q$. It has been shown that treating input points $P_i \in E(\mathbb{F}_q)$ in combination is indeed much faster (with negligible error probability) than validating independently every point P_i. And when the cofactor $h_1 = 3e_1^2$ (or the value e_1) is less smooth, this tendency is clearer. Moreover, the greater the number of points, the more significant the performance gain. Furthermore, two new BLS12 curves have been generated for which $e_1/2$ (and the other cofactor h_2) is prime. These curves are especially well suited for using the (re)invented batch SMT. Bearing in mind potential adaptation of the curves in future blockchain projects, each of them also enjoys an embedded 2-cycle consisting of two plain prime-order curves of j-invariant 0 over highly 2-adic fields.

The batch SMT is generalized to any pair $\mathbb{G} \subset \mathbb{H}$ of groups and to any basic algorithm answering the question $P \in_? \mathbb{G}$ given an element $P \in \mathbb{H}$. The most relevant subgroups are $\mathbb{G}_2$, $\mathbb{G}_T$ of pairing-friendly curves and that of Curve25519 with cofactor 8 (the non-batch Koshelev test works well for other real-world curves). Certainly, there are peculiarities in each concrete case. For instance, even in the case of the BLS12 family (and alternative curve families), one cannot guarantee that $f \mid q^2 - 1$ for a number $f \leqslant 16$ such that $f^2 \mid h_2$. The reason is in the realizable situation $E_2[f] \not\subset E_2(\mathbb{F}_{q^2})$. As a consequence, the preliminary Koshelev test, i.e., Step 1 is not applicable and hence one must restrict to the case $p \leqslant f$. On the other hand, the problem of such a type obviously does not exist in the case of $\mathbb{G}_T$. Lastly, the state-of-the-art Pornin test [63] for Curve25519 is batchable with $p = 2$ analogously to the curve BLS12-377.

Acknowledgements. The authors express their gratitude to Antonio Sanso for attracting attention to the problem of batch subgroup membership testing and to Gautam Botrel for helping with software optimizations.

Dimitri Koshelev acknowledges the strategic project “Advances in post-quantum cryptography applied to the development of a coupon system” (C039/24), resulting from an agreement between the Spanish National Cybersecurity Institute (INCIBE) and University of Lleida. The initiative is carried out in the scope of the funds from the Recovery, Transformation and Resilience Plan, funded by the EU (Next Generation). He also acknowledges the R&D+i project PID2021-124613OB-I00 funded by MICIU/AEI/10.13039/501100011033 and FEDER, EU. Besides, the author was supported by Ethereum Foundation through the grant FY25-1896. Georgios Fotiadis acknowledges the financial support from the European Defence Fund 2024 Programme (EDF-2024-LS-RA-DIS) under the project ORQESTRA (GA No. 101224573-ORQESTRA-EDF-2024-LS).

A Comparison of BLS12-381 and New BLS12 Curves

In Table 5 we compare the new curves BLS12-377 and BLS12-376 to the widely-used one BLS12-381 with respect to common elliptic curve operations. The benchmarks use the same AWS `c7a.8xlarge` single-threaded setup as in Sect. 4. The performance on the two new curves stays close to BLS12-381 for $\mathbb{G}_1$ operations, while $\mathbb{G}_2$ MSMs and pairings remain somewhat faster on BLS12-381 because of its very small seed Hamming weight.

Table 5. Benchmarks (in milliseconds) of common operations on the curve BLS12-381 and on the new ones BLS12-377, BLS12-376

Operation	BLS12-381	new BLS12-377	new BLS12-376
$\mathbb{G}_1$ GLV scalar multiplication	0.100	0.105	0.103
$\mathbb{G}_2$ GLV scalar multiplication	0.221	0.264	0.274
$\mathbb{G}_1$ MSM ($N = 2^5$)	3.730	3.502	3.678
$\mathbb{G}_1$ MSM ($N = 2^{21}$)	202908.167	202353.391	201448.995
$\mathbb{G}_2$ MSM ($N = 2^5$)	7.718	9.122	9.238
$\mathbb{G}_2$ MSM ($N = 2^{21}$)	433099.839	514019.652	511662.283
Pairing	0.668	0.952	0.962
Pairing product ($N = 2$)	0.831	1.207	1.198
Pairing product ($N = 4$)	1.205	1.685	1.666
Pairing product ($N = 10$)	2.371	3.170	3.072

B The Miller Functions $f_{11,Q_{11}}$ and $f_{11,Q'_{11}}$

Consider the points $Q_{11} := (x_{11}, y_{11})$ and $Q'_{11} := (x'_{11}, y'_{11})$ on BLS12-381 with the coordinates

$$
\begin{aligned}
x_{11} &= \texttt{0x19b3e2c8c6bbf59d3c326b531fc1e639d29200c28624ac604f251a12908c9}\\
&\quad \texttt{b7f735318617f625954cc71cdf03229b1ef},\\
y_{11} &= \texttt{0x42fcc94d6c6440d3c0a01177616b72eb6972d90e36e88b5981a05a52ab48c}\\
&\quad \texttt{e3e22fa88d10f6de85a7d386aad66c0ca8},\\
x'_{11} &= \texttt{0xb9529a7b23788075a6c33c7b77b3dcf4da4f58af5310f32e739a6c653a5a8}\\
&\quad \texttt{f7cf7f19a297bd6a8f3f19ea82cf9419},\\
y'_{11} &= \texttt{0x2ecc645926cbd45f215b3fa17df0d7a50e5814f9631c502f2b2c245792608}\\
&\quad \texttt{9a452bd11bf89ee72baa1981f99f88acb2}.
\end{aligned}
$$

They were generated by clearing the cofactor $er/11$ for $(4, 2\sqrt{17})$ and $(5, \sqrt{129})$, the curve points with the smallest x-coordinates, whose orders are divided by 11. Moreover, the points Q_{11}, Q'_{11} form a basis of $E[11]$, since their Weil pairing is non-trivial. The precomputed lines $\ell_{i,j}$, v_i related to Q_{11} are as follows:

$$
\begin{aligned}
\ell_{1,1} &= \texttt{0x52084a813637c846209a6bd185637a4f3064ed2a6842bf0bd880b1f59b0c20bd8}\\
&\quad \texttt{49bfe974d911a8298449f291164bdd} \cdot x + y + \texttt{0x177945f53bd9ccccf92efbde018f02}\\
&\quad \texttt{31394f35d08d5ec12f3ada6582e07b503ffbd3ef06b5897d39ebb8659179e2d724},\\
\ell_{4,1} &= \texttt{0x13c891a2eb0efb385efd6c30a970b8ba2476e5e336ca503655a3f4639afa20ee9}\\
&\quad \texttt{3a66bc4e3292af389c08375b7f7ca11} \cdot x + y + \texttt{0x12fe29f8433353a1efbb127d92e74}\\
&\quad \texttt{b33ef62de088fd63e32e371dc7fdb8fe8c441f43f2e23f272ee147fe8159079192c},\\
\ell_{2,2} &= \texttt{0x1629665baebce7a5e15fd940a207d30b892abbf11839e597e88111ed040ef83e2}\\
&\quad \texttt{28aa158afea8d4b940e1a333d1a330f} \cdot x + y + \texttt{0x18afe2760ca5e1821765ba9f63fb6}\\
&\quad \texttt{95f6141bf348af097618f548b48bc366430475070563872 25d782990d74698b2245},\\
\ell_{5,5} &= \texttt{0xc56f430391b7b504419357c8377df95e6852c5c4dde312c11da4caa0fbb894aa9}\\
&\quad \texttt{ae785edebb1da4425ad3738fc71d9e} \cdot x + y + \texttt{0xe6dd0ee7e55161d51c168b1a4dc8}\\
&\quad \texttt{4a7cde75831ceec4bf58416295c6b483568bbaa2a4d5c4f2f7fc984c70320156fec},\\
v_2 &= x + \texttt{0x175870c9f78d5b3c808076977 1854a65aee01f4ce1c7bab7a8e07219383b0}\\
&\quad \texttt{dd70bf3b6672721aa6c965c809e3129aef2},\\
v_4 &= x + \texttt{0x12f69088512349670c11c7ce2b1917bc1a8e981440a99f9f235bc0f987fd0}\\
&\quad \texttt{0e719a4d68437eb80c91ace7614fa08578d},\\
v_5 &= x + \texttt{0x29cbec7fa11916ea27cafdf2e570b2821d1457fa9fe5f4a06cbd0d7964735}\\
&\quad \texttt{f364f671311150a5d43a425438208a5534}.
\end{aligned}
$$

In turn, the precomputed lines $\ell_{i,j}$, v_i related to Q'_{11} are as follows:

$$\begin{aligned}
\ell_{1,1} = {} & \texttt{0xe86fb44c035add8d5bd0c1bbc00746b8f5948f53d19e6f1463e1c2116aee} \\
& \texttt{7d8e1e5e52f4243d92e30d81016615a4d8f} \cdot x + y + \texttt{0x19e29d77082445f62426e681d21} \\
& \texttt{64313f0938233dc212252d18bd59fa843866de644e19c23fdca39d4caf5a21b6218ef}, \\
\ell_{4,1} = {} & \texttt{0x143a9f359b2e91fde880b224bb02eabe251998d5b9fac7e99344a5f591b} \\
& \texttt{e3c87307b0d8d34066ed312a406df7a3a7de2} \cdot x + y + \texttt{0xdea366ab1f6dad2b4e86d4e09} \\
& \texttt{2d3c60a78cb23409b43afe97572f7c8ea087b37861e527e1074263ceb03442c00c83a5}, \\
\ell_{2,2} = {} & \texttt{0xd90c951049c94a6ed1bd28a9478fbf9832e538012959dc03beda2f2db93} \\
& \texttt{b8d2ad8f118632faa008092f1bd63dbe79ad} \cdot x + y + \texttt{0x8a7c2874b1186be6a04eaa25f} \\
& \texttt{518a805eee85220d647ca6ca7b55367e283de6f5d2827f8bc139d33d399d7b5eaface}, \\
\ell_{5,5} = {} & \texttt{0xe7ffc6cda09c9a1836d575029f4f18ef073d1f62da3e9966afd7d4c8d} \\
& \texttt{6393c67d0ed253d72414922367c7096429c8ca} \cdot x + y + \texttt{0x861494ad62ca8ff789de6c651} \\
& \texttt{0352d4f507d3f52aa71432b6d2675f600318b237ce30295749ac0525a141e0b38b2ea1}, \\
v_2 = {} & x + \texttt{0x1980d2dd2f8125ffb528b941ae1970c1a315247876b662c4e1c9e95f304527} \\
& \texttt{03b0396aa158a04cd163b11cdf62987e06}, \\
v_4 = {} & x + \texttt{0xe1636df6805a24e45371392a93bd29875131d336ed3525c9bc2a5d299241291} \\
& \texttt{8c898f91b13450ebd925f8d6d2e36887}, \\
v_5 = {} & x + \texttt{0x1314a66019d8da69008ff230b23b95e951d0ae4ea9dca5a58f5678b10105345} \\
& \texttt{fa00b065f5c465df9d71d7ea84d702b13}.
\end{aligned}$$

C Notation

Table 6. Symbols and their meanings

Symbol	Meaning
$E/\mathbb{F}_q$	Pairing-friendly elliptic curve (of j-invariant 0) over a finite field
t	Frobenius trace of E
λ	Security level of E
k	Embedding degree of E
$E_2/\mathbb{F}_{q^d}$	Twist of E of degree k/d for some $d \in \mathbb{N}$
$\mathbb{G}_1, \mathbb{G}_2, \mathbb{G}_T$	Subgroups for a type-III pairing on E
r	Identical prime order of the pairing groups
ρ	Ratio $\lceil \log_2(q) \rceil / \lceil \log_2(r) \rceil$
Φ_k	k-th cyclotomic polynomial
μ_i	All the i-th roots of unity (for $i \in \mathbb{N}$) in some extension of $\mathbb{F}_q$
$\mathbb{H}_1, \mathbb{H}_2, \mathbb{H}_T$	Groups $E(\mathbb{F}_q)$, $E_2(\mathbb{F}_{q^d})$, and $\mu_{\Phi_k(q)}$
h_i	Cofactors $\#\mathbb{H}_i/r$ for $i \in \{1, 2, T\}$
z	Seed of the BLS12 family
w	Hamming weight of the NAF representation of z
e_1	Parameter $\sqrt{h_1/3} \in \mathbb{N}$ for BLS12 curves
e	Exponent $3e_1$ of the subgroup of $E(\mathbb{F}_q)$ complementary to $\mathbb{G}_1$
t_e	Reduced Tate pairing $E(\mathbb{F}_q)[e] \times E(\mathbb{F}_q) \to \mu_e \subset \mathbb{F}_q^*$

(*continued*)

Table 6. (*continued*)

Symbol	Meaning
$(\frac{x}{q})_i$	Power residue symbol $x^{(q-1)/i}$ for $x \in \mathbb{F}_q^*$ and $i \mid q-1$
ω	Primitive cubic root of unity in $\mathbb{F}_q^*$
$[\omega]$	Automorphism $(x, y) \mapsto (\omega x, y)$ on E
P_i	Input points from $E(\mathbb{F}_q)$
N	Number of the points P_i
$c_{i,j}$	Random coefficients for batch SMT
S_j	Sums $\sum_{i=1}^{N} c_{i,j} P_i$
m	Upper bound on the coefficients $c_{i,j}$
N'	Expected number $N(m-1)/m$ of nonzero terms in each S_j
$\mathbb{P}$	Error probability of batch SMT
μ	Security parameter such that $\mathbb{P} \leqslant 1/2^{\mu}$
n	Number $\lceil \mu/\log_2(m) \rceil$ of rounds, i.e., of sums S_j
π	Product $2^4 \cdot 3^2 \cdot 5 \cdot 7 \cdot 11 \cdot 13$
π'	Greatest common divisor $\gcd(\pi, e)$
e'	Reduced exponent $e/\pi' \in \mathbb{N}$
p	Smallest prime divisor of e'
$\mathbb{G}_1'$	Intermediate subgroup $E(\mathbb{F}_q)[re']$ occurring in Step 1
$f_{s,Q}$	Miller function associated to $s \in \mathbb{Z}$ and $Q \in E$
$\ell_{i,j}, v_i$	Precomputed general and vertical lines for Miller functions
$\nu_2(u)$	2-adic valuation for $u \in \mathbb{Z}$
$\nu_2^*(u)$	Value $\nu_2(u-1)$ replaced for compactness
p_ℓ	Certain prime of bit length ℓ
$E_e/\mathbb{F}_r$	Embedded curve with respect to E
r'	Prime subgroup order for E_e
h	Cofactor of E_e
D	CM discriminant of E_e
$E_e'/\mathbb{F}_{r'}$	Embedded curve with respect to E_e when $h = 1$
v	Identical 2-adicity for both fields $\mathbb{F}_r$ and $\mathbb{F}_{r'}$
z'	Auxiliary seed $(z+1)/2^v \in \mathbb{Z}$ for finding the new BLS12 curves

References

1. The decaf377 group. https://protocol.penumbra.zone/main/crypto/decaf377.html
2. Aranha, D.F., Salling Hvass, B., Spitters, B., Tibouchi, M.: Faster constant-time evaluation of the Kronecker symbol with application to elliptic curve hashing. In: CCS 2023: ACM SIGSAC Conference on Computer and Communications Security, pp. 3228–3238. Association for Computing Machinery, New York (2023). https://doi.org/10.1145/3576915.3616597
3. Aumasson, J.P., Nguyen, Q.T.M., Sanso, A.: Security of BLS batch verification (2021). https://ethresear.ch/t/security-of-bls-batch-verification/10748
4. Barbulescu, R., Duquesne, S.: Updating key size estimations for pairings. J. Cryptol. **32**(4), 1298–1336 (2019). https://doi.org/10.1007/s00145-018-9280-5
5. Barreto, P.S.L.M., Costello, C., Misoczki, R., Naehrig, M., Pereira, G.C.C.F., Zanon, G.: Subgroup security in pairing-based cryptography. In: Lauter, K., Rodríguez-Henríquez, F. (eds.) LATINCRYPT 2015. LNCS, vol. 9230, pp. 245–265. Springer, Cham (2015). https://doi.org/10.1007/978-3-319-22174-8_14
6. Barreto, P.S.L.M., Lynn, B., Scott, M.: Constructing elliptic curves with prescribed embedding degrees. In: Cimato, S., Persiano, G., Galdi, C. (eds.) Security in Communication Networks. SCN 2002. Lecture Notes in Computer Science, vol. 2576,

pp. 257–267. Springer, Berlin, Heidelberg (2003). https://doi.org/10.1007/3-540-36413-7_19
7. Barreto, P.S.L.M., Naehrig, M.: Pairing-friendly elliptic curves of prime order. In: Preneel, B., Tavares, S. (eds.) SAC 2005. LNCS, vol. 3897, pp. 319–331. Springer, Heidelberg (2006). https://doi.org/10.1007/11693383_22
8. Bellare, M., Garay, J.A., Rabin, T.: Fast batch verification for modular exponentiation and digital signatures. In: Nyberg, K. (ed.) EUROCRYPT 1998. LNCS, vol. 1403, pp. 236–250. Springer, Heidelberg (1998). https://doi.org/10.1007/BFb0054130
9. Bernstein, D.J., Doumen, J., Lange, T., Oosterwijk, J.J.: Faster batch forgery identification. In: Galbraith, S., Nandi, M. (eds.) Progress in Cryptology – INDOCRYPT 2012. Lecture Notes in Computer Science, vol. 7668, pp. 454–473. Springer, Berlin, Heidelberg (2012). https://doi.org/10.1007/978-3-642-34931-7_26
10. Boneh, D., et al.: BLS signatures (2025). https://datatracker.ietf.org/doc/draft-irtf-cfrg-bls-signature
11. Boneh, D., Drijvers, M., Neven, G.: Compact multi-signatures for smaller blockchains. In: Peyrin, T., Galbraith, S. (eds.) ASIACRYPT 2018. LNCS, vol. 11273, pp. 435–464. Springer, Cham (2018). https://doi.org/10.1007/978-3-030-03329-3_15
12. Boneh, D., Franklin, M.: Identity-based encryption from the Weil pairing. In: Kilian, J. (ed.) CRYPTO 2001. LNCS, vol. 2139, pp. 213–229. Springer, Heidelberg (2001). https://doi.org/10.1007/3-540-44647-8_13
13. Boneh, D., Gentry, C., Lynn, B., Shacham, H.: Aggregate and verifiably encrypted signatures from bilinear maps. In: Biham, E. (ed.) EUROCRYPT 2003. LNCS, vol. 2656, pp. 416–432. Springer, Heidelberg (2003). https://doi.org/10.1007/3-540-39200-9_26
14. Boneh, D., Lynn, B., Shacham, H.: Short signatures from the Weil pairing. J. Cryptol. **17**(4), 297–319 (2004). https://doi.org/10.1007/s00145-004-0314-9
15. Botrel, G., Piellard, T., El Housni, Y., Tabaie, A., Gutoski, G., Kubjas, I.: Consensys/gnark-crypto: v0.19.2 (2025). https://doi.org/10.5281/zenodo.5815453
16. Bowe, S.: BLS12-381: New zk-SNARK elliptic curve construction (2017). https://electriccoin.co/blog/new-snark-curve
17. Bowe, S.: Switch from BN254 to BLS12-381 (2017). https://github.com/zcash/zcash/issues/2502
18. Bowe, S.: Faster subgroup checks for BLS12-381 (2019). https://eprint.iacr.org/2019/814
19. Bowe, S., Chiesa, A., Green, M., Miers, I., Mishra, P., Wu, H.: Zexe: enabling decentralized private computation. In: 2020 IEEE Symposium on Security and Privacy (SP), pp. 947–964. IEEE, New York (2020). https://doi.org/10.1109/SP40000.2020.00050
20. Boyd, C., Pavlovski, C.: Attacking and repairing batch verification schemes. In: Okamoto, T. (ed.) ASIACRYPT 2000. LNCS, vol. 1976, pp. 58–71. Springer, Heidelberg (2000). https://doi.org/10.1007/3-540-44448-3_5
21. Brier, E., Géraud-Stewart, R., Joye, M., Naccache, D.: Primary elements in cyclotomic fields with applications to power residue symbols, and more (2021). https://eprint.iacr.org/2021/1106
22. Brier, E., Naccache, D.: The thirteenth power residue symbol (2019). https://eprint.iacr.org/2019/1176

23. Budroni, A., Pintore, F.: Efficient hash maps to $\mathbb{G}_2$ on BLS curves. Appl. Algebra Eng. Commun. Comput. **33**(3), 261–281 (2022). https://doi.org/10.1007/s00200-020-00453-9
24. Chen, L., Moody, D., Regenscheid, A., Robinson, A., Randall, K.: Recommendations for discrete logarithm-based cryptography: elliptic curve domain parameters (NIST Special Publication 800-186) (2023). https://csrc.nist.gov/publications/detail/sp/800-186/final
25. Chen, Y., Peng, C., Dai, Y., Luo, M., He, D.: Load-balanced parallel implementation on GPUs for multi-scalar multiplication algorithm. IACR Trans. Cryptographic Hardware Embed. Syst. **2024**(2), 522–544 (2024). https://doi.org/10.46586/tches.v2024.i2.522-544
26. Clarisse, R., Duquesne, S., Sanders, O.: Curves with fast computations in the first pairing group. In: Krenn, S., Shulman, H., Vaudenay, S. (eds.) CANS 2020. LNCS, vol. 12579, pp. 280–298. Springer, Cham (2020). https://doi.org/10.1007/978-3-030-65411-5_14
27. Dai, Y., He, D., Koshelev, D., Peng, C., Yang, Z.: Revisiting subgroup membership testing on pairing-friendly curves via the tate pairing. In: Public-Key Cryptography – PKC 2026: 29th IACR International Conference on Practice and Theory of Public-Key Cryptography, West Palm Beach, FL, USA, May 25–28, 2026, Proceedings, Part III, pp. 92–120. Springer-Verlag, Berlin, Heidelberg (2026). https://doi.org/10.1007/978-3-032-26737-5_4
28. Dai, Y., Lin, K., Zhao, C.A., Zhou, Z.: Fast subgroup membership testings for $\mathbb{G}_1$, $\mathbb{G}_2$ and $\mathbb{G}_T$ on pairing-friendly curves. Designs, Codes Crypt. **91**(10), 3141–3166 (2023). https://doi.org/10.1007/s10623-023-01223-7
29. El Housni, Y., Guillevic, A.: Optimized and secure pairing-friendly elliptic curves suitable for one layer proof composition. In: Krenn, S., Shulman, H., Vaudenay, S. (eds.) CANS 2020. LNCS, vol. 12579, pp. 259–279. Springer, Cham (2020). https://doi.org/10.1007/978-3-030-65411-5_13
30. El Housni, Y., Guillevic, A., Piellard, T.: Co-factor clearing and subgroup membership testing on pairing-friendly curves. In: Batina, L., Daemen, J. (eds.) Progress in Cryptology – AFRICACRYPT 2022. Lecture Notes in Computer Science, vol. 13503, pp. 518–536. Springer, Cham (2022). https://doi.org/10.1007/978-3-031-17433-9_22
31. Electric Coin Company: What is Jubjub?. https://bitzecbzc.github.io/technology/jubjub
32. Fan, X., Kuchta, V., Sica, F., Xu, L.: Speeding up multi-scalar multiplications for pairing-based zkSNARKs. J. Cryptol. **38**(2), 21 (2025). https://doi.org/10.1007/s00145-025-09540-x
33. Faraoun, K.M.: Why not BLS12-461 with equivalent performance? (2019). https://github.com/zcash/zcash/issues/4065
34. Gabizon, A.: Possible improvements in subgroup testing (2018). https://github.com/zcash/zcash/issues/3470
35. Galbraith, S.D.: Mathematics of public key cryptography. Cambridge University Press, New York (2012). https://doi.org/10.1017/CBO9781139012843
36. Guillevic, A., Masson, S.: Embedded curves and embedded families for SNARK-friendly curves (2024). https://eprint.iacr.org/2024/1737
37. Guillevic, A., Singh, S.: On the alpha value of polynomials in the tower number field sieve algorithm. Trans. Math. Cryptol. **1**(1), 1–39 (2021). https://journals.flvc.org/mathcryptology/article/view/125142
38. Haboeck, U.: Security estimates of pairing-friendly curves (2020). https://github.com/arkworks-rs/algebra/issues/732

39. Haddaji, W., Ghammam, L., El Mrabet, N., Ben Abdelghani, L.: On computing the multidimensional scalar multiplication on elliptic curves (2024). https://eprint.iacr.org/2024/038
40. Hamburg, M.: Computing the Jacobi symbol using Bernstein–Yang (2021). https://eprint.iacr.org/2021/1271
41. Harn, L.: Batch verifying multiple RSA digital signatures. Electron. Lett. **34**(12), 1219–1220 (1998). https://doi.org/10.1049/el:19980833
42. Henry, R.: Pippenger's multiproduct and multiexponentiation algorithms (2010). https://cacr.uwaterloo.ca/techreports/2010/cacr2010-26.pdf
43. Hopwood, D.E.: Understand the concrete security level of the BN_128 curve in libsnark (2024). https://github.com/zcash/zcash/issues/714
44. Jiang, R., Peng, C., Luo, M., Chen, R., He, D.: SimdMSM: SIMD-accelerated multi-scalar multiplication framework for zkSNARKs. IACR Trans. Crypt. Hardware Embed. Syst. **2025**(2), 681–704 (2025). https://doi.org/10.46586/tches.v2025.i2.681-704
45. Joux, A.: A one round protocol for tripartite Diffie–Hellman. J. Cryptol. **17**(4), 263–276 (2004). https://doi.org/10.1007/s00145-004-0312-y
46. Joye, M., Lapiha, O., Nguyen, K., Naccache, D.: The eleventh power residue symbol. J. Math. Cryptol. **15**(1), 111–122 (2021). https://doi.org/10.1515/jmc-2020-0077
47. Keilty, A.P., Aranha, D.F., Pagnin, E., Rodríguez-Henríquez, F.: That's AmorE: amortized efficiency for pairing delegation. In: Tauman Kalai, Y., Kamara, S.F. (eds.) Advances in Cryptology – CRYPTO 2025. Lecture Notes in Computer Science, vol. 16007, pp. 211–246. Springer, Cham (2025). https://doi.org/10.1007/978-3-032-01913-4_7
48. Kim, T., Barbulescu, R.: Extended tower number field sieve: a new complexity for the medium prime case. In: Robshaw, M., Katz, J. (eds.) CRYPTO 2016. LNCS, vol. 9814, pp. 543–571. Springer, Heidelberg (2016). https://doi.org/10.1007/978-3-662-53018-4_20
49. Koshelev, D.: Subgroup membership testing on elliptic curves via the Tate pairing. J. Crypt. Eng. **13**(1), 125–128 (2023). https://doi.org/10.1007/s13389-022-00296-9
50. Koshelev, D.: Correction to: subgroup membership testing on elliptic curves via the Tate pairing. J. Crypt. Eng. **14**(1), 127–128 (2024). https://doi.org/10.1007/s13389-023-00331-3
51. Koshelev, D.: Application of Mordell–Weil lattices with large kissing numbers to acceleration of multiscalar multiplication on elliptic curves. J. Math. Crypt. **19**(1), 20240034 (2025). https://doi.org/10.1515/jmc-2024-0034
52. Koshelev, D., El Housni, Y., Fotiadis, G.: Batch-subgroup-membership-testing (2025). https://github.com/yelhousni/batch-subgroup-membership-testing
53. Koshelev, D., Sanso, A.: Endomorphisms for faster cryptography on elliptic curves of moderate CM discriminants. In: Capuano, L., Civino, R., Romeo, F., Santilli, G. (eds.) CIFRIS25 ACTA. De Cifris Koine, vol. 7, pp. 97–121. De Cifris Press, Milano (2025). https://doi.org/10.69091/koine/vol-7-W09
54. Lim, C.H., Lee, P.J.: A key recovery attack on discrete log-based schemes using a prime order subgroup. In: Kaliski, B.S. (ed.) CRYPTO 1997. LNCS, vol. 1294, pp. 249–263. Springer, Heidelberg (1997). https://doi.org/10.1007/BFb0052240
55. Lin, J., Robert, D., Zhao, C.A., Zheng, Y.: Biextensions in pairing-based cryptography. Designs, Codes Crypt. **94**(1), 5 (2026). https://doi.org/10.1007/s10623-025-01762-1

56. Masson, S., Sanso, A., Zhang, Z.: Bandersnatch: a fast elliptic curve built over the BLS12-381 scalar field. Designs, Codes Crypt. **92**(12), 4131–4143 (2024). https://doi.org/10.1007/s10623-024-01472-0
57. Moody, D., Peralta, R., Perlner, R., Regenscheid, A., Roginsky, A., Chen, L.: Report on pairing-based cryptography. J. Res. National Inst. Standards Technol. **120**, 11–27 (2015). https://doi.org/10.6028/jres.120.002
58. Naccache, D., M'Raïhi, D., Vaudenay, S., Raphaeli, D.: Can D.S.A. be improved? Complexity trade-offs with the digital signature standard. In: De Santis, A. (ed.) Advances in Cryptology – EUROCRYPT 1994. Lecture Notes in Computer Science, vol. 950, pp. 77–85. Springer, Berlin, Heidelberg (1995). https://doi.org/10.1007/BFb0053426
59. Pastuszak, J., Michałek, D., Pieprzyk, J., Seberry, J.: Identification of bad signatures in batches. In: Imai, H., Zheng, Y. (eds.) PKC 2000. LNCS, vol. 1751, pp. 28–45. Springer, Heidelberg (2000). https://doi.org/10.1007/978-3-540-46588-1_3
60. Pastuszak, J., Pieprzyk, J., Seberry, J.: Codes identifying bad signatures in batches. In: Roy, B., Okamoto, E. (eds.) INDOCRYPT 2000. LNCS, vol. 1977, pp. 143–154. Springer, Heidelberg (2000). https://doi.org/10.1007/3-540-44495-5_13
61. Pope, G., Reijnders, K., Robert, D., Sferlazza, A., Smith, B.: Simpler and faster pairings from the Montgomery ladder. IACR Commun. Crypt. **2**(2), 29 (2025). https://doi.org/10.62056/ah2i893y6
62. Pornin, T.: X25519 implementation for ARM Cortex-M0/M0+ (2020). https://github.com/pornin/x25519-cm0
63. Pornin, T.: Point-halving and subgroup membership in twisted Edwards curves (2022). https://eprint.iacr.org/2022/1164
64. Pottier, X., de Ruijter, T., Bertels, J., Legiest, W., Van Beirendonck, M., Verbauwhede, I.: OPTIMSM: FPGA hardware accelerator for zero-knowledge MSM. IACR Trans. Crypt. Hardware Embed. Syst. **2025**(2), 489–510 (2025). https://doi.org/10.46586/tches.v2025.i2.489-510
65. Robert, D.: Fast pairings via biextensions and cubical arithmetic (2024). https://eprint.iacr.org/2024/517
66. Sanso, A.: Fast $\mathbb{G}_2$ subgroup check in BN254 (2022). https://ethresear.ch/t/fast-mathbb-g-2-subgroup-check-in-bn254/13974
67. Sanso, A.: The return of torus based cryptography: Whisk and Curdleproof in the target group (2023). https://ethresear.ch/t/the-return-of-torus-based-cryptography-whisk-and-curdleproof-in-the-target-group/16678
68. Sanso, A., El Housni, Y.: Families of prime-order endomorphism-equipped embedded curves on pairing-friendly curves. J. Crypt. **37**(4), 37 (2024), https://doi.org/10.1007/s00145-024-09514-5
69. Scott, M.: Unbalancing pairing-based key exchange protocols (2013). https://eprint.iacr.org/2013/688
70. Scott, M.: Pairing implementation revisited (2019). https://eprint.iacr.org/2019/077
71. Scott, M.: A note on group membership tests for $\mathbb{G}_1$, $\mathbb{G}_2$ and $\mathbb{G}_T$ on BLS pairing-friendly curves (2021). https://eprint.iacr.org/2021/1130
72. Shlomovits, O.: Baby sharks: injecting small order points to threshold EdDSA (2020). https://medium.com/zengo/baby-sharks-a3b9ceb4efe0
73. Spagni, R.: Disclosure of a major bug in CryptoNote based currencies (2017). https://www.getmonero.org/2017/05/17/disclosure-of-a-major-bug-in-cryptonote-based-currencies.html
74. Straus, E.G.: Addition chains of vectors (problem 5125). Am. Math. Monthly **71**(7), 806–808 (1964). https://doi.org/10.2307/2310929

75. Teruya, T.: A note on subgroup security in discrete logarithm-based cryptography. IEICE Trans. Fundam. Electron. Commun. Comput. Sci. **E104-A**(1), 104–120 (2021). https://doi.org/10.1587/transfun.2020CIP0019
76. Valenta, L., et al.: Measuring small subgroup attacks against Diffie–Hellman (2016). https://eprint.iacr.org/2016/995
77. Vlasov, A.: EIP-2537 (BLS12 precompile) discussion thread (2020). https://ethereum-magicians.org/t/eip-2537-bls12-precompile-discussion-thread/4187
78. Vlasov, A.: EIP-2539: BLS12-377 curve operations (2020). https://eips.ethereum.org/EIPS/eip-2539
79. Wang, J.: BN254 for the rest of us (2024). https://hackmd.io/@jpw/bn254
80. Zaverucha, G.M., Stinson, D.R.: Group testing and batch verification. In: Kurosawa, K. (ed.) Information Theoretic Security. ICITS 2009. Lecture Notes in Computer Science, vol. 5973, pp. 140–157. Springer, Berlin, Heidelberg (2010). https://doi.org/10.1007/978-3-642-14496-7_12
81. Zhu, X., He, H., Yang, Z., Deng, Y., Zhao, L., Hou, R.: Elastic MSM: a fast, elastic and modular preprocessing technique for multi-scalar multiplication algorithm on GPUs. IACR Trans. Crypt. Hardware Embed. Syst. **2024**(4), 258–284 (2024). https://doi.org/10.46586/tches.v2024.i4.258-284

A New Attack on an RSA Variant with Primes Sharing Most Significant Bits

Brahim Chnioune[1(✉)], Mohammed Rahmani[1], Abderrahmane Nitaj[2], and Mhammed Ziane[1]

[1] ACSA Laboratory, Department of Mathematics, Sciences Faculty, Mohammed I University, 60000 Oujda, Morocco
{brahim.chnioune.d24,mohammed.rahmani,m.ziane}@ump.ac.ma
[2] Université Caen Normandie, CNRS, Normandie Univ, LMNO UMR6139, 14000 Caen, France
abderrahmane.nitaj@unicaen.fr

Abstract. At ISPEC 2022, Cotan and Teşeleanu introduced an RSA-like cryptosystem in which the modulus is a standard RSA integer $N = pq$ where p and q are primes of equal bit-length, and the public and private exponents e and d satisfy $ed \equiv 1 \pmod{\frac{(p^n-1)(q^n-1)}{(p-1)(q-1)}}$. In this paper, we propose a novel attack on this scheme when the difference between the primes is sufficiently small. By exploiting Coppersmith's technique in conjunction with lattice basis reduction, our method recovers the RSA primes in polynomial time and further improves the existing bounds for small private exponent attacks in cases where the primes share a portion of their most significant bits.

Keywords: RSA variants · Factoring · Coppersmith's method · Lattice basis reduction

1 Introduction

Introduced in 1978 by Rivest, Shamir, and Adleman [17], the RSA cryptosystem represents the first practical public-key encryption scheme. Its emergence marked a turning point in modern cryptography, and it remains one of the most widely deployed cryptographic systems worldwide. The security of RSA relies on the presumed computational intractability of certain number-theoretic problems, most notably the factorization of large composite integers. In practice, the RSA modulus N is constructed as the product $N = pq$, where p and q are large prime numbers of comparable bit-length. An integer $e < N$ is selected as the public exponent under the condition that $\gcd(e, \varphi(N)) = 1$, where $\varphi(N) = (p-1)(q-1)$, and the private exponent $d < N$ is defined as the modular inverse of e modulo $\varphi(N)$, i.e., $ed \equiv 1 \pmod{\varphi(N)}$. The pair (N, e) forms the public key and (N, d) the corresponding secret key. For any plaintext $m < N$, the RSA encryption produces the ciphertext $c \equiv m^e \pmod N$, and the decryption retrieves the message

N. El Mrabet et al. (Eds.): AFRICACRYPT 2026, LNCS 16832, pp. 316–337, 2026.
https://doi.org/10.1007/978-3-032-31130-6_13

by computing $m \equiv c^d \pmod{N}$. When the modular exponentiation is implemented using standard fast algorithms, the encryption step can be carried out in approximately $O\left((\log N)^2 \log e\right)$ bit operations, whereas the decryption step requires on the order of $O\left((\log N)^2 \log d\right)$ bit operations to retrieve the original message. Notwithstanding the widespread adoption of RSA, its computational cost remains substantial due to arithmetic over large integers. Hence, employing a small private exponent may initially seem to be a natural approach for reducing the decryption overhead. However, in 1990, Wiener [23] demonstrated that RSA becomes insecure when the private exponent satisfies $d < \frac{1}{3}N^{1/4}$. This bound was subsequently improved by Boneh and Durfee [1], who extended the attack to the range $d < N^{0.292}$. These results motivated extensive research aimed at enhancing both the efficiency and the security of RSA, leading to the proposal of numerous variants. Some constructions retain a modulus of the form $N = pq$, including CRT-RSA [16], Rebalanced RSA [23], and KMOV [8]. Other approaches adopt alternative modulus structures, such as Multi-Prime RSA [22], Prime-Power RSA [20], and Prime-Power KMOV [2].

In 2018, Murru and Saettone [11] proposed an RSA-like scheme based on the cubic Pell equation $x^3 + sy^3 + s^2z^3 - 3sxyz = 1$, where s is a cubic non-residue modulo N. The scheme uses a classical RSA modulus $N = pq$, with the public key (N, e) and the private key (N, d) satisfying a new key equation of the form $ed \equiv 1 \pmod{(p^2 + p + 1)(q^2 + q + 1)}$. The authors claimed that this construction is secure against Wiener's attack; however, it has since been subjected to extensive cryptanalysis, as documented in [5,18,24]. In 2022, Cotan and Teşeleanu [4] generalized this scheme by considering a modulus $N = pq$, a public exponent e, and a private exponent d satisfying

$$ed \equiv 1 \pmod{\frac{(p^n - 1)(q^n - 1)}{(p-1)(q-1)}}, \quad n \geq 2. \tag{1}$$

Notably, the case $n = 3$ corresponds to the original scheme of Murru and Saettone. The authors also proposed an attack on this generalized variant, showing that if $d = N^\delta$, $e = N^\alpha$ with $\alpha \leq n - \frac{1}{2}$ and $\delta < \frac{1}{4}(2n - 2\alpha - 1)$, then the scheme can be efficiently broken.

In 2024, Nitaj et al. [14] proposed an improved attack on the Cotan-Teşeleanu scheme. They showed that if $e = N^\theta$, $d = N^\delta$, with $\frac{n-1}{2} \leq \theta \leq 2(n-1)$ and

$$\delta < n - 1 - \frac{\sqrt{2}}{2}\sqrt{(n-1)\theta},$$

then the modulus N can be factored in polynomial time.

In this paper, we present an extended attack targeting the key relation (1). Specifically, given an RSA modulus $N = pq$ and a public exponent $e = N^\theta$, we show that if $d < N^\delta$ and the prime difference satisfies $|p - q| < N^\sigma$, then the prime factors p and q can be efficiently recovered whenever $0 \leq \theta < \frac{n-1}{\sigma}$, and

$$\delta < n - 1 - \sqrt{\theta\sigma(n-1)}. \tag{2}$$

Furthermore, we note the following two observations.

- By fixing $\sigma = \frac{1}{2}$, the upper bound in (2) reduces to

$$\delta < n - 1 - \frac{\sqrt{2}}{2}\sqrt{(n-1)\theta},$$

which recovers the optimal bound previously established by Nitaj et al. [14].
- In scenarios where the prime factors share a portion of their most significant bits, the prime difference may satisfy $|p - q| < N^\sigma$ for some $\sigma < \frac{1}{2}$. In this case, our method extends the feasible range for the secret exponent to

$$d > N^{n-1-\frac{\sqrt{2}}{2}\sqrt{(n-1)\theta}},$$

which cannot be achieved by existing methods.

The organization of the paper is as follows. In Sect. 2, we review the necessary preliminaries. Section 3 introduces a novel method for the cryptanalysis of the Cotan-Teşeleanu scheme. In Sect. 4, we compare the proposed attack with existing approaches. Section 5 presents a detailed numerical example that validates the effectiveness of our method, and Sect. 6 concludes the paper.

2 Preliminaries

2.1 Useful Lemmas

Let $N = pq$ be an RSA modulus such that $q < p < 2q$. The result below provides explicit expressions bounding p and q in terms of N (see [13, Lemma 1]).

Lemma 1. *Let $N = pq$ denote the product of two unknown integers with $q < p < 2q$. Then*

$$\frac{\sqrt{2}}{2}\sqrt{N} < q < \sqrt{N} < p < \sqrt{2}\sqrt{N}.$$

The following lemma establishes an approximation for q as well as $p+q$ based on a given approximation of p (see [5, Lemma 3]).

Lemma 2. *Let $N = pq$ be an RSA modulus with $q < p < 2q$, and let p_0 be an approximation of p such that $|p - p_0| = N^\sigma$. Setting $q_0 = \left\lfloor \frac{N}{p_0} \right\rfloor$, we obtain an approximation of q satisfying*

$$|q - q_0| < N^\sigma, \quad |p + q - p_0 - q_0| < 2\,N^\sigma.$$

For the scheme of Cotan and Teşeleanu [4], the generalized totient function associated with $N = pq$ and $n \geq 2$ is defined by

$$\psi_n(N) = \frac{(p^n - 1)\,(q^n - 1)}{(p-1)(q-1)}.$$

The result below establishes explicit upper and lower bounds for $\psi_n(N)$ (see [19, Lemma 3]).

Lemma 3. *For any modulus $N = pq$, and $n \geq 2$, one finds that*

$$N^{n-1} < \psi_n(N) < 4N^{n-1}.$$

The following result gives a way to recursively compute $\psi_n(N)$ (see [14, Lemma 4]).

Lemma 4. *Let $N = pq$ and denote $S = p + q$. Then one has*

$$\psi_1(N) = 1, \qquad \psi_2(N) = N + 1 + S,$$

and for all integers $n \geq 3$, the sequence satisfies the recurrence relation

$$\psi_n(N) = N^{n-1} + 1 + S\,\psi_{n-1}(N) - N\,\psi_{n-2}(N).$$

The following result establishes that, for arbitrary integers p_0 and q_0, the function $\psi_n(N)$ can be represented as a polynomial in $p + q - p_0 - q_0$ (see [19, Lemma 6] for $M = p_0 + q_0$).

Lemma 5. *Let $N = pq$ be an RSA modulus satisfying $q < p < 2q$, and let p_0, q_0 be integers. For $n \geq 2$, there exist integer coefficients $\alpha_{n-2}, \ldots, \alpha_0$, depending only on N, n, p_0, and q_0, such that*

$$\psi_n(N) = (p + q - p_0 - q_0)^{n-1} + \sum_{j=0}^{n-2} \alpha_j (p + q - p_0 - q_0)^j.$$

2.2 The Cotan-Teşeleanu scheme

Before introducing the cryptosystem, we recall some algebraic structures that will be used throughout the construction. Let $(\mathbb{F}, +, \cdot)$ be a field, let n be a positive integer, and let $a \in \mathbb{F}$ be such that the polynomial $x^n - a$ is irreducible over $\mathbb{F}[x]$. We define the quotient

$$\mathbb{A}_n = \mathbb{F}[x]/(x^n - a),$$

whose elements can be represented as

$$\mathbb{A}_n = \{a_0 + a_1 x + \cdots + a_{n-1}x^{n-1} \mid a_0, \ldots, a_{n-1} \in \mathbb{F}\}.$$

For two elements

$$a(x) = \sum_{i=0}^{n-1} a_i x^i \quad \text{and} \quad b(x) = \sum_{i=0}^{n-1} b_i x^i,$$

in $\mathbb{A}_n$, multiplication is performed by considering the relation $x^n = a$. Explicitly, their product is given by

$$a(x) \circ \mathrm{b(x)} = \sum_{i=0}^{n-2} \left(\sum_{j=0}^{i} a_j b_{i-j} + a \sum_{j=i+1}^{n-1} a_j b_{i-j+n} \right) x^i + \sum_{j=0}^{n-1} a_j b_{n-1-j} x^{n-1}.$$

Let $\mathbb{A}_n^*$ denote the multiplicative group of invertible elements of $\mathbb{A}_n$. We consider the quotient group

$$\mathbb{B}_n = \mathbb{A}_n^*/\mathbb{F}^*.$$

An element of $\mathbb{B}_n$ is therefore an equivalence class of the form

$$[a_0 + \cdots + a_{n-1}x^{n-1}] = \{\gamma a_0 + \cdots + \gamma a_{n-1}x^{n-1} \mid \gamma \in \mathbb{F}^*\}.$$

Moreover, the set $\mathbb{B}_n$ admits the decomposition

$$\mathbb{B}_n = \bigcup_{k=0}^{n-1} \mathbb{B}_k,$$

where

$$\mathbb{B}_k = \{a_0 + a_1 x + \cdots + a_{k-1}x^{k-1} + x^k \mid a_0, \dots, a_{k-1} \in \mathbb{F}\}, \quad 0 \le k \le n-1.$$

In addition, the subsets $\mathbb{B}_i$ and $\mathbb{B}_j$ are disjoint whenever $i \neq j$.

Assume now that p is a prime number and let $\mathbb{F} = \mathbb{F}_p$. In this setting, $\mathbb{A}_n$ is the finite field with p^n elements. The quotient group $\mathbb{B}_n$ is cyclic and has cardinality

$$|\mathbb{B}_n| = \sum_{k=0}^{n-1} p^k = \frac{p^n - 1}{p - 1}.$$

For any positive integer m and any element $y \in \mathbb{B}_n$, we denote by y^m the repeated product of y with itself m times inside $\mathbb{B}_n$. Consequently, an analogue of Fermat's little theorem holds:

$$[a(x)]^{|\mathbb{B}_n|} \equiv 1 \pmod{p}, \qquad \forall\, [a(x)] \in \mathbb{B}_n.$$

Let $N = pq$, where p and q are two distinct prime numbers. The previous constructions and computations can then be naturally extended to the ring $\mathbb{Z}/N\mathbb{Z}$. In this case,

$$\psi_n(N) := |\mathbb{B}_n| = \frac{(p^n - 1)(q^n - 1)}{(p-1)(q-1)}.$$

Furthermore, every element $[a(x)] \in \mathbb{B}_n$ satisfies

$$[a(x)]^{|\mathbb{B}_n|} \equiv 1 \pmod{N}.$$

The cryptosystem proposed by Cotan and Teşeleanu is described below.

Key Generation

1. Choose an integer $n > 1$ together with a security parameter λ.
2. Generate two distinct prime numbers p and q, each having size approximately λ bits.
3. Compute

$$N = pq \quad \text{and} \quad \psi_n(N) = \frac{(p^n - 1)(q^n - 1)}{(p-1)(q-1)}.$$

4. Select an integer a such that the polynomial $x^n - a$ is irreducible over
$$\mathbb{Z}/p\mathbb{Z}[x], \qquad \mathbb{Z}/q\mathbb{Z}[x], \qquad \text{and} \qquad \mathbb{Z}/N\mathbb{Z}[x].$$
5. Choose a public exponent e satisfying
$$\gcd(e, \psi_n(N)) = 1,$$
and compute the private exponent d such that
$$ed \equiv 1 \pmod{\psi_n(N)}.$$
6. Publish the tuple (N, n, a, e) as the public key, while (p, q, d) forms the private key.

Encryption

1. Encode the plaintext as
$$m(x) = m_0 + m_1 x + \cdots + m_{n-2}x^{n-2} + x^{n-1} \in \mathbb{B}_n.$$
2. Compute the ciphertext
$$c(x) \equiv [m(x)]^e \pmod{N},$$
replacing x^n with a during the computation.
3. Output $c(x)$.

Decryption.

To recover the original message, compute
$$m(x) \equiv [c(x)]^d \pmod{N},$$
replacing x^n with a during the computation.

2.3 Lattice Reduction and Coppersmith's Method

Let λ and n be positive integers with $\lambda \leq n$, and let $x_1, x_2, \ldots, x_\lambda$ be linearly independent vectors in $\mathbb{R}^n$. The lattice $\mathcal{L} \subset \mathbb{R}^n$ generated by these vectors is defined as the set of all integer linear combinations of $x_1, \ldots, x_\lambda$, namely
$$\mathcal{L} = \mathbb{Z}x_1 + \mathbb{Z}x_2 + \cdots + \mathbb{Z}x_\lambda.$$
The lattice $\mathcal{L}$ generated by $x_1, \ldots, x_\lambda$ can be represented by a matrix $B \in \mathbb{R}^{\lambda \times n}$ whose rows consist of the vectors $x_1, \ldots, x_\lambda$. The ambient dimension of $\mathcal{L}$ is n, while its rank is λ. The determinant of the lattice is defined by $\det(\mathcal{L}) = \sqrt{\det(B^t B)}$, where B^t denotes the transpose of B.

In the common case where $\lambda = n$, the lattice $\mathcal{L}$ is said to be full-rank. In this situation, the determinant simplifies to $\det(\mathcal{L}) = |\det(B)|$.

A lattice $\mathcal{L}$ admits infinitely many distinct bases, and determining a basis consisting of relatively short vectors becomes computationally difficult as the dimension increases. In 1982, Lenstra, Lenstra, and Lovász [9] introduced the LLL algorithm, a polynomial-time lattice basis reduction algorithm that produces a reduced basis with provably short vectors. The following result (see [10, Theorem 4]) is commonly used to estimate the quality of the basis returned by the LLL algorithm.

Theorem 1. *Let $\mathcal{L}$ be a lattice generated by a basis $(x_1, x_2, \ldots, x_\lambda)$. The LLL algorithm outputs a reduced basis $(y_1, y_2, \ldots, y_\lambda)$ such that*

$$\|y_1\| \leq \cdots \leq \|y_i\| \leq 2^{\frac{\lambda(\lambda-1)}{4(\lambda+1-i)}} \det(\mathcal{L})^{\frac{1}{\lambda+1-i}}, \qquad \textit{for } i = 1, \ldots, \lambda.$$

2.4 Coppersmith's Method

In 1996, Coppersmith [3] introduced a technique to determine small integer solutions of univariate polynomial congruences $R(x) \equiv 0 \pmod{M}$, where M is a given integer. This approach has since then been generalized to multivariate polynomials of the form

$$R(x_1, x_2, \ldots, x_n) = \sum_{i_1, i_2, \ldots, i_n} \eta_{i_1, i_2, \ldots, i_n} x_1^{i_1} x_2^{i_2} \cdots x_n^{i_n}, \quad \eta_{i_1, i_2, \ldots, i_n} \in \mathbb{Z}.$$

For such polynomials, the Euclidean norm is defined as

$$\|R(x_1, \ldots, x_n)\| = \sqrt{\sum_{i_1, i_2, \ldots, i_n} \eta^2_{i_1, i_2, \ldots, i_n}}.$$

In 1997, Howgrave-Graham [6] presented a simplified formulation of Coppersmith's method, summarized in the following result (see [12, Theorem 4.2]).

Theorem 2 (Howgrave-Graham). *Let $R(x_1, x_2, \ldots, x_n) \in \mathbb{Z}[x_1, x_2, \ldots, x_n]$ be a multivariate polynomial with at most λ nonzero monomials, and let e and κ be positive integers. Suppose that there exist positive real numbers $X_1, \ldots, X_n$ and integers $r_1, \ldots, r_n$ such that*

1. $R(r_1, r_2, \ldots, r_n) \equiv 0 \pmod{e^\kappa}$.
2. $|r_i| < X_i$, $i = 1, \ldots, n$.
3. $\|R(x_1X_1, x_2X_2, \ldots, x_nX_n)\| < \frac{e^\kappa}{\sqrt{\lambda}}$.

Then $R(r_1, r_2, \ldots, r_n) = 0$ holds over the integers.

When the polynomial involves more than two variables, Coppersmith-based methods become heuristic in nature. In this work, we adopt the following widely used assumption [1,7,24].

Assumption 1. The polynomials $f_1, f_2, \ldots, f_\lambda$, whose coefficients are the components of the reduced vectors obtained from the LLL algorithm, are assumed to be algebraically independent. That is, the only polynomial P in $\mathbb{Z}[x_1, \ldots, x_\lambda]$ that satisfies $P(f_1, f_2, \ldots, f_\lambda) = 0$ is $P = 0$.

Under the preceding assumption, the common root $(r_1, r_2, \ldots, r_n)$ of the system of polynomial equations $f_i(x_1, x_2, \ldots, x_n) = 0$, $i = 1, \ldots, \lambda$, can be efficiently recovered using Gröbner basis methods or resultant-based techniques.

3 The Novel Lattice-Based Attack

In this section, we present a novel attack on the Cotan-Teşeleanu scheme [4], which is defined by the key equation $ed - k\,\psi_n(N) = 1$, under the assumption that the difference between the primes is sufficiently small.

Theorem 3. *Let (N, e) be an RSA modulus with $N = pq$, where $q < p < 2q$ and $|p - q| < N^\sigma$ for some positive parameter $\sigma \le \frac{1}{2}$. Suppose there exist positive integers k and d such that $ed - k\,\psi_n(N) = 1$, $\psi_n(N) = \frac{(p^n-1)(q^n-1)}{(p-1)(q-1)}$, with $e = N^\theta$ and $d \le N^\delta$. If $\theta \le \frac{n-1}{\sigma}$, and*

$$\delta < n - 1 - \sqrt{\theta\sigma(n-1)},$$

then, under Assumption 1, the modulus N can be factored in polynomial time.

Proof. Assume that the prime difference $p - q$ is sufficiently small and satisfies $p - q < N^\sigma$. By Lemma 1, the inequality $q < \sqrt{N} < p$ implies

$$0 < p - \sqrt{N} < p - q < N^\sigma,$$

which shows that $p_0 = \lfloor \sqrt{N} \rfloor \approx \sqrt{N}$ provides an approximation of p.

Applying Lemma 2, the prime q can then be approximated by

$$q_0 = \left\lfloor \frac{N}{p_0} \right\rfloor \approx \sqrt{N}.$$

Consequently, an approximation of the sum $p + q$ is given by

$$p_0 + q_0 \approx 2\sqrt{N},$$

and moreover,

$$|p + q - p_0 - q_0| < 2N^\sigma.$$

On the other hand, by applying Lemma 5, we obtain the expansion

$$\psi_n(N) = (p + q - p_0 - q_0)^{n-1} + \sum_{j=0}^{n-2} \alpha_j (p + q - p_0 - q_0)^j,$$

where the coefficients α_j are integers for $0 \leq j \leq n-2$. Setting

$$y_0 = p + q - p_0 - q_0,$$

we may rewrite $\psi_n(N)$ in the form $\psi_n(N) = B(y_0)$, where

$$B(y) = y^{n-1} + \sum_{j=0}^{n-2} \alpha_j y^j.$$

Assume that $ed - k\psi_n(N) = 1$. It follows that the triple $(z_0, x_0, y_0) = (d, k, y_0)$ is a solution to the equation $ez - xB(y) = 1$. To solve this equation and recover (d, k, y_0), we apply a variant of Coppersmith's method. We first rewrite the key equation in the reduced form

$$\xi(x, y) = xB(y) + 1 \equiv 0 \pmod{e},$$

and derive suitable bounds for each component of the small root.

Assume that $d < N^{\delta}$ and $e = N^{\theta}$. By Lemma 3, we have $\psi_n(N) > N^{n-1}$, which implies

$$|x_0| = \left| \frac{ed - 1}{\psi_n(N)} \right| < N^{\delta+\theta-n+1}.$$

Moreover, from the approximation of the prime sum, we obtain $|y_0| < 2N^{\sigma}$. Expanding $\xi(x, y)$, we get

$$\xi(x, y) = xB(y) + 1 = xy^{n-1} + x(\alpha_{n-2}y^{n-2} + \cdots + \alpha_1 y + \alpha_0) + 1.$$

We introduce the auxiliary variable $w = xy^{n-1} + 1$, so that $\xi(x, y)$ can be rewritten as the polynomial

$$\zeta(x, y, w) = w + x(\alpha_{n-2}y^{n-2} + \cdots + \alpha_1 y + \alpha_0).$$

Consequently, the corresponding value $w_0 = x_0 y_0^{n-1} + 1$ satisfies the bound

$$|w_0| < 2^{n-1} N^{\theta+\delta+(n-1)(\sigma-1)}.$$

Therefore, with the above parameters, the bounds on the small root (x_0, y_0, w_0) can be expressed in terms of N as

$$X = N^{\theta+\delta-n+1}, \; Y = 2N^{\sigma}, \; W = 2^{n-1} N^{\theta+\delta+(n-1)(\sigma-1)}. \tag{3}$$

In accordance with Coppersmith's method [3], we fix a positive integer κ together with a real parameter $\tau \in [0, 1]$, whose optimal value will be determined later. Next, we form the lattice $\mathcal{L}$ by taking the matrix whose rows are the coefficient vectors associated with the polynomials $\varrho_{a_1,a_2,a_3}(Xx, Yy, Ww)$, where

$$\varrho_{a_1,a_2,a_3}(x, y, w) = x^{a_2} y^{a_3} \zeta(x, y, w)^{a_1} e^{\kappa - a_1}, \quad (a_1, a_2, a_3) \in \mathcal{I}_1 \cup \mathcal{I}_2,$$

the term xy^{n-1} is replaced by $w-1$, and

$$\mathcal{I}_1 = \{(a_1, a_2, a_3) \mid a_1 = 0, \dots, \kappa - 1,\ a_2 = 1, \dots, \kappa - a_1,\ a_3 = 0, \dots, n-2\},$$
$$\mathcal{I}_2 = \{(a_1, a_2, a_3) \mid a_1 = 0, \dots, \kappa,\ a_2 = 0,\ a_3 = 0, \dots, \tau a_1\}.$$

Since $\zeta(x_0, y_0, w_0) \equiv 0 \pmod{e}$, it follows that

$$\varrho_{a_1,a_2,a_3}(x_0, y_0, w_0) \equiv 0 \pmod{e^\kappa},$$

for all index triples $(a_1, a_2, a_3) \in \mathcal{I}_1 \cup \mathcal{I}_2$.

In order to compute the lattice determinant efficiently, it is convenient to arrange the lattice basis matrix in triangular form. This configuration is obtained by carefully ordering the rows and columns. We follow the construction proposed in [7], which yields a lower triangular lattice basis matrix. With this structure, every row of the basis corresponds to a polynomial of the following type $\varrho_{a_1,a_2,a_3}(Xx, Yy, Ww)$. The polynomials $\varrho_{a_1,a_2,a_3}(Xx, Yy, Ww)$ are ordered so that $\varrho_{a_1,a_2,a_3}(Xx, Yy, Ww) \prec \varrho_{a'_1,a'_2,a'_3}(Xx, Yy, Ww)$ if $a_1 < a'_1$, or if $a_1 = a'_1$ and $a_2 < a'_2$, or if $a_1 = a'_1$, $a_2 = a'_2$ and $a_3 < a'_3$. In a similar manner, the columns, corresponding to the monomials $x^{a_2} y^{a_3} w^{a_1}$, are arranged according to the same lexicographic order on (a_1, a_2, a_3).

For illustration, Table 1 shows the structure of the lattice basis matrix for the parameters $\kappa = 2$, $\tau = 1$, and $n = 4$, where the symbol $\star$ denotes the positions of the nonzero entries.

Table 1. The lattice basis matrix corresponding to the parameters $(n, \kappa, \tau) = (4, 2, 1)$.

ϱ_{a_1,a_2,a_3}	1	x	xy	xy^2	x^2	x^2y	x^2y^2	w	yw	xw	xyw	xy^2w	w^2	yw^2	y^2w^2
$\varrho_{0,0,0}$	e^2	0	0	0	0	0	0	0	0	0	0	0	0	0	0
$\varrho_{0,1,0}$	0	e^2X	0	0	0	0	0	0	0	0	0	0	0	0	0
$\varrho_{0,1,1}$	0	0	e^2XY	0	0	0	0	0	0	0	0	0	0	0	0
$\varrho_{0,1,2}$	0	0	0	e^2XY^2	0	0	0	0	0	0	0	0	0	0	0
$\varrho_{0,2,0}$	0	0	0	0	e^2X^2	0	0	0	0	0	0	0	0	0	0
$\varrho_{0,2,1}$	0	0	0	0	0	e^2X^2Y	0	0	0	0	0	0	0	0	0
$\varrho_{0,2,2}$	0	0	0	0	0	0	$e^2X^2Y^2$	0	0	0	0	0	0	0	0
$\varrho_{1,0,0}$	0	$\star$	$\star$	$\star$	0	0	0	eW	0	0	0	0	0	0	0
$\varrho_{1,0,1}$	$\star$	0	$\star$	$\star$	0	0	0	$\star$	eYW	0	0	0	0	0	0
$\varrho_{1,1,0}$	0	0	0	0	$\star$	$\star$	$\star$	0	0	eXW	0	0	0	0	0
$\varrho_{1,1,1}$	0	$\star$	0	0	0	$\star$	$\star$	0	0	$\star$	$eXYW$	0	0	0	0
$\varrho_{1,1,2}$	0	$\star$	$\star$	0	0	0	$\star$	0	0	$\star$	$\star$	eXY^2W	0	0	0
$\varrho_{2,0,0}$	0	$\star$	$\star$	0	$\star$	$\star$	$\star$	0	0	$\star$	$\star$	$\star$	W^2	0	0
$\varrho_{2,0,1}$	0	$\star$	$\star$	$\star$	0	$\star$	$\star$	$\star$	0	$\star$	$\star$	$\star$	$\star$	YW^2	0
$\varrho_{2,0,2}$	$\star$	$\star$	$\star$	$\star$	0	0	$\star$	$\star$	$\star$	$\star$	$\star$	$\star$	$\star$	$\star$	Y^2W^2

By construction, the lattice basis matrix is lower triangular. Consequently, its determinant is equal to the product of the entries along the main diagonal.

It follows that the determinant of the lattice can be expressed in the form

$$\det(\mathcal{L}) = X^{n_X} Y^{n_Y} W^{n_W} e^{n_e}, \tag{4}$$

where the exponents are given by

$$\begin{aligned}
n_X &= \sum_{(a_1,a_2,a_3)\in\mathcal{I}_1} a_2 + \sum_{(a_1,a_2,a_3)\in\mathcal{I}_2} a_2,\\
n_Y &= \sum_{(a_1,a_2,a_3)\in\mathcal{I}_1} a_3 + \sum_{(a_1,a_2,a_3)\in\mathcal{I}_2} a_3,\\
n_W &= \sum_{(a_1,a_2,a_3)\in\mathcal{I}_1} a_1 + \sum_{(a_1,a_2,a_3)\in\mathcal{I}_2} a_1,\\
n_e &= \sum_{(a_1,a_2,a_3)\in\mathcal{I}_1} (\kappa - a_1) + \sum_{(a_1,a_2,a_3)\in\mathcal{I}_2} (\kappa - a_1).
\end{aligned}$$

or simply by

$$\begin{aligned}
n_X &= \sum_{a_1=0}^{\kappa-1}\sum_{a_2=1}^{\kappa-a_1}\sum_{a_3=0}^{n-2} a_2,\\
n_Y &= \sum_{a_1=0}^{\kappa-1}\sum_{a_2=1}^{\kappa-a_1}\sum_{a_3=0}^{n-2} a_3 + \sum_{a_1=0}^{\kappa}\sum_{a_3=0}^{\tau a_1} a_3,\\
n_W &= \sum_{a_1=0}^{\kappa-1}\sum_{a_2=1}^{\kappa-a_1}\sum_{a_3=0}^{n-2} a_1 + \sum_{a_1=0}^{\kappa}\sum_{a_3=0}^{\tau a_1} a_1,\\
n_e &= \sum_{a_1=0}^{\kappa-1}\sum_{a_2=1}^{\kappa-a_1}\sum_{a_3=0}^{n-2} (\kappa - a_1) + \sum_{a_1=0}^{\kappa}\sum_{a_3=0}^{\tau a_1} (\kappa - a_1).
\end{aligned}$$

Additionally, the dimension of the lattice, denoted by λ, is equal to the number of shift polynomials $\varrho_{a_1,a_2,a_3}(Xx, Yy, Ww)$ indexed by $(a_1, a_2, a_3) \in \mathcal{I}_1 \cup \mathcal{I}_2$. In other words, λ is the cardinality of the index set $\mathcal{I}_1 \cup \mathcal{I}_2$. Since $\mathcal{I}_1 \cap \mathcal{I}_2 = \emptyset$, we find that

$$\begin{aligned}
\lambda &= |\mathcal{I}_1 \cup \mathcal{I}_2| = |\mathcal{I}_1| + |\mathcal{I}_2|,\\
&= \sum_{a_1=0}^{\kappa-1}\sum_{a_2=1}^{\kappa-a_1}\sum_{a_3=0}^{n-2} 1 + \sum_{a_1=0}^{\kappa}\sum_{a_3=0}^{\tau a_1} 1,\\
&= (n-1)\sum_{a_1=0}^{\kappa-1} (\kappa - a_1) + \sum_{a_1=0}^{\kappa} (1 + \tau a_1).
\end{aligned}$$

It is then straightforward to verify that for sufficiently large κ, we have

$$\begin{aligned}
n_X &= \frac{1}{6}(n-1)\kappa^3 + o(\kappa^3),\\
n_Y &= \frac{1}{6}\tau^2\kappa^3 + o(\kappa^3),\\
n_W &= \frac{1}{6}(n+2\tau-1)\kappa^3 + o(\kappa^3),\\
n_e &= \frac{1}{6}(2n+\tau-2)\kappa^3 + o(\kappa^3),\\
\lambda &= \frac{1}{2}(n+\tau-1)\kappa^2 + o(\kappa^2).
\end{aligned} \tag{5}$$

By applying the LLL algorithm to the lattice $\mathcal{L}$, we obtain λ reduced polynomials

$$f_l(Xx, Yy, Ww), \quad l = 1, \ldots, \lambda,$$

which satisfy

$$f_l(x_0, y_0, w_0) \equiv 0 \pmod{e^\kappa}.$$

Noting that the determinant remains invariant under LLL reduction, we employ Theorem 2 together with Theorem 1 for $i = 3$ to extract integer solutions to the system $f_l(x, y, w) = 0$ by appropriately setting

$$2^{\frac{\lambda(\lambda-1)}{4(\lambda-2)}} \det(\mathcal{L})^{\frac{1}{\lambda-2}} < \frac{e^\kappa}{\sqrt{\lambda}}.$$

By virtue of (4), the expression simplifies to

$$X^{n_X} Y^{n_Y} W^{n_W} e^{n_e - \kappa(\lambda-2)} < \frac{1}{\lambda^{\frac{\lambda-2}{2}} 2^{\frac{\lambda(\lambda-1)}{4}}} < 1.$$

By applying the bounds (3) together with the dominant parts in (5), and omitting negligible contributions, we get

$$\begin{aligned}
&\sigma\tau^2 + 2(\sigma n + \delta - \sigma - n + 1)\tau + \theta n\\
&\qquad + 2\delta n - 2\sigma n - 2n^2 - \theta - 2\delta + \sigma + 4n - 2 + \sigma n^2 < 0.
\end{aligned} \tag{6}$$

The minimum of the left-hand side occurs at

$$\tau_0 = \frac{(1-\sigma)n - \delta + \sigma - 1}{\sigma}.$$

Inserting τ_0 into (6) yields

$$-\delta^2 + 2\delta(n-1) - \theta\sigma + \theta\sigma \, \mathrm{n} - n^2 + 2n - 1 < 0.$$

Solving the previous inequality for the variable δ leads to

$$\delta < n - 1 - \sqrt{\sigma\theta(n-1)}.$$

To guarantee that δ remains positive, we need

$$n - 1 - \sqrt{\sigma\theta(n-1)} > 0,$$

which leads to the constraint

$$\theta < \frac{n-1}{\sigma}.$$

Assuming that Assumption 1 is satisfied, the small root (x_0, y_0, w_0) can be computed by solving the integer system

$$f_1(x, y, w) = 0, \quad f_2(x, y, w) = 0, \quad f_3(x, y, w) = 0,$$

comprising three reduced, algebraically independent polynomials. This can be accomplished using Gröbner basis methods or resultants. Finally, the decryption exponent d is then determined via

$$d = \frac{1 + x_0 B(y_0)}{e}.$$

This completes the proof. □

Remark 1. The cryptanalytic attack presented in the proof of Theorem 3 relies on two fundamental computational tools. First, lattice basis reduction is carried out using the LLL algorithm, which enables the construction of short vectors from the underlying lattice. Second, once suitable polynomial relations are obtained from the reduced basis vectors, their solutions are recovered via Gröbner basis techniques. It is well known that the LLL algorithm runs in polynomial time with respect to both the lattice dimension and the size of the largest coefficients appearing in the basis matrix [15]. In contrast, the cost of computing a Gröbner basis is influenced by the total degree of the involved polynomials as well as the number of indeterminates. In the present setting, the derived polynomial system involves three indeterminates and remains of relatively low degree. Consequently, for smaller lattice dimensions, the use of Gröbner basis computations remains practical.

4 Comparison with Prior Cryptanalytic Attacks

4.1 Comparison with the Attack of Cotan-Teşeleanu

In 2022, Cotan and Teşeleanu [4] investigated an RSA variant defined by the key equation

$$ed - k\psi_n(N) = 1,$$

and demonstrated that, for parameters $e = N^\theta$ and $d = N^\delta$, the system becomes insecure whenever

$$\theta \leq n - \frac{1}{2} \quad \text{and} \quad \delta < \frac{2n-1}{4} - \frac{1}{2}\theta.$$

Setting $\sigma = \frac{1}{2}$ in Theorem 3, and denoting by $\mathfrak{D}$ the difference between our bound and theirs with respect to δ, a direct computation shows that

$$\mathfrak{D} = (n-1) - \sqrt{\frac{\theta(n-1)}{2}} - \frac{2n-1}{4} + \frac{\theta}{2}$$
$$= \frac{2n-3+2\theta}{4} - \sqrt{\frac{\theta(n-1)}{2}}.$$

To establish that $\mathfrak{D} \geq 0$, it suffices to show that

$$\frac{2n-3+2\theta}{4} \geq \sqrt{\frac{\theta(n-1)}{2}},$$

or equivalently

$$\left(\frac{2n-3+2\theta}{4}\right)^2 \geq \left(\sqrt{\frac{\theta(n-1)}{2}}\right)^2.$$

This means that

$$(2n-3+2\theta)^2 \geq 8\theta(n-1).$$

We define the difference $\mathfrak{D}'$ as follows:

$$\begin{aligned}\mathfrak{D}' &= (2n-3+2\theta)^2 - 8\theta(n-1)\\ &= 4\theta^2 + 4\theta(2n-3) + (2n-3)^2 - 8\theta(n-1)\\ &= 4\theta^2 + 4\theta[(2n-3) - 2(n-1)] + (2n-3)^2\\ &= 4\theta^2 - 4\theta + (2n-3)^2\\ &= 4(\theta - \frac{1}{2})^2 + (2n-3)^2 - 1.\end{aligned}$$

This ensures that $\mathfrak{D}' \geq 0$, and hence $\mathfrak{D} \geq 0$, and shows that our bound is larger than the bound of Cotan and Teşeleanu.

4.2 Comparison with the Attack of Nitaj et al.

In 2024, Nitaj et al. [14] proposed a new attack on the scheme of Cotan and Teşeleanu, improving the bound obtained in [4]. They showed that the scheme can be broken for parameters $e = N^\theta$ and $d = N^\delta$ whenever

$$\frac{n-1}{2} \leq \theta \leq 2(n-1) \quad \text{and} \quad \delta < n - 1 - \frac{\sqrt{2}}{2}\sqrt{(n-1)\theta}.$$

By setting $\sigma = \frac{1}{2}$ in Theorem 3, one recovers their bound on δ, which indicates that their method arises as a particular case of our general framework.

Furthermore, for $\sigma < \frac{1}{2}$, let $\mathfrak{D}$ denote the difference between our bound and theirs with respect to δ. Then

$$\begin{aligned}\mathfrak{D} &= \left(n - 1 - \sqrt{\sigma\theta(n-1)}\right) - \left(n - 1 - \frac{\sqrt{2}}{2}\sqrt{(n-1)\theta}\right) \\ &= \left(\sqrt{\frac{1}{2}} - \sqrt{\sigma}\right)\sqrt{\theta(n-1)} > 0.\end{aligned}$$

This shows that our bound is strictly stronger than the bound established by Nitaj et al. when $\sigma < \frac{1}{2}$.

5 A Detailed Numerical Experiment

In this section, we validate the effectiveness of our proposed attack described in Theorem 3 and demonstrate that previous attacks fail to compromise the scheme under our experimental instances. We also observe that our approach achieves improved bounds as the proportion of shared most significant bits between the primes increases.

The experiment was conducted using SageMath 10.4 on a PC running Ubuntu 22.04.3 LTS with an Intel(R) Core(TM) i5-4460 CPU @ 3.20 GHz × 4 and 8 GB of RAM.

For $n = 4$, we consider

$$\begin{aligned}N =\, &4848704785999048826669152526146177165177734809337416779859809908\backslash\\ &7280317660610696782639272393880426132527549645941971193562236436\backslash\\ &3916058967180141263132709044977419824570038605026526074450183613\backslash\\ &8940078076859173363415047635293069773986191316186413659016412619\backslash\\ &833244348082741252206762692533746870312537861,\\ e =\, &3981159396268734835229476383263156542809828632236010854524454332\backslash\\ &3397355485690267430027087485845085382657276013126454119469674521\backslash\\ &6594360582033924641057323275436463537971653262757996099557069208\backslash\\ &5620285124297940984861957832587259940115967082673998228013770587\backslash\\ &5496615568729821073662864990219394845108064865510565394873549108\backslash\\ &0578486947494040342765998094234598705729073441023001543650650883\backslash\\ &6890538519318401965549427750299108746806746139951609207918211582\backslash\\ &8627290202936290707415119521402498477402443292235702037672500409\backslash\\ &6177565057859331504433398189186644355879953723886707488750902146\backslash\\ &6576822241843132371335886040272430958799909599893269236473363901\backslash\\ &8189171449835207932278795984472468936455021631184173590721908241\backslash\\ &0990709415763765200946476759782948452294222000924218056427780395\backslash\\ &6783094057818671857176529012068073189547704763381373965709050011\backslash\\ &4766942481258423512684111534278154338379272062030607588259417263\backslash\\ &920943.\end{aligned}$$

Then $e = N^\theta$, where $\theta \approx 2.9756$.

The objective is to recover the unknown parameters p, q, k, and d in the key equation

$$ed - k\psi_n(N) = 1.$$

To achieve this, we adopt the approach outlined in the proof of Theorem 3. Specifically, we transform the key equation into the modular relation

$$\xi(x_0, y_0) \equiv 0 \pmod{e},$$

or equivalently,

$$\zeta(x_0, y_0, w_0) \equiv 0 \pmod{e},$$

where, following the derivation in Theorem 3, we define

$$\begin{aligned}
p_0 &= \lfloor\sqrt{N}\rfloor, \\
q_0 &= \left\lfloor \frac{N}{p_0} \right\rfloor, \\
x_0 &= k, \\
y_0 &= p + q - p_0 - q_0, \\
w_0 &= x_0 y_0^{n-1} + 1, \\
\xi(x, y) &= x(y^3 + \alpha_2 y^2 + \alpha_1 y + \alpha_0) + 1, \\
\zeta(x, y, w) &= w + x(\alpha_2 y^2 + \alpha_1 y + \alpha_0).
\end{aligned}$$

The coefficients α_j are determined according to Lemma 4, namely

$$\begin{aligned}
\alpha_2 &= N + 3p_0 + 3q_0 + 1, \\
\alpha_1 &= N^2 + 2Np_0 + 3p_0^2 + 2Nq_0 + 6p_0q_0 + 3q_0^2 - 2N + 2p_0 + 2q_0 + 1, \\
\alpha_0 &= N^2p_0 + Np_0^2 + p_0^3 + N^2q_0 + 2Np_0q_0 + 3p_0^2q_0 + Nq_0^2 + 3p_0q_0^2 + q_0^3 \\
&\quad + N^3 - N^2 - 2Np_0 + p_0^2 - 2Nq_0 + 2p_0q_0 + q_0^2 - N + p_0 + q_0 + 1.
\end{aligned}$$

Assume that $d < N^\delta$ and $p - q < N^\sigma$. We choose the parameters $\delta = 0.9$ and $\sigma = 0.33$ such that all the conditions of Theorem 3 are satisfied, namely

$$\delta < n - 1 - \sqrt{(n-1)\theta\sigma} \approx 1.2769, \qquad \theta < \frac{n-1}{\sigma} \approx 9.0909\,.$$

Under these constraints, the hypotheses of Theorem 3 hold. We then proceed to construct the corresponding lattice by selecting the bounds

$$
\begin{aligned}
X = \lfloor 2N^{\theta+\delta-n+1} \rfloor = {} & 41438835115406797877264277170136056443443231151 48\backslash\\
& 32993080556764740462116419510221258972565452025786338663019673 9030\backslash\\
& 84838297616284838077410542107453140120643378144713605700492109 9404\backslash\\
& 88581410539913420473549518950769012609490823301483930042522743 2525\backslash\\
& 6488405133806526854594 56,\\
Y = \lfloor 2N^{\sigma} \rfloor = {} & 33673362901327055438056522249422095220282925319332732 54\backslash\\
& 77340812249970375315472417758746433244102 6560,\\
W = XY^{n-1} = {} & 158222051367489799589732746010050837113651760048105017\backslash\\
& 545763470801704088375581102597227080520497239523681837857294309905\backslash\\
& 643763125973155551470075561791138363153338671473545439927967355300\backslash\\
& 150162034904910856740209551928521109279839830636813345834473544864\backslash\\
& 028886015832697075060309159564179117993424041861200808579618176787\backslash\\
& 547507780469887505807728763474311065434672801044196889463100459611\backslash\\
& 898151422502539183948661525563685136280887887989149369464991012709\backslash\\
& 823348206610323143099099705145111462651891262108036311612663739657\backslash\\
& 1568058831540532022614308183052579022485444320296960 00.
\end{aligned}
$$

For the parameter choices $\kappa = 3$ and $\tau = 1$, the resulting lattice $\mathcal{L}$ has dimension $\lambda = 28$. Its basis is formed from the coefficient vectors of the polynomials

$$\varrho_{a_1,a_2,a_3}(x, y, w) = x^{a_2} y^{a_3} \zeta(x, y, w)^{a_1} e^{\kappa - a_1}, \quad (a_1, a_2, a_3) \in \mathcal{I}_1 \cup \mathcal{I}_2,$$

where

$$
\begin{aligned}
\mathcal{I}_1 &= \{(a_1, a_2, a_3) \mid a_1 = 0, \ldots, \kappa - 1,\ a_2 = 1, \ldots, \kappa - a_1,\ a_3 = 0, \ldots, n - 2\},\\
\mathcal{I}_2 &= \{(a_1, a_2, a_3) \mid a_1 = 0, \ldots, \kappa,\ a_2 = 0,\ a_3 = 0, \ldots, \tau a_1\},
\end{aligned}
$$

and replacing each occurrence xy^{n-1} with $w - 1$.

Applying the LLL algorithm, we obtain 28 reduced polynomials. Subsequently, using Gröbner basis techniques, we select three of them and solve the resulting system over the integers. This leads to the following solution:

$$\begin{aligned}
x_0 =& 2381357243776933994468971902156088954114935486574798813622993268 1\backslash\\
&3411046460184157870152784791631932433179335159769437703094786328 1\backslash\\
&1888212889909138280829378464838768415615334622873887244478849954 0\backslash\\
&5121459359061420629325691880345204979666410529315756404901331613 3\backslash\\
&68405550534,\\
y_0 =& 123941673600612791873306526748843874559613869604,\\
w_0 =& 4533948892374561207701307186293883388285555277147712077999778963 5\backslash\\
&8166704352980014303721688518011869523680586057196285271725314716 6\backslash\\
&1801476789326144421621871288190317298030103060691912398841782886 9\backslash\\
&4532729928131552567484713310465221646057176208678121407102354610 1\backslash\\
&1292138505890686543467783684524708905309392230580842922493757271 8\backslash\\
&2429758978478268908041812300644129920075776981831792778118019917 7\backslash\\
&7197963513275382101377.
\end{aligned}$$

The value of d can then be computed using

$$d = \frac{x_0(y_0^3 + b_2 y_0^2 + b_1 y_0 + b_0) + 1}{e},$$

that is

$$\begin{aligned}
d =& 6818552900909234572287137633080273392142664246599377056532326306 4\backslash\\
&7878501565470809736102994082829546579164059067436281967725814676 6\backslash\\
&7001094540529556450451012037134510342460311787424059729439359618 2\backslash\\
&1446715543301535226255501868669761952179120519108517935422184917 9\backslash\\
&13301493807.
\end{aligned}$$

The combined execution time of the LLL algorithm and the Gröbner basis method was under 18 s. From $N = pq$ and $y_0 + p_0 + q_0 = p + q$, we compute

$$\begin{aligned}
p =& 2201977471728321026754660426798983897495233445464842369585727161 22\backslash\\
&3775769202344372649186482556030085158205483918350011995468348927 97\backslash\\
&1437579471943773673,\\
q =& 2201977471728321026754660426798983897495233445464841324756988894 79\backslash\\
&5450448433565617224844452794713269270255373503135335642142979974 55\backslash\\
&1096014931975674557.
\end{aligned}$$

Observe that the condition derived by Cotan and Teşeleanu [4] for breaking the system is

$$d < N^{\frac{2n-1}{4} - \frac{1}{2}\theta}.$$

In our numerical example, however, we obtain

$$\frac{d}{N^{\frac{2n-1}{4}-\frac{1}{2}\theta}} \approx 3.2504 \times 10^{195},$$

which is significantly greater than 1. Hence, the attack of Cotan and Teşeleanu does not succeed for this instance.

Similarly, the optimal bound on small decryption exponent attacks is established by Nitaj et al. [14] and is

$$d < N^{n-1-\frac{\sqrt{2}}{2}\sqrt{(n-1)\theta}}.$$

For our parameters, we find

$$\frac{d}{N^{n-1-\frac{\sqrt{2}}{2}\sqrt{\theta(n-1)}}} \approx 3.31919 \times 10^{6},$$

which again far exceeds 1. Therefore, the method of Nitaj et al. is likewise ineffective for this example.

More examples illustrating Theorem 3 for large values of N and e are provided in Appendix A.

6 Conclusion

In this paper, we presented a lattice-based attack on the RSA variant, propose by Cotan and Teşeleanu, which is defined by the key equation $ed \equiv 1 \pmod{\frac{(p^n-1)(q^n-1)}{(p-1)(q-1)}}$. Our approach is built upon Coppersmith's method and lattice basis reduction techniques. When the difference between the primes was sufficiently small, especially when the prime factors shared a significant portion of their most significant bits, the proposed attack enabled the factorization of the RSA modulus $N = pq$ in polynomial time, thereby compromising the scheme of Cotan and Teşeleanu. Moreover, we demonstrated that our results extended previous attacks in the literature, particularly those targeting small private exponents, by establishing improved bounds under comparable parameter settings.

A Experiments for Theorem 3 with Large Values of *N* and *e*

We implemented the attack described in Theorem 3 for the case $n = 4$, using large public keys (N, e). In each experiment, we solve the equation

$$ed - k\psi_4(N) = 1,$$

using the same approach as described in Sect. 5. We show that, in all instances, a lattice of dimension 28 ($m = 3$ and $\tau = 1$) enables the recovery of the factorization $N = pq$ within a practical running time. The results of our experiments are presented in Table 2. While the optimal bound for small private exponent attacks on such variants is given by Nitaj et al. [14], namely

$$d < N^{n-1-\frac{\sqrt{2}}{2}\sqrt{(n-1)\theta}},$$

in our instances we also have

$$d > N^{n-1-\frac{\sqrt{2}}{2}\sqrt{(n-1)\theta}},$$

which means that existing attacks cannot be applied to break the system in these cases.

The parameters appearing in the table are defined as follows.

- $\text{len}(x) = \lfloor \log_2(x) \rfloor + 1$ denotes the binary length of the integer x.
- δ is the parameter satisfying $d < N^{\delta}$.
- α is determined from $e = N^{\theta}$.
- σ satisfies $|p - q| \leq N^{\sigma}$.
- Time 1 is the running time (in seconds) required for the LLL reduction phase.
- Time 2 is the running time (in seconds) required for the Gröbner basis computations.

Table 2. Experimental results corresponding to different public keys (N, e).

len(N)	len(e)	δ	θ	σ	Time 1	Time 2
1024	3068	0.8982	2.997	0.3028	14	6
1100	3294	0.8916	2.998	0.2899	18	7
1200	3599	0.9161	2.999	0.2982	17	7
1300	3898	0.8850	2.999	0.3062	19	8
1400	4194	0.8940	2.999	0.3121	26	10
1500	4497	0.9001	2.999	0.3168	27	10
1600	4795	0.9064	2.998	0.3245	31	12
1700	5099	0.9113	2.999	0.3235	32	12
1800	5396	0.9172	2.999	0.3219	37	13
1900	5696	0.9214	2.999	0.3210	36	14
2048	6142	0.9035	2.999	0.3279	42	15

References

1. Boneh, D., Durfee, G.: Cryptanalysis of RSA with private key d less than $N^{0.292}$. In: Stern, J. (ed.) EUROCRYPT 1999. LNCS, vol. 1592, pp. 1–11. Springer, Heidelberg (1999). https://doi.org/10.1007/3-540-48910-X_1
2. Boudabra, M., Nitaj, A.: A new generalization of the KMOV cryptosystem. J. Appl. Math. Comput. **57**(12), 229–245 (2018)

3. Coppersmith, D.: Small solutions to polynomial equations, and low exponent RSA vulnerabilities. J. Cryptol. **10**(4), 233–260 (1997)
4. Cotan, P., Teşeleanu, G.: Continued fractions applied to a family of RSA-like cryptosystems. In: Su, C., Gritzalis, D., Piuri, V. (eds.) Information Security Practice and Experience. ISPEC 2022. LNCS, vol. 13620, pp. 589–605. Springer, Cham (2022). https://doi.org/10.1007/978-3-031-21280-2_33
5. Feng, Y., Nitaj, A., Pan, Y.: Partial prime factor exposure attacks on some RSA variants. Theoret. Comput. Sci. **999**, 114549 (2024)
6. Howgrave-Graham, N.: Finding small roots of univariate modular equations revisited. In: Darnell, M. (ed.) Cryptography and Coding 1997. LNCS, vol. 1355, pp. 131–142. Springer, Heidelberg (1997). https://doi.org/10.1007/BFb0024458
7. Jochemsz, E., May, A.: A strategy for finding roots of multivariate polynomials with new applications in attacking RSA variants. In: Lai, X., Chen, K. (eds.) ASIACRYPT 2006. LNCS, vol. 4284, pp. 267–282. Springer, Heidelberg (2006). https://doi.org/10.1007/11935230_18
8. Koyama, K., Maurer, U.M., Okamoto, T., Vanstone, S.A.: New public-key schemes based on elliptic curves over the ring Z_n. In: Feigenbaum, J. (ed.) CRYPTO 1991. LNCS, vol. 576, pp. 252–266. Springer, Heidelberg (1992). https://doi.org/10.1007/3-540-46766-1_20
9. Lenstra, A.K., Lenstra, H.W., Lovász, L.: Factoring polynomials with rational coefficients. Math. Ann. **261**, 513–534 (1982)
10. May, A.: New RSA vulnerabilities using lattice reduction methods. Ph.D. thesis, University of Paderborn (2003)
11. Murru, N., Saettone, F.M.: A novel RSA-like cryptosystem based on a generalization of the Rédei rational functions. In: Kaczorowski, J., Pieprzyk, J., Pomykała, J. (eds.) NuTMiC 2017. LNCS, vol. 10737, pp. 91–103. Springer, Cham (2018). https://doi.org/10.1007/978-3-319-76620-1_6
12. Nitaj, A.: Diophantine and lattice cryptanalysis of the RSA cryptosystem. In: Artificial Intelligence, Evolutionary Computing and Metaheuristics: In the Footsteps of Alan Turing, pp. 139–168. Springer, Heidelberg (2013). https://doi.org/10.1007/978-3-642-29694-9_7
13. Nitaj, A.: Another generalization of Wiener's attack on RSA. In: Vaudenay, S. (ed.) AFRICACRYPT 2008. LNCS, vol. 5023, pp. 174–190. Springer, Heidelberg (2008). https://doi.org/10.1007/978-3-540-68164-9_12
14. Nitaj, A., Adenan, N.N.H., Ariffin, M.R.K.: Cryptanalysis of a new variant of the RSA cryptosystem. In: Vaudenay, S., Petit, C. (eds.) AFRICACRYPT 2024. LNCS, vol. 14861, pp. 327–345. Springer, Cham (2024). https://doi.org/10.1007/978-3-031-64381-1_15
15. Nguyen, P.Q., Stehlé, D.: An LLL algorithm with quadratic complexity. SIAM J. Comput. **39**, 874–903 (2009)
16. Quisquater, J.J., Couvreur, C.: Fast decipherment algorithm for RSA public-key cryptosystem. Electron. Lett. **18**(21), 905–907 (1982)
17. Rivest, R., Shamir, A., Adleman, L.: A Method for Obtaining digital signatures and public-key cryptosystems. Commun. ACM **21**(2), 120–126 (1978)
18. Rahmani, M., Nitaj, A., Ziane, M.: Further cryptanalysis of some variants of the RSA cryptosystem. J. Appl. Math. Comput, 1–31 (2024)
19. Rahmani, M., Nitaj, A., Ziane, M.: Partial exposure attacks on new RSA variant. Cryptography **8**(44), 2024 (2024)
20. Takagi, T.: A fast RSA-type public-key primitive modulo $p^k q$ using Hensel lifting. IEICE Trans. Fundam. Electron. Commun. Comput. Sci. **87**(1), 94–101 (2004)

21. Teseleanu, G.: A lattice attack against a family of RSA-like cryptosystems. Cryptology ePrint Archive, Report 2024/1313 (2024)
22. Collins, T., Hopkins, D., Langford, S., Sabin, M.: Public key cryptographic apparatus and Method. US Patent #5,848,159, January 1997 (1997)
23. Wiener, M.: Cryptanalysis of short RSA secret exponents. IEEE Trans. Inf. Theory **36**(3), 553–558 (1990)
24. Zheng, M., Kunihiro, N., Yao, Y.: Cryptanalysis of the RSA variant based on cubic Pell equation. Theor. Comput. Sci. **889**, 135–144 (2021)

Advanced Signatures

On the Properties of HighBits and LowBits Functions and Their Applications

Alice Pellet-Mary[1](✉) and Michel Seck[2]

[1] Univ Bordeaux, CNRS, Inria, Bordeaux INP, IMB, UMR 5251, Talence, France
alice.pellet-mary@math.u-bordeaux.fr
[2] Ecole Polytechnique de Thies, CRISIN'2D, LTISI, Thies, Senegal
mseck@ept.edu.sn

Abstract. ML-DSA is a lattice-based signature scheme that has recently been standardized by NIST as FIPS 204. Among the many subroutines used by ML-DSA are the high bits (Hb) and low bits (Lb) functions, which, as their name suggest, return only the higher bits or the lower bits of some integer. Recently, Seck and Roux-Langlois (IACR CiC 2025) conjectured that the high bits of a sum of two integers t and r can be expressed as the sum of the high bits of each integer, plus an error term that can take at most seven different values. In this paper, we study the properties of the functions Hb and Lb and we prove that the conjecture of Seck and Roux-Langlois holds. In addition, we provide a complete characterization of the error term. As an application, we explain how these properties can be used to design lattice-based signature schemes with advanced features.

Keywords: HighBits · LowBits · ML-DSA · Advanced Signature Schemes

1 Introduction

Most of the widely used public-key cryptographic schemes in the last decades such as ECDSA [16] and RSA [21] are based on the hardness of problems like integer factorization and discrete logarithm. However, these two problems can be efficiently solved using Shor's algorithm [23] on a sufficiently large quantum computer. To address this issue, new cryptographic schemes have been developed, with the hope that they would remain secure against quantum attacks: this is known as post-quantum cryptography. Since December 2016, NIST (National Institute of Standards and Technology) [17] has been leading an effort to standardize post-quantum cryptographic algorithms. In 2024, they announced the selection of several algorithms for standardization, including ML-DSA [18], a lattice-based signature scheme build on top of CRYSTALS-Dilithium [1,9,12], as a winner of the signature category and ML-KEM [19], a lattice-based key

N. El Mrabet et al. (Eds.): AFRICACRYPT 2026, LNCS 16832, pp. 341–362, 2026.
https://doi.org/10.1007/978-3-032-31130-6_14

encapsulation mechanism build on top of CRYSTALS-Kyber [5], as a winner of the KEM category.

In the NIST's standard ML-DSA [18], a function high bits (which we will denote Hb in this article, and corresponds to the first part of the function Power2Round in [1, Fig. 3]) is used to compress the public key. More precisely, a public key pk is in the form $(\rho, \mathsf{Hb}(t))$ instead of (ρ, t) where $t = \mathbf{A}s_1 + s_2$ is an instance of Module learning with errors (MLWE) problem and ρ is a seed used to generate the matrix $\mathbf{A}$. This compression technique was introduced by Bai and Galbraith [2] and is used in many other lattice-based signature schemes such as HAETAE [8] a winner of the KpqC [3] competition, and Racoon [20], that was submitted to the NIST's standardization process for additional post-quantum primitives. The high bits and low bits functions are also used in the design of signature schemes with advanced features such as signature schemes with rerandomizable keys [22] and threshold signatures [4,11].

In 2023, Boudgoust and Takahashi [6] pointed out some vulnerabilities in the Dilithium based multi-signature scheme by Fukumitsu and Hasegawa [15], describing how to mount a (partial) secret-key recovery attack. They proposed a fix to this attack using the high bits function Hb but the non-linearity of Hb (i.e. $\mathsf{Hb}(t+r) \neq \mathsf{Hb}(t) + \mathsf{Hb}(r)$ in general) introduced other challenges. In 2024, Snetkov *et al.* [24] designed an efficient lattice-based two party threshold signature scheme on top of Dilithium, thanks to the properties of the high bits functions.

Recently, Seck and Roux-Langlois [22] constructed Dilithium-RK, an advanced signature scheme build on top of Dilithium with non-compressed public keys. For the compression of the public keys, they conjectured that

$$\mathsf{Hb}(t + r) = \mathsf{Hb}((\mathsf{Hb}(t) + \mathsf{Hb}(r))\alpha) + \varepsilon, \tag{1}$$

where ε is an error term that can take at most seven different values, and where α is a parameter of the Hb function (the low bits of an integer t correspond to $t \bmod {}^{\pm}(\alpha)$). In this paper, we study the properties of the functions Hb and Lb and give a positive answer to the conjecture of Seck and Roux-Langlois [22]. Note that the function Hb depends on the choice of two parameters q and α, which are chosen respectively as a prime integer and a power-of-two in Dilithium. Our proof holds for arbitrary positive integers q and α, as long as $q > \alpha$.

Contributions. Our main contributions can be summarized as follows:

1. We prove in Lemma 3.1 that the high bits (resp. the low bits) of a sum of two integers can be expressed as the sum of the high bits (resp. the low bits) of each integer, plus an error term that can take at most six different values. More precisely, we show that for any integers t and r, we have $\mathsf{Hb}(t + r) = \mathsf{Hb}(t) + \mathsf{Hb}(r) + t^h$ and $\mathsf{Lb}(t + r) = \mathsf{Lb}(t) + \mathsf{Lb}(r) + t^l$, where t^h

and t^l can take at most the six different values, which we specify depending on the choice of the parameters q and α. We extend this result to the case of a sum of n integers $t_1, t_2, \ldots, t_n$ in Theorems 3.3 and 3.4.

2. We prove in Theorem 3.6 that the conjecture of Seck and Roux-Langlois [22] holds. More specifically, $\mathsf{Hb}(t+r) = \mathsf{Hb}((\mathsf{Hb}(t) + \mathsf{Hb}(r))\alpha) + \varepsilon$ where ε is an error term that can take at most seven different values. Furthermore, we provide a complete characterization of the error term ε depending on the choice of the parameters q and α.

3. We show how these properties can be used to design a lattice-based signature scheme with advanced features such as rerandomization of both public and secret keys on top of ML-DSA.

Paper Organization. The rest of the paper is organized as follows. In Sect. 2, we introduce necessary notations and definitions used in the paper. In Sect. 3, we present our main contributions. First, we prove some properties of the Hb and Lb functions and then we prove that the conjecture of Seck and Roux-Langlois [22] holds. The last Sect. 4 is dedicated to one application of these properties in the design of a lattice-based signature scheme with rerandimizable keys.

2 Preliminaries

For two finite sets of integers S_1 and S_2, we define $S = S_1 + S_2$ as the set

$$S = \{s_1 + s_2 \mid s_1 \in S_1, s_2 \in S_2\}.$$

Let $n > 0$ be an integer. For an integer r, we define $r' = r \bmod {}^{\pm}(n)$ to be the unique integer r' in the interval $(-\frac{n}{2}, \frac{n}{2}]$ such that $r' \equiv r \pmod{n}$. We also define $r' = r \bmod {}^{+}(n)$ to be the unique integer r' in the range $0 \leq r' < n$ such that $r' \equiv r \pmod{n}$.

Definition 2.1 (Power2Round, Hb, and Lb). *Let q, α be two positive integers such that $q > \alpha$. For any integer $r \in \mathbb{Z}$, we define the function lower bits $\mathsf{Lb}_{q,\alpha}(r) = r_0 := r_q \bmod {}^{\pm}(\alpha)$, where $r_q = r \bmod {}^{+}(q)$. We also define the function higher bits $\mathsf{Hb}_{q,\alpha}(r) = r_1 := (r_q - r_0)/\alpha$, where r_q and r_0 are as before. The function $\mathsf{Power2Round}_{q,\alpha} : \mathbb{Z} \to \mathbb{Z} \times \mathbb{Z}$ is defined as*

$$\mathsf{Power2Round}_{q,\alpha}(r) = (\mathsf{Hb}_{q,\alpha}(r), \mathsf{Lb}_{q,\alpha}(r))$$

If the parameters q and α are clear from the context, we simply denote these functions by Hb, Lb *and* Power2Round *respectively.*

Remark 2.2. Notice that if we have two integers $r, r' \in \mathbb{Z}$ such that $r = r' \bmod q$, then $\mathsf{Hb}_{q,\alpha}(r) = \mathsf{Hb}_{q,\alpha}(r')$ and $\mathsf{Lb}_{q,\alpha}(r) = \mathsf{Lb}_{q,\alpha}(r')$. So we can extend the functions $\mathsf{Hb}_{q,\alpha}(\cdot)$ and $\mathsf{Lb}_{q,\alpha}(\cdot)$ to elements of $\mathbb{Z}_q$.

It is important to observe that the functions Hb and Lb defined above are *not* the same as the functions HighBits and LowBits from Dilithium [1, Fig. 3]. Indeed, Dilithium uses two very similar high-bits/low-bits decomposition functions, which differ only on a border case: the Power2Round and the Decompose functions. The functions HighBits and LowBits from [1, Fig. 3] correspond to the two components of the function Decompose. However, in this article, we are interested in the function Power2Round (which is the one used to compress the public key), and what we call Hb and Lb are the two components of this slightly different function.

3 Properties of Hb and Lb Functions

3.1 Hb and Lb of a Sum

In this section, we explore some important properties of the $\mathsf{Hb}(\cdot)$ and $\mathsf{Lb}(\cdot)$ functions from Definition 2.1. These properties will be useful in the design of advanced signature schemes based on the Dilithium framework. We are mainly interested in the relationship between $\mathsf{Hb}_{q,\alpha}(\sum t_i)$ (resp. $\mathsf{Lb}_{q,\alpha}(\sum t_i)$) and $\sum \mathsf{Hb}_{q,\alpha}(t_i)$ (resp. $\sum \mathsf{Lb}_{q,\alpha}(t_i)$) for a set of integers $\{t_i\}$.

Sum of 2 Elements. We start by proving a result in the case where we sum over two t_i's only. This will serve as the base case for the more general results stated in Theorems 3.3 and 3.4.

Lemma 3.1. *Let q and α be two positive integers such that $q > \alpha$. Define $q_0 = q \bmod {}^{\pm}(\alpha)$ and $q_1 = \frac{q-q_0}{\alpha}$ (i.e. $q = q_1\alpha + q_0$). For any integers $t, \hat{t} \in \mathbb{Z}$, the following properties hold:*

$$\mathsf{Hb}(t+\hat{t}) = \mathsf{Hb}(t) + \mathsf{Hb}(\hat{t}) + \varepsilon^h \textit{ and } \mathsf{Lb}(t+\hat{t}) = \mathsf{Lb}(t) + \mathsf{Lb}(\hat{t}) + \varepsilon^l,$$

where

$$\varepsilon^h \in \{-1, 0, 1, -q_1-1, -q_1, -q_1+1\} \textit{ and } \varepsilon^l \in \{-\alpha, 0, \alpha, -q_0-\alpha, -q_0, -q_0+\alpha\}.$$

Proof. Since $\mathsf{Hb}_{q,\alpha}(\cdot)$ and $\mathsf{Lb}_{q,\alpha}(\cdot)$ are invariant when we add integer multiples of q, we can assume without loss of generality that $t, \hat{t} \in [0, q)$. Define the sum $S = t + \hat{t} \bmod {}^{+}(q)$. We can write:

$$t = t_1\alpha + t_0, \quad \hat{t} = \hat{t}_1\alpha + \hat{t}_0,$$

where $t_1 = \mathsf{Hb}(t)$, $t_0 = \mathsf{Lb}(t)$, $\hat{t}_1 = \mathsf{Hb}(\hat{t})$ and $\hat{t}_0 = \mathsf{Lb}(\hat{t})$. Then, we have:

$$t + \hat{t} = (t_1 + \hat{t}_1)\alpha + (t_0 + \hat{t}_0).$$

Moreover, we have $t + \hat{t} \in [0, 2q)$, so there is an $\varepsilon \in \{0, 1\}$ such that

$$S = t + \hat{t} - \varepsilon q = (t_1 + \hat{t}_1 - \varepsilon q_1)\alpha + (t_0 + \hat{t}_0 - \varepsilon q_0).$$

Now, we need to consider the possible values of $A := t_0 + \hat{t}_0 - \varepsilon q_0 \in \left(-\frac{3\alpha}{2}, \frac{3\alpha}{2}\right)$:

– If $-\frac{\alpha}{2} < A \leq \frac{\alpha}{2}$, then

$$\mathsf{Hb}(S) = t_1 + \hat{t}_1 - \varepsilon q_1, \quad \mathsf{Lb}(S) = t_0 + \hat{t}_0 - \varepsilon q_0.$$

Then $\varepsilon^h = -\varepsilon q_1$ and $\varepsilon^l = -\varepsilon q_0$. Since $\varepsilon \in \{0, 1\}$, we have $\varepsilon^h \in \{0, -q_1\}$ and $\varepsilon^l \in \{0, -q_0\}$.

– If $\frac{\alpha}{2} < A \leq \frac{3\alpha}{2}$, then we will shift down A by α and get

$$S = (t_1 + \hat{t}_1 - \varepsilon q_1 + 1)\alpha + (t_0 + \hat{t}_0 - \varepsilon q_0 - \alpha).$$

Thus,

$$\mathsf{Hb}(S) = t_1 + \hat{t}_1 - \varepsilon q_1 + 1, \quad \mathsf{Lb}(S) = t_0 + \hat{t}_0 - \varepsilon q_0 - \alpha.$$

Then $\varepsilon^h = 1 - \varepsilon q_1$ and $\varepsilon^l = -\alpha - \varepsilon q_0$. Since $\varepsilon \in \{0, 1\}$, we have $\varepsilon^h \in \{1, 1 - q_1\}$ and $\varepsilon^l \in \{-\alpha, -\alpha - q_0\}$.

– If $-\frac{3\alpha}{2} < A \leq -\frac{\alpha}{2}$, then we will shift up A by α and get

$$S = (t_1 + \hat{t}_1 - \varepsilon q_1 - 1)\alpha + (t_0 + \hat{t}_0 - \varepsilon q_0 + \alpha).$$

Thus,

$$\mathsf{Hb}(S) = t_1 + \hat{t}_1 - \varepsilon q_1 - 1, \quad \mathsf{Lb}(S) = t_0 + \hat{t}_0 - \varepsilon q_0 + \alpha.$$

Then $\varepsilon^h = -1 - \varepsilon q_1$ and $\varepsilon^l = \alpha - \varepsilon q_0$. Since $\varepsilon \in \{0, 1\}$, we have $\varepsilon^h \in \{-1, -1 - q_1\}$ and $\varepsilon^l \in \{\alpha, \alpha - q_0\}$.

Combining all the cases, we conclude that

$$\varepsilon^h \in \{-1, 0, 1, -q_1 - 1, -q_1, -q_1 + 1\} \text{ and } \varepsilon^l \in \{-\alpha, 0, \alpha, -q_0 - \alpha, -q_0, -q_0 + \alpha\}.$$

□

Corollary 3.2 (Dilithium parameters). *Let d be a positive integer and q be a prime such that $q \equiv 1 \mod \alpha$ with $\alpha = 2^d$. For any integers $t, \hat{t} \in \mathbb{Z}_q$, the following properties hold:*

$$\mathsf{Hb}(t + \hat{t}) = \mathsf{Hb}(t) + \mathsf{Hb}(\hat{t}) + \varepsilon^h \text{ and } \mathsf{Lb}(t + \hat{t}) = \mathsf{Lb}(t) + \mathsf{Lb}(\hat{t}) + \varepsilon^l,$$

where

$$\varepsilon^h \in \left\{-1, 0, 1, \frac{1-q}{2^d}, \frac{1-q}{2^d} - 1, \frac{1-q}{2^d} + 1\right\}$$

and

$$\varepsilon^l \in \left\{-2^d, 0, 2^d, -2^d - 1, -1, 2^d - 1\right\}.$$

In particular, for Dilithium parameters where $d = 13$ and $q = 8380417$, we have

$$\varepsilon^h \in \{-1, 0, 1, -1024, -1023, -1022\} \text{ and } \varepsilon^l \in \{-8193, -8192, -1, 0, 8191, 8192\}.$$

Numerical Experiments. We ran some numerical experiments to verify the correctness of Lemma 3.1 and Corollary 3.2. For Lemma 3.1, We generated 10 random pairs (α, q), with $\alpha \leq 100$ and $200 \leq q \leq 500$. We also generated 8 additional pairs where α is a power-of-two and $q = 1 \bmod \alpha$. We then verified experimentally that for these pairs, the values of ε^h and ε^l achieved by running over all pairs $(t, \hat{t})$ in $[0, q) \times [0, q)$ were all contained in the sets described in Lemma 3.1. For Corollary 3.2, since it was too costly to check for all pairs $(t, \hat{t})$ in $[0, q) \times [0, q)$, we picked 10^5 random pairs $(t, \hat{t})$, and verified that for those pairs, ε^h and ε^l were indeed in the sets described in Corollary 3.2. All the tests were successful. The code used to perform these tests is available at https://github.com/funibus/africacrypt-2026-supplementary-material.git.

Sum of *n* Elements. Now that we have proven Lemma 3.1 for the sum of two elements, we can state and prove a more general result, where we sum over an arbitrary number n of elements.

Theorem 3.3. *Let q and α be two positive integers such that $q > \alpha$. Define $q_0 = q \bmod^{\pm}(\alpha)$ and $q_1 = \frac{q - q_0}{\alpha}$ (i.e. $q = q_1\alpha + q_0$). For any integers $t_1, t_2, \ldots, t_n \in \mathbb{Z}$, the following property holds:*

$$\mathsf{Hb}(\sum_{i=1}^{n} t_i) = \sum_{i=1}^{n} \mathsf{Hb}(t_i) + E_n^h$$

where

$$E_n^h \in \{-(n-1), \ldots, 0, \ldots, (n-1)\} + \{0, -q_1, -2q_1, \ldots, -(n-1)q_1\}\,.$$

Proof. We prove the theorem by induction on n.

- **Base case:** For $n = 2$, the result holds by the previous Lemma 3.1.
- **Inductive step:** Assume the result holds for some $k \geq 2$. We need to show it holds for $k + 1$.
  Let $t_1, t_2, \ldots, t_{k+1} \in \mathbb{Z}_q$. By the inductive hypothesis, we have:

  $$\mathsf{Hb}(\sum_{i=1}^{k} t_i) = \sum_{i=1}^{k} \mathsf{Hb}(t_i) + E_k^h,$$

  where

  $$E_k^h \in \{-(k-1), \ldots, 0, \ldots, (k-1)\} + \{0, -q_1, -2q_1, \ldots, -(k-1)q_1\}\,.$$

  Now, consider:

  $$\mathsf{Hb}(\sum_{i=1}^{k+1} t_i) = \mathsf{Hb}(\left(\sum_{i=1}^{k} t_i\right) + t_{k+1}).$$

  Applying the previous lemma to $\sum_{i=1}^{k} t_i$ and t_{k+1}, we get:

  $$\mathsf{Hb}(\sum_{i=1}^{k+1} t_i) = \mathsf{Hb}(\sum_{i=1}^{k} t_i) + \mathsf{Hb}(t_{k+1}) + \varepsilon^h,$$

where

$$\varepsilon^h \in \{-1, 0, 1, -q_1, -q_1 - 1, -q_1 + 1\}.$$

Substituting the inductive hypothesis into this equation gives:

$$\mathsf{Hb}(\sum_{i=1}^{k+1} t_i) = \left(\sum_{i=1}^{k} \mathsf{Hb}(t_i) + E_k^h\right) + \mathsf{Hb}(t_{k+1}) + \varepsilon^h.$$

Thus,

$$\mathsf{Hb}(\sum_{i=1}^{k+1} t_i) = \sum_{i=1}^{k+1} \mathsf{Hb}(t_i) + (E_k^h + \varepsilon^h) = \sum_{i=1}^{k+1} \mathsf{Hb}(t_i) + E_{k+1}^h.$$

Now, we need to analyze the term $E_{k+1}^h = E_k^h + \varepsilon^h$. Since

$$E_k^h \in \{-(k-1), \ldots, (k-1)\} + \{0, -q_1, -2q_1, \ldots, -(k-1)q_1\}$$

and

$$\varepsilon^h \in \{-1, 0, 1\} + \{0, -q_1\},$$

therefore, we have as desired

$$E_{k+1}^h \in \{-k, \ldots, k\} + \{0, -q_1, -2q_1, \ldots, -kq_1\}$$

□

Theorem 3.4. *Let q and α be two positive integers such that $q > \alpha$. Define $q_0 = q \bmod {}^{\pm}(\alpha)$ and $q_1 = \frac{q-q_0}{\alpha}$ (i.e. $q = q_1\alpha + q_0$). For any integers $t_1, t_2, \ldots, t_n \in \mathbb{Z}$, the following property holds:*

$$\mathsf{Lb}(\sum_{i=1}^{n} t_i) = \sum_{i=1}^{n} \mathsf{Lb}(t_i) + E^l$$

where

$$E^l \in \{-(n-1)\alpha, \ldots, 0, \ldots, (n-1)\alpha\} + \{0, -q_0, -2q_0, \ldots, -(n-1)q_0\}.$$

Proof. The proof is similar to that of Theorem 3.3, using the second part of Lemma 3.1 instead. □

3.2 On the Conjecture of Seck and Roux-Langlois

In this section, we study the conjecture of Seck and Roux-Langlois in [22] regarding the behavior of the Hb function when applied to sums of two elements of $\mathbb{Z}_q$. The conjecture states that for any $t, r \in \mathbb{Z}_q$, the high bits of their sum can be closely approximated by using the sum of their individual high bits, with a bounded error term ε which can take at most seven different values. More formally, the conjecture is as follows.

Conjecture 3.5 (Seck and Roux-Langlois [22]). Let q be a prime number and $\alpha = 2^d$ for some positive integer d. For any $t, r \in \mathbb{Z}_q$, the following holds:

$$\mathsf{Hb}(t + r) = \mathsf{Hb}((\mathsf{Hb}(t) + \mathsf{Hb}(r))\alpha) + \varepsilon$$

where ε is an error term that can take at most seven different values. More precisely,

$$\varepsilon \in \{-1, 0, 1, e_4, e_5, e_6, e_7\} \mod q,$$

for some integers e_4, e_5, e_6 and e_7.

Notice that this conjecture is a more sophisticated variant of Lemma 3.1. While in Lemma 3.1, the error term ε can take at most six different values depending on the parameters q and α, in the conjecture of Seck and Roux-Langlois, it is suggested that the error term ε can take up to seven different values, and, for some values of q and α, it can take exactly seven different values. For instance, when $q = 3236147$ and $\alpha = 131072$ (i.e. $d = 17$), the error term ε can take the following seven different values:

$$\varepsilon \in \{-1, 0, 1, -24, 23, 24, 25\} \mod q.$$

In the following, we analyze this conjecture and prove that it holds for arbitrary positive integers q and α such that $q > \alpha$. Depending on the value of $q \bmod {}^{\pm}(\alpha)$, we show that the error term ε can take at most 5, 6 or 7 different values (when t and r vary). More precisely, we prove the following theorem.

Theorem 3.6. *Let q and α be two positive integers such that $q > \alpha$. Define $q_0 = q \bmod {}^{\pm}(\alpha)$ and $q_1 = \frac{q - q_0}{\alpha}$ (i.e., $q = q_1\alpha + q_0$ with $q_0 \in (-\alpha/2, \alpha/2]$). For any integers $t, r \in [0, q)$, the following property hold:*

$$\mathsf{Hb}(t + r) = \mathsf{Hb}((\mathsf{Hb}(t) + \mathsf{Hb}(r)) \cdot \alpha) + \varepsilon,$$

where ε belongs to one of the following sets

1. $\{-1, 0, 1, -q_1 + 1, q_1 - 2, q_1 - 1, q_1\}$, *if* $q_0 \in (-\alpha/2, -\alpha/4)$;
2. $\{-1, 0, 1, -q_1 + 1, q_1 - 1, q_1\}$, *if* $q_0 \in [-\alpha/4, 0]$;
3. $\{-1, 0, 1, -q_1, -q_1 + 1, q_1 - 1\}$, *if* $q_0 \in (0, \alpha/2)$;
4. $\{-1, 0, 1, -q_1, q_1\}$, *if* $q_0 = \alpha/2$.

In the case where $q \equiv 1 \pmod{\alpha}$, one obtains the following corollary.

Corollary 3.7. *Let q and α be two positive integers such that $q \equiv 1 \pmod{\alpha}$. Let $t, r \in [0, q)$, and $\varepsilon = \mathsf{Hb}(t + r) - \mathsf{Hb}((\mathsf{Hb}(t) + \mathsf{Hb}(r))\alpha)$. Then*

$$\varepsilon \in \{-1, 0, 1, -\frac{q-1}{\alpha}, -\frac{q-1}{\alpha} + 1, \frac{q-1}{\alpha} - 1\}.$$

Proof. This is a direct consequence of Theorem 3.6 and the fact that if $q \equiv 1 \pmod{\alpha}$, then $q_0 = 1$ and $q_1 = (q - 1)/\alpha$. □

The rest of this section is devoted to the proof of Theorem 3.6. This proof being a bit technical, we will present it as a succession of smaller lemmas, in order to ease readability. Let us first fix some notations.

Definition 3.8. *Let $q > \alpha$ be integers, let $q_0, q_1 \in \mathbb{Z}$ be such that $q = q_0 + q_1\alpha$ with $q_0 \in (-\alpha/2, \alpha/2]$ (as in the theorem statement). Let t, r be any integers in $[0, q)$, and write them similarly as $t = t_0 + t_1\alpha$ and $r = r_0 + r_1\alpha$ for some t_0, t_1, r_0, r_1 integers with $t_0, r_0 \in (-\alpha/2, \alpha/2]$.*

Define $S = t + r \bmod {}^+(q)$, and let $\varepsilon_S \in \mathbb{Z}$ be such that $S = t + r - \varepsilon_S q$. Define also $X = (t_1 + r_1) \cdot \alpha \bmod {}^+(q)$, and let similarly $\varepsilon_X \in \mathbb{Z}$ be such that $X = (t_1 + r_1) \cdot \alpha - \varepsilon_X q$. Finally, let $S = S_0 + S_1\alpha$ and $X = X_0 + X_1\alpha$ with S_0, S_1, X_0, X_1 integers and $S_0, X_0 \in (-\alpha/2, \alpha/2]$.

We first give a lemma that motivates these definitions and notations.

Lemma 3.9. *Using the notations from Definition 3.8, we have* $\mathsf{Hb}(t + r) = S_1$ *and* $\mathsf{Hb}((\mathsf{Hb}(t) + \mathsf{Hb}(r)) \cdot \alpha) = X_1$.

Proof. This follows from the definition of $\mathsf{Hb}(\cdot)$. Note that since t and r are in $[0, q)$, then $t = t \bmod {}^+(q)$ and $r = r \bmod {}^+(q)$, so that $t_1 = \mathsf{Hb}(t)$ and $r_1 = \mathsf{Hb}(r)$. Similarly, we have $X_1 = \mathsf{Hb}(X)$ and $S_1 = \mathsf{Hb}(S)$ (since X and S are in $[0, q)$). We conclude using the definition of $X = (t_1 + r_1) \cdot \alpha \bmod {}^+(q)$ and $S = t + r \bmod {}^+(q)$, and the fact that $\mathsf{Hb}(x) = \mathsf{Hb}(y)$ if $x = y \bmod q$. □

Using Lemma 3.9, we see that in order to prove Theorem 3.6, one needs to study the difference $S_1 - X_1$. Before giving an explicit description of this difference (depending on the value of q_0), we start by a few auxiliary lemmas. The first one below is a simple observation that the quantities t_1 and r_1 live in some bounded interval, a result which will be helpful multiple times during the proof.

Lemma 3.10. *We have* $\max(0, \frac{t}{\alpha} - \frac{1}{2}) \leq t_1 < \frac{t}{\alpha} + \frac{1}{2}$ *and similarly* $\max(0, \frac{r}{\alpha} - \frac{1}{2}) \leq r_1 < \frac{r}{\alpha} + \frac{1}{2}$.

Proof. Let us do the proof for t_1, the proof for r_1 is obtained similarly. First, note that $t_1 = \frac{t - t_0}{\alpha}$. Since $t_0 > -\alpha/2$ by assumption, then $-t_0/\alpha < 1/2$, and we obtain the desired upper bound $t_1 < t/\alpha + 1/2$. Using similarly the upper bound $t_0 \leq \alpha/2$, we obtain $t_1 \geq t/\alpha - 1/2$. For the bound $t_1 \geq 0$, observe that since $t_0 = t \bmod {}^{\pm}(\alpha)$ and $t \geq 0$, then we always have $t \geq t_0$. Hence we obtain $t_1 = \frac{t - t_0}{\alpha} \geq \frac{t_0 - t_0}{\alpha} = 0$. □

We now provide two lemmas that make explicit the values that can be taken by the quantities ε_S and ε_X.

Lemma 3.11. *We have*

$$\varepsilon_S = \begin{cases} 0 \text{ if } t + r < q, \\ 1 \text{ if } t + r \geq q. \end{cases}$$

Proof. Since t and r are both in $[0, q)$, then $t + r \in [0, 2q)$, and so we have only two possibilities: either $t + r \in [0, q)$, in which case $S = t + r \bmod {}^{+}(q) = t + r$ and $\varepsilon_S = 0$; or $t + r \in [q, 2q)$, in which case $S = t + r \bmod {}^{+}(q) = t + r - q$ and $\varepsilon_S = 1$. □

Lemma 3.12. *We have*

$$\varepsilon_X = \begin{cases} 0 \text{ if } t_1 + r_1 < q/\alpha, \\ 1 \text{ if } t_1 + r_1 \in [q/\alpha, 2q/\alpha), \\ 2 \text{ if } t_1 + r_1 \geq 2q/\alpha. \end{cases}$$

Proof. Using Lemma 3.10, we know that $t_1 + r_1 \geq 0$ and that $t_1 + r_1 < (r + t)/\alpha + 1$. Using the fact that r and t are both $< q$ and that $q/\alpha \geq 1$, we see that $t_1 + r_1 < 2q/\alpha + 1 \leq 3q/\alpha$. This implies that $(t_1 + r_1) \cdot \alpha \in [0, 3q)$.

From this and the definition of ε_X, we conclude that ε_X can take only 3 values. Namely $\varepsilon_X = 0$ if $(t_1 + r_1) \cdot \alpha \in [0, q)$, i.e., if $t_1 + r_1 < q/\alpha$; $\varepsilon_X = 1$ if $(t_1 + r_1) \cdot \alpha \in [q, 2q)$, i.e., if $t_1 + r_1 \in [q/\alpha, 2q/\alpha)$; and $\varepsilon_X = 2$ if $(t_1 + r_1) \cdot \alpha \in [2q, 3q)$, i.e., if $t_1 + r_1 \geq 2q/\alpha$. □

We note that the case $\varepsilon_X = 2$ is quite extreme, and cannot happen for some values of q_0, as stated in the following lemma.

Lemma 3.13. *If* $\varepsilon_X = 2$*, then* $\varepsilon_S = 1$ *and* $q_0 \in (-\alpha/2, 0]$.

Proof. Assume that $\varepsilon_X = 2$. Then from Lemma 3.12, we know that $t_1 + r_1 \geq 2q/\alpha$. Let us first prove that $\varepsilon_S = 1$. By Lemma 3.10, we know that $t_1 + r_1 < (t + r)/\alpha + 1$. Said differently, we have $t + r > (t_1 + r_1) \cdot \alpha - \alpha$. By the lower bound on $t_1 + r_1$, this implies that $t + r > 2q - \alpha \geq q$ (since $q \geq \alpha$). From Lemma 3.11, this then implies that $\varepsilon_S = 1$.

Let us now prove that $q_0 \in (-\alpha/2, 0]$. Since $t_1 + r_1 \geq 2q/\alpha$, then at least one of t_1 or r_1 must be $\geq q/\alpha$. Let us assume without loss of generality that $t_1 \geq q/\alpha$. From Lemma 3.10, we know that $t_1 < t/\alpha + 1/2 \leq q/\alpha + 1/2$. Moreover, t_1 is an integer. Combining everything, this means that the set $[q/\alpha, q/\alpha + 1/2) \cap \mathbb{Z}$ is non-empty (since it contains t_1). Recall that $q = q_0 + q_1 \cdot \alpha$, hence $q/\alpha = q_1 + q_0/\alpha$, with q_1 an integer. Since the set $[q_1 + q_0/\alpha, q_1 + q_0/\alpha + 1/2) \cap \mathbb{Z}$ is non empty, then it must be that $q_0/\alpha \in (-1/2, 0]$. This implies that $q_0 \in (-\alpha/2, 0]$. □

Now that we know what values can be taken by ε_X and ε_S, we will provide a collection of lemmas, one for each possible choice of the pair $(\varepsilon_X, \varepsilon_S)$, that describe the possible values taken by $X_1 - S_1$ for this choice of $(\varepsilon_X, \varepsilon_S)$.

Lemma 3.14. *If* $\varepsilon_S = \varepsilon_X = 0$*, then* $X_1 - S_1 \in \{-1, 0, 1\}$.

Proof. Since $\varepsilon_X = 0$, we know that $X = (t_1 + r_1) \cdot \alpha$. By the definition of X_1 and X_0, it must be that $X_1 = t_1 + r_1$ and $X_0 = 0$.

Let us now consider the case of S_1. Since $\varepsilon_S = 0$, then $S = t + r = (t_1 + r_1) \cdot \alpha + (t_0 + r_0)$. Moreover, $t_0 + r_0 \in (-\alpha, \alpha]$, by choice of t_0 and r_0. We now distinguish three cases.

1. If $t_0 + r_0 \in (-\alpha, -\alpha/2]$, then $S = (t_1 + r_1 - 1) \cdot \alpha + (t_0 + r_0 + \alpha)$ and $(t_0 + r_0 + \alpha) \in (0, \alpha/2] \subseteq (-\alpha/2, \alpha/2]$. From which we conclude that $S_0 = (t_0 + r_0 + \alpha)$ and $S_1 = t_1 + r_1 - 1$.
2. If $t_0 + r_0 \in (-\alpha/2, \alpha/2]$, then $S = (t_1 + r_1) \cdot \alpha + (t_0 + r_0)$ and $(t_0 + r_0) \in (-\alpha/2, \alpha/2]$. From which we conclude that $S_0 = (t_0 + r_0)$ and $S_1 = t_1 + r_1$.
3. If $t_0 + r_0 \in (\alpha/2, \alpha]$, then $S = (t_1 + r_1 + 1) \cdot \alpha + (t_0 + r_0 - \alpha)$ and $(t_0 + r_0 - \alpha) \in (-\alpha/2, 0] \subseteq (-\alpha/2, \alpha/2]$. From which we conclude that $S_0 = (t_0 + r_0 - \alpha)$ and $S_1 = t_1 + r_1 + 1$.

Combining the possible values for X_1 and S_1, we obtain as desired that $X_1 - S_1 \in \{-1, 0, 1\}$. □

Lemma 3.15. *If $\varepsilon_S = \varepsilon_X = 1$, then $X_1 - S_1 \in \{-1, 0, 1\}$.*

Proof. To simplify this proof, let us consider a slightly different decomposition of $q = q'_0 + q'_1 \cdot \alpha$ with $q'_0 \in [-\alpha/2, \alpha/2)$ (instead of $q_0 \in (-\alpha/2, \alpha/2]$ as above). Since $\varepsilon_X = 1$, we know that $X = (t_1 + r_1) \cdot \alpha - q = (t_1 + r_1 - q'_1) \cdot \alpha - q'_0$. By choice of q'_0, we know that $-q'_0 \in (-\alpha/2, \alpha/2]$, and so we obtain that $X_0 = -q'_0$ and that $X_1 = t_1 + r_1 - q'_1$.

Let us now consider the case of S_1. Since $\varepsilon_S = 1$, then $S = t + r - q = (t_1 + r_1 - q'_1) \cdot \alpha + (t_0 + r_0 - q'_0)$. Moreover, $t_0 + r_0 - q'_0 \in (-3\alpha/2, 3\alpha/2]$, by choice of t_0, r_0 and q'_0. We now distinguish three cases.

1. If $t_0 + r_0 - q'_0 \in (-3\alpha/2, -\alpha/2]$, then $S = (t_1 + r_1 - q'_1 - 1) \cdot \alpha + (t_0 + r_0 - q'_0 + \alpha)$ and $(t_0 + r_0 - q'_0 + \alpha) \in (-\alpha/2, \alpha/2]$. From which we conclude that $S_0 = (t_0 + r_0 - q'_0 + \alpha)$ and $S_1 = t_1 + r_1 - q'_1 - 1$.
2. If $t_0 + r_0 - q'_0 \in (-\alpha/2, \alpha/2]$, then $S = (t_1 + r_1 - q'_1) \cdot \alpha + (t_0 + r_0 - q'_0)$ and $(t_0 + r_0 - q'_0) \in (-\alpha/2, \alpha/2]$. From which we conclude that $S_0 = (t_0 + r_0 - q'_0)$ and $S_1 = t_1 + r_1 - q'_1$.
3. If $t_0 + r_0 - q'_0 \in (\alpha/2, 3\alpha/2]$, then $S = (t_1 + r_1 - q'_1 + 1) \cdot \alpha + (t_0 + r_0 - q'_0 - \alpha)$ and $(t_0 + r_0 - q'_0 - \alpha) \in (-\alpha/2, \alpha/2]$. From which we conclude that $S_0 = (t_0 + r_0 - q'_0 - \alpha)$ and $S_1 = t_1 + r_1 - q'_1 + 1$.

Combining the possible values for X_1 and S_1, we obtain as desired that $X_1 - S_1 \in \{-1, 0, 1\}$. □

Lemma 3.16. *If $\varepsilon_S = 0$ and $\varepsilon_X = 1$, then*

$$X_1 - S_1 \in \begin{cases} \{-q_1, -q_1 + 1\} & \text{if } q_0 \in (-\alpha/2, 0] \\ \{-q_1 + 1\} & \text{if } q_0 \in (0, \alpha/2) \\ \{-q_1\} & \text{if } q_0 = \alpha/2 \end{cases}$$

Proof. In this case, we know that $t + r < q$ (since $\varepsilon_S = 0$) and $t_1 + r_1 \geq q/\alpha$ (since $\varepsilon_X = 1$). Moreover, by Lemma 3.10, we also know that $t_1 + r_1 < (t + r)/\alpha + 1 < q/\alpha + 1$. This means that $t_1 + r_1$ is an integer in the interval $[q/\alpha, q/\alpha + 1)$. There is a unique possibility for $t_1 + r_1$, which is $t_1 + r_1 = \lceil q/\alpha \rceil$. We now make a remark that will be useful later: if $q_0 \in (0, \alpha/2]$, then $t_1 + r_1 \geq q/\alpha + 1/2$. Indeed, we know that $q/\alpha = q_1 + q_0/\alpha$ and, if $q_0 \in (0, \alpha/2]$, then we have that

$q_0/\alpha \in (0, 1/2]$, so the rounding up operation increases the quantity by at least 1/2.

Regarding X, since $\varepsilon_X = 1$, we have that $X = (t_1+r_1)\cdot\alpha - q = (t_1+r_1-q_1)\cdot\alpha - q_0$. If $q_0 \in (-\alpha/2, \alpha/2)$, then $X_0 = -q_0$ and $X_1 = t_1 + r_1 - q_1$. If $q_0 = \alpha/2$, then $X_0 = \alpha/2 = \alpha - q_0$ and $X_1 = t_1 + r_1 - q_1 - 1$.

Regarding S, since $\varepsilon_S = 0$, we have that $S = t + r = (t_1 + r_1) \cdot \alpha + (t_0 + r_0)$. Notice that $t_0 + r_0 < 0$. Indeed, we have $t_0 + r_0 = t + r - (t_1 + r_1) \cdot \alpha < q - q = 0$, where we used the fact that $t + r < q$ and $t_1 + r_1 \geq q/\alpha$. This implies that we have either $S_1 = t_1 + r_1$ (if $t_0 + r_0 \in (-\alpha/2, 0)$) or $S_1 = t_1 + r_1 - 1$ (if $t_0 + r_0 \in (-\alpha, -\alpha/2]$).

Let us now consider the three cases from the statement, depending on the value of q_0.

1. If $q_0 \in (-\alpha/2, 0]$, then from the previous discussion we have $X_1 = t_1 + r_1 - q_1$ and $S_1 = t_1 + r_1$ or $S_1 = t_1 + r_1 - 1$. This implies that $X_1 - S_1$ belongs to $\{-q_1, -q_1 + 1\}$, as desired.
2. If $q_0 \in (0, \alpha/2)$, then, from the previous discussion we have $X_1 = t_1 + r_1 - q_1$. Let us be a little bit finer for the value of S_1. We have seen at the beginning of the proof that when $q_0 \in (0, \alpha/2]$, then $t_1 + r_1 \geq q/\alpha + 1/2$. This implies that
$$t_0 + r_0 = t + r - (t_1 + r_1) \cdot \alpha < q - (q/\alpha + 1/2) \cdot \alpha = -\alpha/2.$$
From this, we conclude that $S_1 = t_1 + r_1 - 1$ is the only option for S_1 (see discussion above). Hence, we see that $X_1 - S_1 = -q_1 + 1$ as desired.
3. If $q_0 = \alpha/2$, then, from the previous discussion we have $X_1 = t_1 + r_1 - q_1 - 1$. The computation for S_1 is the same as in the case $q_0 \in (0, \alpha/2)$, so we have $S_1 = t_1 + r_1 - 1$. We conclude that $X_1 - S_1$ is always equal to $-q_1$. This concludes the proof.

□

Lemma 3.17. *If $\varepsilon_S = 1$ and $\varepsilon_X = 0$, then*

$$X_1 - S_1 \in \begin{cases} \{q_1 - 1\} & \text{if } q_0 \in (-\alpha/2, 0] \\ \{q_1, q_1 - 1\} & \text{if } q_0 \in (0, \alpha/2) \\ \{q_1\} & \text{if } q_0 = \alpha/2 \end{cases}$$

Proof. In this case, we know that $t+r \geq q$ (since $\varepsilon_S = 1$) and $t_1+r_1 < q/\alpha$ (since $\varepsilon_X = 0$). Moreover, by Lemma 3.10, we also know that $t_1 + r_1 \geq (t+r)/\alpha - 1 \geq q/\alpha - 1$. This means that $t_1 + r_1$ is an integer in the interval $[q/\alpha - 1, q/\alpha)$. There is a unique possibility for $t_1 + r_1$, which is $t_1 + r_1 = \lceil q/\alpha - 1 \rceil$. We now make a remark that will be useful later: if $q_0 \in (-\alpha/2, 0]$, then $t_1 + r_1 < q/\alpha - 1/2$. Indeed, we know that $q/\alpha - 1 = q_1 - 1 + q_0/\alpha$ and, if $q_0 \in (-\alpha/2, 0]$, then we have $q_0/\alpha \in (-1/2, 0]$, so the rounding up operation increases the quantity by $< 1/2$.

Regarding X, since $\varepsilon_X = 0$, we have that $X = (t_1+r_1)\cdot\alpha$, and so $X_1 = t_1+r_1$.

Regarding S, since $\varepsilon_S = 1$, we have that $S = t + r - q = (t_1 + r_1 - q_1) \cdot \alpha + (t_0 + r_0 - q_0)$. Notice that $t_0 + r_0 - q_0 > -\alpha/2$. Indeed, we have $(t_0 + r_0) - q_0 = t + r - (t_1 + r_1) \cdot \alpha - q_0 > q - q - \alpha/2 = -\alpha/2$, where we used the fact that $t + r \geq q$, that $t_1 + r_1 < q/\alpha$, and that $q_0 \leq \alpha/2$. This implies that we have either $S_1 = t_1 + r_1 - q_1$ (if $t_0 + r_0 - q_0 \in (-\alpha/2, \alpha/2]$) or $S_1 = t_1 + r_1 - q_1 + 1$ (if $t_0 + r_0 - q_0 \in (\alpha/2, 3\alpha/2]$).

Let us now consider the three cases from the statement, depending on the value of q_0.

1. If $q_0 \in (0, \alpha/2)$, then from the previous discussion we have $X_1 = t_1 + r_1$ and $S_1 = t_1 + r_1 - q_1$ or $S_1 = t_1 + r_1 - q_1 + 1$. This implies that $X_1 - S_1$ belongs to $\{q_1, q_1 - 1\}$, as desired.
2. If $q_0 \in (-\alpha/2, 0]$, we still have $X_1 = t_1 + r_1$. Let us be a little bit finer for the value of S_1. We have seen at the beginning of the proof that when $q_0 \in (-\alpha/2, 0]$, then $t_1 + r_1 < q/\alpha - 1/2$. This implies that

$$t_0 + r_0 - q_0 \geq t_0 + r_0 = t + r - (t_1 + r_1) \cdot \alpha > q - (q/\alpha - 1/2) \cdot \alpha = \alpha/2.$$

   From this, we conclude that $S_1 = t_1 + r_1 - q_1 + 1$ is the only option for S_1 (see discussion above). Hence, we see that $X_1 - S_1 = q_1 - 1$ as desired.
3. If $q_0 = \alpha/2$, we still have $X_1 = t_1 + r_1$. Moreover, in this case, we have $(t_0 + r_0) - q_0 \leq \alpha/2 + \alpha/2 - \alpha/2 = \alpha/2$. From this, we conclude that $S_1 = t_1 + r_1 - q_1$, and we obtain $X_1 - S_1 = q_1$. This concludes the proof.

□

Lemma 3.18. *If* $\varepsilon_X = 2$, *then*

$$X_1 - S_1 \in \begin{cases} \{-q_1 + 1, -q_1 + 2\} & \text{if } q_0 \in (-\alpha/2, -\alpha/4) \\ \{-q_1, -q_1 + 1\} & \text{if } q_0 \in [-\alpha/4, 0] \end{cases}$$

Proof. First of all, let us recall that from Lemma 3.13, when $\varepsilon_X = 2$, then it must be that $\varepsilon_S = 1$ and that $q_0 \in (-\alpha/2, 0]$. So we only have to consider these cases for the choice of q_0.

Let us first prove that $t_1 + r_1 = 2q_1$. To see this, observe that, by assumption, we have $t_1 + r_1 \geq 2q/\alpha$ (because $\varepsilon_X = 2$), and $t_1 + r_1 < \frac{t+r}{\alpha} + 1 \leq 2q/\alpha + 1$ by Lemma 3.10. So $t_1 + r_1$ is the unique integer in the interval $[2q/\alpha, 2q/\alpha + 1)$, i.e., it is equal to $\lceil 2q/\alpha \rceil$. But $\frac{2q}{\alpha} = 2q_1 + \frac{2q_0}{\alpha}$. Since $q_0 \in (-\alpha/2, 0]$ by assumption, then $\frac{2q_0}{\alpha} \in (-1, 0]$, from which we conclude that $t_1 + r_1 = \lceil 2q_1 + \frac{2q_0}{\alpha} \rceil = 2q_1$, as desired.

Let us use this observation to compute X_1. We have, that $X = (t_1 + r_1) \cdot \alpha - 2q$ since $\varepsilon_X = 2$. Using the formula for $t_1 + r_1$, we obtain $X = 2q_1\alpha - 2q = -2q_0$. If $q_0 \in [-\alpha/4, 0]$, then $-2q_0 \in [0, \alpha/2]$, and we conclude that $X_1 = 0$. On the other hand, if $q_0 \in (-\alpha/2, -\alpha/4)$, then we have $-2q_0 \in (\alpha/2, \alpha)$, and so we have $X_1 = 1$.

Regarding S_1, recall that $\varepsilon_S = 1$, so that $S = t + r - q = (t_1 + r_1 - q_1) \cdot \alpha + (t_0 + r_0 - q_0) = q_1\alpha + (t_0 + r_0 - q_0)$, where we used that $t_1 + r_1 = 2q_1$. Moreover,

$$t_0 + r_0 = t + r - (t_1 + r_1)\alpha = t + r - 2q_1 \cdot \alpha < 2q - 2q_1\alpha = 2q_0.$$

From this, we see that $t_0 + r_0 - q_0 < q_0 \leq 0$. Hence, we have either $S_1 = q_1$ if $t_0 + r_0 - q_0 \in (-\alpha/2, 0]$, or $S_1 = q_1 - 1$ if $t_0 + r_0 - q_0 \in (-3\alpha/2, -\alpha/2]$.

Overall, we see that $X_1 - S_1$ belongs either to the set $\{-q_1, -q_1 + 1\}$ if $q_0 \in [-\alpha/4, 0]$ (i.e., $X_1 = 0$), or to the set $\{-q_1+1, -q_1+2\}$ if $q_0 \in (-\alpha/2, -\alpha/4)$ (i.e., $X_1 = 1$). □

Combining all these lemmas, we can finally prove Theorem 3.6.

Proof of Theorem 3.6. Let α, q, q_0 and q_1 be as in the theorem statement. Let us fix two integers $t, r \in [0, q)$. From Lemma 3.9, we know that

$$\varepsilon = \mathsf{Hb}(t + r) - \mathsf{Hb}((\mathsf{Hb}(t) + \mathsf{Hb}(r))\alpha) = S_1 - X_1.$$

The result then follows by inspection of Lemmas 3.14, 3.15, 3.16, 3.17, and 3.18. Note that these lemmas indeed cover all the possible cases, thanks to Lemma 3.11, 3.12, and 3.13. □

Numerical Experiments. We ran some numerical experiments to verify the correctness of Theorem 3.6. For each of the four possible interval choices for q_0, we generated 10 random pairs (α, q) with q_0 in the desired interval. We then verified experimentally that for these pairs, the values of ε achieved by running over all pairs (t, r) in $[0, q) \times [0, q)$ were all contained in the sets described in Theorem 3.6. All the 40 tests were successful. The code used to perform these tests is available at https://github.com/funibus/africacrypt-2026-supplementary-material.git.

4 Applications

In this section, we show how one can use our results to construct an efficient signature scheme with rerandomizable keys [14] on top of ML-DSA [18], a recently standardized lattice-based signature scheme by NIST. Signature schemes with rerandomizable keys are cryptographic primitives that can be used in various applications such as deterministic wallets [10] for cryptocurrencies, Tor hidden services [25], etc. Before describing our construction, we will first recall the definition of signature schemes and signature schemes with rerandomizable keys, and the ML-DSA algorithms.

4.1 Signature Schemes with Rerandomizable Keys

Definition 4.1 (signature scheme). *A signature scheme Σ is a tuple of algorithms* $(\Sigma.\mathsf{KGen}, \Sigma.\mathsf{Sign}, \Sigma.\mathsf{Verify})$ *defined as follows.*

- $\Sigma.\mathsf{KGen}(1^\lambda) \to (pk, sk)$: *is a randomized key generation algorithm which takes as input a security parameter 1^λ and outputs a key pair (pk, sk) with pk a public verification key and sk a secret signing key.*
- $\Sigma.\mathsf{Sign}(sk, m) \to \sigma$: *is a randomized (or deterministic) signing algorithm to sign a message m using sk and, producing a signature σ of m.*

- $\Sigma.\mathsf{Verify}(pk, m, \sigma) \rightarrow m$: *is a deterministic verification algorithm that takes as input a message* m*, a signature* σ *and a public key* pk*, and returns* 1 *(valid) or* 0 *(invalid).*

Definition 4.2 (Correctness of a signature scheme). *A signature scheme* $\Sigma := (\Sigma.\mathsf{KGen}, \Sigma.\mathsf{Sign}, \Sigma.\mathsf{Verify})$ *is correct if the following condition holds for all* 1^λ*:*

$$\Pr\left[\Sigma.\mathsf{Verify}\left(pk, m, \Sigma.\mathsf{Sign}(sk, m)\right) = 1 \,\middle|\, \begin{array}{l} m \leftarrow \{0,1\}^*, \\ (pk, sk) \leftarrow \Sigma.\mathsf{KGen}(1^\lambda) \end{array}\right] = 1$$

Definition 4.3 (signature scheme with rerandomizable keys [14]). *A signature scheme with rerandomizable keys (SWRK)* Σ_{RK} *is a tuple of algorithms* $(\Sigma_{\mathsf{RK}}.\mathsf{KGen}, \Sigma_{\mathsf{RK}}.\mathsf{Sign}, \Sigma_{\mathsf{RK}}.\mathsf{Verify}, \Sigma_{\mathsf{RK}}.\mathsf{RandSk}, \Sigma_{\mathsf{RK}}.\mathsf{RandPk})$ *where* $(\Sigma_{\mathsf{RK}}.\mathsf{KGen}, \Sigma_{\mathsf{RK}}.\mathsf{Sign}, \Sigma_{\mathsf{RK}}.\mathsf{Verify})$ *are the standard algorithms of a signature scheme and the two others algorithms are defined over a randomness space* $\mathcal{R}$ *as follows.*

- $\Sigma_{\mathsf{RK}}.\mathsf{RandSk}(sk, \rho) \rightarrow sk'$: *is a deterministic algorithm to update a private key which accepts as input* sk *and a randomness* $\rho \in \mathcal{R}$*, and produces as output a rerandomized secret key* sk'*.*
- $\Sigma_{\mathsf{RK}}.\mathsf{RandPk}(pk, \rho) \rightarrow pk'$: *is a deterministic algorithm to update a public key which accepts as input* pk *and a randomness* $\rho \in \mathcal{R}$*, and produces as output a rerandomized public key* pk'*.*

Definition 4.4 (Correctness of Σ_{RK}). *A signature scheme with rerandomizable keys* $\Sigma_{RK} = (\Sigma_{\mathsf{RK}}.\mathsf{KGen}, \Sigma_{\mathsf{RK}}.\mathsf{Sign}, \Sigma_{\mathsf{RK}}.\mathsf{Verify}, \Sigma_{\mathsf{RK}}.\mathsf{RandSk}, \Sigma_{\mathsf{RK}}.\mathsf{RandPk})$ *is correct if the following two conditions holds:*

$$\Pr\left[\Sigma_{\mathsf{RK}}.\mathsf{Verify}\left(pk, m, \Sigma_{\mathsf{RK}}.\mathsf{Sign}(sk, m)\right) = 1 \,\middle|\, \begin{array}{l} m \leftarrow \{0,1\}^*, \\ (pk, sk) \leftarrow \Sigma_{\mathsf{RK}}.\mathsf{KGen}(1^\lambda) \end{array}\right] = 1$$

and for all $(pk, sk) \leftarrow \Sigma_{\mathsf{RK}}.\mathsf{KGen}(1^\lambda)$

$$\mathbb{P}\left[\Sigma_{\mathsf{RK}}.\mathsf{Verify}\left(pk', m, \Sigma_{\mathsf{RK}}.\mathsf{Sign}(sk', m)\right) = 1 \,\middle|\, \begin{array}{l} m \leftarrow \{0,1\}^*, \rho \leftarrow \mathcal{R} \\ pk' := \Sigma_{\mathsf{RK}}.\mathsf{RandPk}(pk, \rho) \\ sk' := \Sigma_{\mathsf{RK}}.\mathsf{RandSk}(sk, \rho) \end{array}\right] = 1$$

4.2 ML-DSA Algorithms

ML-DSA [18] is a lattice-based signature scheme that was recently standardized by NIST as FIPS 204. It is derived from the Dilithium signature scheme [1,12], and its security is related to the Module Learning With Errors (MLWE) problem. Let us recall the parameters and functions used in ML-DSA algorithms.

Parameters and Sets: In this section, we suppose that q is a prime such that $q \equiv 1 \pmod{\alpha}$ with $\alpha = 2\gamma_2 = 2^d$ for some positive integers γ_2 and d, where d denotes the number of dropped bits in the public key. We also denote by $\mathcal{R} = \mathbb{Z}[X]/(X^{256}+1)$ and the quotient ring $\mathcal{R}_q = \mathcal{R}/(q\mathcal{R})$. For an element $y \in \mathcal{R}^k$ we denote by $\| y \|_\infty$ the infinity norm of the $256k$−dimensional vector of the coefficients of the polynomials of y. The scheme also uses an eXtendable-Output Function H instantiated by SHAKE-256.

Supporting Algorithms: In addition to the function Hb and Power2Round, the signature ML-DSA uses the following algorithms:

- ExpandA(ρ): is a deterministic algorithm that takes as input a seed ρ and outputs a matrix $\mathbf{A} \in \mathcal{R}_q^{k\times l}$.
- ExpandS(ρ'): is a deterministic algorithm that takes as input a seed ρ' and outputs a couple of vectors $(s_1, s_2) \in \mathcal{S}_\eta^l \times \mathcal{S}_\eta^k$ each with polynomial coordinates whose coefficients are in the range $[-\eta, \eta]$.
- HighBits(r, α): returns the corrected high bits of r i.e. r_1 if $r_1 \neq (q-q_0)/\alpha$ and 0 otherwise, where $r_1 = \mathsf{Hb}_{q,\alpha}(r)$ and $q_0 = q \bmod^{\pm}(\alpha)$. If the parameters q and α are clear from the context, we simply denote this function by HighBits(r).
- LowBits(r, α): returns the corrected low bits of r i.e. r_0 if $r_1 \neq (q-q_0)/\alpha$ and $r_0 - 1$ otherwise. We denote this function by LowBits(r) if the parameters q and α are clear from the context.
- MakeHint(z, r): returns a hint $h \in \{0,1\}$ to recover the high bits of $z+r$ from the high bits r.
- UseHint(h, r): returns the high bits of $r+z$ using the binary hint h and the high bits of r.
- ExpandMask(ρ, κ): outputs a vector $y \in \mathcal{R}^l$ such that each polynomial of the components y has coefficients between $-\gamma_1+1$ and γ_1.
- SampleInBall(ρ): is a deterministic algorithm that takes as input a seed ρ and outputs a polynomial $c \in \mathcal{R}$ such that the coefficients of c are in $\{-1,0,1\}$ and their hamming weight τ is at most 60.
- pkEncode(ρ, t_1): encodes the public key components for ML-DSA into a bit string.
- pkDecode(pk): decodes the public key bit string back into its components.
- skEncode($\rho, K, tr, s_1, s_2, t_0$): encodes the secret key components for ML-DSA into a bit string.
- skDecode(sk): decodes the secret key bit string back into its components.
- sigEncode(c, z, h): encodes the signature components for ML-DSA into a bit string.
- sigDecode(σ): decodes the signature bit string back into its components.

We recall the key generation, signing and verification algorithms of ML-DSA in the following (Fig. 1). We refer the reader to [18] for more details about the scheme and its security analysis.

```
ML-DSA.KGen(pp = ζ ∈ {0,1}^256) :
(ρ, ρ', K) := H(ζ);
(s1, s2) ∈ S_η^l × S_η^k := ExpandS(ρ');
A ~ R_q^{k×l} := ExpandA(ρ);
t := A s1 + s2;
(t1, t0) := Power2Round(t);
tr := H(ρ, t1, 64);
pk := pkEncode(ρ, t1);
sk := skEncode(ρ, K, tr, s1, s2, t0);
return (pk, sk)
```

```
ML-DSA.Verify(m, pk, σ) :
A ~ R_q^{k×l} := ExpandA(ρ);
(ρ, t1) := pkDecode(pk);
(c, z, h) := sigDecode(σ);
tr := H(ρ, t1); μ := H(tr, m);
c := SampleInBall(c);
w1' := UseHint(h, Az − c t1 · α);
b1 := [|| z ||∞ ≤ γ1 − β];
b2 := [c = H(μ, w1')];
b3 := [|h|_{hj=1} ≤ ω];
return b1 ∧ b2 ∧ b3
```

```
ML-DSA.Sign(m, sk) :
A ~ R_q^{k×l} := ExpandA(ρ);
(ρ, K, tr, s1, s2, t0) := skDecode(sk);
μ := H(tr, m);
κ := 0; (z, h) := ⊥;
ρ' := H(K, μ);                          ▷ (or ρ' ← {0,1}^512)
while (z, h) = ⊥ do
    y ∈ S_{γ1−1}^l := ExpandMask(ρ', κ);
    w := Ay;
    w1 := HighBits(w);
    c ∈:= H(μ, w1);
    c ∈ B_τ := SampleInBall(c);
    z := y + c s1;
    r0 := LowBits(w − c s2);
    if || z ||∞ ≥ γ1 − β or || r0 ||∞ ≥ γ2 − β then
        (z, h) := ⊥;
    else
        h := MakeHint(−c t0, w − c s2 + c t0);
        if || c t0 ||∞ > γ2 or |h|_{hj=1} > ω then
            (z, h) := ⊥;
    κ := κ + 1
return σ = sigEncode(c, z, h)
```

Fig. 1. ML-DSA: key generation, signature and verification algorithms.

4.3 A SWRK from ML-DSA

By Corollary 3.7, we have $\mathsf{Hb}(t+r) = \mathsf{Hb}((\mathsf{Hb}(t)+\mathsf{Hb}(r))\cdot\alpha) + t^h$ with $t^h \in \{-1, 0, 1, -q_1, -q_1+1, q_1-1\}$ for any $t, r \in [0, q)$. We will use this result to construct an efficient lattice-based signature scheme with rerandomizable keys on top of ML-DSA. Our construction is similar to DilithiumRKC proposed by Seck and Roux-Langlois [22], but for the sake of completeness, we will give the details of the different algorithms of our scheme. We first describe the encoding and decoding algorithms for the hint t^h in the following (Fig. 2). Notice that the hint t^h can be encoded with 3 bits since it takes at most 6 different values.

```
hintEncode(t^h, q, α) :
q0 := q mod ±(α);
q1 = (q − q0)/α;
If t^h = −1 : return 010;
If t^h = 0 : return 000;
If t^h = 1 : return 001;
If t^h = −q1 + 1 : return 011;
If t^h = −q1 : return 100;
If t^h = q1 − 1 : return 101;
```

```
hintDecode(hint, q, α) :
q0 := q mod ±(α);
q1 = (q − q0)/α;
If hint = 010 : return −1;
If hint = 000 : return 0;
If hint = 001 : return 1;
If hint = 011 : return −q1 + 1;
If hint = 100 : return −q1;
If hint = 101 : return q1 − 1;
```

Fig. 2. Encoding and decoding algorithms for the hint t^h.

Now, let us describe the encoding and decoding functions for ML-DSA-RK.

- $\mathsf{pkEncode}'(\rho, t_1')$: outputs a bit string encoding the public key for ML-DSA-RK.
- $\mathsf{pkDecode}'(pk)$: outputs the components ρ and t_1' of a public key for ML-DSA-RK.
- $\mathsf{skEncode}'(\rho, K, tr, s_1, s_2, t_0, t^h)$: outputs a bit string encoding the secret key for ML-DSA-RK. Notice that

$$\mathsf{skEncode}'(\rho, K, tr, s_1, s_2, t_0, t^h) := \mathsf{skEncode}(\rho, K, tr, s_1, s_2, t_0) \| \mathsf{hintEncode}(t^h, q, \alpha)$$

  where skEncode is the secret key encoding function of ML-DSA.
- $\mathsf{skDecode}'(sk)$: outputs the components ρ, K, tr, s_1, s_2, t_0 and t^h of a secret key for ML-DSA-RK.
- $\mathsf{sigEncode}'(c, z, h, t^h)$: outputs a bit string encoding the signature for ML-DSA-RK. Notice that

$$\mathsf{sigEncode}'(c, z, h, t^h) := \mathsf{sigEncode}(c, z, h) \| \mathsf{hintEncode}(t^h, q, \alpha)$$

  where sigEncode is the signature encoding function of ML-DSA.
- $\mathsf{sigDecode}'(\sigma)$: outputs the components c, z, h and t^h of a signature for ML-DSA-RK.

In the following, we define the randomized algorithms RandPk and RandSk for our SWRK for updating the public and private keys (Fig. 3).

$\underline{\mathsf{RandSk}(sk, \mu):}$

$(\rho, K, tr, s_1, s_2, t_0, \_) := \mathsf{skDecode}(sk);$
$\mathbf{A} \sim R_q^{k \times l} := \mathsf{ExpandA}(\rho);$
$t_1 := \mathsf{Hb}(\mathbf{A}s_1 + s_2);$
$\rho_\mu := \mathsf{H}(\rho, t_1, \mu);$
$(s_1', s_2') := \mathsf{ExpandS}(\rho_\mu);$
$r := \mathbf{A}s_1' + s_2';\ r_1 := \mathsf{Hb}(r);$
$s_1^+ := s_1 + s_1';\ s_2^+ := s_2 + s_2';$
$t^+ := \mathbf{A}s_1^+ + s_2^+;$
$(t_1^+, t_0^+) := \mathsf{Power2Round}(t^+);$
$tr' := \mathsf{H}(\rho, t_1^+, 64);$
$t^h := t_1^+ - \mathsf{Hb}((t_1 + r_1) \cdot \alpha);$
$sk' := \mathsf{skEncode}'(\rho, K, tr', s_1^+, s_2^+, t_0^+, t^h);$
return sk'

$\underline{\mathsf{RandPk}(pk, \mu):}$

$(\rho, t_1) := \mathsf{pkDecode}(pk);$
$\mathbf{A} \sim R_q^{k \times l} := \mathsf{ExpandA}(\rho);$
$\rho_\mu := \mathsf{H}(\rho, t_1, \mu);$
$(s_1', s_2') := \mathsf{ExpandS}(\rho_\mu);$
$r := \mathbf{A}s_1' + s_2';$
$r_1 := \mathsf{Hb}(r);$
$t_1' := \mathsf{Hb}((t_1 + r_1) \cdot \alpha);$
$pk' := \mathsf{pkEncode}'(\rho, t_1');$
return pk'

$\underline{\mathsf{KGen}(\zeta \in \{0,1\}^{256}):}$

$(pk, \widehat{sk}) := \mathsf{ML\text{-}DSA.KGen}(\zeta);$
$t^h := 0 \in \mathcal{R}_q^k;\ sk := (\widehat{sk}, t^h);$
return (pk, sk)

Fig. 3. Key generation, public and private keys rerandomization algorithms of ML-DSA-RK.

Remark 4.5. Notice that the value $pk' := (\rho, t_1')$ obtained from the randomized public key algorithm is not the correct public key corresponding to the rerandomized secret key $sk' := (\rho, K, tr', s_1^+, s_2^+, t_0^+, t^h)$. Concretely, the correct public key corresponding to sk' is $(\rho, t_1' + t^h)$. However, the hint t^h cannot be publicly computed from pk and the randomness μ since it depends on the secret elements s_1 and s_2. To handle this problem, the hint t^h which is included in the rerandomized secret key sk' is encoded using the hintEncode algorithm and will be included as a part of the signature. During the verification, the hint will be decoded using the hintDecode algorithm and added to t_1' to obtain the correct public key corresponding to sk'.

Now let us describe the signing and verification algorithms of our SWRK (Fig. 4).

$\underline{\textsf{ML-DSA-RK.Sign}(m, sk):}$

1: $(\rho, K, tr, s_1, s_2, t_0, t^h) := \textsf{skDecode}'(sk)$;
2: $sk' := \textsf{skEncode}(\rho, K, tr, s_1, s_2, t_0)$;
3: $(c, z, h) := \textsf{ML-DSA.Sign}(m, sk')$;
4: $h' := (h, t^h)$;
5: $\sigma := \textsf{sigEncode}'(c, z, h')$;
6: **return** σ

$\underline{\textsf{ML-DSA-RK.Verify}(m, \sigma, pk):}$

1: $(\rho, t_1) := \textsf{pkDecode}'(pk)$;
2: $(c, z, (h, t^h)) := \textsf{sigDecode}'(\sigma)$;
3: $\sigma' := \textsf{sigEncode}(c, z, h)$;
4: $pk' := \textsf{pkEncode}'(\rho, t_1 + t^h)$;
5: $b := \textsf{ML-DSA.Verify}(m, \sigma', pk')$;
6: **return** b

Fig. 4. Signing and verification algorithms of ML-DSA-RK constructed from the sign and verify algorithms of ML-DSA.

Impact of the Hint on Security

After updating the secret key using the RandSk algorithm, the hint t^h is included in the signature and becomes publicly available. The hint t^h is computed using MLWE samples derived from the secret key and the randomness used for rerandomization, i.e.:

$$t^h = \textsf{Hb}(t + r) - \textsf{Hb}((\textsf{Hb}(t) + \textsf{Hb}(r)) \cdot \alpha)$$

where $t = \mathbf{A}s_1 + s_2$ is a master public key component computed from master secret elements s_1 and s_2, and r is an MLWE sample computed from the randomness used for rerandomization.

One may wonder whether the hint t^h could leak information about the secret key, or be used by an adversary to forge signatures or break the unlinkability property. Unlinkability [7,13] ensures that randomized public keys cannot be linked to the master public keys.

- **Impact of t^h on secret key recovery:** Assuming the hardness of the MLWE problem, an adversary cannot recover any information about the secret elements s_1 and s_2 when given as input the element t. Therefore, the hint t^h, which is computed from t and an independent randomness, cannot leak any information about the secret key.

- **Impact of t^h on signature forgery:** In the unforgeability game (see [22, Fig. 2]), the adversary is given a master public key pk (and thus t) and is asked to find a valid randomness r, a message $m^\star$, and a signature $\sigma^\star$ such that $\mathsf{ML\text{-}DSA\text{-}RK.Verify}(m^\star, \sigma^\star, \mathsf{RandPk}(pk, r)) = 1$. Since t^h is computed from t and r, both of which are accessible to the adversary, this hint does not provide any additional advantage for forging signatures. Moreover, t is considered to be public in the security analysis of ML-DSA. Hence, without loss of generality, we can assume t is publicly available in the security analysis of ML-DSA-RK. In this case, it is trivial to see that no further information is learned from t^h.

– **Impact of t^h on unlinkability:** In the game of unlinkability, the adversary is given two session public keys pk_r and $pk_{\hat{r}}$ and is asked to guess whether they are derived from the same master public key or not. The adversary can also ask for signatures on messages of its choice that verify under the session public keys. Then the adversary has access to the hints t^h and $\hat{t}^h$ corresponding to the two session public keys. Suppose that the randomness r and $\hat{r}$ used for deriving the two session public keys are sampled uniformly at random over the randomness space and are not known to the adversary. Then the distributions of the hints t^h and $\hat{t}^h$ computed from (t, r) (i.e. $t^h = \mathsf{Hb}(t+r) - \mathsf{Hb}((\mathsf{Hb}(t) + \mathsf{Hb}(r)) \cdot \alpha))$ and $(\hat{t}, \hat{r})$ (i.e. $\hat{t}^h = \mathsf{Hb}(\hat{t}+\hat{r}) - \mathsf{Hb}((\mathsf{Hb}(\hat{t}) + \mathsf{Hb}(\hat{r})) \cdot \alpha))$ respectively are indistinguishable even if t and $\hat{t}$ are the same. Therefore, the hints t^h and $\hat{t}^h$ do not leak any additional advantage to an adversary attempting to break the unlinkability property.

Remark 4.6. The security analysis of a signature scheme with rerandomizable keys built on top of a simplified version of ML-DSA was presented in [22]. We refer the reader to [22] for further details.

Acknowledgments. Alice Pellet-Mary is supported by the France 2030 program, managed by the French National Research Agency (ANR-22-PETQ-0008 PQ-TLS). Michel Seck is supported by the French National Research Organization CNRS through the CNRS-Afrique project DIALS (2025–26).

References

1. Bai, S., et al.: CRYSTALS–dilithium: algorithm specification and supporting documentation (version 3.1). Round-3 submission to the NIST Post-Quantum Cryptography Standardization Project (2021). https://pq-crystals.org/dilithium/data/dilithium-specification-round3-20210208.pdf
2. Bai, S., Galbraith, S.D.: An improved compression technique for signatures based on learning with errors. In: Benaloh, J. (ed.) CT-RSA 2014. LNCS, vol. 8366, pp. 28–47. Springer, Cham (2014). https://doi.org/10.1007/978-3-319-04852-9_2
3. Bernstein, D.J., et al.: Report on evaluation of KpqC round-2 candidates. Cryptology ePrint Archive, Paper 2024/2077 (2024). https://eprint.iacr.org/2024/2077
4. Borin, G., Celi, S., del Pino, R., Espitau, T., Niot, G., Prest, T.: Threshold signatures reloaded: ML-DSA and enhanced raccoon with identifiable aborts. Cryptology ePrint Archive, Paper 2025/1166 (2025). https://eprint.iacr.org/2025/1166

5. Bos, J., et al.: CRYSTALS–kyber: a CCA-secure module-lattice-based KEM. In: 2018 IEEE European Symposium on Security and Privacy (EuroS&P), pp. 353–367. IEEE (2018). https://doi.org/10.1109/EuroSP.2018.00032
6. Boudgoust, K., Takahashi, A.: Sequential half-aggregation of lattice-based signatures. In: European Symposium on Research in Computer Security, pp. 270–289. Springer (2023). https://doi.org/10.1007/978-3-031-50594-2_14
7. Celi, S., Griffy, S., Hanzlik, L., Perez-Kempner, O., Slamanig, D.: SoK: signatures with randomizable keys. In: Clark, J., Shi, E. (eds.) Financial Cryptography and Data Security. LNCS, pp. 160–187. Springer, Cham (2025). https://doi.org/10.1007/978-3-031-78679-2_9
8. Cheon, J.H., et al.: HAETAE: shorter lattice-based Fiat-Shamir signatures. IACR Trans. Cryptogr. Hardw. Embed. Syst. **2024**(3), 25–75 (2024). https://doi.org/10.46586/tches.v2024.i3.25-75
9. Coron, J.S., Gérard, F., Trannoy, M., Zeitoun, R.: Improved gadgets for the high-order masking of dilithium. IACR Trans. Cryptogr. Hardw. Embed. Syst. **2023**(4) (2023). https://doi.org/10.46586/tches.v2023.i4.110-145
10. Das, P., Faust, S., Loss, J.: A formal treatment of deterministic wallets. In: Proceedings of the 2019 ACM SIGSAC Conference on Computer and Communications Security, pp. 651–668. (2019). https://doi.org/10.1145/3319535.3354236
11. Del Pino, R., Katsumata, S., Maller, M., Mouhartem, F., Prest, T., Saarinen, M.J.: Threshold raccoon: practical threshold signatures from standard lattice assumptions. In: Annual International Conference on the Theory and Applications of Cryptographic Techniques, pp. 219–248. Springer (2024). https://doi.org/10.1007/978-3-031-58723-8_8
12. Ducas, L., et al.: Crystals-dilithium: a lattice-based digital signature scheme. IACR Trans. Cryptogr. Hardw. Embed. Syst., 238–268 (2018). https://doi.org/10.13154/tches.v2018.i1.238-268
13. Eaton, E., Lepoint, T., Wood, C.A.: Security analysis of signature schemes with key blinding. Cryptology ePrint Archive, Paper 2023/380 (2023). https://eprint.iacr.org/2023/380
14. Fleischhacker, N., Krupp, J., Malavolta, G., Schneider, J., Schröder, D., Simkin, M.: Efficient unlinkable sanitizable signatures from signatures with re-randomizable keys. In: Cheng, C.M., Chung, K.M., Persiano, G., Yang, B.Y. (eds.) Public-Key Cryptography - PKC 2016. LNCS, vol. 9614, pp. 301–330. Springer, Heidelberg (2016). https://doi.org/10.1007/978-3-662-49384-7_12
15. Fukumitsu, M., Hasegawa, S.: A lattice-based provably secure multisignature scheme in quantum random oracle model. In: Nguyen, K., Wu, W., Lam, K.Y., Wang, H. (eds.) ProvSec 2020. LNCS, vol. 12505, pp. 45–64. Springer, Cham (2020). https://doi.org/10.1007/978-3-030-62576-4_3
16. Miller, V.S.: Use of elliptic curves in cryptography. In: Williams, H.C. (ed.) CRYPTO 1985. LNCS, vol. 218, pp. 417–426. Springer, Heidelberg (1986). https://doi.org/10.1007/3-540-39799-X_31
17. National Institute of Standards and Technology: Call for proposals for public-key post-quantum cryptographic algorithms. Federal Register Notice (2016). https://csrc.nist.gov/csrc/media/projects/post-quantum-cryptography/documents/call-for-proposals-final-dec-2016.pdf
18. National Institute of Standards and Technology (NIST): Module-Lattice-Based Digital Signature Standard. Federal Information Processing Standards Publication 204, U.S. Department of Commerce (2024). https://csrc.nist.gov/pubs/fips/204/final

19. National Institute of Standards and Technology (NIST): Module-Lattice-Based Key-Encapsulation Mechanism Standard (ML-KEM). Federal Information Processing Standards Publication 203, U.S. Department of Commerce (2024). Standardization of CRYSTALS-Kyber
20. del Pino, R., Katsumata, S., Prest, T., Rossi, M.: Raccoon: a masking-friendly signature proven in the probing model. In: Annual International Cryptology Conference, pp. 409–444. Springer (2024). https://doi.org/10.1007/978-3-031-68376-3_13
21. Rivest, R.L., Shamir, A., Adleman, L.: A method for obtaining digital signatures and public-key cryptosystems. Commun. ACM **21**(2), 120–126 (1978). https://doi.org/10.1145/359340.359342
22. Seck, M., Roux-Langlois, A.: Towards post-quantum bitcoin blockchain using dilithium signature. IACR Commun. Cryptol. **2**(3) (2025). https://doi.org/10.62056/ak5wom2hd
23. Shor, P.W.: Algorithms for quantum computation: discrete logarithms and factoring. In: Proceedings 35th Annual Symposium on Foundations of Computer Science, FOCS 1994, pp. 124–134. IEEE Computer Society (1994). https://doi.org/10.1109/SFCS.1994.365700
24. Snetkov, N., Vakarjuk, J., Laud, P.: TOPCOAT: towards practical two-party crystals-dilithium. Discov. Comput. **27**(1), 18 (2024). https://doi.org/10.1007/s10791-024-09449-2
25. The Tor Project: Tor rendezvous specification - version 3. Technical report, The Tor Project (2025). https://spec.torproject.org/rend-spec/

Aggregate Signature Using Lattice

Meenakshi Kansal(✉)

Rashtriya Raksha University, Lavad, Gujarat, India
meenakshi.kansal@rru.ac.in

Abstract. Damgård, Orlandi, Takahashi and Tibouchi [DOTT] in JoC 2022 used a trapdoor commitment scheme with homomorphic properties to provide the long-standing unavailable construction of round optimal multi-signature under the lattice setting. In this work, we extend their multi-signature scheme to an aggregate signature scheme. This extension is different from the already known extension given by Bellare and Neven [BN] in ACM CCS 2006, which can be obtained by generating a message by concatenating all the messages involved in the signatures aggregation. As given in [BN], the messages $m_1, m_2, \ldots, m_n$ can be exchanged in the first round of communication between the signers, and then each signer will sign the obtained concatenated message $m = m_1||m_2||\ldots||m_n$ following the underlying secure multi-signature scheme. This may increase the rounds of communication if, in case, the signers are utilizing messages before the first round of communication. Our proposed aggregate signature scheme has the same number of rounds as the multi-signature scheme of [DOTT]. Moreover, the signers in our construction do not sign the concatenated message m but each signer i signs their own message m_i.

To obtain an aggregate signature scheme with such properties, we have proposed a trapdoor commitment scheme with homomorphic properties motivated by the homomorphic trapdoor function of Gorbunov, Vaikuntanathan and Wichs [GVW] in STOC 2015 and the trapdoor commitment scheme of DOTT. We are introducing public keys in the commitment scheme. These public keys are different from the commitment keys, and the trapdoor will be generated corresponding to the public key rather than the commitment key. Our scheme is unforgeable-chosen message attack secure under the assumptions of module-short integer solution and module-learning with errors assumptions. The signature size is independent of the number of signatures involved in the aggregation.

Our proposed scheme is a backbone for storage-efficient post-quantum secure cryptocurrency. Each transaction is associated with a digital signature, and these digital signatures can be aggregated using our construction. The size of our aggregated signature is the same as that of a single digital signature. Thus, the storage space needed to store digital signatures in cryptocurrency can be significantly reduced.

Keywords: aggregate signatures · trapdoor commitment schemes · Fiat-Shamir with aborts · lattice-based cryptography

N. El Mrabet et al. (Eds.): AFRICACRYPT 2026, LNCS 16832, pp. 363–380, 2026.
https://doi.org/10.1007/978-3-032-31130-6_15

1 Introduction

An aggregate signature scheme enables n digital signatures $\sigma_1, \sigma_2, \ldots, \sigma_n$ produced on n messages $m_1, m_2, \ldots, m_n$ by n signers $U_1, U_2, \ldots, U_n$ to combine into a signature σ such that the size of the produced aggregated signature σ is independent of n and the verification of σ confirms whether $\{(m_i, \sigma_i)\}_{i=1}^{n}$ are valid message-signature pair or not. Aggregate signature has various applications. One of its applications can be realized in where the data is large but the storage is limited for instance in cryptocurrency. In cryptocurrency, users produce signatures for each transaction and these signatures can be aggregated using aggregate signature resulting in improved storage efficiency.

Aggregate signatures can be viewed as the generalization of multi-signatures. In multi-signatures, n signatures on the same message by n distinct signers are combined into a single short signature. There have been a number of lattice based multi-signature constructions in the literature but most of them were either fall short of security proofs or are dependent on non-standard heuristic assumptions. For more details refer to [7]. Recently, in the Journal of Cryptology 2022, Damgård et al. [7] proposed a two-round multi-signature scheme secure under lattice assumptions. They have designed a commitment scheme with trapdoor and homomorphic properties that is utilized along with the Fiat-Shamir with Aborts (FSwA) technique to achieve several distributed signing protocols with low round complexity. The commitment scheme proposed in [7] cannot be directly plugged into our construction because the signatures we aggregate are on distinct messages and that makes the commitment keys different for all the users. Thus, we required a commitment scheme with all the features of the commitment scheme of [7] along with a new feature: aggregation must be possible with different commitment keys, while trapdoor generation must be feasible. To obtain such a commitment scheme, we have tweaked [7] by introducing the public key in our commitment scheme. So our commitment scheme has two keys namely public key and commitment key. In the security game, the simulator simulates the trapdoor based on the public key and this trapdoor will be used to compute the randomness that was used to commit.

1.1 Prior Work on Lattice Based Aggregate Signature

We put in a nutshell the state of the art below.

Aggregate signatures were introduced by Boneh et al. [3]. Since then there are very few works that derive their security under the hardness of lattice problems. The first such attempt was made by Doroz et al. [8]. In [8] authors have given aggregate signature schemes MMSA, MMSAT and MMSATK. The construction MMSA is secure under the hardness of partial Fourier recovery problem. There are some shortcomings in these constructions such as the size of the aggregated signature in MMSA is more than the concatenation of all the involved signatures. Authors are utilizing a linear transformation to obtain MMSAT with improved signature size. The used linear transformation is prone to simple forgery attack and thus this makes the scheme insecure. Another issue is that the paper does not provide security proofs for MMSAT and MMSATK. All these shortcomings have been discussed in detail in [5,6]. The construction in [5] presents a half-aggregation signature scheme under the hardness of module-short integer solution problem and module-learning with errors problem and the aggregated signature size is more than the size of the concatenation of all the signatures. The authors have utilized forking lemma twice for security proof. Using the forking lemma twice incurs a significant loss in the reduction. Another effort towards lattice based aggregate signature was made by Boneh and Kim [4]. In this work authors have presented two constructions secure under the hardness of standard SIS problem in the random oracle model. The signature size is atmost logarithmic in the number of signatures being aggregated. That is, the signature size is $O(\log n)$ where n is the number of signers involved. The first construction supports public aggregation for one-time signature and the second construction is a many-time signature scheme which requires three rounds of communication. The scheme here does not handle the abort executions and this may cause serious security concerns as discussed in [7]. Bansarkhani and Buchmann [9] proposed a sequential aggregate signature scheme (SAS). A sequential aggregate signature scheme allows a group of signers to sequentially combine their signatures produced on distinct messages into a single signature such that the size of the obtained signature is much smaller than the concatenation of all the signatures. A lattice based digital signature falls into either the FSwA paradigm or the Hash-then-Sign paradigm. Falcon is a lattice based signature scheme which follows the hash-then-sign paradigm. In [1], a non-interactive aggregate signature scheme for Falcon is proposed and it is obtained by utilizing LaBRADOR. Table 1 gives a comparison of all the prior works. In Table 1, n specifies the number of signatures.

1.2 Our Contribution and Techniques

Our construction for obtaining an aggregate signature is highly motivated by the construction of multi-signature scheme by Damgård et al. [7]. The challenge for us was to design a trapdoor commitment scheme having homomorphic properties with respect to distinct commitment keys.

Highlights of our construction are as follows:

- It is different from the already known extension of multi-signature scheme to aggregate signature scheme given by Bellare and Neven [2] which can be obtained by generating a message by concatenating all the messages involved in the aggregation. As given in [2], the messages $m_1, m_2, \ldots, m_n$ can be exchanged in the first round of communication between the signers and then each signer will sign the obtained concatenated message $m = m_1||m_2||\ldots||m_n$ following the underlying secure multi-signature scheme. This may increase the rounds of communication in case the signers are utilizing messages before the first round of communication. In contrast, our proposed aggregate signature scheme has the same number of rounds as the multi-signature scheme of [7].

Table 1. Comparative summary of lattice based aggregate signature schemes

Scheme	Functionality achieved	# Rounds	Signature size	Assumption	Secure
[9]	sequential aggregate signature	–	independent of n	collision-resistant preimage sampleable function	yes
[4]	one-time and many-time aggregate signature	3	$O(\log n)$	SIS	no
MMSA [8] MMSAT [8]	aggregate signature	non interactive	$O(n)$	partial Fourier recovery problem	no
MMSATK [8]	aggregate signature & public key aggregation	non interactive	$O(n)$	partial Fourier recovery problem	no
[5]	half aggregation	non interactive	$O(n)$	M-SIS/M-LWE	yes
[11]	aggregate signature	non interactive	$O(n)$	M-SIS/M-LWE	yes
[1]	aggregate signature for Falcon	non interactive	independent of n	M-SIS	yes
ours	aggregate signature	2	independent of n	M-SIS/M-LWE	yes

Moreover, the signers in our construction do not sign the concatenated message m but each signer i signs their own message m_i.

- It requires only two rounds of communication. Note that realizing an aggregate signature in less than two rounds is practically impossible in Fiat-Shamir with aborts (FSwA) technique. As it is discussed in [7], the first round is required to obtain the commitments com_i from the users those are involved in the signature generation. This is because the sum of the commitments $com = \sum_{j=1}^{n} com_j$ will be hashed along with the message to generate a challenge in the Σ-protocol. The second round is necessary to receive the randomness from each user so that the commitment can be opened.
- The homomorphic property of the trapdoor commitment scheme has a dual effect. It not only helps us to obtain round optimal aggregate signature scheme but at the same time it also assists in addressing the leakage due to aborted commitments. In any distributed signature scheme constructed using the FSwA technique the first step is that each user must reveal their commit message. As noted in the previous point that the challenge is then obtained by combining all the commitments $com = f(com_i)$. Consequently, the commitments are revealed in every execution irrespective of whether the execution will abort or not. These aborted executions may reveal some knowledge about the secrets. Since there is no existing literature that proves the

security of a sigma protocol in FSwA. This is a serious security concern and thus it forces us not to disclose the aborted executions. Therefore, following the techniques of [7] we use homomorphic commitment scheme. We are actually committing the commitment $\mathbf{w}_j$ so that the hiding property of the commitment scheme will reveal no useful information about $\mathbf{w}_j$'s. The homomorphic property (specifically additive property) will be useful in summing the new commitments - i.e., $com = \sum_{i=1}^{n} com_j$ and obtaining the challenge by hashing com and the message m_j.

- The messages are not chosen statically at the setup phase. Each signer chooses their message m_j during the signature generation and the message is sent in the first round of communication along with the commitment com_j.
- The construction is secure in the unforgeability under chosen message attack model. This is noteworthy because, in this model, the simulator, at the beginning of the security game hands over the public key of the honest user (to which adversary will forge) pk_n, the public parameters of the aggregate signature scheme PP, public parameters of the commitment scheme ppc and the public key of the commitment scheme cpk to the adversary. Thus by choosing ppc and cpk the simulator is kind of fixing the commitment scheme for the security game.
- The trapdoor commitment scheme with homomorphic properties is inspired by the homomorphic trapdoor function of Gorbunov et al. [10] and the trapdoor commitment scheme of Damgård et al. [7]. Our commitment scheme has public key and commitment key as two different keys. The public key is chosen uniformly at random from the specified domain and the commitment key is message dependent. The commitment key was simulated in [7] as each signer is signing the same message. In our aggregate signature construction, the simulator simulates the public key and not the commitment key because each signer signs a different message and thus the commitment key for each signer is different. Therefore, we required a key which is same for all the users which motivated us to have commitment key and public key as two different keys. Also for the same reason that the public key gets simulated and at the same time it must be same for all the users the public key of the commitment scheme is simulated at the beginning of the security game by the simulator. The simulator generates the trapdoor corresponding to the simulated public key which will be utilized to derive the randomness when the commitment is not honestly generated.

2 Preliminaries

In this section we give notations and definitions required for this paper.

Notations. We use λ to denote a security parameter. Upper case bold letters denote matrices, lower case bold letters denote vectors and $[n]$ denotes the set

$\{1, 2, 3, \ldots, n\}$. The notation $\mathbf{I}_k$ specifies an identity matrix of $k \times k$ size. Let $N \in \mathbb{N}$ be a power of 2 and $f(x) = x^N + 1$ is a polynomial in x of degree N. The ring $R[x] = \mathbb{Z}[x]/ < f(x) >$ and $R_q[x] = \mathbb{Z}_q[x]/ < f(x) >$.

Definition 1. (Module-Short Integer Solution Problem (M-SIS$_{q,k,l,\beta}$)). *Let $\boldsymbol{A} \in R_q^{k\times l}$ be a matrix. The M-SIS$_{q,k,l,\beta}$ problem is to find $\boldsymbol{x} \in R_q^{l+k}$ so that $[\boldsymbol{A}|\boldsymbol{I}_k]\cdot\boldsymbol{x} = 0$ and $0 < ||\boldsymbol{x}||_2 \leq \beta$.*

Definition 2. (Module-Learning with Errors Problem (M-LWE$_{q,k,l,\eta}$)). *Let $\boldsymbol{A} \in R_q^{k\times l}$ be a matrix and a vector $\boldsymbol{t} \in R_q^k$. The M-LWE$_{q,k,l,\eta}$ problem is to decide whether $(\boldsymbol{A}, \boldsymbol{t})$ are generated uniformly at random from the set $R_q^{k\times l} \times R_q^k$ or $\boldsymbol{t}$ is generated as $\boldsymbol{t} = [\boldsymbol{A}|\boldsymbol{I}] \cdot \boldsymbol{s}$ for any $\boldsymbol{s} \leftarrow_\$ S_\eta^l \times S_\eta^k$.*

Definition 3. (Discrete Gaussian Distribution). *The discrete Gaussian distribution for $\boldsymbol{x} \in R^m$ with mean $\boldsymbol{u} \in R^m$ and variance $s \in R$ is denoted by $D^m_{\boldsymbol{u},s}(\boldsymbol{x})$ and is defined as*

$$D^m_{\boldsymbol{u},s}(\boldsymbol{x}) := \rho_{\boldsymbol{u},s}(\boldsymbol{x})/\rho_{\boldsymbol{u},s}(R^m)$$

where $\rho_{\boldsymbol{u},s}(\boldsymbol{x}) = exp(-\pi||\boldsymbol{x} - \boldsymbol{u}||_2^2)$ is the Gaussian function of $\boldsymbol{u}$ and s and $\rho_{\boldsymbol{u},s}(R^m) = \sum_{\boldsymbol{x}\in R^m} \rho_{\boldsymbol{u},s}(\boldsymbol{x})$. If $\boldsymbol{u} = 0$ then the discrete Gaussian distribution is denoted by $D^m_s(\boldsymbol{x})$.

Let $\{\mathbf{x}_i\}_{i\in[n]}$ for be n independent samples sampled from the distribution D^m_s. When s exceeds the smoothing parameter by a factor ≥ 2 then the distribution of $\mathbf{x} = \sum_{i=1}^{n} \mathbf{x}_i$ is statistically close to the Gaussian distribution $D^m_{s\sqrt{n}}$.

2.1 Generalized Forking Lemma

Let us consider an input generator randomized algorithm denoted by iGen and let H be any set with $|H| \geq 2$. Let Q denotes the number of maximum queries. Let a randomized algorithm $\mathcal{H}$ takes input $x, h_1, h_2, \ldots, h_Q$ and it returns output (i, out). Here $i \in [0, Q]$ is an index and *out* is a side output. Let $\mathcal{G}$ be a forking algorithm (specified in Algorithm 1) with access to $\mathcal{H}$ as a black box. Then

$frk := \Pr[b = 1 : x \leftarrow \text{iGen}(1^\lambda); (b, out, \widehat{out}) \leftarrow \mathcal{G}_{\mathcal{H}}(x)] \geq acc\cdot\left(\frac{acc}{Q} - \frac{1}{|H|}\right)$ and

$acc := \Pr[i \neq 0 : x \leftarrow \text{iGen}(1^\lambda); h_1, h_2, \ldots, h_Q \leftarrow_\$ H; (i, out) \leftarrow \mathcal{H}(x, h_1, h_2, \ldots, h_Q)] \quad \leq \frac{Q}{|H|} + \sqrt{Q \cdot frk}.$

2.2 Trapdoor Commitment Scheme

In this section we define a new trapdoor commitment scheme ComTrap=(SetupC, GenC, Commit, OpenC, GenTC, CommitT, Equiv) having seven polynomial time algorithms.

Algorithm 1. Working of the Algorithm $\mathcal{G}_{\mathcal{H}}(x)$

Input x with access to the randomized algorithm $\mathcal{H}$ as a black box
1. pick ρ, a random coin;
2. sample $h_1, h_2, \ldots, h_Q \leftarrow_\$ H$;
3. generate $(i, out) \leftarrow \mathcal{H}(x, h_1, h_2, \ldots, h_Q; \rho)$;
4. if $i = 0$
5. return $(0, \perp, \perp)$;
6. sample $\widehat{h}_i, \widehat{h}_{i+1}, \ldots, \widehat{h}_Q \leftarrow_\$ H$;
7. generate $(i, out) \leftarrow \mathcal{H}(x, h_1, h_2, \ldots, h_{i-1}, \widehat{h}_i, \widehat{h}_{i+1}, \ldots, \widehat{h}_Q; \rho)$;
8. if $i = \widehat{i}$ and $h_i \neq \widehat{h}_i$
9. return $(1, \perp, \perp)$;
10. else
11. return $(0, \perp, \perp)$.

Definition 4. (Trapdoor Commitment Scheme). *A trapdoor commitment scheme denoted by* ComTrap *has the following polynomial time algorithms.*
$(ppc, pk) \leftarrow \mathsf{SetupC}(1^\lambda)$. *On receiving a security parameter* λ, *the setup algorithm outputs the public parameter ppc which consists of the details of the commitment key space* $\mathcal{F}_{ck}$, *message space* $\mathcal{F}_m$, *randomness space* $\mathcal{F}_r$, *public key space* $\mathcal{F}_{pk}$, *trapdoor space* $\mathcal{F}_{td}$ *and commitment space* $\mathcal{F}_{com}$. *It also outputs the distribution of the randomness* $D(\mathcal{F}_r)$ *and the public key pk.*
$ck \leftarrow \mathsf{GenC}(ppc)$. *A commitment key* $\mathsf{ck} \in \mathcal{F}_{ck}$ *gets generated by the key generation algorithm.*
$com \leftarrow \mathsf{Commit}_{pk,ck}(m; r)$. *The commitment algorithm generates the commitment* $com \in \mathcal{F}_{com}$ *on the message* $m \in \mathcal{F}_m$ *with the randomness* $r \in \mathcal{F}_r$.
$b \in \{0, 1\} \leftarrow \mathsf{OpenC}_{pk,ck}(com, r, m)$. *If* $b = 1$, *the input is a valid tuple, otherwise invalid.*
$(ppc, tpk, td) \leftarrow \mathsf{SetupTC}(1^\lambda)$. *On input the security parameter* λ, *the trapdoor key generation algorithm outputs public parameter ppc, a trapdoor public key* $tpk \in \mathcal{F}_{pk}$ *and a trapdoor* $td \in \mathcal{F}_{td}$.
$com \leftarrow \mathsf{CommitT}_{tpk,ck}(td)$. *On receiving a commitment key ck and a trapdoor public key tpk with a corresponding trapdoor td, a commitment* $com \in \mathcal{F}_{com}$ *is an output of the trapdoor commitment algorithm.*
$r \leftarrow \mathsf{Equiv}_{tpk,ck}(td, com, m)$. *It is an equivocation algorithm and it outputs a randomness* $r \in \mathcal{F}_r$ *associated with the given input such that* $1 \leftarrow \mathsf{OpenC}_{pk,ck}(com, r, m)$.

Correctness. *The above defined* ComTrap *is correct if*

$$\Pr\Big[1 \leftarrow \mathsf{OpenC}_{pk,ck}(com, r, m) : (ppc, pk) \leftarrow \mathsf{SetupC}(1^\lambda), r \leftarrow_\$ D(\mathcal{F}_r), ck \leftarrow \mathsf{GenC}(ppc), com \leftarrow \mathsf{Commit}_{pk,ck}(m; r)\Big] = 1.$$

Hiding. *The above defined* ComTrap *is statistically hiding if for all probabilistic adversary* $\mathcal{A}$ *the following holds.*

$$\epsilon_1 = \Big| \Pr\Big[b = b' : (ppc, pk) \leftarrow \mathsf{SetupC}(1^\lambda); ck \leftarrow \mathsf{GenC}(ppc); (m_0, m_1) \leftarrow \mathcal{A}(ppc, pk, ck);$$

$$b \leftarrow_{\$} \{0,1\}; com \leftarrow \mathsf{Commit}_{pk,ck}(m_b; r);$$
$$b' \leftarrow \mathcal{A}(com)\Big] - \tfrac{1}{2}\Big| < negl(\lambda).$$

Note that if the adversary $\mathcal{A}$ is a probabilistic polynomial time algorithm then the above defined ComTrap *is computationally hiding.*

Binding. *The above defined* ComTrap *is statistically binding if for all probabilistic adversary $\mathcal{A}$ the following holds.*

$$\epsilon_2 = \Pr\Big[m \neq m' \text{ and } 1 = \mathsf{OpenC}_{pk,ck}(com, r, m) \text{ and } 1 = \mathsf{OpenC}_{pk,ck}(com, r', m') : (ppc, pk) \leftarrow \mathsf{SetupC}(1^\lambda); ck \leftarrow \mathsf{GenC}(ppc) \; (com, m, r, m', r') \leftarrow \mathcal{A}(pk, ck)\Big] < negl(\lambda).$$

Note that if the adversary $\mathcal{A}$ is a probabilistic polynomial time algorithm then the above defined ComTrap *is computationally binding.*

Secure Trapdoor. *The trapdoor commitment scheme* ComTrap *has a secure trapdoor if the statistical distance between the two tuples (pk, ck, m, com, r) and (tpk, ck, m, com', r') (for every m) is negligible in λ where $(ppc, pk) \leftarrow$ $\mathsf{SetupC}(1^\lambda); ck \leftarrow \mathsf{GenC}(ppc); r \xleftarrow{\$} \mathcal{F}_r; com \leftarrow \mathsf{Commit}_{pk,ck}(m; r)$; $(ppc, tpk, td) \leftarrow \mathsf{SetupTC}(1^\lambda)$; $com' \leftarrow \mathsf{CommitT}_{tpk,ck}(td)$ and $r' \leftarrow$ $\mathsf{Equiv}_{tpk,ck}(td, com', m)$.*

Additive Homomorphism. ComTrap *is additively homomorphic if*

$$\Pr\Big[1 \leftarrow \mathsf{OpenC}_{pk,ck}(com + com', r + r', m + m') : (ppc, pk) \leftarrow \mathsf{SetupC}(1^\lambda); ck \leftarrow \mathsf{GenC}(ppc) ; r, r' \leftarrow_{\$} \mathcal{F}_r; com \leftarrow \mathsf{Commit}_{pk,ck}(m; r); com' \leftarrow \mathsf{Commit}_{pk,ck}(m'; r')\Big] = 1.$$

Definition 5. (Aggregate Signature Scheme). *Any aggregate signature scheme has four polynomial time algorithms namely* Agg=(setup, gen, sign, verify). *The working of each algorithm is explained below. Let n number of users are coming together to generate aggregate signature.*

$PP \leftarrow$Agg-setup(1^λ). *It takes input as the security parameter λ and outputs the public parameters PP of the aggregate signature scheme.*

$(pk, sk) \leftarrow$Agg-gen(PP). *On receiving a public parameter PP, it generates the public key pk and the corresponding secret key sk.*

$\sigma_{agg} \leftarrow$Agg-sign$(PP, pk_n, P = \{pk_i\}_{i \in [n-1]}, sk_n, m_n)$. *The signing algorithm is an interactive protocol. Each user U_n runs this algorithm with the public key pk_n, secret key sk_n, message m_n along with the public keys P of all the co-signers. Finally, the algorithm outputs an aggregated signature σ_{agg}.*

$(1 \text{ or } 0) \leftarrow$Agg-verify$(\sigma_{agg}, P = \{pk_i\}_{i=1}^n, M = \{m_i\}_{i=1}^n)$. *This algorithm checks whether the produced aggregated signature on a set of messages M by the set of users holding public keys P is correct or not. If it is correct, it outputs 1, otherwise it outputs 0.*

Security. *An aggregate signature scheme is said to be secure under unforgeable-chosen message attack if the advantage $Adv_{AS}^{UF-CMA}(\mathcal{A})$ of the adversary in $Exp_{AS}^{UF-CMA}(\mathcal{A})$ experiment given in Fig. 1 is negligible in λ.*

1. **Setup** The algorithm $\mathcal{A}$ is provided with a public key pk_n and public parameters generated by the simulator.
2. **Queries** Adversary $\mathcal{A}$ may requests signature queries adaptively with pk_n on messages of his choice.
3. **Response** At the end, adversary $\mathcal{A}$ outputs $n-1$ public keys and n messages. On these $\{(pk_i, m_i)\}_{i\in[n]}$, $\mathcal{A}$ will output a forgery σ.

The adversary wins the game if

1. σ is a valid forgery on messages $(m_1, m_2, \ldots, m_n)$ under keys $(pk_1, pk_2, \ldots, pk_n)$ and
2. σ is non-trivial.

Fig. 1. $Exp_{AS}^{UF-CMA}(\mathcal{A})$

3 Lattice Based Trapdoor Commitment Scheme

In this section, we propose a trapdoor based commitment scheme given in Fig. 2. The proposed trapdoor commitment scheme is computationally binding and statistically hiding. It also satisfies certain homomorphic property that will help us in obtaining aggregate signature.

Computationally Binding. If an adversary can produce a commitment $\mathbf{v}$ on message-randomness pair $(m, \mathbf{r})$ and $(m', \mathbf{r}')$ with $m \neq m'$ then there are two cases.
Case 1: Commit$_{pk,ck}(m; \mathbf{r})$=Commit$_{pk,ck}(m'; \mathbf{r}')$.
Let $\mathbf{A}_0 = \begin{bmatrix} \widehat{\mathbf{A}}_{01} \\ \widehat{\mathbf{A}}_{02} \end{bmatrix}$ and $\mathbf{A}_1 = \begin{bmatrix} \widehat{\mathbf{A}}_{11} \\ \widehat{\mathbf{A}}_{12} \end{bmatrix}$ then $\widehat{\mathbf{A}}_{11}(\mathbf{r} - \mathbf{r}') = 0 \bmod q$. Also by the correctness of the commitment scheme it follows that $||\mathbf{r} - \mathbf{r}'|| \leq 2B$ and $\mathbf{r} \neq \mathbf{r}'$. Thus $\mathbf{r} - \mathbf{r}'$ is a solution to the M-SIS$_{q,1,l+2w,2B}$ problem with $\widehat{\mathbf{A}}_{11}$ as the public key. The way $\widehat{\mathbf{A}}_{11}$ is generated i.e., as the $(1, 1)$ cell of $\widehat{\mathbf{A}}_{11}$ is invertible, it can be expressed as $[\mathbf{A}|\mathbf{I}]$. The selection of such $\widehat{\mathbf{A}}_{11}$ helps us to write it directly in the form of M-SIS problem specified in Definition 1.

Strong Computationally Binding. Our proposed trapdoor commitment scheme will provide strong computationally binding if the commitment key $\mathbf{u} \xleftarrow{\$} R_r^{l+2w}$ is chosen to be a short length vector.
Case 2: Commit$_{pk,ck_1}(m; \mathbf{r})$=Commit$_{pk,ck_2}(m'; \mathbf{r}')$. Then $\widehat{\mathbf{A}}_{01}(\mathbf{u} - \mathbf{u}') + \widehat{\mathbf{A}}_{11}(\mathbf{r} - \mathbf{r}') = 0 \bmod q$. That means $[\widehat{\mathbf{A}}_{01} \ \ \widehat{\mathbf{A}}_{11}] \cdot \begin{bmatrix} \mathbf{u} - \mathbf{u}' \\ \mathbf{r} - \mathbf{r}' \end{bmatrix} = 0 \bmod q$. Also by the correctness of the commitment scheme it follows that $||\mathbf{r} - \mathbf{r}'|| \leq 2B$, $||\mathbf{u} - \mathbf{u}'|| \leq 2B$ and

$\mathbf{r} \neq \mathbf{r}'$, $\mathbf{u} \neq \mathbf{u}'$. Thus, $\begin{bmatrix} \mathbf{u} - \mathbf{u}' \\ \mathbf{r} - \mathbf{r}' \end{bmatrix}$ is a solution to the M-SIS$_{q,1,2l+4w,4B}$ problem with $[\widehat{\mathbf{A}}_{01} \ \ \widehat{\mathbf{A}}_{11}]$ as the public key.

Statistically Hiding. By [13], Corollary 7.5, we know that by picking $s > 2Nq^{(2+2/N)/(l+2w)}$ we will have $\mathbf{A} \cdot D_s^{l+2w} \approx_s U(R_q^2)$ with high probability. This gives that the commitment $\mathbf{v}$ is statistically indistinguishable from a uniform vector.
Note that our commitment scheme satisfies a special binding property along with the regular binding property. Informally, the regular binding property says that for one commitment key, it is not possible to find two distinct randomness and two distinct messages which will compute the same commitment. In our special binding property, adversary even have choice on selection of distinct commitment keys and still he will not be able to break the binding property provided the commitment key $\mathbf{u}$ is also a short vector. The proposed commitment scheme is a strong commitment scheme and can be of independent interest.

Indistinguishability of the Trapdoor. Note that [[13], Corollary 7.5] ensures that the public key generated by SetupC and SetupTC are indistinguishable by setting the parameters $s > 2Nq^{(2+2/N)/(l+2w)}$.

Equivocability. The computed randomness $\mathbf{r}$ follows the same distribution as the regular commitment algorithm by choosing the standard deviation of the Gaussian distribution to be $s = \theta(N^{3/2} \log^2 N)$.

Theorem 1. *Let $\epsilon > 0$ and $q = N^{2+\epsilon}$ be a prime. Let us set the parameters to be $\bar{s} = \theta(N)$, $s = \theta(N^{3/2} \log^2 N)$, $B = \theta(N^2 \log^3 N)$, $l = w = \lceil \log_2 q \rceil$. With this setting up of parameters, the newly constructed commitment scheme given in Fig. 2 is a secure trapdoor commitment scheme assuming the M-SIS$_{q,1,l+2w,2B}$ problem is hard.*

$\mathsf{SetupC}(1^\lambda)$ outputs the public parameter $ppc = (q, B, N, l, w)$ and the public key $cpk = (\mathbf{A}_0, \mathbf{A}_1) \in R_q^{2\times(l+2w)} \times R_q^{2\times(l+2w)}$. It samples uniform and invertible elements $b_{1,1}, c_{1,1} \leftarrow R_q^\times$ and rest all elements $b_{1,j}, c_{1,j} \leftarrow R_q$ for $j = 2, 3, \ldots, l + 2w$ and $b_{2,j}, c_{2,j} \leftarrow R_q$ for $j = 3, 4, \ldots, l + 2w$ are chosen uniformly random from R_q. It sets the public key as $\mathbf{A}_0 = \begin{bmatrix} b_{1,1} & b_{1,2} & b_{1,3} & \cdots & b_{1,l+2w} \\ 0 & 1 & b_{2,3} & \cdots & b_{2,l+2w} \end{bmatrix}$ and $\mathbf{A}_1 = \begin{bmatrix} c_{1,1} & c_{1,2} & c_{1,3} & \cdots & c_{1,l+2w} \\ 0 & 1 & c_{2,3} & \cdots & c_{2,l+2w} \end{bmatrix}$.

$\mathsf{GenC}(ppc)$ samples a commitment key $\mathbf{u} \leftarrow R_q^{l+2w}$ and outputs the commitment key $ck = \mathbf{u}$.

$\mathsf{Commit}_{(\mathbf{A}_0,\mathbf{A}_1),\mathbf{u}}(x)$ takes a message $x \in R_q$ and samples a randomness $\mathbf{r} \leftarrow R_q^{l+2w}$ following discrete Gaussian distribution with $||\mathbf{r}|| \leq B$. It computes the commitment on a message x as $\mathbf{v} = \mathbf{A}_0\mathbf{u} + \mathbf{A}_1\mathbf{r} + \begin{bmatrix} 0 \\ x \end{bmatrix}$ and finally outputs the commitment $\mathbf{v}$.

$\mathsf{OpenC}_{(\mathbf{A}_0,\mathbf{A}_1),\mathbf{u}}(\mathbf{v}, \mathbf{r}, x)$ verifies that $\mathbf{v} = \mathbf{A}_0\mathbf{u} + \mathbf{A}_1\mathbf{r} + \begin{bmatrix} 0 \\ x \end{bmatrix}$ and $||\mathbf{r}|| \leq B$.

$\mathsf{SetupTC}(1^\lambda)$ generates the public parameter $ppc = (q, B, N, l, w)$ and samples a matrix $\mathbf{R} \leftarrow D_s^{l\times 2w}$ following Gaussian distribution and two matrices $\mathbf{A}_0 \xleftarrow{\$} R_q^{2\times(l+2w)}, \mathbf{A} \xleftarrow{\$} R_q^{2\times l}$ of the form $\mathbf{A}_0 = \begin{bmatrix} b_{1,1} & b_{1,2} & b_{1,3} & \cdots & b_{1,l+2w} \\ 0 & 1 & b_{2,3} & \cdots & b_{2,l+2w} \end{bmatrix}$ and $\mathbf{A} = \begin{bmatrix} a_{1,1} & a_{1,2} & a_{1,3} & \cdots & a_{1,l} \\ 0 & 1 & a_{2,3} & \cdots & a_{2,l} \end{bmatrix}$ where $b_{1,1}, a_{1,1} \xleftarrow{\$} R_q^\times$ and rest all elements $b_{1,j}, a_{1,k} \xleftarrow{\$} R_q$ for $j = 2, 3, \ldots, l + 2w$, $k = 2, 3, \ldots, l$ and $b_{2,j}, a_{2,k} \xleftarrow{\$} R_q$ for $j = 3, 4, \ldots, l + 2w$, $k = 3, 4, \ldots, l$ are chosen uniformly random from R_q. Now it sets $\bar{\mathbf{A}}_1 = [\mathbf{A}|\mathbf{G} - \mathbf{A}\mathbf{R}]$. Here $\mathbf{G} = \begin{bmatrix} 1 \; 2 \; \ldots \; 2^{w-1} & 0 \; 0 \; \ldots 0 \\ 0 \; 0 \ldots 0 & 1 \;\; 2 \ldots 2^{w-1} \end{bmatrix}$. The matrix $\mathbf{R}$ with small entries is the trapdoor td. It outputs the public parameters ppc, public key $tcpk = (\mathbf{A}_0, \bar{\mathbf{A}}_1)$ and the trapdoor td.

$\mathsf{CommitT}_{(\mathbf{A}_0,\bar{\mathbf{A}}_1),\mathbf{u}}(td)$ returns a uniformly random commitment $\mathbf{v} \in R_q^{2\times 1}$.

$\mathsf{Equiv}_{(\mathbf{A}_0,\bar{\mathbf{A}}_1),\mathbf{u}}(\mathbf{R}, \mathbf{v}, x)$ outputs a randomness $\mathbf{r} \in R_q^{l+2w}$ with $||\mathbf{r}|| \leq B$ satisfying $\mathbf{v} = \mathbf{A}_0\mathbf{u} + \bar{\mathbf{A}}_1\mathbf{r} + \begin{bmatrix} 0 \\ x \end{bmatrix}$. This can be found using a technique given in [14] as follows. Notice that $\bar{\mathbf{A}}_1 \cdot \begin{bmatrix} \mathbf{R} \\ \mathbf{I} \end{bmatrix} = \mathbf{G}$. Let $\mathbf{d} = \mathbf{v} - \mathbf{A}_0\mathbf{u} - \begin{bmatrix} 0 \\ x \end{bmatrix}$ then we need to find $\mathbf{r}$ such that $\bar{\mathbf{A}}_1\mathbf{r} = \mathbf{d} \bmod q$. Choose a vector $\mathbf{p} = \begin{bmatrix} \mathbf{p}_1 \\ \mathbf{p}_2 \end{bmatrix} \leftarrow D_s^{l+2w}$ and set $\bar{\mathbf{w}} = \mathbf{A}(\mathbf{p}_1 - \mathbf{R}\mathbf{p}_2)$ and $\mathbf{w} = \mathbf{G}\mathbf{p}_2$. Let $\mathbf{f} = \mathbf{d} - \bar{\mathbf{A}}_1\mathbf{p}$. Choose a vector $\mathbf{z} \xleftarrow{\$} D_s^{2w}$ such that $\mathbf{G}\mathbf{z} = \mathbf{f}$. Then a small normed vector $\mathbf{r} = \mathbf{p} + \begin{bmatrix} \mathbf{R} \\ \mathbf{I} \end{bmatrix} \mathbf{z}$ satisfies the condition $\bar{\mathbf{A}}_1\mathbf{r} = \mathbf{d}$.

Fig. 2. Trapdoor Commitment Scheme: a variant of DOTT [7].

4 Aggregate Signature Scheme

In this section we propose a two round lattice based aggregate signature scheme using a homomorphic trapdoor commitment scheme given in Sect. 3. To obtain this result, we are utilizing the above proposed trapdoor commitment scheme 2 with homomorphic property.

$PP \leftarrow$Agg-setup(1^λ). It takes input as the security parameter λ and outputs the public parameter $PP = (cpk, pp)$ where $cpk \leftarrow \mathsf{SetupC}(1^\lambda)$ is generated utilizing Lattice based Trapdoor Commitment Scheme given in Fig. 3 and $pp = (n, q, k, l, N, S_\eta, \kappa, \sigma, \beta, \mathbf{A}, H_0, H_1)$ as specified below.

- n is the number of signers involved in signature aggregation.
- q is the prime modulus.
- k and l are respectively the number of rows and columns in a matrix.
- For any $\gamma > 1$, $\Pr[||\mathbf{z}||_2 > \gamma\sigma\sqrt{(l+k)N} : \mathbf{z} \leftarrow_\$ D_s^{l+k}] < \gamma^{(l+k)N} e^{(l+k)N(1-\gamma^2)/2}$. Here γ is chosen such that the probability $\gamma^{(l+k)N} e^{(l+k)N(1-\gamma^2)/2}$ is negligible. This result stated here is taken from [7] and it is originally given in [12].
- $f(x) = x^N + 1$ where N is power of two.
- $R[x] = \mathbb{Z}[x]/ < f(x) >$ and $R_q[x] = \mathbb{Z}_q[x]/ < f(x) >$.
- $S_\eta = \{x \in R : ||x||_\infty \leq \eta\}_{\eta \geq 0}$ is the collection from which the secret keys are picked.
- κ is the L^1-bound on a challenge vector $c \in C = \{c \in R : ||c||_\infty = 1 \wedge ||c||_1 = \kappa\}_{\kappa \geq 0}$.
- $\sigma = s/\sqrt{2\pi} = \alpha T$ is the standard deviation of the discrete Gaussian distribution. Here $T = \kappa\eta\sqrt{N(l+k)}$.
- $\beta = \gamma\sigma\sqrt{N(l+k)}$ is the L^2-upper bound on a signature share and $\beta_n = \sqrt{n}\beta$ is the L^2-upper bound on n aggregated signature.
- $M = e^{t/\alpha + 1/2\alpha^2}$ is the average number of restarts in interactive signature protocol of our proposed construction. Here $t = \omega(\sqrt{\log((l+k)N)}) \wedge t = o(\log((l+k)N))$.
- $\mathbf{A} = [\bar{\mathbf{A}}|\mathbf{I}_k]$ with $\bar{\mathbf{A}} \in R_q^{k \times l}$.
- $H_0 : \{0,1\}^* \to \{0,1\}^{l_0}$ and $H_1 : \{0,1\}^* \to \{0,1\}^{l_1}$ are the cryptographically secure hash functions. The hash function H_0 is modeled as random oracle.

$(pk, sk) \leftarrow$Agg-gen(PP). Each user U_i chooses a secret key $sk_i = \mathbf{s}_i$ and computes a public key $pk_i = \mathbf{t}_i = \mathbf{A} \cdot \mathbf{s}_i \bmod q$.
$\sigma_{agg} \leftarrow$Agg-sign$(PP, pk_n, P = \{pk_j\}_{j \in [n-1]}, sk_n, m_n)$. Let n users come together to run this interactive aggregate signature generation protocol. Each user performs the steps given below. For simplicity we are writing the working of n-th user U_n.

1. (a) Computes the commitment key $ck_n = H_1(m_n, P)$.
   (b) Samples $\mathbf{y}_n \leftarrow D_s^{l+k}$ and sets $\mathbf{w}_n = \mathbf{A} \cdot \mathbf{y}_n \bmod q$.
   (c) Computes $com_n = \mathsf{Commit}_{cpk, ck_n}(\mathbf{w}_n; \mathbf{r}_n)$.
   (d) return (com_n, m_n).
2. After obtaining $\{(com_j, m_j)\}_{j \in [n-1]}$, compute a share of the signature as given below.
   (a) $com = \sum_{j \in [n]} com_j$.
   (b) Derive a challenge $c_n \leftarrow H_0(t_n, com, m_n, \{m_k\}_{k \in [n-1]}, P)$.
   (c) Computes $\mathbf{z}_n = c_n \mathbf{s}_n + \mathbf{y}_n$.

(d) Apply rejection sampling on input $(c_n\mathbf{s}_n, \mathbf{z}_n)$ i.e., with probability $\min(1, D_s^{l+k}(\mathbf{z}_n)/(M \cdot D_{c_n\mathbf{s}_n,s}^{l+k}(\mathbf{z}_n)))$ and return $(\mathbf{z}_n, \mathbf{r}_n)$; else restart from step 1.

3. After collecting $(\mathbf{z}_j, r_j)$ for all $j \in [n-1]$ verify each signature $\mathbf{z}_j$ as below.
   (a) For each $j \in [n-1]$ derive $c_j \leftarrow H_0(t_j, com, m_j, \{m_k\}_{k\in[n],k\neq j}, P)$, $ck_j \leftarrow H_1(m_j, P)$ and reconstruct $\mathbf{w}_j = \mathbf{A}\mathbf{z}_j - c_j\mathbf{t}_j$ and finally verify $||\mathbf{z}_j||_2 \leq \beta$ and $\mathsf{OpenC}_{cpk,ck_j}(\mathbf{v}_j, \mathbf{r}_j, \mathbf{w}_j) = 1$. If any of these conditions fail, send out ABORT.
   (b) Computes the combined signature as follows: $\mathbf{z} = \sum_{j\in[n]} \mathbf{z}_j, \mathbf{r} = \sum_{j\in[n]} \mathbf{r}_j$ and $ck = \sum_{j\in[n]} ck_j$.
   (c) Each user U_i outputs a signature $\sigma_{agg} = (\mathbf{z}, \mathbf{r}, ck, com)$.

(1 or 0) $\leftarrow$Agg-verify$(\sigma_{agg}, P = \{pk_i\}_{i\in[n]}, M = \{m_i\}_{i\in[n]})$. The Verifier does the following.

1. For each user U_j,
   (a) derive $c_j \leftarrow H_0(t_j, com, m_j, \{m_k\}_{k\in[n],k\neq j}, P)$ and
   (b) reconstruct $\mathbf{w} = \mathbf{A}\mathbf{z} - \sum_{j\in[n]} c_j\mathbf{t}_j$.
2. Accepts the aggregated signature σ_{agg} if $||\mathbf{z}|| \leq \beta$ and $\mathsf{OpenC}_{cpk,ck}(com, \mathbf{r}, \mathbf{w}) = 1$

4.1 Security Proof of the Aggregated Signature Scheme Given in Sect. 4

Theorem 2. *The Aggregated Signature Scheme given in Sect. 4 is UF-CMA secure under M-SIS$_{q,k,l+1,\beta}$ and M-LWE$_{q,k,l,\eta}$ assumptions.*

Proof. Let $\mathcal{A}$ be an adversary to our proposed construction 4. Without loss of generality let us assume that $\mathcal{B}$ is a simulator that simulates the transcripts of the honest user U_n without honestly generated secret key sk_n. The simulator $\mathcal{B}$ maintains two lists LIST$_0$ and TD respectively for H_0 and commitment trapdoor. We will define indistinguishable games Sim-i below for $i = 0, 1, 2$. Let Pr[Sim-i] denotes the probability that the simulator $\mathcal{B}$ does not abort or output $\perp$ in Sim-i. Let $D = \{h_1, h_2, \ldots, h_{Q_h+Q_s+1}\}$ be a set of random samples that the simulator $\mathcal{B}$ receives.

In our security model, the adversary will make the hash function H_0 query to $\mathcal{B}$. Thus, our proposed scheme is secure in the random oracle model.

Sim-0: The simulator $\mathcal{B}$ will generate $(ppc, cpk = (\mathbf{A}_0, \mathbf{A}_1)) \leftarrow$SetupC$(1^\lambda)$, $PP \leftarrow$ Agg-setup(1^κ) and $(pk_n, sk_n) = (\mathbf{t}_n, \mathbf{s}_n) \leftarrow$ Agg-gen(PP) and send (ppc, PP, cpk, pk_n) to the adversary $\mathcal{A}$. In this simulation game H_0 queries are honestly answered by $\mathcal{B}$. The signature share of the n-th user U_n with (pk_n, sk_n) is generated by $\mathcal{B}$ as follows.

Generation of Signature Share $(\mathbf{z}_n, \mathbf{r}_n)$.

1. (a) Computes the commitment key $ck_n = H_1(m_n, P)$.
   (b) Samples $\mathbf{y}_n \leftarrow D_s^{l+k}$ and sets $\mathbf{w}_n = \mathbf{A} \cdot \mathbf{y}_n \bmod q$.
   (c) Computes $com_n = \mathsf{Commit}_{cpk,ck_n}(\mathbf{w}_n; \mathbf{r}_n)$ by choosing a randomness $\mathbf{r}_n$.
   (d) Return (com_n, m_n).
2. After obtaining com_j and $\{m_j\}_j$ for every $j \in [n-1]$ computes the following.
   (a) $com = \sum_{j\in[n]} com_j$.
   (b) Compute a challenge $c_n \leftarrow H_0(t_n, com, m_n, \{m_k\}_{k\in[n-1]}, P)$.
   (c) Computes a signature share $\mathbf{z}_n = c_n\mathbf{s}_n + \mathbf{y}_n$.
   (d) Apply rejection sampling on input $(c_n\mathbf{s}_n, \mathbf{z}_n)$ i.e., with probability $\min(1, D_s^{l+k}(\mathbf{z}_n)/(M \cdot D_{c_n\mathbf{s}_n,s}^{l+k}(\mathbf{z}_n)))$ and send out $(\mathbf{z}_n, \mathbf{r}_n)$; else go to 1.

Simulator is behaving just as a real signer in this game. Thus the probability that the simulator $\mathcal{B}$ outputs $(0, \perp)$ in Sim-0 is the advantage in the security game 1. That is $\Pr[\text{Sim-0}] = Adv_{AS}^{UF-CMA}(\mathcal{A})$.

Sim-1: In this game the simulator $\mathcal{B}$ does the following changes to Sim-0.
The simulator $\mathcal{B}$ will generate $(ppc, tcpk = (\mathbf{A}_0, \mathbf{A}_1), td) \leftarrow$SetupTC$(1^\lambda)$, $PP \leftarrow$ Agg-setup(1^κ) and $(pk_n, sk_n) = (\mathbf{t}_n, \mathbf{s}_n) \leftarrow$ Agg-gen(PP) and send (ppc, PP, cpk, pk_n) to the adversary $\mathcal{A}$.

H_0 **Query.** The H_0 query is answered as given in 3.
The signature share $(\mathbf{z}_n, \mathbf{r}_n)$ is generated as below.

Generation of Signature Share $(\mathbf{z}_n, \mathbf{r}_n)$.

1. (a) Computes the commitment key $ck_n = H_1(m_n, P)$.
   (b) Samples $\mathbf{y}_n \leftarrow D_s^{l+k}$ and sets $\mathbf{w}_n = \mathbf{A} \cdot \mathbf{y}_n \bmod q$.
   (c) Computes $com_n = \mathsf{CommitT}_{tcpk,ck_n}(td)$.

Let (x, D) be an input.

1. Parse x as (t, com, m, L).
2. Initialize $ctr = 0$.
3. If $t = t_n$ and $t \in P$ then increment the counter ctr and set $\text{LIST}_0[t, com, m, L] := h_{ctr}$.
4. If $(t \neq t_n) \vee ((t = t_n) \wedge (t \notin P))$ then set $\text{LIST}_0[t, com, m, L] \leftarrow_\$ C$.
5. return the list LIST_0.

Fig. 3. Random Oracle H_0 query.

   (d) Return (com_n, m_n).
2. After obtaining com_j and $\{m_j\}_j$ for every $j \in [n-1]$ compute the followings.
   (a) $com = \sum_{j\in[n]} com_j$.

(b) Compute a challenge $c_n \leftarrow H_0(t_n, com, m_n, \{m_k\}_{k\in[n-1]}, P)$.
(c) Computes $\mathbf{z}_n = c_n\mathbf{s}_n + \mathbf{y}_n$. Extract randomness $\mathbf{r}_n \leftarrow \mathsf{Equiv}_{tcpk,ck_n}(\mathbf{R}, \mathbf{v}, x)$.
(d) Apply rejection sampling on input $(c_n\mathbf{s}_n, \mathbf{z}_n)$ i.e., with probability $\min(1, D_s^{l+k}(\mathbf{z}_n)/(M \cdot D_{c_n\mathbf{s}_n,s}^{l+k}(\mathbf{z}_n)))$ and return $(\mathbf{z}_n, \mathbf{r}_n)$; else go to step 1.

Note that Sim-0 and Sim-1 are indistinguishable under the security of the trapdoor commitment scheme 3.

Sim-2: In this game the simulator $\mathcal{B}$ does the following changes to Sim-1.

Generation of Signature Share $(\mathbf{z}_n, \mathbf{r}_n)$.

1. (a) Computes the commitment key $ck_n = H_1(m_n, P)$.
   (b) Does not perform this step.
   (c) Computes $com_n = \mathsf{CommitT}_{tcpk,ck_n}(td)$.
   (d) Return (com_n, m_n).
2. After obtaining com_j and $\{m_j\}_j$ for $j \in [n-1]$ compute the followings.
   (a) $com = \sum_{j\in[n]} com_j$.
   (b) Compute a challenge $c_n \leftarrow H_0(t_n, com, m_n, \{m_k\}_{k\in[n-1]}, P)$.
   (c) Samples $\mathbf{z}_n \leftarrow D_s^{l+k}$. Extract randomness $\mathbf{r}_n \leftarrow \mathsf{Equiv}_{tcpk,ck_n}(\mathbf{R}, \mathbf{v}, x)$.
   (d) Return $(\mathbf{z}_n, \mathbf{r}_n)$ with probability $\frac{1}{M}$; else go to step 1.

Note that Sim-1 and Sim-2 are statistically indistinguishable using Lemma [[7], Lemma 4] that the output distribution of 2(d) in Sim-1 is within statistical distance of $\frac{\epsilon}{M}$ of output distribution of 2(d) in Sim-2. Here $M = e^{\frac{t}{\alpha}+\frac{1}{2\alpha^2}}$, $\epsilon = 2e^{-t^2/2}$.

Sim-3: In this game the simulator $\mathcal{B}$ does the following changes to Sim-2. Observe that in the signature generation of Sim-2, the secret key $\mathbf{s}_n$ is not utilized. That is $\mathbf{z}_n$ is independent of the secret key $\mathbf{s}_n$. Thus at this stage the simulator $\mathcal{B}$ chooses a public key $\mathbf{t}_n$ randomly in-place of the real public key setup $\mathbf{t}_n = \mathbf{A}\mathbf{s}_n \bmod q$. Here $\mathbf{A}$ follows the uniform distribution and thus the adversary cannot distinguish between Sim-2 and Sim-3 and the indistinguishability comes from the hardness of M-LWE$_{q,k,l,\eta}$. Hence we have $|\Pr[\text{Sim-2}] - \Pr[\text{Sim-3}]| \leq Adv_{M-LWE_{q,k,l,\eta}}$.

The simulated signature share is given in Fig. 4.

It utilizes the random oracle H_0 queries given in Fig 3.

1. (a) Same as real 1(a).
   (b) Does nothing.
   (c) Computes $com_n = \mathsf{CommitT}_{tcpk,ck_n}(td)$.
   (d) Return (com_n, m_n).
2. After obtaining com_j and m_j for $j \in [n-1]$ compute the followings.
   (a) $com = \sum_{j\in[n]} com_j$.
   (b) Compute a challenge $c_n \leftarrow H_0(t_n, com, m_n, \{m_j\}_{j\in[n-1]}, P)$ by calling the random oracle H_0 given in Fig 3.
   (c) Samples a simulated signature share $\mathbf{z}_n \leftarrow D_s^{l+k}$ and obtains randomness $\mathbf{r}_n \leftarrow \mathsf{Equiv}_{tcpk,ck_n}(\mathbf{R}, \mathbf{v}, x)$.
   (d) Return $(\mathbf{z}_n, \mathbf{r}_n)$ with probability $\frac{1}{M}$; else go to 1.
3. If received restart from any of the parties involved in the signature generation then go to step 1; otherwise compute the aggregated signature as specified below.
   (a) For each $j \in [n-1]$, derive $c_j \leftarrow H_0(t_j, com, m_j, \{m_k\}_{k\in[n-1],k\neq j}, P)$, $ck_j \leftarrow H_1(m_j, P)$ and reconstruct $\mathbf{w}_j = \mathbf{A}\mathbf{z}_j - c_j\mathbf{t}_j$ and finally verify $||\mathbf{z}_j||_2 \leq \beta$ and $\mathsf{OpenC}_{cpk,ck_j}(\mathbf{v}_j, \mathbf{r}_j, \mathbf{w}_j) = 1$. If any of these conditions fail, send out ABORT.
   (b) After verifying U_i computes the combined signature as follows: $\mathbf{z} = \sum_j \mathbf{z}_j, \mathbf{r} = \sum_j \mathbf{r}_j$ and $ck = \sum_j ck_j$.
   (c) User U_n outputs a signature $\sigma_{agg} = (\mathbf{z}, \mathbf{r}, ck, com)$ if none of the steps fails.

Fig. 4. Simulated Signature Generation Process

Forking Lemma. Now we construct another randomized algorithm $\mathcal{G}$ utilizing the above designed algorithm $\mathcal{B}$ as a black box as in Fig. 1. The algorithm $\mathcal{G}$ invokes $\mathcal{B}$ on $x = (m_n, ck_n, \mathbf{A}, \mathbf{t}_n)$. Now due to forking lemma, with probability frk we get two forgeries $forge_1 = (i_f, out_1 = (com^*, \{c_j^*\}_{j\in[n-1]}, c_n^*, \mathbf{z}^*, \mathbf{r}^*, \mu^*, P^*, ck_n^*))$ and $forge_2 = (i_f, out_1 = (\widehat{com}^*, \{\widehat{c}_j^*\}_{j\in[n-1]}, \widehat{c}_n^*, \widehat{\mathbf{z}}^*, \widehat{\mathbf{r}}^*, \widehat{\mu}^*, \widehat{P}^*, \widehat{ck}_n^*))$. Here frk satisfies $\Pr[\text{Sim-3}] = acc \leq \frac{Q_h+Q_s+1}{|C|} + \sqrt{(Q_h+Q_s+1)\cdot frk}$. As the randomness ρ is same on invocation of both $\mathcal{B}$ and $\mathcal{G}$, we get: $com^* = \widehat{com}^*, m_j^* = \widehat{m}_j^*, n^* = \widehat{n}^*, P^* = \widehat{P}^*, c_j^* = \widehat{c}_j^*$ for each $j \in [n^*-1]$ and $c_n^* \neq \widehat{c}_n^*$. Thus the adversary's view is identical till the forking point. Note that $ck_j^* = \widehat{ck}_j^* = ck_j$. This is because of the simulation of the random oracle H_0. Since both forgeries are under the same commitment key ck_j^*, we get $||\mathbf{z}^*||_2 \leq \beta_n \wedge ||\widehat{\mathbf{z}}^*||_2 \leq \beta_n$ and $\mathsf{OpenC}_{cpk,ck}(com^*, \mathbf{r}^*, \mathbf{A}\mathbf{z}^* - \sum_{j\in[n^*-1]} c_j^*\mathbf{t}_j^* - c_n^*\mathbf{t}_n) = 1$ and $\mathsf{OpenC}_{cpk,ck}(com_1^*, \mathbf{r}_1^*, \mathbf{A}\widehat{\mathbf{z}}^* - \sum_{j\in[n^*-1]} c_j^*\mathbf{t}_j^* - \widehat{c}_n^*\mathbf{t}_n) = 1$. If $\mathbf{A}\mathbf{z}^* - c_n^*\mathbf{t}_n \neq \mathbf{A}\mathbf{z}_1^* - c_{n,1}^*\mathbf{t}_n$ then $\mathcal{G}$ breaks the computationally binding with respect to ck_j. The probability of happening of this is ϵ_2. If $\mathbf{A}\mathbf{z}^* - c_n^*\mathbf{t}_n =$

$\mathbf{A}\widehat{\mathbf{z}}^* - \widehat{c}_n^*\mathbf{t}_n$ then $[\mathbf{A}|\mathbf{I}|\mathbf{t}_n] \cdot \begin{bmatrix} \mathbf{z}^* - \widehat{\mathbf{z}}^* \\ c_n^* - \widehat{c}_n^* \end{bmatrix} = 0$. Thus we have found a correct solution $\begin{bmatrix} \mathbf{z}^* - \widehat{\mathbf{z}}^* \\ c_n^* - \widehat{c}_n^* \end{bmatrix}$ to an $\mathsf{M\text{-}SIS}_{q,k,l+1,\beta}$ problem. This is because $||\mathbf{z}^* - \widehat{\mathbf{z}}^*|| \leq 2\beta_n$ and $||c_n^* - \widehat{c}_n^*|| \leq \sqrt{4\kappa}$ only if $\beta = \sqrt{(2\beta_n)^2 + 4\kappa}$. From both the cases we get $frk \leq \epsilon_2 + Adv_{M-SIS_{q,k,l+1,\beta}}$.

5 Conclusion

In this paper, we present a two round secure aggregate signature scheme under the hardness of lattice assumptions by utilizing a trapdoor commitment scheme with homomorphic properties. It remains an interesting open problem to achieve quantum secure round-optimal aggregation of class of Fiat-Shamir with Aborts signatures without utilizing homomorphic trapdoor commitment scheme on distinct messages by distinct signers such that the size of the aggregated signature is independent of the number of signatures involved.

Acknowledgments. The author would like to acknowledge the project entitled 'Design and Implementation of a Cryptographically Secure Random Number Generator' awarded by Indian Space Research Organisation, Department of Space, Government of India.

References

1. Aardal, M.A., Aranha, D.F., Boudgoust, K., Kolby, S., Takahashi, A.: Aggregating falcon signatures with LaBRADOR. In: Reyzin, L., Stebila, D. (eds.) CRYPTO 2024. LNCS, vol. 14920, pp. 71–106. Springer, Heidelberg (2024). https://doi.org/10.1007/978-3-031-68376-3_3
2. Bellare, M., Neven, G.: Multi-signatures in the plain public key model and a general forking lemma. In: Proceedings of the 13th ACM conference in Computer and Communications Security, pp. 390–399. Association for Computing Machinery, Alexandria Virginia USA (2006). https://doi.org/10.1145/1180405
3. Boneh, D., Gentry, C., Lynn, B., Shacham, H.: Aggregate and verifiably encrypted signatures from bilinear maps. In: Biham, E. (ed.) EUROCRYPT 2003. LNCS, vol. 2656, pp. 416–432. Springer, Heidelberg (2003). https://doi.org/10.1007/3-540-39200-9_26
4. Boneh, D., Kim, S.: One-Time and interactive aggregate signatures from lattices. crypto.stanford.edu/ skim13/agg_ots.pdf
5. Boudgoust, K., Roux-Langlois, A.: Overfull: too large aggregate signature based on lattices. Comput. J. **67**, 719–727 (2024)
6. Boudgoust, K., Roux-Langlois, A.: Compressed linear aggregate signatures based on module lattices (2021). https://eprint.iacr.org/2021/263.pdf
7. Damgård, I., Orlandi, C., Takahashi, A., Tibouchi, M.: Two-round n-out-of-n and multi-signatures and trapdoor commitment from lattices. J. Cryptology **35**(14) (2022)

8. Doröz, Y., Hoffstein, J., Silverman, J.H., Sunar, B.: A scheme for multimessage multiuser signature aggregation (2020). https://eprint.iacr.org/2020/520.pdf
9. El Bansarkhani, R., Buchmann, J.: Towards lattice based aggregate signatures. In: Pointcheval, D., Vergnaud, D. (eds.) AFRICACRYPT 2014. LNCS, vol. 8469, pp. 336–355. Springer, Cham (2014). https://doi.org/10.1007/978-3-319-06734-6_21
10. Gorbunov, S., Vaikuntanathan, V., Wichs, D.: Leveled fully homomorphic signatures from standard lattices. In: proceedings of the 47th annual ACM symposium on Theory of computing, pp. 469–477. Association for Computing Machinery, New York, USA (2015)
11. Jeudy, C., Roux-Langlois, A., Sanders, O.: Phoenix: hash-and-sign with aborts from lattice gadgets. In: Saarinen, MJ., Smith-Tone, D. (eds.) PQCrypto 2024, LNCS, vol. 17771, pp. 265–299. Springer, Heidelberg (2024). https://doi.org/10.1007/978-3-031-62743-9_9
12. Lyubashevsky, V.: Lattice signatures without trapdoors. In: Pointcheval, D., Johansson, T. (eds.) EUROCRYPT 2012. LNCS, vol. 7237, pp. 738–755. Springer, Heidelberg (2012). https://doi.org/10.1007/978-3-642-29011-4_43
13. Lyubashevsky, V., Peikert, C., Regev, O.: A toolkit for Ring-LWE cryptography. In: Johansson, T., Nguyen, P.Q. (eds.) EUROCRYPT 2013. LNCS, vol. 7881, pp. 35–54. Springer, Heidelberg (2013). https://doi.org/10.1007/978-3-642-38348-9_3
14. Micciancio, D., Peikert, C.: Trapdoors for lattices: simpler, tighter, faster, smaller. In: Pointcheval, D., Johansson, T. (eds.) EUROCRYPT 2012. LNCS, vol. 7237, pp. 700–718. Springer, Heidelberg (2012). https://doi.org/10.1007/978-3-642-29011-4_41

Dual-Type Quotable Signatures with Adaptive Unforgeability and Complete Context-Hiding

Masahito Ishizaka[1(✉)] and Kazuhide Fukushima[2]

[1] National Institute of Information and Communications Technology, Tokyo, Japan
ishimasa@nict.go.jp
[2] KDDI Research, Inc., Saitama, Japan
ka-fukushima@kddi.com

Abstract. In the standard digital signatures, we cannot modify a signed message while keeping the validity of the signature. In P-homomorphic signatures (P-HS), from a signature on a message, we can derive a new signature on another message satisfying the predicate P. In the dual-type (DT) P-HS, each signature is either a homomorphic Type-I signature or a non-homomorphic Type-II signature. Any Type-I signature can be irreversibly transformed into a Type-II signature. DT property has some advantages such that a Type-II signature can be much more efficient than a Type-I signature in terms of signature-size and verification-time. Quotable signatures (QS) are a subclass of P-HS and allow us to extract a substring of the signed message. In this paper, we propose the first two DTQS schemes achieving the strongest security notions, i.e., adaptive unforgeability and complete context-hiding, under the DLIN and q-SFP assumptions in the standard model. In the first (resp. second) scheme, the sizes of a Type-I/Type-II signature on a message of length n are approximately $\mathcal{O}(n \log_c n)$ and $\mathcal{O}(c \log_c n)$ (resp. $\mathcal{O}(nc \log_c n)$ and $\mathcal{O}(\log_c n)$), where $c \geq 2$ is an integer parameter. In the case when $c > n$, the first (resp. second) scheme becomes a balanced (resp. unbalanced) scheme whose sizes of a Type-I/Type-II signature are both $\mathcal{O}(n)$ (resp. $\mathcal{O}(n^2)$ and $\mathcal{O}(1)$).

Keywords: Dual-type quotable signatures · Adaptive unforgeability · Complete context-hiding · Homomorphic signatures

1 Introduction

P-Homomorphic Signatures. In digital signatures, we cannot modify a signed message while keeping the validity of the message. For some applications of the digital signatures, it is desirable that we can partially modify a signed message. The digital signatures do not distinguish a malicious *falsification* from an

M. Ishizaka—This work was partially carried out while the author was affiliated with KDDI Research, Inc.

N. El Mrabet et al. (Eds.): AFRICACRYPT 2026, LNCS 16832, pp. 381–406, 2026.
https://doi.org/10.1007/978-3-032-31130-6_16

appropriate *alteration*, and equally prohibit any kind of modification. In contrast, homomorphic signatures (HS) distinguish the two types of modification, and allow only the latter. Formally, given a predicate $P : \mathcal{M} \times \mathcal{M} \to 1/0$ with message space $\mathcal{M}$, P-HS [3] allow any user who has a valid signature on a message $\mathbf{M}$ to derive a valid signature on any message $\mathbf{M}'$ satisfying P, i.e., $1 \leftarrow P(\mathbf{M}, \mathbf{M}')$[1]. For security, as the standard digital signatures, unforgeability is required. Privacy is also required in the sense that the derived signature on $\mathbf{M}'$ has no more information about the original $\mathbf{M}$ than the fact that $1 \leftarrow P(\mathbf{M}, \mathbf{M}')$.

Various subclasses of P-HS have been proposed. In quotable signatures (QS) [3], each message is a list of (sub-)messages, and the derivation succeeds if $\mathbf{M}'$ is a substring of $\mathbf{M}$. In redactable signatures (RS) [15,18], any user can partially redact or black-out a signed message. Append-only signatures (AOS) [16] can add any sub-message m to the tail of the original message $\mathbf{M}$, i.e., $\mathbf{M}' = \mathbf{M} \| m$. In HS for subset predicates (HSSB) [3], each message is a set of sub-messages, and the derivation succeeds if $\mathbf{M}'$ is a subset of $\mathbf{M}$. History-hiding AOS (H2AOS) [8] are the superset analogue of HSSB. In HS for subset and superset mixed predicates (HSSM) [13], each message consists of two sets, i.e., $\mathbf{M} = (M, W)$, and a signature on $\mathbf{M}$ successfully derives a signature on $\mathbf{M}' = (M', W')$ if M' is a subset of M and W' is a superset of W[2].

QS vs RS. QS and RS are closely-related primitives. The biggest difference lies in whether the traces of deleted information remain or not.

RS are applicable to scenarios where the amount and position of the redacted information are of significant importance. For instance, in a democratic country, citizens equally have the "Right to Know", and they can ask a government agency to disclose an official document. Before disclosing, the government agency must redact sensitive information such as national secrets, private information about a citizen. RS can be a good choice for this application because citizens can monitor whether information has not been overly redacted.

QS are applicable to scenarios where the traces of deleted information may leak some sensitive information. For instance, consider the following scenario. An employee of company X, Alice, pays in advance for business-related expenses (e.g., academic conference registration fees, airfare, and hotel accommodation). After completing the business trip, she submits the necessary documents - such as receipts and her monthly credit card statement - to the accounting department of company X for reimbursement. As shown in Fig. 1, Alice receives a digitally signed monthly credit card statement from credit card company Y. She deletes all entries except those related to the relevant business activities, and submits the modified statement to the accounting department. If RS are used in this process, traces of the deleted entries remain visible. As a result, sensitive information

[1] This definition is uni-variate. The original definition by Ahn et al. [3] is multi-variate. Formally, given a predicate $P : 2^{\mathcal{M}} \times \mathcal{M} \to 1/0$, where $2^{\mathcal{M}}$ is the power set of $\mathcal{M}$, any user who has collected k number of valid signatures $\{\sigma_i\}_{i=1}^{k}$ on messages $\{\mathbf{M}_i\}_{i=1}^{k}$ successfully derives a signature σ' on any message $\mathbf{M}'$ s.t. $1 \leftarrow P(\{\mathbf{M}_i\}_{i=1}^{k}, \mathbf{M}')$.

[2] More formally, if $M' \subseteq M$ and $W' \supseteq W$.

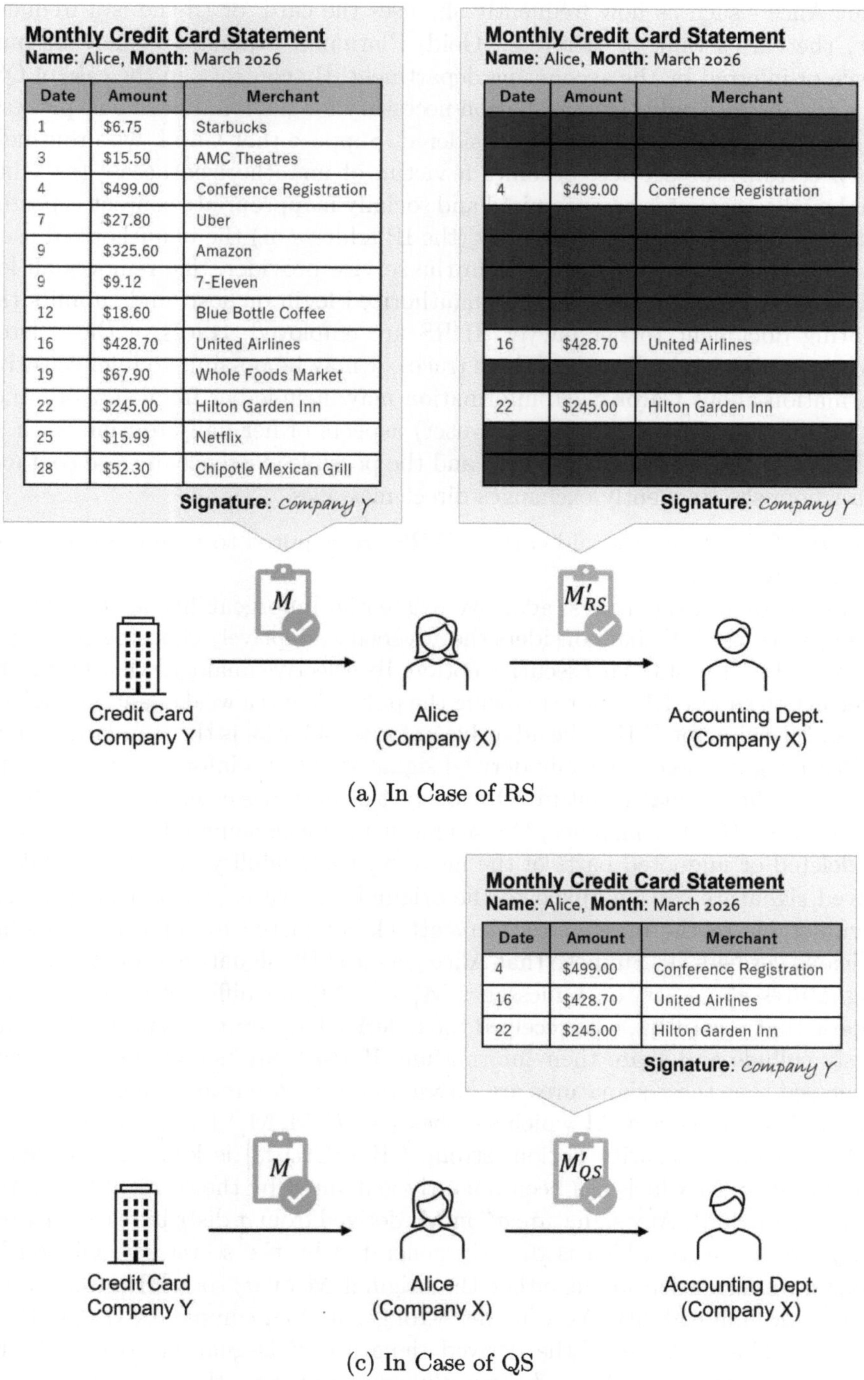

Fig. 1. Alice submits a modified monthly credit card statement to get the reimbursement of business-related expenses

about Alice - such as how frequently she uses the card, or (if she is a frequent user) the card's rank or tier (e.g., Gold, Platinum, Standard) - may become known or inferred by the accounting department. By contrast, in the case of QS, Alice can disclose only the information necessary for the reimbursement process.

Another scenario can also be considered. Suppose that Carol, who routinely uses a certain web service, becomes a victim of unauthorized access (e.g., her social media account is compromised and socially inappropriate content is posted under her name). In order to identify (the IP address of) the unauthorized user, Carol obtains a signed audit log from the service provider. She removes all log entries except those related to the unauthorized login or post, and submits the resulting document to her lawyer. If RS are employed, traces of the deleted entries remain visible. Based on these traces, it may be possible to infer sensitive information about Carol. Such information may include her frequency of use of the web service; (if she is a frequent user) aspects of her daily routine, such as typical meal times or sleeping hours; and the possible existence of close contacts with whom she frequently exchanges direct messages.

Security of P-HS. As we said earlier, P-HS are required to be unforgeable and at least private.

For the digital signatures, adaptive existential unforgeability against chosen messages attacks [11] that considers the adversary adaptively choosing the target message $\mathbf{M}^*$ is the standard security notion. Its selective analogue that forces the adversary to choose $\mathbf{M}^*$ before knowing the public-key is a weaker and unrealistic notion. Likewise, for P-HS, the adaptive unforgeability [3] is the standard notion.

Privacy guarantees that any derived signature has no information about the message of the original signature. Obviously, this notion is essential especially for *deletion*-type HS. For instance, QS lacking it may leak some information about the deleted or unquoted parts of the message. Unlinkability guarantees that no derived signature can be linked to the original signature. P-HS lacking it may be vulnerable to the message-recovery attack conducted by multiple colluding malicious verifiers [4]. Suppose that Alice gets a P-HS signature σ on $\mathbf{M}$, derives n signatures $\sigma'_1, \cdots, \sigma'_n$ on n messages $\mathbf{M}'_1, \cdots, \mathbf{M}'_n$ for different purposes. Also suppose that n verifiers, who received the n derived signatures respectively, maliciously collude and share their information. If P-HS are not unlinkable, it can be guessed that the n signatures are *linked* and originate from a single signature on an unknown message $\mathbf{M}$ which satisfies $1 \leftarrow P(\mathbf{M}, \mathbf{M}'_i)$ for all $i \in [1, n]$.

As a stronger security notion, strong CH (SCH) [3] is known. Consider a signature σ on $\mathbf{M}$ which has been honestly generated by the secret-key (via the signing algorithm). Any signature σ' on $\mathbf{M}'$ derived from σ distributes identically to a *fresh* signature which is directly generated by the secret-key. Obviously, σ' has no information about either the original $\mathbf{M}$ or σ, so SCH implies both privacy and unlinkability. As a further stronger notion, complete CH (CCH) [5] is known. The freshness of the derived signature σ' is guaranteed even if the original signature σ has been *dishonestly* generated, e.g., the randomness used to generate the signature was arbitrarily chosen from the designated randomness space. The only condition that the original signature satisfies is that it is valid.

Since by correctness any signature which has been honestly generated by the secret-key is valid, CCH implies SCH. An advantage of CCH lies in its ability to weaken the trust assumption placed on the source (entity) of the original signature. In CCH, even if the signature has dishonestly generated by the source, just by honestly deriving the next signature, its privacy and unlinkability are guaranteed. By contrast, in SCH, the (deriving) user must trust the source and believe that the signature has never been generated or derived dishonestly. The significance of the CCH property is evident from the application scenarios described above. It must be impossible for Alice or Carol to fully trust the credit card company Y or the service provider.

Dual-Type vs Single-Type P-HS. Two types of P-HS have been implicitly considered, which should be called *dual*-type (DT) and *single*-type (ST). The former allows us to *castrate* a signature in the sense that the message of a castrated signature is fixed. In DT P-HS, each signature is either a Type-I homomorphic signature or a Type-II non-homomorphic signature. Any Type-I signature can be irreversibly transformed into a Type-II signature. ST P-HS have no such castrating ability, and there are only Type-I non-homomorphic signatures.

DT property is desirable for many applications. For instance, in the application scenarios described above, the QS signature submitted by Alice or Carol to the verifier is intended to be final, and she does not wish it to be modified any further. It is possible that Carol's lawyer, without obtaining her consent, removes log entries that could serve as decisive evidence of the unauthorized login, thereby making it more difficult to identify the unauthorized user.

CDH property also has a benefit in terms of efficiency. Because a Type-II signature is less functional than a Type-I signature, it can be more efficient in terms of signature-size and verification-time. For instance, we propose a DTQS scheme whose size of a Type-I (resp. Type-II) signature on a message of length n is $\mathcal{O}(n^2)$ (resp. $\mathcal{O}(1)$).

Our Contribution. To the best of our knowledge, there exist only two QS schemes satisfying SCH security, the one by Ahn et al. [3] and the one by Attrapadung et al. [6]. The former QS scheme by Ahn et al. is of dual-type, and has Type-I signature of length $\mathcal{O}(n \cdot \log n)$ and Type-II signatures of length $\mathcal{O}(\log n)$. It is SCH unconditionally and selectively unforgeable under the computational DH assumption in the random oracle model. The latter QS scheme by Attrapadung et al. is of single-type, and has Type-I signatures of length $\mathcal{O}(n)$. It is CCH unconditionally and adaptively unforgeable under the DLIN and q-SFP [2] assumptions in the standard model. As a result, we pose the following problem as an open problem which has been an important missing piece in the area of HS-related research: *How can we construct a dual-type QS scheme achieving the strongest security notions, i.e., adaptive unforgeability and complete CH, under the standard assumptions?*

We solve the open problem by proposing two DTQS schemes based on the HSSM scheme by Ishizaka and Fukushima (IF HSSM) [13] that are in a trade-off relationship in terms of efficiency. In the first one, denoted by $\Pi_{\mathrm{DTQS},c}$ in

Table 1. Comparison of features among our QS schemes and existing ones.

Schemes	DT?	Type I signature size	Type II sig. size	UNF	CH	Assum.	Model
ABC+12 [3]	Yes	$\mathcal{O}(n \cdot \log n)\lvert g\rvert$	$\mathcal{O}(\log n)\lvert g\rvert$	Selec.	Strong	CDH	RO
ALP13 [6]	No	$\mathcal{O}(n)\lvert g\rvert$	N/A	Adap.	Comp.	q-SFP	STD
$\Pi_{\mathrm{DTQS},c}$ (w/ $n \le c$)	Yes	$\mathcal{O}\left(n\left(\log_c n + \log N\right)\right)\lvert g\rvert$	$\mathcal{O}\left(c \log_c n \cdot \log N\right)\lvert g\rvert$	Adap.	Comp.	DLIN, q-SFP	STD
$\Pi_{\mathrm{DTQS},c}$ (w/ $n > c$)	Yes	$\mathcal{O}\left(n \log N\right)\lvert g\rvert$	$\mathcal{O}\left(n \log N\right)\lvert g\rvert$	Adap.	Comp.	DLIN, q-SFP	STD
$\Pi'_{\mathrm{DTQS},c}$ (w/ $n \le c$)	Yes	$\mathcal{O}\left(n\left(c \log_c n + \log N\right)\right)\lvert g\rvert$	$\mathcal{O}\left(\log_c n \cdot \log N\right)\lvert g\rvert$	Adap.	Comp.	DLIN, q-SFP	STD
$\Pi'_{\mathrm{DTQS},c}$ (w/ $n > c$)	Yes	$\mathcal{O}\left(n\left(n + \log N\right)\right)\lvert g\rvert$	$\mathcal{O}(\log N)\lvert g\rvert$	Adap.	Comp.	DLIN, q-SFP	STD

Note: DT, Assump., UNF, RO and STD mean dual-type, assumptions, unforgeability, random oracle (model) and standard (model). $n \le N$ is the length of a signed message.

Table 1, the size of a Type-I (resp. Type-II) signature on a message of length $n \le N$ is $\mathcal{O}(n(\log_c n + \log N))|g|$ (resp. $\mathcal{O}(c \log_c n \cdot \log N)$), where $c \ge 2$ is an integer parameter, and $|g|$ is the length of an element in the group of a symmetric bilinear pairing. In the specific case that $c > n$, the sizes of a Type-I/Type-II signature are both $\mathcal{O}(n \log N)|g|$.

The second scheme, denoted by $\Pi'_{\mathrm{DTQS},c}$ in Table 1, reinforces the imbalance between the Type-I and Type-II signature sizes in the first one. The size of a Type-I (resp. Type-II) signature is $\mathcal{O}(n(c \log_c n + \log N))|g|$ (resp. $\mathcal{O}(\log_c n \cdot \log N)|g|$). Roughly speaking, if we ignore the term of $\log N$, they become c-times and $1/c$-times of the sizes in the first scheme, respectively. In the specific case that $c > n$, the size of a Type-I (resp. Type-II) signature is $\mathcal{O}(n(n + \log N))|g|$ (resp. $\mathcal{O}(\log N)|g|$). Both of the schemes are secure under the DLIN and q-SFP assumptions in the standard model. At a high level, they adopt the same approach that first proposes an *insecure* generic transformation from HSSM to DTQS, and instantiates it by the IF HSSM scheme, and then modifies it to a secure one.

High-Level Idea of Our Schemes. Since our constructions are somewhat complex, we introduce only the simplest one here, i.e., our first scheme in the case $c > n$. Consider the following transformation from HSSM to DTQS. A Type-I DTQS signature $\sigma_{\mathsf{A:E}}$ on $M_{\mathsf{A:E}} := (\mathsf{A}, \mathsf{B}, \mathsf{C}, \mathsf{D}, \mathsf{E})$ is produced as an HSSM signature on the set pair

$$(\{d_1||\mathsf{A}, d_2||\mathsf{B}, d_3||\mathsf{C}, d_4||\mathsf{D}, d_5||\mathsf{E}\}, \emptyset),$$

where the variables $d_1, \cdots, d_5$ prevent any reordering of the sub-messages. For example, we may set $d_i := i$. To derive a Type-II signature on (B, C), we derive an HSSM signature on

$$(\{d_2||\mathsf{B}, d_3||\mathsf{C}\}, \{\mathsf{B}||\mathsf{C}\}).$$

By the properties of HSSM, the latter set $\{\mathsf{B}||\mathsf{C}\}$ is immutable, and hence the message (B, C) is fixed. Although conceptually simple, this transformation fails to achieve even unlinkability because the relationship between the index d_i and the corresponding sub-message is permanently fixed and publicly known. We address this issue by incorporating the NIWI technique of Groth and Sahai [12].

The size of an IF HSSM signature on a set pair (M, W) linearly grows with $|\mathsf{M}|$ and $|\mathsf{W}|$. Hence, the resulting DTQS Type-I/Type-II signatures on a message of length n in this transformation have sizes both roughly $\mathcal{O}(n)$ (more precisely, $\mathcal{O}(n \log N)$).

Related Works. For any *addition*-type P-HS, there is a simple transformation which transforms a single-type (ST) scheme into a dual-type (DT) scheme. For instance, a ST H2AOS scheme is transformed into a DT H2AOS scheme as follows [17]. The signer generates a Type-I DT H2AOS signature σ on $\mathbf{M} = \{m_1, \cdots, m_k\}$ as a Type-I ST H2AOS signature on $\widetilde{\mathbf{M}} = \{0 \parallel m_1, \cdots, 0 \parallel m_k\}$. To castrate it, we derive a Type-I ST H2AOS signature σ' on $\widetilde{\mathbf{M}}' = \widetilde{\mathbf{M}} \cup \{1 \parallel k\}$. Because the element $1 \parallel k$ prevents any new sub-message m_{k+1} from being added, the H2AOS signature σ' is properly castrated. The same technique works for the other addition-type P-HS such as AOS and HSSM.

For *deletion*-type P-HS, e.g., HSSB, RS and QS, such a "ST-to-DT" transformation has not been known. But fortunately for HSSB and RS, there exist useful primitives named disclosure-controllable HSSB (DCHSSB) [13] and disclosure-controllable RS (DCRS) [13]. In the standard HSSB, for a signature on a set M, any sub-message $m \in M$ can be deleted any time. By contrast, in DCHSSB, any deletable sub-message m can be made undeletable. DCHSSB can be transformed from HSSM [13], and DCRS can be transformed from DCHSSB [14]. DCHSSB can be transformed into DT HSSB in a simple way. Similarly, DCRS can be transformed into DT RS.

Paper Organization. We explain some notations and define three computational assumptions in Sect. 2. We define P-HS and DTQS in Sect. 3. We propose our first scheme for any integer parameter $c > 2$ in Sect. 4, prove its security, and analyze its efficiency. We propose our second scheme for any $c > 3$[3] in Sect. 5.

2 Preliminaries

Notations. For $\lambda \in \mathbb{N}$, 1^λ denotes a security parameter. A function $f : \mathbb{N} \rightarrow \mathbb{R}$ is negligible if for every $c \in \mathbb{N}$, there exists $x_0 \in \mathbb{N}$ such that for every $x \geq x_0$, $f(x) \leq x^{-c}$. PPT means probabilistic polynomial-time. For a set A, $a \xleftarrow{\text{U}} A$ means that an element a is chosen uniformly at random from A. For a set A, $|A|$ denotes its cardinality. For an integer N, $\log N$ denotes $\log_2 N$.

$\mathcal{G}$ takes a security parameter 1^λ with $\lambda \in \mathbb{N}$ and outputs a group description $(p, \mathbb{G}, \mathbb{G}_T, e, g)$. p is a prime with length λ. $\mathbb{G}$ and $\mathbb{G}_T$ are multiplicative groups with order p. g is a generator of $\mathbb{G}$. $e : \mathbb{G} \times \mathbb{G} \rightarrow \mathbb{G}_T$ is an efficiently-computable function which satisfies both of the following conditions, namely (1) bilinearity: for any $a, b \in \mathbb{Z}_p$, $e(g^a, g^b) = e(g, g)^{ab}$, and (2) non-degeneracy: $e(g, g) \neq 1_{\mathbb{G}_T}$, where $1_{\mathbb{G}_T}$ denotes the unit element of $\mathbb{G}_T$.

We define three computational hardness assumptions.

[3] When $c = 2$, both of our two schemes are identical.

Definition 1. *The computational Diffie-Hellman (CDH) assumption holds on the group* $\mathbb{G}$ *if for every PPT* $\mathcal{A}$*, its advantage* $\mathit{Adv}^{\mathit{CDH}}_{\mathcal{A},\mathbb{G}}(\lambda) := \Pr[g^{ab} \leftarrow \mathcal{A}(g, g^a, g^b)]$ *(with* $a, b \xleftarrow{\text{U}} \mathbb{Z}_p$*) is negligible.*

Definition 2. *The decisional linear (DLIN) assumption holds on the group* $\mathbb{G}$ *if for every PPT* $\mathcal{A}$*, its advantage* $\mathit{Adv}^{\mathit{DLIN}}_{\mathcal{A},\mathbb{G}}(\lambda) := |\Pr[1 \leftarrow \mathcal{A}(g^a, g^b, g^{ab}, g^{bd}, g^{c+d})] - \Pr[1 \leftarrow \mathcal{A}(g^a, g^b, g^{ab}, g^{bd}, g^z)]|$ *(with* $a, b, c, d, z \xleftarrow{\text{U}} \mathbb{Z}_p$*) is negligible.*

Definition 3. *The q-simultaneous flexible pairing (q-SFP) problem [2] relative to the group* $\mathbb{G}$ *is given* $g_z, h_z, g_r, h_r, a, \tilde{a}, b, \tilde{b} \in \mathbb{G}$ *and q tuples* $\{(z_j, r_j, s_j, t_j, u_j, v_j, w_j) \in \mathbb{G}^7\}_{j=1}^{q}$ *such that for each* $j \in [1, q]$*,*

$$e(a, \tilde{a}) = e(g_z, z_j) \cdot e(g_r, r_j) \cdot e(s_j, t_j), \quad e(b, \tilde{b}) = e(h_z, z_j) \cdot e(h_r, u_j) \cdot e(v_j, w_j), \quad (1)$$

to find a new tuple $(z^\star, r^\star, s^\star, t^\star, u^\star, v^\star, w^\star) \in \mathbb{G}^7$ *satisfying the conditions (1) and the condition* $z^\star \notin \{1_{\mathbb{G}}, z_1, \cdots, z_q\}$*. The q-SFP assumption holds if for any PPT* $\mathcal{A}$*, its advantage* $\mathit{Adv}^{q\text{-}\mathit{SFP}}_{\mathcal{A},\mathbb{G}}(\lambda)$ *to solve the above problem is negligible.*

3 Dual-Type Quotable Signatures (DTQS)

We firstly define the general P-homomorphic signatures (P-HS) [3], and then define HSSM and DTQS as subclasses of P-HS.

P-HS consists of the following four polynomial-time algorithms.

Key-Generation `KGen`**:** Take 1^λ, then output a public-key pk and a secret-key sk. $(pk, sk) \leftarrow \mathtt{KGen}(1^\lambda)$

Signing `Sig`**:** Take a secret-key sk and a message $\mathbf{M} \in \mathcal{M}$, then output a signature σ. $\sigma \leftarrow \mathtt{Sig}(sk, \mathbf{M})$

Derivation `Derive`**:** Take a public-key pk, a message $\mathbf{M}$, a signature σ and a message $\mathbf{M}' \in \mathcal{M}$, then output a signature σ'. $\sigma' \leftarrow \mathtt{Derive}(pk, \mathbf{M}, \sigma, \mathbf{M}')$

Verification `Ver`**:** Take a public-key pk, a message $\mathbf{M} \in \mathcal{M}$ and a signature σ, then output 1 (meaning *accept*) or 0 (*reject*). $1/0 \leftarrow \mathtt{Ver}(pk, \mathbf{M}, \sigma)$

Every P-HS scheme must satisfy the correctness property: $\forall \lambda \in \mathbb{N}$, $\forall (pk, sk) \leftarrow \mathtt{KGen}(1^\lambda)$, $\forall \mathbf{M} \in \mathcal{M}$, $\forall \mathbf{M}' \in \mathcal{M}$ *s.t.* $1 \leftarrow P(\mathbf{M}, \mathbf{M}')$, *both* $1 \leftarrow \mathtt{Ver}(pk, \mathbf{M}, \mathtt{Sig}(sk, \mathbf{M}))$ *and* $1 \leftarrow \mathtt{Ver}(pk, \mathbf{M}', \mathtt{Derive}(pk, \mathbf{M}, \mathtt{Sig}(sk, \mathbf{M}), \mathbf{M}'))$ *hold.*

We define context-hiding (CH) and unforgeability.

CH is a privacy-related security notion which guarantees that any honestly derived signature looks like a fresh signature. Two concrete notions for CH, namely strong CH (`SCH`) [3] and complete CH (`CCH`) [5], are defined as follows.

Definition 4. *A scheme satisfies* `SCH` *(resp.* `CCH`*) if for any* $\lambda \in \mathbb{N}$*, any* $(pk, sk) \leftarrow \mathtt{KGen}(1^\lambda)$*, any* $\mathbf{M} \in \mathcal{M}$*, any* $\sigma \leftarrow \mathtt{Sig}(sk, \mathbf{M})$ *(resp. any* σ *s.t.* $1 \leftarrow \mathtt{Ver}(pk, \mathbf{M}, \sigma)$*) and any* $\mathbf{M}' \in \mathcal{M}$ *s.t.* $1 \leftarrow P(\mathbf{M}, \mathbf{M}')$*,* $\mathtt{Derive}(pk, \mathbf{M}, \sigma, \mathbf{M}')$ *distributes identically to* $\mathtt{Sig}(sk, \mathbf{M}')$*.*

CCH implies SCH since the correctness property guarantees that any signature which has been honestly generated from sk is a valid one.

For an unforgeability notion UNF, we define the following experiment.

$\boldsymbol{Expt}^{\texttt{UNF}}_{\Sigma_{\text{P-HS}},\mathcal{A}}(1^\lambda)$:

1. $(pk, sk) \leftarrow \texttt{KGen}(1^\lambda)$. Initialize $Q := \emptyset$. $(\sigma^*, \mathbf{M}^* \in \mathcal{M}) \leftarrow \mathcal{A}^{\mathsf{Sign}}(pk)$

- $\mathsf{Sign}(\mathbf{M} \in \mathcal{M})$: $\sigma \leftarrow \texttt{Sig}(sk, \mathbf{M})$. Update $Q := Q \cup \{\sigma\}$. **Rtrn** σ

2. **Rtrn** 1 if (1) $1 \leftarrow \texttt{Ver}(pk, \mathbf{M}^*, \sigma^*)$ and (2) $0 \leftarrow P(\mathbf{M}, \mathbf{M}^*)$ for all $\mathbf{M} \in Q$. **Rtrn** 0

The adversary $\mathcal{A}$ receives public-key pk, and then can arbitrarily access the signing oracle which takes a message then returns a signature. $\mathcal{A}$ wins the experiment if it succeeds in forging a signature σ^* on $\mathbf{M}^*$, i.e., σ^* is a valid one and $\mathbf{M}^*$ cannot be reached from any message which has been sent to the signing oracle.

Definition 5. *A scheme $\Sigma_{\text{P-HS}}$ is UNF if for any $\lambda \in \mathbb{N}$ and any PPT algorithm $\mathcal{A}$, its advantage $\boldsymbol{Adv}^{\mathit{UNF}}_{\Sigma_{\text{P-HS}},\mathcal{A}}(\lambda) := \Pr[1 \leftarrow \boldsymbol{Expt}^{\mathit{UNF}}_{\Sigma_{\text{P-HS}},\mathcal{A}}(1^\lambda)]$ is negligible.*

HSSM [13] are a subclass of P-HS. Each message consists of a set-pair $(M, W) \in 2^{\{0,1\}^L} \times 2^{\{0,1\}^L}$ with $L \in \mathbb{N}$. The predicate P takes two set-pairs (M, W) and (M', W'), then outputs 1 if (1) $M' \subseteq M$ and (2) $W' \supseteq W$.

DTQS are a subclass of P-HS. Each message $\mathbf{M} = (t, M)$ consists of a symbol $t \in \{\text{I}, \text{II}\}$ indicating its Type and a message list $M = (m_1, \cdots, m_n)$, where $m_i \in \{0,1\}^L$ and $n \leq N$ for some $L, N \in \mathbb{N}$. The predicate P takes two messages $\mathbf{M}, \mathbf{M}' \in \mathcal{M}$, where $\mathbf{M}' = (t', M') = (t', (m'_1, \cdots, m'_{n'}))$ for some $n' \leq N$, and outputs 1 if one of the following two conditions is satisfied.

- $t = \text{II} \bigwedge t' = \text{II} \bigwedge n = n' \bigwedge_{i=1}^{n} m_i = m'_i$: This condition guarantees that for any Type-II signature, the message $\mathbf{M} = (t, M)$ is permanently fixed.
- $t = \text{I} \bigwedge n' \leq n \bigwedge \left[\exists \delta \in [0, n - n'] \text{ s.t. } \bigwedge_{i=1}^{n'} m'_i = m_{\delta+i}\right]$: This guarantees that for any Type-I signature on $\mathbf{M} = (t, M)$, the message list M can be modified to any substring of M, and its type t can be changed to Type-II.

4 Our First DTQS Scheme

First, we introduce a generic transformation $\mathsf{H2D}_c$ from HSSM to DTQS parameterized by an integer $c \geq 2$. It is insecure but necessary to understand our concrete DTQS scheme $\Pi_{\text{DTQS},c}$, which is fully described in Subsect. 4.1.

Insecure Transformation $\mathsf{H2D}_c$. A signer generates a DTQS signature on $\mathbf{M} = (t, M) = (t, (m_1, \cdots, m_n))$ as follows. n consecutive integers $d_1, \cdots, d_n$ whose values are in $[0, N-1]$ are assigned to the n sub-messages respectively. Initially, they are set to $d_1 := 0, \cdots, d_n := n - 1$. The type t is either I or II.

If $t = \text{I}$: For each $i \in [1, n]$, among all the substrings of M, select the substrings whose leftmost sub-message is m_i and whose length is an exponentiation of c. Concretely, they are m_i of length 1, $m_i \parallel \cdots \parallel m_{i+c-1}$ of length c,

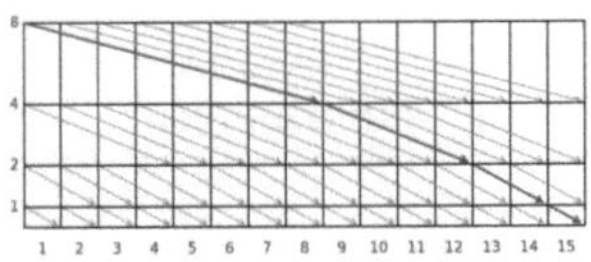

(a) H2D$_c$ with $c = 2$, $n = 15$

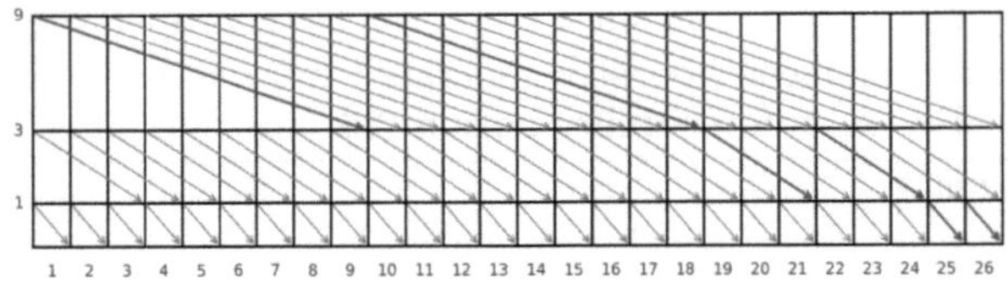

(b) H2D$_c$ with $c = 3$, $n = 26$

(c) H2D$_c$ with $c > n$ ($n = 10$)

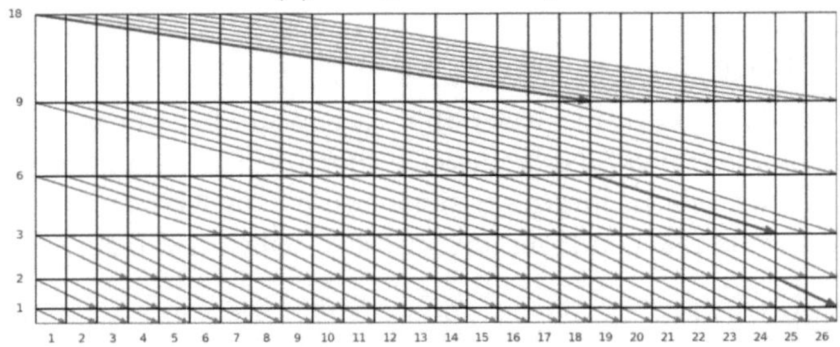

(d) H2D$'_c$ with $c = 3$, $n = 26$

Fig. 2. Visualizing the selected substrings

$m_i \parallel \cdots \parallel m_{i+c^2-1}$ of length c^2, $\cdots$, $m_i \parallel \cdots \parallel m_{i+c^{\lfloor \log_c(n-i+1) \rfloor}-1}$ of the maximal length $c^{\lfloor \log_c(n-i+1) \rfloor}$. Generate an HSSM signature on $(F_{\mathrm{I}}(M, d_1), \emptyset)$, where $F_{\mathrm{I}}(M, d_1) := \bigcup_{i \in [1,n]} \bigcup_{j \in [0, \lfloor \log_c(n-i+1) \rfloor]} \{d_i \parallel j \parallel m_i \parallel \cdots \parallel m_{i+c^j-1}\}$.

For instance, when (c, n) is $(2, 15)$ or $(3, 26)$, the selected substrings are visualized as gray arrows in Fig. 2a and Fig. 2b, respectively. Thicker blue arrows denote the substrings selected for a Type-II signature, which will be explained below. At this point, consider them as standard gray arrows.

Consider the case $c > n$. Because there is no M's substring whose length is c or longer, for each $i \in [1, n]$, only the substring m_i of length 1 is selected. When $n = 10$, if we visualize all the selected substrings as arrows, we obtain Fig. 2c.

If $t = \mathrm{II}$: Divide M under the condition that total number of the substrings is minimal and each substring has a length of an exponentiation of c. The first *stepping stone* is set to $s_1 := 1$. Among all the substrings of M which starts from m_{s_1} and whose length is an exponentiation of c, select the unique one whose length is maximal, i.e., $m_{s_1} \parallel \cdots \parallel m_{s_1+c^{\lfloor \log_c n \rfloor}-1}$ of length $c^{\lfloor \log_c n \rfloor} (= c^{\lfloor \log_c(n-s_1+1) \rfloor})$. Then, set the next stepping stone to the index of the leftmost sub-message which has not been selected yet, i.e., $s_2 := s_1 + c^{\lfloor \log_c n \rfloor}$. Among all the substrings of M which starts from m_{s_2} and whose length is an exponentiation of c, select the unique one whose length is maximal, i.e., $m_{s_2} \parallel \cdots \parallel m_{s_2+c^{\lfloor \log_c(n-s_2+1) \rfloor}-1}$ of length $c^{\lfloor \log_c(n-s_2+1) \rfloor}$. Then, let $s_3 := s_2 + c^{\lfloor \log_c(n-s_2+1) \rfloor}$. Repeat the above procedures until a substring which ends with m_n is selected. Let $S := \{s_1, s_2, \cdots, s_L\}$ with some $L \in \mathbb{N}^4$. Generate an HSSM signature on $(F_{\mathrm{II}}(M, d_1), \{m_1\|\cdots\|m_n\})$, where $F_{\mathrm{II}}(M, d_1) := \bigcup_{i\in[1,L]}\{d_{s_i} \parallel \lfloor\log_c(n - s_i + 1)\rfloor \parallel m_{s_i} \parallel \cdots \parallel m_{s_i+c^{\lfloor\log_c(n-s_i+1)\rfloor}-1}\}$.

When $(c, n) = (2, 15)$, the four substrings which have been visualized as the four thick blue arrows in Fig. 2a are selected. When $c \geq 3$, it is possible that substrings of the same length are consecutively selected multiple times. For instance, when $(c, n) = (3, 26)$, substrings of length 9, 3 and 1 are selected twice, respectively, and they have been visualized as the 6 thick blue arrows in Fig. 2b. Careful readers would notice that how $\mathsf{H2D}_c$ divides a string composed of n sub-messages for a Type-II signature can be explained by the base-c representation of n. Specifically, Theorem 1 holds. Because of the page limit, its proof is presented in the full version of this paper.

Theorem 1. *Let the base-c representation of n be* $[l_{\lfloor\log_c n\rfloor} l_{\lfloor\log_c n\rfloor-1}\cdots l_1 l_0]_c$, *where* $l_{\lfloor\log_c n\rfloor}$ *is the most significant digit (MSD),* l_0 *is the least significant digit (LSD), and each digit value* l_i *is in* $[0, c-1]$. $\mathsf{H2D}_c$ *divides the original string of length n into:* l_i *number of substrings of length* c^{l_i} *for each* $i \in [0, \lfloor\log_c n\rfloor]$. *Naturally, there are* $\sum_{i=0}^{\lfloor\log_c n\rfloor} l_i$ *substrings in total.*

For instance, base-2 representation of 15 is $[1111]_2$, and $\mathsf{H2D}_2$ divides a string of length 15 into four substrings of lengths 8, 4, 2 and 1. Base-3 representation of 26 is $[222]_3$, and $\mathsf{H2D}_3$ divides a string of length 26 into a total of six substrings, consisting of two substrings of each length 9, 3 and 1.

Consider the case $c > n$. Analogously to the case $t = \mathrm{I}$, for each $i \in [1, n]$, only the substring m_i of length 1 is selected. Each stepping stone is placed at an interval of one from the previous one, i.e., $S = \{1, 2, \cdots, n\}$. For instance, when $n = 10$, the selected substrings can be visualized as the ten arrows in Fig. 2c.

4.1 Formal Description of $\varPi_{\mathbf{DTQS},c}$

$\mathsf{H2D}_c$ is obviously insecure. Concretely, it cannot be SCH-secure because the relation between m_i and d_i is permanently fixed and publicly known. We instantiate it by the HSSM scheme by Ishizaka and Fukushima (IF HSSM) [13], and then modify it to a CCH-secure one. We formally describe the CCH-secure one later in this subsection. Before that, we introduce non-interactive witness-indistinguishable proof system by Groth and Sahai (GS NIWI) [12] and IF HSSM scheme.

GS NIWI Proof [12]. In the GS NIWI proof, based on a symmetric bilinear pairing $e : \mathbb{G}^2 \to \mathbb{G}_T$, a CRS consists of three vectors $\vec{f}_1, \vec{f}_2, \vec{f}_3 \in \mathbb{G}^3$, where $\vec{f}_1 = (f_1, 1_{\mathbb{G}}, g)$ and $\vec{f}_2 = (1_{\mathbb{G}}, f_2, g)$ with $f_1, f_2 \in \mathbb{G}$. A commitment $\vec{C}$ to an element $\mathcal{X} \in \mathbb{G}$ is given as $(1_{\mathbb{G}}, 1_{\mathbb{G}}, \mathcal{X}) \cdot \vec{f}_1^{\,r} \cdot \vec{f}_2^{\,s} \cdot \vec{f}_3^{\,t}$ with $r, s, t \xleftarrow{U} \mathbb{Z}_p$. The CRS has two settings, which are hard to distinguish under the DLIN assumption. In the perfect soundness setting, where the vector $\vec{f}_3$ is chosen outside the span of the other vectors $\vec{f}_1$ and $\vec{f}_2$, any commitment is perfectly hiding. In the perfect

[4] By Theorem 1 (given below), L is the sum of all of the digits of the base-c representation $[l_{\lfloor\log_c n\rfloor}\cdots l_1 l_0]_c$ of n. Formally, $L = \sum_{i\in[0,\lfloor\log_c n\rfloor]} l_i$.

witness-indistinguishability (WI) setting, the CRS satisfies $\vec{f}_3 = \vec{f}_1^{\xi_1} \cdot \vec{f}_2^{\xi_2}$ with $\xi_1, \xi_2 \in \mathbb{Z}_p$, and from a commitment $\vec{C} = (f_1^{r+\xi_1 t}, f_2^{s+\xi_2 t}, \mathcal{X} \cdot g^{r+s+t(\xi_1+\xi_2)})$ which distributes identically to a ciphertext of $\mathcal{X}$ in Boneh-Boyen-Shacham (BBS) encryption [9], $\mathcal{X}$ is extracted by using $\beta_1 = \log_g(f_1)$ and $\beta_2 = \log_g(f_2)$.

Given n variables $\mathcal{X}_1, \cdots, \mathcal{X}_n \in \mathbb{G}$, a prover computes a commitment $\vec{C}_{\mathcal{X}_i} \in \mathbb{G}^3$ to each $\mathcal{X}_i$ with randomness $r_i, s_i, t_i \xleftarrow{U} \mathbb{Z}_p$, then computes a proof $\vec{\pi}$ for a pairing-product equation (PPE) in a general form of $\prod_{i=1}^{n} e(\mathcal{A}_i, \mathcal{X}_i) \cdot \prod_{i=1}^{n} \prod_{j=1}^{n} e(\mathcal{X}_i, \mathcal{X}_j)^{a_{ij}} = t_T$ with constants $\mathcal{A}_i \in \mathbb{G}$, $a_{ij} \in \mathbb{Z}_p$ and $t_T \in \mathbb{G}_T$. If the PPE is linear in a simpler form of $\prod_{i=1}^{n} e(\mathcal{A}_i, \mathcal{X}_i) = t_T$, its proof $\vec{\pi} \in \mathbb{G}^3$ is simply $(\prod_{i=1}^{n} \mathcal{A}_i^{r_i}, \prod_{i=1}^{n} \mathcal{A}_i^{s_i}, \prod_{i=1}^{n} \mathcal{A}_i^{t_i})$. Each commitment $\vec{C}_{\mathcal{X}_i}$ is publicly and perfectly re-randomized to $\vec{C}_{\mathcal{X}_i} \cdot \vec{f}_1^{r_i'} \cdot \vec{f}_2^{s_i'} \cdot \vec{f}_3^{t_i'}$ with $r_i', s_i', t_i' \xleftarrow{U} \mathbb{Z}_p$. A proof $\vec{\pi} \in \mathbb{G}^3$ for the linear PPE is updated to $\vec{\pi} \cdot (\prod_{i=1}^{n} \mathcal{A}_i^{r_i'}, \prod_{i=1}^{n} \mathcal{A}_i^{s_i'}, \prod_{i=1}^{n} \mathcal{A}_i^{t_i'})$. A proof $\vec{\pi} \in \mathbb{G}^9$ for the general (or quadratic) PPE can be updated in a manner suggested in [7].

IF HSSM Scheme [13]. It is a simple combination of the HSSB scheme [5] and the H2AOS scheme [17]. Its underlying building blocks are GS NIWI proof [12], Waters signatures [19] (described in Sect. B), structure-preserving signatures (SPS) by Abe-Haralambiev-Ohkubo (AHO) [1,2] (described in Sect. C) with message-space $\mathbb{G}^2$, and Boneh-Lynn-Shacham (BLS) signatures [10] whose hash function is instantiated by Waters programmable hash function [19], i.e., $H_{\mathbb{G}}$. In key-generation, a signer generates a long-term AHO key-pair.

In generation of a signature on a set-pair (M, W), the signer independently generates one-time key-pairs of Waters signatures and BLS signatures, i.e., (X, x) and (Y, y), where $X := g^x$ and $Y := g^y$ with $x, y \xleftarrow{U} \mathbb{Z}_p$. For each $m \in M$, the signer generates a Waters signature $(\sigma_{m,1}, \sigma_{m,2}) \in \mathbb{G}^2$ on m. On the other hand, the signer divides the BLS secret-key y into $|W|$ shares by $|W|$-out-of-$|W|$ secret sharing. Specifically, the signer randomly chooses $\{\gamma_w \in \mathbb{Z}_p\}_{w \in W}$ s.t. $\sum_{w \in W} \gamma_w = y \pmod p$. For each $w \in W$, the signer computes $(\sigma_{w,1}, \sigma_{w,2}) := (H_{\mathbb{G}}(w)^{\gamma_w}, g^{\gamma_w}) \in \mathbb{G}^2$, where $\sigma_{w,1}$ is the BLS signature on w under the *pseudo* BLS public-key $\sigma_{w,2}$. The signer needs to generates an AHO signature $(\theta_1, \cdots, \theta_7) \in \mathbb{G}^7$ on (X, Y). Finally, the signer computes GS commitments to X, Y, $\{\sigma_{m,1}\}_{m \in M}, \{\sigma_{w,1}, \sigma_{w,2}\}_{w \in W}, \theta_1, \theta_2, \theta_5 \in \mathbb{G}$, then computes GS proofs that (1) *the AHO signature* $(\theta_1, \cdots, \theta_7)$ *on the message* (X, Y) *is valid*, (2) *the Waters signature* $(\sigma_{m,1}, \sigma_{m,2})$ *on the message* m *under the public-key* X *is valid for each* $m \in M$, (3) *the BLS signature* $\sigma_{w,1}$ *on the message* w *under the pseudo public-key* $\sigma_{w,2}$ *is valid for each* $w \in W$, and (4) *the* $|W|$ *pseudo BLS public-keys correctly recover the original BLS public-key, i.e.,* $\prod_{w \in W} \sigma_{w,2} = Y$.

In derivation of a signature on a set-pair (M', W'), for each deleted sub-message m from M, i.e., $m \in M \setminus M'$, we delete all the elements related to the Waters signature on m included in the original HSSM signature. On the other hand, we need to randomly choose $\{\gamma_w' \in \mathbb{Z}_p\}_{w \in W'}$ s.t. $\sum_{w \in W'} \gamma_w' = 0 \pmod p$. For each added element w in W', i.e., $w \in W' \setminus W$, we compute $(\sigma_{w,1}, \sigma_{w,2}) := (H_{\mathbb{G}}(w)^{\gamma_w'}, g^{\gamma_w'})$ and their GS commitments. For each inherited element w in W', i.e., $w \in W' \cap W$, we update the committed variables $\sigma_{w,1}, \sigma_{w,2} \in \mathbb{G}$ to

$\sigma_{w,1} \cdot H_{\mathbb{G}}(w)^{\gamma'_w}$ and $\sigma_{w,2} \cdot g^{\gamma'_w}$, respectively. All the remaining GS commitments and proofs are perfectly re-randomized and naturally updated, respectively.

Formal Description. For each sub-message index d_i, we prove, while hiding its value, that its relation to the other hidden indices d_j is appropriate. Concretely, we compute a GS commitment to each d_i, and then, if the difference between d_i and d_j is k, i.e., $d_j - d_i = k$, we compute a GS proof of this fact. In the signature derivation, they are perfectly re-randomized, just like the other existing ones.

$\boxed{\mathtt{KGen}(1^\lambda, L, N):}$ $(p, \mathbb{G}, \mathbb{G}_T, e, g) \leftarrow \mathcal{G}(1^\lambda)$. Conduct the following three steps.

1. Generate the public parameter of the Waters signatures with message length $\mathsf{len} := LN+1$ by choosing $h, u', u_1, \cdots, u_{\mathsf{len}} \xleftarrow{\text{U}} \mathbb{G}$. The Waters programmable hash function $H_{\mathbb{G}} : \{0,1\}^{\mathsf{len}} \rightarrow \mathbb{G}$ takes a binary string $m = m[1] \| \cdots \| m[\mathsf{len}] \in \{0,1\}^{\mathsf{len}}$, then outputs $u' \prod_{i=1}^{\mathsf{len}} u_i^{m[i]} \in \mathbb{G}$.
2. Generate a key-pair $(pk_{\mathsf{s}}, sk_{\mathsf{s}})$ of AHO SPS with message space $\mathbb{G}^2$.
3. Generate a CRS $\boldsymbol{f} = (\vec{f}_1, \vec{f}_2, \vec{f}_3)$ for the perfect WI setting of the GS NIWI proof. Concretely, $\vec{f}_1 := (f_1, 1, g)$, $\vec{f}_2 := (1, f_2, g)$ and $\vec{f}_3 := \vec{f}_1^{\xi_1} \cdot \vec{f}_2^{\xi_2} \cdot (1,1,g)^{-1}$, where $f_1, f_2 \xleftarrow{\text{U}} \mathbb{G}$ and $\xi_1, \xi_2 \xleftarrow{\text{U}} \mathbb{Z}_p$.

Output (pk, sk), where $pk := (g, h, u', \{u_i\}_{i=1}^{\mathsf{len}}, pk_{\mathsf{s}}, \boldsymbol{f})$ and $sk := sk_{\mathsf{s}}$.

$\boxed{\mathtt{Sig}(sk, \mathbf{M}):}$ Parse $\mathbf{M}$ as $(t, M) = (t, (m_1, \cdots, m_n))$ for some $t \in \{\text{I}, \text{II}\}$ and $n \leq N$. Firstly, conduct the following six steps.

1. Choose $x, y \xleftarrow{\text{U}} \mathbb{Z}_p$. Let $X := g^x$ and $Y := g^y$.
2. Generate an AHO signature $\sigma_{\mathsf{AHO}} = (\theta_1, \cdots, \theta_7)$ on $(X, Y) \in \mathbb{G}^2$.
3. If $t = \text{I}$, let $\gamma_{\mathsf{null}} := y$ and compute $(\sigma_{\mathsf{null},1}, \sigma_{\mathsf{null},2}) := (H_{\mathbb{G}}(0)^{\gamma_{\mathsf{null}}}, g^{\gamma_{\mathsf{null}}})$[5].
   If $t = \text{II}$, choose $\gamma_{\mathsf{null}} \xleftarrow{\text{U}} \mathbb{Z}_p$, and compute $\gamma_{\mathsf{full}} := y - \gamma_{\mathsf{null}}$, $(\sigma_{\mathsf{null},1}, \sigma_{\mathsf{null},2}) := (H_{\mathbb{G}}(0)^{\gamma_{\mathsf{null}}}, g^{\gamma_{\mathsf{null}}})$ and $(\sigma_{\mathsf{full},1}, \sigma_{\mathsf{full},2}) := (H_{\mathbb{G}}(1 \| m_1 \| \cdots \| m_n)^{\gamma_{\mathsf{full}}}, g^{\gamma_{\mathsf{full}}})$.
4. For each $i \in [1, n]$, define $d_i := i - 1$, and then do:
   For each $j \in [0, \lfloor \log_c (n - i + 1) \rfloor]$, generate a Waters signature on $d_i \| j \| m_i \| \cdots \| m_{i+c^j-1}$, i.e., $\sigma_{i,j} := (\sigma_{i,j,1}, \sigma_{i,j,2}) := (h^x \cdot H_{\mathbb{G}}(d_i \| j \| m_i \| \cdots \| m_{i+c^j-1})^{\chi_{ij}}, g^{\chi_{ij}})$ with $\chi_{ij} \xleftarrow{\text{U}} \mathbb{Z}_p$. Note that when $c > n$, for any $i \in [1, n]$, $\lfloor \log_c (n - i + 1) \rfloor$ is 0 and only one Waters signature $\sigma_{i,0} \in \mathbb{G}^2$ is generated.
5. Compute GS commitments to all the following group elements, namely (X, $Y, \theta_1, \theta_2, \theta_5, \{g^{d_i}\}_{i\in[1,n]}, \{\sigma_{i,j,1}, \sigma_{i,j,2}\}_{i\in[1,n], j\in[0,\lfloor \log_c (n-i+1)\rfloor]}$, $\{g^{d_i[j]}, g^{1-d_i[j]}, u_j^{d_i[j]}\}_{i\in[1,n], j\in[0,\lceil \log N \rceil]}$) and additionally either $(\sigma_{\mathsf{null},1}, \sigma_{\mathsf{null},2})$ if $t = \text{I}$ or $(\sigma_{\mathsf{null},1}, \sigma_{\mathsf{null},2}, \sigma_{\mathsf{full},1}, \sigma_{\mathsf{full},2})$ if $t = \text{II}$. For each committed variable $Z \in \mathbb{G}$, its GS commitment is denoted by $\vec{C}_Z \in \mathbb{G}^3$.
6. Compute GS proofs for all the following PPEs. Note that the PPEs surrounded by a grey rectangle are quadratic and the others are linear, and that the variable $\vec{\pi}_Z$ for some $Z \in \{0,1\}^*$ placed in front of each PPE indicates the computed GS proof for the PPE.

[5] Hereafter, $H_{\mathbb{G}}$ often takes a binary string $a \in \{0,1\}^{|a|}$ whose length is shorter than the specified length, i.e., $|a| < \mathsf{len}$. In this case, the latter part of the input a is filled with 0, i.e., $H_{\mathbb{G}}(a)$ is equivalent to $H_{\mathbb{G}}(a \| 0^{\mathsf{len}-|a|})$.

$\mathsf{StSt}_c(n)$: // $n, c \in \mathbb{N}$
  $i := 1$. While $i \leq n$, do: $S := S \cup \{i\}$. $i := i + c^{\lfloor \log_c (n-i+1) \rfloor}$.
  Rtrn S.

$\mathsf{StSt}'_c(n)$: // $n, c \in \mathbb{N}$
  $i := 1$. While $i \leq n$, do:
    $S := S \cup \{i\}$. $a_i := \lfloor \log_c (n - i + 1) \rfloor$.
    Let $l_{i,a_i} \in [1, c-1]$ denote the MSD of the base-c representation of $n - i + 1$.
    $i := i + l_{i,a_i} \cdot c^{a_i}$.
  Rtrn S.

Fig. 3. The functions *stepping stones* StSt_c, StSt'_c

$$[\vec{\pi}_A:]\ A \cdot e(\theta_3, \theta_4)^{-1} = e(g_z, \theta_1) \cdot e(g_r, \theta_2) \cdot e(g_1, X) \cdot e(g_2, Y)$$
$$[\vec{\pi}_B:]\ B \cdot e(\theta_6, \theta_7)^{-1} = e(h_z, \theta_1) \cdot e(h_r, \theta_5) \cdot e(h_1, X) \cdot e(h_2, Y)$$
$$[\vec{\pi}_{i,j,\mathsf{Wat}}:]\ e(\sigma_{i,j,1}, g) = e(X, h) \cdot e(\sigma_{i,j,2}, H_{\mathbb{G}}(0^{\lfloor \log N \rfloor + 1} \parallel j \parallel m_i \parallel \cdots \parallel m_{i+c^j-1})) \cdot \prod_{k=1}^{\lfloor \log N \rfloor} e(\sigma_{i,j,2}, u_k^{d_i[k]}) \quad (\text{For } i \in [1,n],\ j \in [0, \lfloor \log_c (n-i+1) \rfloor])$$
$$[\vec{\pi}_{i,j,\mathsf{mul}}:]\ e(g^{d_i[j]}, g^{1-d_i[j]}) = 1_{\mathbb{G}_T} \quad (\text{For } i \in [1,n],\ j \in [0, \lfloor \log N \rfloor])$$
$$[\vec{\pi}_{i,j,\mathsf{sum}}:]\ e(g^{d_i[j]}, g) \cdot e(g^{1-d_i[j]}, g) = e(g, g) \quad (\text{For } i \in [1,n],\ j \in [0, \lfloor \log N \rfloor])$$
$$[\vec{\pi}_{i,j,\mathsf{exp}}:]\ e(g^{d_i[j]}, u_j) = e(g, u_j^{d_i[j]}) \quad (\text{For } i \in [1,n],\ j \in [0, \lfloor \log N \rfloor])$$
$$[\vec{\pi}_{i,\mathsf{bin}}:]\ e(g^{d_i}, g) = \prod_{j=0}^{\lfloor \log N \rfloor} e(g^{d_i[j]}, g^{2^j}) \quad (\text{For } i \in [1,n])$$
$$[\vec{\pi}_{i,j,\mathsf{dif}}:]\ e(g^{d_{i+c^j}}, g) = e(g^{d_i}, g) \cdot e(g^{c^j}, g) \quad (\text{For } i \in [1,n-1],\ j \in [0, \lfloor \log_c (n-i+1) \rfloor])$$
$$[\vec{\pi}_{\mathsf{null}}:]\ e(\sigma_{\mathsf{null},1}, g) = e(\sigma_{\mathsf{null},2}, H_{\mathbb{G}}(0))$$
$$[\vec{\pi}_{\mathsf{full}}:]\ e(\sigma_{\mathsf{full},1}, g) = e(\sigma_{\mathsf{full},2}, H_{\mathbb{G}}(1 \parallel m_1 \parallel \cdots \parallel m_n)) \quad (\text{If } t = \mathrm{II})$$
$$[\vec{\pi}_Y:]\ e(Y, g) = e(\sigma_{\mathsf{null},2}, g) \quad (\text{If } t = \mathrm{I})$$
$$[\vec{\pi}_Y:]\ e(Y, g) = e(\sigma_{\mathsf{null},2}, g) \cdot e(\sigma_{\mathsf{full},2}, g) \quad (\text{If } t = \mathrm{II})$$

Lastly, output a DTQS signature σ. If $t = \mathrm{I}$, it consists of

$$\left(\begin{array}{l} \vec{C}_X, \vec{C}_Y, \{\vec{C}_{\theta_i}\}_{i \in \{1,2,5\}}, \{\theta_i\}_{i \in \{3,4,6,7\}}, \vec{\pi}_A, \vec{\pi}_B, \vec{C}_{\sigma_{\mathsf{null},1}}, \vec{C}_{\sigma_{\mathsf{null},2}}, \vec{\pi}_{\mathsf{null}}, \vec{\pi}_Y, \\ \{\{\vec{\pi}_{i,j,\mathsf{dif}}\}_{j=0}^{l_i}\}_{i=1}^{n-1}, \left\{ \begin{array}{l} \vec{C}_{g^{d_i}}, \vec{\pi}_{i,\mathsf{bin}}, \underbrace{\left\{ \vec{C}_{\sigma_{i,j,1}}, \vec{C}_{\sigma_{i,j,2}}, \vec{\pi}_{i,j,\mathsf{Wat}} \right\}_{j=0}^{l_i}}_{①}, \\ \underbrace{\left\{ \vec{C}_{g^{d_i[j]}}, \vec{C}_{g^{1-d_i[j]}}, \vec{C}_{u_j^{d_i[j]}}, \vec{\pi}_{i,j,\mathsf{mul}}, \vec{\pi}_{i,j,\mathsf{sum}}, \vec{\pi}_{i,j,\mathsf{exp}} \right\}_{j=0}^{\lfloor \log N \rfloor}}_{②} \end{array} \right\}_{i=1}^{n} \end{array} \right), \tag{2}$$

where $l_i := \lfloor \log_c (n - i + 1) \rfloor$[6]. Else if $t = \mathrm{II}$, we compute the set of *stepping stones* $S = (s_1, \cdots, s_L)$ for some $L \in \mathbb{N}$ as $S := \mathsf{StSt}_c(n)$ under the function StSt_c which is formally defined in Fig. 3, then construct σ as follows.

---

[6] The underlined parts with ①, ② and ③ will be referred in efficiency analysis..

$$\left(\begin{array}{l}\vec{C}_X, \vec{C}_Y, \{\vec{C}_{\theta_i}\}_{i\in\{1,2,5\}}, \{\theta_i\}_{i\in\{3,4,6,7\}}, \vec{\pi}_A, \vec{\pi}_B, \vec{C}_{\sigma_{\mathsf{null},1}}, \vec{C}_{\sigma_{\mathsf{null},2}}, \vec{\pi}_{\mathsf{null}}, \vec{\pi}_Y, \\ \{\vec{\pi}_{s_i,t_i,\mathsf{dif}}\}_{i=1}^{L-1}, \vec{C}_{\sigma_{\mathsf{full},1}}, \vec{C}_{\sigma_{\mathsf{full},2}}, \vec{\pi}_{\mathsf{full}}, \left\{\vec{C}_{g^{d_{s_i}}}, \vec{\pi}_{s_i,\mathsf{bin}}, \vec{C}_{\sigma_{s_i,t_i,1}}, \vec{C}_{\sigma_{s_i,t_i,2}}, \vec{\pi}_{s_i,t_i,\mathsf{Wat}}, \right. \\ \left. \underbrace{\left\{\vec{C}_{g^{d_{s_i}[j]}}, \vec{C}_{g^{1-d_{s_i}[j]}}, \vec{C}_{u_j^{d_{s_i}[j]}}, \vec{\pi}_{s_i,j,\mathsf{mul}}, \vec{\pi}_{s_i,j,\mathsf{sum}}, \vec{\pi}_{s_i,j,\mathsf{exp}}\right\}_{j=0}^{\lfloor\log N\rfloor}}_{③}\right\}_{i=1}^{L}\end{array}\right), \tag{3}$$

where $t_i := \lfloor \log_c (n - s_i + 1)\rfloor$ for $i \in [1, L]$(see footnote 6).

Derive$(pk, \mathbf{M}, \sigma, \mathbf{M}')$: Parse $\mathbf{M}$ as above in Sig. Parse $\mathbf{M}'$ as $(t', M') = (t', (m'_1, \cdots, m'_{n'}))$ for some $t' \in \{\mathrm{I}, \mathrm{II}\}$ and $n' \le N$. Since $1 \leftarrow P(\mathbf{M}, \mathbf{M}')$, (t, t') is either one of the three patters, namely (I, I), (I, II) and (II, II).

If $(t, t') = (\mathrm{I}, \mathrm{I})$: Parse σ as (2). Conduct the following four steps.

1. Since $1 \leftarrow P(\mathbf{M}, \mathbf{M}')$, $n' \le n \bigwedge \exists \delta \in [0, n - n']$ s.t. $\bigwedge_{i=1}^{n'} m'_i = m_{\delta+i}$.
2. Re-randomize the (partially GS-committed) AHO signature $(\theta_1, \cdots, \theta_7) \in \mathbb{G}^7$ in the same way as [1,2,5,13]. Choose $\eta_2, \eta_5, \mu, \nu \xleftarrow{\mathrm{U}} \mathbb{Z}_p$, then

$$\vec{C}'_{\theta_1} := \vec{C}_{\theta_1} \cdot \vec{f}_1^{r'_{\theta_1}} \cdot \vec{f}_2^{s'_{\theta_1}} \cdot \vec{f}_3^{t'_{\theta_1}},$$
$$\vec{C}'_{\theta_2} := \vec{C}_{\theta_2} \cdot \iota_{\mathbb{G}}(\theta_4^{\eta_2}) \cdot \vec{f}_1^{r'_{\theta_2}} \cdot \vec{f}_2^{s'_{\theta_2}} \cdot \vec{f}_3^{t'_{\theta_2}}, \quad \theta'_3 := (\theta_3 \cdot g_r^{-\eta_2})^{1/\mu}, \quad \theta'_4 := \theta_4^{\mu},$$
$$\vec{C}'_{\theta_5} := \vec{C}_{\theta_5} \cdot \iota_{\mathbb{G}}(\theta_7^{\eta_5}) \cdot \vec{f}_1^{r'_{\theta_5}} \cdot \vec{f}_2^{s'_{\theta_5}} \cdot \vec{f}_3^{t'_{\theta_5}}, \quad \theta'_6 := (\theta_6 \cdot h_r^{-\eta_5})^{1/\nu}, \quad \theta'_7 := \theta_7^{\nu},$$

   where $r'_{\theta_i}, r'_{\theta_i}, t'_{\theta_i} \xleftarrow{\mathrm{U}} \mathbb{Z}_p$ for each $i \in \{1, 2, 5\}$. Visit Sect. C to see how to re-randomize a normal, i.e., non GS-committed, AHO signature.
3. Re-randomize all the required GS commitments, namely $\vec{C}_X, \vec{C}_Y, \vec{C}_{\sigma_{\mathsf{null},1}}, \vec{C}_{\sigma_{\mathsf{null},2}}, \{\vec{C}_{g^{d_{i+\delta}}}, \{\vec{C}_{\sigma_{i+\delta,j,1}}, \vec{C}_{\sigma_{i+\delta,j,2}}\}_{j=0}^{\lfloor \log_c (n'-i+1)\rfloor},$ $\{\vec{C}_{g^{d_{i+\delta}[j]}}, \vec{C}_{g^{1-d_{i+\delta}[j]}}, \vec{C}_{u_j^{d_{i+\delta}[j]}}\}_{j=0}^{\lfloor \log N\rfloor}\}_{i=1}^{n'}$. Each commitment $\vec{C}_Z$ with $Z \in \mathbb{G}$ is updated to $\vec{C}'_Z := \vec{C}_Z \cdot \vec{f}_1^{r'_Z} \cdot \vec{f}_2^{s'_Z} \cdot \vec{f}_3^{t'_Z}$, where $r'_Z, s'_Z, t'_Z \xleftarrow{\mathrm{U}} \mathbb{Z}_p$.
4. Re-randomize all the required GS proofs for linear PPEs in the manner explained earlier in this section, namely $\vec{\pi}_A, \vec{\pi}_B, \vec{\pi}_{\mathsf{null}}, \vec{\pi}_Y, \{\{\vec{\pi}_{i+\delta,j,\mathsf{dif}}\}_{j=0}^{\lfloor \log_c (n'-i+1)\rfloor}\}_{i=1}^{n'-1}, \{\vec{\pi}_{i+\delta,\mathsf{bin}}, \{\vec{\pi}_{i+\delta,j,\mathsf{sum}}, \vec{\pi}_{i+\delta,j,\mathsf{exp}}\}_{j=0}^{\lfloor \log N\rfloor}\}_{i=1}^{n'}$. Then, re-randomize all the required GS proofs for quadratic PPEs in the manner suggested in [7], namely $\{\{\vec{\pi}_{\sigma_{i+\delta,j,\mathsf{Wat}}}\}_{j=0}^{\lfloor \log_c (n'-i+1)\rfloor}, \{\vec{\pi}_{i+\delta,j,\mathsf{mul}}\}_{j=0}^{\lfloor \log N\rfloor}\}_{i=1}^{n'}$. For the GS proof $\vec{\pi}_Z$ with some $Z \in \{0,1\}^*$, let $\vec{\pi}'_Z$ denote the re-randomized one.

Output a signature composed of

$$\left(\begin{array}{l}\vec{C}'_X, \vec{C}'_Y, \{\vec{C}'_{\theta_i}\}_{i\in\{1,2,5\}}, \{\theta'_i\}_{i\in\{3,4,6,7\}}, \vec{\pi}'_A, \vec{\pi}'_B, \vec{C}'_{\sigma_{\mathsf{null},1}}, \vec{C}'_{\sigma_{\mathsf{null},2}}, \vec{\pi}'_{\mathsf{null}}, \vec{\pi}'_Y, \\ \{\{\vec{\pi}'_{i+\delta,j,\mathsf{dif}}\}_{j=0}^{l'_i}\}_{i=1}^{n'-1}, \left\{\vec{C}'_{g^{d_{i+\delta}}}, \vec{\pi}'_{i+\delta,\mathsf{bin}}, \left\{\vec{C}'_{\sigma_{i+\delta,j,1}}, \vec{C}'_{\sigma_{i+\delta,j,2}}, \vec{\pi}'_{i+\delta,j,\mathsf{Wat}}\right\}_{j=0}^{l'_i}, \right. \\ \left. \left\{\vec{C}'_{g^{d_{i+\delta}[j]}}, \vec{C}'_{g^{1-d_{i+\delta}[j]}}, \vec{C}'_{u_j^{d_{i+\delta}[j]}}, \vec{\pi}'_{i+\delta,j,\mathsf{mul}}, \vec{\pi}'_{i+\delta,j,\mathsf{sum}}, \vec{\pi}'_{i+\delta,j,\mathsf{exp}}\right\}_{j=0}^{\lfloor\log N\rfloor}\right\}_{i=1}^{n'}\end{array}\right),$$

where $l'_i := \lfloor \log_c (n'-i+1)\rfloor$.

$\boxed{\text{If } (t,t') = (\text{I}, \text{II}):}$ Parse σ as (2). Conduct the first two steps in the case $(t,t') = (\text{I}, \text{I})$. Then, conduct the following three steps.

1. Derive the set of stepping stones $S' = \{s_1, \cdots, s_{L'}\} := \mathsf{StSt}_c(n')$.
2. Re-randomize all the required GS commitments except for $\vec{C}_{\sigma_{\mathsf{null},1}}$ and $\vec{C}_{\sigma_{\mathsf{null},2}}$, namely $\vec{C}_X, \vec{C}_Y, \{\vec{C}_{g^{d_{s_i+\delta}}}, \{\vec{C}_{\sigma_{s_i+\delta,j,1}}, \vec{C}_{\sigma_{s_i+\delta,j,2}}\}_{j=0}^{\lfloor\log_c (n'-s_i+1)\rfloor}, \{\vec{C}_{g^{d_{s_i+\delta}[j]}}, \vec{C}_{g^{1-d_{s_i+\delta}[j]}}, \vec{C}_{u_j^{d_{s_i+\delta}[j]}}\}_{j=0}^{\lfloor\log N\rfloor}\}_{i=1}^{L'}$. Choose $\gamma'_{\mathsf{null}} \xleftarrow{\text{U}} \mathbb{Z}_p$, then set $\gamma'_{\mathsf{full}} := -\gamma_{\mathsf{null}}$. Update $(\vec{C}_{\sigma_{\mathsf{null},1}}, \vec{C}_{\sigma_{\mathsf{null},2}})$ to $(\vec{C}_{\sigma_{\mathsf{null},1}} \cdot \iota_{\mathbb{G}}(H_{\mathbb{G}}(0)^{\gamma'_{\mathsf{null}}}), \vec{C}_{\sigma_{\mathsf{null},2}} \cdot \iota_{\mathbb{G}}(g^{\gamma'_{\mathsf{null}}}))$, then re-randomize them. As above, $\vec{C}'_Z$ (with the apostrophe mark) denotes the re-randomized GS proof. Lastly, we set $(\sigma_{\mathsf{full},1}, \sigma_{\mathsf{full},2}) := (H_{\mathbb{G}}(1\|m'_1\|\cdots\|m'_{n'})^{\gamma'_{\mathsf{full}}}, g^{\gamma'_{\mathsf{full}}})$, then compute GS commitments for them, i.e., $\vec{C}_{\sigma_{\mathsf{full},i}} := \iota_{\mathbb{G}}(\sigma_{\mathsf{full},i}) \cdot \vec{f}_1^{\,r_{\sigma_{\mathsf{full},i}}} \cdot \vec{f}_2^{\,s_{\sigma_{\mathsf{full},i}}} \cdot \vec{f}_3^{\,t_{\sigma_{\mathsf{full},i}}}$ for each $i \in \{1,2\}$, where $r_{\sigma_{\mathsf{full},i}}, s_{\sigma_{\mathsf{full},i}}, t_{\sigma_{\mathsf{full},i}} \xleftarrow{\text{U}} \mathbb{Z}_p$.
3. Re-randomize all the required GS proofs for linear or quadratic PPEs except for $\vec{\pi}_Y$, namely $\vec{\pi}_A, \vec{\pi}_B, \vec{\pi}_{\mathsf{null}}, \{\vec{\pi}_{s_i+\delta,\mathsf{bin}}, \vec{\pi}_{s_i+\delta,t_i,\mathsf{Wat}}, \vec{\pi}_{s_i+\delta,t_i,\mathsf{dif}}, \{\vec{\pi}_{s_i+\delta,j,\mathsf{mul}}, \vec{\pi}_{s_i+\delta,j,\mathsf{sum}}, \vec{\pi}_{s_i+\delta,j,\mathsf{exp}}\}_{j=}^{\lfloor\log N\rfloor}\}_{i=1}^{L'}$. As above, $\vec{\pi}'_Z$ (being added an apostrophe mark) denotes the re-randomized one. Additionally, we need to compute the GS proof $\vec{\pi}_{\mathsf{full}} \in \mathbb{G}^3$ for the PPE $e(\sigma_{\mathsf{full},1}, g) = e(\sigma_{\mathsf{full},2}, H_{\mathbb{G}}(1 \| m'_1 \| \cdots \| m'_{n'}))$ and update the GS proof $\vec{\pi}_Y \in \mathbb{G}^3$ to $\vec{\pi}'_Y := \vec{\pi}_Y \cdot (g^{-r_{\sigma_{\mathsf{full},2}}}, g^{-s_{\sigma_{\mathsf{full},2}}}, g^{-t_{\sigma_{\mathsf{full},2}}})$.

Output a signature composed of

$$\left(\begin{array}{l}\vec{C}'_X, \vec{C}'_Y, \{\vec{C}'_{\theta_i}\}_{i\in\{1,2,5\}}, \{\theta'_i\}_{i\in\{3,4,6,7\}}, \vec{\pi}'_A, \vec{\pi}'_B, \vec{C}'_{\sigma_{\mathsf{null},1}}, \vec{C}'_{\sigma_{\mathsf{null},2}}, \vec{\pi}'_{\mathsf{null}}, \vec{\pi}'_Y, \\ \{\vec{\pi}'_{s'_i,t_i,\mathsf{dif}}\}_{i=1}^{L'-1}, \vec{C}_{\sigma_{\mathsf{full},1}}, \vec{C}_{\sigma_{\mathsf{full},2}}, \vec{\pi}_{\mathsf{full}}, \left\{\vec{C}'_{g^{d_{s'_i}}}, \vec{\pi}'_{s'_i,\mathsf{bin}}, \vec{C}'_{\sigma_{s'_i,t_i,1}}, \vec{C}'_{\sigma_{s'_i,t_i,2}}, \vec{\pi}'_{s'_i,t_i,\mathsf{Wat}}, \right. \\ \left. \left\{\vec{C}'_{g^{d_{s'_i}[j]}}, \vec{C}'_{g^{1-d_{s'_i}[j]}}, \vec{C}'_{u_j^{d_{s'_i}[j]}}, \vec{\pi}'_{s'_i,j,\mathsf{mul}}, \vec{\pi}'_{s'_i,j,\mathsf{sum}}, \vec{\pi}'_{s'_i,j,\mathsf{exp}}\right\}_{j=0}^{\lfloor\log N\rfloor}\right\}_{i=1}^{L'}\end{array}\right),$$

where $t_i := \lfloor \log_c (n'-s_i+1)\rfloor$ and $s'_i := s_i + \delta$ for $i \in [1, L']$.

$\boxed{\text{If } (t,t') = (\text{II}, \text{II}):}$ Parse σ as (3). Since $1 \leftarrow P(\mathbf{M}, \mathbf{M}')$, $n' = n \bigwedge_{i=1}^{n} m'_i = m_i$. Re-randomize all of the AHO signature, GS commitments and GS proofs in σ in the same manner as the above two cases, then output it.

$\boxed{\mathtt{Ver}(pk, \mathbf{M}, \sigma):}$ Parse $\mathbf{M}$ as above in $\mathtt{Sig}$. Parse σ either as (2) if $t = \text{I}$ or (3) if $t = \text{II}$. Each GS proof $\vec{\pi}_Z \in \mathbb{G}^3$ with some $Z \in \{0,1\}^*$ is parsed as $(\pi_Z[1], \pi_Z[2],$

$\pi_Z[3]$). Each GS proof $\vec{\pi}_Z \in \mathbb{G}^9$ with some $Z \in \{0,1\}^*$ is parsed as $(\vec{\pi}_Z[1], \vec{\pi}_Z[2], \vec{\pi}_Z[3])$ with $\vec{\pi}_Z[k] \in \mathbb{G}^3$ for each $k \in \{1,2,3\}$. For any element $Z \in \mathbb{G}$, $\iota_{\mathbb{G}}(Z)$ denotes $(1_{\mathbb{G}}, 1_{\mathbb{G}}, Z) \in \mathbb{G}^3$. For any element $Z \in \mathbb{G}_T$, $\iota_{\mathbb{G}_T}(Z)$ denotes $(1_{\mathbb{G}_T}, 1_{\mathbb{G}_T}, Z) \in \mathbb{G}_T^3$. For any $h, g_1, g_2, g_3 \in \mathbb{G}$, $E(h,(g_1,g_2,g_3))$ denotes $(e(h,g_1), e(h,g_2), e(h,g_3)) \in \mathbb{G}_T^3$. For any $\vec{X} = (X_1,X_2,X_3) \in \mathbb{G}^3$ and $\vec{Y} = (Y_1,Y_2,Y_3) \in \mathbb{G}^3$, $F(\vec{X},\vec{Y}) := \tilde{F}(\vec{X},\vec{Y})^{1/2} \cdot \tilde{F}(\vec{Y},\vec{X})^{1/2} \in \mathbb{G}_T^{3\times 3}$, where $\tilde{F}(\vec{X},\vec{Y}) \in \mathbb{G}_T^{3\times 3}$ contains $e(X_i,Y_j)$ as the (i,j)-th element for all $i,j \in \{1,2,3\}$.

If $t = \mathrm{I}$, output 1 when all the following ten equations hold.

$[\vec{\pi}_A$:] $\iota_{\mathbb{G}_T}(A \cdot e(\theta_3,\theta_4)^{-1}) = E(g_z, \vec{C}_{\theta_1}) E(g_r, \vec{C}_{\theta_2}) E(g_1, \vec{C}_X) E(g_2, \vec{C}_Y) \prod_{k=1}^{3} E(\pi_A[k], \vec{f}_k)$

$[\vec{\pi}_B$:] $\iota_{\mathbb{G}_T}(B \cdot e(\theta_6,\theta_7)^{-1}) = E(h_z, \vec{C}_{\theta_1}) E(h_r, \vec{C}_{\theta_5}) E(h_1, \vec{C}_X) E(h_2, \vec{C}_Y) \prod_{k=1}^{3} E(\pi_B[k], \vec{f}_k)$

$[\vec{\pi}_{i,j,\mathsf{Wat}}$:] $F(\iota_{\mathbb{G}}(g), \vec{C}_{\sigma_{i,j,1}}) = F(\iota_{\mathbb{G}}(g), \vec{C}_X) \cdot \prod_{k=0}^{\lfloor \log N \rfloor} F(\vec{C}_{\sigma_{i,j,2}}, \vec{C}_{u_k^{d_i[k]}})$
$\cdot F(\iota_{\mathbb{G}}(H_{\mathbb{G}}(0^{\lfloor \log N \rfloor+1} \parallel j \parallel m_i \parallel \cdots \parallel m_{i+c^j-1})), \vec{C}_{\sigma_{i,j,2}}) \cdot \prod_{k=1}^{3} F(\vec{\pi}_{i,j,\mathsf{Wat}}[k], \vec{f}_k)$
(For $i \in [1,n]$, $j \in [0, \lfloor \log_c(n-i+1) \rfloor]$)

$[\vec{\pi}_{i,j,\mathsf{mul}}$:] $F(\vec{C}_{g^{d_i[j]}}, \vec{C}_{g^{1-d_i[j]}}) = \prod_{k=1}^{3} F(\vec{\pi}_{i,j,\mathsf{mul}}[k])$

$[\vec{\pi}_{i,j,\mathsf{sum}}$:] $E(g, \vec{C}_{g^{d_i[j]}}) \cdot E(g, \vec{C}_{g^{1-d_i[j]}}) = \iota_{\mathbb{G}_T}(e(g,g)) \cdot \prod_{k=1}^{3} E(\pi_{i,j,\mathsf{sum}}[k], \vec{f}_k)$
(For $i \in [1,n]$ and $j \in [0, \lfloor \log N \rfloor]$)

$[\vec{\pi}_{i,j,\mathsf{exp}}$:] $E(g, \vec{C}_{g^{d_i[j]}}) = E(g, \vec{C}_{u_j^{d_i[j]}}) \cdot \prod_{k=1}^{3} E(\pi_{i,j,\mathsf{exp}}[k], \vec{f}_k)$
(For $i \in [1,n]$ and $j \in [0, \lfloor \log N \rfloor]$)

$[\vec{\pi}_{i,\mathsf{bin}}$:] $E(g, \vec{C}_{g^{d_i}}) = \prod_{j=0}^{\lfloor \log N \rfloor} E(g^{2^{j-1}}, \vec{C}_{g^{d_i[j]}}) \cdot \prod_{k=1}^{3} E(\pi_{i,\mathsf{bin}}[k], \vec{f}_k)$
(For $i \in [1,n]$)

$[\vec{\pi}_{i,j,\mathsf{dif}}$:] $E(g, \vec{C}_{g^{d_{i+c^j}}}) = E(g, \vec{C}_{g^{d_i}}) \cdot \iota_{\mathbb{G}_T}(e(g^{c^j}, g)) \cdot \prod_{k=1}^{3} E(\pi_{i,j,\mathsf{dif}}[k], \vec{f}_k)$
(For $i \in [1, n-1]$, $j \in [0, \lfloor \log_c(n-i+1) \rfloor]$)

$[\vec{\pi}_{\mathsf{null}}$:] $E(g, \vec{C}_{\sigma_{\mathsf{null},1}}) = E(H_{\mathbb{G}}(0), \vec{C}_{\sigma_{\mathsf{null},2}}) \cdot \prod_{k=1}^{3} E(\pi_{\mathsf{null}}[k], \vec{f}_k)$

$[\vec{\pi}_Y$:] $E(g, \vec{C}_Y) = E(g, \vec{C}_{\sigma_{\mathsf{null},2}}) \cdot \prod_{k=1}^{3} E(\pi_Y[k], \vec{f}_k)$

If $t = \mathrm{II}$, output 1 if all the following equations hold. Let $S = \{s_1, \cdots, s_L\} := \mathsf{StSt}_c(n)$ for some $L \in \mathbb{N}$.

$[\vec{\pi}_A$, $\vec{\pi}_B$, $\vec{\pi}_{\mathsf{null}}$:] *Unchanged from the case of* $t = \mathrm{I}$.

$[\vec{\pi}_{s_i,j,\mathsf{Wat}}$:] $F(\iota_{\mathbb{G}}(g), \vec{C}_{\sigma_{s_i,j,1}}) = F(\iota_{\mathbb{G}}(g), \vec{C}_X) \cdot \prod_{k=0}^{\lfloor \log N \rfloor} F(\vec{C}_{\sigma_{s_i,j,2}}, \vec{C}_{u_k^{d_{s_i}[k]}})$
$\cdot F(\iota_{\mathbb{G}}(H_{\mathbb{G}}(0^{\lfloor \log N \rfloor+1} \parallel j \parallel m_{s_i} \parallel \cdots \parallel m_{s_i+c^j-1})), \vec{C}_{\sigma_{s_i,j,2}}) \cdot \prod_{k=1}^{3} F(\vec{\pi}_{s_i,j,\mathsf{Wat}}[k], \vec{f}_k)$
(For $i \in [1,L]$, $j \in [0, \lfloor \log_c(n-s_i+1) \rfloor]$)

$[\vec{\pi}_{s_i,j,\mathsf{mul}}$:] $F(\vec{C}_{g^{d_{s_i}[j]}}, \vec{C}_{g^{1-d_{s_i}[j]}}) = \prod_{k=1}^{3} F(\vec{\pi}_{s_i,j,\mathsf{mul}}[k])$

$[\vec{\pi}_{s_i,j,\mathsf{sum}}$:] $E(g, \vec{C}_{g^{d_{s_i}[j]}}) \cdot E(g, \vec{C}_{g^{1-d_{s_i}[j]}}) = \iota_{\mathbb{G}_T}(e(g,g)) \cdot \prod_{k=1}^{3} E(\pi_{s_i,j,\mathsf{sum}}[k], \vec{f}_k)$
(For $i \in [1,L]$ and $j \in [0, \lfloor \log N \rfloor]$)

$[\vec{\pi}_{s_i,j,\mathsf{exp}}$:] $E(g, \vec{C}_{g^{d_{s_i}[j]}}) = E(g, \vec{C}_{u_j^{d_{s_i}[j]}}) \cdot \prod_{k=1}^{3} E(\pi_{s_i,j,\mathsf{exp}}[k], \vec{f}_k)$
(For $i \in [1,L]$ and $j \in [0, \lfloor \log N \rfloor]$)

$[\vec{\pi}_{i,\mathsf{bin}}$:] $E(g, \vec{C}_{g^{d_{s_i}}}) = \prod_{j=0}^{\lfloor \log N \rfloor} E(g^{2^{j-1}}, \vec{C}_{g^{d_{s_i}[j]}}) \cdot \prod_{k=1}^{3} E(\pi_{s_i,\mathsf{bin}}[k], \vec{f}_k)$
(For $i \in [1,L]$)

$[\vec{\pi}_{s_i,t_i,\mathsf{dif}}$:] $E(g, \vec{C}_{g^{d_{s_i+c^{t_i}}}}) = E(g, \vec{C}_{g^{d_{s_i}}}) \cdot \iota_{\mathbb{G}_T}(e(g^{c^{t_i}}, g)) \cdot \prod_{k=1}^{3} E(\pi_{s_i,t_i,\mathsf{dif}}[k], \vec{f}_k)$
(For $i \in [1, L-1]$. Let $t_i := \lfloor \log_c(n-s_i+1) \rfloor$)

$[\vec{\pi}_{\mathsf{full}}$:] $E(g, \vec{C}_{\sigma_{\mathsf{full},1}}) = E(H_{\mathbb{G}}(1 \parallel m_1 \parallel \cdots \parallel m_n), \vec{C}_{\sigma_{\mathsf{full},2}}) \cdot \prod_{k=1}^{3} E(\pi_{\mathsf{full}}[k], \vec{f}_k)$

$[\vec{\pi}_Y$:] $E(g, \vec{C}_Y) = E(g, \vec{C}_{\sigma_{\mathsf{null},2}}) \cdot E(g, \vec{C}_{\sigma_{\mathsf{full},2}}) \cdot \prod_{k=1}^{3} E(\pi_Y[k], \vec{f}_k)$

Security Analysis. Its security is guaranteed by the following theorem.

Theorem 2. *The scheme is unconditionally* CCH. *Let* $q \in \mathtt{poly}(\lambda)$ *denote the maximal number of times that the signing oracle can be accessed. The scheme is* UNF *under the DLIN assumption w.r.t the group* $\mathbb{G}$ *and the q-SFP assumption.*

Proof. First is CCH. Let σ' denote the signature on $\mathbf{M}'$ derived from the original signature σ on $\mathbf{M}$. Let σ^* denote the signature on $\mathbf{M}'$ produced by sk. It is obvious that at deriving σ', all the GS commitments and GS proofs are perfectly re-randomized. Since the GS proof is WI, all the GS commitments, GS proofs and the AHO signature elements $\{\theta'_i\}_{i\in\{3,4,6,7\}}$ included in σ' distribute identically to the corresponding ones included in σ^*. Thus, the scheme is CCH.

Next is UNF. We define the following four experiments. Each experiment is obtained by partially modifying the previous one.

- ***Expt***$_0$**:** The standard UNF experiment. The DTQS message $\mathbf{M}^*$ for the forged signature σ is parsed as $(t^*, M^*) = (t^*, (m_1^*, \cdots, m_{n^*}^*))$ for some $n^* \le N$.
- ***Expt***$_1$**:** The GS CRS $\boldsymbol{f} = (\vec{f}_1, \vec{f}_2, \vec{f}_3)$ is generated as a perfectly sound one. Specifically, $\vec{f}_1 := (f_1, 1_{\mathbb{G}}, g)$, $\vec{f}_2 := (1_{\mathbb{G}}, f_2, g)$ and $\vec{f}_3 := \vec{f}_1^{\xi_1} \cdot \vec{f}_2^{\xi_2}$, where $f_1 := g^{\phi_1}$ and $f_2 := g^{\phi_2}$ with $\phi_1, \phi_2, \xi_1, \xi_2 \overset{\text{U}}{\longleftarrow} \mathbb{Z}_p$. Note that in this and the subsequent experiments, all GS commitments are perfectly binding. From the forged GS commitments, we can extract all the committed variables by using the BBS decryption keys (ϕ_1, ϕ_2). Since the forged GS proofs are perfectly sound, the extracted variables satisfy all the PPEs defined in the sixth step in the signing algorithm Sig.
- ***Expt***$_2$**:** For each $\kappa \in [1, q]$, $\mathbf{M}_\kappa$ denotes the κ-th DTQS message queried to the signing oracle. $\mathbf{M}_\kappa$ is parsed as $(t_\kappa, M_\kappa) = (t_\kappa, (m_{\kappa,1}, \cdots, m_{\kappa,n_\kappa}))$ for some $n_\kappa \le N$. Additionally, $(X_\kappa, Y_\kappa) \in \mathbb{G}^2$ denote the group elements (X, Y) chosen for the κ-th signing query. It aborts if the group elements (X^*, Y^*) extracted from the forgery are a new pair, i.e., do not match any of the group elements (X_κ, Y_κ). Formally, it aborts if $\nexists \kappa \in [1, q]$ s.t. $(X_\kappa, Y_\kappa) = (X^*, Y^*)$.
- ***Expt***$_3$**:** It aborts if $\exists \kappa \in [1, q]$ s.t. $(X_\kappa, Y_\kappa) = (X^*, Y^*) \wedge t_\kappa = \text{II}$.

S_i denotes that ***Expt***$_i$ outputs 1. We obtain $\mathtt{Adv}^{\mathtt{UNF}}_{\Pi_{\text{DTQS},c},\mathcal{A}}(\lambda) = \Pr[S_0] \le \sum_{i=1}^{3} |\Pr[S_{i-1}] - \Pr[S_i]| + \Pr[S_3]$, which is negligible under the DLIN and q-SFP assumptions[7] by the following four lemmas. Because of the page limit, the proofs for Lemma 2, Lemma 3 and Lemma 4 are presented in the full version of this paper. □

Lemma 1. $|\Pr[S_0] - \Pr[S_1]|$ *is negligible under the DLIN assumption.*

Proof. The two settings of the GS CRS are hard to distinguish under the DLIN assumptions. □

Lemma 2. $\Pr[S_1] - \Pr[S_2]$ *is negligible under the q-SFP assumption.*

Lemma 3. $\Pr[S_2] - \Pr[S_3]$ *is negligible under the CDH assumption.*

Lemma 4. $\Pr[S_3]$ *is negligible under the CDH assumption.*

[7] The CDH assumption is implied by the DLIN and q-SFP assumptions.

Efficiency Analysis. We calculate the asymptotic length of a Type-I/II signature.

First is the Type-I case. At deriving the asymptotic length of a Type-I signature parsed as (2), the variables underlined with ① and ② dominate in size, and the others can be ignored. If we denote the numbers of elements in $\mathbb{G}$ included in the dominant variables by $\mathbf{N}_{①}$ and $\mathbf{N}_{②}$ respectively, they can be calculated as follows: $\mathbf{N}_{①} = \sum_{i=1}^{n} \sum_{j=0}^{\lfloor \log_c (n-i+1) \rfloor} 15 \leq \sum_{i=1}^{n} \sum_{j=0}^{\lfloor \log_c n \rfloor} 15 = 15(\lfloor \log_c n \rfloor + 1) \cdot n = \mathcal{O}(n \log_c n)$, $\mathbf{N}_{②} = \sum_{i=1}^{n} \sum_{j=0}^{\lfloor \log N \rfloor} 24 = 24(\lfloor \log N \rfloor + 1) \cdot n = \mathcal{O}(n \log N)$.

By summing them, the size of a Type-I signature is $\mathcal{O}(n(\log_c n + \log N))|g|$, where $|g|$ is the length of an element in $\mathbb{G}$. Although not explicitly mentioned, the above analysis assumes that $c \leq n$. When $c > n$, because $\lfloor \log_c (n-i+1) \rfloor = 0$ for any $i \in [1, n]$, $\mathbf{N}_{①}$ is re-calculated and becomes $15n = \mathcal{O}(n)$. $\mathbf{N}_{②}$ is unchanged. The size of a Type-I signature (when $c > n$) is $\mathcal{O}(n \log N)|g|$.

Next is the Type-II case. For a Type-II signature parsed as (3), the variables with ③ dominate. Their number of group elements is $\mathbf{N}_{③} = \sum_{i=1}^{L} \sum_{j=0}^{\lfloor \log N \rfloor} 24 = 24L \cdot (\lfloor \log N \rfloor + 1)$. By Theorem 1, if the base-c representation of n is $[l_{\lfloor \log_c n \rfloor} \cdots l_1 l_0]_c$, the total number of stepping stones L is equal to $\sum_{i=0}^{\lfloor \log_c n \rfloor} l_i$, and its upper bound is $(c-1) \cdot (\lfloor \log_c n \rfloor + 1)$. Hence, $\mathbf{N}_{③} \leq 24(c-1)(\lfloor \log_c n \rfloor + 1)(\lfloor \log N \rfloor + 1)$. Thus, the asymptotic size of a Type-II signature (when $c \leq n$) is $\mathcal{O}(c \cdot \log_c n \cdot \log N)|g|$. When $c > n$, as we explained in Sect. 4, L is always equal to n. Hence, $\mathbf{N}_{③} = 24n \cdot (\lfloor \log N \rfloor + 1)$ and the size of a Type-II signature when $c > n$ is $\mathcal{O}(n \log N)|g|$.

We compare our first DTQS scheme with two existing QS schemes [3,6] and our second DTQS scheme (given in Sect. 5) in Table 1.

5 Our Second DTQS Scheme

We propose another DTQS scheme. Roughly speaking, the length of a Type-I (resp. Type-II) signature in the 2nd scheme is c-times (resp. $1/c$-times) that in our 1st one. When $c > n$, they are n-times and $1/n$-times, respectively. As our first scheme, we start with an insecure transformation $\mathsf{H2D}'_c$ based on HSSM.

Transformation $\mathsf{H2D}'_c$. A signature on $\mathbf{M} = (t, M) = (t, (m_1, \cdots, m_n))$ is generated as follows. The n integers $d_1, \cdots, d_n$ are defined analogously to $\mathsf{H2D}_c$.

$\boxed{\text{If } t = \text{I:}}$ For each $i \in [1, n]$, among all the substrings of M, select the substrings whose leftmost sub-message is m_i and whose length is a constant multiple of an exponentiation of c, where the constant is at most $c - 1$. Concretely, they are

$$\begin{array}{lll}
\underbrace{m_i}_{1}, & \underbrace{m_i \parallel m_{i+1}}_{2}, & \cdots\ \underbrace{m_i \parallel \cdots \parallel m_{i+(c-1)-1}}_{c-1}, \\
\underbrace{m_i \parallel \cdots \parallel m_{i+c-1}}_{c}, & \cdots & \cdots\ \underbrace{m_i \parallel \cdots \parallel m_{i+(c-1)\cdot c-1}}_{(c-1)\cdot c}, \\
\vdots & & \vdots \\
\underbrace{m_i \parallel \cdots \parallel m_{i+c^{a_i-1}-1}}_{c^{a_i-1}}, & \cdots & \cdots\ \underbrace{m_i \parallel \cdots \parallel m_{i+(c-1)\cdot c^{a_i-1}-1}}_{(c-1)\cdot c^{a_i-1}}, \\
\underbrace{m_i \parallel \cdots \parallel m_{i+c^{a_i}-1}}_{c^{a_i}}, & \cdots & \cdots\ \underbrace{m_i \parallel \cdots \parallel m_{i+l_{i,a_i}\cdot c^{a_i}-1}}_{l_{i,a_i}\cdot c^{a_i}},
\end{array}$$

where $a_i := \lfloor \log_c (n-i+1) \rfloor$ and $l_{i,a_i} \in [1, c-1]$ is the MSD of the base-c representation of $n-i+1$, i.e., $[l_{i,a_i} l_{i,a_i-1} \cdots l_{i,1} l_{i,0}]_c$ for some $l_{i,j} \in [0, c-1]$. Generate an HSSM signature σ on the set-pair $(F'_{\mathrm{I}}(M, d_1), \emptyset)$, where $F'_{\mathrm{I}}(M, d_1) := \bigcup_{i \in [1,n]} \bigcup_{j \in [0,a_i], k \in [1,c-1] \text{ s.t. } j \leq a_i - 1 \vee k \leq l_{i,a_i}} \{d_i \| j \| k \| m_i \| \cdots \| m_{i+k\cdot c^j-1}\}$.

For instance, when $(c, n) = (3, 26)$, the selected substrings are visualized as the gray arrows in Fig. 2d. When $c > n$, for any $i \in [1, n]$, since $n - i + 1 \leq c - 1$, any M's substring whose leftmost sub-message is m_i satisfies the required condition and is selected. Thus, literally all the M's substrings are selected.

If $t = \mathrm{II}$: Divide M under the condition that total number of the substrings is minimal and each substring has a length of a constant multiple of an exponentiation of c, where the constant is equal to or less than $c-1$. Let $s_1 := 1$. Among all the M's substrings which start with m_{s_1} and whose length is a constant multiple of an exponentiation of c, select the longest one. Concretely, if the MSD of $n - s_1 + 1$ is $l_{s_1, \lfloor \log_c (n-s_1+1) \rfloor} \in [1, c-1]$, then $m_{s_1} \parallel \cdots \parallel m_{s_1 + l_{s_1, \lfloor \log_c (n-s_1+1) \rfloor} \cdot c^{\lfloor \log_c (n-s_1+1) \rfloor} - 1}$ is selected. Let $s_2 := s_1 + l_{s_1, \lfloor \log_c (n-s_1+1) \rfloor} \cdot c^{\lfloor \log_c (n-s_1+1) \rfloor}$. Among all the M's substrings which start from m_{s_2} and whose length is a constant multiple of an exponentiation of c, select the longest one, i.e., $m_{s_2} \parallel \cdots \parallel m_{s_2 + l_{s_2, \lfloor \log_c (n-s_2+1) \rfloor} \cdot c^{\lfloor \log_c (n-s_2+1) \rfloor} - 1}$, where $l_{s_2, \lfloor \log_c (n-s_2+1) \rfloor}$ is the MSD of $n - s_2 + 1$. Then, let $s_3 := s_2 + l_{s_2, \lfloor \log_c (n-s_2+1) \rfloor} \cdot c^{\lfloor \log_c (n-s_2+1) \rfloor}$. Repeat the above procedures until a substring which ends with m_n is selected. Let $S := \{s_1, s_2, \cdots, s_L\}$ with some $L \in \mathbb{N}$[8]. Generate an HSSM signature on a set-pair $(F'_{\mathrm{II}}(M, d_1), \{m_1 \| \cdots \| m_n\})$, where $F'_{\mathrm{II}}(M, d_1) := \bigcup_{i \in [1,L]} \{d_{s_i} \parallel \lfloor \log_c (n - s_i + 1) \rfloor \parallel l_{s_i, \lfloor \log_c (n-s_i+1) \rfloor} \parallel m_{s_i} \parallel \cdots \parallel m_{s_i + l_{s_i, \lfloor \log_c (n-s_i+1) \rfloor} \cdot c^{\lfloor \log_c (n-s_i+1) \rfloor} - 1}\}$.

When $(c, n) = (3, 26)$, the three substrings which are visualized as the three thick blue arrows in Fig. 2d are selected. Theorem 3 is derived from Theorem 1.

Theorem 3. *Let* $n = [l_{\lfloor \log_c n \rfloor} l_{\lfloor \log_c n \rfloor - 1} \cdots l_1 l_0]_c$. $\mathsf{H2D}'_c$ *divides the original string of length* n *into: a single substring of length* $l_i \cdot c^{l_i}$ *for each* $i \in [0, \lfloor \log_c n \rfloor]$. *Naturally, the number of substrings is equivalent to the number of non-zero digits of the base-c representation of* n, *i.e.,* $\sum_{i \in [0, \lfloor \log_c n \rfloor] \text{ s.t. } l_i \neq 0} 1$.

[8] By Theorem 3, $L = \sum_{i \in [0, \lfloor \log_c n \rfloor] \text{ s.t. } l_i \neq 0} 1$.

For instance, the base-3 representation of 26 is $[222]_3$, and $\mathsf{H2D}'_3$ divides a string of length 26 into three substrings of lengths $18(= 2{\cdot}3^2)$, $6(= 2{\cdot}3^1)$ and $2(= 2{\cdot}3^0)$, respectively. As Theorem 1 states, $\mathsf{H2D}_c$ divides a string of length n into l_i number of substrings of length c^{l_i} for all $i \in [0, \lfloor \log_c n \rfloor]$. We can say that for each i, $\mathsf{H2D}'_c$ aggregates l_i number of substrings of length c^{l_i} into a single substring of length $l_i \cdot c^{l_i}$. As a result, the total number of substrings is reduced. When all of the digits of the base-c representation of n are $c-1$, the number is reduced the most, and becomes $\frac{1}{c-1}$-times that of $\mathsf{H2D}_c$. Actually, as we observed earlier, when $(c, n) = (3, 26)$, the former is 3 and the latter is 6.

When $c > n$, analogously to $t = \mathrm{I}$, all the M's substrings whose leftmost sub-message is m_1 satisfy the required condition. Among them, the original string itself, i.e., $m_1 \parallel \cdots \parallel m_n$ is the longest. The set S is the smallest one $\{1\}$.

5.1 Formal Description of $\Pi'_{\mathrm{DTQS},c}$

Because of the page limit, we describe only the signing algorithms. The other algorithms are basically the same as and can be guessed from the corresponding ones of our first scheme.

$\boxed{\mathtt{Sig}(sk, \mathrm{M}):}$ Conduct the first three steps in the signing algorithm of our first scheme. After that, conduct the following three steps.

4. For each $i \in [1, n]$, let $d_i := i-1$ and $a_i := \lfloor \log_c (n-i+1) \rfloor$ then do: Let the base-c representation of $n-i+1$ be $[l_{i,a_i} \cdots l_{i,1} l_{i,0}]_c$ for $l_{i,j} \in [0, c-1]$. For each $j \in [0, a_i]$ and $k \in [1, c-1]$ s.t. $j \le a_i - 1 \bigvee k \le l_{i,a_i}$, generate a Waters signature on $d_i \parallel j \parallel k \parallel m_i \parallel \cdots \parallel m_{i+k\cdot c^j-1}$, i.e., $\sigma_{i,j,k} := (\sigma_{i,j,k,1}, \sigma_{i,j,k,2}) := (h^x \cdot H_{\mathbb{G}}(d_i \parallel j \parallel k \parallel m_i \parallel \cdots \parallel m_{i+k\cdot c^j-1})^{\chi_{ijk}}, g^{\chi_{ijk}})$ with $\chi_{ijk} \xleftarrow{\mathrm{U}} \mathbb{Z}_p$. Note that if $c > n$, Waters signatures for all the M's substrings are generated.
5. Compute GS commitments to all the following group elements, namely $X, Y, \theta_1, \theta_2, \theta_5, \{g^{d_i}\}_{i\in[1,n]}, \{\{\sigma_{i,j,k,1}, \sigma_{i,j,k,2}\}_{j\in[0,a_i-1],k\in[1,c-1]}, \{\sigma_{i,a_i,k,1}, \sigma_{i,a_i,k,2}\}_{k\in[1,l_{i,a_i}]}\}_{i\in[1,n]}$, $\{g^{d_i[j]}, g^{1-d_i[j]}, u_j^{d_i[j]}\}_{i\in[1,n],j\in[0,\lceil \log N \rceil]}$, and either $(\sigma_{\mathsf{null},1}, \sigma_{\mathsf{null},2})$ if $t = \mathrm{I}$ or $(\sigma_{\mathsf{null},1}, \sigma_{\mathsf{null},2}, \sigma_{\mathsf{full},1}, \sigma_{\mathsf{full},2})$ if $t = \mathrm{II}$.
6. Compute GS proofs for all the following PPEs.
   $[\vec{\pi}_A, \vec{\pi}_B$:] *The same as the ones in our first scheme.*
   $[\vec{\pi}_{i,j,k,\mathsf{Wat}}$:] $e(\sigma_{i,j,k,1}, g) = e(X, h) \cdot \prod_{l=1}^{\lfloor \log N \rfloor} e(\sigma_{i,j,k,2}, u_k^{d_i[l]}) \cdot e(\sigma_{i,j,k,2}, H_{\mathbb{G}}(0^{\lfloor \log N \rfloor+1} \parallel j \parallel k \parallel m_i \parallel \cdots \parallel m_{i+k\cdot c^j-1}))$ (For $i \in [1, n]$, $j \in [0, a_i - 1]$, $k \in [1, c-1]$)
   $[\vec{\pi}_{i,a_i,k,\mathsf{Wat}}$:] $e(\sigma_{i,a_i,k,1}, g) = e(X, h) \cdot \prod_{l=1}^{\lfloor \log N \rfloor} e(\sigma_{i,a_i,k,2}, u_k^{d_i[l]}) \cdot e(\sigma_{i,a_i,k,2}, H_{\mathbb{G}}(0^{\lfloor \log N \rfloor+1} \parallel a_i \parallel k \parallel m_i \parallel \cdots \parallel m_{i+k\cdot c^{a_i}-1}))$ (For $i \in [1, n]$, $k \in [1, l_{i,a_i}]$)
   $[\vec{\pi}_{i,j,\mathsf{mul}}, \vec{\pi}_{i,j,\mathsf{sum}}, \vec{\pi}_{i,j,\mathsf{exp}}, \vec{\pi}_{i,\mathsf{bin}}$:] *The same as the ones in our first scheme.*
   $[\vec{\pi}_{i,j,k,\mathsf{dif}}$:] $e(g^{d_{i+k\cdot c^j}}, g) = e(g^{d_i}, g) \cdot e(g^{k\cdot c^j}, g)$ (For $i \in [1, n-1]$, $j \in [0, a_i - 1]$, $k \in [1, c-1]$)
   $[\vec{\pi}_{i,a_i,k,\mathsf{dif}}$:] $e(g^{d_{i+k\cdot c^{a_i}}}, g) = e(g^{d_i}, g) \cdot e(g^{k\cdot c^{a_i}}, g)$ (For $i \in [1, n-1]$, $k \in [1, l_{i,a_i}]$)

[$\vec{\pi}_{\mathsf{null}}$, $\vec{\pi}_{\mathsf{full}}$, $\vec{\pi}_Y$:] *The same as the ones in our first scheme.*

Lastly, output a DTQS signature σ. If $t = \mathrm{I}$, it consists of

$$\left(\begin{array}{l} \vec{C}_X, \vec{C}_Y, \{\vec{C}_{\theta_i}\}_{i\in\{1,2,5\}}, \{\theta_i\}_{i\in\{3,4,6,7\}}, \vec{\pi}_A, \vec{\pi}_B, \vec{C}_{\sigma_{\mathsf{null},1}}, \vec{C}_{\sigma_{\mathsf{null},2}}, \vec{\pi}_{\mathsf{null}}, \vec{\pi}_Y, \\ \left\{\{\vec{\pi}_{i,j,k,\mathsf{dif}}\}_{j\in[0,a_i],k\in[1,c-1]\ s.t.\ j\le a_i-1 \vee k\le l_{i,a_i}}\right\}_{i\in[1,n-1]}, \\ \left\{\begin{array}{l} \vec{C}_{g^{d_i}}, \vec{\pi}_{i,\mathsf{bin}}, \underbrace{\left\{\vec{C}_{\sigma_{i,j,k,1}}, \vec{C}_{\sigma_{i,j,k,2}}, \vec{\pi}_{i,j,k,\mathsf{Wat}}\right\}_{j\in[0,a_i],k\in[1,c-1]\ s.t.\ j\le a_i-1\vee k\le l_{i,a_i}}}_{④}, \\ \underbrace{\left\{\vec{C}_{g^{d_i[j]}}, \vec{C}_{g^{1-d_i[j]}}, \vec{C}_{u_j^{d_i[j]}}, \vec{\pi}_{i,j,\mathsf{mul}}, \vec{\pi}_{i,j,\mathsf{sum}}, \vec{\pi}_{i,j,\mathsf{exp}}\right\}_{j\in[0,\lfloor\log N\rfloor]}}_{⑤} \end{array}\right\}_{i\in[1,n]}, \end{array}\right). \tag{4}$$

Else if $t = \mathrm{II}$, we compute $S = (s_1, \cdots, s_L)$ for some $L \in \mathbb{N}$ as $S := \mathsf{StSt}'_c(n)$ under StSt'_c defined in Fig. 3, then construct σ as follows.

$$\left(\begin{array}{l} \vec{C}_X, \vec{C}_Y, \{\vec{C}_{\theta_i}\}_{i\in\{1,2,5\}}, \{\theta_i\}_{i\in\{3,4,6,7\}}, \vec{\pi}_A, \vec{\pi}_B, \vec{C}_{\sigma_{\mathsf{null},1}}, \vec{C}_{\sigma_{\mathsf{null},2}}, \vec{\pi}_{\mathsf{null}}, \vec{\pi}_Y, \\ \{\vec{\pi}_{s_i,a_{s_i},l_{s_i,a_{s_i}},\mathsf{dif}}\}_{i=1}^{L-1}, \vec{C}_{\sigma_{\mathsf{full},1}}, \vec{C}_{\sigma_{\mathsf{full},2}}, \vec{\pi}_{\mathsf{full}}, \\ \left\{\begin{array}{l} \vec{C}_{g^{d_{s_i}}}, \vec{\pi}_{s_i,\mathsf{bin}}, \vec{C}_{\sigma_{s_i,a_{s_i},l_{s_i,a_{s_i}},1}}, \vec{C}_{\sigma_{s_i,a_{s_i},l_{s_i,a_{s_i}},2}}, \vec{\pi}_{s_i,a_{s_i},l_{s_i,a_{s_i}},\mathsf{Wat}}, \\ \underbrace{\left\{\vec{C}_{g^{d_{s_i}[j]}}, \vec{C}_{g^{1-d_{s_i}[j]}}, \vec{C}_{u_j^{d_{s_i}[j]}}, \vec{\pi}_{s_i,j,\mathsf{mul}}, \vec{\pi}_{s_i,j,\mathsf{sum}}, \vec{\pi}_{s_i,j,\mathsf{exp}}\right\}_{j=0}^{\lfloor\log N\rfloor}}_{⑥} \end{array}\right\}_{i=1}^{L} \end{array}\right). \tag{5}$$

The following theorem can be proven in the same manner as Theorem 2.

Theorem 4. *The scheme is unconditionally* CCH. *Let $q \in \mathtt{poly}(\lambda)$ denote the maximal number of times that the signing oracle can be accessed. The scheme is* UNF *under the DLIN assumption w.r.t the group $\mathbb{G}$ and the q-SFP assumption.*

Efficiency Analysis. We calculate the length of a Type-I/II signature.

For a Type-I signature parsed as (4), the variables underlined with ④ and ⑤ dominate in size. Let $\mathbf{N}_{④}$ and $\mathbf{N}_{⑤}$ denote their numbers of group elements, respectively. Since $\mathbf{N}_{⑤} = \mathbf{N}_{②}$[9], $\mathbf{N}_{⑤} = \mathcal{O}(n \log N)$. $\mathbf{N}_{④}$ are calculated as

$$\begin{aligned}
\mathbf{N}_{④} &= \sum_{i=1}^{n} \sum_{\substack{j\in[0,a_i],k\in[1,c-1]\ s.t.\\ j\le a_i-1 \bigvee k\le l_{i,a_i}}} 15 = \sum_{i=1}^{n}\left(\sum_{j=0}^{a_i-1}\sum_{k=1}^{c-1} 15 + \sum_{k=1}^{l_{i,a_i}} 15\right) \\
&= 15\sum_{i=1}^{n}(a_i\cdot(c-1)+l_{i,a_i}) \le 15\sum_{i=1}^{n}(\lfloor\log_c n\rfloor\cdot(c-1)+c-1) \\
&= 15n\cdot(c-1)\cdot(\lfloor\log_c n\rfloor+1) = \mathcal{O}(nc\cdot\log_c n).
\end{aligned}$$

The intermediate inequality is derived because for any $i \in [1, n]$, $a_i (= \lfloor \log_c(n-i+1) \rfloor) \le \lfloor \log_c n \rfloor$ and $l_{i,a_i} \le c-1$. Hence, the length of a Type-I signature is $\mathcal{O}(n\cdot(c\log_c n + \log N))|g|$. When $c > n$, since for any $i \in [1, n]$, $a_i = 0$ and $l_{i,a_i} = n-i+1$, $\mathbf{N}_{④} = \sum_{i=1}^{n}\sum_{k=1}^{l_{i,a_i}} 15 = 15\sum_{i=1}^{n} l_{i,a_i} = 15\sum_{i=1}^{n} n-i+1 = \mathcal{O}(n^2)$. The length of a Type-I signature when $c > n$ is $\mathcal{O}(n\cdot(n+\log N))|g|$.

For a Type-II signature parsed as (5), the variables underlined with ⑥ are dominant. Let $\mathbf{N}_{⑥}$ denote their number of group elements. In the same manner as $\mathbf{N}_{③}$(see footnote 9), $\mathbf{N}_{⑥}$ is calculated as $\mathbf{N}_{⑥} = 24L\cdot(\lfloor\log N\rfloor+1)$. By Theorem 3, if the base-c representation of n is $[l_{\lfloor\log_c n\rfloor}\cdots l_1 l_0]_c$, L is equal to $\sum_{i\in[0,\lfloor\log_c n\rfloor]\ s.t.\ l_i\neq 0} 1 \le \lfloor\log_c n\rfloor+1$. Hence, $\mathbf{N}_{⑥} \le 24\cdot(\lfloor\log_c n\rfloor+1)\cdot(\lfloor\log N\rfloor+1)$. Thus, the asymptotic length of a Type-II signature (when $c \le n$) is $\mathcal{O}(\log_c n\cdot\log N)$. When $c > n$, as we explained in Sect. 5, L is always 1. Hence, $\mathbf{N}_{⑥} = 24\cdot(\lfloor\log N\rfloor+1)$ and the length of a Type-II signature when $c > n$ is $\mathcal{O}(\log N)|g|$.

A Digital Signatures

Syntax. A digital signatures scheme consists of the following three polynomial time algorithms. Note that `Ver` is deterministic and the others are probabilistic.

Key-Generation `KGen`: It takes a security parameter 1^λ for $\lambda \in \mathbb{N}$, then outputs a public-parameter *pp*, public-key *pk* and secret-key *sk*. $\mathcal{M}$ denotes space of messages. Assume that *pp* is implicitly inputted to the signing and verification algorithms. $(pp, pk, sk) \leftarrow \mathtt{KGen}(1^\lambda)$

Siging `Sig`: It takes a secret-key *sk* and a message $\mathbf{M} \in \mathcal{M}$, then outputs a signature σ. $\sigma \leftarrow \mathtt{Sig}(sk, \mathbf{M})$

Verification `Ver`: It takes a public-key *pk*, a message $\mathbf{M} \in \mathcal{M}$ and a signature σ, then outputs 1 or 0. $1/0 \leftarrow \mathtt{Ver}(pk, \mathbf{M}, \sigma)$

We require every digital signatures scheme to be correct. A scheme is correct if for every $\lambda \in \mathbb{N}$, every $(pp, pk, sk) \leftarrow \mathtt{KGen}(1^\lambda)$, every $\mathbf{M} \in \mathcal{M}$, every $\sigma \leftarrow \mathtt{Sig}(sk, \mathbf{M})$, it holds that $1 \leftarrow \mathtt{Ver}(pk, \mathbf{M}, \sigma)$.

[9] For $\mathbf{N}_{②}$ and $\mathbf{N}_{③}$, refer to efficiency analysis in Sect. 4..

Security. The most standard unforgeability notion for digital signatures is (weak) existential unforgeability against chosen messages attacks (EUF-CMA) [11]. We consider an experiment for a PPT adversary $\mathcal{A}$ defined as follows.

$\boldsymbol{Expt}^{\mathtt{EUF\text{-}CMA}}_{\Sigma_{\mathrm{DS}},\mathcal{A}}(1^\lambda)$: // $\boldsymbol{Expt}^{\mathtt{EUF\text{-}CMA}}_{\Sigma_{\mathrm{DS}},\mathcal{A}}$
$(pp, pk, sk) \leftarrow \mathtt{KGen}(1^\lambda)$. $Q := \emptyset$. $(\mathbf{M}^* \in \mathcal{M}, \sigma^*) \leftarrow \mathcal{A}^{\mathsf{Sign}}(pp, pk)$

- $\mathsf{Sign}(\mathbf{M} \in \mathcal{M})$: $\sigma \leftarrow \mathtt{Sig}(sk, \mathbf{M})$. $Q := Q \cup \{\mathbf{M}\}$. **Rtrn** σ

Rtrn 1 if $1 \leftarrow \mathtt{Ver}(pk, \mathbf{M}^*, \sigma^*) \wedge \mathbf{M}^* \notin Q$.

Definition 6. *A scheme Σ_{DS} is EUF-CMA if for any $\lambda \in \mathbb{N}$ and any PPT algorithm $\mathcal{A}$, its advantage $\boldsymbol{Adv}^{\mathit{EUF\text{-}CMA}}_{\Sigma_{\mathrm{DS}},\mathcal{A}}(\lambda) := \Pr[1 \leftarrow \boldsymbol{Expt}^{\mathit{EUF\text{-}CMA}}_{\Sigma_{\mathrm{DS}},\mathcal{A}}(1^\lambda)]$ is negligible.*

B Waters Signatures [19]

Their scheme is based on a symmetric bilinear paring $e : \mathbb{G} \times \mathbb{G} \rightarrow \mathbb{G}_T$ with prime order p and generator $g \in \mathbb{G}$.

$\mathtt{KGen}(1^\lambda, L)$**:** $L \in \mathbb{N}$ denotes bit length of a message. Generate $pp := (h, u', u_1, \cdots, u_L)$, where $h, u', u_1, \cdots, u_L \xleftarrow{\mathrm{U}} \mathbb{G}$. The programmable hash function $H_{\mathbb{G}} : \{0,1\}^L \rightarrow \mathbb{G}$ takes $\mathbf{M}$ then outputs $u' \cdot \prod_{i=1}^{L} u_i^{m[i]} \in \mathbb{G}$. Generate $(pk, sk) := (X, x)$, where $X := g^x$ with $x \xleftarrow{\mathrm{U}} \mathbb{Z}_p$. Output (pp, pk, sk).

$\mathtt{Sig}(sk, \mathbf{M})$**:** Choose $r \xleftarrow{\mathrm{U}} \mathbb{Z}_p$. Output $\sigma := (h^x \cdot H_{\mathbb{G}}(m)^r, g^r)$.

$\mathtt{Ver}(pk, \mathbf{M}, \sigma)$**:** Parse σ as (A, B). Output 1 if $e(A, g) = e(X, h) \cdot e(H_{\mathbb{G}}(m), B)$. Output 0 otherwise.

Theorem 5. *Waters signatures scheme is EUF-CMA under the CDH assumption w.r.t. the group $\mathbb{G}$.*

C Abe-Haralambiev-Ohkubo (AHO) SPS [1,2]

Their scheme is based on a symmetric bilinear paring $e : \mathbb{G} \times \mathbb{G} \rightarrow \mathbb{G}_T$ with prime order p and generator $g \in \mathbb{G}$.

$\mathtt{KGen}(1^\lambda, n)$**:** $n \in \mathbb{N}$ denotes the maximal number of group elements to be signed.
Choose generators $g_r, h_r \xleftarrow{\mathrm{U}} \mathbb{G}$. Let $pp := (g_r, h_r)$.
Choose elements $\gamma_z, \delta_z, \alpha_a, \alpha_b \xleftarrow{\mathrm{U}} \mathbb{Z}_p$ and $\gamma_i, \delta_i \xleftarrow{\mathrm{U}} \mathbb{Z}_p$ for $i \in [1, n]$. Compute $g_z := g_r^{\gamma_z}$, $h_z := h_r^{\delta_z}$, $A := e(g_r, g^{\alpha_a})$, $B := e(h_r, g^{\alpha_b})$, and $g_i := g_r^{\delta_i}$ and $h_i := h_r^{\delta_i}$ for $i \in [1, n]$. Output (pp, pk, sk), where $pk := (g_z, h_z, \{g_i, h_i\}_{i=1}^n, A, B)$ and $sk := (\alpha_a, \alpha_b, \gamma_z, \delta_z, \{\gamma_i, \delta_i\}_{i=1}^n)$.

$\mathtt{Sig}(sk, (\mathbf{M}_1, \cdots, \mathbf{M}_n))$: Choose $\eta, \rho_a, \rho_b, \omega_a, \omega_b \xleftarrow{\mathrm{U}} \mathbb{Z}_p$. Compute $\theta_1 := g^{\eta}$ and

$$\theta_2 := g^{\rho_a - \gamma_z \eta} \cdot \prod_{i=1}^{n} \mathbf{M}_i^{\gamma_i}, \quad \theta_3 := g_r^{\omega_a}, \quad \theta_4 := g^{(\alpha_a - \rho_a)/\omega_a},$$
$$\theta_5 := g^{\rho_b - \delta_z \eta} \cdot \prod_{i=1}^{n} \mathbf{M}_i^{\delta_i}, \quad \theta_6 := h_r^{\omega_b}, \quad \theta_7 := g^{(\alpha_b - \rho_b)/\omega_b}.$$

Output a signature $\sigma := (\theta_1, \cdots, \theta_7)$.

$\mathtt{Ver}(pk, (\mathbf{M}_1, \cdots, \mathbf{M}_n), \sigma)$: Output 1 if both of the following two equations hold, namely $A = e(g_z, \theta_1) \cdot e(g_r, \theta_2) \cdot e(\theta_3, \theta_4) \cdot \prod_{i=1}^{n} e(g_i, \mathbf{M}_i)$ and $B = e(h_z, \theta_1) \cdot e(h_r, \theta_5) \cdot e(\theta_6, \theta_7) \cdot \prod_{i=1}^{n} e(h_i, \mathbf{M}_i)$.

As shown in [1,2], any signature $\sigma = (\theta_1, \cdots, \theta_n)$ can be publicly randomized as follows. The first element is unchanged, i.e., $\theta_1' := \theta_1$. We choose $\eta_2, \eta_5, \mu, \nu \xleftarrow{\mathrm{U}} \mathbb{Z}_p$ then compute

$$\theta_2' := \theta_2 \cdot \theta_4^{\eta_2}, \quad \theta_3' := (\theta_3 \cdot g_r^{-\eta_2})^{1/\mu}, \quad \theta_4' := \theta_4^{\mu},$$
$$\theta_5' := \theta_5 \cdot \theta_7^{\eta_5}, \quad \theta_6' := (\theta_6 \cdot h_r^{-\eta_5})^{1/\nu}, \quad \theta_7' := \theta_7^{\nu}.$$

According to [1,2], $(\theta_2', \theta_3', \theta_4') \in \mathbb{G}^3$ uniformly distribute under a restriction that $e(g_r, \theta_2') \cdot e(\theta_3', \theta_4') = e(g_r, \theta_2) \cdot e(\theta_3, \theta_4)$, and $(\theta_5', \theta_6', \theta_7') \in \mathbb{G}^3$ uniformly distribute under a restriction that $e(h_r, \theta_5') \cdot e(\theta_6', \theta_7') = e(h_r, \theta_5) \cdot e(\theta_6, \theta_7)$.

Theorem 6. *Let $q \in \mathtt{poly}(\lambda)$ denote the maximal number of signing queries. The signature scheme is EUF-CMA under the q-SFP assumption.*

References

1. Abe, M., Fuchsbauer, G., Groth, J., Haralambiev, K., Ohkubo, M.: Structure-preserving signatures and commitments to group elements. In: Rabin, T. (ed.) CRYPTO 2010. LNCS, vol. 6223, pp. 209–236. Springer, Heidelberg (2010). https://doi.org/10.1007/978-3-642-14623-7_12
2. Abe, M., Haralambiev, K., Ohkubo, M.: Signing on elements in bilinear groups for modular protocol design. Cryptology ePrint Archive: Report 2010/133 (2010)
3. Ahn, J.H., Boneh, D., Camenisch, J., Hohenberger, S., Shelat, A., Waters, B.: Computing on authenticated data. In: Cramer, R. (ed.) TCC 2012. LNCS, vol. 7194, pp. 1–20. Springer, Heidelberg (2012). https://doi.org/10.1007/978-3-642-28914-9_1
4. Ateniese, G., Chou, D.H., De Medeiros, B., Tsudik, G.: Sanitizable signatures. In: ESORICS (2005)
5. Attrapadung, N., Libert, B., Peters, T.: Computing on authenticated data: new privacy definitions and constructions. In: Wang, X., Sako, K. (eds.) ASIACRYPT 2012. LNCS, vol. 7658, pp. 367–385. Springer, Heidelberg (2012). https://doi.org/10.1007/978-3-642-34961-4_23

6. Attrapadung, N., Libert, B., Peters, T.: Efficient completely context-hiding quotable and linearly homomorphic signatures. In: Kurosawa, K., Hanaoka, G. (eds.) PKC 2013. LNCS, vol. 7778, pp. 386–404. Springer, Heidelberg (2013). https://doi.org/10.1007/978-3-642-36362-7_24
7. Belenkiy, M., Camenisch, J., Chase, M., Kohlweiss, M., Lysyanskaya, A., Shacham, H.: Randomizable proofs and delegatable anonymous credentials. In: Halevi, S. (ed.) CRYPTO 2009. LNCS, vol. 5677, pp. 108–125. Springer, Heidelberg (2009). https://doi.org/10.1007/978-3-642-03356-8_7
8. Bethencourt, J., Boneh, D., Waters, B.: Cryptographic methods for storing ballots on a voting machine. In: NDSS 2007 (2007)
9. Boneh, D., Boyen, X., Shacham, H.: Short group signatures. In: Franklin, M. (ed.) CRYPTO 2004. LNCS, vol. 3152, pp. 41–55. Springer, Heidelberg (2004). https://doi.org/10.1007/978-3-540-28628-8_3
10. Boneh, D., Lynn, B., Shacham, H.: Short signatures from the Weil pairing. In: Boyd, C. (ed.) ASIACRYPT 2001. LNCS, vol. 2248, pp. 514–532. Springer, Heidelberg (2001). https://doi.org/10.1007/3-540-45682-1_30
11. Goldwasser, S.,Micali, S., Rivest, R.L.: A digital signature scheme secure against adaptive chosen-message attacks. SIAM J. Comput
12. Groth, J., Sahai, A.: Efficient non-interactive proof systems for bilinear groups. In: Smart, N. (ed.) EUROCRYPT 2008. LNCS, vol. 4965, pp. 415–432. Springer, Heidelberg (2008). https://doi.org/10.1007/978-3-540-78967-3_24
13. Ishizaka, M., Fukushima, K.: Homomorphic signatures for subset and superset mixed predicates and its applications. In: Simpson, L., Rezazadeh Baee, M.A. (eds.) ACISP 2023. LNCS, vol. 13915, pp. 291–319. Springer, Cham (2023). https://doi.org/10.1007/978-3-031-35486-1_14
14. Ishizaka, M., Fukushima, K., Kiyomoto, S.: Trapdoor sanitizable and redactable signatures with unlinkability, invisibility and strong context-hiding. In: Seo, SH., Seo, H. (eds.) ICISC 2022. LNCS, vol. 13849, pp. 337–362. Springer, Cham (2022). https://doi.org/10.1007/978-3-031-29371-9_17
15. Johnson, R., Molnar, D., Song, D., Wagner, D.: Homomorphic signature schemes. In: Preneel, B. (ed.) CT-RSA 2002. LNCS, vol. 2271, pp. 244–262. Springer, Heidelberg (2002). https://doi.org/10.1007/3-540-45760-7_17
16. Kiltz, E., Mityagin, A., Panjwani, S., Raghavan, B.: Append-only signatures. In: Caires, L., Italiano, G.F., Monteiro, L., Palamidessi, C., Yung, M. (eds.) ICALP 2005. LNCS, vol. 3580, pp. 434–445. Springer, Heidelberg (2005). https://doi.org/10.1007/11523468_36
17. Libert, B., Joye, M., Yung, M., Peters, T.: Secure efficient history-hiding append-only signatures in the standard model. In: Katz, J. (ed.) PKC 2015. LNCS, vol. 9020, pp. 450–473. Springer, Heidelberg (2015). https://doi.org/10.1007/978-3-662-46447-2_20
18. Steinfeld, R., Bull, L., Zheng, Y.: Content extraction signatures. In: Kim, K. (ed.) ICISC 2001. LNCS, vol. 2288, pp. 285–304. Springer, Heidelberg (2002). https://doi.org/10.1007/3-540-45861-1_22
19. Waters, B.: Efficient identity-based encryption without random oracles. In: Cramer, R. (ed.) EUROCRYPT 2005. LNCS, vol. 3494, pp. 114–127. Springer, Heidelberg (2005). https://doi.org/10.1007/11426639_7

Cryptographic Models and Applications

Post-quantum Secure Non-committing Registered Functional Encryption

Ramprasad Sarkar(✉)

Cryptology and Security Research Unit, R C Bose Centre for Cryptology and Security Indian Statistical Institute Kolkata, Kolkata 700108, India
rpsarkar123@gmail.com

Abstract. Non-committing encryption (NCE) is a key primitive for proving security against adaptive corruptions, enabling simulators to generate ciphertexts before the encrypted message is known. Existing non-committing constructions for attribute-based encryption primitives [Hiroka *et al.*, ASIACRYPT 2021; Goyal *et al.*, PKC 2025] typically rely on centralized trust that generate users' secret keys. However, modern cryptographic systems increasingly aim to eliminate such trust assumptions through decentralized frameworks such as registered encryption, where users independently generate and register their own keys.

In this work, we initiate the study of *non-committing registered functional encryption* (NC-RFE) as a generalization of non-committing attribute-based encryption in the decentralized framework. We formalize the notion of NC-RFE by adapting classical non-committing security to the registered setting. We then present a generic construction based on indistinguishability obfuscation and zero-knowledge arguments, and prove its security assuming a secure underlying registered functional encryption (RFE) scheme. We further provide a lattice-based instantiation, yielding a post-quantum secure NC-RFE scheme based on the hardness of the plain LWE and equivocal LWE assumptions.

Keywords: Functional Encryption · Non-committing Security · Registered Cryptography · Post-quantum Security

1 Introduction

Modern cryptographic protocols are often deployed in dynamic environments where parties may become corrupted over time. Achieving security in such settings requires strong simulation techniques that allow a simulator to generate protocol transcripts before all inputs are known. A fundamental primitive enabling such simulations is *non-committing encryption* (NCE), introduced by Canetti *et al.* [6]. Informally, an NCE scheme allows a simulator to generate a public key and a ciphertext without committing to the encrypted message. Later, once the message is determined, the simulator can generate suitable explanations, typically in the form of randomness or keys, showing that the same

N. El Mrabet et al. (Eds.): AFRICACRYPT 2026, LNCS 16832, pp. 409–433, 2026.
https://doi.org/10.1007/978-3-032-31130-6_17

ciphertext corresponds to an encryption of that message. This flexibility allows protocol transcripts to remain consistent even when the simulator learns new information after earlier messages have already been generated. Over the years, several variants and relaxations of non-committing encryption [4,8,9,21,26,31] have been studied. One particularly useful notion is *receiver non-committing encryption* (RNCE) [17], where the simulator only needs to explain the secret key corresponding to a public key, rather than all the randomness used during encryption [17,22]. This notion has proven sufficient for many applications, including secure multiparty computation [6,7], adaptive secure attribute-based encryption for Turing Machines [17], selective opening secure schemes [20] and more. This naturally raises the following question:

Can non-committing security be extended to advanced encryption primitives that provide more expressive forms of access control?

Non-committing encryption beyond PKE. Early work on NCE [6,7,9,21,26] mainly focused on standard public-key encryption. In contrast, several widely studied encryption paradigms provide more expressive mechanisms for controlling access to encrypted data, including identity-based encryption (IBE) [28], attribute-based encryption (ABE) [18,27], and functional encryption (FE) [3]. These primitives allow flexible control over encrypted data: decryption capabilities may depend on identities, attributes, or even functions applied to the encrypted message.
Motivated by this growing importance of expressive encryption, recent works [16, 22] has begun exploring non-committing variants of such primitives [18,27,28]. In 2021, Hiroka *et al.* [22] introduced non-committing attribute-based encryption in the context of quantum encryption with certified deletion. More recently, Goyal *et al.* [16] studied receiver non-committing identity-based encryption (RNC-IBE), providing constructions under standard assumptions and highlighting connections to incompressible cryptography. These works suggest that extending non-committing security beyond classical public-key encryption is both a natural and important research direction.

Decentralization and the Registered Model. At the same time, another important direction in cryptographic research is the removal of centralized trust assumptions. In most advanced encryption systems [3,18,27,28], a central authority generates and distributes secret keys to users. Although convenient, this approach introduces key-escrow risks and creates a single point of failure.
Registration-based encryption (RBE) [14] addresses the above-mentioned limitations by decentralizing key generation procedure. In the RBE setting, users generate their own key pairs and register only their public keys, while a curator aggregates them into a master public key without holding any private information. This model eliminates the problem of central key escrow while maintaining global encryptability. Building on this foundation, registered attribute-based encryption (RABE) [23] extends decentralization to attribute-controlled settings: users independently register both their keys and attributes, and encryption policies are evaluated relative to the registered attributes.

Towards Non-committing Security in Advanced Encryption. Despite progress in both non-committing encryption and decentralized cryptographic frameworks, most existing works on non-committing encryption [6,7,9,16,21, 22,26] still rely on centralized setup assumptions. This reliance becomes particularly restrictive when considering highly expressive primitives such as functional encryption. A notable exception is the recent work of Murshid *et al.* [25], which proposes non-committing registered attribute-based encryption in the context of certified deletion without requiring a centralized authority.
Functional encryption (FE) [3] allows users to compute specific functions on encrypted data without revealing the underlying message. In an FE scheme, a trusted authority holds a master secret key and issues function-specific secret keys sk_f to users. Given a ciphertext that encrypts a message m, a user possessing sk_f can only learn the value $f(m)$. Due to its generality, functional encryption subsumes many existing encryption paradigms, including IBE, ABE, and predicate encryption. Recently, Datta *et al.* [12,13] extended this idea to the decentralized setting by introducing registered functional encryption (RFE). These developments naturally lead to the following motivating question:

Can we achieve non-committing security in a decentralized functional encryption setting where no trusted authority exists?

Combining these two directions introduces several conceptual and technical challenges. In a registered system, users independently generate and register public keys, while encryption depends on a global aggregation of these registrations. Achieving non-committing security requires a simulator capable of generating consistent global parameters, ciphertexts, and registration states without knowing the encrypted message in advance. Later, the simulator must reconcile these objects with a valid set of secret keys corresponding to registered functions. Ensuring such consistency across registration, key generation, and encryption becomes highly non-trivial due to the intricate dependencies between these components.

Our Contribution. In this work, we initiate the study of *non-committing registered functional encryption* (NC-RFE). Our main contributions are summarized below.

- We introduce the notion of *non-committing registered functional encryption* (NC-RFE) and formalize its security definition. Our formulation extends the classical non-committing security framework of [6,7] to the registered encryption setting. Informally, the definition requires that a simulator can generate master public parameters and ciphertexts without knowing the encrypted message in advance, and later produce consistent user secret keys and helper decryption keys when users are adaptively corrupted. At the same time, the definition preserves the fundamental property of registered encryption: honest users independently generate their own keys, and the key curator does not possess any secret information. This notion naturally extends non-committing security to a decentralized functional encryption framework and provides a

useful foundation for building adaptively secure protocols in distributed environments where users manage their own cryptographic keys.
- We present a generic construction of NC-RFE based on indistinguishability obfuscation and zero-knowledge arguments. Our design shows how to achieve non-committing security in the registered functional encryption setting while maintaining decentralized key generation.
- We prove that our construction satisfies non-committing security assuming the security of the underlying RFE scheme, the existence of indistinguishability obfuscation for P/poly, and an interactive zero-knowledge argument system for NP. Our proof demonstrates that the simulator can consistently explain previously generated parameters and ciphertexts even in the presence of adaptive corruptions.
- Finally, we present a lattice-based instantiation of NC-RFE based on the hardness of plain LWE, and Equivocal LWE assumptions. This instantiation provides post-quantum security for the proposed framework and shows that non-committing security can be achieved in decentralized functional encryption systems.

Organisation. The rest of the paper is structured as follows. In Sect. 2, we provide a high-level technical overview of our construction. Section 3 introduces the required preliminaries. In Sect. 4, we describe the system model and security definition for NC-RFE, and present its generic construction together with correctness and compactness properties. The security analysis of the proposed NC-RFE scheme is given in Sect. 5. Section 6 presents a lattice-based instantiation of our construction. Finally, Sect. 7 concludes the paper.

2 Technical Overview

We first introduce the notation used throughout the paper and then present a high-level technical overview of our constructions for non-committing registered functional encryption.

Notations. The notation $x \leftarrow X$ denotes that x is selected uniformly at random from a finite set X. If A is an algorithm (which may be classical, probabilistic, or quantum), then $y \leftarrow A(x)$ represents the output of A on input x, and we write $y \leftarrow A(x; r)$ when A uses explicit randomness r. Let λ and τ be a security parameter and a policy-family parameter. For a distribution D, we write $x \leftarrow D$ to denote sampling according to D. The assignment $y := z$ indicates that the variable y is set or defined to be equal to z. For a positive integer n, we denote the set $\{1, 2, \ldots, n\}$ by $[n] := \{1, \ldots, n\}$. The symbol λ denotes the security parameter. For classical strings x and y, their concatenation is written as $x \| y$. For a bit string $s \in \{0,1\}^n$, both s_i and $s[i]$ refer to its i-th bit. A function $f : \mathbb{N} \rightarrow \mathbb{R}$ is said to be negligible if, for every constant $c > 0$, there exists $\lambda_0 \in \mathbb{N}$ such that $f(\lambda) < \lambda^{-c}$ for all $\lambda > \lambda_0$. We use the notation $f(\lambda) \leq \mathsf{negl}(\lambda)$ to express that f is a negligible function. For a bit string x, we write x_j to mean the j-th bit of x.

Starting Point. As a preliminary step toward our construction, we revisit the notion of non-committing attribute-based encryption (NCABE) [22]. This primitive provides the simulation-based properties necessary to achieve non-committing security within the attribute-based encryption framework. An NCABE is defined over a message space $\mathcal{M}$, an attribute space $\mathcal{X}$, and a policy space $\mathcal{P}$ with the following algorithms.

- **Setup**: Given the security parameter 1^λ, the setup algorithm outputs a master public key mpk and a master secret key msk.
- **KeyGen**: On input of msk and a policy P, the key generation algorithm generates the corresponding secret key sk_P.
- **Encryption**: Using mpk, an attribute X, and a message μ, the encryption algorithm produces a ciphertext ct.
- **Decryption**: The decryption algorithm recovers μ' from ct using sk_P, or outputs $\perp$ in case of failure.
- **FakeSetup**: The fake setup algorithm produces a mpk together with auxiliary information aux, serving as an alternative to the real setup.
- **FakeCT**: Given mpk, aux, and an attribute X, the fake encryption algorithm outputs a fake ciphertext $\widetilde{\mathsf{ct}}$.
- **FakeSK**: The fake key generation algorithm generates a fake secret key $\widetilde{\mathsf{sk}}$ corresponding to policy P.
- **Reveal**: On input of mpk, aux, $\widetilde{\mathsf{ct}}$, and μ, the reveal algorithm outputs a fake master secret key $\widetilde{\mathsf{msk}}$.

These algorithms allow the simulator to generate protocol transcripts without committing to plaintext during encryption.

First Step: Towards NCFE from NCABE. Our first step is to extend the NCABE framework to support non-committing functional encryption (NCFE). Because functional encryption itself generalizes attribute-based encryption, the syntax of NCFE can be viewed as a natural extension of the algorithms used in NCABE. The key difference lies in the structure of the keys and the decryption functionality. In particular, the following changes are required:

- **KeyGen**: On input of msk and a function f, the key generation algorithm generates the corresponding secret key sk_f.
- **Encryption**: Using mpk, and a message m, the encryption algorithm produces a ciphertext ct.
- **Decryption**: The decryption algorithm recovers $f(m)$ from ct using sk_f.
- **FakeCT**: Given mpk, aux, the fake encryption algorithm outputs a fake ciphertext $\widetilde{\mathsf{ct}}$.
- **FakeSK**: The fake key generation algorithm generates a fake secret key $\widetilde{\mathsf{sk}}$ corresponding to function f.

Second Step: Towards NC-RFE from NCFE. Having established NCFE as an intermediate building block, we next extend the NCFE to the registered setting.

In the NCFE, a trusted authority holds the master secret key msk and is responsible for generating user secret keys. However, the registered model imposes a crucial restriction: the curator responsible for managing registrations must remain transparent and publicly verifiable. Consequently, the curator cannot hold or access any secret information. This restriction makes a direct adaptation of NCFE to the registered setting infeasible. The main challenge for this extended framework, non-committing registered functional encryption (NC-RFE), is therefore to redesign the NCFE framework so that the functionality previously provided by the trusted authority can be simulated without relying on any hidden secret state.

Third Step: Architecture of NC-RFE. To overcome this challenge, we can integrate simulation procedures directly into the registered functional encryption (RFE) framework. In this perspective, we can be viewed as an RFE scheme augmented with additional algorithms that enable non-committing simulation. These simulation procedures are used only within the security experiment and therefore do not affect the correctness of the scheme. The resulting primitive, which we call non-committing registered functional encryption (NC-RFE), introduces several additional algorithms that allow the simulator to generate public keys, simulate registrations, produce ciphertexts, and later reconcile them with appropriate secret keys. At a high level, the simulator maintains auxiliary state information that records the simulated registration history. Using this state, it can generate ciphertexts that are independent of the underlying message. When the message is eventually revealed, the simulator produces secret keys that ensure the simulated ciphertext is consistently decrypted. The NC-RFE framework therefore augments the standard RFE algorithms with the following five simulation algorithms.

- **SimKeyGen**: Given crs, aux, and an ancillary dictionary B (possibly empty) indexed by public keys, the simulator runs the key-generation procedure to produce a simulated public key $\widetilde{\mathsf{pk}}$ along with an updated B.
- **SimRegPK**: The simulated registration procedure takes as input crs, aux, pk, and f, and outputs a simulated master public key $\widetilde{\mathsf{mpk}}$ together with an updated auxiliary state $\widetilde{\mathsf{aux}}$.
- **SimCorrupt**: The simulated corrupt algorithm, on input crs, pk, and B, returns a simulated secret key $\widetilde{\mathsf{sk}}$ corresponding to pk.
- **SimCT**: Given $\widetilde{\mathsf{mpk}}$, aux, and B, the ciphertext simulation algorithm produces a simulated ciphertext $\widetilde{\mathsf{ct}}$.
- **Reveal**: On input of $\widetilde{\mathsf{pk}}$, B, $\widetilde{\mathsf{ct}}$, and a target message m, the reveal algorithm outputs a simulated secret key $\widetilde{\mathsf{sk}}$ that decrypts $\widetilde{\mathsf{ct}}$ to μ.

Now, we need to argue for the security of NC-RFE, which we discuss in the following.

Security for NC-RFE. The security foundation of NC-RFE builds upon a receiver non-committing security framework that combines indistinguishability obfuscation with zero-knowledge arguments possessing statistical soundness and computational zero-knowledge properties. The security analysis employs a sequence of hybrid transformations that systematically transition from real-world operations to ideal-world simulations, ensuring that no polynomial-time adversary can distinguish between these worlds with non-negligible probability. The proof methodology begins with the original NC-RFE security experiment, where all cryptographic operations are performed according to their original algorithms. The analysis then progressively introduces simulation components through computationally indistinguishable transformations. The first transformation replaces left-or-right decryption circuits embedded within obfuscated programs with left-only variants, thereby eliminating the scheme's dependence on the random selector string z, which determines the bit representation to use for each message position. This change relies on the security properties of indistinguishability obfuscation, which ensures that functionally equivalent circuits remain computationally indistinguishable when obfuscated.

Next, to integrate zero-knowledge arguments within the registered framework, we consider constructions that rely on a common reference string crs. In such settings, each new user registration would necessitate an update of the crs. Our initial attempt was to realize NC-RFE using existing NIZK schemes with updatable common reference strings [1,19]. However, these schemes either fail to achieve statistical soundness or depend on pairing-based assumptions that are potentially insecure against quantum polynomial-time (QPT) adversaries.

To overcome these limitations, we employ a zero-knowledge argument system that does not require any common reference string, while still guaranteeing soundness and zero-knowledge properties against QPT adversaries. The analysis transitions to simulated ZKA components, where challenge proofs are generated using simulation algorithms: $\widetilde{\pi} \leftarrow \langle Sim \rangle(d^*, y)$, where d^*, y are the statement and a polynomial-length bit string over $\{0,1\}$, respectively. This transformation leverages the computational zero-knowledge property of the ZKA protocol to ensure that the simulated proofs are indistinguishable from the real ones. This makes the proof components independent of the actual challenge message.

Another hybrid transformation introduces asymmetric encryption patterns that break the symmetry in how different message bits are encrypted. For each bit position i, the construction encrypts different values depending on the selector bit $z[i]$: $\mathsf{ct}^*_{i,z[i]} \leftarrow \mathsf{RFE.Encrypt}(\widetilde{\mathsf{mpk}}_{i,z[i]}, m[i])$ encrypts the actual message bit, while $\mathsf{ct}^*_{i,1-z[i]} \leftarrow \mathsf{RFE.Encrypt}(\widetilde{\mathsf{mpk}}_{i,1-z[i]}, 1 - m[i])$ encrypts its complement, where z, m are a polynomial-length bitstring over $\{0,1\}$ and a target message, respectively. This asymmetric approach is validated through a position-by-position hybrid argument that relies on the semantic security of the underlying RFE scheme.

Finally, the analysis achieves complete independence from the target message m employing a new random string $z^* \leftarrow \{0,1\}^{\ell_m}$ and encrypting fixed values: $\mathsf{ct}^*_{i,z^*[i]} \leftarrow \mathsf{RFE.Encrypt}(\widetilde{\mathsf{mpk}}_{i,z^*[i]}, 0)$ and $\mathsf{ct}^*_{i,1-z^*[i]} \leftarrow \mathsf{RFE.Encrypt}\ (\widetilde{\mathsf{mpk}}_{i,1-z^*[i]}, 1)$. This systematic elimination of dependencies, from the random selector string z, through real ZKA proofs, to the target message m itself, combined with the computational indistinguishability of consecutive transformations, establishes that no polynomial-time adversary can distinguish between real and ideal executions with non-negligible probability.

3 Preliminaries

We briefly recall the cryptographic preliminaries that are required in our construction.

3.1 NP Languages

In computational complexity theory, NP represents a non-deterministic polynomial time machine [11,29] (*i.e.*, a machine that can move more than one state from a given configuration). A language $\mathcal{L}$ over an alphabet Σ is called an NP languages iff there exists a $k \in \mathbb{N}$ and a polynomial checking relation $R_{\mathcal{L}} \subseteq \Sigma^* \times \Sigma^*$ such that for all strings $x \in \Sigma^*$, $x \in \mathcal{L} \iff \exists y\ (|y| \leq |x|^k$ and $R_{\mathcal{L}}(x,y))$,

where $|x|$ and $|y|$ are the lengths of the strings x and y, respectively.

3.2 Indistinguishability Obfuscation

Let $\{\mathcal{C}_\lambda\}_{\lambda \in \mathbb{N}}$ be a family of circuits. A PPT algorithm $i\mathcal{O}$ is an indistinguishability obfuscator for the circuit class if it satisfies the following:

- **Correctness:** For every security parameter $\lambda \in \mathbb{N}$, every circuit $C \in \mathcal{C}_\lambda$, and every input x, the obfuscated circuit preserves functionality:

$$\Pr[C'(x) = C(x) \mid C' \leftarrow i\mathcal{O}(C)] = 1.$$

- **Indistinguishability:** For any QPT distinguisher $\mathcal{D}$ and any pair of functionally equivalent circuits $C_0, C_1 \in \mathcal{C}_\lambda$ such that $C_0(x) = C_1(x)$ for all inputs x and $|C_0| = |C_1|$, the obfuscations are computationally indistinguishable:

$$\big|\Pr[\mathcal{D}(i\mathcal{O}(C_0)) = 1] - \Pr[\mathcal{D}(i\mathcal{O}(C_1)) = 1]\big| \leq \mathsf{negl}(\lambda).$$

In recent literature, candidates for indistinguishability obfuscation secure against QPT adversaries have been proposed [5,15,30]. Moreover, the work of [10] proposes a post-quantum $i\mathcal{O}$ candidate based on the NTRU assumption and a novel Equivocal LWE problem, employing a trapdoor-based Gaussian hint-release mechanism that ensures correctness while preventing structural leakage, with security proven against QPT adversaries.

3.3 Zero-Knowledge Arguments

We define a zero-knowledge argument system (ZKA) as an interactive protocol between two parties. Let $\langle A(w), B(z)\rangle(x)$ denote the interaction between interactive machines A and B on a common input x, where A receives auxiliary input w and B receives auxiliary input z. We refer to the protocol as $\prod_{\mathsf{ZKA}} = \langle A, B\rangle$.

Definition 1 (Classical Proof and Argument Systems for NP). *Let (P, V) be a protocol with an honest PPT prover P and an honest PPT verifier V for a language $\mathcal{L} \in \mathsf{NP}$, satisfying:*

Perfect Completeness: *For any $x \in \mathcal{L}$, $R_{\mathcal{L}}(x, w)$ and $z \in \{0,1\}^*$,*

$$\Pr[\langle P(w), V(z)\rangle(x) = 1] = 1.$$

Soundness: *For any quantum polynomial-size prover $P^* = \{P_\lambda^*, \rho_\lambda\}_{\lambda \in \mathbb{N}}$, there exists a negligible function $\mu(\cdot)$ such that for any security parameter $\lambda \in \mathbb{N}$ and any $x \in \{0,1\}^\lambda \setminus \mathcal{L}$ and $z \in \{0,1\}^*$, $\Pr[\langle P_\lambda^*(\rho_\lambda), V(z)\rangle(x) = 1] \leq \mu(\lambda)$. A protocol with computational soundness is called an* argument.

Zero Knowledge: *There exists a quantum polynomial-time simulator* Sim *such that for any quantum polynomial-size verifier $V^* = \{V_\lambda^*, \rho_\lambda\}_{\lambda \in \mathbb{N}}$,*

$$\left\{\langle P(w), V_\lambda^*(\rho_\lambda)\rangle(x)\right\}_{\lambda,x,w} \overset{c}{\approx} \left\{\mathsf{Sim}(x, V_\lambda^*, \rho_\lambda)\right\}_{\lambda,x},$$

where $\lambda \in \mathbb{N}$, $x \in \mathcal{L} \cap \{0,1\}^\lambda$, and $R_{\mathcal{L}}(x, w)$. If V^* is a classical circuit, then the simulator is computable by a classical polynomial-time algorithm.

$$\{\langle P(w), V^*(z)\rangle(x)\}_{x,w,z} \overset{c}{\approx} \{\langle \mathsf{Sim}\rangle(x, z)\}_{x,z}$$

when the distinguishing gap is considered as a function of $|x|$.

If the LWE assumption holds against quantum polynomial-size adversaries, then there exists a post-quantum zero-knowledge interactive argument system $\langle P, V\rangle$ for all languages in NP [2].

3.4 Registered Functional Encryption

We now recall the notion of Registered Functional Encryption (RFE) [12,13]. Let $\mathcal{U}_F = \{F_\lambda\}_{\lambda \in \mathbb{N}}$ denote a family of function classes indexed by the security parameter, and let $\mathcal{M}$ be the associated message space. A registered functional encryption scheme for function universe $\mathcal{U}_F$ and message space $\mathcal{M}$ consists of a collection of efficient algorithms RFE = (Setup, KeyGen, RegPK, Encrypt, Update, Dec), which operate as described below.

$\mathsf{Setup}(1^\lambda, 1^{\ell_f})$**:** On input the security parameter λ and an upper bound ℓ_f on the description length of functions in $\mathcal{U}_F$, this algorithm generates and outputs a common reference string crs.

$\mathsf{KeyGen}(\mathsf{crs}, \mathsf{aux})$**:** Given the common reference string crs and auxiliary state information aux (which may be empty), this algorithm outputs a public/secret key pair (pk, sk).

$\mathsf{RegPK}(\mathsf{crs}, \mathsf{aux}, \mathsf{pk}, f_{\mathsf{pk}})$**:** Given the reference string crs, the current auxiliary state aux, a public key pk, and an associated function $f_{\mathsf{pk}} \in F_\lambda$, this deterministic algorithm outputs an updated master public key mpk together with updated auxiliary state aux′.

$\mathsf{Encrypt}(\mathsf{mpk}, m)$: On input a master public key mpk and a message $m \in \mathcal{M}$, this algorithm produces a ciphertext ct.
$\mathsf{Update}(\mathsf{crs}, \mathsf{aux}, \mathsf{pk})$: Given the reference string crs, auxiliary state aux, and a public key pk, this deterministic procedure outputs a helper decryption key hsk.
$\mathsf{Dec}(\mathsf{sk}, \mathsf{hsk}, \mathsf{ct})$: On input a secret key sk, a helper decryption key hsk, and a ciphertext ct, this deterministic algorithm outputs a message m', the failure symbol $\perp$, or the instruction $\mathsf{GetUpdate}$ indicating that an updated helper secret key is required.

The algorithms are required to satisfy the following properties.

Correctness and Efficiency. For every security parameter $\lambda \in \mathbb{N}$, every message $m \in \mathcal{M}$, and every function $f \in F_\lambda$, consider the following experiment between an adversary $\mathcal{A}$ and a challenger.

- **Setup phase.** The challenger first samples a common reference string $\mathsf{crs} \leftarrow \mathsf{Setup}(1^\lambda, 1^{\ell_f})$. It initializes the auxiliary state $\mathsf{aux} \leftarrow \perp$ and the initial master public key $\mathsf{mpk}_0 \leftarrow \perp$. Furthermore, it initializes the counters $\mathsf{ctr}[\mathsf{reg}] \leftarrow 0, \mathsf{ctr}[\mathsf{enc}] \leftarrow 0$, which track the number of registration and encryption queries, respectively. The challenger also sets $\mathsf{ctr}[\mathsf{reg}]^* \leftarrow \infty$ to denote the index of the target key. Finally, the challenger sends crs to $\mathcal{A}$.
- **Query phase.** During this phase, $\mathcal{A}$ may issue the following queries.

- **Register non-target key query.** $\mathcal{A}$ submits a public key pk and a function $f \in \mathcal{U}_F$. The challenger increments the counter $\mathsf{ctr}[\mathsf{reg}] \leftarrow \mathsf{ctr}[\mathsf{reg}] + 1$, and registers the key by computing $(\mathsf{mpk}_{\mathsf{ctr}[\mathsf{reg}]}, \mathsf{aux}') \leftarrow \mathsf{RegPK}(\mathsf{crs}, \mathsf{aux}, \mathsf{pk}, f)$. The auxiliary state is updated as $\mathsf{aux} \leftarrow \mathsf{aux}'$, and the challenger returns $(\mathsf{ctr}[\mathsf{reg}], \mathsf{mpk}_{\mathsf{ctr}[\mathsf{reg}]}, \mathsf{aux})$ to $\mathcal{A}$.
- **Register target key query.** $\mathcal{A}$ specifies a function $f^* \in \mathcal{U}_F$. If a target-key registration query was previously issued, the challenger outputs $\perp$. Otherwise, the challenger increment the registration counter $\mathsf{ctr}[\mathsf{reg}] \leftarrow \mathsf{ctr}[\mathsf{reg}] + 1$. It sample a key pair $(\mathsf{pk}^*, \mathsf{sk}^*) \leftarrow \mathsf{KeyGen}(\mathsf{crs}, \mathsf{aux})$, and register the key $(\mathsf{mpk}_{\mathsf{ctr}[\mathsf{reg}]}, \mathsf{aux}') \leftarrow \mathsf{RegPK}(\mathsf{crs}, \mathsf{aux}, \mathsf{pk}^*, f^*)$. It then compute the helper decryption key $\mathsf{hsk}^* \leftarrow \mathsf{Update}(\mathsf{crs}, \mathsf{aux}, \mathsf{pk}^*)$. The challenger updates $\mathsf{aux} \leftarrow \mathsf{aux}'$ and records the target index $\mathsf{ctr}[\mathsf{reg}]^* \leftarrow \mathsf{ctr}[\mathsf{reg}]$. Finally it returns $(\mathsf{ctr}[\mathsf{reg}], \mathsf{mpk}_{\mathsf{ctr}[\mathsf{reg}]}, \mathsf{aux}, \mathsf{pk}^*, \mathsf{hsk}^*, \mathsf{sk}^*)$ to $\mathcal{A}$.
- **Encryption query.** $\mathcal{A}$ submits an index $\mathsf{ctr}[\mathsf{reg}]^* \leq i \leq \mathsf{ctr}[\mathsf{reg}]$ together with a message $m_{\mathsf{ctr}[\mathsf{enc}]} \in \mathcal{M}$. If the target key has not yet been registered, the challenger returns $\perp$. Otherwise it increments the encryption counter $\mathsf{ctr}[\mathsf{enc}] \leftarrow \mathsf{ctr}[\mathsf{enc}] + 1$ and computes $\mathsf{ct}_{\mathsf{ctr}[\mathsf{enc}]} \leftarrow \mathsf{Encrypt}(\mathsf{mpk}_i, m)$. The challenger replies with $(\mathsf{ctr}[\mathsf{enc}], \mathsf{ct}_{\mathsf{ctr}[\mathsf{enc}]})$.
- **Decryption query.** $\mathcal{A}$ provides a ciphertext index $1 \leq j \leq \mathsf{ctr}[\mathsf{enc}]$. The challenger computes $m'_j \leftarrow \mathsf{Dec}(\mathsf{sk}^*, \mathsf{hsk}^*, \mathsf{ct}_j)$. If $m'_j = \mathsf{GetUpdate}$, the challenger updates the helper key $\mathsf{hsk}^* \leftarrow \mathsf{Update}(\mathsf{crs}, \mathsf{aux}, \mathsf{pk}^*)$, and recomputes the decryption. If $m'_j \neq f^*(m_j)$, the experiment terminates with output $b = 1$.

If $\mathcal{A}$ completes all queries and the experiment has not halted, the experiment outputs $b = 0$.
The scheme RFE is said to be correct and efficient if every adversary making a polynomial number of queries satisfies the following properties.

- **Correctness.** There exists a negligible function $\mathsf{negl}(\cdot)$ such that $\Pr[b = 1] = \mathsf{negl}(\lambda)$. The scheme achieves *perfect correctness* if $\Pr[b = 1] = 0$.
- **Compactness.** Let N denote the number of registration queries. There exists a polynomial poly$(\cdot)$ such that for every $i \in$, $|\mathsf{mpk}_i| = \text{poly}(\lambda, \ell_f, \log i)$. Moreover the helper key size satisfies $|\mathsf{hsk}^*| = \text{poly}(\lambda, \ell_f, \log N)$.
- **Update efficiency.** Let N be the number of registrations. Throughout the experiment the challenger invokes Update at most $O(\log N)$ times, and each invocation runs in time poly$(\log N)$ in the RAM model.

Security. Let $b \in \{0, 1\}$ be a bit. We define the following security experiment $\mathsf{Exp}_A^{\mathsf{RFE}}(1^\lambda, b)$ between an adversary $\mathcal{A}$ and a challenger.

- **Setup phase.** The challenger samples a common reference string $\mathsf{crs} \leftarrow \mathsf{Setup}(1^\lambda, 1^{\ell_f})$. It initializes the auxiliary state $\mathsf{aux} \leftarrow \perp$ and the master public key $\mathsf{mpk} \leftarrow \perp$. It also sets a counter $\mathsf{ctr} \leftarrow 0$ that records the number of honest-key registration queries made by $\mathcal{A}$. Furthermore, it initializes an empty set of corrupted keys $C \leftarrow \emptyset$ and an empty dictionary $\mathsf{D} \leftarrow \emptyset$ that maps public keys to the functions registered for them. For convenience, if a public key $\mathsf{pk} \notin \mathsf{D}$ then we define $\mathsf{D}[\mathsf{pk}] := \emptyset$. Finally, the challenger gives crs to $\mathcal{A}$.
- **Query phase.** During this phase, the adversary $\mathcal{A}$ may issue the following queries.

  - **Registered corrupted key query.** $\mathcal{A}$ specifies a public key pk and a function $f \in \mathcal{U}_F$. The challenger registers this key by computing $(\mathsf{mpk}', \mathsf{aux}') \leftarrow \mathsf{RegPK}(\mathsf{crs}, \mathsf{aux}, \mathsf{pk}, f)$. It then updates its internal state by setting $\mathsf{mpk} \leftarrow \mathsf{mpk}'$ and $\mathsf{aux} \leftarrow \mathsf{aux}'$, adds pk to the corrupted set C, and records the function by updating $\mathsf{D}[\mathsf{pk}] \leftarrow \mathsf{D}[\mathsf{pk}] \cup \{f\}$. Finally, it returns $(\mathsf{mpk}', \mathsf{aux}')$ to $\mathcal{A}$.
  - **Registered honest key query.** $\mathcal{A}$ submits a function $f \in \mathcal{U}_F$. The challenger first increments the counter $\mathsf{ctr} \leftarrow \mathsf{ctr}+1$ and generates a fresh key pair $(\mathsf{pk}_{\mathsf{ctr}}, \mathsf{sk}_{\mathsf{ctr}}) \leftarrow \mathsf{KeyGen}(\mathsf{crs}, \mathsf{aux})$. It then registers the public key by computing $(\mathsf{mpk}', \mathsf{aux}') \leftarrow \mathsf{RegPK}(\mathsf{crs}, \mathsf{aux}, \mathsf{pk}_{\mathsf{ctr}}, f)$. The challenger updates $\mathsf{mpk} \leftarrow \mathsf{mpk}'$ and $\mathsf{aux} \leftarrow \mathsf{aux}'$, records the function via $\mathsf{D}[\mathsf{pk}_{\mathsf{ctr}}] \leftarrow \mathsf{D}[\mathsf{pk}_{\mathsf{ctr}}] \cup \{f\}$, and returns $(\mathsf{ctr}, \mathsf{mpk}', \mathsf{aux}', \mathsf{pk}_{\mathsf{ctr}})$ to $\mathcal{A}$.
  - **Corrupt honest query.** $\mathcal{A}$ specifies an index $1 \leq i \leq \mathsf{ctr}$. Let $(\mathsf{pk}_i, \mathsf{sk}_i)$ denote the key pair generated in the i-th honest-key registration query. The challenger adds pk_i to the corrupted set C and returns the secret key sk_i to $\mathcal{A}$.

- **Challenge phase.** $\mathcal{A}$ outputs two challenge messages $m_0^*, m_1^* \in \mathcal{M}$. The challenger responds with the challenge ciphertext $\mathsf{ct}^* \leftarrow \mathsf{Encrypt}(\mathsf{mpk}, m_b^*)$.

- **Output phase.** Finally, $\mathcal{A}$ outputs a bit $b' \in \{0,1\}$, which is taken as the output of the experiment.

Let $S = \{f_{\mathsf{pk}} \in \mathsf{D}[\mathsf{pk}] : \mathsf{pk} \in C\}$. We say that an adversary $\mathcal{A}$ is *admissible* if for every corrupted slot function $f_{\mathsf{pk}} \in S$, it holds that $f_{\mathsf{pk}}(m_0^*) = f_{\mathsf{pk}}(m_1^*)$.
The registered functional encryption scheme RFE is considered secure if for every admissible adversary $\mathcal{A}$ there exists a negligible function $\mathsf{negl}(\cdot)$ such that for all $\lambda \in \mathbb{N}$, $|\Pr[\mathsf{Exp}_{\mathcal{A}}^{\mathsf{RFE}}(1^\lambda, 0) = 1] - \Pr[\mathsf{Exp}_{\mathcal{A}}^{\mathsf{RFE}}(1^\lambda, 1) = 1]| = \mathsf{negl}(\lambda)$.

4 Non-committing Registered Functional Encryption

In this section, we first introduce the system model for *non-committing registered functional encryption* (NC-RFE) and formalize its security definition through a security game. We then present a generic construction of our NC-RFE scheme by modularly combining registered functional encryption, zero-knowledge arguments, and indistinguishability obfuscation. Finally, we discuss the correctness of our construction as well as its compactness and update efficiency properties.

4.1 System Model of NC-RFE

A NC-RFE scheme with function universe $\mathcal{U}_F$, and message space $\mathcal{M}$ is a tuple of efficient algorithms $\prod_{\mathsf{NC\text{-}RFE}} =$ (Setup, KeyGen, RegPK, Encrypt, Update, Decrypt, SimKeyGen, SimRegPK, SimCT, SimCorrupt, Reveal) with the following syntax:

- $(\mathsf{crs}) \leftarrow \mathsf{Setup}(1^\lambda, 1^{\ell_f})$. On input the security parameter λ and an upper bound ℓ_f on the description length of functions in $\mathcal{U}_F$, this algorithm generates and outputs a common reference string crs.
- $(\mathsf{pk}, \mathsf{sk}) \leftarrow \mathsf{KeyGen}(\mathsf{crs}, \mathsf{aux})$. Given the common reference string crs and auxiliary state information aux (which may be empty), this algorithm outputs a public/secret key pair (pk, sk).
- $(\mathsf{mpk}, \mathsf{aux}') \leftarrow \mathsf{RegPK}(\mathsf{crs}, \mathsf{aux}, \mathsf{pk}, f_{\mathsf{pk}})$. Given the reference string crs, the current auxiliary state aux, a public key pk, and an associated function $f_{\mathsf{pk}} \in F_\lambda$, this deterministic algorithm outputs an updated master public key mpk together with updated auxiliary state aux′.
- $(\mathsf{ct}) \leftarrow \mathsf{Encrypt}(\mathsf{mpk}, m)$. On input a master public key mpk and a message $m \in \mathcal{M}$, this algorithm produces a ciphertext ct.
- $(\mathsf{hsk}) \leftarrow \mathsf{Update}(\mathsf{crs}, \mathsf{aux}, \mathsf{pk})$. This algorithm outputs a helper secret key hsk given crs, aux, and pk as inputs.
- $(m') \leftarrow \mathsf{Decrypt}(\mathsf{sk}, \mathsf{hsk}, \mathsf{ct})$. On input a secret key sk, a helper decryption key hsk, and a ciphertext ct, this deterministic algorithm outputs a message m'.
- $(\mathsf{pk}, \mathsf{B}) \leftarrow \mathsf{SimKeyGen}(\mathsf{crs}, \mathsf{aux}, \mathsf{B})$. Given crs, aux, and an ancillary dictionary B (possibly empty) indexed by public keys, the simulated key generation algorithm outputs pk together with an updated ancillary dictionary B.
- $(\widetilde{\mathsf{mpk}}, \widetilde{\mathsf{aux}}) \leftarrow \mathsf{SimRegPK}(\mathsf{crs}, \mathsf{aux}, \mathsf{pk}, f_{\mathsf{pk}})$. The simulated key registration algorithm, given crs, aux, pk, and f_{pk}, produces a simulated master public key $\widetilde{\mathsf{mpk}}$ and an updated auxiliary state $\widetilde{\mathsf{aux}}$.

- $(\widetilde{\mathsf{sk}}) \leftarrow \mathsf{SimCorrupt}(\mathsf{crs}, \mathsf{pk}, \mathsf{B})$. The simulated corruption algorithm takes as input crs, pk and B to return a simulated secret key $\widetilde{\mathsf{sk}}$ corresponding to pk.
- $(\widetilde{\mathsf{ct}}) \leftarrow \mathsf{SimCT}(\widetilde{\mathsf{mpk}}, \mathsf{aux}, \mathsf{B})$. The simulated ciphertext generation algorithm simulates the entire encryption algorithm using the simulated master public key $\widetilde{\mathsf{mpk}}$, aux, and B, and outputs a simulated ciphertext $\widetilde{\mathsf{ct}}$.
- $(\widetilde{\mathsf{sk}}) \leftarrow \mathsf{Reveal}(\mathsf{pk}, \mathsf{B}, \widetilde{\mathsf{ct}}, m)$. Given pk, B, $\widetilde{\mathsf{ct}}$, and a target message m, this algorithm generates a simulated secret key $\widetilde{\mathsf{sk}}$.

Correctness and Update Efficiency of NC-RFE. The NC-RFE protocol preserves the same correctness and efficiency guarantees as the underlying RFE scheme.

Compactness: Let N denote the number of registration queries. There exists a universal polynomial $\mathsf{poly}(\cdot,\cdot,\cdot)$ such that for all $i \in [N]$,

$$|\mathsf{mpk}_i|, |\widetilde{\mathsf{mpk}_i}| = \mathsf{poly}(\lambda, |\mathcal{U}_F|, \log i), \quad |\mathsf{hsk}^*| = \mathsf{poly}(\lambda, |\mathcal{U}_F|, \log N).$$

4.2 Security Model for NC-RFE

Let a non-committing registered functional encryption scheme $\prod_{\mathsf{NC\text{-}RFE}} =$ (Setup, KeyGen, RegPK, Encrypt, Update, Decrypt, SimKeyGen, SimRegPK, SimCT, SimCorrupt, Reveal) be defined over a function universe $\mathcal{U}_F$ and message space $\mathcal{M}$. For a security parameter λ, a bit $b \in \{0, 1\}$, and an adversary $\mathcal{A}$, we define the following security game $\mathsf{Exp}_{\mathcal{A}}^{\mathsf{NC\text{-}RFE}}(\lambda, b)$ between $\mathcal{A}$ and a challenger:

- **Setup.** The challenger begins by generating $\mathsf{crs} \leftarrow \mathsf{Setup}(1^\lambda, 1^{\ell_f})$. It initializes its internal variables as follows: $\mathsf{aux} \leftarrow \perp$, $\mathsf{mpk} \leftarrow \perp$, and a counter $\mathsf{ctr} \leftarrow 0$ to track the number of honestly registered keys. Additionally, two empty sets $C \leftarrow \emptyset$ and $H \leftarrow \emptyset$ are initialized to store corrupted and honest public keys, respectively. The challenger also initializes empty dictionaries, $\mathsf{D} \leftarrow \emptyset$ and $\mathsf{B} \leftarrow \emptyset$, indexed by the public keys. For ease of notation, it is assumed that if $\mathsf{pk} \notin \mathsf{D}$, then $\mathsf{D}[\mathsf{pk}] := \emptyset$ and same for B. Finally, the challenger sends crs to $\mathcal{A}$.
- **Query Phase:** During this phase, $\mathcal{A}$ is allowed to make the following types of queries:

- **Register corrupted key query.** Upon receiving pk and $f \in \mathcal{U}_F$ from $\mathcal{A}$, the challenger proceeds as follows:

$$(\mathsf{mpk}', \mathsf{aux}') \leftarrow \begin{cases} \mathsf{RegPK}(\mathsf{crs}, \mathsf{aux}, \mathsf{pk}, f), & \text{if } b = 0 \\ \mathsf{SimRegPK}(\mathsf{crs}, \mathsf{aux}, \mathsf{pk}, f), & \text{if } b = 1 \end{cases}$$

It then updates its internal state as:

$$\mathsf{mpk} \leftarrow \mathsf{mpk}', \mathsf{aux} \leftarrow \mathsf{aux}', C \leftarrow C \cup \{\mathsf{pk}\}, \mathsf{D}[\mathsf{pk}] \leftarrow \mathsf{D}[\mathsf{pk}] \cup \{f\}.$$

The challenger returns $(\mathsf{mpk}', \mathsf{aux}')$ to $\mathcal{A}$.

- **Register honest key query:** When $\mathcal{A}$ specifying a function $f \in \mathcal{U}_F$, the challenger increments its counter $\mathsf{ctr} \leftarrow \mathsf{ctr} + 1$, and performs the following based on the bit b:

$$\left.\begin{array}{r}(\mathsf{pk}_{\mathsf{ctr}}, \mathsf{sk}_{\mathsf{ctr}}) \leftarrow \mathsf{KeyGen}(\mathsf{crs}, \mathsf{aux}) \\ (\mathsf{mpk}', \mathsf{aux}') \leftarrow \mathsf{RegPK}(\mathsf{crs}, \mathsf{aux}, \mathsf{pk}_{\mathsf{ctr}}, f)\end{array}\right\} \quad \text{if} \quad b = 0$$

$$\left.\begin{array}{r}(\mathsf{pk}_{\mathsf{ctr}}, \mathsf{B}') \leftarrow \mathsf{SimKeyGen}(\mathsf{crs}, \mathsf{aux}, \mathsf{B}) \\ (\mathsf{mpk}', \mathsf{aux}') \leftarrow \mathsf{SimRegPK}(\mathsf{crs}, \mathsf{aux}, \mathsf{pk}_{\mathsf{ctr}}, f)\end{array}\right\} \quad \text{if} \quad b = 1.$$

It then updates:

$$\mathsf{mpk} \leftarrow \mathsf{mpk}', \mathsf{aux} \leftarrow \mathsf{aux}', H \leftarrow H \cup \{\mathsf{pk}_{\mathsf{ctr}}\},$$
$$\mathsf{D}[\mathsf{pk}_{\mathsf{ctr}}] \leftarrow \mathsf{D}[\mathsf{pk}_{\mathsf{ctr}}] \cup \{f\}, B \leftarrow B'.$$

It then replies with $(\mathsf{ctr}, \mathsf{mpk}', \mathsf{aux}', \mathsf{pk}_{\mathsf{ctr}})$.

- **Corrupt honest key query:** $\mathcal{A}$ may request the corruption of an honest key by specifying an index i such that $1 \leq i \leq \mathsf{ctr}$. The challenger responds based on the bit b:
(a) If $b = 0$, it returns the actual secret key sk_i.
(b) If $b = 1$, it computes a simulated secret key $\widetilde{\mathsf{sk}}_i \leftarrow \mathsf{SimCorrupt}(\mathsf{crs}, \mathsf{pk}_i, \mathsf{B})$.
In either case, pk_i is removed from H and added to C.

- **Challenge phase:** $\mathcal{A}$ selects $m \in \mathcal{M}$ subject to the following restriction that for all $f \in S$, $f(m)$ is fixed and consistent with the adversary's view, where $S = \{f \in \mathsf{D}[\mathsf{pk}] \mid \mathsf{pk} \in C\}$. The challenger then prepares the challenge ciphertext as follows:

$$\mathsf{ct}^* \leftarrow \begin{cases} \mathsf{Encrypt}(\mathsf{mpk}, m) & \text{if } b = 0, \\ \mathsf{SimCT}(\mathsf{mpk}, \mathsf{aux}, \mathsf{B}) & \text{if } b = 1. \end{cases}$$

For every honest public key $\mathsf{pk}_i \in H$, the challenger generates the corresponding secret and helper keys as follows:

$$\mathsf{sk}_i^* \leftarrow \begin{cases} \mathsf{sk}_i & \text{if } b = 0, \\ \mathsf{Reveal}(\mathsf{pk}_i, \mathsf{B}, \mathsf{ct}^*, m) & \text{if } b = 1, \end{cases}$$
$$\mathsf{hsk}_i \leftarrow \mathsf{Update}(\mathsf{crs}, \mathsf{aux}, \mathsf{pk}_i).$$

The challenger then returns to $\mathcal{A}$ the tuple: $(\mathsf{ct}^*, \{\mathsf{sk}_i^*\}_{\mathsf{pk}_i \in H}, \{\mathsf{hsk}_i\}_{\mathsf{pk}_i \in H})$. The post-challenge query is redundant beacuse the adversary already has maximum information after the challenge phase.

- **Output phase:** $\mathcal{A}$ finally outputs a bit $b' \in \{0, 1\}$.

A NC-RFE scheme is said to be secure if for every efficient quantum polynomial-time (QPT) adversary $\mathcal{A}$, there exists a negligible function $\mathsf{negl}(\cdot)$ such that for all $\lambda \in \mathbb{N}$,

$$\left|\Pr\left[\mathsf{Exp}_{\mathcal{A}}^{\mathsf{NC\text{-}RFE}}(\lambda, 0) = 1\right] - \Pr\left[\mathsf{Exp}_{\mathcal{A}}^{\mathsf{NC\text{-}RFE}}(\lambda, 1) = 1\right]\right| \leq \mathsf{negl}(\lambda).$$

4.3 Generic Construction of NC-RFE Protocol

In this section, we construct NC-RFE scheme with message space $\{0,1\}^{\ell_m}$, and function universe $\mathcal{U}_F$, where ℓ_m are some polynomials. Our construction builds upon the following cryptographic components:

- A registered functional encryption scheme with the tuple of algorithms $\prod_{\mathsf{RFE}} = \mathsf{RFE}.(\mathsf{Setup}, \mathsf{KeyGen}, \mathsf{RegPK}, \mathsf{Encrypt}, \mathsf{Update}, \mathsf{Decrypt})$ defined over the same $\mathcal{U}_F$.
- A zero-knowledge argument given by the interactive machines $\langle \mathcal{P}, \mathcal{V} \rangle$ for an NP language $\mathcal{L}$ characterized by the relation R defined as:

$$R := \big\{ \big(\big(\{\mathsf{mpk}_{i,0}, \mathsf{mpk}_{i,1}\}_{i\in[\ell_m]}, \{\mathsf{ct}_{i,0}, \mathsf{ct}_{i,1}\}_{i\in[\ell_m]} \big), \{(m[i], r_{i,0}, r_{i,1})\}_{i\in[\ell_m]} \big) \\ : \forall i \in [\ell_m],\ \forall b \in \{0,1\},\ \mathsf{ct}_{i,b} = \mathsf{RFE}.\mathsf{Encrypt}(\mathsf{mpk}_{i,b}, m[i]; r_{i,b}) \big\}.$$

  Each $r_{i,b}$ is sampled uniformly from the randomness space of the RFE.Encrypt algorithm.
- An indistinguishability obfuscator $i\mathcal{O}$ for polynomial-size circuits.

The algorithms of NC-RFE are detailed below.

$\mathsf{Setup}(1^\lambda, 1^{\ell_f})$:
- For every $i \in [\ell_m]$ and $b \in \{0,1\}$, generate $\mathsf{crs}_{i,b} \leftarrow \mathsf{RFE}.\mathsf{Setup}(1^\lambda, 1^{\ell_f})$.
- Sample $y \leftarrow \{0,1\}^{\ell_m}$ uniformly at random.
- Output $\mathsf{crs} := (\{\mathsf{crs}_{i,b}\}_{i\in[\ell_m],\ b\in\{0,1\}}, y)$.

$\mathsf{KeyGen}(\mathsf{crs}, \mathsf{aux})$:
- Parse $\mathsf{crs} = (\{\mathsf{crs}_{i,b}\}_{i,b}, y)$.
- Sample $z \leftarrow \{0,1\}^{\ell_m}$ uniformly at random.
- For all $i \in [\ell_m]$, $b \in \{0,1\}$, generate $(\mathsf{pk}_{i,b}, \mathsf{sk}_{i,b}) \leftarrow \mathsf{RFE}.\mathsf{KeyGen}(\mathsf{crs}_{i,b}, \mathsf{aux}_{i,b})$.
- Set $\mathsf{pk} := (\{\mathsf{pk}_{i,b}\}_{i,b})$.
- Construct the secret key $\mathsf{sk} := i\mathcal{O}(\mathcal{D}[\{\mathsf{sk}_{i,z[i]}\}_i, z])$ where the circuit is defined in Fig. 1.
- Output $(\mathsf{pk}, \mathsf{sk})$.

$\mathsf{RegPK}(\mathsf{crs}, \mathsf{aux}, \mathsf{pk}, f)$:
- Parse $\mathsf{crs} = (\{\mathsf{crs}_{i,b}\}_{i,b}, y)$ and $\mathsf{pk} = (\{\mathsf{pk}_{i,b}\}_{i,b})$.
- If $\mathsf{aux} = \perp$, initialize $\mathsf{aux}_{i,b} := \perp$ for all i, b.
- For each i, b, compute $(\mathsf{mpk}_{i,b}, \mathsf{aux}'_{i,b}) \leftarrow \mathsf{RFE}.\mathsf{RegPK}(\mathsf{crs}_{i,b}, \mathsf{aux}_{i,b}, \mathsf{pk}_{i,b}, f)$.
- Set $\mathsf{mpk} := (\{\mathsf{mpk}_{i,b}\}_{i,b}, y)$ and $\mathsf{aux}' := \{\mathsf{aux}'_{i,b}\}_{i,b}$.
- Output $(\mathsf{mpk}, \mathsf{aux}')$.

$\mathsf{Encrypt}(\mathsf{mpk}, m)$:
- Parse $\mathsf{mpk} = (\{\mathsf{mpk}_{i,b}\}_{i,b}, y)$
- For each i, b, compute $\mathsf{ct}_{i,b} \leftarrow \mathsf{RFE}.\mathsf{Encrypt}(\mathsf{mpk}_{i,b}, m[i]; r_{i,b})$.
- Let $d := (\{\mathsf{mpk}_{i,b}, \mathsf{ct}_{i,b}\}_{i,b})$ and $w := (m, \{r_{i,b}\}_{i,b})$.
- Compute $\pi \leftarrow \langle \mathcal{P}(w), \mathcal{V}(y) \rangle (d)$.
- Output $\mathsf{ct} := (\{\mathsf{ct}_{i,b}\}_{i,b}, \pi)$.

Left or Right Decryption Circuit $\mathcal{D}$

Input: hsk, ct
Hardcoded: $\{\mathsf{sk}_{i,z[i]}\}_{i\in[\ell_m]}$, $z \in \{0,1\}^{\ell_m}$

1. Parse $\mathsf{ct} = (\{\mathsf{ct}_{i,0}, \mathsf{ct}_{i,1}\}_{i\in[\ell_m]}, \pi)$
2. Parse $\mathsf{hsk} = (\{\mathsf{hsk}_{i,0}, \mathsf{hsk}_{i,1}\}_{i\in[\ell_m]})$
3. If $\pi \neq 1$, then output $\perp$
4. For each $i \in [\ell_m]$, compute:

$$m'[i] \leftarrow \mathsf{RFE.Decrypt}(\mathsf{sk}_{i,z[i]}, \mathsf{hsk}_{i,z[i]}, \mathsf{ct}_{i,z[i]})$$

5. Output: $m' := m'[1] \,\|\, m'[2] \,\|\, \cdots \,\|\, m'[\ell_m]$

Fig. 1. Left or Right Decryption Circuit.

$\mathsf{Update}(\mathsf{crs}, \mathsf{aux}, \mathsf{pk})$:
- Parse $\mathsf{crs} = (\{\mathsf{crs}_{i,b}\}_{i,b}, y)$, $\mathsf{aux} = \{\mathsf{aux}_{i,b}\}_{i,b}$, and $\mathsf{pk} = \{\mathsf{pk}_{i,b}\}_{i,b}$.
- For each $i \in [\ell_m]$, $b \in \{0,1\}$, compute $\mathsf{hsk}_{i,b} \leftarrow \mathsf{RFE.Update}(\mathsf{crs}_{i,b}, \mathsf{aux}_{i,b}, \mathsf{pk}_{i,b})$.
- Output $\mathsf{hsk} := \{\mathsf{hsk}_{i,b}\}_{i,b}$.

$\mathsf{Decrypt}(\mathsf{sk}, \mathsf{hsk}, \mathsf{ct})$:
- Parse $\mathsf{sk} = \mathcal{D}_e$ and $\mathsf{hsk} = \{\mathsf{hsk}_{i,b}\}_{i,b}$.
- Compute and return $m' := \mathcal{D}_e(\mathsf{hsk}, \mathsf{ct})$.

$\mathsf{SimKeyGen}(\mathsf{crs}, \mathsf{aux}, \mathsf{B})$:
- Parse $\mathsf{crs} = (\{\mathsf{crs}_{i,b}\}_{i,b}, y)$.
- For all $i \in [\ell_m], b \in \{0,1\}$, compute $(\mathsf{pk}_{i,b}, \mathsf{sk}_{i,b}) \leftarrow \mathsf{RFE.KeyGen}(\mathsf{crs}_{i,b}, \mathsf{aux}_{i,b})$.
- Sample $z^*_{\mathsf{pk}} \leftarrow \{0,1\}^{\ell_m}$ uniformly at random.
- Set $\mathsf{pk} := (\{\mathsf{pk}_{i,b}\}_{i,b})$ and update $\mathsf{B}[\mathsf{pk}] = (\{\mathsf{sk}_{i,b}\}_{i,b}, z^*_{\mathsf{pk}})$.
- Output $(\widetilde{\mathsf{pk}}, \mathsf{B})$.

Left Decryption Circuit $\mathcal{D}_0$

Input: hsk, ct
Hardcoded: $\{\mathsf{sk}_{i,0}\}_{i\in[\ell_m]}$

1. Parse $\mathsf{ct} = (\{(\mathsf{ct}_{i,0}, \mathsf{ct}_{i,1})\}_{i\in[\ell_m]}, \pi)$
2. Parse $\mathsf{hsk} = (\{\mathsf{hsk}_{i,0}, \mathsf{hsk}_{i,1}\}_{i\in[\ell_m]})$
3. If $\pi \neq 1$, output $\perp$
4. For each $i \in [\ell_m]$, compute:

$$m'[i] \leftarrow \mathsf{RFE.Decrypt}(\mathsf{sk}_{i,0}, \mathsf{hsk}_{i,0}, \mathsf{ct}_{i,0})$$

5. Output: $m' = m'[1] \,\|\, m'[2] \,\|\, \cdots \,\|\, m'[\ell_m]$

Fig. 2. Left Decryption Circuit.

$\mathsf{SimRegPK}(\mathsf{crs}, \mathsf{aux}, \mathsf{pk}, f)$:
- Parse $\mathsf{crs} = (\{\mathsf{crs}_{i,b}\}_{i,b}, y)$ and $\mathsf{pk} = (\{\mathsf{pk}_{i,b}\}_{i,b})$.
- For each i, b, compute $(\widetilde{\mathsf{mpk}}_{i,b}, \widetilde{\mathsf{aux}}_{i,b}) \leftarrow \mathsf{RFE.RegPK}(\mathsf{crs}_{i,b}, \mathsf{aux}_{i,b}, \mathsf{pk}_{i,b}, f)$.

– Set $\widetilde{\mathsf{mpk}} := (\{\widetilde{\mathsf{mpk}}_{i,b}\}_{i,b}, y)$ and $\widetilde{\mathsf{aux}} := \{\widetilde{\mathsf{aux}}_{i,b}\}_{i,b}$.
– Output $(\widetilde{\mathsf{mpk}}, \widetilde{\mathsf{aux}})$.

SimCorrupt(crs, pk, B):
– Parse $\mathsf{pk} = (\{\mathsf{pk}_{i,b}\}_{i,b})$ and $\mathsf{B}[\mathsf{pk}] = (\{\mathsf{sk}_{i,b}\}_{i,b}, z^*_{\mathsf{pk}})$.
– Compute $\widetilde{\mathsf{sk}} := i\mathcal{O}(\mathcal{D}_0[\{\mathsf{sk}_{i,0}\}_i])$, where the circuit is defined in Fig. 2.
– Output $\widetilde{\mathsf{sk}}$.

SimCT($\widetilde{\mathsf{mpk}}$, aux, B):
– Parse $\widetilde{\mathsf{mpk}} = (\{\widetilde{\mathsf{mpk}}_{i,b}\}_{i,b}, y)$.
– Compute $z^* := \bigoplus_{\mathsf{pk} \in \mathsf{B}} z^*_{\mathsf{pk}}$ where $\mathsf{B}[\mathsf{pk}] = (\{\mathsf{sk}_{i,b}\}_{i,b}, z^*_{\mathsf{pk}})$.
– For each $i \in [\ell_m]$, compute:

$$\mathsf{ct}^*_{i,z^*[i]} \leftarrow \mathsf{RFE.Encrypt}(\widetilde{\mathsf{mpk}}_{i,z^*[i]}, 0),$$
$$\mathsf{ct}^*_{i,1-z^*[i]} \leftarrow \mathsf{RFE.Encrypt}(\widetilde{\mathsf{mpk}}_{i,1-z^*[i]}, 1).$$

– Define $d^* := (\{\mathsf{mpk}_{i,0}, \mathsf{mpk}_{i,1}, \mathsf{ct}^*_{i,0}, \mathsf{ct}^*_{i,1}\}_i)$.
– Compute $\widetilde{\pi} \leftarrow \langle \mathsf{Sim} \rangle (d^*, y)$.
– Output $\widetilde{\mathsf{ct}} := (\{\mathsf{ct}^*_{i,b}\}_{i,b}, \widetilde{\pi})$.

Reveal(pk, B, $\widetilde{\mathsf{ct}}$, m):
– Parse $\mathsf{B}[\mathsf{pk}] = (\{\mathsf{sk}_{i,b}\}_{i,b}, z^*_{\mathsf{pk}})$.
– Parse $m = m[1] \parallel m[2] \parallel \cdots \parallel m[\ell_m]$.
– Compute $z^* := \bigoplus_{\mathsf{pk} \in \mathsf{B}} z^*_{\mathsf{pk}}$ where $\mathsf{B}[\mathsf{pk}] = (\{\mathsf{sk}_{i,b}\}_{i,b}, z^*_{\mathsf{pk}})$.
– Compute $\widetilde{\mathsf{sk}} := i\mathcal{O}(\mathcal{D}[\{\mathsf{sk}_{i,z^*[i]\oplus m[i]}\}_i, z^* \oplus m])$.
– Output $\widetilde{\mathsf{sk}}$.

Theorem 1. *The NC-RFE protocol is correct, update-efficient, and compact.*

Proof. The correctness of the NC-RFE protocol follows directly from the correctness of RFE and the perfect completeness of $\prod_{\mathsf{ZKA}}$. The simulated algorithms, SimKeyGen, SimRegPK, SimCT, SimCorrupt, Reveal, play no role in establishing correctness; they affect only the security properties of the protocol. Moreover, NC-RFE inherits the update-efficiency and compactness properties of $\prod_{\mathsf{RFE}}$.

5 Security Proof

We now analyze the security of our NC-RFE construction and prove the following theorem.

Theorem 2. *If $\prod_{RFE}$ is secure and assuming the existence of an indistinguishability obfuscator $i\mathcal{O}$ for P/poly, and an interactive zero-knowledge argument system $\prod_{\mathsf{ZKA}}$ for NP language, then the NC-RFE construction is secure.*

Proof. We define a sequence of hybrid experiments to transition between real and ideal security games.

Hyb_0: This corresponds precisely to the security experiment $\mathsf{Exp}_{\mathcal{A}}^{\mathsf{NC\text{-}RFE}}(\lambda, 0)$. Throughout the analysis, m refers to the target message chosen by $\mathcal{A}$.

Hyb_1: This hybrid modifies Hyb_0 by altering the generation of secret keys during the query phase. Instead of using the left-or-right decryption circuit $\mathcal{D}[\{\mathsf{sk}_{i,z[i]}\}_{i\in[\ell_m]}, z]$, the challenger now employs the left-only decryption circuit $\mathcal{D}_0[\{\mathsf{sk}_{i,0}\}_{i\in[\ell_m]}]$. Consequently, for each key-generation query, it provides $\widetilde{\mathsf{sk}} = i\mathcal{O}\left(\mathcal{D}_0[\{\mathsf{sk}_{i,0}\}_{i\in[\ell_m]}]\right)$, instead of $\mathsf{sk} = i\mathcal{O}\left(\mathcal{D}[\{\mathsf{sk}_{i,z[i]}\}_{i\in[\ell_m]}, z]\right)$. As a result, the secret keys in this hybrid no longer depend on the random selection bit string z (Fig. 3) and (Table 1).

Hyb_2: This game is the same as Hyb_1 apart from the fact that it transitions from real to simulated machine $\langle Sim \rangle$ of an interactive proof system given by the interactive machines $\langle \mathcal{P}, \mathcal{V} \rangle$ for an NP language $\mathcal{L}$ characterized by the relation R in the ciphertext.

Hyb_3: This game is the same as Hyb_2 except that it introduces asymmetric encryption patterns in the challenge ciphertext. Rather than encrypting the same message bit under both master public keys, the challenger now generates position-dependent encryptions. For the combined randomness $z := \bigoplus z_{\text{user}}$, where z_{user} is sampled in KeyGen for every user and each bit position $i \in [\ell_m]$, it computes:

$$\mathsf{ct}^*_{i,z[i]} \leftarrow \mathsf{RFE.Encrypt}(\widetilde{\mathsf{mpk}}_{i,z[i]}, m[i]),$$
$$\mathsf{ct}^*_{i,1-z[i]} \leftarrow \mathsf{RFE.Encrypt}(\widetilde{\mathsf{mpk}}_{i,1-z[i]}, 1 - m[i]).$$

Hyb_4: This game is the same as Hyb_3, except that it is completely independent of the target message m. The challenger uses the same combined randomness $z^* := \bigoplus z^*_{\text{user}}$, where z^*_{user} is sampled in KeyGen for every user and generates challenge ciphertexts according to:

$$\mathsf{ct}^*_{i,z^*[i]} \leftarrow \mathsf{RFE.Encrypt}(\widetilde{\mathsf{mpk}}_{i,z^*[i]}, 0),$$
$$\mathsf{ct}^*_{i,1-z^*[i]} \leftarrow \mathsf{RFE.Encrypt}(\widetilde{\mathsf{mpk}}_{i,1-z^*[i]}, 1).$$

When revealing secret keys in the final phase, the challenger computes for each honest user with randomness z^*_{user}:

$$\mathsf{sk} := i\mathcal{O}(\mathcal{D}[\{\mathsf{sk}_{i,z^*_{\text{user}}[i]\oplus m[i]}\}_{i\in[\ell_m]}, z^*_{\text{user}} \oplus m]).$$

Note that the game Hyb_4 is identical to the simulated experiment $\mathsf{Exp}_{\mathcal{A}}^{\mathsf{NC\text{-}RFE}}$ $(\lambda, 1)$.

Let the distribution of the output of an execution of Hyb_j, with $\mathcal{A}$, be denoted as $\mathsf{Hyb}_j(\mathcal{A})$. We establish computational indistinguishability between consecutive hybrid games through the reductions.

Lemma 1. *Suppose that $\prod_{\mathsf{RFE}}$ satisfies perfect correctness, $\prod_{\mathsf{ZKA}}$ achieves soundness property, and the indistinguishability obfuscator $i\mathcal{O}$ ensures security under indistinguishability. Then, the following holds,*

$$|\Pr[\mathsf{Hyb}_0(\mathcal{A}) = 1] - \Pr[\mathsf{Hyb}_1(\mathcal{A}) = 1]| \leq \mathsf{negl}(\lambda).$$

Table 1. Hybrid sequence for the security proof of NC-RFE

Hybrid	Secret Keys	uNIZK Proofs	Challenge Ciphertext	Dependence on m
Hyb_0	$i\mathcal{O}(\mathcal{D}[\{\mathsf{sk}_{i,z[i]}\}_{i\in[\ell_m]}, z])$	Real proofs	$\mathsf{ct}^*_{i,0}, \mathsf{ct}^*_{i,1}$ encrypt $m[i]$	Yes (depends on m)
	$i\mathcal{O}(\mathcal{D}_0[\{\mathsf{sk}_{i,0}\}_{i\in[\ell_m]}])$	↓	↓	↓
	↓	Simulated proofs using $\langle Sim \rangle$	↓	↓
	↓	↓	Asymmetric encryptions: $\mathsf{ct}^*_{i,z[i]}, \mathsf{ct}^*_{i,1-z[i]}$	↓
	$i\mathcal{O}(\mathcal{D}[\{\mathsf{sk}_{i,z^*_{\mathsf{user}}[i]\oplus m[i]}\}, z^*_{\mathsf{user}} \oplus m])$	↓	Encrypt fixed bits 0/1 under z^* randomness	No (independent of m)

Simulated proof $\langle Sim \rangle$ appears in Hyb_2, and asymmetric challenge ciphertexts are introduced in Hyb_3.
In Hyb_4, the ciphertext becomes entirely independent of the challenge message m.
Arrows (↓) indicate no change from the previous hybrid.

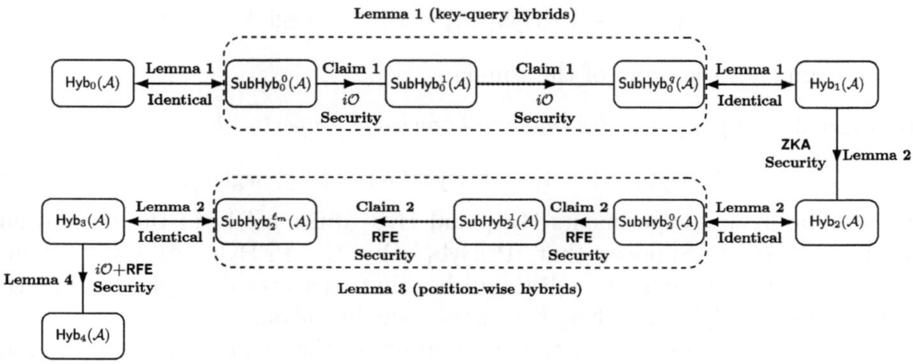

Fig. 3. Hybrid argument for the security proof.

Proof. We employ a hybrid argument over the adversary's key-generation queries. Let q denote the total number of such queries made by $\mathcal{A}$. Now, we define a sequence of hybrid sub-experiments SubHyb_0^j for each $j \in [0, q]$, where the challenger responds to the adversary's key queries as follows:

- For queries $k \in [j+1, q]$, the challenger returns $\mathsf{sk} = i\mathcal{O}\left(\mathcal{D}\left[\{\mathsf{sk}_{i,z[i]}\}_{i\in[\ell_m]}, z\right]\right)$.
- For queries $k \in [1, j]$, the challenger returns $\widetilde{\mathsf{sk}} = i\mathcal{O}\left(\mathcal{D}_0\left[\{\mathsf{sk}_{i,0}\}_{i\in[\ell_m]}\right]\right)$.

We observe that $\mathsf{SubHyb}_0^0(\mathcal{A}) = \mathsf{Hyb}_0(\mathcal{A})$, and $\mathsf{SubHyb}_0^q(\mathcal{A}) = \mathsf{Hyb}_1(\mathcal{A})$.
Let $\mathsf{Invalid}$ denote the event that there exists a statement $d^\dagger \notin \mathcal{L}$ such that for $\langle \mathcal{P}(w), \mathcal{V}(y)\rangle(d) = 1$. By the soundness of $\prod_{\mathsf{ZKA}}$, it holds that $\Pr[\mathsf{Invalid}] \leq \mathsf{negl}(\lambda)$.
Conditioned on the event $\neg\mathsf{Invalid}$, the circuits $\mathcal{D}$ and $\mathcal{D}_0$ are functionally equivalent on all valid inputs. This equivalence follows from their construction and the perfect correctness of the underlying RFE scheme. We now formalize the indistinguishability of adjacent subgames.
Claim 1. For every $j \in [1, q]$, the distinguishing advantage between hybrid subexperiments $\mathsf{SubHyb}_0^{j-1}(\mathcal{A})$ and $\mathsf{SubHyb}_0^j(\mathcal{A})$ is negligible, *i.e.*,

$$\left|\Pr[\mathsf{SubHyb}_0^{j-1}(\mathcal{A}) = 1] - \Pr[\mathsf{SubHyb}_0^j(\mathcal{A}) = 1]\right| \leq \mathsf{negl}(\lambda).$$

Proof. Consider the transition between hybrid sub-experiments SubHyb_0^{j-1} and SubHyb_0^{j}, which differ only in the j-th key query. In SubHyb_0^{j-1}, the response is $\mathsf{sk} = i\mathcal{O}\left(\mathcal{D}\left[\{\mathsf{sk}_{i,z[i]}\}_{i\in[\ell_m]}, z\right]\right)$, while in SubHyb_0^{j}, the response is $\widetilde{\mathsf{sk}} = i\mathcal{O}(\mathcal{D}_0\left[\{\mathsf{sk}_{i,0}\}_{i\in[\ell_m]}\right])$. Under the assumption $\neg\mathsf{Invalid}$, the two circuits $\mathcal{D}$ and $\mathcal{D}_0$ are functionally equivalent. Hence, by the security of indistinguishability obfuscator $i\mathcal{O}$, any QPT distinguisher can distinguish between these responses with at most negligible probability.

Applying the hybrid sub-experiments argument across the q key queries and invoking the above claim repeatedly, we conclude that

$$|\Pr[\mathsf{Hyb}_0(\mathcal{A}) = 1] - \Pr[\mathsf{Hyb}_1(\mathcal{A}) = 1]| \le q \cdot \mathsf{negl}(\lambda) = \mathsf{negl}(\lambda),$$

which completes the proof of the lemma.

Lemma 2. *If $\prod_{ZKA}$ satisfies the zero-knowledge property, then*

$$|\Pr[\mathsf{Hyb}_1(\mathcal{A}) = 1] - \Pr[\mathsf{Hyb}_2(\mathcal{A}) = 1]| \le \mathsf{negl}(\lambda).$$

Proof. The hybrid experiments Hyb_1 and Hyb_2 differ solely in the generation of the ciphertext. Suppose that $|\Pr[\mathsf{Hyb}_1(\mathcal{A}) = 1] - \Pr[\mathsf{Hyb}_2(\mathcal{A}) = 1]|$ is non-negligible. Then there exists a distinguisher that separates the ciphertext distributions used in Hyb_1 and Hyb_2 with non-negligible advantage.
This would further imply that the distributions of the real and simulated proof, namely $\langle\mathcal{P}(w), \mathcal{V}(y)\rangle(d)$ and $\langle\mathsf{Sim}\rangle(d^*, y)$, are computationally distinguishable. Such a distinguisher contradicts the zero-knowledge property of $\prod_{\mathsf{ZKA}}$, since it would allow one to efficiently distinguish the real view of the verifier from a simulated one for instances of size $|y|$ with non-negligible advantage.
Hence, by the zero-knowledge property, the advantage $\big|\Pr[\mathsf{Hyb}_1(\mathcal{A}) = 1] - \Pr[\mathsf{Hyb}_2(\mathcal{A}) = 1]\big|$ must be negligible.

Lemma 3. *If the underlying $\prod_{RFE}$ scheme is secure, then*

$$|\Pr[\mathsf{Hyb}_2(\mathcal{A}) = 1] - \Pr[\mathsf{Hyb}_3(\mathcal{A}) = 1]| \le \mathsf{negl}(\lambda).$$

Proof. We employ a position-by-position hybrid argument across the message bits. For each position $i \in [\ell_m]$, we demonstrate that modifying the encryption pattern at position i introduces at most a negligible distinguishing advantage.
We now define the hybrid sub-experiments games SubHyb_2^{j} for $j \in [0, \ell_m]$, where the challenger responds as follows:

- For positions $i \in [j+1, \ell_m]$, both ciphertexts encrypt the same message bit.

$$\mathsf{ct}^*_{i,b} \leftarrow \mathsf{RFE.Encrypt}(\widetilde{\mathsf{mpk}}_{i,b}, m[i]) \text{ for } b \in \{0,1\}$$

- For positions $i \in [1, j]$, the ciphertexts are generated using the following computation.

$$\mathsf{ct}^*_{i,1-z[i]} \leftarrow \mathsf{RFE.Encrypt}(\widetilde{\mathsf{mpk}}_{i,1-z[i]}, 1 - m[i]),$$
$$\mathsf{ct}^*_{i,z[i]} \leftarrow \mathsf{RFE.Encrypt}(\widetilde{\mathsf{mpk}}_{i,z[i]}, m[i])$$

By construction, $\mathsf{SubHyb}_2^0(\mathcal{A}) = \mathsf{Hyb}_2(\mathcal{A})$ and $\mathsf{SubHyb}_2^{\ell_m}(\mathcal{A}) = \mathsf{Hyb}_3(\mathcal{A})$. To complete the proof, we introduce the following claim.

Claim 2. For every $j \in [1, \ell_m]$, the hybrids $\mathsf{SubHyb}_2^{j-1}(\mathcal{A})$ and $\mathsf{SubHyb}_2^{j}(\mathcal{A})$ are computationally indistinguishable under the security of the RFE scheme.

Proof. To show that adjacent games SubHyb_2^{j-1} and SubHyb_2^{j} for $i \in [1, \ell_m]$, are computationally indistinguishable, we define a reduction $\mathcal{B}_{\mathsf{RFE}}$ against the security of the underlying RFE scheme. $\mathcal{B}_{\mathsf{RFE}}$ receives master public key $\widetilde{\mathsf{mpk}}$ from the RFE challenger of $\mathsf{Exp}_{\mathcal{A}}^{\mathsf{RFE}}(\lambda, b')$ for $b' \in \{0,1\}$ and sets $\widetilde{\mathsf{mpk}}_{j,1-z[j]} := \widetilde{\mathsf{mpk}}$. For all other public keys, $(i, b) \neq (j, 1 - z[j])$, it generates $\widetilde{\mathsf{mpk}}_{i,b}$ itself. It then compiles the overall master public key as $\mathsf{mpk} := \left(\{\widetilde{\mathsf{mpk}}_{i,b}\}_{i\in[\ell_m],b\in\{0,1\}}, y\right)$,

which is given to $\mathcal{A}$. Similar to before, $\mathcal{B}_{\mathsf{RFE}}$ receives $\mathsf{sk}_{j,1-z[j]}$ from the RFE challenger, and locally generates all other secret keys. Since these keys are never used in any decryption or response, the simulation remains indistinguishable. $\mathcal{B}_{\mathsf{RFE}}$ then constructs $\widetilde{\mathsf{sk}} := iO\left(\mathcal{D}_0[\{\mathsf{sk}_{i,0}\}_{i\in[\ell_m]}]\right)$.

At the challenge phase, $\mathcal{A}$ submits m to the $\mathcal{B}_{\mathsf{RFE}}$ and it sends the message pair $(m[j], 1 - m[j])$ to the RFE challenger. It then computes $\mathsf{ct}^*_{j,z[j]} \leftarrow \mathsf{RFE.Encrypt}$ $(\widetilde{\mathsf{mpk}}_{j,z[j]}, m[j])$, and all remaining ciphertexts $\mathsf{ct}^*_{i,b}$ for $i \neq j$, as in the hybrids SubHyb_2^{j-1} and SubHyb_2^{j}. Finally, it outputs whatever $\mathcal{A}$ outputs.
The reduction proceeds as follows:

- If $b' = 0$, then $\mathsf{ct}^*_{j,1-z[j]} \leftarrow \mathsf{RFE.Encrypt}(\widetilde{\mathsf{mpk}}_{j,1-z[j]}, m[j])$, which implies that $\mathcal{B}_{\mathsf{RFE}}$ perfect simulation of the hybrid sub-experiment SubHyb_2^{j-1}.
- If $b' = 1$, then $\mathsf{ct}^*_{j,1-z[j]} \leftarrow \mathsf{RFE.Encrypt}(\widetilde{\mathsf{mpk}}_{j,1-z[j]}, 1 - m[j])$, which implies that $\mathcal{B}_{\mathsf{RFE}}$ perfect simulation of the hybrid sub-experiment SubHyb_2^{j-1}.

Hence, any non-negligible advantage by $\mathcal{A}$ in distinguishing between SubHyb_2^{j-1} and SubHyb_2^{j} can be used to break the security of the RFE scheme. Therefore, the hybrid sub-experiments are computationally indistinguishable.

Applying the hybrid sub-experiment argument to all ℓ_m positions and using the above claim iteratively, we conclude that

$$|\Pr[\mathsf{Hyb}_2(\mathcal{A}) = 1] - \Pr[\mathsf{Hyb}_3(\mathcal{A}) = 1]| \leq \ell_m \cdot \mathsf{negl}(\lambda) = \mathsf{negl}(\lambda).$$

This concludes the proof of Lemma 3.

Lemma 4. *The hybrid games satisfy perfect indistinguishability:*

$$\Pr\left[\mathsf{Hyb}_3(\mathcal{A}) = 1\right] = \Pr\left[\mathsf{Hyb}_4(\mathcal{A}) = 1\right].$$

Proof. This hybrid transition is a purely formal change that preserves the adversary's view. Specifically, the two games become identical under the variable substitution $z := z^* \oplus m$.

In game Hyb_3, the challenge ciphertexts are given by: $\mathsf{ct}^*_{i,1-z[i]}$ encrypts $1-m[i]$, and $\mathsf{ct}^*_{i,z[i]}$ encrypts $m[i]$.

After applying the substitution $z := z^* \oplus m$, the ciphertexts in Hyb_4 take the form $\mathsf{ct}^*_{i,z^*[i]}$ encrypts 0, $\mathsf{ct}^*_{i,1-z^*[i]}$ encrypts 1.
Since the secret keys are generated independently of the selection string z in both hybrids, this change of variables does not affect the underlying distributions. Consequently, the adversary's view is identical across the two hybrids, and we conclude that $\Pr[\mathsf{Hyb}_3(\mathcal{A}) = 1] = \Pr[\mathsf{Hyb}_4(\mathcal{A}) = 1]$. This concludes the lemma.

Consequently, by combining Lemmas 1, 2, 3, and 4, we conclude that the NC-RFE construction satisfies security against all quantum polynomial-time adversaries.

6 Instantiation of NC-RFE from Lattices

Our generic construction of NC-RFE, presented in Sect. 4.3, is fully modular and can be instantiated from any secure registered FE scheme which satisfy perfect correctness, zero-knowledge argument system, and indistinguishability obfuscation. In this section, we give a concrete lattice-based instantiation of each component, resulting in a quantum-secure NC-RFE scheme under the hardness of plain LWE, equivocal LWE assumption.
We instantiate our generic framework using the following state-of-the-art lattice-based primitives:

- **Registered FE Component:** We employ the registered FE scheme for general function of Datta *et al.* [12,13]. This scheme supports an arbitrary number of users from indistinguishability obfuscation [10] and somewhere statistically binding hash functions [24].
- **ZKA Component:** We utilize the post-quantum secure zero-knowledge argument system of Bitansky *et al.* [2] for arbitrary NP languages. Their construction achieves soundness and zero-knowledge under the plain LWE assumption against quantum adversaries.
- **Indistinguishability Obfuscation Component:** We utilize the lattice-based $i\mathcal{O}$ construction of Cini *et al.* [10], which provides post-quantum security under the equivocal LWE assumption in conjunction with standard NTRU lattice assumptions. This represents the first plausibly post-quantum secure $i\mathcal{O}$ construction from well-studied lattice problems.

Adapting the above-mentioned component as a building block, we can construct a post-quantum secure NC-RFE protocol from lattices.

7 Conclusion

In this work, we introduced non-committing registered functional encryption (NC-RFE), extending non-committing security to the registered setting. We presented a generic construction of NC-RFE based on indistinguishability obfuscation and zero-knowledge arguments, and proved its security under a secure underlying registered functional encryption scheme. In addition, we presented a lattice-based instantiation, yielding a post-quantum secure realization of NC-RFE. An interesting direction for future research is to design more efficient NC-RFE schemes from standard assumptions such as LWE, without relying on indistinguishability obfuscation.

Acknowledgements. This study is funded by the Information Security Education and Awareness (ISEA) Project Phase-III initiatives of the Ministry of Electronics and Information Technology (MeitY) under Grant No. F.No. L-14017/1/2022-HRD. I would also like to express my sincere gratitude to Shayeef Murshid for the valuable discussions and insights.

References

1. Abdolmaleki, B., Ramacher, S., Slamanig, D.: Lift-and-shift: obtaining simulation extractable subversion and updatable snarks generically. In: Proceedings of the 2020 ACM SIGSAC Conference on Computer and Communications Security, pp.1987–2005 (2020)
2. Bitansky, N., Shmueli, O.: Post-quantum zero knowledge in constant rounds. In: Proceedings of the 52nd Annual ACM SIGACT Symposium on Theory of Computing, pp. 269–279 (2020)
3. Boneh, D., Sahai, A., Waters, B.: Functional encryption: definitions and challenges. In: Theory of Cryptography Conference, pp. 253–273. Springer (2011)
4. Brakerski, Z., Branco, P., Döttling, N., Garg, S., Malavolta, G.: Constant ciphertext-rate non-committing encryption from standard assumptions. In: Theory of Cryptography Conference, pp. 58–87. Springer (2020)
5. Brakerski, Z., Döttling, N., Garg, S., Malavolta, G.: Factoring and pairings are not necessary for io: circular-secure LWE suffices. Cryptology ePrint Archive (2020)
6. Canetti, R., Feige, U., Goldreich, O., Naor, M.: Adaptively secure multi-party computation. In: Proceedings of the Twenty-eighth Annual ACM Symposium on Theory of Computing, pp. 639–648 (1996)
7. Canetti, R., Halevi, S., Katz, J.: Adaptively-secure, non-interactive public-key encryption. In: Theory of Cryptography Conference, pp. 150–168. Springer (2005)
8. Canetti, R., Poburinnaya, O., Raykova, M.: Optimal-rate non-committing encryption. In: International Conference on the Theory and Application of Cryptology and Information Security, pp. 212–241. Springer (2017)
9. Choi, S.G., Dachman-Soled, D., Malkin, T., Wee, H.: Improved non-committing encryption with applications to adaptively secure protocols. In: International Conference on the Theory and Application of Cryptology and Information Security, pp. 287–302. Springer (2009
10. Cini, V., Lai, R.W., Woo, I.K.: Lattice-based obfuscation from NTRU and Equivocal LWE. Cryptology ePrint Archive (2025). https://link.springer.com/chapter/10.1007/978-3-032-01907-3_2
11. Cook, S.: The P versus NP problem. Clay Math. Institute **2** (2000). https://www.claymath.org/wp-content/uploads/2022/06/pvsnp.pdf
12. Datta, P., Pal, T.: Registration-based functional encryption. IACR Cryptol. ePrint Arch. **2023**, 457 (2023)

13. Datta, P., Pal, T., Yamada, S.: Registered FE beyond predicates: (attribute-based) linear functions and more. In: International Conference on the Theory and Application of Cryptology and Information Security, pp. 65–104. Springer (2024)
14. Garg, S., Hajiabadi, M., Mahmoody, M., Rahimi, A.: Registration-based encryption: removing private-key generator from IBE. In: Theory of Cryptography Conference, pp. 689–718. Springer (2018)
15. Gay, R., Pass, R.: Indistinguishability obfuscation from circular security. In: Proceedings of the 53rd Annual ACM SIGACT Symposium on Theory of Computing, pp. 736–749 (2021)
16. Goyal, R., Kitagawa, F., Koppula, V., Nishimaki, R., Rajasree, M.S., Yamakawa, T.: Non-committing identity based encryption: constructions and applications. In: IACR International Conference on Public-Key Cryptography, pp. 158–193. Springer (2025)
17. Goyal, R., Syed, R., Waters, B.: Bounded collusion ABE for TMS from IBE. In: International Conference on the Theory and Application of Cryptology and Information Security, pp. 371–402. Springer (2021)
18. Goyal, V., Pandey, O., Sahai, A., Waters, B.: Attribute-based encryption for fine-grained access control of encrypted data. In: Proceedings of the 13th ACM conference on Computer and communications security. pp. 89–98 (2006). https://doi.org/10.1145/1180405.1180418
19. Groth, J., Kohlweiss, M., Maller, M., Meiklejohn, S., Miers, I.: Updatable and universal common reference strings with applications to ZK-snarks. In: Annual International Cryptology Conference, pp. 698–728. Springer (2018)
20. Hazay, C., Patra, A., Warinschi, B.: Selective opening security for receivers. In: International Conference on the Theory and Application of Cryptology and Information Security, pp. 443–469. Springer (2015)
21. Hemenway, B., Ostrovsky, R., Richelson, S., Rosen, A.: Adaptive security with quasi-optimal rate. In: Theory of Cryptography Conference, pp. 525–541. Springer (2015)
22. Hiroka, T., Morimae, T., Nishimaki, R., Yamakawa, T.: Quantum encryption with certified deletion, revisited: public key, attribute-based, and classical communication. In: International Conference on the Theory and Application of Cryptology and Information Security, pp. 606–636. Springer (2021)
23. Hohenberger, S., Lu, G., Waters, B., Wu, D.J.: Registered attribute-based encryption. In: Annual International Conference on the Theory and Applications of Cryptographic Techniques, pp. 511–542. Springer (2023)
24. Koppula, V., Lewko, A.B., Waters, B.: Indistinguishability obfuscation for turing machines with unbounded memory. In: Proceedings of the Forty-seventh Annual ACM Symposium on Theory of Computing, pp. 419–428 (2015)
25. Murshid, S., Sarkar, R., Mandal, M.: Registered attribute-based encryption with publicly verifiable certified deletion, everlasting security, and more. Cryptology ePrint Archive (2025)
26. Nielsen, J.B.: Separating random oracle proofs from complexity theoretic proofs: the non-committing encryption case. In: Annual International Cryptology Conference, pp. 111–126. Springer (2002)
27. Sahai, A., Waters, B.: Fuzzy identity-based encryption. In: Annual international Conference on the Theory and Applications of Cryptographic Techniques, pp. 457–473. Springer (2005). https://doi.org/10.1007/11426639_27
28. Shamir, A.: Identity-based cryptosystems and signature schemes. In: Workshop on the theory and application of cryptographic techniques, pp. 47–53. Springer (1984)

29. Turing, A.M.: On computable numbers, with an application to the entscheidungsproblem. Proc. London Math. Soc. **s2-42**(1), 230–265 (1936). https://doi.org/10.1112/plms/s2-42.1.230
30. Wee, H., Wichs, D.: Candidate obfuscation via oblivious LWE sampling. In: Annual International Conference on the Theory and Applications of Cryptographic Techniques, pp. 127–156. Springer (2021)
31. Yoshida, Y., Kitagawa, F., Tanaka, K.: Non-committing encryption with quasioptimal ciphertext-rate based on the DDH problem. In: International Conference on the Theory and Application of Cryptology and Information Security, pp. 128–158.Springer (2019)

Deterministic Random-Walk Leader Election for Blockchains

Durgesh Pandey(✉) and Kannan Srinathan

International Institute of Information Technology, Hyderabad, India
durgesh.pandey@research.iiit.ac.in, srinathan@iiit.ac.in

Abstract. We present a publicly verifiable, VDF-free leader-election protocol for blockchain consensus that eliminates per-hop grinding over participant-chosen randomness. The protocol realizes a deterministic random walk over the roster using a transcript-bound BLS relay chain: at hop k, party i_k signs the canonical message $m_k = (\mathsf{DST}, M_{e,r}, \Sigma_{k-1}, i_k)$, updates Σ_k, and evaluates domain-separated hashes on the new state for leadership testing and successor selection. The first hop whose leadership coin falls below the threshold is the first *eligible* leader; if a designated successor or an eligible leader withholds, the protocol uses timeout-certified deterministic failover until a final *accepted* leader is produced.

In the random-oracle model, deterministic BLS fixes each hop signature and the evolving aggregate Σ_k yields fresh transcript-bound inputs, so the per-hop eligibility bits are i.i.d. Bernoulli(p). Hence the first eligible hop count is geometric with mean $1/p$. Under Δ-bounded synchrony, the corresponding no-withholding delay satisfies $\mathbb{E}[T] \leq \Delta/p$ and $T_\varepsilon \leq \Delta \lceil \ln(\varepsilon)/\ln(1-p) \rceil$; under exact per-hop latency Δ, these bounds are equalities. Under withholding, realized-output fairness is over the effective non-withholding set, and if an attempted hop is honest and responsive with probability h, then the accepted-leader attempt count is geometric with parameter hp, giving $\mathbb{E}[T] = (h\Delta_h + (1-h)\Delta_b)/(hp)$.

Phase I supplies a public epoch seed and governance threshold key, and epoch transitions use verifiable re-sharing of the same governance secret without public-key rotation. The relay supports transparent replay and a succinct proof mode, making the auditability/bandwidth tradeoff explicit. We prove ROM guarantees and give a scoped UC realization of the relay abstraction.

Keywords: Blockchain consensus · Leader election · Random-walk relay · Transcript binding · BLS signatures · Dynamic membership · ROM/UC security

1 Introduction

Leader election under adversaries must be *unpredictable* before finalization, *bias-resistant* once fixed, and *publicly verifiable* after execution. Blockchains and other replicated ledgers additionally require accountable progress, transparent setup,

N. El Mrabet et al. (Eds.): AFRICACRYPT 2026, LNCS 16832, pp. 434–459, 2026.
https://doi.org/10.1007/978-3-032-31130-6_18

and auditable election transcripts, with succinct verification desirable when transcripts become long. The election primitive should also compose with governance actions such as timeouts, slashing, and validator reconfiguration. Existing approaches based on VRFs, VDFs, or public beacons address different parts of these requirements, but expose different tradeoffs in timing, auditability, and bias surfaces. We study a VDF-free leader-election primitive that realizes these requirements through transcript-bound deterministic state evolution: each hop extends a unique BLS-certified prefix, derives fresh random-oracle coins from the resulting aggregate, and either terminates or advances to the next roster identity by a public rule. The resulting protocol is a deterministic random-walk relay with transparent setup, public replayability, anti-grinding by construction, and accountable failover.

The construction has two phases. Phase I outputs a public epoch seed $S^{(e)}$ and a governance threshold key $Y^{(e)}$ using transparent setup, gated recovery, dealerless DKG, and verifiable redistribution for future roster changes. Phase II uses the public round context $M_{e,r}$ to run one election round: the relay signs canonical BLS messages, maintains the aggregate state Σ_k, derives domain-separated leadership and successor coins, and applies timeout-certified failover when a successor or eligible leader withholds. The sequential cost is parameterized directly: p controls the expected signed-path length, while under withholding h controls retry pressure and the final accepted-output law.

1.1 Problem Statement and Contributions

Problem and Objective. We seek a Byzantine-resilient, VDF-free leader-election primitive for blockchains and replicated ledgers that is unpredictable before the accepted output is fixed, bias-resistant, publicly verifiable in transparent or succinct mode, compatible with transparent setup and dynamic membership, and accompanied by explicit latency and bandwidth tradeoffs. We formalize a relay-based election primitive whose randomness is transcript-bound, whose accepted execution is publicly replayable, and whose failover behavior is deterministic and accountable. The main design objective is to remove per-hop grinding while keeping the sequential relay cost explicit through p, h, and the timeout parameters.

Contributions. First, we define a deterministic BLS relay chain: each hop signs $m_k = (\mathsf{DST}, M_{e,r}, \Sigma_{k-1}, i_k)$, updates Σ_k, derives the leadership coin $h_k = \mathcal{H}_2(\mathsf{DST}_{\text{lead}} \parallel pk_{i_k} \parallel M_{e,r} \parallel \Sigma_k)$, and, on non-success, derives the ordinary successor seed $u_k = \mathcal{H}_3(\mathsf{DST}_{\text{next}} \parallel pk_{i_k} \parallel M_{e,r} \parallel \Sigma_k)$. BLS uniqueness eliminates intra-hop grinding. Second, we give exact random-oracle probability bounds: the first eligible success is geometric with realized parameter $p = \tau_L/2^{\ell}$, while under withholding the final accepted output is governed by parameter hp. Third, Phase I supplies a public epoch seed $S^{(e)}$ and governance key $Y^{(e)}$, with gated recovery, admission controls, and verifiable re-sharing that preserves the governance public key across epochs. Fourth, the protocol supports transparent replay and a succinct proof mode for accepted-path accountability. Finally, we prove random-oracle guarantees for unpredictability, initiator and first-eligible fairness, realized final-output fairness over the effective non-withholding set, accountability, and liveness, and we give a scoped UC realization of the relay abstraction.

Claims and Limits. We analyze three random objects: the initiator $I_{e,r}$, the first eligible leader $\widetilde{L}_{e,r}$, and the final accepted leader $L_{e,r}$. The theorem set gives exact uniform public indexing for $I_{e,r}$, uniform fairness of $\widetilde{L}_{e,r}$, public verifiability and accountability of accepted transcripts, and geometric liveness with dependence on p and, under withholding, on h. For $L_{e,r}$, the realized output law is uniform over the fixed effective non-withholding set $E_{e,r}$. A stake-weighted extension requires replacing every use of INDEX by a canonical public weighted sampler and is outside the main theorem. The analysis is for a single authenticated roster per epoch and a sequential relay with explicit latency and bandwidth costs; federated multi-roster deployments and same-round full-roster final-output fairness under Byzantine withholding are outside this model.

1.2 Intuition and Background

Deterministic Randomness from Deterministic Inputs. Let $\mathcal{H} : \{0,1\}^* \to \{0,1\}^\ell$ be modeled as a random oracle with explicit domain separation. For epoch e and round r, let $M_{e,r}$ be the public round context and let Σ_k be the aggregate relay state after hop k, with $\Sigma_{-1} := \mathsf{neutral}$. A leadership query has the form $h_k = \mathcal{H}(\mathsf{DST}_{\text{lead}} \parallel pk_{i_k} \parallel M_{e,r} \parallel \Sigma_k)$. Once Σ_k is fixed by the transcript, h_k is uniform and publicly recomputable; before Σ_k exists, it is unpredictable. The task is therefore to evolve Σ_k by a public deterministic rule, leaving no local resampling freedom, and to ensure signature uniqueness for the messages that advance it. We realize this with a BLS relay chain whose canonical hop message binds $M_{e,r}$, the previous aggregate Σ_{k-1}, and the current identity i_k.

Relay Mechanics. Fix the epoch roster $\mathcal{P}_e = \{0, \dots, n_e - 1\}$ with BLS keys (pk_i, sk_i). The public context is $M_{e,r} = (\mathsf{DST}, e, r, S^{(e)}, \mathsf{ctx}_{e,r})$, where $S^{(e)}$ is the Phase I seed and $\mathsf{ctx}_{e,r}$ binds the roster and public parameters. The initiator is $i_0 := \text{INDEX}(\mathcal{H}_3(\mathsf{DST}_{\text{idx}} \parallel M_{e,r}), n_e)$, using rejection sampling to remove modulo bias. Hop j signs $m_j = (\mathsf{DST}, M_{e,r}, \Sigma_{j-1}, i_j)$, obtains $\sigma_{i_j} = \mathsf{Sign}(sk_{i_j}, m_j)$, and updates $\Sigma_j = \Sigma_{j-1} \cdot \sigma_{i_j}$. BLS determinism gives a unique signature for fixed m_j, so each valid prefix determines a unique aggregate state and admits no intra-hop grinding.

Leadership, Successor Selection, and Verification. At hop k, party i_k computes $h_k := \mathcal{H}_2(\mathsf{DST}_{\text{lead}} \parallel pk_{i_k} \parallel M_{e,r} \parallel \Sigma_k)$. With threshold τ_L, the realized per-hop success probability is $p = \tau_L / 2^\ell$. If $\mathsf{ToInt}(h_k) < \tau_L$, the hop is eligible to terminate. Otherwise, the ordinary successor is derived from the separate seed $u_k := \mathcal{H}_3(\mathsf{DST}_{\text{next}} \parallel pk_{i_k} \parallel M_{e,r} \parallel \Sigma_k)$, giving $i_{k+1} = \text{INDEX}(u_k, n_e)$. If the designated successor does not acknowledge, failover proceeds under $\mathsf{DST}_{\text{fail}}$. The transcript is self-verifying: anyone recomputes m_j, verifies σ_{i_j}, recomputes h_j and u_j, and checks that ordinary or failover successors follow the public rule.

First Eligible Leader and Random-Walk Law. Under the random-oracle model and BLS uniqueness, the leadership inputs are fresh and domain-separated, so the per-hop indicators $\mathcal{I}_k := \mathbf{1}(\mathsf{ToInt}(h_k) < \tau_L)$ are i.i.d. Bernoulli(p). Hence the number of tests until first eligibility is geometric with mean $1/p$. Under Δ-bounded synchrony, no-withholding latency is bounded by the corresponding geometric tail; exact formulas and numerical instantiations are given in Sect. 4.

Withholding and Failover. Cycles, revisits, and self-loops are allowed; verification checks rule compliance, not acyclicity. If successors or eligible leaders withhold, timeout certificates activate deterministic failover under $\mathsf{DST}_{\mathsf{fail}}$. With effective honest/responsive rate h, final completion is governed by parameter hp, while realized final-output fairness is only over the effective non-withholding set. Timeout certificates provide objective evidence for slashing or expulsion, but do not restore full-roster fairness in the same round.

1.3 Organization

Sect. 2 reviews related work. Sections 3–7 give the model, probability analysis, Phase I setup, Phase II relay protocol, and ROM/UC security analysis.

2 Related Work

Leader election in BFT and blockchain protocols is usually coupled to consensus or public randomness. Classical partial synchrony was formalized by Dwork–Lynch–Stockmeyer [1]; PBFT [2], HotStuff [3], and Narwhal–Tusk [4] illustrate the evolution from quadratic communication to pipelined and DAG-based designs. In blockchain settings, Algorand uses VRF-based cryptographic sortition [5], while Ouroboros and Praos analyze stake-weighted leader schedules [6,7]. These approaches motivate the same requirements as ours: unpredictability before fixing the leader, limited bias, and public auditability.

Random walks have been studied as abstract leader-election mechanisms. Alsmeyer, Kabluchko, and Marynych analyze leader election using random walks as a probabilistic/asymptotic process [33]. Their model does not address transcript binding, public verification of each transition, Byzantine withholding, timeout certificates, or governed blockchain membership. Our random walk is cryptographic: transitions are induced by deterministic BLS state evolution, ordinary successor selection is domain-separated from leadership testing, and accepted transcripts are publicly verifiable.

Public randomness beacons based on threshold cryptography or PVSS, such as RandHound/RandHerd [10], SCRAPE [11], HydRand [12], and drand [13], provide verifiable randomness but require threshold coordination per beacon. Commit–reveal beacons such as RANDAO are simple but face selective-abort and last-revealer bias [15,16]; HashRand gives an asynchronous hash-based beacon under a different trust and communication model [14]. Our Phase I uses transparent setup and gated recovery for an epoch seed, while Phase II is not a beacon: it is a transcript-bound relay election.

VDFs provide sequentially hard outputs with succinct proofs [19–21], but impose evaluator cost and timing assumptions. VRFs [8,9] support cheap local eligibility tests, but the relevant attack surfaces include key grinding, immediate computability after seed revelation, and seed influence through chain state. Our relay removes per-hop resampling: BLS signatures are deterministic on canonical messages, random-oracle inputs are transcript-bound, and exact rejection sampling removes modulo bias in initiator and successor selection.

The setup/governance layer follows dynamic proactive secret-sharing ideas. CHURP [17] and COBRA [18] study reconfiguration and churn-robust secret sharing for blockchain-style or BFT settings. We use this line only for governance: the public epoch seed is not re-shared, while the governance secret is redistributed across epochs without reconstruction. BLS signatures [22,23], proof-of-possession techniques [25], and hashing-to-curve standards [24] provide the signature layer; standard succinct proof systems [30,31] can compress verification of a valid accepted path. Our analysis uses the random-oracle methodology [28] and UC composition [29].

3 Security Model

We specify the execution model, adversary, cryptographic assumptions, target security properties, and UC functionalities for the BLS-relay election. The security parameter is λ, and hash outputs have length $\ell = \Theta(\lambda)$, defaulting to $\ell = \lambda$. We write $\mathcal{H}_1$ for the BLS hash-to-curve map. The maps $\mathcal{H}_2, \mathcal{H}_3, \mathcal{H}_4$ are domain-separated interfaces to the same random oracle $\mathcal{H}$; equivalently, each call is a call to $\mathcal{H}$ with a disjoint role tag. We use domain-separation tags $\mathsf{DST}, \mathsf{DST}_{\text{lead}}, \mathsf{DST}_{\text{next}}, \mathsf{DST}_{\text{idx}}, \mathsf{DST}_{\text{fail}}, \mathsf{DST}_{\text{timeout}}, \mathsf{DST}_{\text{commit}}, \mathsf{DST}_{\text{unseal}}, \mathsf{DST}_{\text{seed}}, \mathsf{DST}_{\text{evolve}}, \mathsf{DST}_{\text{gov}}$ for canonical hop messages, leadership, ordinary successor selection, indexing, failover, timeout statements, and Phase I/governance messages. Phase I outputs the epoch seed $S^{(e)}$; round r in epoch e uses public context $M_{e,r} = (\mathsf{DST}, e, r, S^{(e)}, \mathsf{ctx}_{e,r})$ and UC session identifier $\mathsf{sid} := (\mathsf{DST}, e, r)$. By default, Phase II uses $M_{e,r}$ directly; an implementation may additionally bind a lagged ledger digest $D_{e,r}$ derived from $M_{e,r}$ and a previously finalized block header. The model has one authenticated roster $\mathcal{P}_e$ per epoch. Membership changes occur only at epoch boundaries and affect future contexts. Federated or cross-jurisdictional aggregation is outside the theorem set.

3.1 System and Network Model

Parties and Keys. In epoch e, governance maintains the authenticated roster $\mathcal{P}_e = \{P_i : i \in [n_e]\}$, where $[n_e] = \{0, \ldots, n_e - 1\}$. Each party is PPT, has identity id_i, and holds a BLS key pair (sk_i, pk_i) registered through the ledger/PKI with a proof of possession to prevent rogue-key attacks under aggregation.
Partial Synchrony. Communication is over authenticated channels. There

exists an unknown global stabilization time GST and an unknown but fixed delay bound $\Delta > 0$ such that after GST, any honest-to-honest message is delivered within Δ; before GST, no timing guarantee holds. Liveness is stated post-GST, while safety and accountability are timing-agnostic.

Timing and Threshold. After GST, honest relay steps complete within $\Delta_h \leq \Delta$, while timeout steps use $\Delta_b \geq \Delta_h$. For a target per-hop leadership probability $p^\star \in (0,1)$, set $\tau_L := \max\{1, \lfloor p^\star 2^\ell \rfloor\}$ and write $p := \tau_L/2^\ell$ for the realized threshold probability. Then $1 \leq \tau_L \leq 2^\ell - 1$ and $|p - p^\star| < 2^{-\ell}$. All geometric laws use the realized probability p.

3.2 Adversarial Model

The adversary $\mathcal{A}$ is PPT, rushing within each round, and controls the network scheduler subject to partial synchrony. Corruptions may be static or adaptive; upon corruption, the keys and local state of the party are revealed and arbitrary deviation is allowed.

Capabilities. $\mathcal{A}$ may delay, drop, or reorder messages, pre-GST arbitrarily and post-GST within the synchrony bound. It may instruct corrupted parties to equivocate, withhold relays, suppress halting broadcasts, or attempt key/message grinding before key registration.

Limitations. $\mathcal{A}$ cannot forge signatures under honest keys, cannot predict or bias random-oracle outputs on fresh inputs, and cannot bias public index selection because rejection sampling is exact, except for negligible random-oracle or collision events. Post-GST, the scheduler respects the delay bound Δ.

Honesty Rate. Let $h \in (0,1]$ be a lower bound on the per-attempt probability that the designated next hop is honest and responsive under the uniform public Index distribution. If $E_{e,r}$ is a fixed honest/responsive subset, then $h = |E_{e,r}|/n_e$. Liveness and final-output fairness are conditional on this effective responsiveness bound; adaptive corruptions are allowed only subject to maintaining such a bound. The election primitive itself does not require $n_e \geq 3t+1$; such thresholds arise when it is composed with a BFT consensus or governance layer.

3.3 Cryptographic Assumptions

Random Oracle. A hash $\mathcal{H} : \{0,1\}^* \to \{0,1\}^\ell$ is modeled as a random oracle: distinct inputs map to independent uniform outputs, and repeated inputs replay the same output. Distinct uses are domain-separated by DST-tags. In the ROM we treat $\mathcal{H}$ as ideal; in UC we use a global $\mathcal{F}_{\mathsf{RO}}$.

BLS Signatures. Let $(\mathbb{G}_1, \mathbb{G}_2, e)$ be bilinear groups of prime order $q = \Theta(2^\lambda)$ with generator $g \in \mathbb{G}_1$. Hash-to-curve follows RFC 9380; messages are canonically serialized and domain-separated. We assume EUF-CMA security, deterministic uniqueness for fixed (pk, m), and aggregation soundness for the per-hop product relation used by the relay. Proofs of possession at registration preclude rogue-key attacks under aggregation.

Threshold Encryption (Phase I Recovery Only). The gated recovery path in Phase I assumes a threshold-encryption scheme with public key $\mathsf{TEPK}^{(e)}$, correctness of decryption from any $2t_e + 1$ valid shares, and semantic security against coalitions smaller than that threshold. Publicly verifiable decryption-share proofs are assumed when recovery is invoked. This primitive is used only to release missing committed seed contributions after an authorized unseal step and does not affect the Phase II relay law.

Index Selection. The main protocol uses uniform public selection. The next hop is computed by a public map $\mathsf{Index} : \{0,1\}^\ell \times [n_e] \rightarrow [n_e]$ implemented by random-oracle-based rejection sampling: let $A = \lfloor 2^\ell / n_e \rfloor n_e$, return $\mathsf{ToInt}(x) \bmod n_e$ if $\mathsf{ToInt}(x) < A$, and otherwise resample on $x' = \mathcal{H}_3(\mathsf{DST}_{\text{idx}} \parallel x \parallel n_e)$. This yields exact uniformity on $[n_e]$ and expected trials $< 1/(1 - n_e/2^\ell)$. A stake-weighted variant requires replacing Index everywhere by a canonical weighted sampler; it is not part of the main theorem.

Freshness Implies i.i.d. Leadership Tests. For hop k, the canonical message is $m_k = (\mathsf{DST}, M_{e,r}, \Sigma_{k-1}, i_k)$, or its $D_{e,r}$-bound variant when ledger binding is enabled. Deterministic BLS fixes a unique σ_{i_k} for m_k, so each valid transcript prefix determines a unique aggregate $\Sigma_k = \prod_{j=0}^{k} \sigma_{i_j}$. The leadership coin $h_k := \mathcal{H}(\mathsf{DST}_{\text{lead}} \parallel pk_{i_k} \parallel M_{e,r} \parallel \Sigma_k)$ is therefore random-oracle uniform on a fresh transcript-bound input at each hop, except with negligible repeated-input probability over polynomially many valid hops. The success indicators $\mathbf{1}(\mathsf{ToInt}(h_k) < \tau_L)$ are i.i.d. Bernoulli(p). Ordinary successor selection uses the separate seed $u_k := \mathcal{H}(\mathsf{DST}_{\text{next}} \parallel pk_{i_k} \parallel M_{e,r} \parallel \Sigma_k)$, while failover uses $\mathsf{DST}_{\text{fail}}$; thus leadership testing, ordinary successor selection, and failover are domain-separated.

3.4 Security Properties

We formalize unpredictability, fairness, liveness, and accountability. Probabilities are over random-oracle answers and $\mathcal{A}$'s coins; timing statements hold post-GST.

Leader Variables. For round (e, r), let $I_{e,r}$ be the initiator selected by the public indexing rule. Since protocol hops are indexed from 0, let $\widetilde{X}_{e,r} := \inf\{x \geq 1 : \mathsf{ToInt}(h_{x-1}) < \tau_L\}$ be the number of leadership tests until the first eligible success, let $\widetilde{K}_{e,r} := \widetilde{X}_{e,r} - 1$ be the corresponding hop index, and let $\widetilde{L}_{e,r} := i_{\widetilde{K}_{e,r}}$. Thus $\widetilde{L}_{e,r}$ is the first eligible identity, ignoring withholding. For the realized output, let $K_{e,r}$ be the terminal hop index of the first publicly accepted transcript, and let $L_{e,r} := i_{K_{e,r}}$. Thus $L_{e,r}$ is the final accepted leader output by the protocol. The attempt count $N_{e,r}$, used in the liveness analysis, is defined separately and counts retries/timeouts; $K_{e,r}$ counts signed hops in the accepted transcript. If withholding is absent, then $\widetilde{K}_{e,r} = K_{e,r}$ and $\widetilde{L}_{e,r} = L_{e,r}$. Let $E_{e,r} \subseteq \mathcal{P}_e$ denote the effective subset of identities that, if selected at a successful hop, do not suppress the outcome; conservatively, one may take $E_{e,r}$ to be the honest/responsive subset.

Unpredictability. Consider the game where $\mathcal{A}$ outputs a guess $\widehat{L}_{e,r}$ before any honest party has computed the accepted-leader transcript prefix $\Sigma_{K_{e,r}}$. The protocol is ε-unpredictable if $\Pr(\widehat{L}_{e,r} = L_{e,r}) \leq \max_{i \in \mathcal{P}_e} \Pr(L_{e,r} = i) + \varepsilon$. Thus the

adversary's advantage over the best a priori single identity is at most ε.
Fairness / bias resistance. Let $\mu_i^{\mathsf{init}} := \Pr(I_{e,r} = i)$, $\mu_i^{\mathsf{elig}} := \Pr(\widetilde{L}_{e,r} = i)$, and $\mu_i^{\mathsf{real}} := \Pr(L_{e,r} = i)$. For the uniform protocol, we require $\max_{i \in \mathcal{P}_e} |\mu_i^{\mathsf{init}} - 1/n_e| \le \delta$ and $\max_{i \in \mathcal{P}_e} |\mu_i^{\mathsf{elig}} - 1/n_e| \le \delta$. For the final accepted leader under withholding, let $E_{e,r} \subseteq \mathcal{P}_e$ be a fixed effective non-withholding set with $|E_{e,r}| > 0$; then $\max_{i \in E_{e,r}} |\mu_i^{\mathsf{real}} - 1/|E_{e,r}|| \le \delta$. Thus final-output fairness under withholding is stated over the effective set, not over identities that can suppress their own successful output.
Liveness. Post-GST, define an attempt as selecting a next hop and either completing at an honest party within Δ_h or timing out at a Byzantine party within Δ_b. Let $N_{e,r}$ be the number of attempts until the protocol outputs a final accepted leader $L_{e,r}$, and let τ_t be the duration of attempt t. Only effective attempts can halt; the per-attempt success probability is hp, so $N_{e,r} \sim \mathrm{Geom}(hp)$ and $\Pr(N_{e,r} > t) = (1 - hp)^t$. If each attempt lasts at most Δ, where $\Delta \ge \max\{\Delta_h, \Delta_b\}$, then $T = \sum_{t=1}^{N_{e,r}} \tau_t \le \Delta N_{e,r}$, and therefore $\Pr(T > \Delta t) \le (1 - hp)^t$. The $(1-\varepsilon)$-time quantile is $T_\varepsilon \le \Delta \lceil \ln(\varepsilon)/\ln(1-hp) \rceil$. If attempts have common mean $\mathbb{E}[\tau_t] \le \bar{\Delta}$ and are independent of future survival events, Wald's identity gives $\mathbb{E}[T] = \bar{\Delta}/(hp)$.

Accountability. There exists a polynomial-time public verifier $\mathcal{V}$ that accepts exactly transcripts where: (i) the initiator is obtained by public Index; (ii) each hop signature verifies on $m_j = (\mathsf{DST}, M_{e,r}, \Sigma_{j-1}, i_j)$, or on the $D_{e,r}$-bound variant; (iii) each non-final ordinary transition follows $i_{j+1} = \mathsf{Index}(u_j, n_e)$, with $u_j = \mathcal{H}(\mathsf{DST}_{\text{next}} \parallel pk_{i_j} \parallel M_{e,r} \parallel \Sigma_j)$; (iv) failover transitions match the active timeout count in $\mathsf{TOLog}_{e,r}$, use target-bound timeout certificates, and follow the $\mathsf{DST}_{\text{fail}}$-derived fallback rule; and (v) only the last accepted hop satisfies $\mathsf{ToInt}(h_j) < \tau_L$. Any invalid signature, wrong successor, stale timeout branch, early success, or timeout without response yields transferable evidence. Cycles are allowed; verification checks rule compliance, not acyclicity.

Sanity Check. In the ROM, the leadership coins are i.i.d. uniform on fresh inputs, hence the number of leadership tests until first eligibility satisfies $\widetilde{X}_{e,r} \sim \mathrm{Geom}(p)$, $\mathbb{E}[\widetilde{X}_{e,r}] = 1/p$, and $\mathrm{Var}(\widetilde{X}_{e,r}) = (1-p)/p^2$. With withholding, the protocol output is governed by the accepted-leader attempt count $N_{e,r} \sim \mathrm{Geom}(hp)$, so all final time and tail bounds use hp rather than p.

3.5 Ideal Functionalities for UC Analysis

We work in UC with global setup. For a fixed epoch roster and round context, Phase II is analyzed in the $(\mathcal{F}_{\mathsf{RO}}, \mathcal{F}_{\mathsf{BLS}})$-hybrid. The full dynamic protocol, including epoch-transition re-sharing, is analyzed in the $(\mathcal{F}_{\mathsf{RO}}, \mathcal{F}_{\mathsf{BLS}}, \mathcal{F}_{\mathsf{VSR}})$-hybrid. The session identifier is $\mathsf{sid} = (\mathsf{DST}, e, r)$.

$\mathcal{F}_{\mathsf{RO}}$ is a global programmable random oracle: on first query (sid, x), it samples an ℓ-bit value and returns the same value on repeated queries. All role tags, including $\mathsf{DST}_{\text{lead}}, \mathsf{DST}_{\text{next}}, \mathsf{DST}_{\text{idx}}, \mathsf{DST}_{\text{fail}}$, are part of x. $\mathcal{F}_{\mathsf{BLS}}$ abstracts deterministic signing and public verification for registered BLS keys, relying on EUF-

CMA security, proof of possession, and aggregation soundness. $\mathcal{F}_{\mathsf{RELAY}}$ abstracts the canonical relay transcript with timeout-log failover. It samples the initiator from the public uniform Index rule, samples independent leadership coins and successor seeds for each hop, records adversarial delivery or withholding choices, records timeout events in the public timeout log, follows the deterministic $\mathsf{DST}_{\text{fail}}$-based failover rule after certified timeouts, and outputs the first accepted successful transcript. Thus the functionality outputs the final accepted leader, not necessarily the first eligible leader. It verifies that all strict prefixes are non-successes, all timeout-log branches are canonical, and all transitions follow the public rule. $\mathcal{F}_{\mathsf{LE}}$ wraps $\mathcal{F}_{\mathsf{RELAY}}$ and outputs the final accepted leader and transcript. $\mathcal{F}_{\mathsf{VSR}}$ abstracts the epoch-transition procedure of Sect. 5.2: on a valid governance certificate, it updates the future roster, redistributes fresh shares of the same governance secret to the new roster, preserves the public key $Y = g^{\kappa}$, and leaves the public epoch seed and any already fixed round context unchanged.

For a fixed $M_{e,r}$, the real Phase II protocol maps to $\mathcal{F}_{\mathsf{RELAY}}$ by binding each prefix to Σ_k with deterministic BLS, obtaining leadership coins under $\mathsf{DST}_{\text{lead}}$, ordinary successor seeds under $\mathsf{DST}_{\text{next}}$, indexing recursion under $\mathsf{DST}_{\text{idx}}$, and failover seeds under $\mathsf{DST}_{\text{fail}}$, and computing successors through the public Index rule. If ledger binding is enabled, the public digest $D_{e,r}$ is an additional deterministic input and does not change the realization argument. By UC composition, the dynamic protocol realizes $\mathcal{F}_{\mathsf{LE}}$ in the $(\mathcal{F}_{\mathsf{RO}}, \mathcal{F}_{\mathsf{BLS}}, \mathcal{F}_{\mathsf{VSR}})$-hybrid, with the simulator argument given in Sect. 7.

4 Mathematical Model

This section gives the probability model used for the latency, withholding, and fairness bounds. We distinguish two random quantities. First, X is the number of leadership tests until the first eligible success; this governs the no-withholding signed-path length. Second, N is the number of attempts until a final accepted leader is produced under withholding; this governs realized completion time and depends on the effective honesty rate h.

4.1 Protocol-Specific Probability Model

We model $\mathcal{H} : \{0,1\}^* \to \{0,1\}^{\ell}$ as a random oracle: distinct inputs give independent uniform outputs, while repeated queries are consistent. Domain separation uses disjoint tags $(\mathsf{DST}, \mathsf{DST}_{\text{lead}}, \mathsf{DST}_{\text{next}}, \mathsf{DST}_{\text{idx}}, \mathsf{DST}_{\text{fail}})$. In a fixed election round (e, r) with public context $M_{e,r}$, hop k signs the canonical message $m_k = (\mathsf{DST}, M_{e,r}, \Sigma_{k-1}, i_k)$, producing a deterministic BLS signature $\sigma_{i_k} = \mathsf{Sign}(sk_{i_k}, m_k)$ and aggregate state $\Sigma_k = \prod_{j=0}^{k} \sigma_{i_j}$, with $\Sigma_{-1} := \mathsf{neutral}$.

The leadership coin and ordinary successor seed are derived from separate domain-separated inputs: $h_k := \mathcal{H}(\mathsf{DST}_{\text{lead}} \parallel pk_{i_k} \parallel M_{e,r} \parallel \Sigma_k)$, and $u_k := \mathcal{H}(\mathsf{DST}_{\text{next}} \parallel pk_{i_k} \parallel M_{e,r} \parallel \Sigma_k)$. The leadership test is $\mathsf{ToInt}(h_k) < \tau_L$, while ordinary successor selection uses $i_{k+1} = \textsc{Index}(u_k, n_e)$, with rejection-sampling recursion under $\mathsf{DST}_{\text{idx}}$ as specified by $\textsc{Index}$. Since deterministic BLS fixes the signature on each canonical hop message, each valid transcript prefix determines a unique aggregate state. Thus, under the random-oracle model and the uniqueness/aggregation assumptions from Sect. 3.3, leadership inputs are fresh across valid hops, including revisits. The indicators $\mathcal{I}_k := \mathbf{1}(\mathsf{ToInt}(h_k) < \tau_L)$ are therefore i.i.d. Bernoulli(p), where $p := \tau_L/2^\ell$ is the realized threshold probability fixed by the integer threshold τ_L. Dynamic membership and verifiable re-sharing occur only between epochs, so the analysis below is conditional on a fixed epoch roster $\mathcal{P}_e$, fixed public context $M_{e,r}$, and fixed public parameters.

4.2 First Eligible Leader and No-Withholding Delay

Let X denote the number of leadership tests until the first eligible success, with $X = 1$ if the first tested hop succeeds: $X := \inf\{x \geq 1 : \mathcal{I}_{x-1} = 1\}$. Then $X \sim \mathrm{Geom}(p)$, so $\Pr(X = x) = (1-p)^{x-1}p$, $\mathbb{E}[X] = \frac{1}{p}$, $\Pr(X > t) = (1-p)^t$. For $\varepsilon \in (0,1)$, the $(1-\varepsilon)$-quantile of X is $x_\varepsilon = \left\lceil \frac{\ln(\varepsilon)}{\ln(1-p)} \right\rceil$. Let $\Delta > 0$ be a post-GST per-hop latency bound. Under Δ-bounded synchrony, the no-withholding time $\widetilde{T}$ to the first eligible success satisfies $\widetilde{T} \leq \Delta X$, hence $\mathbb{E}[\widetilde{T}] \leq \frac{\Delta}{p}$, $\Pr(\widetilde{T} > \Delta t) \leq (1-p)^t$, $\widetilde{T}_\varepsilon \leq \Delta x_\varepsilon$. Under exact-$\Delta$ synchrony, these become equalities: $\widetilde{T} = \Delta X$, $\mathbb{E}[\widetilde{T}] = \frac{\Delta}{p}$, $\widetilde{T}_\varepsilon = \Delta x_\varepsilon$. Rows 1–2 of Table 1 instantiate these no-withholding formulas. With withholding, the final accepted leader is governed by the attempt count N, not by X.

4.3 Withholding and Final Accepted Leader

Let $E_{e,r} \subseteq \mathcal{P}_e$ be a fixed effective set of identities that release a successful output, chosen independently of the fresh leadership coins, and let $h := |E_{e,r}|/n_e$. Model attempt t by a responsiveness bit $R_t \sim \mathrm{Bernoulli}(h)$ and an independent leadership bit $I_t \sim \mathrm{Bernoulli}(p)$. The attempt produces a final accepted leader exactly when $R_t I_t = 1$. Hence the effective success probability is hp, the attempt count satisfies $N \sim \mathrm{Geom}(hp)$, and $\mathbb{E}[N] = 1/(hp)$ with tail $\Pr(N > t) = (1-hp)^t$.

Let a responsive attempt take Δ_h and a withholding attempt time out in Δ_b, where $\Delta_h \leq \Delta_b$. A first-step calculation gives $\mathbb{E}[T] = (h\Delta_h + (1-h)\Delta_b)/(hp)$. For $\varepsilon \in (0,1)$, define $n_\varepsilon := \lceil \ln(\varepsilon)/\ln(1-hp) \rceil$. Since at most $n_\varepsilon - 1$ failed attempts precede the successful one, $T_\varepsilon \leq \Delta_b(n_\varepsilon - 1) + \Delta_h$. A simpler conservative form is $n_\varepsilon \leq \lceil \ln(1/\varepsilon)/(hp) \rceil$, giving $T_\varepsilon \leq \Delta_b \lceil \ln(1/\varepsilon)/(hp) \rceil$.

The same model gives the final-output law. For any $i \in E_{e,r}$, the per-attempt probability of outputting i is p/n_e, while the total halting probability is $p|E_{e,r}|/n_e$. Therefore $\Pr(L_{e,r} = i) = 1/|E_{e,r}|$, so the final accepted leader is uniform over the effective non-withholding set. More generally, if identity i releases an eligible output with probability $a_i \in [0,1]$, independently of the fresh leadership coin, then the realized law is proportional to a_i: $\Pr(L_{e,r} = i) = a_i/A$, where $A := \sum_j a_j > 0$. Timeout certificates and slashing provide accountability and liveness pressure, but they do not restore full-roster fairness within the same round.

4.4 Numerical Parameter Instantiations

Table 1 instantiates the closed-form latency formulas. Rows 1–2 use the no-withholding first-eligible model $X \sim \mathrm{Geom}(p)$. Rows 3–4 use the withholding model $N \sim \mathrm{Geom}(hp)$ with $T_{99} \leq \Delta_b(N_{0.01} - 1) + \Delta_h$. The table gives formula-level latency instantiations rather than implementation measurements; communication costs are quantified in Sect. 6.5.

Table 1. Representative latency instantiations. Rows 1–2 use $X \sim \mathrm{Geom}(p)$; rows 3–4 use $N \sim \mathrm{Geom}(hp)$.

p	h	Δ_h	Δ_b	mean count	$\mathbb{E}[T]$	T_{99}
1/16	1.0	1.0s	–	16	16.0s	72.0s
1/8	1.0	0.5s	–	8	4.0s	17.5s
1/16	0.8	0.5s	2.0s	20	16.0s	178.5s
1/16	0.4	0.5s	2.0s	40	56.0s	362.5s

5 Phase I: Transparent Setup

Phase I runs once per epoch e. It outputs an epoch seed $S^{(e)}$, used in $M_{e,r}$, and a governance public key $Y^{(e)} = g^{\kappa^{(e)}}$, whose secret is threshold-shared among the epoch roster. The seed supplies public entropy for round contexts; the governance key authorizes timeout certificates, unseal certificates, admission decisions, slashing, and roster updates. All messages use canonical encodings and explicit domain separation.

5.1 Seed Generation with Gated Recovery

Let $\mathcal{P}_e = \{P_i : i \in [n_e]\}$ with $n_e \geq 3t_e + 1$. Each P_i commits to $r_i \leftarrow \{0,1\}^\ell$ by $c_i = \mathcal{H}(\mathsf{DST}_{\mathsf{commit}} \parallel e \parallel i \parallel r_i)$, signs the commitment, and later reveals r_i with a reveal signature. Anyone accepts a reveal only if the signatures verify and the commitment opens correctly.

To guarantee output, each dealer also posts encrypted recovery material for r_i: a verifiable sharing of r_i whose evaluations are encrypted under the epoch threshold-encryption key $\mathsf{TEPK}^{(e)}$. If P_i withholds past the reveal deadline, parties first record a $2t_e + 1$ unseal certificate on $\mathsf{serialize}(\mathsf{DST}_{\mathsf{unseal}}, e, i)$. Only then are threshold decryption shares accepted, and r_i is reconstructed from $t_e + 1$ valid evaluations. This prevents a $t_e + 1$ coalition from reconstructing contributions before the authorized fallback step.

Let $\mathcal{V}_e$ be the set of indices whose contributions are revealed or recovered. The epoch seed is $S^{(e)} := \mathcal{H}(\mathsf{DST}_{\mathsf{seed}} \parallel e \parallel \mathsf{serialize}((i, r_i)_{i \in \mathcal{V}_e}^{\uparrow i}))$. Round contexts

may instead use $S_r^{(e)} := \mathcal{H}(\mathsf{DST}_{\mathsf{evolve}} \parallel e \parallel r \parallel S^{(e)})$; this only changes the public context and not the Phase II analysis.
Security and Cost. If at least one honest r_i remains hidden until the seed input is fixed, then $S^{(e)}$ is pseudorandom in the random-oracle model. Missing contributions are recovered only after the $2t_e + 1$ unseal step. Commit–reveal costs $O(n_e \ell)$ bits in the common case; the gated fallback and DKG have the usual $O(n_e^2)$ epoch-level overhead, amortized over all Phase II rounds.

5.2 Governance Key and Verifiable Re-Sharing

Independently of seed generation, the roster runs a standard dealerless DKG with Pedersen/Feldman commitments [26,27,32], producing a $(t_e + 1)$-of-n_e sharing of a governance secret $\kappa^{(e)}$ and public key $Y^{(e)} = g^{\kappa^{(e)}}$. No party learns $\kappa^{(e)}$; threshold attestations under this sharing authorize timeout, admission, unseal, slashing, and reconfiguration actions.

A roster update from epoch e to epoch $e + 1$ is triggered by a governance ballot $\mathsf{ballot} := (\mathsf{DST}_{\mathsf{gov}} \parallel e \parallel \mathsf{serialize}(\mathcal{J}, \mathcal{L}, \mathcal{K}, \theta_e, \beta_e, d_{\mathsf{act}}, B_e))$, where $\mathcal{J}$, $\mathcal{L}$, and $\mathcal{K}$ are the join, leave, and kick sets. The update is valid only if it satisfies the admission controls below and carries a $2t_e + 1$ threshold certificate Cert_e under $Y^{(e)}$. Approved updates activate only in future epoch contexts.

At the epoch transition, verifiable secret re-sharing redistributes the same governance secret to the new roster without reconstructing it. Let the old shares be $y_i = f(\alpha_i)$ for a degree-t_e polynomial f with $f(0) = \kappa^{(e)}$. A deterministic public rule selects a live old subset $U_e \subseteq \mathcal{P}_e$ of size $t_e + 1$, and let $\lambda_i^{(0)}$ be the Lagrange coefficient at zero for α_i in U_e. Each $i \in U_e$ computes $c_i := \lambda_i^{(0)} y_i$, samples a degree-$t_{e+1}$ polynomial $g_i(Y)$ with $g_i(0) = c_i$, broadcasts commitments to g_i, and privately sends encrypted evaluations $g_i(\beta_j)$ to each $P_j \in \mathcal{P}_{e+1}$ with public consistency proofs. Each new party sets $y'_j := \sum_{i \in U_e} g_i(\beta_j)$. For $G(Y) := \sum_{i \in U_e} g_i(Y)$, we have $G(0) = \sum_{i \in U_e} \lambda_i^{(0)} f(\alpha_i) = f(0) = \kappa^{(e)}$, so the new shares are a t_{e+1}-threshold sharing of the same secret and $Y^{(e+1)} := Y^{(e)} = g^{\kappa^{(e)}}$.

The re-sharing transcript contains public commitments, encrypted evaluations, consistency proofs, the authorizing certificate Cert_e, and a digest $\mathsf{VSR\_tx}_e$ recorded by the ledger together with the new roster metadata. Malformed shares are detected by the public proofs and handled by complaint resolution and slashing. These epoch-transition costs are separate from Phase II: they update future signer/relayer sets and future contexts $M_{e+1,r}$, but do not change the relay law of any already fixed round (e, r).
Governance Controls for Roster Updates. Roster changes obey five admission controls: a $2t_e + 1$ supermajority certificate under $Y^{(e)}$; stake θ_e and operational bond β_e for joining identities; activation delay $d_{\mathsf{act}} \geq 1$; per-epoch join budget B_e and roster cap $n_{\max}$; and rate-limited finalization every R_{min} blocks. These controls are not needed for the correctness of a fixed round, but they bound setup/re-sharing workload and prevent admission churn from modifying the relay law inside an election round.

6 Phase II: One-Round Deterministic Leader Election

We specify the VDF-free relay election run in each round (e, r). The protocol extends a BLS-certified transcript, derives leadership and successor coins from fresh transcript-bound random-oracle inputs, and outputs either a transparent transcript or a succinct proof of a valid accepted path.

6.1 Objects, Parameters, and Context

Let $\mathcal{P}_e = \{0, \ldots, n_e - 1\}$ be the authenticated epoch roster, with BLS keys (sk_i, pk_i) and proofs of possession. The public round context is $M_{e,r} := (\mathsf{DST}, e, r, S^{(e)}, \mathsf{ctx}_{e,r})$, where $S^{(e)}$ is the epoch seed from Phase I and $\mathsf{ctx}_{e,r}$ canonically binds $(\mathsf{serialize}(\mathcal{P}_e), \mathrm{params}_{e,r})$. The main analysis treats $\mathcal{P}_e$ as fixed throughout epoch e; roster changes are applied only at epoch boundaries and affect future contexts. After $k \geq 0$ accepted relay hops, the transparent transcript prefix is $\mathsf{st}_k = ((i_0, \sigma_{i_0}, \mathcal{C}_0), \ldots, (i_k, \sigma_{i_k}, \mathcal{C}_k))$, where $\mathcal{C}_j$ is the ordered timeout-certificate list for hop j. The aggregate is $\Sigma_k := \prod_{j=0}^{k} \sigma_{i_j} \in \mathbb{G}_1$, with $\Sigma_{-1} := \mathsf{neutral}$. Hop j signs $m_j = (\mathsf{DST}, M_{e,r}, \Sigma_{j-1}, i_j)$, producing $\sigma_{i_j} = \mathsf{Sign}(sk_{i_j}, m_j)$. BLS determinism fixes the signature on each canonical message and prevents per-hop resampling. Fix random-oracle output length ℓ and target per-hop leadership probability $p^\star \in (0, 1)$. Set $\tau_L := \max\{1, \lfloor p^\star 2^\ell \rfloor\}$ and write $p := \tau_L / 2^\ell$ for the realized per-hop success probability. At hop k, the leadership coin and ordinary successor seed are $h_k := \mathcal{H}_2(\mathsf{DST}_{\mathrm{lead}} \parallel pk_{i_k} \parallel M_{e,r} \parallel \Sigma_k)$ and $u_k := \mathcal{H}_3(\mathsf{DST}_{\mathrm{next}} \parallel pk_{i_k} \parallel M_{e,r} \parallel \Sigma_k)$. The leadership test is $\mathsf{ToInt}(h_k) < \tau_L$; on non-success, the ordinary successor is $\textsc{Index}(u_k, n_e)$.

Ledger Binding. By default, hop messages exclude block data, so per-hop coins do not depend on mutable ledger contents. If an instantiation requires ledger anchoring, use a lagged public digest $D_{e,r}$ derived from $M_{e,r}$ and a previously finalized block header fixed before round (e, r) begins, and replace the hop message by $m_j = (\mathsf{DST}, M_{e,r}, D_{e,r}, \Sigma_{j-1}, i_j)$. The initiator remains block-free: $i_0 = \textsc{Index}(\mathcal{H}_3(\mathsf{DST}_{\mathrm{idx}} \parallel M_{e,r}), n_e)$. This prevents the current round leader from grinding current block contents to bias the current relay.

Verification Mode. In transparent mode, the accepted leader broadcasts the full transcript st_K, and verifiers replay every signature, leadership test, timeout certificate, timeout-log branch, and successor transition. In succinct final-broadcast mode, relayers still exchange enough prefix material to run prefix validation, but the accepted leader may replace the final full-transcript broadcast by (i_K, Σ_K, π), where π proves knowledge of a valid accepted first-success path satisfying the NP relation below. A fully recursive succinct relay, in which every hop carries a proof of prefix validity, is a separate optimization and is not used in the main analysis.

Succinct NP Relation. The public input to the relation includes the timeout-board snapshot $\mathsf{TOLog}_{e,r}$. There exists a sequence $((i_j, \sigma_{i_j}, \mathcal{C}_j))_{j=0}^{K}$, with $K \geq 0$, such that:

1. $i_0 = \textsc{Index}(\mathcal{H}_3(\mathsf{DST}_{\mathrm{idx}} \parallel M_{e,r}), n_e)$.

2. For all j, $\mathsf{Verify}(pk_{i_j}, m_j, \sigma_{i_j}) = 1$, where $m_j = (\mathsf{DST}, M_{e,r}, \Sigma_{j-1}, i_j)$, $\Sigma_j = \Sigma_{j-1} \cdot \sigma_{i_j}$, and the public keys are taken from $\mathsf{serialize}(\mathcal{P}_e)$ inside $M_{e,r}$.
3. For each $j < K$, letting $h_j = \mathcal{H}_2(\mathsf{DST}_{\text{lead}} \parallel pk_{i_j} \parallel M_{e,r} \parallel \Sigma_j)$ and $u_j = \mathcal{H}_3(\mathsf{DST}_{\text{next}} \parallel pk_{i_j} \parallel M_{e,r} \parallel \Sigma_j)$, one has $\mathsf{ToInt}(h_j) \geq \tau_L$. Let $t_j = |\mathcal{C}_j|$, and require $t_j = \mathsf{ActiveTO}(\mathsf{TOLog}_{e,r}, e, r, \Sigma_j, i_j)$. If $t_j = 0$, then $i_{j+1} = \textsc{Index}(u_j, n_e)$. If $t_j > 0$, then for each $\rho = 1, \ldots, t_j$, the target $q_{j,\rho-1}$ is computed as $q_{j,0} = \textsc{Index}(u_j, n_e)$ for $\rho = 1$, and $q_{j,\rho-1} = \textsc{Index}(\mathcal{H}_3(\mathsf{DST}_{\text{fail}} \parallel i_j \parallel \Sigma_j \parallel (\rho - 1)), n_e)$ for $\rho > 1$; every $C_{j,\rho}$ verifies under $Y^{(e)}$ against $\mathsf{TO\_stmt}(e, r, \Sigma_j, i_j, q_{j,\rho-1}, \rho)$, and $i_{j+1} = \textsc{Index}(\mathcal{H}_3(\mathsf{DST}_{\text{fail}} \parallel i_j \parallel \Sigma_j \parallel t_j), n_e)$.
4. The last hop is the first accepted success: $\mathsf{ToInt}(h_K) < \tau_L$, where $h_K = \mathcal{H}_2(\mathsf{DST}_{\text{lead}} \parallel pk_{i_K} \parallel M_{e,r} \parallel \Sigma_K)$.
5. The aggregate pairing equation holds: $e(\Sigma_K, g_2) = \prod_{j=0}^{K} e(\mathcal{H}_1(m_j), pk_{i_j})$.

6.2 Exact Indexing and Deterministic Initiator

Algorithm 1 implements exact public indexing: it outputs a uniform index in $\{0, \ldots, n-1\}$, has expected trials $< 1/(1 - n/2^\ell)$, and is used for the initiator, ordinary successor selection, and failover retargeting.

Algorithm 1. $\textsc{Index}(z, n)$ – map a hash value to a party index

Require: $z \in \{0,1\}^\ell$, $1 \leq n \leq 2^\ell$
Ensure: $\mathtt{idx} \in \{0, \ldots, n-1\}$
$A \leftarrow \lfloor 2^\ell / n \rfloor \cdot n$
if $\mathsf{ToInt}(z) < A$ **then**
  return $\mathsf{ToInt}(z) \bmod n$
$z' \leftarrow \mathcal{H}_3(\mathsf{DST}_{\text{idx}} \parallel z \parallel n)$
return INDEX(z',n)

6.3 Relay Mechanics and Timeout Failover

For hop j with sender i_j and prefix aggregate Σ_j, let the ordinary target be $q_{j,0} := \textsc{Index}(u_j, n_e)$. After $\rho \geq 1$ certified timeouts, let the failover target be $q_{j,\rho} := \textsc{Index}(\mathcal{H}_3(\mathsf{DST}_{\text{fail}} \parallel i_j \parallel \Sigma_j \parallel \rho), n_e)$. Define $\theta_{j,\rho} := (\mathsf{DST}_{\text{timeout}}, e, r, \Sigma_j, i_j, q_{j,\rho-1}, \rho)$, certifying that the previously active target $q_{j,\rho-1}$ failed to make valid progress. The timeout certificate is $C_{j,\rho} := \mathsf{TSig}_{\kappa^{(e)}}(\theta_{j,\rho})$, verifiable under $Y^{(e)} = g^{\kappa^{(e)}}$. Timeout certificates are posted to a public timeout board $\mathsf{TOLog}_{e,r}$. Let $a_j := \mathsf{ActiveTO}(\mathsf{TOLog}_{e,r}, e, r, \Sigma_j, i_j)$ be the largest $t \geq 0$ such that the board contains a contiguous valid sequence $C_{j,1}, \ldots, C_{j,t}$ for this prefix. A valid extension of (e, r, Σ_j, i_j) must go to q_{j,a_j}. Thus, once $C_{j,\rho}$ is active, any later extension by $q_{j,\rho-1}$ is stale and rejected. The transcript list $\mathcal{C}_j = [C_{j,1}, \ldots, C_{j,t_j}]$ is accepted only if $t_j = a_j$ and every $C_{j,\rho}$ verifies against $\theta_{j,\rho}$.

Algorithm 2. Initiator Hop

Require: $M_{e,r}$, initiator i_0, key pair (sk_{i_0}, pk_{i_0}), threshold τ_L, timeout Δ_{to}, governance key $Y^{(e)}$

Ensure: $\langle\mathsf{LEADER}\rangle$ broadcast or $\langle\mathsf{RELAY}\rangle$ forwarded

$\Sigma_{-1} \leftarrow \mathsf{neutral}$; $\mathcal{C}_0 \leftarrow [\,]$

$m_0 \leftarrow (\mathsf{DST}, M_{e,r}, \Sigma_{-1}, i_0)$; $\sigma_{i_0} \leftarrow \mathsf{Sign}(sk_{i_0}, m_0)$; $\Sigma_0 \leftarrow \sigma_{i_0}$

$h_0 \leftarrow \mathcal{H}_2(\mathsf{DST}_{\text{lead}} \parallel pk_{i_0} \parallel M_{e,r} \parallel \Sigma_0)$

if $\mathsf{ToInt}(h_0) < \tau_L$ **then**

  Broadcast $\langle\mathsf{LEADER}, e, r, i_0, ((i_0, \sigma_{i_0}, \mathcal{C}_0))\rangle$; **return**

$u_0 \leftarrow \mathcal{H}_3(\mathsf{DST}_{\text{next}} \parallel pk_{i_0} \parallel M_{e,r} \parallel \Sigma_0)$; $\rho \leftarrow 0$

while true **do**

$$j \leftarrow \begin{cases} \textsc{Index}(u_0, n_e), & \rho = 0 \\ \textsc{Index}(\mathcal{H}_3(\mathsf{DST}_{\text{fail}} \parallel i_0 \parallel \Sigma_0 \parallel \rho), n_e), & \rho \geq 1 \end{cases}$$

  Send $\langle\mathsf{RELAY}, e, r, ((i_0, \sigma_{i_0}, \mathcal{C}_0))\rangle$ **to** j

  $\mathsf{ok} \leftarrow \mathsf{WaitProgressOrTimeout}(j, \Delta_{\text{to}})$

  if $\mathsf{ok} = \mathsf{true}$ **then**

    return

  $\rho \leftarrow \rho + 1$; $C_{0,\rho} \leftarrow \mathsf{ObtainTimeoutCert}(\Sigma_0, i_0, j, \rho)$; post $C_{0,\rho}$ to $\mathsf{TOLog}_{e,r}$; append $C_{0,\rho}$ to $\mathcal{C}_0$

Local Prefix Validation Before Extension. Before extending a relay, an honest party runs $\textsc{ValidatePrefix}$ on the received prefix. This check is the prefix version of public verification: it recomputes the initiator, verifies all included hop signatures, checks that every included hop is non-final, verifies ordinary successor transitions using $u_j = \mathcal{H}_3(\mathsf{DST}_{\text{next}} \parallel pk_{i_j} \parallel M_{e,r} \parallel \Sigma_j)$, verifies timeout certificates against $\mathsf{TOLog}_{e,r}$, checks the active $\mathsf{DST}_{\text{fail}}$-based failover branch, and returns the expected next identity $i_k^\star$. The relayer signs only if $i_k^\star$ equals its own identity. Invalid prefixes are discarded and never extended. This local validation is the prefix-restricted form of Algorithm 4 to enforce the same public transition rules on the prefix that get extended.

Timeout Counters. At hop j, let $t_j = |\mathcal{C}_j|$ be the number of timeouts before valid progress. If each candidate successor is honest and responsive with probability h, then t_j is geometric on $\{0, 1, 2, \dots\}$ with success probability h, so $\Pr(t_j = \rho) = h(1-h)^\rho$, $\mathbb{E}[t_j] = (1-h)/h$, and $\mathrm{Var}(t_j) = (1-h)/h^2$. These counters affect retry traffic and timeout evidence, but not the distribution of leadership coins on accepted signed hops.

Cycles. Revisits and self-loops are allowed. No de-duplication of $(i_0, \dots, i_k)$ is enforced. Implementations that skip revisits must publish the rule, and verifiers must replay it for consensus.

Succinct Verification. In succinct final-broadcast mode, the verifier computes $i_0^\star = \textsc{Index}(\mathcal{H}_3(\mathsf{DST}_{\text{idx}} \parallel M_{e,r}), n_e)$, sets $\mathsf{pub}_{e,r} := (M_{e,r}, Y^{(e)}, \mathsf{TOLog}_{e,r}, \tau_L, n_e, i_0^\star, i_K, \Sigma_K)$, and accepts iff $\mathsf{NIZK.Verify}(\pi; \mathsf{pub}_{e,r}) = 1$. This checks the same public relation as Algorithm 4, with the path, signatures, timeout evidence, timeout-log branch, and aggregate relation supplied as the proof witness.

Algorithm 3. Relayer Hop

Require: $\langle \mathsf{RELAY}, e, r, \mathsf{st}_{k-1} \rangle$, public $M_{e,r}$, timeout log $\mathsf{TOLog}_{e,r}$, current identity i_k, key pair (sk_{i_k}, pk_{i_k}), threshold τ_L, timeout Δ_{to}, governance key $Y^{(e)}$

Ensure: $\langle \mathsf{LEADER} \rangle$ broadcast or $\langle \mathsf{RELAY} \rangle$ forwarded

$(\mathsf{ok}, \Sigma_{k-1}, i_k^\star) \leftarrow \textsc{ValidatePrefix}(e, r, M_{e,r}, Y^{(e)}, \mathsf{TOLog}_{e,r}, \mathsf{st}_{k-1}, \tau_L, n_e)$

Reject unless $\mathsf{ok} = 1$ and $i_k = i_k^\star$

$\mathcal{C}_k \leftarrow [\,]$

$m_k \leftarrow (\mathsf{DST}, M_{e,r}, \Sigma_{k-1}, i_k)$; $\sigma_{i_k} \leftarrow \mathsf{Sign}(sk_{i_k}, m_k)$; $\Sigma_k \leftarrow \Sigma_{k-1} \cdot \sigma_{i_k}$

$h_k \leftarrow \mathcal{H}_2(\mathsf{DST}_{\text{lead}} \parallel pk_{i_k} \parallel M_{e,r} \parallel \Sigma_k)$

if $\mathsf{ToInt}(h_k) < \tau_L$ **then**

  Broadcast $\langle \mathsf{LEADER}, e, r, i_k, \mathsf{st}_{k-1} \| (i_k, \sigma_{i_k}, \mathcal{C}_k) \rangle$; **return**

$u_k \leftarrow \mathcal{H}_3(\mathsf{DST}_{\text{next}} \parallel pk_{i_k} \parallel M_{e,r} \parallel \Sigma_k)$; $\rho \leftarrow 0$

while true **do**

  $j \leftarrow \begin{cases} \textsc{Index}(u_k, n_e), & \rho = 0 \\ \textsc{Index}(\mathcal{H}_3(\mathsf{DST}_{\text{fail}} \parallel i_k \parallel \Sigma_k \parallel \rho), n_e), & \rho \geq 1 \end{cases}$

  Send $\langle \mathsf{RELAY}, e, r, \mathsf{st}_{k-1} \| (i_k, \sigma_{i_k}, \mathcal{C}_k) \rangle$ **to** j

  $\mathsf{ok} \leftarrow \mathsf{WaitProgressOrTimeout}(j, \Delta_{\text{to}})$

  if $\mathsf{ok} = \mathsf{true}$ **then**

    return

  $\rho \leftarrow \rho + 1$; $C_{k,\rho} \leftarrow \mathsf{ObtainTimeoutCert}(\Sigma_k, i_k, j, \rho)$; post $C_{k,\rho}$ to $\mathsf{TOLog}_{e,r}$; append $C_{k,\rho}$ to $\mathcal{C}_k$

6.4 Leadership Proof and Public Verification

Theorem 1 (Verification soundness and completeness). *Honest transparent transcripts pass Algorithm 4. Conversely, any deviation in initiator selection, hop signature validity, strict-prefix non-success, ordinary successor selection, timeout-log branch selection, failover certification, or final leadership success is rejected.*

Proof. The initiator is fixed by exact public indexing. BLS verification fixes each hop signature on $m_j = (\mathsf{DST}, M_{e,r}, \Sigma_{j-1}, i_j)$, hence fixes the aggregate prefix Σ_j. The random-oracle inputs under $\mathsf{DST}_{\text{lead}}$, $\mathsf{DST}_{\text{next}}$, and $\mathsf{DST}_{\text{fail}}$ then determine, respectively, the leadership test, ordinary successor, and failover successor. Algorithm 4 rejects any strict prefix with $\mathsf{ToInt}(h_j) < \tau_L$, requires the last hop to satisfy $\mathsf{ToInt}(h_K) < \tau_L$, checks the active timeout-log count, and verifies every timeout certificate before accepting a failover transition. Thus every accepted transcript is exactly a valid first-success path under the public rules.

Round Flow and Grinding Resistance. The relay is grinding-resistant because every accepted hop is fixed by public deterministic rules. BLS gives a unique signature on the canonical message $m_k = (\mathsf{DST}, M_{e,r}, \Sigma_{k-1}, i_k)$, or on $m_k = (\mathsf{DST}, M_{e,r}, D_{e,r}, \Sigma_{k-1}, i_k)$ when ledger binding is enabled. The message binds the prior prefix, and the fresh aggregate Σ_k determines both the leadership coin $h_k = \mathcal{H}_2(\mathsf{DST}_{\text{lead}} \parallel pk_{i_k} \parallel M_{e,r} \parallel \Sigma_k)$ and the ordinary successor seed $u_k = \mathcal{H}_3(\mathsf{DST}_{\text{next}} \parallel pk_{i_k} \parallel M_{e,r} \parallel \Sigma_k)$. Thus a party cannot resample a hop locally

Algorithm 4. $\textsc{VerifyLeader}(e, r, M_{e,r}, Y^{(e)}, \mathsf{TOLog}_{e,r}, \mathsf{st}_K, \tau_L)$

Require: $\mathsf{st}_K = ((i_0, \sigma_{i_0}, \mathcal{C}_0), \ldots, (i_K, \sigma_{i_K}, \mathcal{C}_K))$, public context $M_{e,r}$, governance key $Y^{(e)}$, timeout log $\mathsf{TOLog}_{e,r}$, threshold τ_L, roster size n_e
Ensure: accept iff the claim is valid

$i_0^\star \leftarrow \textsc{Index}(\mathcal{H}_3(\mathsf{DST}_{\text{idx}} \parallel M_{e,r}), n_e)$; **reject** if $i_0 \neq i_0^\star$
$\Sigma_{-1} \leftarrow \mathsf{neutral}$
for $j = 0$ **to** K **do**
  $m_j \leftarrow (\mathsf{DST}, M_{e,r}, \Sigma_{j-1}, i_j)$; **reject** if $\mathsf{Verify}(pk_{i_j}, m_j, \sigma_{i_j}) \neq 1$
  $\Sigma_j \leftarrow \Sigma_{j-1} \cdot \sigma_{i_j}$; $h_j \leftarrow \mathcal{H}_2(\mathsf{DST}_{\text{lead}} \parallel pk_{i_j} \parallel M_{e,r} \parallel \Sigma_j)$
  if $j < K$ **and** $\mathsf{ToInt}(h_j) < \tau_L$ **then**
    reject
if $\mathsf{ToInt}(h_K) \geq \tau_L$ **then**
  reject
if $\mathcal{C}_K \neq [\,]$ **then**
  reject
for $j = 0$ **to** $K - 1$ **do**
  Let $\mathcal{C}_j = [C_{j,1}, \ldots, C_{j,t_j}]$; set $u_j \leftarrow \mathcal{H}_3(\mathsf{DST}_{\text{next}} \parallel pk_{i_j} \parallel M_{e,r} \parallel \Sigma_j)$
  $\hat{t}_j \leftarrow \mathsf{ActiveTO}(\mathsf{TOLog}_{e,r}, e, r, \Sigma_j, i_j)$; **reject** if $t_j \neq \hat{t}_j$
  for $\rho = 1$ **to** t_j **do**
    $$q_{j,\rho-1} \leftarrow \begin{cases} \textsc{Index}(u_j, n_e), & \rho = 1 \\ \textsc{Index}(\mathcal{H}_3(\mathsf{DST}_{\text{fail}} \parallel i_j \parallel \Sigma_j \parallel (\rho - 1)), n_e), & \rho > 1 \end{cases}$$
    reject if $\mathsf{TSigVerify}_{Y^{(e)}}(C_{j,\rho}, \mathsf{TO\_stmt}(e, r, \Sigma_j, i_j, q_{j,\rho-1}, \rho)) \neq 1$
  $$i_{j+1}^\star \leftarrow \begin{cases} \textsc{Index}(u_j, n_e), & t_j = 0 \\ \textsc{Index}(\mathcal{H}_3(\mathsf{DST}_{\text{fail}} \parallel i_j \parallel \Sigma_j \parallel t_j), n_e), & t_j > 0 \end{cases}$$
  if $i_{j+1} \neq i_{j+1}^\star$ **then**
    reject
accept

or change the successor without failing public verification. A round proceeds as follows: all parties compute $i_0 = \textsc{Index}(\mathcal{H}_3(\mathsf{DST}_{\text{idx}} \parallel M_{e,r}), n_e)$; the initiator starts the relay; each responsive relayer validates the received prefix, signs m_k, updates Σ_k, and either broadcasts leadership or forwards to the public successor; if the successor does not acknowledge, timeout evidence certifies a deterministic $\mathsf{DST}_{\text{fail}}$-based failover; finally, verifiers check either the full accepted transcript or its succinct proof. Governance updates are finalized only between epochs and affect future contexts $M_{e+1,r}$, not the relay law of the fixed round (e, r).

6.5 Complexity and Operational Interpretation

Let $p \in (0, 1)$ be the per-hop leadership probability and $h \in (0, 1]$ the probability that a designated next hop is honest and responsive. Let $K \in \{0, 1, 2, \ldots\}$ be the number of non-final signed hops before the final accepted leader hop. Since only responsive hops appear in the signed relay transcript, the signed-path length is governed by first eligible success rather than by timeout retries. Thus $\Pr(K = k) = (1 - p)^k p$, $\mathbb{E}[K] = (1 - p)/p$, and $\mathbb{E}[K + 1] = 1/p$.

For each non-final hop $j < K$, the timeout counter t_j has $\mathbb{E}[t_j] = (1-h)/h$ and $\mathbb{E}[t_j+1] = 1/h$. Let $b_{\text{sig}} = O(\lambda)$ be one BLS signature, $b_{\text{idx}} = \lceil \log_2 n_e \rceil$, $b_{\text{ent}} := b_{\text{sig}} + b_{\text{idx}} + O(1)$, and $b_{\text{cert}} = O(\lambda)$ be one timeout certificate.

Transparent Mode. The final leader broadcast contains all $K+1$ signed hops and all timeout certificates from the non-final hops, so its size is $(K+1)b_{\text{ent}} + (\sum_{j=0}^{K-1} t_j)b_{\text{cert}}$. Therefore $\mathbb{E}[\text{leader broadcast}] = b_{\text{ent}}/p + ((1-p)/p)((1-h)/h)b_{\text{cert}}$. Relay traffic before the final broadcast accounts for repeated timeout sends. At each non-final hop j, there are t_j+1 transmissions carrying the current prefix, giving $\mathbb{E}[\text{relay traffic}] = ((1-p)/p^2)(b_{\text{ent}}/h + ((1-h)/h^2)b_{\text{cert}})$. Transparent mode is therefore fully auditable but grows with the revealed path and retry evidence.

Succinct Final-Broadcast Mode. In the protocol analyzed here, succinctness compresses the accepted leader broadcast, not every relay message. Relayers still receive enough prefix data to run ValidatePrefix, so relay traffic follows the transparent-mode expression above. The accepted broadcast is reduced from $(K+1)b_{\text{ent}} + (\sum_{j=0}^{K-1} t_j)b_{\text{cert}}$ to $O(\lambda + |\pi|)$, where $|\pi|$ is the proof size. A fully recursive succinct relay could carry (i_k, Σ_k, π_k) at every hop and reduce per-hop relay payloads, but that optimization requires recursive prefix-validity proofs and is left outside the current model.

Interpretation. The parameter p controls the expected number of signed relay extensions before eligibility; h controls retry pressure and timeout evidence. These costs are sequential by construction. The numerical instantiations in Sect. 4.4 make the latency tradeoff explicit, while the formulas above separate transparent audit cost from final-broadcast proof compression.

6.6 Dynamic Membership Interface

Dynamic membership is applied at epoch boundaries, not during a fixed election round. The epoch seed $S^{(e)}$ is public and is not re-shared. Joins, leaves, and expulsions affect only the governance sharing and the roster used in future contexts. At the transition $e \to e+1$, the governance layer applies the controls and verifiable re-sharing procedure of Sect. 5.2 to redistribute the same governance secret κ from $(\mathcal{P}_e, t_e)$ to $(\mathcal{P}_{e+1}, t_{e+1})$, without reconstructing κ and without rotating the public key: $Y^{(e+1)} = Y^{(e)} = g^{\kappa}$. The ledger records the new roster metadata, the authorizing governance certificate, and a digest of the re-sharing transcript. Thus membership changes update future round contexts $M_{e+1,r}$, while the intra-round relay law, freshness argument, and verification rules for the already fixed context $M_{e,r}$ remain unchanged.

7 Security Analysis

We analyze Phase II in the random-oracle model and in the UC framework. Notation and ideal functionalities follow Sects. 3 and 6. For round (e, r), the public context is $M_{e,r}$, the epoch roster is $\mathcal{P}_e$ of size n_e, the leadership threshold is $\tau_L \in \{1, \dots, 2^{\ell}-1\}$, and the per-hop success probability is the realized threshold probability $p := \Pr(\mathsf{ToInt}(h_k) < \tau_L) = \tau_L/2^\ell$. We use $I_{e,r}$ for the initiator, $\widetilde{L}_{e,r}$ for the first eligible leader ignoring withholding, and $L_{e,r}$ for the final accepted leader output by the protocol. Under withholding, $\widetilde{L}_{e,r}$ and $L_{e,r}$ may differ. The effective per-attempt success probability for the final accepted output is hp, where $h \in (0,1]$ is the effective honest/responsive rate. Cycles, revisits, and self-loops are allowed; verification checks local rule compliance, not acyclicity.

7.1 ROM Analysis: Indexing, Freshness, Unpredictability, Fairness, Accountability, and Liveness

Lemma 1 (Exact public indexing). *Let* $1 \le n \le 2^\ell$, *let* $A := \lfloor 2^\ell/n \rfloor n$, *and let* INDEX$(z, n)$, *for* $z \in \{0,1\}^\ell$, *set* $u := \mathsf{ToInt}(z)$, *accept iff* $u < A$, *output* $u \bmod n$, *and otherwise recurse on* $z' = \mathcal{H}_3(\mathsf{DST}_{\mathrm{idx}} \parallel z \parallel n)$. *Then the output is exactly uniform on* $\{0, \ldots, n-1\}$, *and the expected number of trials is at most* $1/(1 - n/2^\ell)$.

Proof. Each residue class modulo n has exactly A/n representatives in $\{0, \ldots, A-1\}$, so conditioned on acceptance the output is uniform. The acceptance probability is $A/2^\ell \ge 1 - n/2^\ell$, and the number of trials is geometric with that success probability. Each rejection uses a fresh domain-separated input, so the recursive trials are independent in the ROM.

Lemma 2 (Fresh leadership and successor inputs; no intra-hop grinding). *For hop* k, *let* $m_k = (\mathsf{DST}, M_{e,r}, \Sigma_{k-1}, i_k)$, $\sigma_{i_k} = \mathsf{Sign}(sk_{i_k}, m_k)$, $\Sigma_k = \Sigma_{k-1} \cdot \sigma_{i_k}$, $h_k := \mathcal{H}_2(\mathsf{DST}_{\mathrm{lead}} \parallel pk_{i_k} \parallel M_{e,r} \parallel \Sigma_k)$, *and* $u_k := \mathcal{H}_3(\mathsf{DST}_{\mathrm{next}} \parallel pk_{i_k} \parallel M_{e,r} \parallel \Sigma_k)$. *If ledger binding is enabled,* m_k *is replaced by its* $D_{e,r}$*-bound variant. Under deterministic BLS on canonical encodings, each valid transcript prefix determines a unique aggregate state* Σ_k, *and a signer has no alternative valid signature with which to resample the same hop. Over any polynomial number of valid hops, except with negligible probability that two hops repeat the same transcript-bound random-oracle input, the leadership inputs are fresh, including under identity revisits. Hence the values* h_k *are independent uniform* ℓ*-bit strings, the indicators* $\mathbf{1}(\mathsf{ToInt}(h_k) < \tau_L)$ *are i.i.d. Bernoulli*(p), *and the ordinary successor seeds* u_k *are independent of the leadership coins by domain separation.*

Proof. For a fixed canonical message m_k, deterministic BLS gives a unique valid signature under pk_{i_k}. Thus a party cannot locally resample σ_{i_k} to search for a favorable leadership coin or successor seed, and any alternative encoding or invalid signature is rejected by public verification. Once a valid prefix is fixed, the aggregate Σ_k and the random-oracle inputs under $\mathsf{DST}_{\mathrm{lead}}$ and $\mathsf{DST}_{\mathrm{next}}$ are fixed public strings.

An identity revisit does not by itself repeat a random-oracle input, because the input also contains the current aggregate Σ_k. A repeated leadership input would require the same tuple $(\mathsf{DST}_{\mathrm{lead}}, pk_{i_k}, M_{e,r}, \Sigma_k)$ to occur twice, and similarly for the successor input under $\mathsf{DST}_{\mathrm{next}}$. Over polynomially many valid hops, such repeated transcript-bound inputs occur only with negligible probability under the group/hash collision assumptions used for the BLS aggregate state. Conditioned on no such repeat, the random oracle returns independent uniform values on these fresh inputs. The same reasoning applies to failover inputs $\mathsf{DST}_{\mathsf{fail}} \parallel i_k \parallel \Sigma_k \parallel \rho$, where the retry counter ρ gives a fresh public input for each certified failover attempt at the same prefix. Since $\mathsf{DST}_{\mathsf{lead}}$ and $\mathsf{DST}_{\mathsf{next}}$ are distinct tags, leadership testing and ordinary successor selection are independent random-oracle calls.

Unpredictability. Consider the game where the adversary outputs $\widehat{L}_{e,r}$ before any honest party has produced the transcript prefix certifying the final accepted leader $L_{e,r}$.

Theorem 2 (Unpredictability). *For every PPT adversary,* $\Pr(\widehat{L}_{e,r} = L_{e,r}) \leq \max_{i \in \mathcal{P}_e} \Pr(L_{e,r} = i) + \mathrm{negl}(\lambda)$.

Proof. Replace concrete hashes by the ROM and concrete signing by the ideal signing abstraction. By Lemma 2, before the accepted-leader transcript exists, future leadership coins and successor seeds depend on unseen random-oracle values at fresh transcript-bound inputs. Any advantage beyond the best a priori identity probability therefore implies prediction of a fresh random-oracle output, a successful manipulation of a public indexing seed, or an honest-key signature forgery, each of which has negligible probability under the stated assumptions.

Fairness Variables. We distinguish initiator fairness for $I_{e,r}$, first-eligible fairness for $\widetilde{L}_{e,r}$, and realized fairness for the final accepted leader $L_{e,r}$. Under Byzantine withholding, an eligible identity may suppress its own output, so the support of $L_{e,r}$ is the effective non-withholding set $E_{e,r} \subseteq \mathcal{P}_e$, conservatively the honest/responsive set.

Theorem 3 (Fairness / bias resistance). *Assume the uniform* INDEX *rule. Let $E_{e,r} \subseteq \mathcal{P}_e$ be fixed before the relevant fresh leadership coins are sampled, and suppose identities in $E_{e,r}$ release successful outputs while identities outside $E_{e,r}$ suppress them. Except with negligible aggregate-collision or random-oracle collision probability, the following hold:* (i) $\Pr(I_{e,r} = i) = 1/n_e$ *for every* $i \in \mathcal{P}_e$*;* (ii) $\Pr(\widetilde{L}_{e,r} = i) = 1/n_e$ *for every* $i \in \mathcal{P}_e$*; and* (iii) $\Pr(L_{e,r} = i) = 1/|E_{e,r}|$ *for every* $i \in E_{e,r}$*. More generally, if identity i releases an eligible output with probability* $a_i \in [0, 1]$*, independently of the fresh leadership coin, then* $\Pr(L_{e,r} = i) = a_i/A$*, where* $A := \sum_j a_j > 0$.

Proof. Write $n := n_e$, $E := E_{e,r}$, $\widetilde{L} := \widetilde{L}_{e,r}$, and $L := L_{e,r}$. Lemma 1 gives exact uniformity for the initiator, so $\Pr(I_{e,r} = i) = 1/n$. For the first eligible leader, Lemma 2 gives that each leadership bit is independent of the ordinary successor seed. Conditional on non-success, the next identity is therefore again uniform by the INDEX rule. Hence every tested identity has uniform marginal law, independent of the stopping event, and $\Pr(\widetilde{L} = i) = \sum_{t \geq 1} (1 - p)^{t-1} p/n = 1/n$.

For the final accepted leader under the fixed effective set E, an attempt outputs $i \in E$ exactly when the current identity is i, the leadership test succeeds, and the output is released. This has probability p/n, while the total accepted-output probability per attempt is $p|E|/n$. Thus $\Pr(L=i)=\sum_{t\geq 1}(1-p|E|/n)^{t-1}p/n = 1/|E|$. The a_i-release formula follows identically: the per-attempt output probability for i is pa_i/n, the total halting probability is pA/n, and hence $\Pr(L = i) = a_i/A$.

Accountability. The transparent verifier replays the accepted transcript hop by hop; the succinct verifier checks a proof of knowledge of a valid accepted path. In both modes, accountability is for the public verification relation of the accepted transcript: signatures, leadership tests, successor transitions, timeout certificates, and final success.

Theorem 4 (Soundness and completeness of public verification). *In transparent mode, every honestly generated accepted transcript passes Algorithm 4. Conversely, any malformed transcript accepted by the transparent verifier implies either a BLS forgery, an invalid threshold timeout certificate accepted as valid, a stale timeout-log branch accepted as active, or an inconsistency with the public random-oracle outputs, except with negligible probability. In succinct mode, the same statement holds under completeness and knowledge soundness of the proof system.*

Proof. In transparent mode, the verifier recomputes the initiator from $\mathcal{H}_3(\mathsf{DST}_{\text{idx}} \parallel M_{e,r})$, checks every hop signature on $m_j = (\mathsf{DST}, M_{e,r}, \Sigma_{j-1}, i_j)$, or on the corresponding ledger-bound message if $D_{e,r}$ is enabled, recomputes Σ_j, $h_j = \mathcal{H}_2(\mathsf{DST}_{\text{lead}} \parallel pk_{i_j} \parallel M_{e,r} \parallel \Sigma_j)$, and $u_j = \mathcal{H}_3(\mathsf{DST}_{\text{next}} \parallel pk_{i_j} \parallel M_{e,r} \parallel \Sigma_j)$. It rejects any strict prefix with $\mathsf{ToInt}(h_j) < \tau_L$, requires the final hop to satisfy $\mathsf{ToInt}(h_K) < \tau_L$, checks ordinary successors using $\textsc{Index}(u_j, n_e)$, checks that $|\mathcal{C}_j|$ matches the active timeout count in $\mathsf{TOLog}_{e,r}$, and checks failover successors using the certificates in $\mathcal{C}_j$ together with the $\mathsf{DST}_{\text{fail}}$-derived fallback rule. Thus an accepted transcript that violates the public relation must contain an honest-key signature forgery, an invalid timeout certificate accepted under $Y^{(e)}$, or a transition inconsistent with the public random-oracle values. In succinct mode, completeness accepts honestly generated witnesses, and knowledge soundness ensures that any accepting proof yields a witness satisfying the same public relation; the transparent argument then applies to that witness. Hidden eligible hops suppressed by Byzantine parties are not part of the accepted transcript; they affect realized fairness and liveness, not transcript verification.

Liveness Variables. The number of leadership tests until the first eligible success is governed by *p*. The final accepted output under withholding is governed by *hp*.

Theorem 5 (Liveness). *Let* $X := \widetilde{X}_{e,r} := \inf\{x \geq 1 : \mathsf{ToInt}(h_{x-1}) < \tau_L\}$ *be the number of leadership tests until first eligibility, let* $N := N_{e,r}$ *be the number of attempts until a final accepted leader is output, and set* $q := hp$*. Then:* (i)

$X \sim \mathrm{Geom}(p)$, *so* $\Pr(X > t) = (1-p)^t$, $\mathbb{E}[X] = 1/p$, *and* $\mathrm{Var}(X) = (1-p)/p^2$*;* (ii) *if attempts are i.i.d. with effective success probability* q*, then* $N \sim \mathrm{Geom}(q)$, $\Pr(N > t) = (1-q)^t$, $\mathbb{E}[N] = 1/q$, *and* $\mathrm{Var}(N) = (1-q)/q^2$*;* (iii) *if attempts are* Δ*-bounded after* GST, *then* $T \le \Delta N$ *and* $T_\varepsilon \le \Delta\lceil \ln(\varepsilon)/\ln(1-q)\rceil$*;* (iv) *if a responsive attempt takes* Δ_h *and a withholding attempt times out in* Δ_b*, then* $\mathbb{E}[T] = (h\Delta_h + (1-h)\Delta_b)/(hp)$*; and* (v) *if the effective honesty rate varies by attempt but is always at least* $h_{\min} > 0$*, then* N *is stochastically dominated by* $\mathrm{Geom}(h_{\min}p)$.

Proof. Lemma 2 gives i.i.d. Bernoulli(p) leadership indicators $\mathbf{1}(\mathsf{ToInt}(h_k) < \tau_L)$. Since $\widetilde{X}_{e,r}$ counts tests starting with hop 0, it is geometric with parameter p, proving (i). For withholding, model attempt t by a responsiveness indicator $R_t \sim \mathrm{Bernoulli}(h)$ and an independent leadership indicator $I_t \sim \mathrm{Bernoulli}(p)$. The attempt outputs a final accepted leader exactly when $R_t I_t = 1$, so the per-attempt success probability is hp. Therefore $N_{e,r} \sim \mathrm{Geom}(hp)$, proving (ii). If every attempt lasts at most Δ, then $T \le \Delta N_{e,r}$. Combining this with $\Pr(N_{e,r} > t) = (1-hp)^t$ gives $T_\varepsilon \le \Delta\lceil \ln(\varepsilon)/\ln(1-hp)\rceil$, proving (iii). For (iv), let F denote the expected remaining completion time at the start of an attempt. With probability hp, the attempt is responsive and successful and costs Δ_h. With probability $h(1-p)$, it is responsive but not successful and costs $\Delta_h + F$. With probability $1-h$, it times out and costs $\Delta_b + F$. Thus $F = hp\Delta_h + h(1-p)(\Delta_h + F) + (1-h)(\Delta_b + F)$, so $hpF = h\Delta_h + (1-h)\Delta_b$, and $\mathbb{E}[T] = F = (h\Delta_h + (1-h)\Delta_b)/(hp)$. Finally, if the responsiveness probability in each attempt is at least $h_{\min}$, then each attempt succeeds with probability at least $h_{\min}p$. Coupling each attempt with an independent Bernoulli($h_{\min}p$) success event shows that $N_{e,r}$ is stochastically dominated by $\mathrm{Geom}(h_{\min}p)$, proving (v).

7.2 UC Security

We use the ideal functionalities from Sect. 3.5. For a fixed epoch roster and round context, Phase II realizes the relay abstraction in the $(\mathcal{F}_{\mathsf{RO}}, \mathcal{F}_{\mathsf{BLS}})$-hybrid. The full dynamic protocol, including epoch-transition re-sharing, is analyzed in the $(\mathcal{F}_{\mathsf{RO}}, \mathcal{F}_{\mathsf{BLS}}, \mathcal{F}_{\mathsf{VSR}})$-hybrid, and the leader-election functionality $\mathcal{F}_{\mathsf{LE}}$ is obtained by composition.

Theorem 6 (Scoped UC realization). *For a fixed epoch roster and round context, the Phase II protocol of Sect. 6 realizes the relay abstraction* $\mathcal{F}_{\mathsf{RELAY}}$ *in the* $(\mathcal{F}_{\mathsf{RO}}, \mathcal{F}_{\mathsf{BLS}})$*-hybrid, with timeout-log failover modeled as above. With epoch-transition re-sharing modeled by* $\mathcal{F}_{\mathsf{VSR}}$*, the dynamic protocol realizes the same relay abstraction across valid epoch transitions. By the UC composition theorem, the relay wrapper realizes* $\mathcal{F}_{\mathsf{LE}}$*. This statement is scoped to the leader-election relay and is not an end-to-end consensus proof.*

Proof (Proof sketch). Fix a PPT adversary $\mathcal{A}$ and environment $\mathcal{Z}$. The simulator $\mathcal{S}$ internally runs $\mathcal{A}$, forwards corrupted-party messages, obtains honest signatures from $\mathcal{F}_{\mathsf{BLS}}$, and schedules delivery consistently with the partial-synchrony restrictions from Sect. 3.2. The proof proceeds through the following hybrids.

H0 (real world). This is the real protocol with concrete hashes, BLS signatures, timeout certificates, and epoch-transition handling.

H1 (global random oracle). Replace all random-oracle calls by $\mathcal{F}_{\mathsf{RO}}$ on the same domain-separated inputs. The view is unchanged relative to the ROM, except that the simulator can explicitly record and program first-use points.

H2 (ideal signatures). Replace concrete BLS signing and verification by $\mathcal{F}_{\mathsf{BLS}}$. Honest signatures are obtained from the functionality, and public verification queries are answered consistently. Any distinguisher between H1 and H2 gives an EUF-CMA or aggregation-soundness violation for deterministic BLS.

H3 (ideal epoch transition). Replace concrete governance re-sharing by $\mathcal{F}_{\mathsf{VSR}}$. This only updates future rosters and threshold material; for a fixed round (e, r), it affects the relay only through the public context $M_{e,r}$.

H4 (ideal relay transcript by fresh-point programming). When honest parties start round (e, r), $\mathcal{S}$ obtains the ideal relay transcript from $\mathcal{F}_{\mathsf{RELAY}}$, including the sequence of identities, leadership coins, successor seeds, timeout-log entries, timeout counters, and the final accepted leader. For each hop j, $\mathcal{S}$ obtains or forwards the hop signature and computes the corresponding Σ_j. For every strict prefix $j < K$, it programs the fresh leadership point $x_j^L := \mathsf{DST}_{\text{lead}} \parallel pk_{i_j} \parallel M_{e,r} \parallel \Sigma_j$ to a value y_j with $\mathsf{ToInt}(y_j) \geq \tau_L$. If the transition is ordinary, it programs the fresh successor point $x_j^N := \mathsf{DST}_{\text{next}} \parallel pk_{i_j} \parallel M_{e,r} \parallel \Sigma_j$, together with any $\mathsf{DST}_{\text{idx}}$-tagged rejection-sampling recursion points used by INDEX, so that the ordinary successor is i_{j+1}. If the transition is a certified failover with counter ρ, it programs the corresponding failover point $x_{j,\rho}^F := \mathsf{DST}_{\text{fail}} \parallel i_j \parallel \Sigma_j \parallel \rho$, again including any $\mathsf{DST}_{\text{idx}}$-tagged recursion points, so that the failover successor is i_{j+1}, and simulates the timeout certificate under the governance interface. At the final hop K, it programs $x_K^L := \mathsf{DST}_{\text{lead}} \parallel pk_{i_K} \parallel M_{e,r} \parallel \Sigma_K$ to a value y_K with $\mathsf{ToInt}(y_K) < \tau_L$. By Lemma 2, these programmed points are fresh except with negligible repeated-input probability, including under identity revisits.

H5 (delivery schedule). Finally, $\mathcal{S}$ releases messages according to any schedule permitted by the adversary and partial synchrony. Rushing and withholding choices are reflected either in the delivered transcript or in timeout/failover certificates. Delivery order does not alter the programmed random-oracle values, signatures, or public verification relation.

The transition H0–H1 is by random-oracle idealization; H1–H2 is by BLS security; H2–H3 is by the idealized correctness and privacy guarantees of $\mathcal{F}_{\mathsf{VSR}}$ for epoch-transition re-sharing; H3–H4 is by fresh-point random-oracle programming; and H4–H5 is schedule transparency under the same partial-synchrony constraints. Thus the environment's view is indistinguishable from the ideal relay execution. Composing $\mathcal{F}_{\mathsf{RELAY}}$ with the wrapper $\mathcal{F}_{\mathsf{LE}}$ yields the leader-election claim.

Scope of the UC idealization. $\mathcal{F}_{\mathsf{LE}}$ models the protocol's final accepted leader. Initiator and first-eligible fairness are ROM distributional properties of the real transcript law, while final-output fairness under withholding is stated over $E_{e,r}$.

The UC abstraction covers a single authenticated epoch roster and does not model federated multi-roster aggregation.
Dynamic Membership Soundness. $\mathcal{F}_{\mathsf{VSR}}$ is invoked only at epoch transitions: it updates the future roster, redistributes fresh shares of the same governance secret, and preserves $Y = g^{\kappa}$ as in Sect. 5.2. Since $M_{e,r}$, $\mathcal{P}_e$, and the thresholds are fixed before round (e, r), VSR cannot change the intra-round relay law. The same indexing, freshness, unpredictability, fairness, accountability, and liveness arguments then apply after each valid transition with the new epoch parameters.

8 Conclusion

We presented a VDF-free deterministic random-walk leader-election protocol with transparent setup, public auditability, and explicit latency/communication tradeoffs. Each hop signs $m_k = (\mathsf{DST}, M_{e,r}, \Sigma_{k-1}, i_k)$, updates Σ_k, and derives h_k under $\mathsf{DST}_{\text{lead}}$ and u_k under $\mathsf{DST}_{\text{next}}$. BLS determinism removes intra-hop resampling, while Σ_k keeps random-oracle inputs transcript-bound and replayable even under revisits. The relay gives exact indexing, threshold-certified failover, transparent replay, and succinct final-broadcast verification. In the ROM, it gives unpredictability, initiator and first-eligible fairness, final-output fairness over the effective non-withholding set, transcript accountability, and geometric liveness. Phase II realizes the relay abstraction in the $(\mathcal{F}_{\mathsf{RO}}, \mathcal{F}_{\mathsf{BLS}})$-hybrid; with re-sharing, the dynamic protocol is analyzed in the $(\mathcal{F}_{\mathsf{RO}}, \mathcal{F}_{\mathsf{BLS}}, \mathcal{F}_{\mathsf{VSR}})$-hybrid. Phase I supplies $S^{(e)}$ and $Y^{(e)}$, and membership changes preserve the governance public key by verifiable re-sharing. The protocol makes the sequential relay cost explicit while providing deterministic anti-grinding, public replayability, and accountable failover. The numerical study is formula-level and is not an implementation benchmark; implementation-level optimization and benchmarking are left for future work. The present analysis is for a single authenticated roster per epoch; federated deployments, weighted sampling, and parallel relays require independently domain-separated instances and schedule-independent combiners, left for future work.

Disclosure of Interests. The authors have no competing interests to declare that are relevant to the content of this article.

References

1. Dwork, C., Lynch, N., Stockmeyer, L.: Consensus in the presence of partial synchrony. J. ACM **35**(2), 288–323 (1988)
2. Castro, M., Liskov, B.: Practical byzantine fault tolerance. In: OSDI (1999)
3. Yin, M., Malkhi, D., Reiter, M.K., Golan-Gueta, G., Abraham, I.: HotStuff: BFT consensus with linearity and responsiveness. In: *PODC* (2019)
4. Danezis, G., Kokoris-Kogias, E., Sonnino, A., Spiegelman, A.: Narwhal and tusk: a DAG-based mempool and efficient BFT consensus. In: EuroSys (2022)
5. Gilad, Y., Hemo, R., Micali, S., Vlachos, G., Zeldovich, N.: Algorand: scaling byzantine agreements for cryptocurrencies. In: SOSP (2017)

6. Kiayias, A., Russell, A., David, B., Oliynykov, R.: Ouroboros: A Provably Secure Proof-of-Stake Blockchain Protocol. In: CRYPTO (2017)
7. David, B., Gaži, P., Kiayias, A., Russell, A.: Ouroboros Praos: An Adaptively-Secure. EUROCRYPT, Semi-synchronous Proof-of-Stake Protocol. In (2018)
8. Micali, S., Rabin, M., Vadhan, S.: Verifiable random functions. In: FOCS (1999)
9. Goldberg, S., Reyzin, L., Papadopoulos, D., Včelák, J.: Verifiable Random Functions (VRFs). RFC 9381, IRTF (2023)
10. Syta, E., et al.: Scalable bias-resistant distributed randomness. In: IEEE S&P (2017)
11. Cascudo, I., David, B.: SCRAPE: scalable randomness attested by public entities. In: ACNS (2017)
12. Schindler, P., Judmayer, A., Stifter, N., Weippl, E.: HydRand: efficient continuous distributed randomness. In: IEEE S&P (2020)
13. League of Entropy: drand: Distributed Randomness Beacon. Documentation and whitepaper (2019–2024). https://drand.love/
14. Bandarupalli, A., Bhat, A., Bagchi, S., Kate, A., Reiter, M.K.: Random beacons in monte carlo: efficient asynchronous random beacon without threshold cryptography. In: CCS (2024)
15. RANDAO: Verifiable Random Number Generation. Whitepaper, version 0.85 (2017)
16. Alpturer, K., Weinberg, S.M.: Optimal RANDAO manipulation in Ethereum. In: AFT , LIPIcs **316**, 10:1–10:21 (2024)
17. Maram, S.K.D., et al.: CHURP: dynamic-committee proactive secret sharing. In: CCS (2019)
18. Vassantlal, R., Alchieri, E., Ferreira, B., Bessani, A.: COBRA: dynamic proactive secret sharing for confidential BFT services. In: IEEE S&P (2022)
19. Boneh, D., Bonneau, J., Bünz, B., Fisch, B.: Verifiable delay functions. IACR ePrint 2018/601 (2018)
20. Wesolowski, B.: Efficient verifiable delay functions. In: EUROCRYPT (2019)
21. Pietrzak, K.: Simple verifiable delay functions. In: ITCS (2019)
22. Boneh, D., Lynn, B., Shacham, H.: Short Signatures from the Weil Pairing. In: *ASIACRYPT* (2001)
23. Boneh, D., Gentry, C., Lynn, B., Shacham, H.: Aggregate and verifiably encrypted signatures from bilinear maps. In: EUROCRYPT (2003)
24. Faz-Hernández, A., Scott, S., Sullivan, N., Wahby, R.S., Wood, C.A.: Hashing to Elliptic Curves. RFC 9380, IRTF (2023)
25. Ristenpart, T., Yilek, S.: The power of proofs-of-possession: securing multiparty signatures against rogue-key attacks. In: EUROCRYPT (2007)
26. Feldman, P.: A practical scheme for non-interactive verifiable secret sharing. In: FOCS (1987)
27. Pedersen, T.P.: Non-interactive and information-theoretic secure verifiable secret sharing. In: CRYPTO (1991)
28. Canetti, R., Goldreich, O., Halevi, S.: The Random Oracle Methodology. STOC, Revisited. In (1998)
29. Canetti, R.: Universally composable security: a new paradigm for cryptographic protocols. In: FOCS (2001)
30. Groth, J.: On the size of pairing-based non-interactive arguments. In: EUROCRYPT (2016)
31. Ben-Sasson, E., Bentov, I., Horesh, Y., Riabzev, M.: Scalable, Transparent, and Post-Quantum Secure Computational Integrity. IACR ePrint 2018/046 (2018)

32. Gennaro, R., Jarecki, S., Krawczyk, H., Rabin, T.: Secure distributed key generation for discrete-log based cryptosystems. In: EUROCRYPT (1999)
33. Alsmeyer, G., Kabluchko, Z., Marynych, A.: Leader election using random walks. ALEA Lat. Am. J. Probab. Math. Stat. **13**, 1095–1122 (2016)

Security Modeling of Platform-Agnostic Electronic Know Your Customer (e-KYC) System

Yassir Yahaya(✉)

School of Computing, Newcastle University, Newcastle upon Tyne NE4 5TG, UK
y.yahaya2@newcastle.ac.uk

Abstract. Electronic know-your-customer (e-KYC) has in recent years attracted a wave of research interest. These interests have spiraled since the advent of blockchain technology, with most of them focusing on simplifying the KYC process by avoiding repetition and reducing cost associated with it, mitigating the rising scale and sophistication of fraud and identity theft, and addressing regulatory compliance challenges. However, majority of these studies remain tied to specific technologies, particularly blockchain, and do not offer a universal procedure with a formal security model that can be applied across different e-KYC paradigms, including self-sovereign identity, and cloud-based systems. This, in turn, creates practical challenges for regulatory compliance and cross-border interoperability, and it undermines the development of a uniform implementation model or framework that assures consistent security guarantees across different technological building blocks. We introduce PaKYC, a platform-agnostic and cross-sector security model for integrating e-KYC processes across diverse technological and regulatory settings. Our framework provides a formal security framework that abstracts key cryptographic operations to deliver technology-neutral security guarantees. It also supports features such as key recovery, certificate revocation, and user-authorized bi-jurisdictional data sharing; which have hitherto not been formally captured in existing KYC literature from a security-modelling perspective. We utilized game-based security experiments and comparative analysis against other KYC protocols—namely KYChain [12], TrustBlock [19], and AASSI [21]—to show that PaKYC captures the same security guarantees as they do, in addition to providing a broader traceability and accountability, making it a strong foundation for secure, interoperable, and regulatory compliant e-KYC systems.

Keywords: Electronic Know-Your-Customer (e-KYC) · Platform-agnostic security framework · Formal security modeling · Interoperability · Traceability and accountability

1 Introduction

Over time, the Know-Your-Customer (KYC) procedure has evolved into a core prerequisite for accessing many services in modern economies. Initially centered

N. El Mrabet et al. (Eds.): AFRICACRYPT 2026, LNCS 16832, pp. 460–487, 2026.
https://doi.org/10.1007/978-3-032-31130-6_19

on and still dominated by the financial sector ([31] [12] [33] [11] [37] [39]), KYC has increasingly found applicability in many other sectors—such as health [36], real estate [41], and media [27]. Some studies also target multi-sectoral application, including (but not limited to) Pauwels' ZkKYC [35], Sundareswaran et al. [40], Bandara et al. [4], and Lundkvist et al.'s uPort [29], among others. This adoption of KYC on a wider scale is partly driven by the digitization of KYC (e-KYC), and that of service delivery in general. Presently, most organizations have platforms for onboarding customers remotely, accepting electronic documents and biometrics [6]. They also utilize digital workflows to help in reducing cost associated with KYC operations, improving user experience, and scaling operations [5].

However, this new regime for conducting KYC also brings a corresponding shift in the threat landscape. KYC information is sensitive and reusable, making identity verification workflows and KYC datasets attractive targets. Adversarial attacks span multiple points: forged or manipulated documents, synthetic identities [9] (especially with the advent of Artificial Intelligence (AI) [24]), credential and device compromise, abuse of privileged insider access, and exploitation of weaknesses in verification pipelines. The repercussions for the customer include financial losses, identity theft and long-term privacy impacts, while the organization faces regulatory sanctions, reputational harm, and damage to systems.

Additionally, mandatory compliance with obligations like Anti-Money Laundering and Combating the Financing of Terrorism (AML/CFT) [43], and privacy and data-protection regulations such as the EU's General Data Protection Regulation (GDPR) [44] adds another layer of challenge. AML/CFT requires strong customer due diligence and demonstrable accountability, while GDPR frames customer-data handling around principles of purpose limitation, data minimization, storage limitation, integrity/confidentiality, and accountability [15]. In February 2025, for example, the US Department of Justice fined OKX—a cryptocurrency exchange— over $500 million for violating US anti-money laundering laws [42].

Numerous works have proposed different solutions, ranging from protocols to architectures for e-KYC in order to mitigate the aforementioned challenges, particularly since the advent of blockchain and SSI-inspired designs. They are mostly focused on reducing repeated onboarding [12], lowering verification costs [32], improving auditability [5], enhancing compliance with regulatory policies such as GDPR [10], boosting conformity with AML/CFT obligations [23], and improving forgery detection [3]. However, in spite of the myriad of solutions proposed by existing studies to mitigate the aforementioned problems, the e-KYC landscape remains more fragmented than it is unified, as the majority of those solutions remain tied to specific technology stacks, especially blockchain-based deployments. This implies that the guarantees they provide do not translate cleanly across other paradigms, such as cloud-based e-KYC [34] or alternative trust infrastructures [22]. The absence of such guarantees consistently across different KYC building blocks may have some practical consequences during implementation in the following areas:

i. Interoperability: organizations rarely operate within a single homogeneous e-KYC building block and architecture. Activities such as sharing verified KYC data across verifiers are difficult to reason about when each design assumes a different trust and threat model (what is assumed to be reliable, in what way; who the attacker is, their capabilities, what is being protected).
ii. Regulatory Evaluation: complications could arise here as regulators and auditors would require consistent security claims, yet the meaning of a property like confidentiality or traceability can vary across architectures. The question of clearly defined accountability boundaries across disparate KYC verifiers and regulators may arise here, such as which entities are responsible for which checks and controls (e.g., validation, revocation checking, and policy enforcement).
iii. Cross-border Operation: cases of errors in compliance could arise when KYC data is exchanged across jurisdictions, as different regulatory policies may apply. Complying with these policies through ad-hoc integration without pre-existing bi or multi-jurisdictional compliance framework may complicate cross-border operation.

All the listed challenges motivates the need for a formal, platform-agnostic security framework for e-KYC. While a formal model provides a common language for specifying entities, capabilities, security goals, and attacker power, a platform-agnostic framework enables technology-neutral comparison where one can abstract the essential operations responsible for implementing security guarantees rather than tying them to a particular architecture or building block. Without an available explicit adversarial model and well-defined security experiments, it becomes unclear what exactly is being protected, what the attacker is allowed to do, and whether claimed guarantees still hold under realistic compromise scenarios such as key loss, credential theft, or malicious insiders.

Existing works that offer some form of formal security treatment still leave gaps that matter for real deployments. KYChain [12] provides a privacy-preserving certification protocol for blockchain-based e-KYC and models properties such as data confidentiality and certificate compliance, but it does not address post-compromise confidentiality or post on-boarding compliance enforcement via key recovery or certificate revocation. In addition, its modeling scope does not explicitly address interoperability among verifiers within the same jurisdiction or across jurisdictions, which is central to real-world KYC operations. AASSI [21] formalizes multiple properties, including correctness, unforgeability, anonymity, and traceability, but it remains anchored in a blockchain-based SSI setting, limiting portability to other e-KYC paradigms. TrustBlock [19] leverages Ciphertext-Policy Attribute-Based Encryption (CP-ABE) [7] to enforce fine-grained access control in a blockchain-based design, but its formal treatment is largely centred on the underlying primitive and does not provide a unified, game-based model that simultaneously addresses life-cycle requirements such as revocation, replacement, recovery, and cross-verifier sharing under explicit adversarial power. In general, the lack of a single, platform-agnostic framework makes it difficult to express what is shared across these systems, what differs, and which assumptions are necessary for the claimed guarantees.

In this work, we introduce PaKYC, a platform-agnostic and cross-sector e-KYC framework that aims to provide technology-neutral security guarantees and regulatory compliance across diverse e-KYC paradigms. PaKYC abstracts core cryptographic capabilities into agnostic operations (for confidentiality and authentication), and specifies the entities, algorithms, lists, and threat-driven experiments needed to model key stages of the KYC life-cycle (i.e., onboarding, due diligence, suspicious activity reporting, offboarding [16,17]). Beyond modelling, PaKYC explicitly supports operational requirements that are often left informal in prior work, including key revocation and replacement, certificate revocation, and user-authorized cross-verifier data sharing both within a jurisdiction and across jurisdictions, under regulator-governed policies.

Contribution. Our contributions are as follows:

i We propose a formal, platform-agnostic security framework for e-KYC that supports consistent reasoning across disparate e-KYC paradigms and provides a standardization-oriented foundation for secure design.
ii We define a set of security properties using game-based experiments with explicit adversarial capabilities and winning conditions, covering fundamental requirements such as data confidentiality, traceability as well as operational life-cycle requirements such as key replacement, and revocation of keys and credentials. We additionally formalize and analyze cross-verifier data sharing within a jurisdiction and across jurisdictions, capturing the conditions under which a new verifier can accept a user-permissioned shared KYC data without violating confidentiality or policy constraints.
iii We conduct a security-grounded comparative analysis against representative prior works (including KYChain [12], TrustBlock [19], and AASSI [21]), showing that PaKYC captures their shared guarantees while extending coverage to interoperability and life cycle requirements that are not explicitly modelled in those systems.

Organization. The remainder of this paper is structured as follows. Section 2 presents the PaKYC framework, including entities, notations, assumptions, algorithms, and security experiments. Section 3 provides comparative analysis and discusses instantiations, similarities, and how we extend the literature via PaKYC. Section 4 concludes and outlines future directions.

2 PaKYC Security Modeling

2.1 Entities

PaKYC serves as both the definitional framework and a specific instance of the framework. For our modeling specification, we begin by defining the entities responsible for the activities that culminate in the e-KYC process, which we intend to model in the latter part of this paper. In our scheme, each entity is endowed with confidentiality capabilities—represented by the data-sealing operation $\mathcal{S}$ and the data-unsealing operation $\mathcal{S}^{-1}$—and authentication capabilities—represented by the attestation creation operation $\mathcal{A}$ and the proof verification operation $\mathcal{V}^{fy}$. To illustrate the adoption of these agnostic approaches in our framework using public key cryptography, sealing and unsealing abstract over encryption and decryption, whereas attestation creation and proof verification abstract over authentication and verification. While in symmetric encryption, the sealing operation is invertible (can be unsealed) by the holder of the key (call it $\mathcal{K}$), and the same key is used for both sealing and unsealing (i.e., $\mathcal{K} = \mathcal{K}^{-1}$ in that instantiation). In tokenization-based systems, sealing and unsealing operations are represented by the tokenization/detokenization privileges. However, our framework imposes no such restriction, as we leave those critical decisions to the implementers who best understand their own environment.

Each entity X is equipped with two keys that enable it to perform the confidentiality and authentication operations introduced above. For simplicity, we label these as follows: the sealing key—denoted by $\mathcal{K}_X$, where X is the entity that owns the key– is used for sealing and proof verification operation. While the accompanying unsealing key, denoted by $\mathcal{K}_X^{-1}$, is used for unsealing and attestation operations. We define the entities as follows:

- **User:** An individual or a corporate entity intending to access services requiring identity verification. Multiple users can engage the services of one or more verifiers—an entity we will be discussing next. The User, which we denote as '**U**', is subjected to the KYC process directly with the verifying entity it intends to establish a business relationship with. For both the confidentiality and authentication capabilities, **U** is empowered with a key pair consisting of a sealing key $\mathcal{K}_U$, and a unsealing key $\mathcal{K}_U^{-1}$, where $\mathcal{K}_U$ is used for the sealing and proof verification operation, and $\mathcal{K}_U^{-1}$ for unsealing and attestation operations respectively.
- **Regulator:** Responsible for enacting and enforcing policies governing the KYC process, as well as overseeing and monitoring the verifying entity (to be discussed next) to ensure strict compliance with legal requirements. Examples of regulators include central banks, the UK's Financial Conduct Authority (FCA), the US' Financial Crimes Enforcement Network (FinCEN), or any government-appointed agencies as found in other different jurisdictions. In our algorithms discussion, the regulator, denoted as '**R**', is responsible for the policy Ψ_R that serves as the regulatory framework governing the KYC process. Analogously to **U**, '**R**' has a sealing key $\mathcal{K}_R$, and an unsealing key $\mathcal{K}_R^{-1}$.
- **Verifier:** The verifier provides the services requested or needed by the user and verifies their identity before providing a service. It is ultimately responsible for subjecting the user '**U**' to the KYC process and ensuring regulatory compliance in the process. Denote as '**V**' in our framework, the verifier issues KYC certificates (service approval/enrollment) upon a successful KYC pro-

cess outcome. Examples include banks, hospitals, insurance, and telecoms providers. In our framework, we assume the existence of multiple verifiers within the KYC ecosystem. Similarly to the User entity earlier discussed, each **V** possesses a sealing key $\mathcal{K}_V$—for sealing and proof verification operation—and an unsealing key $\mathcal{K}_V^{-1}$—for unsealing and attestation operations. We also denote the verifier responsible for performing the initial KYC process and issuing the root verifiable credential as the **anchor verifier**, which serves as the trust anchor for all subsequent presentations of that credential to other verifiers within the same or different jurisdictions.
- **Issuer:** These are trusted authorities that issue and validate verifiable identities used by a user to carry out a KYC exercise. Passport details, national ID, driver's license, and verifiable credentials in SSI are some of the popular credentials used for KYC. Examples of identity-issuing organizations include government agencies such as passport authorities, interior ministries, driver licensing organizations, and blockchain-based decentralized identity issuers. We denote the issuer by **I** in our framework, backed by a sealing and an unsealing key pair $(\mathcal{K}_I, \mathcal{K}_I^{-1})$ for performing the confidentiality and authentication operations defined earlier, and we assume the existence of multiple issuers in the system.

2.2 Notations

We utilize the following notations in our syntaxes:

- We define Z as a finite set, where $Z \to x$ indicates that x is chosen uniformly at random from Z.
- The notation $A(a) \to b$ denotes an algorithm A where the input a leads to the output b.
- Let the expression $P_{A,B}\langle a, b\rangle \to \langle (c)_A, (d)_B\rangle$ describe an interactive protocol between the entities A and B, where A inputs a and B inputs b. As a result of the protocol, A ends up with c, and B with d.
- Let the expression $P_{A,B}\langle a, b\rangle \to (c)_A$ illustrate interaction between entities A and B, where A inputs a and B inputs b. The outcome results in A getting the output c.
- We formalize policy Ψ_R as a boolean predicate $\Psi_R : \{0,1\}^* \to \{0,1\}$ that evaluates to 1 if the input $Data$, $UPinfo$, keys, or Φ satisfy jurisdictional compliance rules, and 0 otherwise. Compliance checks of the form $(X \models \Psi_R)$ are evaluated by running $\Psi_R(X)$ and verifying the output is 1. The specific contents of Ψ_R are jurisdiction-dependent and are treated as a public, fixed parameter in our model.
- We use the term **object** as a general term for any structured entity in the PaKYC model, including keys $(\mathcal{K}_U, \mathcal{K}_V, \mathcal{K}_R, \mathcal{K}_I)$, identifiers (Uid, Vid), credentials (Φ), policies (Ψ_R), and data payloads. We reserve the term **data** specifically to refer to a user's KYC information payload $UPinfo$ or $Data$, with the latter being the specific object subject to confidentiality protection in the model.

- Let h_X denote a unique non-keyed tag $\mathcal{H}$ of an object X generated via the tagging function $h_X \leftarrow \mathcal{H}\{X\}$, where $\mathcal{H} : \{0,1\}^* \rightarrow \{0,1\}^\lambda$ is modeled as a collision-resistant hash function.
- Let $\mathcal{T}_X$ denote a unique keyed tag $\mathfrak{T}$ of an object X generated via the tagging function $\mathcal{T}_X \leftarrow \mathfrak{T}\{X|\delta_X\}$, where $\mathcal{T}$: $\{0,1\}^*$ x $\{0,1\}^\lambda$ is modeled as a pseudo-random function (PRF), and $\mathfrak{T}\{X|\delta_X\} := \text{PRF}(\delta, X)$ for a key $\delta \leftarrow \{0,1\}^\lambda$ drawn uniformly at random. δ_X is a secret commitment defined explicitly as a uniform random salt $\delta_X \leftarrow \{0,1\}^\lambda$, generated fresh for each KYC data item X. We will also clarify that the purpose of δ_X is to ensure that $\mathcal{T}_X$ is not a deterministic function of X alone, which is essential for GDPR-compatible implementations (e.g., on immutable ledgers where erasure of δ_X renders $\mathcal{T}_X$ unlinkable to X).
- We require $\mathsf{bundle} : \mathsf{object}^* \leftarrow \{0,1\}^*$ to be injective, so that $\mathsf{unbundle} : \{0,1\}^* \leftarrow \mathsf{object}^*$ is well-defined as its left inverse (i.e., $\mathsf{unbundle}(\mathsf{bundle}([A_1, A_2, \ldots, A_n])) = [A_1, A_2, \ldots, A_n]$). In practice, this is realized by standard length-prefixed or delimiter-based serialization formats. For simplicity, we represent bundle and $\mathsf{unbundle}$ with $:=$ and $=:$ respectively.
- We define $\mathcal{K}_{\mathsf{seal}}$ and $\mathcal{K}_{\mathsf{unseal}}$ as the sets of all valid sealing and unsealing keys, respectively, such that for every key $\mathcal{K} \in \mathcal{K}_{\mathsf{seal}}$, there exists a corresponding recovery key $\mathcal{K}^{-1} \in \mathcal{K}_{\mathsf{unseal}}$.
- Let $\mathcal{S} : \mathcal{M} \times \mathcal{K}_{\mathsf{seal}} \rightarrow \mathcal{C}$ be a deterministic or probabilistic sealing algorithm. We let $[M]_{\mathcal{K}} \in \mathcal{C}$ denote the sealed container generated by evaluating $[M]_{\mathcal{K}} \leftarrow \mathcal{S}(M, \mathcal{K})$, where $M \in \mathcal{M}$ represents the payload and $\mathcal{K} \in \mathcal{K}_{\mathsf{seal}}$ is the sealing key.
- Let $\mathcal{S}^{-1} : \mathcal{C} \times \mathcal{K}_{\mathsf{unseal}} \rightarrow \mathcal{M} \cup \{\perp\}$ be a deterministic unsealing algorithm. We let $M \leftarrow \mathcal{S}^{-1}([M]_{\mathcal{K}}, \mathcal{K}^{-1})$ denote the recovery of the original payload M from a sealed container $[M]_{\mathcal{K}}$ using the corresponding private (or symmetric) key $\mathcal{K}^{-1}$, where $M \in \mathcal{M}$ represents the payload and $\mathcal{K}^{-1} \in \mathcal{K}_{\mathsf{unseal}}$ is the unsealing key. The algorithm outputs the error symbol $\perp$ if the container is invalid.
- Let $[\sigma_M]_{\mathcal{K}^{-1}}$ denote an attestation made by an entity on a data M with a key $\mathcal{K}^{-1}$ defined by the attestation creation function $[\sigma_M]_{\mathcal{K}^{-1}} \leftarrow \mathcal{A}(M, \mathcal{K}^{-1})$. $\mathcal{A}$ is defined by $\mathcal{A} : \mathcal{M} \times \mathcal{K}_{\mathsf{unseal}} \rightarrow \mathcal{S}$. For brevity, we write σ_M (or any chosen symbol) in place of $[\sigma_M]_{\mathcal{K}^{-1}}$, as the signing key is always made explicit in the corresponding $\mathcal{A}(M, \mathcal{K}^{-1})$ call that generates the attestation.
- Let $b \in \{0,1\}$ denote the Boolean result of a proof verification operation on the attestation $[\sigma_M]_{\mathcal{K}^{-1}}$ for a message M, using the key $\mathcal{K}$, defined by the proof verification function $b \leftarrow \mathcal{V}^{fy}(\,[\sigma_M]_{\mathcal{K}^{-1}}, M, \mathcal{K})$. $\mathcal{V}^{fy}$ is defined by $\mathcal{V}^{fy} : \mathcal{S} \times \mathcal{M} \times \mathcal{K}_{\mathsf{seal}} \rightarrow \{0,1\}$
- Let $V_{List} \leftarrow Add_V(Vid, \mathcal{K}_V, ts, \mathcal{K}_R^{-1})$ denote an operation performed by the regulator **R** to add a verifier **V** to the verifier list V_{List} maintained by **R**, where Vid denotes **V**'s unique ID, $\mathcal{K}_V$ denotes **V**'s sealing key, ts denotes the timestamp at which the addition is made, and $\mathcal{K}_R^{-1}$ denotes the regulator's unsealing key authorizing the transaction.
- Let $I_{List} \leftarrow Add_I(Iid, \mathcal{K}_I, ts, \mathcal{K}_R^{-1})$ denote an operation performed by the regulator **R** to add an Issuer **I** to the Issuer list I_{List} maintained by **R**,

where Iid denotes **I**'s unique ID, $\mathcal{K}_I$ denotes **I**'s sealing key, ts denotes the timestamp at which the addition is made, and $\mathcal{K}_R^{-1}$ denotes the regulator's unsealing key authorizing the transaction.

- Let $\Psi_{\text{R,R}'}$ denote bi-jurisdictional policy formed by merging policies Ψ_{R}, $\Psi_{\text{R}'}$ between two different jurisdictions A, and B. In the case where A, and B are from the same jurisdiction, then $\Psi_{\text{R,R}'}$ is simply assumed to be the same as Ψ_{R}.
- Let '**if**$(\langle A_1, A_2, \ldots, A_n\rangle \in X_{List})$' for $n \geq 1$ denote a conditional statement that returns **true** if there exists a tuple $t \in X_{List}$ such that $(t.A_1 = A_1 \wedge t.A_2 = A_2 \wedge \cdots \wedge t.A_n = A_n)$, and returns **false** otherwise.
- Likewise, let '**if**$(\langle A_1, A_2, \ldots, A_n\rangle \notin X_{List})$' for $n \geq 1$ denote a conditional statement that returns **true** if there is no tuple $t \in X_{List}$ such that $(t.A_1 = A_1 \wedge t.A_2 = A_2 \wedge \cdots \wedge t.A_n = A_n)$, and returns **false** otherwise.

2.3 Assumptions

While we may mention certain specific assumptions in the subsequent sections of this work, the following general assumptions hold:

1. We assume PaKYC works in a setting where regulatory oversight is required or mandatory.
2. We assume that while a jurisdiction can only have one regulator **R** governed by a single policy Ψ_{R}, it may contain multiple users **U**, verifiers **V**, and issuers **I**.
3. We assume both single jurisdictional policy Ψ_{R} and bi-jurisdictional policy $\Psi_{\text{R,R}'}$ are public knowledge, and for brevity, we omit including them in our syntax inputs requiring compliance checks.
4. We assume certificate revocation by **V**—which signals withdrawal of services to a user **U**—is limited to the verifier's platform the user belongs to. That is, the user's credential is removed only from that specific verifier's platform, and flagging or removing its certificate from list of certified users. Revocation that triggers jurisdiction-wide key blacklisting due to a policy-compliance violation under Ψ_{R} warranting regulatory escalation (e.g., confirmed identity fraud) is treated as a regulator-sanctioned action rather than a unilateral verifier decision. We leave the modelling of such cases for future research.
5. We assume that both the public and private registers in PaKYC of the form X_{List} are incorruptible, cannot be altered illegitimately, and remain consistent across all verifiers and regulators. In practice, the integrity and consistency of public registers ($V_{List}, I_{List}, CU_{List}, CRV_{List}, BLK_{List}$, and SH_{List}) can be realized via append-only authenticated data structures such as merkle trees, certificate transparency logs, or blockchain-based ledgers. The incorruptibility assumption allows us abstract away the specific realization mechanism. Relaxing it to model a Byzantine-fault-tolerant register is an identified direction for future work.

6. We assume that all communication channels between honest parties are secure against eavesdropping and tampering. This assumption is a standard abstraction to isolate the application-layer security properties of PaKYC from transport-layer and network-layer concerns. Where confidential or authenticated transport is required, we assume it is provided by standard secure-channel mechanisms such as TLS or authenticated out-of-band delivery. Modeling network-level channel compromise is outside the scope of this paper.
7. We assume that in cross-jurisdictional scenarios, the PaKYC framework is limited to just two jurisdictions at a given time.
8. We assume that the data (*Data*) used by **U** for the KYC process is issued by a trusted issuer **I** belonging to the same jurisdiction as the verifier **V** that the user intends to engage for their very first verification.
9. We assume each user **U**, verifier **V**, and issuer **I** implicitly keeps verifiable logs ($\mathcal{L}_U$, $\mathcal{L}_V$, $\mathcal{L}_I$, respectively) of all its interactions with the other parties (users, verifiers, and issuers) as well as with the internal regulator **R** and external regulator(s) **R'**.
10. Finally, PaKYC assumes an honest regulator, consistent with the standard approach in PKI-based security models where root certificate authorities are treated as unconditionally trusted. A corrupt regulator would, by design, compromise both traceability (by refusing to unseal $\mathcal{K}_R$ protected payloads) and confidentiality (by leaking them). Modeling regulator corruption and recovery, for example, via threshold secret sharing of $\mathcal{K}_R$ across multiple regulatory authorities, is an important extension for multi-jurisdictional deployments and is identified as future work.

2.4 Algorithms

Setup(λ) $\rightarrow$ pp: A probabilistic polynomial-time (PPT) algorithm run by **R**, whose running time is polynomial in the security parameter λ. The Setup algorithm establishes the e-KYC ecosystem by taking a security parameter λ and outputs a public parameter *pp*. We assume **R** has already generated $\mathcal{K}_R, \mathcal{K}_R^{-1}$ via $\mathsf{KeyGen}_\mathsf{R}(\mathsf{Rid}) \rightarrow (\mathcal{K}_\mathsf{R}, \mathcal{K}_\mathsf{R}^{-1})$. After publishing *pp*, Verifiers (**V**) and Issuers (**I**) generate their own keys via KeyGen_V and KeyGen_I. $\mathtt{Setup}$ requires an initial number of **V**s and **I**s to populate a public verifiers list V_{List} and a public issuers list I_{List}, both maintained by **R**. **R** also creates the public lists: CU_{List} (Certified Users), CRV_{List} (revoked certificates), BLK_{List} (revoked user public keys Pk_U), and SH_{List} (cross-verifier data-sharing requests), and publishes the regulatory policy Ψ_R. Each on-boarded **V** additionally maintains private lists: RU_{List} (registered users) and OBU_{List} (KYC-approved users' private data). Each **V** keeps local copies of CU_{List}, CRV_{List}, BLK_{List}, and SH_{List}, periodically broadcasting updates to **R** for compliance.

KeyGen$_\mathbf{V}$(pp, Vid) $\rightarrow$ ($\mathcal{K}_\mathbf{V}, \mathcal{K}_\mathbf{V}^{-1}$): Generates a verifier's sealing/unsealing key pair, personalised by *pp* and the verifier's unique identifier Vid.

KeyGen$_\mathbf{I}$(pp, Iid) $\rightarrow$ ($\mathcal{K}_\mathbf{I}, \mathcal{K}_\mathbf{I}^{-1}$): Generates an issuer's sealing/unsealing key pair from *pp* and its unique identifier Iid.

KeyGen$_{\mathbf{U}}$**(pp, UPinfo)** $\rightarrow (\mathcal{K}_U, \mathcal{K}_U^{-1})$: Generates the user's key pair from *pp* and personal information *UPinfo*, storing $\mathcal{K}_U^{-1}$ in secure storage.
Issue$_{\mathbf{I,U}}$ $\langle(\mathbf{pp}, \mathcal{K}_I^{-1}, \mathcal{K}_U), (\mathbf{pp}, \mathbf{UPinfo}, \mathcal{K}_U^{-1}, \mathcal{K}_I)\rangle \rightarrow \langle(\mathbf{UPinfo}), (\mathbf{Uid})\rangle$: An interactive algorithm between an issuer **I** and a user **U** that generates **U**'s unique identifier. Both parties attest with their unsealing keys $\mathcal{K}_U^{-1}, \mathcal{K}_I^{-1}$; **U** additionally submits its personally identifiable information *UPinfo* (e.g., SSN, name, date of birth, address) to **I** (identified by $\mathcal{K}_I$). **I** issues Uid and saves *UPinfo* if Ψ_R is satisfied; otherwise it returns $\perp$.
Register$_{\mathbf{U,V}}$ $\langle(\mathbf{pp}, \mathbf{Uid}, \mathcal{K}_I, \mathcal{K}_U^{-1}, \mathcal{K}_V, \mathtt{cc}), (\mathbf{pp}, \mathcal{K}_V^{-1}, \mathcal{K}_U)\rangle \rightarrow \langle(\varrho), (\mathbf{Uid})\rangle/\perp$: An interactive algorithm initiated by **U** to begin the KYC process with **V**. **U** attests with $\mathcal{K}_U^{-1}$ and submits Uid, the issuing authority's $\mathcal{K}_I$, and an out-of-band communication channel cc (e.g., email, SMS, biometric link, push notification) to **V**. **V** attests with $\mathcal{K}_V^{-1}$ and verifies $\langle Iid, \mathcal{K}_I\rangle \in I_{List}$. On success, **V** issues an attested registration token ϱ generated from Uid and the registration timestamp reg-date, and stores $\langle Uid, \mathcal{K}_U, \mathtt{cc}, \varrho\rangle$ in RU_{List}. The execution returns $\perp$ on any failure.
CertifyUpdate$_{\mathbf{U,V}}$ $\langle(\mathbf{pp}, \mathcal{K}_U^{-1}, \mathbf{Uid}, \mathcal{K}_V, \mathbf{op}, \mathbf{dat}), (\mathbf{pp}, \mathcal{K}_V^{-1}, \mathbf{Vid}, \mathcal{K}_U)\rangle \rightarrow \langle(\Theta_1), (\Theta_2)\rangle/\perp$: An interactive algorithm between **U** (authenticated with $\mathcal{K}_U^{-1}$) and **V** (identified by Vid, governed by Ψ_R) handling both initial certification and later KYC-data updates, selected by $op \in \{\mathtt{issue}, \mathtt{update}\}$. When $op = \mathtt{issue}$, **U** submits $dat := [Data, ts_U, \varrho, \pi_U]$, where $Data$ is **U**'s KYC information, ϱ is the registration token from **V**, ts_U is **U**'s timestamp, and $\pi_U \leftarrow \mathcal{A}(req, \mathcal{K}_U^{-1})$ is an attestation over $req := [Uid, Vid, \mathtt{issue}, h_{\mathtt{Data}}, ts_U]$. **V** checks $Data \models \Psi_R$, verifies ϱ under $\mathcal{K}_V$, and verifies π_U under $\mathcal{K}_U$. On success, **V** generates a secret commitment $\delta_{\mathtt{Data}}$, computes $\mathcal{T}_{\mathtt{Data}} \leftarrow \mathfrak{T}\{Data|\delta_{\mathtt{Data}}\}$, issues a unique transaction reference t-ref, and builds $Z := [Data, \delta_{\mathtt{Data}}, ts_U, Uid, Vid]$, $\varphi \leftarrow \mathcal{A}(Z, \mathcal{K}_V^{-1})$, $P := [Z, \varphi]$, $Q \leftarrow \mathcal{S}(P, \mathcal{K}_R)$, and $m := [h_{\mathtt{Uid}}, Q, \mathtt{t\text{-}ref}, \mathcal{T}_{\mathtt{Data}}, ts, \Psi_R]$, where $h_{\mathtt{Uid}}$ is the non-keyed tag of **U**'s ID and ts is **V**'s timestamp at message generation. **V** produces $\sigma_m \leftarrow \mathcal{A}(m, \mathcal{K}_V^{-1})$ and bundles $\Phi := [m, \sigma_m]$. **U** receives $\Theta_1 = (\mathtt{t\text{-}ref}, \Phi, \delta_{\mathtt{Data}})$ and **V** keeps $\Theta_2 = (\Phi, Data, \pi_U, ts_U, \delta_{\mathtt{Data}})$. **V** appends $\langle Uid, \mathtt{t\text{-}ref}, Data, \Phi, \mathcal{T}_{\mathtt{t\text{-}ref}}, ts, ts_U, \delta_{\mathtt{Data}}, \Delta\rangle$ to OBU_{List} (Δ flags the record as new or updated), and saves $\langle\pi_U, h_{\mathtt{t\text{-}ref}}, h_{\mathtt{Uid}}, h_{\mathtt{Vid}}, \mathcal{T}_{\mathtt{Data}}, h_\Phi, ts, \mathcal{K}_U, \mathcal{K}_V\rangle$ in CU_{List}.
When $op = \mathtt{update}$, **U** submits $dat = (Data', ts'_U, \mathtt{t\text{-}ref}, \pi'_U)$ with $\pi'_U \leftarrow \mathcal{A}(req', \mathcal{K}_U^{-1})$ over $req' := [Uid, Vid, \mathtt{update}, h_{\mathtt{Data'}}, ts'_U]$. **V** confirms t-ref appears in OBU_{List}, validates $Data' \models \Psi_R$, verifies π'_U, generates fresh $\delta_{\mathtt{Data'}}$, computes $\mathcal{T}_{\mathtt{Data'}} \leftarrow \mathfrak{T}\{Data'|\delta_{\mathtt{Data'}}\}$, and builds $Z' := [Data', \delta'_{\mathtt{Data}}, ts'_U, Uid, Vid]$, $\varphi' \leftarrow \mathcal{A}(Z', \mathcal{K}_V^{-1})$, $P' := [Z', \varphi']$, $Q' \leftarrow \mathcal{S}(P', \mathcal{K}_R)$, and $m' := [h_{\mathtt{Uid}}, Q', \mathtt{t\text{-}ref}, \mathcal{T}_{\mathtt{Data'}}, ts', \Psi_R]$. **V** produces $\sigma_{m'} \leftarrow \mathcal{A}(m', \mathcal{K}_V^{-1})$ and bundles $\Phi' := [m', \sigma_{m'}]$. **U** receives $\Theta_1 = \Phi', \delta_{\mathtt{Data'}}$; **V** keeps $\Theta_2 = (\Phi', Data', \pi'_U, ts'_U, \delta_{\mathtt{Data'}})$. **V** replaces **U**'s record in OBU_{List} with $\langle Uid, \mathtt{t\text{-}ref}, Data', \Phi', h_{\mathtt{t\text{-}ref}}, ts', ts'_U, \delta_{\mathtt{Data'}}, \Delta'\rangle$ and updates the corresponding $h_{\mathtt{t\text{-}ref}}$ tuple in CU_{List} with $\langle\pi'_U, h_{\mathtt{t\text{-}ref}}, h_{\mathtt{Uid}}, h_{\mathtt{Vid}}, \mathcal{T}_{\mathtt{Data'}}, h_{\Phi'}, ts', \mathcal{K}_U, \mathcal{K}_V\rangle$. The old tuple bearing h_Φ is flagged or removed, and $\langle h_{\mathtt{Uid}}, \Phi, ts_{rev}, \mathcal{K}_V\rangle$ is

appended to CRV_{List}, with ts_{rev} the revocation timestamp. The interactive algorithm returns $\perp$ on any failure in either branch.

Verify(pp, $\mathcal{K}_{V'}^{-1}$, $\mathcal{K}_U$, $\mathcal{K}_V$, t-ref, Φ) $\rightarrow$ (1/0): Lets a new verifier **V'** (assumed to have obtained Φ with **U**'s consent) self-verify the anchor-issued Φ and its `t-ref`. **V'** first checks $\Phi \notin CRV_{List}$, unbundles Φ into σ_m, m, and runs $b \leftarrow \mathcal{V}^{fy}(\sigma_m, m, \mathcal{K}_V)$ to confirm Φ as a valid attestation by the anchor **V**. If $b = 1$, Φ's issuance by the anchor **V** is confirmed and the regulator-sealed payload Q in m is established as untampered, since Q contains $\varphi \leftarrow \mathcal{A}(Z, \mathcal{K}_V^{-1})$ over $Z := [Data, \delta_{\texttt{Data}}, ts_U, Uid, Vid]$, unsealable only by **R**. **V'** then computes h_Φ, $h_{\texttt{t-ref}}$ and confirms they appear together with $\mathcal{K}_U$ in a CU_{List} tuple. The algorithm returns 1 on success, 0 otherwise.

Trace(pp, $\mathcal{K}_R^{-1}$, Φ) $\rightarrow$ (Uid, Vid) / $\perp$: Run by **R**, Trace links a valid KYC credential Φ to its issuing verifier **V** and recipient user **U**. **R** first validates $\Phi \notin CRV_{List}$ and $h_\Phi \in CU_{List}$, then unbundles Φ into m, σ_m, and m into $[h_{\texttt{Uid}}, Q, \texttt{t-ref}, \mathcal{T}_{\texttt{Data}}, ts, \Psi_R]$. **R** unseals Q with $\mathcal{K}_R^{-1}$ to obtain $P := [Z, \varphi]$ where $Z := [Data, \delta_{\texttt{Data}}, ts_U, Uid, Vid]$. From P, Vid is used to retrieve $\mathcal{K}_V$ from V_{List}, and **R** runs $\mathcal{V}^{fy}(\sigma_m, m, \mathcal{K}_V)$ to confirm **V** as legitimate issuer of Φ, and $\mathcal{V}^{fy}(\varphi, Z, \mathcal{K}_V)$ to confirm payload integrity. **R** then computes h_Φ, $h_{\texttt{Uid}}$, $h_{\texttt{Vid}}$, $\mathcal{T}_{\texttt{Data}}$, $h_{\texttt{t-ref}}$ and matches them in a CU_{List} tuple. Outputs (Uid, Vid) on success; otherwise $\perp$.

RevokeKey(pp, $\mathcal{K}_V^{-1}$, Uid, $\mathcal{K}_U$, $\mathcal{K}_V$): When a breach (or other Ψ_R-sanctioned reason) is suspected on a registered user's keys, **V** stops honoring attestations from $\mathcal{K}_U^{-1}$ by appending $\langle h_{\texttt{Uid}}, \mathcal{K}_U, ts_{bl}, \mathcal{K}_V \rangle$ to BLK_{List}, where ts_{bl} is the blacklisting timestamp. **V** authenticates the operation with $\mathcal{K}_V^{-1}$. Returns 1 on success after updating BLK_{List}, $\perp$ otherwise.

RevokeCert(pp, $\mathcal{K}_V^{-1}$, Uid, $\mathcal{K}_U$, Φ, $\mathcal{K}_V$): **V** off-boards **U** by revoking Φ when **U** fails Ψ_R compliance. The algorithm flags or removes the tuple bearing Uid and Φ in OBU_{List}, removes the tuple bearing h_Φ from CU_{List}, and appends $\langle h_{\texttt{Uid}}, \Phi, ts_{rev}, \mathcal{K}_V \rangle$ to CRV_{List}. Returns 1 on success (with updated OBU'_{List}, RU'_{List}, CRV'_{List}, CU'_{List} periodically shared with **R** for compliance), $\perp$ on failure.

GetToken(pp, Uid, $\mathcal{K}_V$, Φ, cc) $\rightarrow$ η / $\perp$: **U** runs this with **V** to obtain a unique token η used by the subsequent RestoreKey call. **V** verifies it issued Φ, checks $Uid \in OBU_{List}$, confirms $h_{\texttt{Uid}} \notin CRV_{List}$, and validates the out-of-band channel cc against RU_{List} for the same Uid. On success, η is delivered to **U** over cc and **V** stores $\langle Uid, \eta, ts_\eta \rangle$ (ts_η being the token's expiry). The algorithm run returns $\perp$ on failure.

RestoreKey$_{U,V}$$\langle$(pp, Uid, η, Φ, $\mathcal{K}'_U$, $\mathcal{K}_V$), (pp, η, $\mathcal{K}_V^{-1}$)$\rangle$ $\rightarrow$ $\langle(\alpha), (\mathcal{K}'_U)\rangle$ / $\perp$: An interactive algorithm sequencing GetToken and handling key replacement on **U**'s key loss/compromise. **U** runs KeyGen$_U$ to generate a fresh pair $({\mathcal{K}'_U}^{-1}, \mathcal{K}'_U)$ and presents $\mathcal{K}'_U$ to **V**. Since the old keys are unavailable, **U** self-identifies with Uid and the credential Φ. **V** attests with $\mathcal{K}_V^{-1}$, validates Uid, η, Φ, and accepts $\mathcal{K}'_U$. On success, **U** receives an acknowledgment α. Returns $\perp$ if any sub-algorithm or validation fails (e.g., a tampered token).

$\mathbf{Share}_{\mathtt{U,V'}}\langle(\mathbf{pp}, \mathcal{K}_{\mathtt{U}}^{-1}, \mathbf{\Phi}, \mathbf{Data}, \delta_{\mathtt{Data}}, \pi_{\mathtt{sh}}, \mathcal{K}_{\mathtt{V'}}), (\mathbf{pp}, \mathcal{K}_{\mathtt{V'}}^{-1}, \mathcal{K}_{\mathtt{U}}, \mathcal{K}_{\mathtt{V}})\rangle$ $\rightarrow \langle(\mathtt{sh\text{-}ref}), (\mathbf{\Phi}, \mathbf{Data}, \delta_{\mathtt{Data}})\rangle\ /\bot$: Lets **U** share KYC data already verified by an anchor verifier **V** with a new verifier **V'** (same or different jurisdiction), avoiding full re-onboarding. **U** sends **V'** the data *Data*, the secret commitment $\delta_{\mathtt{Data}}$, and a consent attestation $\pi_{sh} \leftarrow \mathcal{A}(shr, \mathcal{K}_U^{-1})$ over $shr = [\mathcal{K}_U, \mathcal{K}_{V'}, \mathtt{share}, h_{\mathtt{Data}}, ts_U]$.
V' checks $Data \models \Psi_{\mathtt{R,R'}}$, unbundles Φ into m, σ_m, verifies $1 \leftarrow \mathcal{V}^{fy}(\sigma_m, m, \mathcal{K}_V)$, and unpacks m into $[h_{\mathtt{Uid}}, Q, \mathtt{t\text{-}ref}, \mathcal{T}_{\mathtt{Data}}, ts, \Psi_{\mathtt{R}}]$. To confirm authenticity, **V'** computes $\mathcal{T}_{\tilde{\mathtt{Data}}} \leftarrow \mathfrak{T}\{Data|\delta_{\mathtt{Data}}\}$ and matches it against the $\mathcal{T}_{\mathtt{Data}}$ in m—a match means **U** presented the same *Data* that **V** used to generate Φ. **V'** then issues a sharing reference $\mathtt{sh\text{-}ref}$, on-boards **U**, and appends $\langle \mathcal{K}_{V'}, \mathcal{K}_U, \mathcal{K}_V, ts_{sh}, \Psi_{\mathtt{R,R'}}, \mathcal{T}_{\mathtt{Data}}, \mathtt{sh\text{-}ref}, \pi_{sh}, \delta_{\mathtt{Data}}\rangle$ to SH_{List}. The operation returns $\bot$ on any failure.

2.5 Security Properties

We provide the following security requirements our PaKYC framework aims to satisfy in a given e-KYC system:

a) Data Confidentiality
b) Correctness
c) Traceability
d) Non-frameability
e) Consistent Cross-Verifier Data Sharing
f) Unforgeability
g) Secure Key Recovery

Before we discuss each of the requirements mentioned above, it is noteworthy to highlight some of the assumptions we've put forward that pertains this subsection:

i. We denote $\mathcal{A} = (\mathcal{A}_1, \mathcal{A}_2)$ to be a probabilistic polynomial-time (PPT) adversary whose running time is bounded above by a polynomial in the security parameter λ. It is composed of two parts, where $\mathcal{A}_1$ represent the first stage that gathers information (such as public parameters, keys, and operational behaviors of the PaKYC system), and $\mathcal{A}_2$ represent the adversary's second phase, where it makes its decision after receiving some form of challenge or further input.
ii. We denote $\mathcal{A}_1^{\mathcal{O}}$ and $\mathcal{A}_2^{\mathcal{O}}$ as the first and second stages of a PPT adversary $\mathcal{A} = (\mathcal{A}_1, \mathcal{A}_2)$ with oracle access to $\mathcal{O}$, where $\mathcal{A}_1^{\mathcal{O}}$ adaptively queries the oracles and outputs a challenge, and $\mathcal{A}_2^{\mathcal{O}}$ receives this challenge and continues to query oracles adaptively before producing its final output (such as a guess, attempts to break the security property).
iii. We denote $Storage \leftarrow Save(A)$ as the operation of saving an object A to an external storage, where $A \in \{A_1, A_2, \ldots, A_n\}$.

iv. We denote *corruptDataBits*(*Data*) to be a procedure used by an adversary $\mathcal{A}$ to tamper the bits or structure of a genuine KYC data *Data*.

The oracles in our security games model the behavior of honest parties in the real protocol. Input validity checks within an oracle (such as *valid*($\mathcal{K}_U$) or *Data* $\models \Psi_R$) reflect checks that the corresponding honest party (verifier, issuer, or user) would perform before proceeding in the real execution. This ensures the adversary's queries correspond to valid protocol sessions; malformed inputs that no honest party would accept are simply rejected (returning $\perp$), consistent with the real protocol's behavior.

Furthermore, our oracles are designed so that the adversary provides the inputs from its controlled side of the interaction, while the honest party generates its responses internally. For example, in $\mathcal{O}Register_{U,V}$, the adversary (acting as user **U**) supplies $(Uid, \mathcal{K}_I, \mathcal{K}_U^{-1}, \mathcal{K}_V, \mathsf{cc})$. The verifier **V** generates its response (the registration token ϱ) honestly using $\mathcal{K}_V^{-1}$. We present below the oracles that $\mathcal{A}$ can interact with in our experiments:

- $\mathcal{O}$**KeyGen**$_{\mathbf{U}}$**(pp, UPinfo)** : Generates $\mathcal{K}_U$, $\mathcal{K}_U^{-1}$, and shares only the $\mathcal{K}_U$ with $\mathcal{A}$.
- $\mathcal{O}$**KeyGen**$_{\mathbf{V}}$**(pp, Vid)** : Generates $\mathcal{K}_V$, $\mathcal{K}_V^{-1}$, and shares only the $\mathcal{K}_V$ with $\mathcal{A}$.
- $\mathcal{O}$**KeyGen**$_{\mathbf{I}}$**(pp, Iid)** : Generates $\mathcal{K}_I$, $\mathcal{K}_I^{-1}$, and shares only the $\mathcal{K}_I$ with $\mathcal{A}$.
- $\mathcal{O}\mathbf{Issue}_{\mathbf{I,U}}\langle(\mathbf{pp}, \mathcal{K}_{\mathbf{I}}^{-1}, \mathcal{K}_{\mathbf{U}}), (\mathbf{pp}, \mathbf{UPinfo}, \mathcal{K}_{\mathbf{U}}^{-1}, \mathcal{K}_{\mathbf{I}})\rangle$: Allows $\mathcal{A}$ to successfully obtain a *Uid* from an Issuer.
- $\mathcal{O}\mathbf{Register}_{\mathbf{U,V}}\langle(\mathbf{pp}, \mathbf{Uid}, \mathcal{K}_I, \mathcal{K}_{\mathbf{U}}^{-1}, \mathcal{K}_V, \mathsf{cc}), (\mathbf{pp}, \mathcal{K}_{\mathbf{V}}^{-1}, \mathcal{K}_{\mathbf{U}})\rangle$: Allows the adversary $\mathcal{A}$ to register as a User **U** in the adversarial game by submitting *Uid* and $\mathcal{K}_U$ to $\mathcal{C}$, and obtaining the signature ϱ as a proof of successful registration. Otherwise, the oracle returns an error $\perp$ if the execution fails.
- $\mathbf{CertifyUpdate}_{\mathbf{U,V}}\langle(\mathbf{pp}, \mathcal{K}_{\mathbf{U}}^{-1}, \mathbf{Uid}, \mathcal{K}_{\mathbf{V}}, \mathbf{op}, \mathbf{dat}), (\mathbf{pp}, \mathcal{K}_{\mathbf{V}}^{-1}, \mathbf{Vid}, \mathcal{K}_{\mathbf{U}})\rangle$: Invokes $CertifyUpdate_{\mathrm{U,V}}$, which enables the adversary to either submit its KYC data for on-boarding or update its data with the challenger.
- $\mathcal{O}$**Cor**$_{\mathbf{U}}$**(pp, UPinfo,** $\mathcal{K}_{\mathbf{U}}$**)** : Allows the adversary to retrieve the unsealing key $\mathcal{K}_U^{-1}$ of a user **U** from *Storage*, where the tuple $\langle UPinfo, \mathcal{K}_U^{-1}, \mathcal{K}_U\rangle$ exists.
- $\mathcal{O}$**Cor**$_{\mathbf{V}}$**(pp, Vid,** $\mathcal{K}_{\mathbf{V}}$**)** : Allows the adversary to retrieve the unsealing key $\mathcal{K}_V^{-1}$ of a verifier **V** from *Storage*, where the tuple $\langle Vid, \mathcal{K}_V^{-1}, \mathcal{K}_V\rangle$ exists.
- $\mathcal{O}$**CorData(pp, Data)** : Converts a valid *Data* into raw bits, modifies them, and returns a corrupted reassembled version $\widetilde{Data}$.
- $\mathcal{O}\mathbf{RevokeKey}(\mathbf{pp}, \mathcal{K}_{\mathbf{V}}^{-1}, \mathbf{Uid}, \mathcal{K}_{\mathbf{U}}, \mathcal{K}_{\mathbf{V}})$ Enables a verifier identified by $\mathcal{K}_V$ to revoke the sealing key $\mathcal{K}_U$ of a user. If successful, the execution returns 1, otherwise, it returns $\perp$.
- $\mathcal{O}\mathbf{RevokeCert}(\mathbf{pp}, \mathcal{K}_{\mathbf{V}}^{-1}, \mathbf{Uid}, \mathcal{K}_{\mathbf{U}}, \boldsymbol{\Phi}, \mathcal{K}_{\mathbf{V}})$ Enables a verifier identified by $\mathcal{K}_V$ to revoke the KYC attestation credential Φ of a user identified by *Uid*. If successful, the execution returns 1, otherwise, it returns $\perp$.
- $\mathcal{O}\mathbf{GetToken}(\mathbf{pp}, \mathbf{Uid}, \mathcal{K}_{\mathbf{V}}, \boldsymbol{\Phi}, \mathsf{cc})$ Allows $\mathcal{A}$ to request for a unique token, which is then used for key restoration. A token η is returned if it executes successfully, otherwise, it returns $\perp$.

- **$\mathcal{O}$RestoreKey$_{\text{U,V}}\langle(\text{pp}, \text{Uid}, \eta, \Phi, \mathcal{K}'_{\text{U}}, \mathcal{K}_{\text{V}}), (\text{pp}, \eta, \mathcal{K}_{\text{V}}^{-1})\rangle$:** Uses the token η from the *OGetToken* oracle for key replacement. For a successful operation, $\mathcal{A}$ is allowed to provide new key to replace a compromised one. The oracle returns $\perp$ if any of the executions is unsuccessful.
- **$\mathcal{O}$Share$_{\text{U,V}'}\langle(\text{pp}, \mathcal{K}_{\text{U}}^{-1}, \Phi, \text{Data}, \delta_{\text{Data}}, \pi_{\text{sh}}, \mathcal{K}_{\text{V}'}), (\text{pp}, \mathcal{K}_{\text{V}'}^{-1}, \mathcal{K}_{\text{U}}, \mathcal{K}_{\text{V}})\rangle$:** The adversary $\mathcal{A}$ emulates a malicious user **U**, attempting to trick the new verifier **V'** into accepting a *Data* that is different from the one used by the anchor verifier **V** when registering **U** (Figs. 1 and 2).

$\mathcal{O}$KeyGen$_{\text{U}}$(pp, UPinfo)

$(\mathcal{K}_U^{-1}, \mathcal{K}_U) \leftarrow$ generateKey($UPinfo$)
$Storage \leftarrow Save(UPinfo, \mathcal{K}_U^{-1}, \mathcal{K}_U)$
return $\mathcal{K}_U$

$\mathcal{O}$KeyGen$_{\text{V}}$(pp, Vid)

$(\mathcal{K}_V^{-1}, \mathcal{K}_V) \leftarrow$ generateKey(Vid); $Storage \leftarrow Save(Vid, \mathcal{K}_V^{-1}, \mathcal{K}_V)$
return $\mathcal{K}_V$

$\mathcal{O}$KeyGen$_{\text{I}}$(pp, Iid)

$(\mathcal{K}_I^{-1}, \mathcal{K}_I) \leftarrow$ generateKey(Iid); $Storage \leftarrow Save(Iid, \mathcal{K}_I^{-1}, \mathcal{K}_I)$
return $\mathcal{K}_I$

$\mathcal{O}$Issue$_{\text{I,U}}\langle(\text{pp}, \mathcal{K}_{\text{I}}^{-1}, \mathcal{K}_{\text{U}}), (\text{pp}, \text{UPinfo}, \mathcal{K}_{\text{U}}^{-1}, \mathcal{K}_{\text{I}})$

if $(\neg\text{valid}(\mathcal{K}_U) \vee \neg\text{valid}(\mathcal{K}_I) \vee \neg((UPinfo) \models \Psi_{\text{R}})$ **then**
  return $\perp$
end if
$Uid \leftarrow$ generateUID($UPinfo$); $Storage \leftarrow Save(UPinfo)$
return Uid

$\mathcal{O}$CorData(pp, Data)

$\tilde{Data} \leftarrow$ corruptDataBits($Data$)
return $\tilde{Data}$

$\mathcal{O}$Register$_{\text{U,V}}\langle(\text{pp}, \text{Uid}, \mathcal{K}_I, \mathcal{K}_{\text{U}}^{-1}, \mathcal{K}_V, \text{cc}), (\text{pp}, \mathcal{K}_{\text{V}}^{-1}, \mathcal{K}_{\text{U}})\rangle$

if $(\neg\text{valid}(\mathcal{K}_U) \vee \neg\text{valid}(Uid) \vee \neg\text{valid}(cc))$ **then**
  return $\perp$
end if
$Iid \leftarrow IList.Search(\mathcal{K}_I)$
if $((Iid = \perp) \vee (\langle Iid, \mathcal{K}_I\rangle \notin I_{List}))$ **then**
  return $\perp$
end if
if $((\neg verifyID(Uid, \mathcal{K}_I)) \vee (\langle\mathcal{K}_U\rangle \in RU_{List}))$ **then**
  return $\perp$
end if
reg-date $\leftarrow getCurrentTimestamp()$;
$\varrho \leftarrow \mathcal{S}^{-1}([Uid, \text{reg-date}], \mathcal{K}_V^{-1})$
$RU_{List} \leftarrow RU_{List} \cup \langle Uid, \mathcal{K}_U, \text{cc}, \varrho\rangle$
return ϱ

RevokeKey(pp, $\mathcal{K}_{\text{V}}^{-1}$, Uid, $\mathcal{K}_{\text{U}}$, $\mathcal{K}_{\text{V}}$)

if $((\mathcal{K}_U \models \Psi_{\text{R}}) \vee (\langle\mathcal{K}_U\rangle \notin RU_{List}) \vee (\langle\mathcal{K}_U\rangle \in BLK_{List}))$ **then**
  return $\perp$
end if
$ts_{bl} \leftarrow$ genTimeStamp()
$\tau_{\text{Uid}} \leftarrow \mathcal{H}\{Uid\}$; $BLK_{List} \leftarrow BLK_{List} \cup \langle h_{\text{Uid}}, \mathcal{K}_U, ts_{bl}, \mathcal{K}_V\rangle$
$RU_{List} \leftarrow RU_{List}[Uid] \setminus \{\mathcal{K}_U\}$
return 1

$\mathcal{O}$GetToken(pp, Uid, $\mathcal{K}_{\text{V}}$, Φ, cc)

$h_{\text{Uid}} \leftarrow \mathcal{H}\{Uid\}$
if $((\langle h_{\text{Uid}}\rangle \in CRV_{List}) \vee (\langle Uid\rangle \notin OBU_{List}))$ **then**
  return $\perp$
end if
if $((\langle \text{cc}\rangle \notin RU_{List}))$ **then**
  return $\perp$
end if
$\eta \leftarrow$ GenerateToken(); $Save(\eta)$
return SendToken(cc, η)

$\mathcal{O}$CertifyUpdate$_{\text{U,V}}\langle(\text{pp}, \mathcal{K}_{\text{U}}^{-1}, \text{Uid}, \mathcal{K}_{\text{V}}, \text{op}, \text{dat}), (\text{pp}, \mathcal{K}_{\text{V}}^{-1}, \text{Vid}, \mathcal{K}_{\text{U}})\rangle$

if $\neg\text{valid}(\mathcal{K}_U) \vee (\langle\mathcal{K}_U\rangle \notin RU_{List})$ **then**
  return $\perp$
end if
$\Theta_1 \leftarrow \emptyset$; $\Theta_2 \leftarrow \emptyset$
$op \leftarrow$ {issue, update} // — *Input Parameter* —
if (op = issue) **then** // — *Submit-Certify Phase* —
  $(Data, ts_U, \varrho, \pi_U) \leftarrow dat$
  $\mathcal{A}(req, \mathcal{K}_U^{-1}) \leftarrow \pi_U$
  $[Uid, Vid, \text{issue}, h_{\text{Data}}, ts_U] \leftarrow req$
  if $(\neg((Data) \models \Psi_{\text{R}}) \vee (\langle\mathcal{K}_U\rangle \in CU_{List})$
  $\vee(\langle\varrho, \mathcal{K}_U\rangle \notin RU_{List}) \vee (\mathcal{V}^{fy}(\pi_U, req, \mathcal{K}_U) \neq 1))$ **then**
    return $\perp$
  end if
  $ts \leftarrow$ getCurrentTimestamp(); $\delta_{\text{Data}} \leftarrow$ genSecretCommitment()
  t-ref $\leftarrow$ genUniTransRef($\mathcal{K}_U, ts$)
  $\tau_{\text{Data}} \leftarrow \mathcal{T}\{Data|\delta_{\text{Data}}\}$; $h_{\text{Uid}} \leftarrow \mathcal{H}\{Uid\}$
  $Z := [Data, \delta_{\text{Data}}, ts_U, Uid, Vid]$; $\varphi \leftarrow \mathcal{A}(Z, \mathcal{K}_V^{-1})$
  $P := [Z, \varphi]$; $Q \leftarrow \mathcal{S}(P, \mathcal{K}_R)$
  $m := [h_{\text{Uid}}, Q, \text{t-ref}, \tau_{\text{Data}}, ts, \Psi_{\text{R}}]$
  $\sigma_m \leftarrow \mathcal{A}(m, \mathcal{K}_V^{-1})$; $\Phi := [m, \sigma_m]$
  $h_{\text{t-ref}} \leftarrow \mathcal{H}\{\text{t-ref}\}$; $h_\Phi \leftarrow \mathcal{H}\{\Phi\}$
  $h_{\text{Vid}} \leftarrow \mathcal{H}\{Vid\}$
  $OBU_{List} \leftarrow OBU_{List} \cup \langle Uid, \text{t-ref}, Data, \Phi,$
  $h_{\text{t-ref}}, ts, ts_U, \delta_{\text{Data}}, \Delta\rangle$
  $CU_{List} \leftarrow CU_{List} \cup \langle\pi_U, h_{\text{t-ref}}, h_{\text{Uid}}, h_{\text{Vid}},$
  $\tau_{\text{Data}}, h_\Phi, ts, \mathcal{K}_U, \mathcal{K}_V\rangle$
  $\Theta_1 \leftarrow (\text{t-ref}, \Phi, \delta_{\text{Data}})$; $\Theta_2 \leftarrow (\Phi, Data, \pi_U, ts_U, \delta_{\text{Data}})$
end if
if (op = update) **then** // — *Update* Phase —
  $(Data', ts'_U, \text{t-ref}, \pi'_U) \leftarrow dat$
  $\mathcal{A}(req', \mathcal{K}_U^{-1}) \leftarrow \pi'_U$
  $[Uid, Vid, \text{update}, h_{\text{Data}'}, ts'_U] \leftarrow req'$
  $h_{\text{t-ref}} \leftarrow \mathcal{H}\{\text{t-ref}\}$; $h_{\text{Uid}} \leftarrow \mathcal{H}\{Uid\}$
  if $(\neg((Data') \models \Psi_{\text{R}}) \vee (\langle h_{\text{Uid}}, h_{\text{t-ref}}\rangle \notin CU_{List})$
  $\vee(\mathcal{V}^{fy}(\pi'_U, req', \mathcal{K}_U) \neq 1))$ **then**
    return $\perp$
  end if
  $ts' \leftarrow$ getCurrentTimestamp()
  $\delta_{\text{Data}'} \leftarrow$ genSecretCommitment()
  $\tau_{\text{Data}'} \leftarrow \mathcal{T}\{Data'|\delta_{\text{Data}'}\}$
  $Z' := ([Data', \delta_{\text{Data}'}, ts_U, Uid, Vid])$; $\varphi' \leftarrow \mathcal{A}(Z', \mathcal{K}_V^{-1})$
  $P' := [Z', \varphi']$; $Q' \leftarrow \mathcal{S}(P', \mathcal{K}_R)$
  $m' := [h_{\text{Uid}}, Q', \text{t-ref}, \tau_{\text{Data}'}, ts', \Psi_{\text{R}}]$
  $\sigma_{m'} \leftarrow \mathcal{A}(m', \mathcal{K}_V^{-1})$; $\Phi' := [m', \sigma_{m'}]$
  $OBU_{List} \leftarrow OBU_{List}[Uid, \text{t-ref}] \setminus \{Data, \Phi, ts\}$
  $h_{\Phi'} \leftarrow \mathcal{H}\{\Phi'\}$; $h_{\text{Vid}} \leftarrow \mathcal{H}\{Vid\}$
  $ts_{rev} \leftarrow$ getCurrentTimestamp()
  $CRV_{List} \leftarrow CRV_{List} \cup \{\langle h_{\text{Uid}}, \Phi, ts_{rev}, \mathcal{K}_V\rangle\}$
  $OBU_{List} \leftarrow OBU_{List}[Uid, \text{t-ref}] \cup \{Data', \Phi', ts', ts'_U, \delta_{\text{Data}'}, \Delta'\}$
  $CU_{List} \leftarrow CU_{List}[h_{\text{t-ref}}, h_{\text{Uid}}, h_{\text{Vid}}]$
  $\cup\{\pi'_U, \tau_{\text{Data}'}, h_{\Phi'}, ts', \mathcal{K}_U, \mathcal{K}_V\}$
  $\Theta_1 \leftarrow (\Phi', \delta_{\text{Data}'})$; $\Theta_2 \leftarrow (\Phi', Data', \pi'_U, ts'_U, \delta_{\text{Data}'})$
end if
return Θ_1

Fig. 1. Details of Oracles used in the Adversarial Games

$\mathcal{O}$RevokeCert(pp, $\mathcal{K}_{V}^{-1}$, Uid, $\mathcal{K}_{U}$, Φ, $\mathcal{K}_{V}$)

$h_{\mathtt{Uid}} \leftarrow \mathcal{H}\{Uid\}$; $h_{\Phi} \leftarrow \mathcal{H}\{\Phi\}$
if $((\langle h_{\mathtt{Uid}}, \Phi, ts_{rev}, \mathcal{K}_V \rangle \in CRV_{List}) \vee (\neg(\Phi \models \Psi_{\mathrm{R}})))$ **then**
  return $\perp$
end if
if $(\mathcal{O}RevokeKey(.) \neq 1)$ **then**
  return $\perp$
end if
$ts_{rev} \leftarrow$ genTimeStamp()
$OBU_{List} \leftarrow$
$OBU_{List} \setminus \{\langle Uid, \mathtt{t\text{-}ref}, Data, \Phi, \mathcal{T}_{\mathtt{t\text{-}ref}}, ts, ts_U, \delta_{\mathtt{Data}}, \Delta \rangle\}$
$RU_{List} \leftarrow RU_{List} \setminus \{\langle Uid, \mathcal{K}_U, \mathsf{cc}, \varrho \rangle\}$
$CU_{List} \leftarrow CU_{List}[\, h_{\mathtt{t\text{-}ref}}, h_{\mathtt{Uid}}] \setminus \{\langle h_{\Phi} \rangle\}$
$CRV_{List} \leftarrow CRV_{List} \cup \langle h_{\mathtt{Uid}}, \Phi, ts_{rev}, \mathcal{K}_V \rangle$
return 1

$\mathcal{O}$RestoreKey$_{\mathrm{U,V}}$ ⟨(pp, Uid, η, Φ, $\mathcal{K}'_{U}$, $\mathcal{K}_{V}$), (pp, η, $\mathcal{K}_{V}^{-1}$)

$h_{\mathtt{Uid}} \leftarrow \mathcal{H}\{Uid\}$
if $(\neg(valid(\eta) \vee (\langle h_{\mathtt{Uid}} \rangle \in CRV_{List})$
  $\vee(\langle \Phi \rangle \notin OBU_{List}))$ **then**
  return $\perp$
end if
$\Theta_1 \leftarrow \emptyset$
$\Theta_2 \leftarrow \mathcal{K}'_U$
$RU_{List} \leftarrow RU_{List}[Uid] \cup \langle \mathcal{K}'_U \rangle$
$\alpha \leftarrow GenAck()$
$\Theta_1 \leftarrow \alpha$
if $(\langle h_{\mathtt{Uid}} \rangle \in BLK_{List})$ **then**
  $BLK_{List} \leftarrow BLK_{List} \setminus \{BLK_{List}[h_{\mathtt{Uid}}]\}$
end if
return Θ_1

$\mathcal{O}$Share$_{\mathrm{U,V'}}$ (pp, $\mathcal{K}_{U}^{-1}$, Φ, Data, $\delta_{\mathtt{Data}}$, π_{sh}, $\mathcal{K}_{V'}$), (pp, $\mathcal{K}_{V'}^{-1}$, $\mathcal{K}_{U}$, $\mathcal{K}_{V}$)

$h_{\Phi} \leftarrow \mathcal{H}\{\Phi\}$
if $((\langle h_{\Phi} \rangle \notin CU_{List}) \vee (\neg(Data \models \langle \Psi_{\mathrm{R,R'}} \rangle)) \vee (\langle \mathcal{K}_{V'} \rangle \notin V_{List}))$
then
  return $\perp$
end if
$\mathcal{A}(shr, \mathcal{K}_U^{-1}) \leftarrow \pi_{sh}$
$[\mathcal{K}_U, \mathcal{K}_{V'}, \mathtt{share}, \mathcal{T}_{\mathtt{Data}}, ts_U] \leftarrow shr$
if $(\mathcal{V}^{fy}(\pi_{sh}, shr, \mathcal{K}_U) \neq 1)$ **then**
  return $\perp$
end if
$(m, \sigma_m) \leftarrow unbundle(\Phi)$
if $(\mathcal{V}^{fy}(\sigma_m, m, \mathcal{K}_V) \neq 1)$ **then**
  return $\perp$
end if
$[h_{\mathtt{Uid}}, Q, \mathtt{t\text{-}ref}, \mathcal{T}_{\mathtt{Data}}, ts, \Psi_{\mathrm{R}}] =: m$
$\mathcal{T}_{\tilde{\mathtt{Data}}} \leftarrow \mathcal{T}\{Data | \delta_{\mathtt{Data}}\}$
if $(\mathcal{T}_{\tilde{\mathtt{Data}}} \neq \mathcal{T}_{\mathtt{Data}})$ **then**
  return $\perp$
end if
$\mathtt{sh\text{-}ref} \leftarrow genShareRef()$
$SH_{List} \leftarrow$
$SH_{List} \cup \{\langle \mathcal{K}_{V'}, \mathcal{K}_U, \mathcal{K}_V, ts_{sh}, \Psi_{\mathrm{R,R'}}, \mathcal{T}_{\tilde{\mathtt{Data}}}, \mathtt{sh\text{-}ref}, \pi_{sh}, \delta_{\mathtt{Data}} \rangle\}$
return sh-ref

Verify(pp, $\mathcal{K}_{V'}^{-1}$, $\mathcal{K}_{U}$, $\mathcal{K}_{V}$, t-ref*, Φ)

if $(\langle \Phi \rangle \in CRV_{List})$ **then**
  return 0
end if
$[m, \sigma_m] =: \Phi$
$b \leftarrow \mathcal{V}^{fy}(\sigma_m, m, \mathcal{K}_V)$
if $(b \neq 1)$ **then**
  return 0
end if
$[h_{\mathtt{Uid}}, Q, \mathtt{t\text{-}ref}, \mathcal{T}_{\mathtt{Data}}, ts, \Psi_{\mathrm{R}}] =: m$
if $(\mathtt{t\text{-}ref}^* \neq \mathtt{t\text{-}ref})$ **then**
  return 0
end if
$h_{\mathtt{t\text{-}ref}^*} \leftarrow \mathcal{H}\{\mathtt{t\text{-}ref}^*\}$
$h_{\Phi} \leftarrow \mathcal{H}\{\Phi\}$
if $(\langle h_{\Phi}, h_{\mathtt{t\text{-}ref}^*}, \mathcal{K}_U \rangle \notin CU_{List})$ **then**
  return 0
end if
return 1

Trace(pp, $\mathcal{K}_{R}^{-1}$, Φ)

$h_{\Phi} \leftarrow \mathcal{H}\{\Phi\}$
if $((\langle \Phi \rangle \in CRV_{List}) \vee (\langle h_{\Phi} \rangle \notin CU_{List}))$ **then**
  return $\perp$
end if
$[m, \sigma_m] =: \Phi$
$[h_{\mathtt{Uid}}, Q, \mathtt{t\text{-}ref}, \mathcal{T}_{\mathtt{Data}}, ts, \Psi_{\mathrm{R}}] =: m$
$P \leftarrow \mathcal{S}^{-1}(Q, \mathcal{K}_R^{-1})$
if $(P = \perp)$ **then**
  return $\perp$
end if
$[(Z, \varphi)] =: P$
$b \leftarrow \mathcal{V}^{fy}(\varphi, Z, \mathcal{K}_V)$
if $(b = 0)$ **then**
  return $\perp$
end if
$[Data, \delta_{\mathtt{Data}}, ts_U, Uid, Vid] =: Z$
$\mathcal{K}_V \leftarrow VList.Search(Vid)$
if $(\mathcal{K}_V = \perp)$ **then**
  return $\perp$
end if
$b \leftarrow \mathcal{V}^{fy}(\sigma_m, m, \mathcal{K}_V)$
if $(b \neq 1)$ **then**
  return $\perp$
end if
$h_{\mathtt{Uid}} \leftarrow \mathcal{H}\{Uid\}$; $h_{\mathtt{Vid}} \leftarrow \mathcal{H}\{Vid\}$; $\mathcal{T}_{\tilde{\mathtt{Data}}} \leftarrow \mathcal{T}\{Data | \delta_{\mathtt{Data}}\}$
$h_{\mathtt{t\text{-}ref}} \leftarrow \mathcal{H}\{\mathtt{t\text{-}ref}\}$
if $(CUList.Search(\langle h_{\Phi}, h_{\mathtt{Uid}}, h_{\mathtt{Vid}}, \mathcal{T}_{\tilde{\mathtt{Data}}}, h_{\mathtt{t\text{-}ref}} \rangle) = \perp)$ **then**
  return $\perp$
end if
return (Uid, Vid)

Fig. 2. Additional Oracle Details, and the *Verify* and *Trace* Algorithms

i. **Data Confidentiality:**
The Data confidentiality game in PaKYC requires that the certificate Φ and `t-ref` leak no information beyond metadata about the underlying KYC data (*Data*). The PPT adversary $\mathcal{A} = (\mathcal{A}_1, \mathcal{A}_2)$ aims to guess which of two equally-sized payloads $Data_0, Data_1$ was used to generate $\Phi_{\beta}, \mathtt{t\text{-}ref}_{\beta}$, where $\beta \in \{0, 1\}$ is chosen by the challenger $\mathcal{C}$. To prevent the adversary from inferring β via $\delta_{\mathtt{Data}}$ or $\mathcal{T}_{\mathtt{Data}}$, both fields are derived from $Data_{\beta}$ (i.e., $\delta_{\mathtt{Data}_{\beta}}, \mathcal{T}_{\mathtt{Data}_{\beta}}$) in Z, m, and req. $\mathcal{A}$ has access to the $\mathcal{O}KeyGen_U$, $\mathcal{O}Issue_{I,U}$, $\mathcal{O}Register_{U,V}$, $\mathcal{O}CertifyUpdate_{U,V}$, and $\mathcal{O}Cor_U$ oracles. Access to $\mathcal{O}Cor_U$ does not trivialize confidentiality: $Data_{\beta}$ appears only inside the regulator-sealed payload $Q \leftarrow \mathcal{S}(P, \mathcal{K}_R)$ within m, and is undecryptable using $\mathcal{K}_U^{-1}$. PaKYC is data-confidential if $\mathcal{A}$ can do no better than randomly guess $\beta' = \beta$.

Definition 1: PaKYC satisfies data confidentiality if for any PPT adversary $\mathcal{A}$ and any Uid,

$$\mathrm{Adv}^{\mathrm{dc}}_{\mathcal{A},\mathrm{PaKYC}} = \Pr\left[\mathrm{Exp}^{\mathrm{dc},\beta}_{\mathcal{A},\mathrm{PaKYC}}(\mathrm{Uid}, \lambda) = 1\right] \le \frac{1}{2} + \mathrm{negl}(\lambda) \quad (1)$$

ii. **Correctness:**
Correctness guarantees that when entities follow PaKYC as prescribed, every legitimate operation yields a valid outcome. For instance, if **U** registers properly with **V**, submits $Data \models \Psi_{\mathrm{R}}$, and **V** issues an attested credential Φ with `t-ref`, then any other verifier **V'** running $Verify$ must deterministically accept (Φ, `t-ref`). The same guarantee extends to trace, key/certificate revocation, token generation, key recovery, and data sharing.
Definition 2: PaKYC satisfies correctness if for any PPT adversary $\mathcal{A}$,

$$\mathrm{Adv}^{\mathrm{correctness}}_{\mathcal{A},\mathrm{PaKYC}} = \Pr\left[\mathrm{Exp}^{\mathrm{correctness}}_{\mathcal{A},\mathrm{PaKYC}}(\lambda) = 0\right] \le \mathrm{negl}(\lambda) \quad (2)$$

is negligible in λ.

iii **Traceability:**
Traceability ensures that every valid Φ can be traced by **R** to its issuing verifier **V** and recipient user **U**, even with malicious entities and a compromised user. Each valid $\Phi := [m, \sigma_m]$ has $m := [h_{\mathtt{Uid}}, Q, \mathtt{t\text{-}ref}, \mathcal{T}_{\mathtt{Data}}, ts, \Psi_{\mathrm{R}}]$ with $Q \leftarrow \mathcal{S}(P, \mathcal{K}_R)$ and $P = [Z, \varphi]$, $Z := [Data, \delta_{\mathtt{Data}}, ts_U, Uid, Vid]$. The fields sealed inside P ($Uid, Vid, \delta_{\mathtt{Data}}, ts, Data$) can only be revealed by the honest **R**. For accountable tracing, **R** further links the unveiled ($h_{\mathtt{Uid}}$, $h_{\mathtt{Vid}}$) to a CU_{List} tuple binding them with $h_{\mathtt{t\text{-}ref}}$, $\mathcal{T}_{\mathtt{Data}}$, h_{Φ}, and a user-binding π_U verifying under $\mathcal{K}_U$. $\mathcal{A}$ has access to $\mathcal{O}KeyGen_V$, $\mathcal{O}Issue_{I,U}$, $\mathcal{O}Register_{U,V}$, $\mathcal{O}CertifyUpdate_{U,V}$, $\mathcal{O}Cor_U$, and $\mathcal{O}Cor_V$, and may corrupt (but not create) honest users. $\mathcal{A}$ wins if it outputs ($\tilde{\Phi}$, $\mathtt{t\text{-}\tilde{ref}}$) such that $\mathsf{Verify}(\tilde{\Phi}, \mathtt{t\text{-}\tilde{ref}}) = 1$ and Trace returns either (i) a pair ($\tilde{Uid}, \tilde{Vid}$) for which $\langle h_{\tilde{\Phi}}, h_{\mathtt{\tilde{Uid}}}, h_{\mathtt{\tilde{Vid}}}, \mathcal{T}_{\mathtt{\tilde{Data}}}, h_{\mathtt{t\text{-}\tilde{ref}}} \rangle \notin CU_{List}$, or (ii) $\tilde{Vid} \notin V_{List}$. Trace returning $\perp$ for malformed structure, failed unsealing, tag mismatch, revocation, or missing list bindings counts as honest rejection, not adversarial success.
Definition 3: PaKYC satisfies traceability if for any PPT adversary $\mathcal{A}$,

$$\mathrm{Adv}^{\mathrm{trace}}_{\mathcal{A},\mathrm{PaKYC}} = \Pr\left[\mathrm{Exp}^{\mathrm{trace}}_{\mathcal{A},\mathrm{PaKYC}}(\lambda) = 1\right] \le \mathrm{negl}(\lambda) \quad (3)$$

is negligible in λ.

iv. **Non-frameability:**
PaKYC ensures that no adversary $\mathcal{A}$ can produce a valid Φ and `t-ref` linking them to an honest **U** without access to $\mathcal{K}_U^{-1}$, or share **U**'s data with **V'** without consent—preventing fake transactions for certification, update, and data sharing. $\mathcal{A}$ may create dummy users and verifiers but is forbidden from corrupting the honest target **U**. Available oracles: $\mathcal{O}KeyGen_U$, $\mathcal{O}KeyGen_V$, $\mathcal{O}Issue_{I,U}$, $\mathcal{O}Register_{U,V}$, $\mathcal{O}CertifyUpdate_{U,V}$, $\mathcal{O}Cor_U$, $\mathcal{O}Cor_V$, $\mathcal{O}Share_{U,V'}$. $\mathcal{A}$ attempts to forge **U**'s authentication attestations $\tilde{\pi_U}$ and $\tilde{\pi_{sh}}$ used in $\mathcal{O}CertifyUpdate_{U,V}$ and $\mathcal{O}Share_{U,V'}$—essentially an attack on $\mathcal{K}_U^{-1}$. We assume $\mathcal{L}_U$, $\mathcal{L}_V$, $\mathcal{L}_I$ log every transaction, preventing replay.
Definition 4: PaKYC satisfies non-frameability if for any PPT adversary $\mathcal{A}$,

$$\mathrm{Adv}^{\mathrm{nf}}_{\mathcal{A},\mathrm{PaKYC}} = \Pr\left[\mathrm{Exp}^{\mathrm{nf}}_{\mathcal{A},\mathrm{PaKYC}}(\lambda) = 1\right] \leq \mathrm{negl}(\lambda) \tag{4}$$

is negligible in λ.

v. **Consistent Cross-Verifier Data Sharing:**
PaKYC ensures that an adversary $\mathcal{A}$ acting as **U** cannot convince any new verifier $\mathbf{V}'$ to accept KYC data inconsistent with the data the anchor **V** used to issue Φ. Available oracles: $\mathcal{O}KeyGen_U$, $\mathcal{O}Issue_{I,U}$, $\mathcal{O}Register_{U,V}$, $\mathcal{O}CertifyUpdate_{U,V}$, $\mathcal{O}CorData$, $\mathcal{O}Share_{U,V'}$. $\mathcal{A}$ presents Φ and a corrupted $\tilde{Data}$ to **V'**. **V'** unbundles Φ into m, σ_m, runs $1/0 \leftarrow \mathcal{V}^{fy}(\sigma_m, m, \mathcal{K}_V)$ (failing if 0), then extracts $\mathcal{T}_{\mathtt{Data}}$ from m and compares it with $\mathcal{T}_{\tilde{\mathtt{Data}}}$ recomputed from $\tilde{Data}$. $\mathcal{A}$ wins iff $\mathcal{T}_{\mathtt{Data}} = \mathcal{T}_{\tilde{\mathtt{Data}}}$ despite $Data \neq \tilde{Data}$.
Definition 5: PaKYC satisfies consistent cross-verifier data sharing if for any PPT adversary $\mathcal{A}$,

$$\mathrm{Adv}^{\mathrm{ccvds}}_{\mathcal{A},\mathrm{PaKYC}} = \Pr\left[\mathrm{Exp}^{\mathrm{ccvds}}_{\mathcal{A},\mathrm{PaKYC}}(\lambda) = 1\right] \leq \mathrm{negl}(\lambda) \tag{5}$$

is negligible in λ.

vi **Unforgeability:**
Unforgeability ensures that no adversary $\mathcal{A}$ can produce a fresh, valid Φ whose m, σ_m verify under $\mathcal{K}_V$ unless legitimately generated by an honest **V** running *CertifyUpdate*. Available oracles: $\mathcal{O}KeyGen_U$, $\mathcal{O}KeyGen_V$, $\mathcal{O}Issue_{I,U}$, $\mathcal{O}Register_{U,V}$, $\mathcal{O}CertifyUpdate_{U,V}$, $\mathcal{O}Cor_U$, $\mathcal{O}Cor_V$. $\mathcal{A}$ tries to forge a credential appearing to be issued by an honest **V**—an attack on $\mathcal{K}_V^{-1}$ used for σ_m and hence Φ. $\mathcal{A}$ may corrupt users and other verifiers, but is forbidden from corrupting the targeted honest **V**.
Definition 6: PaKYC satisfies unforgeability if for any PPT adversary $\mathcal{A}$,

$$\mathrm{Adv}^{\mathrm{unforge}}_{\mathcal{A},\mathrm{PaKYC}} = \Pr\left[\mathrm{Exp}^{\mathrm{unforge}}_{\mathcal{A},\mathrm{PaKYC}}(\lambda) = 1\right] \leq \mathrm{negl}(\lambda) \tag{6}$$

is negligible in λ.

vii. **Secure Key Recovery:**
This property ensures that even if $\mathcal{K}_U^{-1}$ is lost or compromised, **U** can generate a new key and bind it to their identity without enabling impersonation, token forgery, or unauthorized key replacement. The adversary $\mathcal{A}$ (a malicious user) has access to $\mathcal{O}KeyGen_U, \mathcal{O}Issue_{I,U}, \mathcal{O}Register_{U,V}, \mathcal{O}CertifyUpdate_{U,V}, \mathcal{O}Cor_U$, $\mathcal{O}GetToken$, and $\mathcal{O}RestoreKey_{U,V}$, and aims to forge or guess a fresh token η for RestoreKey without access to the legitimate user's cc. We assume cc is protected and only the genuine owner can access it. $\mathcal{A}$ wins if it did not obtain η via an honest user's cc.
Definition 7: PaKYC satisfies Secure Key Recovery if for any PPT adversary $\mathcal{A}$,

$$\mathrm{Adv}^{\mathrm{skr}}_{\mathcal{A},\mathrm{PaKYC}} = \Pr\left[\mathrm{Exp}^{\mathrm{skr}}_{\mathcal{A},\mathrm{PaKYC}}(\lambda) = 1\right] \le \mathrm{negl}(\lambda) \tag{7}$$

is negligible in λ.

Below, we present the experiments for all the security properties we propose (Fig. 3):

Experiment: $\mathbf{Exp}^{dc,\beta}_{\mathcal{A},PaKYC}(Uid, \lambda)$

$(pp) \leftarrow \mathsf{Setup}(\lambda)$
$RU_{List}, OBU_{List}, CU_{List}, BLK_{List}, CRV_{List}, SH_{List}, V_{List}, V'_{List}, I_{List}, \mathcal{L}_U, \mathcal{L}_V, \mathcal{L}_I \leftarrow \emptyset$
$(\mathcal{K}_V, \mathcal{K}_V^{-1}) \leftarrow \mathsf{KeyGen}_V(pp, Vid)$; $V_{List} \leftarrow Add_V(Vid, \mathcal{K}_V, ts, \mathcal{K}_R^{-1})$
$(\mathcal{K}_{V'}, \mathcal{K}_{V'}^{-1}) \leftarrow \mathsf{KeyGen}_{V'}(pp, Vid')$; $V'_{List} \leftarrow Add_{V'}(Vid', \mathcal{K}_{V'}, ts, \mathcal{K}_{R'}^{-1})$
$(\mathcal{K}_I, \mathcal{K}_I^{-1}) \leftarrow \mathsf{KeyGen}_I(pp, Iid)$; $I_{List} \leftarrow Add_I(Iid, \mathcal{K}_V, ts, \mathcal{K}_R)$
$\mathcal{O} \leftarrow \{\mathcal{O}KeyGen_U, \mathcal{O}Issue_{I,U}, \mathcal{O}Register_{U,V}, \mathcal{O}CertifyUpdate_{U,V}, \mathcal{O}\mathrm{Cor}_U\}$
$(Data_0, Data_1, Uid, \varrho) \leftarrow \mathcal{A}_1^{\mathcal{O}}(pp)$
$(\texttt{t-ref}_\beta, \Phi_\beta, \delta_{\mathtt{Data}_\beta}), (\Phi_\beta, Data_\beta, \pi_U, ts_U, \delta_{\mathtt{Data}_\beta})$
$\quad \leftarrow \mathsf{CertifyUpdate}_{U,V}\langle(\mathrm{pp}, \mathcal{K}_U^{-1}, Uid, \mathcal{K}_V, \mathtt{issue}, \{Data_\beta, ts_U, \varrho, \pi_U\}), (\mathrm{pp}, \mathcal{K}_V^{-1}, Vid, \mathcal{K}_U)\rangle$
$b_{ver} \leftarrow \mathsf{Verify}(pp, \mathcal{K}_{V'}^{-1}, \mathcal{K}_U, \mathcal{K}_V, \texttt{t-ref}_\beta, \Phi_\beta)$ ▷ Verifying the attested credential.
if $(b_{ver} = 0)$ **then** ▷ If verification fails, terminate.
  return $\perp$
end if
$\beta' \leftarrow \mathcal{A}_2^{\mathcal{O}}(\texttt{t-ref}_\beta, \Phi_\beta)$ ▷ $\mathcal{A}$ guesses if $Data_0$ or $Data_1$ was used to obtain Φ_β, $\texttt{t-ref}_\beta$
if $(\beta' = \beta)$ **then**
  return 1 ▷ $\mathcal{A}$ wins if the result from comparing β' and $\beta = 1$
end if
return 0 ▷ Otherwise $\mathcal{C}$ wins if 0

Fig. 3. List of Experiments Utilized

Experiment: $\mathbf{Exp}^{correctness}_{\mathcal{A},PaKYC}(\lambda)$

$(pp) \leftarrow \mathsf{Setup}(\lambda)$

$RU_{List}, OBU_{List}, CU_{List}, BLK_{List}, CRV_{List}, SH_{List}, V_{List}, V'_{List}, I_{List}, \mathcal{L}_U, \mathcal{L}_V, \mathcal{L}_I \leftarrow \emptyset$

$(\mathcal{K}_U, \mathcal{K}_U^{-1}) \leftarrow \mathsf{KeyGen}_U(pp, UPinfo)$; $\mathsf{Storage} \leftarrow \mathsf{Save}(\mathcal{K}_U^{-1})$

$(\mathcal{K}_V, \mathcal{K}_V^{-1}) \leftarrow \mathsf{KeyGen}_V(pp, Vid)$; $V_{List} \leftarrow Add_V(Vid, \mathcal{K}_V, ts, \mathcal{K}_R^{-1})$

$(\mathcal{K}_{V'}, \mathcal{K}_{V'}^{-1}) \leftarrow \mathsf{KeyGen}_{V'}(pp, Vid')$; $V'_{List} \leftarrow Add_{V'}(Vid', \mathcal{K}_{V'}, ts, \mathcal{K}_{R'}^{-1})$

$(\mathcal{K}_I, \mathcal{K}_I^{-1}) \leftarrow \mathsf{KeyGen}_I(pp, Iid)$; $I_{List} \leftarrow Add_I(Iid, \mathcal{K}_V, ts, \mathcal{K}_R^{-1})$

$\langle (Uid), (UPinfo) \rangle \leftarrow \mathsf{Issue}_{I,U}\langle (pp, \mathcal{K}_I^{-1}, \mathcal{K}_U), (pp, UPinfo, \mathcal{K}_U^{-1}, \mathcal{K}_I) \rangle$

if $((Uid = \perp) \vee (UPinfo = \perp))$ **then return** 0

$\langle (\varrho), (\mathrm{Uid}) \rangle \leftarrow \mathsf{Register}_{\mathrm{U,V}}\langle (\mathrm{pp}, \mathrm{Uid}, \mathcal{K}_I, \mathcal{K}_{\mathrm{U}}^{-1}, \mathcal{K}_V, \mathrm{cc}), (\mathrm{pp}, \mathcal{K}_{\mathrm{V}}^{-1}, \mathcal{K}_{\mathrm{U}}) \rangle$

if $\varrho = \perp$ **then return** 0

$(\mathtt{t\text{-}ref}, \Phi, \delta_{\mathtt{Data}}), (\Phi, Data, \pi_U, ts_U, \delta_{\mathtt{Data}}) \leftarrow \mathsf{CertifyUpdate}_{\mathrm{U,V}}\langle (\mathrm{pp}, \mathcal{K}_U^{-1}, \mathcal{K}_V, \mathtt{issue}, \{Data, ts_U, \varrho, \pi_U\}), (\mathrm{pp}, \mathcal{K}_V^{-1}, Vid, \mathcal{K}_U) \rangle$

if $((\Phi = \perp) \vee (\mathtt{t\text{-}ref} = \perp))$ **then return** 0

$(\Phi', \delta_{\mathtt{Data'}}), (\Phi', Data', \pi'_U, ts'_U, \delta_{\mathtt{Data'}}) \leftarrow \mathsf{CertifyUpdate}_{\mathrm{U,V}}\langle (\mathrm{pp}, \mathcal{K}_U^{-1}, \mathcal{K}_V, \mathtt{update}, \{\mathtt{t\text{-}ref}, Data', ts'_U, \pi'_U\}), (\mathrm{pp}, \mathcal{K}_V^{-1}, Vid, \mathcal{K}_U) \rangle$

if $(\Phi' = \perp)$ **then return** 0

$b_{ver} \leftarrow \mathsf{Verify}(pp, \mathcal{K}_{V'}^{-1}, \mathcal{K}_U, \mathcal{K}_V, \mathtt{t\text{-}ref}, \Phi)$

if $b_{ver} \neq 1$ **then return** 0;

$b_{trace} \leftarrow \mathsf{Trace}(pp, \mathcal{K}_R^{-1}, \Phi)$

if $b_{trace} \neq (Uid, Vid))$ **then return** 0;

$b_{revK} \leftarrow \mathsf{RevokeKey}(pp, \mathcal{K}_V^{-1}, Uid, \mathcal{K}_U)$

if $b_{revK} \neq 1$ **then return** 0;

$b_{revC} \leftarrow \mathsf{RevokeCert}(pp, \mathcal{K}_V^{-1}, Uid, \mathcal{K}_U, \Phi)$

if $b_{revC} \neq 1$ **then return** 0;

$\eta \leftarrow \mathsf{GetToken}(pp, Uid, \mathcal{K}_V, \Phi, cc)$

$(\mathcal{K}'_U, \mathcal{K}'^{-1}_U) \leftarrow \mathsf{KeyGen}_U(pp, UPinfo)$ ▷ Generate fresh keys

$\langle (\alpha), (\mathcal{K}'_U) \rangle \leftarrow \mathsf{RestoreKey}_{U,V}\langle (pp, Uid, \eta, \Phi, \mathcal{K}'_U, \mathcal{K}_V), (pp, \eta, \mathcal{K}_V^{-1}) \rangle$

if $\alpha = \perp$ **then return** 0

$\langle (\mathtt{sh\text{-}ref}), (\Phi, Data, \delta_{\mathtt{Data}}) \rangle \leftarrow \mathsf{Share}_{U,V'}\langle (pp, \mathcal{K}_U^{-1}, \Phi, Data, \delta_{\mathtt{Data}}, \pi_{sh}, \mathcal{K}_{V'}), (pp, \mathcal{K}_{V'}^{-1}, \mathcal{K}_U, \mathcal{K}_V) \rangle$

if $\mathtt{sh\text{-}ref} = \perp$ **then return** 0

return 1 ▷ Success: All functionalities behaved as intended

Experiment: $\mathbf{Exp}^{trace}_{\mathcal{A},PaKYC}(Uid, \lambda)$

$(pp) \leftarrow \mathsf{Setup}(\lambda)$

$RU_{List}, OBU_{List}, CU_{List}, BLK_{List}, CRV_{List}, SH_{List}, V_{List}, V'_{List}, I_{List}, \mathcal{L}_U, \mathcal{L}_V, \mathcal{L}_I \leftarrow \emptyset$

$(\mathcal{K}_U, \mathcal{K}_U^{-1}) \leftarrow \mathsf{KeyGen}_U(pp, UPinfo)$

$(\mathcal{K}_V, \mathcal{K}_V^{-1}) \leftarrow \mathsf{KeyGen}_V(pp, Vid)$; $V_{List} \leftarrow Add_V(Vid, \mathcal{K}_V, ts, \mathcal{K}_R^{-1})$

$(\mathcal{K}_{V'}, \mathcal{K}_{V'}^{-1}) \leftarrow \mathsf{KeyGen}_{V'}(pp, Vid')$; $V'_{List} \leftarrow Add_{V'}(Vid', \mathcal{K}_{V'}, ts, \mathcal{K}_R^{-1})$

$(\mathcal{K}_I, \mathcal{K}_I^{-1}) \leftarrow \mathsf{KeyGen}_I(pp, Iid)$; $I_{List} \leftarrow Add_I(Iid, \mathcal{K}_V, ts, \mathcal{K}_R^{-1})$

$\langle (UPinfo), (Uid) \rangle \leftarrow \mathsf{Issue}_{I,U}\langle (pp, \mathcal{K}_I^{-1}, \mathcal{K}_U), (pp, UPinfo, \mathcal{K}_U^{-1}, \mathcal{K}_I) \rangle$

$\mathcal{O} \leftarrow \{\mathcal{O}KeyGen_U, \mathcal{O}KeyGen_V, \mathcal{O}Issue_{I,U}, \mathcal{O}Register_{U,V}, \mathcal{O}CertifyUpdate_{U,V}, \mathcal{O}Cor_U, \mathcal{O}Cor_V\}$

$(\tilde{Vid}, \mathcal{K}_{\tilde{V}}, \tilde{Data}, \delta_{\tilde{\mathtt{Data}}}, \tilde{\pi_U}, \mathtt{t\text{-}\tilde{ref}}, \tilde{\Phi}) \leftarrow \mathcal{A}^{\mathcal{O}}(pp, \mathcal{K}_U)$ ▷ $\mathcal{A}$ outputs a credential $\tilde{\Phi}$ with its reference $\mathtt{t\text{-}\tilde{ref}}$.

$b_{ver} \leftarrow \mathsf{Verify}(pp, \mathcal{K}_{V'}^{-1}, \mathcal{K}_U, \mathcal{K}_{\tilde{V}}, \mathtt{t\text{-}\tilde{ref}}, \tilde{\Phi})$

if $(b_{ver} = 0)$ **then** ▷ Failed verification, though not a traceability break

  return 0 ▷ $\mathcal{C}$ wins, and $\mathcal{A}$ loses because it didn't generate acceptable Φ, $\mathtt{t\text{-}ref}$.

end if

$b_{trace} \leftarrow \mathsf{Trace}(pp, \mathcal{K}_R^{-1}, \tilde{\Phi})$

if $\Big((b_{trace} \neq \perp) \wedge \Big((\langle \tilde{\pi}_U, h_{\mathtt{t\text{-}\tilde{ref}}}, h_{\tilde{\mathtt{Uid}}}, h_{\tilde{\mathtt{Vid}}}, \tau_{\tilde{\mathtt{Data}}}, h_{\tilde{\Phi}}, .\rangle \notin CU_{List}) \vee \Big(\tilde{Vid} \notin V_{List}\Big)\Big)\Big)$ **then**

  return 1 ▷ Adversary wins

end if

return 0 ▷ $\mathcal{C}$ wins (the credential does not match any issuing Vid and receiving Uid)

Fig. 3. *(continued)*

Experiment: $\mathbf{Exp}^{nf,\beta}_{\mathcal{A},PaKYC}(Uid, \lambda)$

$(pp) \leftarrow \mathsf{Setup}(\lambda)$
$RU_{List}, OBU_{List}, CU_{List}, BLK_{List}, CRV_{List}, SH_{List}, V_{List}, V'_{List}, I_{List}, \mathcal{L}_U, \mathcal{L}_V, \mathcal{L}_I \leftarrow \emptyset$
$(\mathcal{K}_U, \mathcal{K}_U^{-1}) \leftarrow \mathsf{KeyGen}_U(pp, UPinfo)$ ▷ Honest User targeted in the game
$(\mathcal{K}_{V'}, \mathcal{K}_{V'}^{-1}) \leftarrow \mathsf{KeyGen}_{V'}(pp, Vid')$; $V'_{List} \leftarrow Add_{V'}(Vid', \mathcal{K}_{V'}, ts, \mathcal{K}_R^{-1})$
$(\mathcal{K}_I, \mathcal{K}_I^{-1}) \leftarrow \mathsf{KeyGen}_I(pp, Iid)$; $I_{List} \leftarrow Add_I(Iid, \mathcal{K}_V, ts, \mathcal{K}_R^{-1})$
$\langle (UPinfo), (Uid) \rangle \leftarrow \mathsf{Issue}_{I,U}\langle (pp, \mathcal{K}_I^{-1}, \mathcal{K}_U), (pp, UPinfo, \mathcal{K}_U^{-1}, \mathcal{K}_I)\rangle$
$\mathcal{O} \leftarrow \{\mathcal{O}KeyGen_U, \mathcal{O}KeyGen_V, \mathcal{O}Issue_{I,U}, \mathcal{O}Register_{U,V}, \mathcal{O}CertifyUpdate_{U,V}, \mathcal{O}Cor_U, \mathcal{O}Cor_V, \mathcal{O}Share_{U,V'}\}$
$(\tilde{\mathcal{K}_V}, \tilde{Data}, \delta_{\tilde{\mathsf{Data}}}, \tilde{\pi_U}, \tilde{\mathtt{t\text{-}ref}}, \tilde{\Phi}, \tilde{\pi_{sh}}, \tilde{\mathtt{sh\text{-}ref}}) \leftarrow \mathcal{A}^{\mathcal{O}}(pp)$ ▷ $\mathcal{A}$ produces some outputs
$b_{ver} \leftarrow \mathsf{Verify}(pp, \mathcal{K}_{V'}^{-1}, \mathcal{K}_U, \mathcal{K}_{\tilde{V}}, \tilde{\mathtt{t\text{-}ref}}, \tilde{\Phi})$
if $(b_{ver} = 0)$ **then** ▷ Failed verification, though not a non-frameability break
  return 0 ▷ $\mathcal{C}$ wins, and $\mathcal{A}$ loses because it didn't generate acceptable Φ, t-ref.
end if
if $\Big((\langle \tilde{\pi_U}, ., h_{\mathsf{Uid}}, . \rangle \notin CU_{List}) \wedge \big(\big(\mathcal{V}^{fy}(\tilde{\pi_U}, \tilde{req}, \mathcal{K}_U)\big) = 1\big) \wedge \big(\big(\mathcal{V}^{fy}(\tilde{\pi_{sh}}, \tilde{shr}, \mathcal{K}_U)\big) = 1\big) \wedge$ ($\mathcal{A}$ did not call $\mathcal{O}Cor_U(., \mathcal{K}_U)) \wedge$ (transaction for $\tilde{\mathtt{t\text{-}ref}}, \tilde{\mathtt{sh\text{-}ref}} \notin \mathcal{L}_U)\Big)$ **then**
  return 1 ▷ $\mathcal{A}$ wins if $\tilde{\pi_U}$, h_{Uid} do not belong to a tuple in CU_{List}, and $\tilde{\pi_U}$ and $\tilde{\pi_{sh}}$ verify under $\mathcal{K}_U$, and $\mathcal{A}$ did not call $\mathcal{O}Cor_U(., \mathcal{K}_U)$, and transactions that generated $\tilde{\mathtt{t\text{-}ref}}$, $\tilde{\mathtt{sh\text{-}ref}}$ are not logged in $\mathcal{L}_U$.
else
  return 0 ▷ $\mathcal{C}$ wins
end if

Experiment: $\mathbf{Exp}^{ccvds}_{\mathcal{A},PaKYC}(\lambda)$

$(pp) \leftarrow \mathsf{Setup}(\lambda)$
$RU_{List}, OBU_{List}, CU_{List}, BLK_{List}, CRV_{List}, SH_{List}, V_{List}, V'_{List}, I_{List}, \mathcal{L}_U, \mathcal{L}_V, \mathcal{L}_I \leftarrow \emptyset$
$(\mathcal{K}_V, \mathcal{K}_V^{-1}) \leftarrow \mathsf{KeyGen}_V(pp, Vid)$; $V_{List} \leftarrow Add_V(Vid, \mathcal{K}_V, ts, \mathcal{K}_R^{-1})$
$(\mathcal{K}_{V'}, \mathcal{K}_{V'}^{-1}) \leftarrow \mathsf{KeyGen}_{V'}(pp, Vid')$; $V'_{List} \leftarrow Add_{V'}(Vid', \mathcal{K}_{V'}, ts, \mathcal{K}_{R'}^{-1})$
$(\mathcal{K}_I, \mathcal{K}_I^{-1}) \leftarrow \mathsf{KeyGen}_I(pp, Iid)$; $I_{List} \leftarrow Add_I(Iid, \mathcal{K}_V, ts, \mathcal{K}_R^{-1})$
$\mathcal{O} \leftarrow \{\mathcal{O}KeyGen_U, \mathcal{O}Issue_{I,U}, \mathcal{O}Register_{U,V}, \mathcal{O}CertifyUpdate_{U,V}, \mathcal{O}Cor_U, \mathcal{O}CorData, \mathcal{O}Share_{U,V'}\}$ ▷ Available oracles
$(\tilde{Uid}, \mathcal{K}_{\tilde{U}}, Data, \delta_{\mathsf{Data}}, \mathtt{t\text{-}ref}, \Phi, \tilde{Data}) \leftarrow \mathcal{A}^{\mathcal{O}}(pp)$ ▷ $\tilde{Data}$ was obtained via $\mathcal{O}CorData$
$\langle(\mathtt{sh\text{-}ref}), (\Phi, \tilde{Data})\rangle \leftarrow \mathsf{Share}_{U,V'}\langle(pp, \mathcal{K}_{\tilde{U}}^{-1}, \Phi, \tilde{Data}, \delta_{\mathsf{Data}}, \pi_{sh}, \mathcal{K}_{V'}), (pp, \mathcal{K}_{V'}^{-1}, \mathcal{K}_{\tilde{U}}, \mathcal{K}_V)\rangle$
if $\Big((\mathtt{sh\text{-}ref} \neq \perp) \wedge (Data \neq \tilde{Data}) \wedge (\mathcal{T}\{Data|\delta_{\mathsf{Data}}\} = \mathcal{T}\{\tilde{Data}|\delta_{\mathsf{Data}}\}) \Big)$ **then**
  return 1 ▷ $\mathcal{A}$ wins
end if
return 0 ▷ $\mathcal{C}$ wins otherwise

Experiment: $\mathbf{Exp}^{unforge}_{\mathcal{A},PaKYC}(Uid, \lambda)$

$(pp) \leftarrow \mathsf{Setup}(\lambda)$
$RU_{List}, OBU_{List}, CU_{List}, BLK_{List}, CRV_{List}, SH_{List}, V_{List}, V'_{List}, I_{List}, \mathcal{L}_U, \mathcal{L}_V, \mathcal{L}_I \leftarrow \emptyset$
$(\mathcal{K}_V, \mathcal{K}_V^{-1}) \leftarrow \mathsf{KeyGen}_V(pp, Vid)$; $V_{List} \leftarrow Add_V(Vid, \mathcal{K}_V, ts, \mathcal{K}_R^{-1})$
$(\mathcal{K}_{V'}, \mathcal{K}_{V'}^{-1}) \leftarrow \mathsf{KeyGen}_{V'}(pp, Vid')$; $V'_{List} \leftarrow Add_{V'}(Vid', \mathcal{K}_{V'}, ts, \mathcal{K}_{R'}^{-1})$
$(\mathcal{K}_I, \mathcal{K}_I^{-1}) \leftarrow \mathsf{KeyGen}_I(pp, Iid)$; $I_{List} \leftarrow Add_I(Iid, \mathcal{K}_V, ts, \mathcal{K}_R)$
$\mathcal{O} \leftarrow \{\mathcal{O}KeyGen_U, \mathcal{O}KeyGen_V, \mathcal{O}Issue_{I,U}, \mathcal{O}Register_{U,V}, \mathcal{O}CertifyUpdate_{U,V}, \mathcal{O}Cor_U, \mathcal{O}Cor_V\}$ ▷ Available oracles but $\mathcal{A}$ cannot corrupt honest **V**
$(\tilde{Uid}, \mathcal{K}_{\tilde{U}}, \tilde{\mathtt{t\text{-}ref}}, \tilde{\Phi}) \leftarrow \mathcal{A}^{\mathcal{O}}(pp)$
$b_{ver} \leftarrow \mathsf{Verify}(pp, \mathcal{K}_{V'}^{-1}, \mathcal{K}_{\tilde{U}}, \mathcal{K}_V, \tilde{\mathtt{t\text{-}ref}}, \tilde{\Phi})$
if $(b_{ver} = 0)$ **then** ▷ Failed verification, though not an unforgeability break
  return 0 ▷ $\mathcal{C}$ wins, and $\mathcal{A}$ loses because it didn't generate acceptable Φ, t-ref.
end if
if $\Big($ ($\mathcal{A}$ did not call $\mathcal{O}Cor_V(., \mathcal{K}_V)) \wedge$ (transaction for $\tilde{\Phi}, \tilde{\mathtt{t\text{-}ref}} \notin \mathcal{L}_V)\Big)$ **then**
  return 1 ▷ $\mathcal{A}$ wins if $\tilde{\mathtt{t\text{-}ref}}$, $\tilde{\Phi}$ pass verification, and $\mathcal{A}$ did not call $\mathcal{O}Cor_V(., \mathcal{K}_V)$, and the transaction that generated $\tilde{\mathtt{t\text{-}ref}}$ is not logged in $\mathcal{L}_V$.
else
  return 0 ▷ $\mathcal{C}$ wins
end if

Fig. 3. *(continued)*

Experiment: $\mathbf{Exp}^{skr}_{\mathcal{A},PaKYC}(\lambda)$

$(pp) \leftarrow \mathsf{Setup}(\lambda)$
$RU_{List}, OBU_{List}, CU_{List}, BLK_{List}, CRV_{List}, SH_{List}, V_{List}, V'_{List}, I_{List}, \mathcal{L}_U, \mathcal{L}_V, \mathcal{L}_I \leftarrow \emptyset$
$(\mathcal{K}_V, \mathcal{K}_V^{-1}) \leftarrow \mathsf{KeyGen}_V(pp, Vid)$; $V_{List} \leftarrow Add_V(Vid, \mathcal{K}_V, ts, \mathcal{K}_R^{-1})$
$(\mathcal{K}_{V'}, \mathcal{K}_{V'}^{-1}) \leftarrow \mathsf{KeyGen}_{V'}(pp, Vid')$; $V'_{List} \leftarrow Add_{V'}(Vid', \mathcal{K}_{V'}, ts, \mathcal{K}_{R'}^{-1})$
$(\mathcal{K}_I, \mathcal{K}_I^{-1}) \leftarrow \mathsf{KeyGen}_I(pp, Iid)$; $I_{List} \leftarrow Add_I(Iid, \mathcal{K}_V, ts, \mathcal{K}_R^{-1})$
$(\mathcal{K}_U, \mathcal{K}_U^{-1}) \leftarrow \mathsf{KeyGen}_U(pp, UPinfo)$ ▷ An honest user
$\langle (Uid), (UPinfo) \rangle \leftarrow \mathsf{Issue}_{I,U}\langle (pp, \mathcal{K}_I^{-1}, \mathcal{K}_U), (pp, UPinfo, \mathcal{K}_U^{-1}, \mathcal{K}_I) \rangle$
$\langle (\varrho), (\mathrm{Uid}) \rangle \leftarrow \mathsf{Register}_{\mathrm{U,V}}\langle (\mathrm{pp}, \mathrm{Uid}, \mathcal{K}_I, \mathcal{K}_{\mathrm{U}}^{-1}, \mathcal{K}_V, \mathtt{cc}), (\mathrm{pp}, \mathcal{K}_{\mathrm{V}}^{-1}, \mathcal{K}_{\mathrm{U}}) \rangle$
$(\mathtt{t\text{-}ref}, \Phi, \delta_{\mathtt{Data}}), (\Phi, Data, \pi_U, ts_U, \delta_{\mathtt{Data}}) \leftarrow \mathsf{CertifyUpdate}_{\mathrm{U,V}}\langle (\mathrm{pp}, \mathcal{K}_U^{-1}, \mathcal{K}_V, \mathtt{issue}, \{Data, ts_U, \varrho, \pi_U\}), (\mathrm{pp}, \mathcal{K}_V^{-1}, Vid, \mathcal{K}_U) \rangle$
if $(b_{ver} = 0)$ **then**
  return 0
end if
$\eta \leftarrow \mathsf{GetToken}(pp, Uid, \mathcal{K}_V, \Phi, \mathtt{cc})$ ▷ Generates the real, authentic token
if $(\eta = \perp)$ **then return** 0
▷ Available oracles
$\mathcal{O} \leftarrow \{\mathcal{O}KeyGen_U, \mathcal{O}Issue_{I,U}, \mathcal{O}Register_{U,V}, \mathcal{O}CertifyUpdate_{U,V}, \mathcal{O}Cor_U, \mathcal{O}GetToken, \mathcal{O}RestoreKey_{U,V}\}$
$(\tilde{\eta}, \mathcal{K}'_{\tilde{U}}) \leftarrow \mathcal{A}^{\mathcal{O}}(pp)$ ▷ A corrupt user
$b_{resK} \leftarrow \mathsf{RestoreKey}_{U,V}\langle (pp, Uid, \tilde{\eta}, \Phi, \mathcal{K}'_{\tilde{U}}, \mathcal{K}_V), (pp, \eta, \mathcal{K}_V^{-1}) \rangle$ ▷ The Challenge
if $\Big((b_{resK} = \big\langle (\alpha), (\mathcal{K}'_{\tilde{U}}) \big\rangle) \wedge (\mathcal{A}$ did not access **U's cc**$) \Big)$ **then**
  return 1 ▷ $\mathcal{A}$ wins if RestoreKey succeeds, and $\mathcal{A}$ did not learn η via $OGetToken$
end if
return 0 ▷ $\mathcal{C}$ wins otherwise

Fig. 3. (*continued*)

2.6 Instantiation and Reduction Sketch

To illustrate how the abstract PaKYC interfaces are realizable, we map each agnostic operation to standard cryptographic primitives. The sealing and unsealing operations $(\mathcal{S}, \mathcal{S}^{-1})$ may be instantiated by any IND-CPA [8] secure encryption scheme. Concrete instantiations include symmetric encryption (e.g., ChaCha20 [1] or Twofish [38]), public-key encryption (e.g., RSA-OAEP [20], ElGamal [14]), and tokenization-based constructions, where sensitive data is replaced by a token issued by a trusted detokenization service that holds the equivalent of the unsealing key. The attestation and verification operations $(\mathcal{A}, V^{fy})$ may be instantiated by any EUF-CMA [18] secure digital signature scheme (e.g., ECDSA [25] or EdDSA [26]), where as in symmetric or tokenization-based deployments, message authentication codes (e.g., HMAC) may serve the analogous role. The non-keyed tagging function $\mathcal{H}$ is instantiated by a collision-resistant hash function (e.g., SHA-256 [2], SHA-3 [13]), and the keyed tagging function $\mathcal{T}$ is instantiated by a pseudorandom function keyed by the secret commitment δ (e.g., HMAC-SHA-256 [28]). This reference instantiation demonstrates that the PaKYC abstraction can be grounded in conventional cryptographic primitives under standard security assumptions.

Table 1 gives a reduction sketch mapping each PaKYC security property to a standard cryptographic assumption, showing that any adversary that violates a PaKYC property can be transformed into one that breaks the corresponding underlying primitive—all of which are assumed computationally hard. Full reductions are left to a follow-up paper.

Table 1. Security Property Reductions to Cryptographic Primitives

Security Property	Mathematical Reduction Goal	Supporting Primitive(s)
Data Confidentiality	**IND-CPA** (Sealing) + **PRF** Security (Tagging)	Π_{Enc}, F
Correctness	Deterministic Completeness	—
Traceability	**EUF-CMA** (Signatures) + **INT-CTXT** (Π_{Enc}) + **PRF**(F)	Π_{Sig}, Π_{Enc}, F
Non-Frameability	**EUF-CMA** of User's unsealing key $\mathcal{K}_U^{-1}$	Π_{Sig}
Consistent Sharing	**PRF** Security (Tag indistinguishability)	F
Unforgeability	**EUF-CMA** of Verifier's unsealing key $\mathcal{K}_V^{-1}$	Π_{Sig}
Secure Key Recovery	**Min-entropy** of η + Authenticated **OOB** channel	η, cc

3 Comparative Analysis

3.1 How Our Framework Compares to Existing Models

Many of the existing e-KYC literature (e.g., Sovrin [30], uPort [29], zkKYC [35], and BBM [10]) do not formalize security properties under an explicit adversarial model. Since our objective here is a security-grounded comparison, we restrict our attention to works that state security properties formally and give an adversarial experiment or equivalent formalization. On that basis, we compare PaKYC against KYChain [12], TrustBlock [19], and AASSI [21], strictly on the security properties they share with PaKYC.

Table 2 summarizes a feature-level comparison, and Table 3 provides the security-grounded side-by-side. In what follows we highlight the most consequential differences that the tables alone do not fully convey.

KYChain⇒Data Confidentiality and Certificate Compliance: Both KYChain and PaKYC use IND-CPA-based confidentiality games; PaKYC additionally relies on PRF security so that $\mathcal{T}_{\texttt{Data}}$ is computationally indistinguishable from random. The key conceptual divergence is the *confidentiality holder*: KYChain's `t-rec` is built around user-controlled access and loses confidentiality once the user's secret key `sk*` leaks, whereas in PaKYC the challenge payload $Data_{\beta}$ sits only inside the regulator-sealed component Q within m, so corrupting $\mathcal{K}_U^{-1}$ via $\mathcal{O}Cor_U$ yields no advantage—only $\mathcal{K}_R^{-1}$ can unseal it. This makes PaKYC's confidentiality *compromise-resilient*, with the regulator as confidentiality holder. PaKYC also broadens the adversary by adding $\mathcal{O}Issue_{I,U}$, capturing identity-forgery attempts on the Uid bound to $Data_{\beta}$. On certificate compliance, KYChain relies on the assumption that honest certifiers issue only to clients meeting Ψ; PaKYC instead enforces Ψ_{R} as an explicit validity check inside $\mathcal{O}CertifyUpdate_{U,V}$ and additionally models post-onboarding enforcement via RevokeCert. We treat this as a modelling extension beyond KYChain's stated compliance scope, not a claim of unconditional cryptographic dominance.

TrustBlock⇒Traceability: TrustBlock's traceability is essentially a blockchain-auditability claim, where all activities lives on-chain as immutable transactions, so FI members and auditors can see who did what. However, traceability in TrustBlock offers no adversarial definition, game-based proof, or formal reduction. PaKYC instead models traceability as a platform-agnostic cryptographic accountability property, with an explicit Trace algorithm, an adversarial definition, and a game with a win condition (see Table 3). At the implementation level, PaKYC's lists/logs can themselves be realized as an append-only ledger, inheriting the audit-trail benefits TrustBlock emphasizes while retaining the game-based traceability definition.

AASSI⇒Traceability and Unforgeability: AASSI offers *user-identity traceability*—the tracer reveals the user behind an otherwise privacy-preserving credential—while PaKYC offers *KYC credential accountability*, tracing both the issuing verifier **V** and the user **U** and enforcing that trace results match CU_{List} records and V_{List} membership. PaKYC therefore subsumes what AASSI provides. The corruption surface also widens: AASSI's adversary corrupts users only, while PaKYC permits corruption of both users ($\mathcal{O}Cor_U$) and non-target verifiers ($\mathcal{O}Cor_V$). On unforgeability, AASSI targets credential/attribute forgery against user credentials (tracked via $HU/CU/ATTR$); PaKYC targets forgery of *verifier*-issued attestations and tightens the win condition with an explicit log non-membership check ($\notin \mathcal{L}_V$) that defeats replay even when verification passes. Our framework therefore captures AASSI's unforgeability intent while offering a stricter adversarial model and explicit replay prevention.

The summary tables (Table 2, and Table 3) follow.

Table 2. Feature-level comparison (✓: supported; ✗: not supported).

Work	Support Multiple Platforms	Credential Post-Compromise Confidentiality	Compliance With Regulation	Post-Onboarding Compliance Enforcement	Data Sharing Within Jurisdiction	Data Sharing Across Jurisdiction	Key Revocation	Key Replacement	Multi-sectoral Applicability
PaKYC	✓	✓	✓	✓	✓	✓	✓	✓	✓
KYChain [12]	✗	✗	✓	✗	✓†	✗	✗	✗	✗
TrustBlock [19]	✗	✗	✗	✗	✓‡	✗	✗	✗	✗
AASSI [21]	✗	✗	✗	✓‡‡	✗	✗	✗	✗	✗

†KYChain supports multi-FI sharing, but it does not model interoperability across jurisdictions.

‡TrustBlock enables CP-ABE access-controlled sharing, but it does not model key revocation/recovery.

‡‡AASSI supports post-issuance selective revocation (revoking offending users/credentials) via dynamic accumulators, but it is not explicitly modeled as post-onboarding KYC compliance enforcement driven by a regulator-policy (as obtain in PaKYC's RevokeCert)

Table 3. PaKYC vs Existing Formal Models: Shared Security Properties

Model	Shared Property	Summary of Features/Limitations	PaKYC Equivalent/Extension
KYChain [12]	Data Confidentiality	i. Limited to blockchain designs; uses an IND-style adversary that guesses which of data_0 or data_1 was used to produce t-rec. ii. To win, the adversary must guess β correctly, not corrupt the user's pk*, and not ask for t-rec to be decrypted via Oprf.	i. Platform-agnostic design; uses an IND-style adversary that guesses which of $Data_0$ or $Data_1$ was used to produce Φ and t-rec, in addition to PRF security for $\tau_{\mathtt{Data}}$. ii. Adds an identity-forgery capability through $\mathcal{O}Issue_{I,U}$, letting the adversary influence the identifier Uid bound to $Data_\beta$. This tests whether confidentiality still holds when the identity layer is tampered with. iii. Winning only needs the adversary to guess β correctly. PaKYC also offers compromise-resilient confidentiality: corrupting the user's $\mathcal{K}_U$ via $\mathcal{O}Cor_U$ to get $\mathcal{K}_U^{-1}$ during the challenge gives no advantage, since $Data_\beta$ sits only inside the regulator-sealed component Q (i.e., $[Data, \delta_{\mathtt{Data}}, ts_U, Uid, Vid]$), which needs $\mathcal{K}_R^{-1}$ to unseal.
KYChain [12]	Certificate Compliance	i. Relies on the assumption that honest certifiers only issue certificates (cert) to authenticated clients that meet the regulatory policy Ψ. ii. Does not model any explicit mechanism for compliance enforcement after onboarding.	i. Enforces policy satisfaction Ψ_R as an explicit validity check inside $\mathcal{O}CertifyUpdate_{U,V}$, which must hold before a certificate Φ is issued. ii. Extends this by modelling ongoing compliance via RevokeCert, which revokes Φ after issuance if the user later breaks Ψ_R (post-onboarding enforcement).
TrustBlock [19]	Traceability	i. Treats traceability as operational blockchain auditability (immutability/audit trail); no explicit adversarial experiment, trace-related oracles, or game-based reduction. ii. Only traces user activities on the blockchain; does not model credential issuance after successful KYC verification, and does not support tracing a credential back to a user.	i. Models traceability as a platform-agnostic cryptographic/accountability property with an explicit Trace algorithm, an adversarial definition, and an experiment with a win condition. ii. Extends the literature by letting the regulator **R** in a given jurisdiction trace any valid issued credential Φ back to both the issuing verifier **V** and the requesting user **U**.
AASSI [21]	Traceability	i. Built on a self-sovereign identity (SSI) design; the adversary has oracles to issue and use credentials, but corruption is limited to users only, so the corruption surface is mostly user-oriented. ii. The only explicit trace oracle appears under the Anonymity security property and only targets the user (i.e., $\mathcal{O}Trace$ calling TraceUser).	i. Supports a multi-platform design; the adversary has oracles to issue and use credentials. Extends AASSI by letting the adversary corrupt both the user and the verifier (credential issuer) via $\mathcal{O}Cor_U$ and $\mathcal{O}Cor_V$, giving a stricter model with a wider corruption surface that covers both user and verifier. ii. Extends the trace target beyond user-only to include both (Uid, Vid) (user and verifier), and enforces accountability by requiring trace outputs to match maintained records (CU_{List}) and verifier membership (V_{List}).
AASSI [21]	Unforgeability	i. $\mathcal{A}$ is built around credential/attribute forgery; it can create honest and corrupt users, get credentials through issuance oracles, and request derivations. Legitimacy is tracked using HU, CU, and the bookkeeping set $ATTR$. ii. $\mathcal{A}$ cannot corrupt a verifier, which limits the attack surface and makes the model relatively lenient. It wins if it outputs a credential that passes verification despite not being legitimately produced through the permitted issuance/derivation interfaces and having no tracked $ATTR$ history.	Frames forgery as producing a *fresh* verifier-issued attestation $\tilde{\Phi}$ that verifies under an honest verifier V without corrupting the target verifier ($\mathcal{O}Cor_V$ forbidden on $\mathcal{K}_V$). ii. Has a similar win condition to AASSI but extends it to block replay attacks by requiring that the generating reference satisfies $\tilde{\Phi}, \tilde{\mathtt{t\text{-}ref}} \notin \mathcal{L}_V$, even if verification passes.

4 Conclusion

We have presented PaKYC, a platform-agnostic framework offering a uniform approach to KYC across different design paradigms, with features including user-authorized bi-jurisdictional data sharing, key revocation, certificate/credential revocation, key replacement, and multi-sectoral applicability. PaKYC also has the following limitations that motivate future research:

- PaKYC suits settings where regulatory oversight is non-negotiable; it may not be preferred where anonymity is. Future work may explore anonymity-compliance without unduly reducing traceability.
- Multi-jurisdictional capability is currently limited to two jurisdictions, keeping the merged-policy $\Psi_{R,R'}$ tractable. Extending to n jurisdictions would require an n-way policy composition function—a non-trivial open problem.
- We compared selected guarantees (Data Confidentiality, Traceability, Unforgeability) but did not provide full game-based reduction proofs; completing these is a natural next step.
- Modelling a corrupt regulator $\mathbf{R}$ and its effect on confidentiality and traceability is another future direction.

We hope PaKYC serves as a foundation for future interoperable, regulator-aligned KYC systems.

Acknowledgement. This work acknowledges the support of Dr. Essam Ghadafi and Dr. Paul Ezhilchevan, both from the School of Computing at Newcastle University, United Kingdom, and Dr. Carlton Shepherd from Durham University's Department of Computer Science. Their unwavering support and guidance have been instrumental in bringing this research to completion.

Funding Information. This research was sponsored by scholarship funds from the Petroleum Technology Development Fund (PTDF), Nigeria.

References

1. Alyas, H.H., Abdullah, A.A.: Enhancement the chacha20 encryption algorithm based on chaotic maps. In: Next Generation of Internet of Things: Proceedings of ICNGIoT 2021, pp. 91–107. Springer (2021)
2. Appel, A.W.: Verification of a cryptographic primitive: Sha-256. ACM Trans. Program. Lang. Syst. (TOPLAS) **37**(2), 1–31 (2015)
3. Babbar, D., Jain, A., Sharma, A., Banerjee, D.: Forgery detection in Aadhaar-based KYC using deep learning. In: Proceedings of the 2024 16th International Conference on Machine Learning and Computing, pp. 244–250 (2024)
4. Bandara, E., Liang, X., Foytik, P., Shetty, S., De Zoysa, K.: A blockchain and self-sovereign identity empowered digital identity platform. In: 2021 International Conference on Computer Communications and Networks (ICCCN), pp. 1–7. IEEE (2021)

5. Bandara, E., et al.: Octopus: privacy preserving peer-to-peer transactions system with interplanetary file system (IPFS). Int. J. Inf. Secur. **22**(3), 591–609 (2023)
6. Bandara, E., et al.: Casper: a blockchain-based system for efficient and secure customer credential verification. J. Banking Finan. Technol. **6**(1), 43–62 (2022)
7. Bethencourt, J., Sahai, A., Waters, B.: Ciphertext-policy attribute-based encryption. In: IEEE symposium on security and privacy (SP'07), pp. 321–334. IEEE (2007)
8. Carstens, T.V., Ebrahimi, E., Tabia, G.N., Unruh, D.: Relationships between quantum IND-CPA notions. In: Theory of Cryptography Conference, pp. 240–272. Springer (2021)
9. Do, T.L., Tran, M.K., Nguyen, H.H., Tran, M.T.: Potential attacks of deepfake on ekyc systems and remedy for ekyc with deepfake detection using two-stream network of facial appearance and motion features. SN Comput. Sci. **3**(6), 464 (2022)
10. Dong, C., Wang, Z., Chen, S., Xiang, Y.: BBM: a blockchain-based model for open banking via self-sovereign identity. In: International Conference on Blockchain, pp. 61–75. Springer (2020)
11. Dong, C., et al.: A blockchain-based self-sovereign identity system for KYC processes. In: Proceedings of the 6th ACM International Symposium on Blockchain and Secure Critical Infrastructure, pp. 1–11 (2024)
12. Drăgan, C.C., Manulis, M.: KYChain: user-controlled KYC data sharing and certification. In: Proceedings of the 35th Annual ACM Symposium on Applied Computing, pp. 301–307 (2020)
13. Dworkin, M.J.: SHA-3 standard: Permutation-based hash and extendable-output functions (2015)
14. ElGamal, T.: A public key cryptosystem and a signature scheme based on discrete logarithms. IEEE Trans. Inf. Theory **31**(4), 469–472 (1985)
15. European Parliament and Council of the European Union: Regulation (EU) 2016/679 (general data protection regulation), article 5: Principles relating to processing of personal data. https://gdpr-info.eu/art-5-gdpr/ (2016). Accessed 05 Mar 2026. Text accessed via gdpr-info.eu
16. EY Advisory Netherlands LLP: how to make your PSP compliant with relevant AML/CFT regulations in the Netherlands? Independent review consulting services report, EY Financial Crime Services, The Netherlands (2021). https://www.ey.com/content/dam/ey-unified-site/ey-com/en-nl/industries/banking-capital-markets/documents/fco/ey-fc-psp-compliant-with-aml-cft-regulations-in-the-netherlands.pdf
17. FIS: master compliance in an era of regulatory change: Introducing the fis®lifecycle manager. Product overview/white paper, FIS Global (2024). https://www.fisglobal.com/-/media/fisglobal/files/pdf/article/fis-investor-services-lifecyle-manager-compliance-article.pdf, accessed: 2026-05-04
18. Fuchsbauer, G., Hanser, C., Slamanig, D.: EUF-CMA-secure structure-preserving signatures on equivalence classes. IACR Cryptol. ePrint Arch. **2014**, 944 (2014)
19. Fugkeaw, S.: Enabling trust and privacy-preserving e-KYC system using blockchain. IEEE Access **10**, 49028–49039 (2022)
20. Fujisaki, E., Okamoto, T., Pointcheval, D., Stern, J.: RSA-OAEP is secure under the RSA assumption. In: Annual International Cryptology Conference, pp. 260–274. Springer (2001)
21. Gao, L., Yu, J., Zhang, J., Tang, Y., Wen, Q.: AASSI: a self-sovereign identity protocol with anonymity and accountability. IEEE Access (2024)

22. Giacobino, A., Grierson, D., Singh, H.P., McHale, P., Maggs, S.: Cosmos cash: public permissionless approach towards SSI and use cases. In: 2022 IEEE International Conference on Blockchain (Blockchain), pp. 462–467. IEEE (2022)
23. He, Y., Chen, J.: Amlchain: supporting anti-money laundering, privacy-preserving, auditable distributed ledger. In: International Symposium on Emerging Information Security and Applications, pp. 50–67. Springer (2021)
24. Jiang, Y., Li, X., Luo, H., Yin, S., Kaynak, O.: Quo vadis artificial intelligence? Discover Artif. Intell. **2**(1), 4 (2022)
25. Johnson, D., Menezes, A., Vanstone, S.: The elliptic curve digital signature algorithm (ECDSA). Int. J. Inf. Secur. **1**(1), 36–63 (2001)
26. Josefsson, S., Liusvaara, I.: Edwards-curve digital signature algorithm (EDDSA) (2017). Technical report
27. Kapsoulis, N., et al.: Know Your Customer (KYC) implementation with smart contracts on a privacy-oriented decentralized architecture. Future Internet **12**(2), 41 (2020)
28. Kelly, S., Frankel, S.: Using HMAC-SHA-256, HMAC-sha-384, and HMAC-SHA-512 with ipsec (2007). Technical report
29. Lundkvist, C., Heck, R., Torstensson, J., Mitton, Z., Sena, M.: Uport: a platform for self-sovereign identity. **128**, 214 (2017). https://whitepaperuport.me/uPort_whitepaper_DRAFT20170221.pdf
30. Naik, N., Jenkins, P.: Sovrin network for decentralized digital identity: analysing a self-sovereign identity system based on distributed ledger technology. In: 2021 IEEE International Symposium on Systems Engineering (ISSE), pp. 1–7. IEEE (2021)
31. Norvill, R., et al.: A security and privacy focused KYC data sharing platform. In: Proceedings of the 2nd ACM International Symposium on Blockchain and Secure Critical Infrastructure, pp. 151–160. (2020)
32. Ostern, N.K., Riedel, J.: Know-Your-Customer (KYC) requirements for initial coin offerings. Bus. Inf. Syst. Eng. **63**(5), 551–567 (2021)
33. Parra Moyano, J., Ross, O.: KYC optimization using distributed ledger technology. Bus. Inf. Syst. Eng. **59**, 411–423 (2017)
34. Patil, S., Pitchai, R., Madhubabu, C.: Know Your Customer (KYC) as a service for Business Process Management (BPM) using cloud computing. In: 2022 International Conference on Innovative Computing, Intelligent Communication and Smart Electrical Systems (ICSES), pp. 1–6. IEEE (2022)
35. Pauwels, P.: zkKYC: a solution concept for KYC without knowing your customer, leveraging self-sovereign identity and zero-knowledge proofs. Cryptology ePrint Archive (2021)
36. Saragih, T.K., Tanuwijaya, E., Wang, G.: The use of blockchain for digital identity management in healthcare. In: 2022 10th International Conference on Cyber and IT Service Management (CITSM), pp. 1–6. IEEE (2022)
37. Schlatt, V., Sedlmeir, J., Feulner, S., Urbach, N.: Designing a framework for digital KYC processes built on blockchain-based self-sovereign identity. Inf. Manage. **59**(7), 103553 (2022)
38. Schneier, B., et al.: Twofish: a 128-bit block cipher. NIST AES Proposal **15**(1), 23–91 (1998)
39. Soltani, R., Nguyen, U.T., An, A.: A new approach to client onboarding using self-sovereign identity and distributed ledger. In: IEEE International Conference on Internet of Things (iThings) and IEEE Green Computing and Communications (GreenCom) and IEEE Cyber, Physical and Social Computing (CPSCom) and IEEE Smart Data (SmartData), pp. 1129–1136. IEEE (2018)

40. Sundareswaran, N., Sasirekha, S., Paul, I.J.L., Balakrishnan, S., Swaminathan, G.: Optimised KYC blockchain system. In: 2020 International Conference on Innovative Trends in Information Technology (ICITIIT), pp. 1–6. IEEE (2020)
41. Tan, V.H., Lim, W.Y.B., Xiong, Z., Niyato, D.: Blockchain for decentralized Know Your Customer (KYC) and Customer Due Diligence (CDD) pipelines in the metaverse. In: 2023 IEEE International Conference on Metaverse Computing, Networking and Applications (MetaCom), pp. 433–440. IEEE (2023)
42. U.S. Attorney's Office, Southern District of New York: OKX pleads guilty to violating U.S. anti-money laundering laws and agrees to pay penalties totaling more than US$500 million (2025). https://www.justice.gov/usao-sdny/pr/okx-pleads-guilty-violating-us-anti-money-laundering-laws-and-agrees-pay-penalties. Accessed 05 Mar 2026
43. Verdugo Yepes, C.: Compliance with the AML/CFT international standard: Lessons from a cross-country analysis (2011)
44. Voigt, P., Von dem Bussche, A.: The EU general data protection regulation (GDPR). A Practical Guide, , vol. 10, no. 3152676, pp. 10–5555, 1st edn. Cham, Springer International Publishing (2017)

Author Index

N. El Mrabet et al. (Eds.): AFRICACRYPT 2026, LNCS 16832, pp. 489–490, 2026.
https://doi.org/10.1007/978-3-032-31130-6

MIX
Papier aus verantwortungsvollen Quellen
Paper from responsible sources
FSC® C105338

If you have any concerns about our products,
you can contact us on
ProductSafety@springernature.com

In case Publisher is established outside the EU,
the EU authorized representative is:
Springer Nature Customer Service Center GmbH
Europaplatz 3, 69115 Heidelberg, Germany

Printed by Libri Plureos GmbH
in Hamburg, Germany